1997–98 Oregon Blue Book

Compiled and published by Phil Keisling, Secretary of State

Credits

Project Manager/Editor: Deborah Smith
Design and Production: Innovative Solutions Group (ISG)
Photo Consultants: Negative Perfection, Carlene Lynch and Jeff Sherwin
Proofreader: Dick Peckham
Printer: Daily Journal of Commerce

PHIL KEISLING
SECRETARY OF STATE

MICHAEL GREENFIELD
DEPUTY SECRETARY OF STATE

STATE OF OREGON
SECRETARY OF STATE
136 STATE CAPITOL
SALEM, OREGON 97310-0722
(503) 986-1500

Dear Oregonians:

Welcome to the 1997-98 *Oregon Blue Book*. Many changes have occurred since publication of the last edition, the most striking being the proliferation of information about our state now available on the World Wide Web. This edition is longer mainly because it contains hundreds of references to web sites and electronic mail addresses for state and federal agencies, cities, counties, and other organizations.

Whether you are just browsing for information about the state of Oregon or looking for some specific data, the best place to start is the Oregon OnLine web site (www.state.or.us). This site is the top level of a rapidly expanding pyramid of information about almost everything in Oregon from down-loadable business registration forms, to economic data, to live camera shots of Keiko the whale in Newport.

Oregon OnLine provides four basic links which cover govern-ment, communities, commerce and education. As much as possible in this edition of the Blue Book we have included the addresses for specific web sites to make it easier to find the information you need.

Another interesting aspect of this Blue Book is that it includes at least one photograph from each of Oregon's 36 counties. The contest to select a cover photo for this year's book attracted almost 200 entrants who submitted more than 1,000 photos. From the many wonderful photos we received we selected 38 to use inside the book. I am pleased with this comprehensive photo coverage of the state, and thank all those who spent time and energy to send in their photos for our consideration.

I hope you find this edition of the Oregon Blue Book informative, interesting and enjoyable. Please let us know how we can make it even more valuable in future years.

Best,

Phil Keisling

Phil Keisling
Secretary of State

Dedication

Adversity often brings out courage and heroism in people who do not know they have it in them. This was certainly the case during the floods of 1996. Oregon was hit hard in February by some of the worst flooding this century and then, just after many people had finished a summer of rebuilding and cleaning up, the state was flooded again in November when rivers rose once more.

During the February 1996 floods, 26 Oregon rivers reached or exceeded flood stage, 18 counties were declared federal disaster areas, and seven Oregonians lost their lives. Despite the raging waters and mudslides throughout the state, people came out to help. They helped with sandbagging, furniture moving, evacuations; where help was needed, Oregonians were there.

Oregon is no stranger to floods. The Christmas week floods of 1964 devastated many parts of the state and claimed almost 50 lives. A 1948 flood on the Columbia River wiped out the city of Vanport, a wartime community built on the river's flood plain. The Heppner flood of 1903, killing 251 residents of this small Morrow County town, is another sad story in Oregon's flood history. Through each of these natural disasters, however, there is a common thread of people helping people—Oregonians helping Oregonians.

This 44th edition of the *Oregon Blue Book* is dedicated to all Oregonians who turned out to help hold back the 1996 floodwaters, who rescued those in immediate danger, and most of all those who participated in the massive clean-up efforts. For weeks after the waters receded, many Oregonians voluntarily worked long and hard to help flood victims clean up the mud and debris left in homes and businesses. The outpouring of community support was also heartwarming with donations of food, clothing and household items in bountiful supply.

Oregon's climate and geography make it inevitable that the state will experience devastating floods again in the future. We can take some comfort in the knowledge that when they are needed most, Oregonians will be there to help each other.

National Guard members and citizens of Lake Oswego passed sandbags along a human chain in an effort to shore up a barricade keeping Lake Oswego from spilling over its banks.
Photo by © Bob Ellis, courtesy of The Oregonian.

Fellow Oregonians:

In the past two years I have had the opportunity to speak with many Oregonians about our state and what they think of it. An underlying theme in all the answers is "quality of life," a term that means something different to everyone. Yet Oregon's quality of life is prized by all residents, whether they love the bustle of the city, the beauty of the coast, or the thrill of world-class skiing.

The *Oregon Blue Book* paints a comprehensive picture of our great state. This picture helps explain the quality of life so precious to state residents. With chapters describing the history, cultural opportunities, educational offerings, economic statistics, natural resources and much more, the Blue Book provides a wealth of information to residents and non-residents alike.

In addition, the Blue Book offers an in-depth explanation of the executive, judicial and legislative branches of government, complete with details about the people who make our government work. The availability of phone and fax numbers, Email addresses and web sites allows concerned citizens to easily contact legislators, state and federal agencies, cities and counties, and other organizations.

As Oregon completes the transition from a natural resource-based economy to one based on high technology and information exchange, it becomes increasingly important to have well-educated and well-informed citizens. The Blue Book provides citizens with much of the information they need about their state and its government to understand the choices that must be made to preserve our quality of life.

To provide information from my office in a timely and accurate manner, I have established a site on the World Wide Web (www.governor.state.or.us) which is regularly updated with news releases, policy reports and other information of interest to state residents. I invite you to visit this web site for the latest information about what is happening in Oregon.

Sincerely,

John A. Kitzhaber
Governor

INTRODUCTION

Offshore rocks and sandy beaches are typical of the beautiful southern Oregon Coast. Photo by Barnett Howard.

FACTS, figures and symbols provide background from which to build our comprehension of the state, its people and its institutions. Symbols like the salmon and the Douglas Fir, along with the father of Oregon, the state dance and the state song, put Oregon in context. These symbols merge past and future with political, cultural, heritage and environmental aspects of Oregon. The almanac rounds out the picture with information about demographics, geography and economics. We hope you enjoy this first glimpse of Oregon.

Symbols of Oregon

State Flag

The Oregon state flag, adopted in 1925, is navy blue with gold lettering and symbols. Blue and gold are the state colors. On the flag's face the legend "STATE OF OREGON" is written above a shield which is surrounded by 33 stars. Below the shield, which is part of the state seal, is written "1859," the year of Oregon's admission to the union as the 33rd state.

The flag's reverse side depicts a beaver. Oregon has the distinction of being the only state in the union whose flag has a different pattern on the reverse side. The dress or parade flag has a gold fringe, and the utility flag has a plain border.

State Motto

"She Flies With Her Own Wings" was adopted by the 1987 Legislature as the state motto. The phrase originated with Judge Jessie Quinn Thornton and was pictured on the territorial seal in Latin: *Alis Volat Propiis*. The new motto replaces "The Union," which was adopted in 1957.

State Seal

The state seal consists of an escutcheon, or shield, supported by 33 stars and divided by an ordinary, or ribbon, with the inscription "The Union." Above the ordinary are the mountains and forests of Oregon, an elk with branching antlers, a covered wagon and ox team, the Pacific Ocean with setting sun, a departing British man-of-war signifying the departure of British influence in the region and an arriving American merchant ship signifying the rise of American power. Below the ordinary is a quartering with a sheaf of wheat, plow and pickax, which represent Oregon's mining and agricultural resources. The crest is the American Eagle. Around the perimeter of the seal is the legend "State of Oregon 1859."

A resolution adopted by the Constitutional Convention in session on September 17, 1857, authorized the president to appoint a committee of three—Benjamin F. Burch, L.F. Grover and James K. Kelly—to report on a proper device for the seal of the state of Oregon. Harvey Gordon created a draft, to which the committee recommended certain additions that are all incorporated in the state seal.

The Name "Oregon"

The first written record of the name "Oregon" comes to us from a 1765 proposal for a journey written by Major Robert Rogers, an English army officer. It reads, "The rout ... is from the Great Lakes towards the Head of the Mississippi, and from thence to the River called by the Indians Ouragon. ..." His proposal rejected, Rogers reapplied in 1772, using the spelling "Ourigan."

The first printed use of the current spelling appeared in Captain Jonathan Carver's 1778 book, "Travels Through the Interior Parts of North America 1766, 1767 and 1768." He listed the four great rivers of the continent, including "the River Oregon, or the River of the West, that falls into the Pacific Ocean at the Straits of Annian."

Father of Oregon

The 1957 Legislature bestowed upon Dr. John McLoughlin the honorary title of "Father of Oregon" in recognition of his great contributions to the early development of the Oregon Country. Dr. McLoughlin originally came to the Northwest region in 1824 as a representative of the Hudson's Bay Company.

Mother of Oregon

Honored by the 1987 Legislature as Mother of Oregon, Tabitha Moffatt Brown "represents the distinctive pioneer heritage and the charitable and compassionate nature of Oregon's people." At 66 years of age, she financed her own wagon for the trip from Missouri to Oregon. The boarding school for orphans

that she established later became known as Tualatin Academy and eventually was chartered as Pacific University.

Historian Laureate

For his years as keeper of Oregon's memory and heritage, the 1989 Legislature named Thomas Vaughan historian laureate of Oregon. His dedicated leadership and distinguished record of professional study and publication have brought worldwide recognition to the Oregon Historical Society and contributed greatly to historical interest and knowledge.

State Animal

The American Beaver (*Castor canadensis*) was named Oregon state animal by the 1969 Legislature. Prized for its fur, the beaver was overtrapped by early settlers and eliminated from much of its original range. Through proper management and partial protection, the beaver has been reestablished in watercourses throughout the state and remains an important economic asset. The beaver has been referred to as "nature's engineer," and its dam-building activities are important to natural water flow and erosion control. Oregon is known as the "Beaver State" and Oregon State University's athletic teams are called the "Beavers."

State Bird

The Western Meadowlark (*Sturnella neglecta*) was chosen state bird in 1927 by Oregon's school children in a poll sponsored by the Oregon Audubon

Society. Native throughout western North America, the bird has brown plumage with buff and black markings. Its underside is bright yellow with a black crescent on the breast; its outer tail feathers are mainly white and are easily visible when it flies. The Western Meadowlark is known for its distinctive and beautiful song.

State Dance

In 1977 the Legislature declared the Square Dance to be the official state dance. The dance is a combination of various steps and figures danced with four couples grouped in a square. The pioneer origins of the dance and the characteristic dress are deemed to reflect Oregon's heritage; the lively spirit of the dance exemplifies the friendly, free nature and enthusiasm that are a part of the Oregon Character.

State Fish

The Chinook Salmon (*Oncorhynchus tshawytscha*), also known as spring, king and tyee salmon, is the largest of the Pacific salmons and the most highly prized for the fresh fish trade. Declared state fish by the 1961 Oregon Legislature, the Chinook Salmon is found from southern California to the Canadian Arctic. Record catches of 53 inches and 126 pounds have been reported.

State Flower

The Legislature designated the Oregon Grape (*Berberis aquifolium*) as the Oregon state flower by resolution in 1899. A low growing

plant, the Oregon Grape is native to much of the Pacific Coast and found sparsely east of the Cascades. Its year-round foliage of pinnated, waxy green leaves resembles holly. The plant bears dainty yellow flowers in early summer and a dark blue berry that ripens late in the fall. The fruit can be used in cooking.

State Gemstone

The 1987 Legislature designated the Oregon sunstone as the official state gemstone. Uncommon in its composition, clarity, and

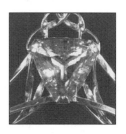

colors, it is a large, brightly colored transparent gem in the feldspar family. The Oregon sunstone attracts collectors and miners and has been identified as a boon to tourism and economic development in southeastern Oregon counties.

State Insect

In 1979 the Legislature designated the Oregon Swallowtail (*Papilio oregonius*) as Oregon's official insect. A true native of the

Northwest, the Oregon Swallowtail is at home in the lower sagebrush canyons of the Columbia River and its tributaries, including the Snake River drainage. This strikingly beautiful butterfly, predominantly yellow, is a wary, strong flier not easily captured.

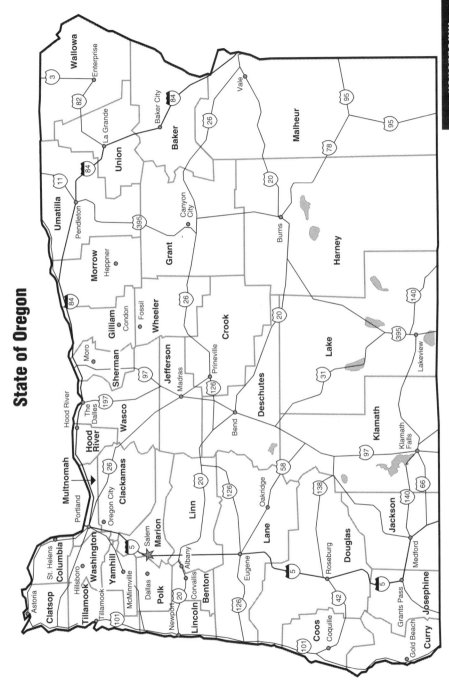

State of Oregon

State Nut

The hazelnut (*Corylus avellana*) was named state nut by the 1989 Legislature. Oregon grows 99 percent of the entire U.S. commercial crop. The Oregon hazelnut, unlike wild varieties, grows on single-trunked trees up to 30 or 40 feet tall. Adding a unique texture and flavor to recipes and products, hazelnuts are preferred by chefs, bakers, confectioners, food manufacturers and homemakers worldwide.

State Rock

The Thunder-egg (geode) was named state rock by the 1965 Legislature after rockhounds throughout Oregon voted it first choice. Thundereggs range in diameter from less than one inch to over four feet. Nondescript on the outside, they reveal exquisite designs in a wide range of colors when cut and polished. They are found chiefly in Crook, Jefferson, Malheur, Wasco and Wheeler counties.

State Seashell

In 1848, a conchologist (shell expert) named Redfield named the *Fusitriton oregonensis* after the Oregon Territory. Commonly called the Oregon hairy triton, the shell is one of the largest found in the state, reaching lengths up to five inches. The shells are found from Alaska to California and wash up on the Oregon coast at high tide. The Legislature named the state shell in 1991.

State Song

J.A. Buchanan of Astoria and Henry B. Murtagh of Portland wrote "Oregon, My Oregon," in 1920. With this song, Buchanan and Murtagh won a statewide competition sponsored by the Society of Oregon Composers, gaining statewide recognition. The song became the official state song in 1927.

State Tree

The Douglas Fir (*Pseudotsuga menziesii*), named for David Douglas, a 19th century Scottish botanist, was designated state tree in 1939. Great strength, stiffness and moderate weight make it an invaluable timber product said to be stronger than concrete. Averaging up to 200' in height and six feet in diameter, heights of 325' and diameters of 15' can also be found.

Oregon Almanac of Facts and Figures

This collection of facts and figures, though in no way complete, offers a cross section of significant information about Oregon and should prove helpful to those embarking on a study of the state.

Abbreviation, Oregon: Ore., Oreg. (traditional), OR (postal)

Airports: 51 (public), 244 (private)

Altitudes:

    Highest: Mt. Hood (Clackamas and Hood River counties) 11,240'

    Lowest: Pacific Ocean, sea level

Apportionment, U.S. House of Representatives:

    1860—1, 1870—1, 1880—1, 1890—2, 1900—2, 1910—3, 1920—3, 1930—3, 1940—4, 1950—4, 1960—4, 1970—4, 1980—5, 1990—5

Architects: (1996)	2,500
Attorneys: active (1996)	10,851

Awards (Nobel, Pulitzer Prizes):

    1934 *Medford Mail Tribune*—Pulitzer, Journalism

    1939 Ronald Callvert, *The Oregonian*—Pulitzer, Editorial Writing

    1954 Linus Pauling—Nobel, Chemistry

    1957 Wallace Turner and William Lambert, *The Oregonian*—Pulitzer, Reporting (No Edition Time)

    1962 Linus Pauling—Nobel, Peace

Births: (1995) 42,715

Borders and Boundaries: Washington on north (1853), California on south (1819), Idaho on east (1863), Pacific Ocean on west, Nevada on southeast

Buildings, Tallest: (Portland)

	Ht.	/Stories
First Interstate Bank Tower	546'	41
U.S. Bancorp Tower	536'	39
KOIN Tower Plaza	509'	35
Standard Insurance Center	367'	27
Pacwest Center	356'	31

Campsites: (1996) Overnight use
Oregonians 55%
Nonresidents 45%

Chiropractic Physicians: (1996) 1,368

Cities, Total: (Incorp.) 240
Largest population: Portland, Eugene, Salem, Gresham, Beaverton, Medford

Counselors, Licensed Professional: (1996) 991

Counties, Total: 36
Largest area, sq. mi.: Harney, Malheur, Lake, Klamath, Douglas
Smallest area, sq. mi.: Multnomah, Hood River, Benton, Columbia, Yamhill
Largest population: Multnomah, Washington, Lane, Clackamas, Marion

Deaths: (1995) 28,190

Dental Hygienists: (1996) 1,887

Dentists: (1996) 2,199

Dissolutions and Annulments: (1995) 15,289

Electoral Votes for President: 7

Geographic Center: Crook (25 miles south-southeast of Prineville)

Geyser: Old Perpetua (60' into air—north edge of Lakeview)

Gorge, Deepest: Hell's Canyon (7,900'—Snake River, Oregon and Idaho)

Hot Springs: (Partial list) Austin, Bagby, Breitenbush, Cove Swimming Pool, Kah-Nee-Ta, Lehman, Radium

Hydropower Projects, Largest:

	Completed	River	U.S. Rank
John Day	1968	Columbia	3
The Dalles	1957	Columbia	6
Bonneville	1937	Columbia	12

Other Major Dams in Oregon
Owyhee (1932), McNary (1954)

Insurance Agents: (1996) 25,123

Jails/Correctional Institutions: (1996) 103 jails; 12 state, 1 federal prison

Judicial Districts: 22

Lake, Deepest: Crater Lake
(deepest in U.S.) 1,932'

Lakes, Total: (Named) 1,400

Legal Holidays and Days of Special Observance:

New Year's Day: Jan. 1, 1997; Jan. 1, 1998; Jan. 1, 1999

Martin Luther King Jr.'s Birthday: Third Monday in January Observed: Jan. 20, 1997; Jan. 19, 1998; Jan. 18, 1999

Presidents Day: Third Monday in February Observed: Feb. 17, 1997; Feb. 16, 1998; Feb. 15, 1999

Memorial Day: Fourth Monday in May Observed: May 26, 1997; May 25 1998; May 24, 1999

Independence Day: Observed: July 4, 1997; July 3, 1998; July 5, 1999

Labor Day: First Monday in September Observed: Sept. 1, 1997; Sept. 7, 1998; Sept. 6, 1999

Veterans Day: Nov. 11, 1997; Nov. 11, 1998; Nov. 11, 1999

Thanksgiving Day: Fourth Thursday in November Observed: Nov. 27, 1997; Nov. 26, 1998; Nov. 25, 1999

Christmas Day: Observed: Dec. 25, 1997; Dec. 25, 1998; Dec. 24, 1999

In addition to the standing holidays described above, other days may be legal holidays in Oregon. These are: every day appointed by the governor as a holiday; and every day appointed by the president of the United States as a day of mourning, rejoicing or other special observance when the governor also appoints that day as a holiday.

If any of the above holiday dates falls on Sunday, the succeeding Monday will be a legal holiday. If the holiday falls on Saturday, the preceding Friday will be a legal holiday. According to law, any act authorized or required to be performed on a holiday may be performed on the next succeeding business day without any liability or loss of rights.

While many school districts do not close on Martin Luther King Day, and many have consolidated the days honoring Presidents Washington and Lincoln, the schools are directed to set aside classroom time to honor these men and their ideals. Teachers and administrators also arrange for activities in honor of Women in History Week, the second week in March, and Arbor Week, the first full week in April.

At various intervals throughout the year, the governor also proclaims days or weeks to give special recognition and attention to individuals or groups and to promote issues and causes.

Lighthouses: Cape Arago, Cape Blanco, Cape Meares, Coquille River, Heceta Head, Umpqua, Yaquina Bay, Yaquina Head

Maritime Pilots: (1996)	70
Marriages: (1995)	25,292

Mileage Distances, Road:
(from Portland)

Albuquerque, New Mexico	1,372
Atlanta, Georgia	2,664
Boise, Idaho	432
Chicago, Illinois	2,117
Denver, Colorado	1,261
Fargo, North Dakota	1,488
Houston, Texas	2,243
Los Angeles, California	962
Miami, Florida	3,257
New York, New York	2,914
Omaha, Nebraska	1,692
Phoenix, Arizona	1,268
Saint Louis, Missouri	2,057
Salt Lake City, Utah	763
San Francisco, California	637
Seattle, Washington	172

Mountains, Major:

Coast Range: (highest elevation, Mary's Peak, 4,097'/1,249 meters) is 200 miles/320 km. long and 30-60 miles/50-100 km. wide, and extends along Oregon's coast in the west

Klamath Mountains: sometimes called the Siskiyou Mountains (highest elevation, Mt. Ashland, 7,533'/2,296 meters) extends southeast from the Coast Range near the California border

Cascade Range: (highest elevation, Mt. Hood, 11,240'/3,426 meters) extends the entire length of Oregon east of the Willamette River valley. The Deschutes-Umatilla plateau (up to 6,900'/2,100 meters) is located east of the Cascades. Northeast of the plateau is the Blue Mountain region, including the Wallowa Mountains and the Elkhorn and Greenhorn ranges. Southeastern Oregon is made up of two distinct surfaces: the high lava plains averaging 4,000'/1,200 meters elevation and, further south, the Basin and Range Province (highest point, Steens Mountain, 9,670'/3,968 meters

Names, Oregon Geographic:
(Language of Origin)

English 81%	Indian 8.3%
made up 2.7%	German 2.1%
French 1.4%	Spanish 1.4%
Norse 0.6%	Greek 0.5%
Hebrew 0.5%	unknown 0.5%
Latin 0.3%	Italian 0.3%
Oriental 0.2%	Portugese 0.1%

National Cemeteries:
Willamette (98,000 veterans); Eagle Point (6,701 veterans and spouses); Roseburg (closed; 5,200 veterans)

National Fish Hatcheries:
Eagle Creek, Warm Springs

National Forests: Deschutes, Fremont, Malheur, Mount Hood, Ochoco, Rogue River, Siskiyou, Siuslaw, Umatilla, Umpqua, Wallowa-Whitman, Willamette, Winema

National Monuments:
John Day Fossil Beds (1974), Newberry National Volcanic Monument (1990), Oregon Caves (1909)

National Park: Crater Lake (1902)

National Recreation Areas: Hell's Canyon (1975), Oregon Dunes (1972)

National Scenic Areas:
Columbia River Gorge

National Trail, Historic: (Oregon Trail) 2,000 miles/3,200 km. from Independence, Missouri (near the Missouri River) to Fort Kearny, Nebraska; up the Platte River and its north branch to Fort Laramie, Wyoming; along the North Platte to its Sweetwater branch; crossed through the South Pass in the Rocky Mountains to the Green River Valley at Fort Bridger, Wyoming; turned northwest to Fort Hall in the Snake River area, and on to Fort Boise, Idaho; crossed the Grande Ronde Valley and the Blue Mountains to Marcus Whitman's mission at Walla Walla, Washington; traveled down the Columbia River to Fort Vancouver and the Willamette Valley of Oregon

National Wildlife Refuges
Ankeny, Bandon Marsh, Baskett Slough, Bear Valley, Cape Mears, Cold Springs, Julia Butler Hansen (Columbian White-tailed Deer), Hart Mountain (Antelope), Klamath Marsh, Lower Klamath, Malheur, McKay Creek, Oregon Islands, Three Arch Rocks, Umatilla Complex, Upper Klamath, William L. Finley

Oregon Olympic Medalists
(1906–1996)

1906

Kerrigan, Bert H.W.	High Jump	Bronze

1908

Gilbert, Alfred C.	Pole Vault	Gold
Kelly, Dan	Long Jump	Silver
Smithson, Forrest	Hurdles	Gold

1912

Hawkins, Martin	Hurdles	Bronze

1920

Balbach, Louis J.	Diving	Bronze
Kuehn, Louis (Hap)	Diving	Gold
Ross, Norman	Swimming	Gold(3)
Samborn-Payne, Thelma	Diving	Bronze
Sears, Robert	Fencing	Bronze

1924

Newton, Chester	Wrestling	Silver
Reed, Robin	Wrestling	Gold

1928

Hamm, Edward B.	Broad Jump	Gold

1932

Graham, Norris	Rowing	Gold
Hill, Ralph	Track and Field	Silver
LaBorde, Henri J.	Discus	Silver

1936

Dunn, Gordon G.	Discus	Silver

1948

Beck, Lewis W. Jr.	Basketball	Gold
Brown, David P.	Rowing	Gold
Gordien, Fortune	Discus	Bronze
Helser (DeMorelos), Brenda	Swimming	Gold
Zimmerman-Edwards, Suzanne	Swimming	Silver

1952

Proctor, Hank	Rowing	Gold
Smith, William T.	Wrestling	Gold

1956

Fifer, James	Rowing	Gold
Gordien, Fortune	Discus	Silver
Tarala, Harold	Ice Hockey	Gold

1960

Dischinger, Terry G.	Basketball	Gold
Imhoff, Darrall	Basketball	Gold

1964

Carr, Ken	Basketball	Gold
Counts, Mel G.	Basketball	Gold
Dellinger, William S.	Track and Field	Bronze
Saubert, Jean M.	Skiing	Silver/Bronze

1968

Fosbury, Richard D.	High Jump	Gold
Garrigus, Thomas I.	Trapshooting	Silver
Sanders, Richard J.	Wrestling	Silver

1972

Peyton McDonald, Kim M.	Swimming	Gold
Sanders, Richard J.	Wrestling	Silver

1976

Peyton McDonald, Kim M.	Swimming	Gold
Wilkins, Mac M.	Discus	Gold

1984

Burke, Douglas L.	Water Polo	Silver
Herland, Douglas J.	Rowing Pairs	Bronze
Huntley (Ruete), Joni	High Jump	Bronze
Johnson, William D.	Skiing	Gold
King (Brown), Judith L.	Track and Field	Silver
Menken-Schaudt, Carol J.	Basketball	Gold
Schultz, Mark P.	Wrestling	Gold
Wilkins, Mac M.	Discus	Silver

1988

Brown, Cynthia L.	Basketball	Gold
Lang, Brent	Swimming	Gold

1992

Jorgenson, Dan	Swimming	Bronze

1994

Street, Picabo	Skiing	Silver

1996

Deal, Lance	Hammer	Silver
MacMillan, Shannon	Soccer	Gold
Milbrett, Tiffany	Soccer	Gold
Schneider, Marcus	Rowing	Bronze
Steding, Katy	Basketball	Gold

Olympic medal information courtesy of Jack Elder, 1998 Nike World Masters Games.

Native Americans: 9 tribes, 6 reservations, 34,496 individuals (1990 census)

Nurse Practitioners: (1996)   1,200

Nurses: (1996)
RN   32,000
LPN   6,000

Nursing Home Administrators:
(1996)   500

Occupational Therapists: (1996)   868

Olympic medalists: (1912-1996)
32 gold, 16 silver, 12 bronze (See table on page 10 for list of Oregon Olympic medalists)

Optometrists: (1996)   571

Parks, State: (1996)   224

Pharmacists: (1996)   2,484

Physical Dimensions:
Rank in area: (United States)   10
Land area:
97,060 sq. mi./251,418 km.
Inland Water area:
889 sq. mi./2,302 km.
Coastline: 296 mi./476 km.

Physical Therapists: (1996)   2,279

Physicians: (1996)   10,793

Pilots: (1996)   8,000

Population:
(in Oregon by Official Census):

1850	12,093	1930	953,786
1860	52,465	1940	1,089,684
1870	90,923	1950	1,521,341
1880	174,768	1960	1,768,687
1890	317,704	1970	2,091,533
1900	413,536	1980	2,633,321
1910	672,765	1990	2,842,321
1920	783,389	1994	3,082,000

Precipitation, Record Maximum:
(24 hours, through 1996)
Measured at Elk River Fish Hatchery, 5 miles east of Port Orford:
11.65" on November 19, 1996
Average yearly precipitation at Salem: 39.16"

Psychologists: (1996)   943

Radiologic Technologists:
(1996)   2,122

Real Estate Appraisers: (1996)   1,300

Real Estate Brokers: (1996)   6,172

Reservoir, Longest: Lake Owyhee

Rivers, Longest:
Columbia   1,243 miles
Willamette   309 miles
Klamath   250 miles

Schools: (1996)
Education Service Districts: 21
School Districts: 220
Students, Public School: 561,500

Shoes, Oldest: 9,000-year-old sandals made of sage brush and bark found at Silver Lake in Central Oregon in 1938

Skiing
Downhill: (Partial list) Mt. Hood Meadows, Cooper Spur, Timberline Lodge, Summit, Ski Bowl, Spout Springs, Anthony Lakes
Cross Country: (National forests) Mt. Hood, Willamette, Deschutes, Ochoco, Malheur, Umatilla, Wallowa-Whitman, Hell's Canyon

Speech/Language Pathologists:
(1996)   1,014

Standard of Time: The state of Oregon has officially adopted the standard of time established by Congress in 1918. The one exception to this occurs every spring when Oregon goes on daylight-saving time. At 2 a.m. on the first Sunday in April (April 6, 1997; April 5, 1998; April 4, 1999) the state "springs forward" one hour. At 2 a.m. on the last Sunday in October (Oct. 26, 1997; Oct. 25, 1998; Oct. 31, 1999) the state "falls back" one hour. Most of the state is in the Pacific Standard Time zone. However, a small portion near the Idaho border is on Mountain Standard Time, one hour ahead.

Tax Preparers: (1996)   1,840

Temperatures, Record:
(High, Low, Average)
Highest: 119° F, 48° C July 29, 1898, in Prineville (elevation 2,868') 119° F, 48° C Aug. 10, 1938 in Pendleton (elevation 1,068')
Lowest: -54° F, -48° C Feb. 9, 1933 in Ukiah (elevation 3,347') -54° F, -48° C Feb. 10, 1933 in Seneca (elevation 4,666')
Average Jan./July temp.:

Burns	Jan. 23.3° F	-4.83° C
	July 66.2° F	19.0° C
Grants Pass	Jan. 40.2° F	4.55° C
	July 71.7° F	22.05° C
Newport	Jan. 43.9° F	6.61° C
	July 57.1° F	13.94° C
Redmond	Jan. 31.4° F	.33° C
	July 65.9° F	18.83° C
Salem	Jan. 39.6° F	4.22° C
	July 66.3° F	19.0° C

Trees, Giant:

Big Leaf Maple: National champion, 34' 11" circumference, 101' tall, located near Jewell near junction of highways 202 and 103.

Black Cottonwood: National champion, 26' 8" circumference, 158' tall, located in Willamette Mission State Park, 8 miles north of Salem

Black Walnut: National champion, 23' 2" circumference, 130' tall, located on Sauvie Island at 22236 NW Gillihan Road.

California White Fir: National champion, 19' 3" circumference, 175' tall, located adjacent to Jefferson Lake Trail near Sisters.

Coastal Douglas Fir: National champion, 36' 6" circumference, 329' tall, located on BLM land northeast of Sitkum.

Ponderosa Pine; National co-champion, 28' 6" circumference, 178' tall, located in La Pine State Park.

Port Orford Cedar: National champion, 37' 7" circumference, 219' tall, located 9.8 miles southeast of Powers on the Elk Creek Road in a picnic area.

Rocky Mountain Douglas Fir: National champion, 24' 7" circumference, 114' tall, located adjacent to Jefferson Lake Trail near Sisters.

Sitka Spruce: National co-champion, 56' 1" circumference, 206" tall, located near the junction of highways 101 and 26 in Clatsop County's Klootchy Creek Park.

Visit the Oregon Department of Forestry's world wide web site for more information about Oregon's biggest trees: www.odf.state.or.us

Veterinarians: (1996)   1,300

Water, Largest Natural Body:
Malheur Lake, south of Burns

Waterfalls, Highest:
Multnomah Falls   620'

EXECUTIVE

A hot air balloon floats lazily over tulip fields near the Willamette Valley community of Mt. Angel. Photo by Albert H. Russell.

THE people of Oregon elect six statewide officials to administer and manage state agencies. The officials comprise the governor, secretary of state, treasurer, attorney general, commissioner of labor and industries and superintendent of public instruction. Every two years, the governor is responsible for submitting a budget to the Legislature covering all state agencies. Together these officials and their departments are considered the executive section of state government.

JOHN A. KITZHABER was born in Colfax, Washington. He graduated from Dartmouth College in 1969. He received his medical training at the University of Oregon and graduated with his medical degree in 1973. Kitzhaber practiced emergency medicine in Roseburg for 13 years. He serves on the faculty of the Estes Park Institute and has been a clinical professor at Oregon Health Sciences University since 1989.

He was elected to the Oregon House of Representatives in 1978 and to the Oregon Senate in 1980, where he served three terms. As Senate president from 1985 to 1993, he oversaw legislation that included the Oregon Health Plan, the Oregon Education Act for the 21st Century and the Oregon Forest Practices Act. In 1994, he was elected Governor.

Kitzhaber received national attention for authoring the groundbreaking Oregon Health Plan. In 1992 he received the American Medical Association's Dr. Nathan Davis Award recognizing his outstanding contributions in health care.

He has also been recognized for his environmental stewardship, as demonstrated by his receipt of the prestigious Neuberger Award given by the Oregon Environmental Council.

Governor John A. Kitzhaber

254 State Capitol, Salem 97310; 503-378-3111

Governor John Kitzhaber, Salem; Democrat; elected 1994; inaugurated January 9, 1995; term expires January 1999.

The governor is elected to a four-year term and is limited to two terms in office. The governor must be a U.S. citizen, at least 30 years old, and an Oregon resident for three years before taking office.

The governor provides leadership, planning and coordination for the executive branch of state government. He appoints many department and agency heads within the executive branch and appoints members to more than 200 policy-making, regulatory and advisory boards and commissions.

The governor proposes a two-year budget to the Legislature, recommends a legislative program to each regular session and may also call special sessions. He reviews all bills passed by the Legislature and may veto measures he believes are not in the public interest.

The governor chairs both the State Land Board, which manages state-owned lands, and the Progress Board, which sets strategic goals for Oregon. The governor directs state government's coordination with local and federal governments and is commander-in-chief of the state's military forces.

The governor appoints judges to fill vacancies in judicial office, has extradition authority and may grant reprieves, commutations and pardons of criminal sentences.

If the office of governor becomes vacant, the office passes, in order, to the secretary of state, state treasurer, president of the Senate and speaker of the House of Representatives.

For additional information, see page 20.

PHIL KEISLING, Oregon's 22nd secretary of state, was born June 23, 1955. He graduated from Beaverton's Sunset High in 1973 and received a B.A. from Yale College in 1977.

Prior to his appointment as secretary of state by Governor Barbara Roberts in 1991, he served as a speechwriter for former Governor Tom McCall; a reporter for Willamette Week newspaper; an editor of the Washington Monthly magazine in Washington, D.C.; and a senior assistant to former House Speaker Vera Katz. He was elected state representative from House District 12 in 1988 and reelected in 1990.

After serving by appointment, Keisling was elected to the secretary of state's position in 1992 and reelected in 1996.

As secretary of state, Phil Keisling completed the 1991 legislative redistricting plan and in 1996 conducted the nation's first Vote-by-Mail election for a federal office. He has also led successful efforts to implement "motor voter" registration; create a "Forest Resource Trust" to rehabilitate Oregon land; establish a one-stop "Central Business Clearinghouse" for start-up businesses; reform campaign finance; and to expand financial and performance-related auditing to ensure government accountability for taxpayer dollars. He and his wife Pam Wiley have two children.

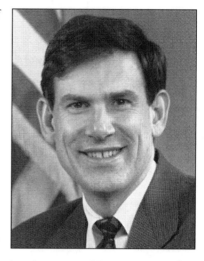

Secretary of State Phil Keisling

136 State Capitol, Salem 97310; 503-986-1500

Phil Keisling, Portland; Democrat; appointed 1991; elected 1992, reelected 1996; term expires January 2001. The secretary of state is the auditor of public accounts and chief elections officer, keeps records of official acts of the Legislature and Executive Department, is custodian of the state seal, has responsibility for the State Archives, and oversees the Corporation Division.

As auditor, the secretary examines and audits accounts of all state boards, commissions and agencies. As chief elections officer, he interprets and applies state election laws and supervises all elections, local and statewide. The secretary codifies, edits, and publishes the administrative rules for state agencies, processes public documents, prepares notarial applications, and serves as filing officer for Uniform Commercial Code financial statements and security agreements.

The Archives Division has custody of state historical documents and other state public records. The secretary of state also publishes the *Oregon Blue Book.*

The Corporation Division registers all domestic and foreign businesses, profit and nonprofit corporations, assumed business names and trade and service marks. The Board of Accountancy licenses and oversees the professional competence of certified public accountants. The Tax Service Examiners Board licenses consultants and paid preparers of income tax returns. These boards are located in the Secretary of State agency for administrative support purposes only.

As a member of the State Land Board, the secretary shares responsibility with the governor and state treasurer in supervising management of state-owned lands, including offshore, grazing and timberlands; coastal estuarine tidelands; and submerged and submersible lands along the state's navigable waterways.

For additional information, see page 20.

JIM HILL was born in Atlanta, Georgia, on April 23, 1947. He attended Our Lady of Lourdes Elementary School in Atlanta and St. Emma Military Academy in Powhatan, Virginia. He graduated from Michigan State University with a B.A. in Economics, 1969 and received a Masters in Business Administration and Doctor of Jurisprudence from Indiana University.

He was elected to the Oregon House in 1982, reelected in 1984; elected to the Oregon Senate in 1986 and reelected 1990. He served as chair of the Senate Committee on Business, Housing and Finance, vice chair of the Senate Committee on the Judiciary and House co-chair of the Joint Committee on Trade and Economic Development. He also held memberships on Senate committees on Trade and Economic Development, Senate Interim Transportation Committee and Senate committees on the Judiciary, Elections, Agriculture, Forestry and Natural Resources.

His professional background includes Corporate Accounts Manager for Latin America, Mentor Graphics Corporation; Director of Marketing, PEN-NOR Inc.; Personnel Specialist and Consultant, State Farm Insurance; Hearings Referee, Oregon Department of Revenue; Assistant Attorney General, Oregon Department of Justice.

State Treasurer Jim Hill

159 State Capitol, Salem 97310-0804; 503-378-4329

Jim Hill, Salem; Democrat; elected 1992; reelected 1996; term expires January 2001. The state treasurer is a constitutional officer and a statewide elected official.

The treasurer serves as the chief financial officer for the state and is responsible for the prudent financial management of state money. The treasurer also serves as the state's chief investment officer, and has the duty of investing the moneys of the Public Employes Retirement Fund, the State Accident Insurance Fund, the Common School Fund and other trust and general funds.

The treasurer serves on a variety of state financial boards and on the State Land Board which is charged with managing natural resources that are under the ownership of the state on behalf of the Common School Fund. The treasurer serves a four-year term and, if reelected, can hold the position for two terms.

Over the years, the Oregon State Treasury has developed into a highly sophisticated organization with a wide range of financial responsibilities, including the issuance of all state debt and serving as the central bank for state agencies. The Treasury is managed like a business, striving to save taxpayers' money and earning the highest risk adjusted return on funds' investments.

The Treasury manages nearly $32 billion. Investments range from common stocks, bonds and Oregon real estate to alternative equity investments, foreign stocks and U.S. Treasuries.

In 1996, the State Treasury had nearly a billion dollars invested in Oregon. That money creates jobs, contributes to a thriving economy and assists economic development.

For additional information, see page 23.

HARDY MYERS was born in Electric Mills, Miss. on October 25, 1939. He was educated in the public schools of Bend and Prineville before graduating from the University of Oregon in 1964 with an LL.B.

Myers served as law clerk to United States District Judge William East from 1964–65. He has been in private law practice with Stoel Rives and predecessor firms since 1965 specializing in labor and employment law and government affairs law. He is a member of the Oregon State Bar and Multnomah County Bar Association.

First elected to the Oregon House of Representatives in 1975, Myers served as a state representative for 10 years and as Speaker of the House from 1979–83. He also served as a Councilor for the Metropolitan Service District from 1985–86.

Other professional activities include serving as co-chair of the Governor's Task Force on State Employee Compensation (1995), chair of the Governor's Task Force on State Employee Benefits (1994), chair of the Oregon Criminal Justice Council (1987–91), chair of the Oregon Jail Project (1984–86) and chair of the Citizen's Task Force on Mass Transit Policy.

Married to Mary Ann Thalhofer of Prineville, the attorney general and his wife live in Portland and have three children.

Attorney General Hardy Myers

Justice Building, Salem 97310; 503-378-6002

Hardy Myers, Portland; Democrat; elected 1996; term expires January 2001. The attorney general is the chief legal officer of the state of Oregon and heads the Department of Justice and its six operating divisions.

The attorney general controls and supervises all court actions and legal proceedings in which the state of Oregon is a party or has an interest. The attorney general also has full charge and control of all legal business of all state departments, boards and commissions that require the services of legal counsel. He prepares ballot titles for measures to be voted upon by the people of Oregon and appoints the assistant attorneys general to act as counsel for the various state departments, boards and commissions.

The attorney general gives written opinions upon any question of law in which the state of Oregon or any public subdivision may have an interest when requested by the governor, any state agency official or any member of the Legislature. The attorney general and his assistants are prohibited by law from rendering opinions or giving legal advice to any other persons or agencies.

Services and responsibilities of the attorney general and the Department of Justice are: representation of the state's interests in all civil and criminal cases before the state and federal courts; consumer protection and information services; supervision of charitable trusts and solicitations; enforcement of state and federal antitrust laws in Oregon; assistance to the state's district attorneys; administration of the state crime victims compensation program; investigations of organized crime and public corruption; and the establishment and enforcement of child support obligations for families who receive public assistance.

The term of office for attorney general is four years. Oregon citizens voted to impose a two-term limit on those holding the office of attorney general.

For additional information, see page 26

JACK ROBERTS was born in Sanford, North Carolina, October 23, 1952. His family moved to Eugene in 1962 where Jack attended Sheldon High School, graduating in 1971. He graduated from the University of Oregon with a bachelor's degree in Journalism in 1975.

He graduated from the University of Oregon School of Law with a J.D. in 1978 and from the New York University School of Law with a Masters of Law in Taxation in 1980, and was admitted to the Oregon State Bar, 1980. He was an attorney in private practice from 1980-89.

Roberts was appointed to the Lane County Board of Commissioners in October, 1989, representing the North Eugene District. He was elected to the Lane County Board of Commissioners in May, 1990, elected chair 1991 and reelected to the board in 1992.

Roberts and his wife, Tammy, have three sons. He was elected labor commissioner in 1994.

Commissioner of Labor and Industries Jack Roberts

800 NE Oregon St., #32, Portland 97232; 503-731-4070

Jack Roberts, Eugene; Republican; elected 1994; term expires January 1999. The commissioner is chief executive of the Oregon Bureau of Labor and Industries. The commissioner also serves as chairperson of the State Apprenticeship and Training Council and executive secretary of the Wage and Hour Commission. The term of the commissioner is four years with a two term limitation.

The commissioner enforces state laws prohibiting discrimination in employment, housing, public accommodation, and vocational, professional and trade schools, and has authority to initiate a "commissioner's complaint" on behalf of victims of discrimination. In addition, he may issue the final order in a contested-case hearing.

Through the Wage and Hour Division, the commissioner administers state laws relating to wages, hours of employment, basic working conditions, child labor and prevailing wage rates, and licenses certain industries to ensure quality

professional services. The division administers the Wage Security Fund which pays workers for wages earned, but not paid in certain business closure situations, and enforces group-health insurance termination-notification provisions.

The commissioner also oversees the state's apprenticeship-training system through the Apprenticeship and Training Division, providing workers with the opportunity to learn a job skill while earning a living. It benefits employers by providing them with a pool of skilled workers to meet business and industry demands.

Through the Office of Administrative Services, the commissioner provides public education programs to help employers comply with the law and conducts administrative hearings. The office also includes a number of support functions such as budget and fiscal control.

For additional information, see page 28.

NORMA PAULUS was born near Belgrade, Nebraska, March 13, 1933. She graduated from Burns High School in 1950, worked as a legal secretary, graduated from Willamette University School of Law in 1962 without attending college and subsequently practiced as an appellate lawyer.

She won election to the Oregon House as Republican representative from Marion County in 1970 and served three terms. She was elected Secretary of State in 1976 and served two terms. In 1986 she was the Republican gubernatorial candidate, and served as an Oregon council member on the Northwest Power Planning Council, 1987-89.

Paulus currently serves on the Willamette University Board of Trustees, is an overseer of Whitman College, and a trustee of the Oregon Graduate Institute of Science and Technology. Awards and honors include: Honorary Doctor of Humane Letters from Lewis and Clark College, 1996; National Assessment Governing Board, 1996; honorary Doctor of Letters from Whitman College, 1990. She was a member of a presidential commission monitoring the 1986 Philippine election; an adjunct professor at Willamette University School of Law; and honorary Doctor of Laws, Linfield College, 1985. She and her husband, Bill, have two adult children.

Superintendent of Public Instruction Norma Paulus

255 Capitol St. NE, Salem 97310; 503-378-3573

Norma Paulus, Salem; Nonpartisan; appointed October 1, 1990; elected in 1990 and 1994; term expires January 1999.

The Oregon Constitution, Article VIII established the office of the State Superintendent of Public Instruction. The superintendent is elected by the people of Oregon every four years and acts as administrative officer of the State Board of Education and executive head of the Department of Education.

The superintendent is responsible for providing statewide leadership for some 561,500 elementary and secondary students in Oregon's 220 school districts. The responsibility also extends to public preschool programs, the state Schools for the Blind and the Deaf, regional programs for children with disabilities and education programs for adjudicated youth. The superintendent recommends policy to the State Board of Education which adopts rules affecting local schools.

The superintendent is in charge of directing the implementation of Oregon's comprehensive school improvement program, the Oregon Education Act for the 21st Century. The 1991 Legislative Assembly created the program to raise academic standards in Oregon schools so students will be ready for the challenges they will face after high school.

In conjunction with the Legislature's actions, the superintendent and State Board of Education set priorities designed to lead the state's efforts in early childhood education; improve education for all students in Oregon's public elementary and secondary schools; reduce unnecessary burdens on classrooms, schools and districts; establish the Department of Education as a research, development and dissemination service; and provide that service with absolute accountability.

For additional information see page 30.

Agencies Headed by Statewide Elected Officials

Public officials, elected statewide, are responsible for the operations of state agencies. The following section describes the operations of the governor's office and the agencies reporting to the other five statewide elected officials.

Office of the Governor

John Kitzhaber, Governor
254 State Capitol, Salem 97310; 503-378-3111; Fax: 503-378-4863; Web: www.governor.state.or.us

Bill Wyatt is Gov. John Kitzhaber's chief of staff. Steve Marks is senior policy adviser. The governor's policy advisers include: Mark Gibson, healthcare, labor and housing; Chip Lazenby, legal counsel; Paula Burgess, natural resources; Olivia Clark, intergovernmental relations; Katy Coba, executive appointments; Roger Bassett, education; Greg Wolf, transportation; Jean Thorne, federal policy; and Al Nunez, advocate for minority and women owned businesses.

Chris Dearth is the legislative director and serves as the liaison to the Legislature. Bob Applegate is communications director. Patty Greenfield is responsible for scheduling. Liz Kiren is the citizen contact coordinator. Sharon Wong is the office manager.

Affirmative Action Office

Raleigh Lewis, Dir.
155 Cottage St. NE, Salem 97310; 503-373-1224; Fax: 503-378-3139

The Affirmative Action Office directs and monitors affirmative action programs in all state agencies, a large portion of which is done on the basis of plans developed by state agencies.

The director of affirmative action works closely with each state agency to assess its recruitment, placement, promotion and training practices with respect to achieving affirmative action goals. The director recommends and participates in affirmative action and Equal Opportunity training for state employees at all levels.

In addition, the director acts as a liaison between the governor's office and several boards and commissions.

Citizens' Representative

Annabelle Jaramillo, Citizens' Representative

State Capitol, Salem 97310; 503-378-4582; Fax: 503-378-4863

The Citizens' Representative Office provides access and help for citizens who have problems, questions, ideas or suggestions about state government. The office uses supervised student interns and volunteer help to work with the heavy volume of mail and telephone calls. The citizens' representative reports regularly to the governor, noting issues in state government that need attention.

The Citizens' Representative Office aims to treat all inquiries fairly, to examine each situation objectively and to respond in a clear and helpful way.

Office of the Secretary of State

Phil Keisling, Secretary of State
Michael Greenfield, Deputy

136 State Capitol, Salem 97310-0722; 503-986-1500; Web: www.sos.state.or.us

The Office of Secretary of State is one of three established at statehood. The secretary is the auditor of public accounts, chief elections officer and manager of the state's records, a role that includes preserving official acts of the Legislative Assembly and the executive branch. The secretary of state serves with the governor and state treasurer on the State Land Board, managing state-owned lands for the benefit of the Common School Fund.

Since the 1995–96 Oregon Blue Book was published, many state agencies have established sites on the World Wide Web to provide information for citizens with access to the Internet. These Web addresses are denoted in the contact information at the top of each agency listing. In addition, many agencies now have Email addresses where questions and requests can be sent.

Executive Division

Michael Greenfield, Deputy
136 State Capitol, Salem 97310-0722;
503-986-1523; Fax: 503-986-1616;
Email: executive-office@sosinet.sos.state.or.us

The Executive Division has management responsibility for the entire agency, and executive staff are responsible for strategic planning, policy development, legislative and press relations, and the publication of the *Oregon Blue Book*.

Archives Division

Roy C. Turnbaugh, State Archivist
800 Summer St. NE, Salem 97310;
503-373-0701; Fax: 503-373-0953;
Email: reference.archives@state.or.us;
Web: arcweb.sos.state.or.us

The Archives Division, founded in 1947, houses and provides access to the permanently valuable records of Oregon government. Oldest documents at the archives include records of the provisional and territorial governments and the Oregon Constitution.

The division provides records management advice and assistance to state agencies and political subdivisions and operates the State Records Center which provides inexpensive storage for inactive state agency records. The division also files, codifies and publishes state agency administrative rules. Statutory authority is ORS 192.001–192.170 and ORS 357.805–357.895.

Historical Records Advisory Board

Roy C. Turnbaugh, State Coord. (Chair)
800 Summer St. NE, Salem 97310; 503-373-0701

The National Historical Records and Publications Commission asked the governor of each state to form an advisory board to review and make recommendations on applications for funding of historical records preservation projects. The NHRPC was set up to locate, identify and arrange for the preservation of historical records of all types: manuscripts, governmental records, private business records, even newspapers. The board meets at the call of the coordinator as requests for grants are received.

Audits Division

John Lattimer, State Auditor
Public Service Bldg., 255 Capitol St. NE,
Suite 500, Salem 97310; 503-986-2255;
Fax: 503-378-6767;
Citizen Hotline: 800-336-8218;
Email: audits.hotline@state.or.us;
Web: www.sos.state.or.us/audits/audithp.htm

The Audits Division has the constitutional and statutory duty to protect the public interest and improve Oregon government by evaluating the financial condition and operations of state agencies. In addition to determining whether public funds are properly accounted for and spent in accordance with legal requirements, the Audits Division works with state agency managers to make government better and more efficient.

The Audits Division also administers the Municipal Audit law, which plays an important role in the public accountability of some 1,700 local governments in Oregon.

In the fall of 1994, the Audits Division began a new outreach effort to encourage citizens and government workers to report waste and misspending of tax dollars. The program includes a Citizen Hotline number that gives citizens a way to offer suggestions on potential audits.

Audit summaries can be found on the division's web site.

Torrential rain in November 1996 caused flooding for the second time that year in the Lane County community of Westfir. High water damaged homes, including property near the historic Workman home.

Photo by John Warner.

Business Services Division

Carol Ann Kirby, CPA, Business Mgr.
Public Service Bldg., 255 Capitol St. NE,
Suite 180, Salem 97310-1342; 503-986-2204;
Fax: 503-378-4991;
Oregon Blue Book Web: www.sos.state.or.us

Bev Mix, Personnel Mgr.
143 State Capitol, Salem 97310-0722;
503-986-1526; Fax: 503-373-0762

Ann Terry, Information Systems Mgr.
Public Service Bldg., 255 Capitol St. NE,
Suite 103, Salem 97310-1360; 503-986-2245;
Fax: 503-378-4991

The Business Services Division is composed of three sections: Business Section, Personnel Resources Section and Information Systems Section. The division provides accounting, budgeting, contracting, personnel resource services, data processing and computer systems development to the Office of the Secretary of State.

Corporation Division

Jan Sullivan, Dir.
Public Service Bldg., 255 Capitol St. NE,
Suite 151, Salem 97310-1327; 503-986-2200;
Fax: 503-986-6355;
Web: www.sos.state.or.us/corporation/corphp.htm

Prior to 1862, an Act of the Oregon Legislature was required to create a corporation. Between 1862 and 1913, corporations were required to file a copy of their charter with the Secretary of State. The Corporation Division was created in 1913 by an Act of the Oregon Legislature.

The Corporation Division now administers four programs: the Business Information Center, Business Registry, Notary Public and Uniform Commercial Code.

The **Business Information Center**, 503-986-2222, is a centralized information site for obtaining information on starting a business in Oregon. The center provides information on state registration and licensing requirements for new businesses. The center mails packets with information and forms for registering a business and refers calls to appropriate agencies or boards for licenses or regulatory information. The *Oregon Business Guide* is available on the Corporation Division's web site.

Business Registry files documents for domestic and foreign corporations, limited partnerships, business trusts, cooperatives, limited liability companies, limited liability partnerships, trade and service marks, and assumed business names doing business in Oregon. It also provides information to the public in the form of copies, certifications, microfilm/fiche, computer-generated reports, computer tapes, and public access through Oregon Ed-Net. Business Registry filing forms are available on the Corporation Division's web site.

Notary Public commissions notaries public, investigates complaints and provides certifications of notarized documents.

Uniform Commercial Code files secured transactions, statutory liens, and administers the Farm Products Program. It performs lien searches and provides information to the public in the form of copies, certifications, microfilm and computer tapes. The UCC database is now available on the Corporation Division's web site.

Elections Division

Colleen Sealock, Dir.
141 State Capitol, Salem 97310; 503-986-1518;
Fax: 503-373-7414;
Web: www.sos.state.or.us/elections/elechp.htm

The Elections Division assures the uniform interpretation and application of Oregon's election laws. The division provides the public, elected officials, candidates, the media and interested parties with advice and assistance in all matters related to elections.

The division receives candidate filings for state offices, initiative and referendum petitions, campaign contribution and expenditure reports, and other election documents. The division publishes and distributes the state Voters' Pamphlet for primary and general elections. Complaints of alleged election law violations are investigated and processed by the Elections Division.

State Treasury

Jim Hill, State Treasurer
Gary H. Bruebaker, Deputy
Rollie Wisbrock, Chief of Staff
159 State Capitol, Salem 97310-0840;
503-378-4329; Fax: 503-373-7051;
Web: www.ost.state.or.us

The office of the State Treasury has grown considerably since it was set out in the original state Constitution in 1859. Today, the Treasury fulfills the functions of banking, savings and investment institutions. Its mission is to provide professional and prudent fiscal management and financial services with the highest degree of proficiency and accountability.

The Treasury:

1. Invests approximately $32 billion in trust funds (principally Public Employes Retirement System and State Accident Insurance Fund monies).
2. Operates an investment pool (similar to a money market fund) for use by state and local governments.
3. Manages contracts with outside money managers charged with investing approximately $14 billion of state trust fund money in common stocks.
4. Provides staff to the Oregon Investment Council.
5. Provides information and assistance to local governments in the issuance of bonds.
6. Oversees the issuance and retirement of bonds and the payment thereon.
7. Implements the Oregon Baccalaureate Bond Program.
8. Receives and processes deposits and other monies acquired by state agencies.
9. Provides an automated banking system to state agencies to help manage daily banking activities.
10. Invests monies that are beyond the state's daily cash needs.
11. Maintains systematic accounting of these transactions.

Debt Management Division

Charles R. Smith, Dir.
100 Labor and Industries Bldg., 350 Winter St. NE, Salem 97310-0840; 503-378-4930

Municipal Debt Advisory Commission

Charles R. Smith, Dir.
Debt Management Div., Sec.
100 Labor and Industries Bldg., 350 Winter St. NE, Salem 97310-0840; 503-378-4930

James P. Shannon, chair, representing public, Portland; Gary H. Bruebaker, Deputy State Treasurer; Gary Cadle, Association of Oregon Counties, Medford; Susan Gill, Oregon School Board Association, Creswell; Mike Lewis,

representing public, Portland; Kenneth Rust, League of Oregon Cities, Portland.

The Municipal Debt Advisory Commission was created in 1975 by ORS 287.030–287.045 to assist local governments in the issuance of municipal debt, to maintain and provide information on such debt and to promote methods of reducing the cost of issuing municipal bonds. The commission maintains a data bank on debt issued by all taxing districts in Oregon.

Baccalaureate Bond Program, Oregon

Charles R. Smith, Dir.
100 Labor and Industries Bldg., 350 Winter St. NE, Salem 97310-0840; 503-378-4930

To assist anyone wishing to save for a child's future educational expenses, the State of Oregon periodically sells Oregon Baccalaureate (ORBAC) Bonds.

ORBAC Bonds are issued as "deferred interest" bonds. Unlike most tax-exempt bonds, which pay interest every six months, ORBAC Bonds pay interest only at maturity (sometimes called zero-coupon bonds).

Interest on ORBAC Bonds is compounded annually at a fixed rate until maturity. At maturity an ORBAC Bond is redeemed at face value.

Tillamook Rock Lighthouse, as seen from Ecola State Park, ceased operating in 1957. After many years of disuse it was purchased in the 1980s and converted to a columbarium—a storage site for cremated remains.

Photo by Jean P. Gammon.

Private Activity Bond Committee

Charles R. Smith, Dir.
Debt Management Div., Sec.
100 Labor and Industries Bldg., 350 Winter St.
NE, Salem 97310-0840; 503-378-4930

The 1986 Tax Reform Act limited the number of bonds that each state may issue for "private activity" purposes. Consisting of a representative of the State Department of Administrative Services, Theresa McHugh; the Oregon State Treasury, Gary H. Bruebaker; and a public member, Fred Elledge, appointed by the governor; the three-member committee allocates to local governments a portion of the state private activity bond limit pursuant to ORS 286.625 and the 1986 Tax Reform Act.

Health, Housing, Educational and Cultural Facilities Authority (HHECFA)

William E. Love, Exec. Dir.
1950 Pacwest Center, 1211 SW 5th Ave.,
Portland 97204-3795; 503-228-6127

Gerry Langeler, chair, Portland, 1997; Ken Lindbloom, vice-chair, Medford, 1999; George Bell, Lake Oswego, 2000; Phyllis Bell, Newport, 1997; Glenn Ford, Portland, 1999.

The Health, Housing, Educational and Cultural Facilities Authority (HHECFA) consists of five Oregon residents appointed by the state treasurer for a term of four years. At least one of the members shall be a person knowledgeable in the field of state and municipal finance and one in the construction field, and not more than three members shall be of the same political party.

HECFA was created by the Legislature in 1989 by Oregon Laws chapter 820 (ORS chapter 289). The 1991 Legislature added the word "health." HHECFA is empowered to assist with the assembling and financing of lands for health, housing, educational and cultural uses and for the construction and financing of facilities for such uses.

All bonds issued by the state treasurer upon recommendation of HHECFA are repaid solely from revenues generated by the projects or from other sources available to the applying institution. Interest on the bonds is tax-exempt from federal income taxes and is also exempt from personal income taxes imposed by the state.

Employee Services

Beryl Anderson, Mgr.
100 Labor and Industries Bldg., 350 Winter St.
NE, Salem 97310-0840; 503-378-4000

Employee Services provides administrative direction and centralized support services for the State Treasury, and is responsible for personnel, staff development and training, purchasing services and supplies, fixed assets, facilities management, mail distribution and records retention.

Executive Services

Rollie Wisbrock, Chief of Staff
Mari Anne Gest, Dir. of Public and Legis. Affairs
Michael Parker, Communications Dir.
Penney Ryan, Exec. Asst.
159 State Capitol, Salem 97310-0840;
503-378-4329

Executive Services coordinates policy development, strategic planning, legislative initiatives, press relations and publication of periodic financial reports for the various trust funds invested by the State Treasury.

The Oregon Constitution mandates that the state treasurer serve on the State Land Board and the Prison Industries Board. In addition, the state treasurer has the following mandates:

- Develop an Oregon Retirement Commission to study the increasing problem of retirement savings in Oregon.
- Implement the Treasury's strategic business plan.
- Increase communication and education of Treasury programs and responsibilities to the people of Oregon and to the Legislature.
- Develop a strategic debt plan in cooperation with the Legislature.
- Implement the Save For America school savings program throughout Oregon.

Finance Division

Darren Q. Bond, Dir.
100 Labor and Industries Bldg., 350 Winter St. NE,
Salem 97310-0840; 503-378-4633

The Finance Division serves as the central bank for all state agencies and provides cash management and investment accounting services. The division maintains an effective working relationship between the banking community and the state, acts as collateral pool manager for some of Oregon's largest banks and redeems general obligation bonds issued by state agencies.

The Finance Division has also championed an outreach program designed to offer cash management consultation to state agencies. The program offers advice on how to increase the efficiencies of state agency operations through increased automation and decreased duplication.

The division also provides agency accounting, payroll, accounts payable, accounts receivable, budgeting and general support to the Treasury.

Bond Valuation Committee

Darren Q. Bond, Dir.
100 Labor and Industries Bldg., 350 Winter St. NE, Salem 97310-0840; 503-378-4633

William Heath, chair; Dan Davis; Warren Hastings; David C. Mann; Patricia Montgomery.

The Bond Valuation Committee is authorized by ORS 295.095 and appointed by the state treasurer. The committee meets once a year or as requested by the state treasurer to determine the value of eligible securities and bonds used as collateral by public officials, pool managers, banks and the state treasurer.

Information Systems Division

Mary Campbell, Mgr.
100 Labor and Industries Bldg., 350 Winter St. NE, Salem 97310-0840; 503-378-4694

The Information Systems Division is the information management center for the Treasury. The division designs, constructs, maintains and enhances information systems and functions, which provide telecommunications services to connect Treasury's multiple office sites as well as connections to state agencies, local governments, banks and other financial firms.

Internal Auditor

Michael Mueller, CPA, Internal Auditor
100 Labor and Industries Bldg., 350 Winter St. NE, Salem 97310-0840; 503-378-4000

The internal auditor reports directly to the state treasurer and is a member of the executive staff. The internal auditor reviews Treasury's compliance with relevant statutes, policies and procedures and assesses qualitative aspects

of Treasury programs. The auditor identifies potential and real risk areas and assists in the development of controls to mitigate those risks.

Investment Council, Oregon

W. Dan Smith, Dir., Investment Div., Sec.
100 Labor and Industries Bldg., 350 Winter St. NE, Salem 97310-0840; 503-378-4111

Gerard K. Drummond, chair, investment/finance expertise, Portland, 1997; Jim Hill, State Treasurer; Fred McDonnal, as director, PERS, ex officio and non voting, Portland; Peter Ozanne, investment/finance expertise, Portland, 1999; Randall Pozdena, investment/finance expertise, Portland, 1998; Warren Rosenfeld, investment/finance expertise, Portland, 1997.

The governor appoints council members to four-year terms, subject to Senate confirmation. The state treasurer serves as chief investment officer.

The Oregon Investment Council is responsible for the investment of all state funds. Monies are invested in accordance with the "Prudent Investor Rule" to achieve the investment objectives of the various funds and to make the monies as productive as possible. The council was created by ORS 293.706.

Investment Division

W. Dan Smith, Dir.
Angela Davis, Asst. Dir.
Gary Combs, Jay Fewel, Bill Unverzagt, Jim Yasutome
100 Labor and Industries Bldg., 350 Winter St. NE, Salem 97310-0840; 503-378-4111, 503-373-7089, 503-378-4113, 503-378-4155

The Investment Division is responsible for the productive and prudent investment of all state funds entrusted to the state for management. Investments supervised by Treasury staff include: trust funds, constitutional bond funds and those funds not necessary to meet current state or local demands and excess funds.

Excess Funds—Monies from the Local Government Investment Pool, the state's General Fund and other cash balances of state agencies are combined and make up the Oregon Short-Term Fund. In addition to providing an attractive investment alternative for short-term funds of local governments, the pool provides participants with such services as direct warrant and inter-fund transfers. These services are particularly helpful when state basic school support payments are made, and for counties when transferring real estate tax proceeds to school districts and cities.

Trust Funds—Included in this category are: Public Employes Retirement System Fund (PERS), State Accident Insurance Fund (SAIF), Common School Fund and Veterans' Bond Fund.

By law a maximum of 50 percent of PERS and SAIF funds, at time of contribution, may be invested in common stock, and no equity purchases may be made by the Treasury. Implementing this statute, the Oregon Investment Council retains outside money management firms to invest in common stocks. One of the council's primary responsibilities is to monitor the progress of these firms, as well as scores of other prospective managers, to obtain the best possible return for the funds.

Justice, Department of

Hardy Myers, Attorney General
Justice Bldg., Salem 97310; 503-378-4400

The Department of Justice, established by statute in 1891, is Oregon state government's law firm. Administered by the attorney general, it represents and advises all state elected and appointed officials, agencies, boards and commissions. The attorney general, by statute, has control and supervision of all court actions in which the state is a party or has an interest.

In addition to legal services, the department has various program-service functions including child-support enforcement, technical and investigative assistance to district attorneys, organized crime investigation, consumer protection and service, charitable trust supervision, and crime-victim compensation. In all, the department and attorney general have responsibility and authority under more than 350 state statutes.

Appellate Division

Virginia Linder, Solicitor General
Justice Bldg., Salem 97310; 503-378-4402

The Appellate Division generally is responsible for representing the state's interests in all civil, criminal and administrative cases before all state and federal appellate courts. Under supervision of the solicitor general, division attorneys articulate and defend the state's legal policies in written briefs and oral arguments before the Oregon Court of Appeals and Supreme Court; and the U.S. Court of Appeals and Supreme Court.

Civil Enforcement Division

David Hicks, Acting Div. Admin.
Justice Bldg., Salem 97310; 503-378-4732

The Civil Enforcement Division handles civil law enforcement. Its purpose is to identify and eliminate violations of laws that regulate the commercial and labor markets. Sections in the division are:

Charitable Activities Section enforces laws regarding charitable trusts and solicitations. It also licenses and regulates bingo and raffle operations.

Credit and Bankruptcy Section is responsible for collecting debts owed to state agencies.

Family Law Section provides legal services to the Support Enforcement Division in establishing and enforcing child support and paternity orders in cases where children are receiving public assistance. It also operates a statewide program to assist the State Office for Services to Children and Families in its Permanent Planning Program.

Financial Fraud Section responsibilities include enforcement of Oregon's antitrust, securities, civil racketeering, unlawful trade practices and charitable solicitations laws. Its purpose is to protect Oregon consumers from predatory marketplace practices.

Consumer Advisory Council

Jan Margosian, Consumer Info. Coord.
Financial Fraud; Justice Bldg., Salem 97310; Consumer Lines: 503-378-4320 (Salem) 503-229-5576 (Portland) M–F: 8:30 a.m.- noon

The council was created in 1971 under the auspices of the Department of Commerce and transferred to the Department of Justice in 1981 when Consumer Services and Consumer Protection merged under ORS 180.520. Appointed by the attorney general, it consists of seven members, two representing business, two representing labor and three representing voluntary consumer agencies. Meetings are held quarterly and are open to the public.

The council was created to assist the Financial Fraud section of the Civil Enforcement Division. Functions include statewide promotion of Consumer Week; working with staff to coordinate state, local and federal agencies; conducting studies and research in consumer services; and advising executive and legislative branches in consumer matters.

Industrial Accident Section provides legal services to a single client, the State Accident Insurance Fund (SAIF).

Medicaid Fraud Unit is part of a federally-subsidized program created to deter and prosecute fraud committed by Medicaid health care service providers. It detects and prosecutes cases of criminal abuse or neglect of patients or residents of health-care facilities who receive Medicaid funds.

Criminal Justice Division

Charles Pritchard, Chief Counsel
Justice Bldg., Salem 97310; 503-378-6347

The Criminal Justice Division serves as a statewide, multipurpose catalyst to the law-enforcement community. Among its many functions is serving as counsel to the Board on Public Safety Standards and Training and providing staff for the Oregon District Attorneys Association and the Governor's Commission on Organized Crime. Each of these functions is closely related and assists in creating a climate of quality law enforcement in Oregon.

Crime Victims' Compensation Program: established to provide certain benefits to innocent victims of violent crimes.

District Attorney Assistance Program: provides to district attorneys and their deputies extensive statewide training in the techniques of criminal prosecution, uniform manuals, forms, case digests, expert trial assistance and other coordinated services.

Organized Crime Section: primary purpose is to prevent infiltration of organized criminal enterprises into Oregon and to detect and combat existing organized criminal activities in the state. The unit also is charged with the specific responsibility of coordinating law-enforcement efforts in organized crime and has established a viable, cooperative network.

Organized Crime, Governor's Commission on

Hardy Myers, Attorney General, chair
Justice Bldg., Salem 97310; 503-378-4400

The commission was established in 1977 by Executive Order 77-9 and continued by EO 83-14 in 1983. It is composed of 17 members designated by virtue of their position in Oregon's law enforcement system. These include: Attorney General, chair; Superintendent, Oregon State Police; Chief of Police, Portland Police Bureau; Multnomah County Sheriff; Multnomah County District Attorney; Administrator of the Oregon Liquor Control Commission; a representative from the Oregon State Sheriff's Association; a representative from the Oregon Association of Chiefs of Police; United States Attorney; Special Agent in Charge of the Federal Bureau of Investigation, Portland; Chief of the Criminal Investigation Division, Internal Revenue Service, Portland; Resident Agent in Charge, Bureau of Alcohol, Tobacco and Firearms, Portland; Resident Agent in Charge, Drug Enforcement Administration, Portland; Special Agent in Charge, U.S. Customs Service, Portland; U.S. Marshal; and the Postal Inspector in Charge, U.S. Postal Service, Portland.

The commission coordinates information on and investigation of organized crime. Services are provided by the staff of the attorney general.

General Counsel Division

Donald C. Arnold, Chief Counsel
Justice Bldg., Salem 97310; 503-378-4620

The General Counsel Division provides a broad range of legal services to state agencies, boards and commissions, including day-to-day legal advice necessary for the state's operation.

The division is composed of the following operating sections, headed by attorneys-in-charge. They are Education; Human Services; Government Services; Natural Resources; Tax and Finance; Public Utility Commission; Business Activities; and Labor and Employment.

Support Enforcement Division

Cynthia A. Chinnock, Admin.
Justice Bldg., Salem 97310; 503-378-4879

The Support Enforcement Division establishes, modifies and enforces

Snowboarding is a year-round sport in Wallowa County where these snowboarding fans have found enough snow to ski every month consecutively for three years. Photo by Gary Fletcher.

child-support obligations for families who receive public assistance. Since its inception in 1957 as the Welfare Recovery Division, the program has grown steadily in size, effectiveness and national stature. The Division's activities are an integral part of Oregon's "Self-Sufficiency Strategy" for low-income families.

Trial Division

Timothy Wood, Acting Chief Counsel
Justice Bldg., Salem 97310; 503-378-6313

The Trial Division represents the state and all of its agencies, boards and commissions in state and federal trial courts in Oregon. In addition, it defends all state officers, officials, employees, agents and all elected officers, judges and legislators from tort claims filed against them for acts within the scope of their official duties.

Bureau of Labor and Industries

Jack Roberts, Commiss. of Labor and Industries
Margo Norton, Deputy Labor Commiss.
*800 NE Oregon St., #32, Portland 97232;
503-731-4070*

The Bureau of Labor and Industries was created by the Legislature in 1903 and the state elected its first labor commissioner in 1906. The bureau was created to oversee the rapidly developing industrial workplace and to protect workers, especially minors. Its original

responsibilities included inspecting mills, factories and schools as well as enforcing pay regulations and helping workers collect wages.

Today the bureau enforces laws banning discrimination in employment, housing, public accommodations and in professional or career schools; administers laws relating to wages, hours and working conditions; and facilitates apprenticeship programs through local volunteer committees.

Commissioner's Office and Program Services

Margo Norton, Deputy Labor Commiss.
*800 NE Oregon St., #32, Portland 97232;
503-731-4896*

The Commissioner's Office and Program Services provides policy direction, resources and accountability to help operating units encourage compliance and enforce wage and hour and civil rights laws and apprenticeship standards.

Administrative services include policy development, strategic planning, intergovernmental relations and public information. Business services include budget management, accounting, data processing and human resources. A Hearings Unit convenes administrative law proceedings in contested case hearings for wage and hour, civil rights and apprenticeship determinations. The Technical Assistance for Employers Program provides a telephone information line; pamphlets, handbooks and printed materials; and public or company-based seminars and workshops to keep the business community informed about employment law. Employers can call 503-731-4073 for immediate answers.

The bureau has regional offices in Bend, Eugene, Medford, Pendleton, Portland and Salem.

Apprenticeship and Training Division

Stephen Simms, Dir.
*800 NE Oregon St., #32, Portland 97232;
503-731-4072*

Under Oregon's apprenticeship training system, apprenticed workers learn on the job while taking related classroom courses. The Apprenticeship and Training Division assists 183 local volunteer committees of employers and employees monitor the progress of 7,634 apprentices. There are more than 488 apprenticeship programs for occupations such as baker, carpenter, heavy equipment operator and culinarian.

The division promotes the development of a highly skilled workforce through partnerships with government, business, labor and education. The division, together with business, assists high schools and community colleges develop curricula to help youth enter various apprenticeship programs.

Also included in division programs are youth apprenticeship, and veterans' and dislocated workers' on-the-job training.

Apprenticeship and Training Council

Stephen Simms, Sec.
800 NE Oregon St., #32, Portland 97232; 503-731-4072

Commissioner Jack Roberts, chair; Constance Ashbrook, Portland, 1998; Vicky L. Bacon, Portland, 2000; Dr. Harvey Bennett, Grants Pass, 1997; Chet Caruthers, Portland, 2000; Ed J. Gormley, McMinnville, 1997; Dan Lacy, The Dalles, 2000; Janet L. Lewis, Tigard, 1998; Robert L. Martinez, Sweet Home, 1998; Ronald S. Sherman, Scappoose, 1998.

The governor appoints 10 members to the council for four-year terms under ORS 660.110. The board sets policy for apprenticeship training and registers individual apprenticeship programs.

Civil Rights Division

Johnnie Bell, Admin.
800 NE Oregon St., #32, Portland 97232; 503-731-4075

The bureau's Civil Rights Division administers and enforces laws that ban discrimination based on race, color, national origin, religion, sex, marital status, disability and age. These laws protect Oregonians against unlawful discrimination in employment, housing, public accommodations and career schools. Oregon workers are also protected at the workplace on the basis of their family relationship and personal association, expunged juvenile record, genetic screening or brain wave tests or polygraph and breathalyzer tests, using (or perceived to be using) the workers' compensation system, reporting patient abuse, giving legislative testimony, reporting workplace safety or health violations, taking family leave, whistle-blowing or reporting criminal activities.

The division also enforces the Portland, Corvallis and Eugene city anti-discrimination ordinances covering source of income and sexual orientation.

Staff investigates and works to resolve complaints alleging unlawful discrimination. The commissioner may hear cases where substantial evidence of discrimination is found and the parties do not settle.

Wage and Hour Division

Christine Hammond, Admin.
800 NE Oregon St., #32, Portland 97232; 503-731-4074

The Wage and Hour Division administers and enforces state laws concerning working conditions, minimum wage, overtime, employment of minors, wage collection and the prevailing wage rate. It licenses and regulates farm and forest labor contractors and private employment agencies. The division also administers the Wage Security Fund, sets the prevailing wage rate on public works projects and enforces group health insurance termination-notification provisions.

Wage and Hour Commission, State

Wage and Hour Division, 800 NE Oregon St., #32, Portland 97232; 503-731-4074

Gene Provonost, chair, Wilsonville, 1997; Gary Lockwood, Salem, 2000; Shelley Olson, Salem, 2000.

Under ORS 653.505 the governor appoints the three members of this commission to four-year terms. The commission sets minimum standards for the working conditions of minors and may grant specific exceptions to child labor laws.

Education, Department of

Norma Paulus, State Supt. of Public Instruction
C. Gregory McMurdo, Deputy Supt.
255 Capitol St. NE, Salem 97310-0203; 503-378-3573; TDD: 503-378-2892; Fax: 503-378-4772; Web: www.ode.state.or.us

The Department of Education, as described in ORS 326.111, is directed by the State Board of Education to implement state policies regarding public kindergarten through community colleges.

The state superintendent of public instruction is the executive head of the Department of Education, serving 220 elementary and secondary school districts and 21 education service districts, which in turn serve some 561,500 elementary and secondary school students. In addition, the department manages the Oregon School for the Blind, Oregon School for the Deaf and education programs for adjudicated youth.

The department carries out educational policies set by the Legislature and State Board of Education and assists districts in complying with applicable statutes and rules.

Education, State Board of

Bob Burns, Deputy Supt. to the State Board
255 Capitol St. NE, Salem 97310-0203;
503-378-3573; TDD: 503-378-2892;
Fax: 503-378-4772

Judy Stiegler, chair, Bend, 1998; Tom McClintock, vice-chair, Corvallis, 1997; Joe Burdic, Ontario, 1999; Wayne Feller, Silverton, 1998; Jill Kirk, Portland, 2000; Susan Massey, North Bend, 2000; Jeana Woolley, Portland, 1997.

In 1951, the Legislature created the State Board of Education, consisting of seven Oregonians appointed by the governor for up to two consecutive four-year terms. One member is selected from each of Oregon's five congressional districts and two members are selected from the state at large. Board members are unsalaried and cannot engage in teaching, school administration or operation while they serve on the board.

The board sets educational policies and standards for Oregon's 220 school districts, 17 community colleges and 21 education service districts. The K-12 system serves some 561,500 students

In September 1996, the State Board of Education adopted new, more rigorous academic standards describing what students should know and be able to do in English, mathematics, science, the social sciences, the arts and a second language. Student progress toward the standards will be measured at grades three, five, eight and 10 through state tests and classroom assignments.

For more information, visit the Department of Education's Web site at www.ode.state.or.us or call 503-378-8004.

and the community college system serves some 335,500 students. School districts, community colleges and education services districts all have their own boards responsible for transacting business within their districts.

In January 1996, the State Board of Education adopted the following major goals for the 1995-97 biennium:

• Improve Oregon's public prekindergartens, K-12 schools and community colleges by implementing the Oregon Educational Act for the 21st Century, expanding education to employment programs, aligning high school certificate and diploma requirements with college entrance requirements and other means;

• Increase accountability for students, staff and schools by setting high academic standards, evaluating student progress toward the standards through state tests, requiring school and district improvement plans and other means;

• Focus on issues that support children and families by strongly supporting early childhood education, working together with other organizations that address children and family issues and other means;

• Use technology for teaching, learning and managing information by building access to technology at schools, offering instruction in the use of technology, increasing opportunities for teachers to improve their technology skills and other means; and

• Build the capacity of schools to deliver quality education by offering specific legislative proposals, working with the State Board of Higher Education on issues of common interest and other means.

The State Board of Education is called upon by the Legislature to implement the Oregon Educational Act for the 21st Century; implement state standards for public schools; adopt rules governing public elementary and secondary schools and community colleges; and distribute state education funds to school districts meeting all state requirements.

Fair Dismissal Appeals Board

C. Gregory McMurdo, Exec. Sec.
255 Capitol St. NE, Salem 97310-0203;
503-378-3573; TDD 503-378-2892;
Fax: 503-378-4772

The 20-member board is appointed by the governor and is subject to confirmation by the Senate. Terms expire on June 30 of the years indicated.

Administrators: Faith Chapel, Lake Oswego, 2000; Robert Eddy, Enterprise, 1998; Dennis Dempsey, Sisters, 1999; Betty Shalhope, Hood River, 1998; Charles Sharps, Coos Bay, 1999.

Board Members: Kenneth Knutson, Sheridan, 1999; Michael Collins, Pendleton, 1998; Duane Johnson, Cannon Beach, 2000; Michael Fox, Eugene, 1997; Craig Smith, Salem, 2000.

Nonaffiliated: Noble Morinaka Jr., Nyssa, 2000; Alfred McDaniel, Springfield, 1997; Kathleen Himmelsbach, Baker City, 1999; Jonathan Ross, Portland, 1997; Alice Meyer, Portland, 1998.

Teachers: Cathy Colburn, Beaver, 1997; Karen Moen, Roseburg, 1999; Larry Wolf, The Dalles, 1998; Linda Pattison, Portland, 2000; Michael Summers, Central Point, 1999.

The Fair Dismissal Law was enacted by the Legislative Assembly in 1971. It replaced the Teacher Tenure Law and established the Fair Dismissal Appeals Board (FDAB). A permanent teacher or administrator dismissed by a school board may appeal that decision to the Fair Dismissal Appeals Board which holds a hearing on the dismissal in accordance with ORS 342.905–342.930.

Other Agencies, Boards and Commissions

This section includes contact names and addresses, together with descriptions of the functions and responsibilities of other state agencies, boards and commissions, which are listed alphabetically by substantive name. For example, the Oregon Department of Human Resources is alphabetized under H for Human Resources rather than under D for Department or O for Oregon.

Often a board or commission falls under the major heading of an agency. The Index, starting on page 469, contains a complete list of each department, division, section, board and commission, as well as key content words.

Administrative Services, Department of (DAS)

Jon Yunker, Dir.
Theresa McHugh, Deputy Dir.
155 Cottage St. NE, Salem 97310-0310;
503-378-3104; Fax: 503-373-7643;
Web: www.state.or.us

The Department of Administrative Services' mission is to provide leadership, direction and service to state government so Oregonians receive responsive, efficient and accountable services.

DAS provides state government with a mixture of pure management and sale of central services. For example, DAS controls central accounting, labor relations and hiring, as "manager." At the same time, it runs the motor pool, central printing plants, office facilities and a variety of other services as a "vendor" to the rest of government. Though primarily responsible to the governor, the agency also assists in administering policies and regulations of other elected officials and branches of government.

Springer Holstein heifers head up a walkway at Pete DeHaan Holsteins operation in McMinnville. Numerous Oregon dairy farmers donated cows to the Tillamook area dairies devastated by the Flood of 1996. Photo by Beth Buglione.

The department was created by the 1993 Legislature by merging the Executive Department and the Department of General Services. The director is appointed by and serves at the pleasure of the governor. Department revenues come almost entirely from fees for services rendered other agencies, or general overhead assessments on those agencies. The 1995-97 operating budget is $57 million.

Director's Office

Jon Yunker, Dir.
503-378-3104

David White, Asst. Dir.
503-378-8267; Fax: 503-373-7643;
Email: oregon.info@state.or.us

Theresa McHugh, Deputy Dir.
503-378-4691

The Director's Office provides central administration, central communication programs and leadership to the department. It also has a strong management and leadership role for the rest of state government.

Economic Analysis, Office of

Paul Warner, State Economist
503-378-3106; Fax: 503-373-7643;
Web: www.oea.das.state.or.us

The Office of Economic Analysis prepares state economic and revenue forecasts. It assesses long-term economic and demographic trends and evaluates their implications, and conducts special economic and demographic studies.

Health Plan Administrator, Office of

Barney Speight, Admin.
255 Capitol St. NE, Fifth Floor, Salem 97310;
503-378-2422; Fax: 503-378-5511;
Web: www.das.state.or.us/ohpa/ohpa.htm

The Office of the Health Plan Administrator advises the Legislature and the governor on the implementation of the Oregon Health Plan. The Plan is contained in a series of laws enacted since 1989. Taken together these laws reflect the unifying goal of ensuring that Oregonians have "universal access to an adequate level of high quality health care at an affordable cost." The Plan established state-run pools for small businesses and persons with pre-existing medical conditions; expanded the Medicaid program; reformed insurance laws; created commissions to develop standard benefit packages and to evaluate medical technologies; and established this office.

The office, which is the state's focal point for health care policy and health reform, is administratively responsible for the Oregon Health Council, the Health Resources Commission and the Health Services Commission. The office also has coordination and oversight responsibilities for Oregon Health Plan programs managed by other departments.

The office collects, analyzes and disseminates data related to health care and health insurance. It has ongoing responsibility for seeking ways to increase the efficiency and effectiveness of health care delivery, contain costs and expand health care coverage. In addition, the office takes on special task forces and other work as assigned by the Legislature or the governor. Two recent examples include the legislatively assigned Mental Health Task Force and the Governor's Task Force on State Employee Benefits.

Oregon Health Council

Bob DiPrete, Dir.
255 Capitol St. NE, Salem 97310; 503-378-2422,
ext. 402; Fax: 503-378-5511;
Web: www.das.state.or.us/ohpa/ohpa.htm

Alan Yordy, chair; John Santa, vice-chair; Michael Bonnazola, Jeanne Bowden, Jean Cowen, Ross Dwinell, Carla Freeman, Amy Klare, Eric Santiago.

The Oregon Health Council is authorized by ORS 442.035. The nine-member council is appointed by the governor. It is charged with identifying and analyzing significant health care issues and making policy recommendations to the governor, Legislature and Oregon Health Plan administrator. It annually revises the state Health Plan and establishes policy for a statewide clearinghouse on health care data.

Health Resources Commission

Daniel M. Harris, Ph.D., Exec. Dir.
255 Capitol St. NE, Salem 97310;
503-378-2422, ext. 415;
Web: www.das.state.or.us/ohpa/ohpa.htm

Dr. Frank Baumeister, chair, 1997; Diane Lovell, vice-chair, 1997; Dr. Steven DeLashmutt, 1996; Elaine Dunda, 1998; Dr. John Hoggard, 1998; Dr. David Noall, 1996; Larry Richards, 1996.

The Health Resources Commission (HRC) was created in 1991 and is authorized by ORS 442.575–584. Commission members are appointed by the governor.

The commission's purpose is to encourage the rational and appropriate allocation and utilization of medical technology used in Oregon to achieve an optimal balance between access, quality and cost.

The HRC's major activity is to conduct a publicly funded Medical Technology Assessment Program (MedTAP) that addresses the introduction, diffusion and utilization of medical technologies. It also serves as a clearinghouse for medical technology information; monitors costs and outcomes associated with the use of assessed technologies in Oregon; addresses deficiencies in information needed for informed decision making; and provides a public forum for discussion of significant emerging issues regarding medical technology.

Health Services Commission

255 Capitol St. NE, Salem 97310;
503-378-2422, ext. 413;
Web: www.das.state.or.us/ohpa/ohpa.htm

David Arnold, Klamath Falls, 1999; Dr. Alan Bates, Central Point, 1999; Marie Deatherage, Portland, 1997; Donalda Dodson, Salem, 2000; Dr. Andrew Glass, Portland, 1998; Amy Klare, Salem, 1999; Dr. Alison Little, Redmond, 2000; Ellen Lowe, Portland, 2000; Kathy Savicki, Salem, 1999; Dr. Kathleen Weaver, Lake Oswego, 1998.

The Health Services Commission was created by the 1989 Legislature (ORS 414.036). Commission members are appointed by the governor with Senate confirmation for four-year terms.

The commission is charged with providing a biennial report to the governor and the Legislature listing health services ranked by priority from the most to least important.

Controller's Division, State

John J. Radford, Admin.
503-378-3156, ext. 226; Fax: 503-378-3518

The State Controller's Division facilitates and provides comprehensive statewide integrated financial systems, procedures and fiscal support services across state agencies, lowering the overall cost of state financial administration.

The division provides accounting, financial reporting, purchasing, and fixed asset systems to all agencies. The division monitors agency follow-up to the findings and recommendations of the Secretary of State's Audits Division; processes approximately 42,000 monthly employee payroll transactions; monitors compliance with federal cash management laws and other federal financial regulations; and prepares the state's Comprehensive Annual Financial Report to citizens and public bodies. The division currently manages a complete integration and overhaul of the state's accounting systems (State Financial Management System project).

Budget and Management Division

Theresa McHugh, Admin.
503-378-4691; Fax: 503-373-7643

The Budget and Management Division prepares the governor's budget recommendations for legislative consideration and implements budget and management policies which reflect the governor's priorities. The division works with state agencies to identify, allocate and expand resources in an efficient manner consistent with state law and policy. The division also includes Criminal Justice Services, which is responsible for administering criminal justice federal grant programs.

Facilities Division

Mike Marsh, Admin.
503-378-4138; Fax: 503-373-7210;
Email: mike.b.marsh@state.or.us

The Facilities Division acquires and maintains space for state agency functions. Its staff plans and manages construction of new facilities and supplies space planning services. The statewide Waste Prevention and Recycling Program provides assistance to all agencies in their efforts to achieve Oregon's resource conservation goals.

The division provides property management, lease negotiation and supervision, parking management, building operations, and landscape maintenance for state agencies.

Human Resource Services Division

Dan Kennedy, Admin.
503-378-3020; Fax: 503-378-4596

The Human Resource Services Division is the state's central personnel system control unit. It develops employee relations systems and policies. The division manages employee pay, benefits, recruitment and personnel records. The division includes the office of the Bargaining Unit Benefits Board (BUBB) and the State Employees' Benefits Board (SEBB), which plan and develop employee benefit programs, including health insurance benefits.

The division manages relations with labor unions representing 22,183 employees. It represents the state in collective bargaining and responds to grievances. It also provides advice and training to state agencies and develops state policy on labor relations.

Information Resource Management Division

Curt Pederson
Admin./Chief Information Officer
503-378-3161; Fax: 503-986-3242;
Email: curt.pederson@state.or.us

The Information Resource Management Division operates the state's information and telecommunications, voice, video and data networks and provides leadership in the use of information technology. It provides statewide planning and policy development for telecommunication and information systems, and works with state agencies to design and implement compatible systems. It operates the state's general government data center, central telephone/data systems, software development and two-way satellite television network (ED-NET).

Geographic Information Systems, State Service Center for (GIS)

Theresa Valentine, Mgr.
503-378-4163; Fax: 503-986-3242;
Email: theresa.j.valentine@state.or.us;
Web: www.sscgis.state.or.us

Geographic Information Systems (GIS) are computer systems that merge automated mapping with database management. The Center provides GIS coordination and services to state, federal, county and local governments as well as private and non-profit organizations. Services include training, data analysis, cartography, database development, custom GIS development, GIS needs assessments, system administration and consulting. A standard fee is charged for all services.

The Service Center also maintains the largest library of GIS data for Oregon. The collection includes data on transportation, environment, natural resources, land ownership, boundaries and demographics. The data is available free of charge through the Center's web site.

Internal Support Division

Coyne Smith, Admin.
503-373-7849; Fax: 503-378-6879

The Internal Support Division provides administrative and operational support to 10 divisions of the Department of

A frozen waterfall turns Wasco County's White River into a winter wonderland.

Photo by Shirley Yost.

Administrative Services as well as the Office of the Governor, select commissions and approximately 30 agencies. Division responsibilities encompass accounting, fiscal management, payroll, information systems, employee services, safety and wellness, and the general administration of agency-wide business operations.

Risk Management Division

Dan Hartman, Admin.
503-378-5526; Fax: 503-373-7337;
Email: risk.management@state.or.us

The Risk Management Division administers Chapter 278, Insurance for Public Bodies, and the state's Insurance Fund. It provides workers' compensation, tort liability, property, dishonesty, inmate injury, volunteer injury and other coverages to state government using a mix of self-insurance and commercial insurance. State managers are provided help and guidance to avoid needless and wasteful costs of loss.

State law allows citizens and entities to assert tort claims against the state, its employees and agents for damage or injury caused by negligence. Written notice of intent to make a claim may be sent to the Risk Management Division.

Transportation, Purchasing and Print Services Division

Cameron Birnie, Admin.
503-378-4643; Fax: 503-373-1626

The Transportation, Purchasing and Print Services Division manages six programs. From its three locations, the **Motor Pool** provides more than 3,800 vehicles to agency drivers on official state business. **Central Mail** distributes interagency and federal mail between state offices. **State Surplus Property** coordinates the distribution of state surplus personal property to state and public agencies, qualified non-profit organizations and the general public. **Federal Surplus Property** obtains surplus federal equipment and material and assigns it to state and public agencies and qualified non-profit organizations. **Purchasing** directs large-scale and large-volume product and service procurements for state agencies, as well as for numerous public agencies through competitive bidding processes. **Print Services** coordinates and

provides, or arranges for, printing and related publishing services through inplant facilities as well as through contracts with private sector providers.

Boards and Commissions

Accountancy, Board of

Karen DeLorenzo, Admin.
3218 Pringle Rd. SE, Suite 110, Salem 97302-6307; 503-378-4181; Fax: 503-378-3575; Email: bd.of.accntcy@state.or.us; Web: www.boa.state.or.us

Robert L. Armstrong, PA, chair, Salem, 1999; David Efurd, CPA, vice-chair, Portland, 1997; Judith Bennington, CPA, secretary-treasurer, Beaverton, 1998; Dennis Donnelly, CPA, Medford, 1999; William Green, CPA, Eugene, 1999; James Houle, Pendleton, CPA, 1999; Nancy Towslee, public member, Salem, 1999.

The Board of Accountancy assures that approximately 7,000 CPAs, PAs and municipal auditors registered to practice in Oregon demonstrate and maintain knowledge of accounting standards and practices to serve the needs of their clients and other users of their services.

The board is authorized by ORS chapter 673 to establish and enforce standards and regulations, examine applicants and register qualified candidates in the field of public accounting. The board conducts a twice-yearly CPA examination.

Bargaining Unit Benefits Board

1730 Commercial St. SE, Salem 97301; 503-373-1174

Charles W. Mendenhall, chair

Authorized by ORS 243.235, this board purchases health, life, dental and other insurance benefits for employees represented by the Oregon Public Employees Union.

Economic Advisors, Governor's Council of

Paul Warner, State Economist
Dave Griffiths, Senior Economist
Sarah Gates, Research Analyst
155 Cottage St. NE, Salem 97310; 503-378-3106; Fax: 503-373-7643

John W. Mitchell, chair, U.S. Bancorp; Ken Choi, K.C. International Ltd.; William B. Conerly, Investment Manager; Patrick Done, Rouse Management,

Inc.; Ann Eike, Port of Portland; Rebecca Johnson, Oregon State University; Thomas McCoy, private farmer; Ham T. Nguyen, Portland General Electric; Tom Potiowsky, Portland State University; Hans Radtke, economic consultant; Ralph Shaw, Shaw Venture Partners.

Council appointments represent academics, business and industry, and financial institution interests. Members serve staggered three-year terms. The Governor's Council of Economic Advisors was formed by executive order on December 2, 1980. The council is charged with reviewing and discussing alternative national economic forecasts; reviewing preliminary state economic forecasts provided by the Office of Economic Analysis; and advising on dissemination methods for the quarterly economic and revenue forecasts. The council meets quarterly.

Employee Suggestion Awards Commission

Robyn MacKillop, Internal Support Division, Prog. Coord.

155 Cottage St. NE, Salem 97310; 503-378-5796; Fax: 503-378-6879

Authorized by ORS 182.310, this commission encourages and rewards employees who submit suggestions that improve effectiveness, efficiency and economy in state government.

Federal Forest and Resource Policy Team, Governor's

Paula Burgess, Dir.

775 Summer St. NE, Salem 97310; 503-986-0091

With the federal government owning more than 50 percent of Oregon, land-management actions by federal agencies have a direct impact on Oregon's people, environment and economy. Established in 1987, the team consists of representatives from appropriate state agencies who meet regularly. The team's director provides information to the governor and the Legislature, reviews and monitors federal land and resource-management actions, and coordinates state agency input and responses to proposed federal actions.

Geographic Information Council

Debora Balsley
State Service Center for GIS, staff

155 Cottage St. NE, Salem 97310; 503-378-4036; Fax: 503-986-3242

Mike Zanon, chair

The council, established by executive order and formerly known as the State Map Advisory Council, provides vision and leadership related to the development and use of geographic information; provides a forum to address state geographic information systems (GIS) issues; develops GIS policies and plans; and promotes coordination and cooperation among state, local and federal government GIS users.

Twelve state agencies are represented on the council, and the governor appoints the chair. Representatives from other state, federal and local governments are encouraged to participate in council discussions.

Public Lands Advisory Committee

Bill Nickleberry, Lands Mgr.

Capital Investment Section, 155 Cottage St. NE, Salem 97310; 503-378-3418; Fax: 503-373-7643

Alvin Brown, Prineville, 1998; Christine Carman, Medford, 1997; Sen. Gene Derfler, Salem, 1999; Richard Elfering, Astoria, 1997; Rep. Bryan Johnston, Salem, 1999; Jon Mangis, Department of Veterans' Affairs, 1997; Scott Taylor, Real Estate Agency, 1999.

The Public Lands Advisory Committee was established by statute to advise the Department of Administrative Services on the management of real property and surplus real property. The advisory committee advises the department on the acquisition, exchange or disposal of real property valued at $100,000 or more.

The seven committee members, appointed by the governor and confirmed by the Senate, are two members of the Legislature, one person licensed as a realtor in the state, two persons who serve in the executive branch of state government, one person qualified as a land-use planner and one person qualified as a real estate management expert. The Department of Administrative Services provides staff support.

Public Officials Compensation Commission

Kate Schmidt
Human Resource Mgmt. Div., staff
155 Cottage St. NE, Salem 97310;
503-378-2766; Fax: 503-373-7684

Geoffrey G. Guilfoy, Linda B. Kozlowski, Jane Leo, Richard Lindsay, Donald W. Scott, Craig Seal, Anne Seiler Jarvis.

All commissioners serve until 2000. The Public Officials Compensation Commission was authorized by the 1983 Legislature under ORS 292.907 to review salaries of all elected officials and to recommend salary adjustments to the Legislature for each succeeding biennium.

Seismic Safety Policy Advisory Commission

595 Cottage St. NE, Salem 97310; 503-378-2911

Peg Reagan, chair
The Seismic Safety Policy Advisory Commission (OSSPAC) is responsible to the governor and Legislative Assembly for review and advice concerning all plans and proposals addressing seismic hazards, for coordination of the design and for implementation and maintenance of an appropriate emergency services system.

State Employees' Benefits Board

155 Cottage St. NE, Salem 97310;
503-378-3020; Fax: 503-378-4596

Dan Kennedy, chair
Authorized by ORS 183.310, the State Employees' Benefits Board determines policy and evaluates and contracts for health, dental and other insurance benefit plans for state employees, except those represented by the Oregon Public Employees Union.

Tax Service Examiners, Board of

Joyce Thorbeck, Admin.
3218 Pringle Rd. SE, Suite 120, Salem 97302-6308; 503-378-4034;
Email: tax.bb@state.or.us

Peggy Dooley, chair, Corvallis, 1999; Dave Kim, vice-chair, Beaverton, 1997; Cheryl Brown, La Grande, 1999; Elaine Elsea, Portland, 1997; Rosalie Ritacco, Newport, 1997; Brian Teller Sr., public member, Beaverton, 1999; Karen Winters, Cottage Grove, 1999. The governor appoints the board members, subject to Senate confirmation, to serve three-year terms.

The Board of Tax Service Examiners examines and licenses persons who prepare, advise or assist in the preparation of personal income tax returns for a fee. Licensed tax preparers are apprentice-level practitioners who must work under supervision of licensed tax consultants.

Advocacy Center, Oregon

Bob Joondeph, Exec. Dir.
620 SW 5th Ave., Fifth Floor,
Portland 97204-1428; 503-243-2081;
toll-free: 1-800-452-1694; TDD: 503-323-9161;
toll-free TDD: 1-800-556-5351;
Fax: 503-243-1738; Email: oradvocacy@aol.com

The Oregon Advocacy Center provides protection and advocacy services to Oregonians with disabilities. The center receives federal funding under the Developmental Disabilities Act, the Protection and Advocacy for Individuals with Mental Illness Act, and the Rehabilitation Act as the officially designated protection and advocacy agency for Oregon. It is the entity to be notified of any sterilization petitions under ORS 436.255(2)(c). The center provides legal representation in matters directly related to disabilities, counseling in legal rights, information and referral services, investigation of reported abuse or neglect of people with developmental disabilities or mental illness and community education on rights of the disabled. Services are free.

The center's **Mental Health Association Program** performs policy analysis, training and advocacy for improved mental health services.

Agriculture, Department of

Bruce Andrews, Dir.
635 Capitol St. NE, Salem 97310-0110;
503-986-4552; Fax: 503-986-4747

The Oregon Department of Agriculture was created in 1931 to provide leadership, service and regulatory functions for food production and processing. Its mission has expanded to ensure food safety at all levels of production, to develop and expand product markets, and to protect the natural-resource base. The director is appointed by the governor, and the department is divided into eight divisions that oversee 36 chapters of Oregon laws.

Agricultural Development and Marketing Division

Jeff Jones, Asst. Dir.
*121 SW Salmon St., Suite 240, Portland
97204-2987; 503-229-6734; Fax: 503-229-6113*

The Agricultural Development and Marketing Division carries out market research and trade missions, serving as a link between buyers and sellers of Oregon agricultural products by creating new marketing opportunities and locating buyers. The division monitors activities, contractual obligations and budget development of all commodity commissions.

Animal Health and Identification Division

Rodger Huffman, Admin.
503-986-4680; Fax: 503-986-4681

The Animal Health and Identification Division is responsible for prevention, control and eradication of livestock diseases harmful to humans or animals. The division also administers brand recording and change-of-ownership inspection of animals throughout the state.

Commodity Inspection Division

Robert Hawkes, Admin.
503-986-4620; Fax: 503-986-4737

The Commodity Inspection Division inspects and grades agricultural products to meet requirements of quality, uniformity and labeling for receiving states and countries. The division is also responsible for controlling certain noxious weeds.

Food Safety Division

Jim Black, Admin.
503-986-4720; Fax: 503-986-4729

The Food Safety Division is responsible for safe, wholesome and properly labeled foods in Oregon. It licenses and inspects all retail food establishments (excluding restaurants), bakeries, dairies, food storage and most processing facilities.

Laboratory Services Division

Norma Corristan, Admin.
503-986-4565; Fax: 503-986-4751

The Laboratory Services Division provides analytical services for the department and other government agencies, and helps Oregon exporters by certifying food for export and providing technical

expertise on foreign food laws through the Export Service Center.

Measurement Standards Division

Kendrick J. Simila, Admin.
503-986-4670; Fax: 503-986-4784

The Measurement Standards Division seeks to prevent consumer fraud and ensure fair competition by making sure that goods such as groceries, fuels and most packaged products are accurately weighed, measured and labeled.

Natural Resources Division

Chuck Craig, Admin.
503-986-4700; Fax: 503-986-4730

The Natural Resources Division provides technical assistance and guidance for the state's 45 local soil and water conservation districts. The division also oversees non-point source water quality problems on agricultural lands, including investigating complaints regarding discharge of animal wastes into streams and rivers from confined livestock operations. The division is also responsible for most field-burning functions.

Plant Division

Dan Hilburn, Admin.
503-986-4644; Fax: 503-986-4786

The Plant Division licenses nursery stock growers and dealers and Christmas tree growers; inspects and certifies nursery stock and Christmas trees for shipment to other states and countries; excludes, detects and controls or eradicates serious pests and plant diseases; inspects and certifies seed crops, fruit trees and other agricultural crops.

Pesticide Regulatory Unit

Chris Kirby, Asst. Admin.
503-986-4635; Fax: 503-986-4735

The Pesticide Regulatory Unit administers the Oregon Pesticide Control Act, and cooperates with USEPA and USDA in the administration of federal pesticide programs in Oregon. Activities include the registration of pesticide products, certification of pesticide consultants and applicators, licensing of pesticide dealers and businesses that apply pesticides, and investigation of compliance with state and federal laws. This unit also regulates the labeling and quality of commercial animal feed, fertilizer, lime, mineral and agricultural amendment products.

Advisory Groups

Agriculture, State Board of

Lois Shafer, Board Sec.

635 Capitol St. NE, Salem 97310-0110; 503-986-4757; Fax: 503-986-4747

Karla Chambers, chair, Salem, 1997

Ten members and two ex officio members are appointed by the governor to four-year terms; not more than five members may be from one political party. Authorized under ORS chapter 561, the board advises the director of the department and assists in determining policies.

Applied Agricultural Research Board, Center for

635 Capitol St. NE, Salem 97310-0110; 503-986-4701

Art Christiansen, chair, Stayton, 1998; Bruce Andrews, Salem, 1998; Dr. Pat Breen, Corvallis, 1998; Sonja Connor, Portland, 1997; Barry Fujishin, Adrian, 1998; Dr. Wesley Jarrell, Beaverton, 1997; Wayne Kizer, Harrisburg, 2000; Jim Landrith, Salem, 1997; Jean Nixon, Junction City, 2000; Phyllis Wustenberg, Bay City, 2000.

The board is comprised of 10 members representing the private sector, research and technology, education, industry, state government and two citizen representatives. It awards grants for applied research on specific problems related to production and food safety and processing. All grants require a match from private industry.

Christmas Tree Advisory Committee

Plant Division

635 Capitol St. NE, Salem 97310-0110; 503-986-4644

This committee, authorized by ORS 571.515, was created to provide close contact between the department and representatives of the Christmas tree industry. It is composed of six members appointed by the director.

New Crops Development Board

Commodity Inspection Division
635 Capitol St. NE, Salem 97310-0110; 503-986-4620

Authorized by ORS chapter 561, the board consists of seven members appointed by the director and one ex officio member. The board's objectives are to identify, endorse and promote worthy new and alternative crops for Oregon and to act as a clearinghouse for new ideas and resources in the development of new crops.

Nursery Research and Regulatory Committee

Plant Division
635 Capitol St. NE, Salem 97310-0110; 503-986-4644

Paul Orson, chair, Tangent

This committee, authorized by ORS 571.025, is composed of seven members appointed by the director. It was created to provide close contact between the department and the nursery industry.

Pesticide Analytical and Response Center

Catherine Thomsen, Health Division
800 NE Oregon St., #21, Portland 97232; 503-731-4025

The Pesticide Analytical and Response Center (PARC) was established in 1978 to coordinate state-agency investigations of health and environmental incidents involving pesticides. PARC serves as a clearinghouse of information and complaints; assesses pesticide incidents; conducts sample analyses; and publishes a yearly report on its findings. PARC is authorized by statute, and the board is composed of representatives from eight agencies plus a citizen representative.

Soil and Water Conservation Commission

John Mellott, Special Asst. to the Dir. for Soil and Water Conservation Districts
635 Capitol St. NE, Salem 97310-0110; 503-986-4705; Fax: 503-373-7210

Tom Straughan, chair, Pendleton.

The Department of Agriculture's Natural Resources Division, through the state Soil and Water Conservation Commission, serves as liaison between the state and the 45 soil and water conservation districts, each of which is administered by five or seven locally elected officials. These 293 elected officials form the Oregon Association of Conservation Districts, responsible for conservation of the state's natural resources as directed in the Oregon Soil and Water Conservation District Laws, chapter 568.

Agricultural Commodity Commissions

Members of 23 of the 29 commodity commissions are appointed by the director of the Department of Agriculture upon recommendations of the industries they represent. Each individual commission has the authority to hire its own employees or contract with individuals or firms to handle administrative duties. Six commissions—Bartlett Pear, Fryer, Highland Bentgrass, Orchardgrass Seed Producers, Ryegrass Growers Seed and Tall Fescue—elect their members as a result of a 1986 amendment that permits this optional method. Each of these must hold an election each year for the terms that expire.

Ex officio members of each commission are the director of the Department of Agriculture and the dean of the School of Agriculture at Oregon State University. In addition, each of the four seafood commissions has an ex officio member representing the Department of Fish and Wildlife. The Wine Advisory Board, technically not a commodity commission, is also listed in this program area.

The commodity commissions are authorized by ORS chapters 576, 577, 578 and 579 and are funded by assessments upon the producers of the commodities. Most commissions conduct promotional, educational, production and market-research projects. The majority are now studying market potential outside the United States.

Alfalfa Seed Commission, 1990

Edith Kressly, Admin.

541-881-1345

Bartlett Pear Commission, 1965

Linda Bailey, Admin.

503-223-8139; Fax: 503-294-1428

Beef Council, 1959

Dianne Byrne, Admin.

503-229-6830; Fax: 503-229-5663

Blueberry Commission, 1985

Jan Marie Schroeder, Admin.

541-758-4043; Fax: 541-758-4553

Clover Commission

John McCulley, Admin.

503-370-7019; Fax: 503-399-8082

Dairy Products Commission, 1943

Sheldon Pratt, Dairy Center Admin.

503-229-5033; Fax: 503-245-7916

Dungeness Crab Commission, 1977

Nick Furman, Admin.

541-267-5810; Fax: 541-267-5772

Fine Fescue Commission, 1955

David S. Nelson, Admin.

503-585-1157; Fax: 503-585-1292

Fryer Commission, 1957

Paul Rains, Admin.

503-256-1151; Fax: 503-257-2774

Grains Commission, 1989

Julie Newtson, Admin.

503-276-4609; Fax: 503-276-5753

Hazelnut Commission, 1951

Polly Owen, Admin.

503-639-3118; Fax: 503-620-9808

Highland Bentgrass Commission, 1959

Bryan Ostlund, Admin.

503-364-2944; Fax: 503-581-6819

Hop Commission, 1964

Susan Hillar, Admin.

503-393-0368; Fax: 503- 393-0677

Mint Commission, 1984

Bryan Ostlund, Admin.

503-364-3346; Fax: 503-581-6819

Orchardgrass Seed Producers Commission, 1962

John McCulley, Admin.
503-370-7019; Fax: 503-399-8082

Potato Commission, 1949

William Wise, Admin.
503-731-3300; Fax: 503-239-4763

Processed Prune and Plum Growers Commission, 1966

Ray Moholt, Admin.
503-292-9305; Fax: 503-292-9305

Processed Vegetable Commission, 1985

John McCulley, Admin.
503-370-7019; Fax: 503-399-8082

Raspberry and Blackberry Commission, 1981(Formerly Oregon Caneberry Commission)

Jan Marie Schroeder, Admin.
541-758-4043; Fax: 541-758-4553

Ryegrass Growers Seed Commission, 1965

Bryan Ostlund, Admin.
503-364-3346; Fax: 503-581-6819

Salmon Commission, 1984

Nancy Fitzgerald, Admin.
541-265-2437; Fax: 541-265-5241

Sea Urchin Producers Commission, 1991

Lisa Charpilloz Hanson, Admin.
503-229-6734; Fax: 503-229-6113

Sheep Commission, 1977

Lisa Charpilloz Hanson, Admin.
503-229-6734; Fax: 503-229-6113

Strawberry Commission, 1967

Jan Marie Schroeder, Admin.
541-758-4043; Fax: 541-758-4553

Sweet Cherry Commission, 1989

Marshall Coba, Admin.
503-585-7716; Fax: 503-399-8082

Tall Fescue Commission, 1969

David S. Nelson, Admin.
503-585-1157; Fax: 503-585-1292

Trawl Commission, 1963

Joe Easley, Admin.
503-325-3384; Fax: 503-325-4416

Western Oregon Onion Commission, 1988

Ed Ross, Admin.
503-378-7349; Fax: 503-378-7349

Wheat Commission, 1947

Tom Winn, Admin.
503-229-6665; Fax: 503-229-6584

Wine Advisory Board, 1984

Christine Pascal, Exec. Dir.
503-228-8336; Fax: 503-228-8337

Architect Examiners, State Board of

Gil Bellamy, Admin.
750 Front St. NE, Suite 260, Salem 97310;
503-378-4270; Fax: 503-378-6091

John Sachs, chair, Portland, 1997; Bill Olsen, vice-chair, Bend, 1998; Darwin Doss, Salem, 1999; Roger Meyer, Portland, 1999; Ted Mularz, Ashland, 2000; Kenneth Nagao, Eugene, 1997; Candace Robertson, Portland, 2000.

The governor appoints the seven board members consisting of five architects and two public members to serve three-year terms which expire in the year indicated.

The State Board of Architect Examiners was created in 1919 and operates under ORS 671.010–671.220 and OAR chapter 806. The board prescribes qualifications for the practice of architecture, conducts examinations to qualify applicants prior to registration, and issues certificates to those who qualify. The board has authority to revoke certificates and assess civil penalties against unregistered individuals practicing architecture without statutory authority.

Approximately 2,500 architects are registered in Oregon, either by examination or by reciprocity.

Taking this picture at just the right moment, A. Paige Baker caught a ship framed neatly by an arched rock along the coast in Tillamook County.

Black Affairs, Commission on

PSU Smith Center, Room M-319, PO Box 751, Portland 97207; 503-725-4646; Fax: 503-725-5899

Linda Hunter, chair, Portland, 1997; Robert Bolden, Eugene, 1999; Anderson DuBoise, Portland, 1998; Sen. Tom Hartung; Bill Isabell, Salem, 1998; Johnny Lake, Salem, 1998; Rep. Frank Shields; Rance Spruill, Portland, 1997; A.J. Talley, Salem, 1998; DeBorah Williams, Portland, 1999.

Created by executive order in October 1980, the Governor's Commission on Black Affairs became a statutory commission in 1983 (ORS 185.410). The commission works for the implementation and establishment of economic, social, legal and political equality for Oregon's African Americans.

The commission monitors existing programs and legislation; identifies and researches concerns and issues affecting the African American community and recommends appropriate action to the governor and to the Legislative Assembly; maintains a liaison between the African American community and Oregon's government; encourages African American representation on state boards and commissions; and serves as analyst, advocate and advisor to the governor, Legislative Assembly, state agencies and officials, and African Americans throughout the state.

The commission also produces and/or assists with the production of events that promote African American heritage and cross-cultural experiences, i.e., Juneteenth Celebration, Martin Luther King Jr. Holiday Recognition, Kwanza Celebration and development of an Oregon Black History Museum.

Blind, Commission for the

Chuck Young, Admin.
535 SE 12th Ave., Portland 97214-2488; 503-731-3221; Fax: 503-731-3230

Steve Hanamura, chair, Portland, 1997; Bill Cardwell, Bend, 1998; Dr. Steven Evers, Madras, 1997; Dr. Jeffery Liegner, Corvallis, 1998; Kae Madera, Portland, 1997; Ralph Policar, Portland, 1997; Jackie Shepherd, Bend, 1997. Four of the seven governor-appointed commissioners must be blind.

The Oregon Commission for the Blind provides vocational rehabilitation and independent living services to Oregonians with severe visual impairments.

Clients learn adaptive skills, including alternative reading, writing and travel techniques, which enable them to live and work independently.

The agency, established in 1937 under ORS 346.120, serves people who are totally blind as well as those with partial vision. There are at least 7,500 legally blind Oregonians. The agency serves individuals statewide from office locations in Portland, Salem, Eugene and Medford.

Services include:

Vocational Rehabilitation. The commission provides a wide range of services to individuals who are legally blind to prepare them for and assist them in securing employment.

Independent Living. Individuals, including older blind Oregonians, are trained to maximize their ability to live independently in their communities and homes and with their families.

Orientation Center. Clients receive training in alternative methods of traveling, reading, cooking and using office equipment.

Business Enterprise Program. Legally blind Oregonians are trained and placed as managers of cafeterias and snack bars in state and federal office buildings.

Industries. Multi-handicapped individuals work in the centers and learn basic job and survival skills.

Summer Work Experience Program. Each summer, 20 to 30 high school students from around the state come to Portland and Salem to work at summer jobs in a variety of fields.

Boundary Commissions

Two Boundary Commissions are established by statute: Lane County Local Government Boundary Commission and Portland Metropolitan Area Local Government Boundary Commission (Clackamas, Multnomah and Washington Counties). Other commissions may be established as provided for by the law governing boundary commissions. Operating under ORS 199.410–199.540, the commission's purpose is to guide the creation and growth of cities, special service districts and privately owned community water and sewer systems.

Lane County Local Government Boundary Commission

Steven C. Gordon, Exec. Officer
North Plaza Level, PSB, 125 E 8th, Eugene 97401-6807; 541-682-4425; Fax: 541-682-4099; Email: ptaylor@lane.cog.or.us

Members appointed by the governor are George Grier, Springfield, 2000; John Lively, Eugene, 2000; Gretchen Miller, Eugene, 1999; Walt Sands, Creswell, 1998; Emily Schue, Eugene, 1998; Don Stewart, Florence, 2000; Ray Walter, Springfield, 2000. The commission was created in 1969.

Portland Metropolitan Area Local Government Boundary Commission

Kenneth S. Martin, Exec. Officer
800 NE Oregon St., #16, Suite 540, Portland 97232-2019; 503-731-4093; Fax: 503-731-8376; Email: pmalgbc@orednet.org

Members appointed by the Metropolitan Service District Executive: Raymond Bartel, Oregon City; Robert Bouneff, Portland; Nathalie Darcy, Portland; Marilyn Helzerman, Hillsboro; Sy Kornbrodt, Portland; Thomas Whittaker, Wilsonville. The commission was created in 1969.

Capitol Planning Commission

Douglas L. Capps, Exec. Dir.
895 Summer St. NE, Salem 97310; 503-378-8163; Fax: 503-378-8948

Carl Myers, chair, public member, Salem; Ruby Brockett, public member, Eugene; Sen. Gene Derfler, Salem (Senate President's designee); Paul Ferder, Salem (Salem Planning Commission representative); Mayor Mike Swaim, Salem; Jeanette M. Launer, public member, Portland; House Speaker's designee; Director of the Department of Administrative Services; Administrator, Facilities Division. The legislative representatives serve as non-voting members of the commission.

The Capitol Planning Commission, established in 1949, is authorized by ORS 276.030–276.043 to establish, adopt and implement a long-range plan of development for state-owned properties within Marion and Polk Counties. The commission also reviews state projects and conducts continuing studies and analysis to determine if capital facility projects are in compliance with adopted policies and plans.

One purpose of these planning and review functions is to coordinate the acquisition of facilities and construction or modification of buildings or building use by the state.

In addition, the state is a major player in land holdings and facilities in the Salem/Keizer area. In reviewing capital projects and facilities, the commission provides a forum for communication and consultation between state and local government agencies. It assures compliance of the state's development plans with local planning guidelines and standards affecting the community.

The commission's makeup provides for fuller appreciation of goals and objectives by key state and local players involved in capital development, facilities planning, community development, and land use and transportation planning. It assures that conflicts between competing interests will be successfully resolved and that capital and community development goals and plans will be mutually supportive.

Children and Families, Commission on/Juvenile Justice Advisory Committee

Lynn N. Fallin, Exec. Dir.
530 Center St. NE, Suite 300, Salem 97310;
503-373-1283; Fax: 503-378-8395

Jonathan Ater, chair, Portland, 1997; Sue Cameron, Tillamook, 1997; Rodney Cook (JJAC), Gladstone, 1998; Randy Franke, Salem, 1997; Don Hamon, Salem, 1999; LeRon Howland (JJAC), Salem, 1998; Terry Leggert (JJAC), Salem, 1998; Robert Lieberman, Grants Pass, 1997; Hilary Miller (JJAC), Salem, 1998; Linda Nishi-Strattner, Tigard, 1999; Juan Ortegon (JJAC), Albany, 1998; State Supt. of Public Instruction Norma Paulus, Salem, by statute; Tiah Sanderson (JJAC), Salem, 1998; Edward Schmidt, The Dalles, 1999; Angela Sherbo, Portland, 1999; Pat Sowers, Halfway, 1997; Lucrecia V. Suarez-Gimenez, Beaverton, 1997; Robin Tompkins, Portland, 1999; John Ward (JJAC), Coos Bay, 1998; Dir. of Department of Human Resources Gary Weeks, Salem, by statute; Janice Yaden, Lake Oswego, 1997.

The Oregon Commission on Children and Families (OCCF) is the largest umbrella advocacy group for children and families in Oregon.

Commission members are appointed by the governor for four-year terms. A majority of them, including the chair, must be lay citizens. The commission is devoted to the mobilization of communities by shifting decision making to the local level. All 36 Oregon counties have local Commissions on Children and Families, which are responsible for major decision making, comprehensive planning, fiscal management and grant making in their communities.

Created by 1993 legislation, the OCCF was built upon the model of the former Oregon Community Children and Youth Services Commission. The Juvenile Justice Advisory Committee (JJAC) was created by executive order in 1994. JJAC membership includes commission members and the governor appoints additional members to meet federal requirements. JJAC participates in the development of Oregon's Juvenile Justice plan, reviews Juvenile Justice grants, receives input from juveniles currently in the system, and actively consults with local government in developing the state plan (two-thirds of federal funds are passed through to local governments).

Programs administered through OCCF/JJAC include: **Great Start**, a community grant program designed to complement and stimulate local efforts to help Oregon's youngest children, from prenatal to six years, to ensure that they reach the first grade with good physical, social, intellectual and emotional development; **Court Appointed Special Advocates** (CASA), citizens appointed to represent the best interests of children who are victims of abuse and neglect on a case-by-case basis in Oregon's juvenile courts; **Oregon's Youth Conservation Corps**, a nationally-acclaimed youth employment program targeting "at-risk" youth ages 16-25, providing life and work-skills training with focus on conservation of natural, human, historical and cultural resources; **Juvenile Justice and Delinquency Prevention** programs, to prevent gang activity and control delinquency by providing for the separation of juveniles from incarcerated adults; **Healthy Start**, a community level collaborative project featuring home visits by paraprofessionals to screen families for risk factors, teach parenting skills and connect families to needed services; **Juvenile Services**, to assure Oregon's youth access to 24-hour intake, family crisis intervention and diversion services; **Student Retention Initiative**, designed to curb the high school dropout rate; and **Child Care and Development Block Grant**, a federal grant to benefit children and working parents by enhancing and stabilizing before- and after-school, and infant and toddler child care.

Chiropractic Examiners, Oregon Board of

Dave McTeague, Exec. Dir.
3218 Pringle Rd. SE, Suite 150, Salem 97302-6311; 503-378-5816; Fax: 503-378-3575

C. Robert Hovenden, DC, president, Roseburg, 1998; Roger Setera, DC, vice-president, Portland, 1996; Bonnie McDowell, DC, secretary, Forest Grove, 1997; James W. Hendry, Portland, 1999; Charles A. Simpson, DC, Cornelius, 1999.

The five-member Board of Chiropractic Examiners, appointed by the governor to three-year terms, is composed of four practicing doctors of chiropractic and one public member.

The Oregon Board of Chiropractic Examiners (OBCE) was created in 1915 and operates under the statutory authority of ORS chapter 684 and OAR 811. Its mission is to protect the public health and safety through examination, licensing and disciplinary programs for chiropractic physicians and chiropractic assistants. All complaints regarding chiropractic should be referred to the OBCE.

Citizens' Utility Board of Oregon

Bob Jenks, Exec. Dir.
921 SW Morrison St., #550, Portland 97205; 503-227-1984; Fax: 503-274-2956; Email: cub@teleport.com

Officers: Kirk Roberts, chair; Margot Beutler, vice-chair; Chuck Mundorff, treasurer; Steve Gorham, secretary.

District 1: Kirk Roberts, Portland, 1998. District 2: DonElla Payne, Grants Pass, 1999; Mark Wilk, Ontario, 2000. District 3: Margot Beutler, Portland, 1998; Tim Goss, Portland, 1997. District 4: Chuck Mundorff, Eugene, 2000. District 5: Joan Cote, Salem, 2000; Steve Gorham, Salem, 1997.

The Citizens' Utility Board of Oregon (CUB) was created by voter initiative in 1984. CUB is an independent, non-profit, public corporation, designed to represent the interests of utility consumers through research and investigation; through appearances before legislative, judicial, and administrative bodies; and by participating in governmental proceedings. It has the same powers and is subject to the same restrictions as other Oregon non-profit corporations and its board meetings are open to the public.

CUB is funded by voluntary membership contributions. Any Oregon resident 18 and older may become a member by making an annual membership contribution of $5 or more. The membership fee may be waived due to financial hardship. The board of governors is elected by CUB members. Any CUB member may run for office.

Clinical Social Workers, State Board of

Elizabeth A. Buys, Admin.
3218 Pringle Rd. SE, Suite 140, Salem 97302-6310; 503-378-5735; Fax: 503-378-3575; Email: elizabeth.buys@state.or.us

Roger A. Kryzanek, LCSW, chair, Bend, 2000; Carole Gray, Portland, 1998; Wm. "Pat" MacKenzie, LCSW, Roseburg, 1998; Virginia Martin, LCSW, Portland, 2000; Kathy Outland, LCSW, Salem, 1999; Agnes Sowle, Portland, 1997; William D. Young, Eugene, 1998.

Created in 1979 and authorized by ORS 675.510–675.600, the Board of Clinical Social Workers is composed of four licensed clinical social workers and three public citizens with an interest in social work. Members are appointed by the governor for four-year terms and are eligible for one reappointment. Terms expire on June 30 of the year indicated.

The mission of the board is to protect the citizens of Oregon through the regulation of clinical social workers. This is done by certifying (Associates) working toward licensure through two-year Plans of Supervision and licensing Licensed Clinical Social Workers (LCSWs) through a national examination with a self-test on Oregon law and rules upon completion of the requirements.

The board audits LCSWs continuing education annually as part of license renewal and exercises disciplinary authority when necessary through Letters of Reprimand, Stipulated Agreements and Revocation of Licenses. The board adopts rules, has the authority to deny, suspend, revoke or refuse to renew a certificate or license. The board holds monthly meetings which are open to the public.

Columbia River Gorge Commission

Jonathan L. Doherty, Exec. Dir.

PO Box 730, White Salmon, WA 98672; 509-493-3323; Fax: 509-493-2229; Email: crgc@gorge.net

Governor appointees: Steve McCarthy, Portland, 2000; Louie Pitt Jr., Warm Springs, 1997; Janice Staver, The Dalles, 1999.

Oregon county appointees: Blair Batson, Multnomah County, 1997; Donald

Etta Conner of Pendleton participates in the 6th Annual Wallowa Band Nez Perce Friendship Feast and Pow Wow. Efforts are underway to establish a permanent home for the Pow Wow at a proposed 60-acre Nez Perce Trail Interpretive Center. Photo by Gary Fletcher.

Dunn, Wasco County, 1999; Joyce Reinig, Hood River County, 2000.

The bi-state Columbia River Gorge Commission was created by the states of Oregon and Washington in 1987. The board has six appointees from each state, three appointed by each governor and three by the local counties. There is also a non-voting member representing the U.S. Secretary of Agriculture.

The commission was created in response to federal legislation that established the 285,000-acre Columbia River Gorge National Scenic Area in 1986. The purposes of the legislation are to protect and provide for the enhancement of the scenic, cultural, recreational and natural resources of the Columbia River Gorge, and to protect and support the area's economy by encouraging growth within existing urban areas and by allowing future economic development elsewhere when consistent with the area's important resources.

The commission is working in partnership with the U.S. Forest Service, six counties and four tribes to implement a regional management plan.

Construction Contractors Board

Kenneth K. Keudell, Admin.

700 Summer St. NE, Suite 300, PO Box 14140, Salem 97309-5052; 503-378-4621; Fax: 503-373-2007

Michael M. Daly, chair, Redmond, 1997; James A. Chaney, vice-chair, Eugene, 1997; Dick Ballard, Milwaukie, 1999; Diana M. Bilyeu, Medford, 2000; Sydney Brewster, Salem, 1999; James Hirte, Dundee, 1999; Mary T. Nolan, Portland, 2000; Jeanne Staton, Eugene, 2000; Gwen M. VanDenBosch, Dallas, 1998.

The governor appoints the nine-member board, subject to Senate confirmation, to serve four-year terms. Six of the board members are contractors, two are public members and one is an elected local official.

The Construction Contractors Board, originally established as the Builders Board by the 1971 Legislative Assembly, is primarily responsible for safeguarding the security and property of the citizens of Oregon by preventing and resolving construction contracting problems, and by ensuring contractors' competency and compliance with the laws of other agencies.

The board administers the Oregon Contractors Law (ORS chapter 701) that provides for registration of all residential and commercial construction contractors and subcontractors, investigation and adjudication of complaints filed against registrants, and assessment of civil penalties against contractors who are not registered. The board also engages in education activities aimed at preventing construction problems and publishes pamphlets that explain its role in helping citizens resolve problems.

Registered contractors have submitted a surety bond and evidence of liability insurance. Contractors who registered after July 1, 1990 are required to complete business and Oregon law classes. More than 38,000 contractors are registered in Oregon.

Consumer and Business Services, Department of

Kerry Barnett, Dir.
Deborah Lincoln, Deputy Dir.
350 Winter St. NE, Salem 97310; 503-378-4100 (voice/TTY); Fax: 503-378-6444; Email: dcbs.director@state.or.us; Web: www.cbs.state.or.us

In an effort to streamline state government, the 1993 Oregon Legislature created the Department of Consumer and Business Services (DCBS). Senate Bill 167 merged the Department of Insurance and Finance with the Appraiser Certification and Licensure Board; the Building Codes Agency; the Office of Minority, Women and Emerging Small Business; and the Oregon Medical Insurance Pool. In 1995 the Department of Energy was merged, becoming the Office of Energy within DCBS.

DCBS is the state's largest regulatory agency and administers the state laws and rules governing workers' compensation, occupational health and safety, real estate appraisal activity, building codes, the operation of insurance companies and financial institutions, and securities offerings.

DCBS has seven regulatory and service divisions: Appraiser Certification and Licensure Board; Energy; Building Codes; Insurance; Finance and Corporate Securities; Occupational Safety and Health (Oregon OSHA); Workers' Compensation; and the Office of Minority, Women and Emerging Small Business, which provides targeted economic opportunities for minority and women-owned businesses. The department has three internal support divisions: Business Administration, Information Management, and the Director's Office. The Oregon Medical Insurance Pool (OMIP) is a health insurance program administered by the department, designed for Oregonians who cannot obtain coverage because of health reasons. The Workers' Compensation Board is an independent adjudicatory body that shares fiscal and management services with the department. DCBS has 1,204 staff positions and a total budget of $489.8 million.

Director, Office of the

Kerry Barnett, Dir.
Deborah Lincoln, Deputy Dir.
350 Winter St. NE, Salem 97310; 503-378-4100 (voice/TTY); Fax: 503-378-6444; Email: dcbs.director@state.or.us; Web: www.cbs.state.or.us

The Office of the Director provides the department with leadership, policy direction and general supervision of all program areas. It is focused on department-wide initiatives aimed at improving agency performance in five critical areas: customer service, public information, regulatory reform, workforce development and use of technology. These initiatives are key to fulfilling its mission and statutory responsibilities.

The Office of the Director serves as liaison to the governor, Legislature, executive branch, and other state agencies on issues of consumer protection, worker safety, and business regulation. The office also serves as ambassador to public interest groups and business organizations in communicating the department's mission and programs.

Appraiser Certification and Licensure Board

Linda Riddell, Admin.
350 Winter St. NE, Salem 97310; 503-373-1505; Fax: 503-378-6576; Email: linda.c.riddell@state.or.us; Web: www.cbs.state.or.us

Roxanne Gillespie, chair

The Appraiser Certification and Licensure Board (ACLB) licenses and certifies real estate appraisers in Oregon and develops and establishes appraisal education and experience requirements in accordance with state and federal law, guidelines and standards.

The 1991 Legislature created the board to implement Title XI of the Federal Financial Institutions Reform Recovery and Enforcement Act of 1989 (Public Law 101-73) in Oregon. The regulatory functions of the board are independent of other realty-related regulatory agencies. The Appraiser Certification and Licensure Board consists of 10 members, nine of whom are appointed by the governor— five of these nine are appraisers, two are from the banking industry, and two are members of the public. The 10th is the DCBS director or designee, who serves as a non-voting member.

Office of Energy

John Savage, Admin.
625 Marion St. NE, Salem 97310; 503-378-4040; toll-free: 1-800-221-8035 (in Oregon); Fax: 503-373-7806; Email: energy.in.internet@state.or.us; Web: www.cbs.state.or.us/external/ooe

The Office of Energy (formerly the Oregon Department of Energy) was created by the 1975 Legislature and operates under ORS 469.010–469.120. Its mission is to protect Oregon's quality of life by saving energy, developing clean and low-cost energy resources, and safely cleaning up nuclear waste. To encourage investments in energy efficiency and conservation, the Office offers loans, rebates, grants and tax credits to households, businesses and public agencies, to finance a portion of the costs of their conservation projects.

The Office also aims to ensure that Oregon develops a mix of energy resources that not only minimize environmental harm but also provide electricity that is affordable, reliable, adequate and safe. The Office of Energy oversees the cleanup and transport of low-level radioactive wastes in Oregon,

As a result of action taken by the 1995 Legislature, the Office of Energy, formerly the Oregon Department of Energy became part of the Department of Consumer and Business Services.

as well as developing and implementing emergency plans for accidents involving radioactive materials.

The Office staffs two energy policy and regulatory boards—the Energy Facility Siting Council (EFSC) and Hanford Waste Board. EFSC is a seven-member board of citizens that determines whether energy facilities may be built in Oregon. The Hanford Waste Board represents the state and protects Oregon's interests relating to the Hanford site in Washington.

Building Codes Division

Joseph A. Brewer III, Admin.
1535 Edgewater St. NW, Salem 97310; 503-378-4133; Fax: 503-378-2322; Email: bcd.webmaster@state.or.us; Web: www.cbs.state.or.us/external/bcd

The mission of the Building Codes Division is to facilitate the construction of safe, accessible and energy efficient structures while promoting a positive business climate.

This division is charged with adopting and enforcing a uniform statewide building code relating to construction, reconstruction, alteration and repair of structures, and to the installation of mechanical, plumbing, and electrical devices and equipment. The administrator is appointed by the director of the Department of Consumer and Business Services.

The division administers seven specialty codes and regulates six other construction industry-related activities. It examines, certifies, registers and licenses 11 professions or trades, and issues operating permits for three industries. In addition to its West Salem headquarters, the division maintains full-service field offices in Coquille, Pendleton and The Dalles. The division works with, provides staff support to, and receives advice and counsel from five boards.

Boiler Rules, Board of

Curt Lundine, Board Sec.
503-373-1216; Email: william.curt.lundine@state.or.us

George Connelly, chair

The governor appoints the board's 11 members to four-year terms, subject to Senate confirmation. Operating under the direction of ORS 480.535, the board assists in adopting, amending, and enforcing rules, certifications, and minimum safety standards for boilers, pressure vessels and pressure piping; approves related division fees and training programs; hears code appeals; and makes scientific and technical findings related to code interpretations.

Building Codes Structures Board

Darin Wilson, Board Sec.
503-373-1354; Email: darin.wilson@state.or.us

John Talbott, chair

Under ORS 455.132, the board assists the DCBS director in the administration of the structural, mechanical, one- and two-family dwelling, prefabricated structure and energy programs described in ORS chapter 455, and programs promoting accessibility for persons with physical disabilities described in ORS 447.210–447.280. The board hears code appeals and makes scientific and technical findings related to code interpretations. The governor appoints the board's 15 members to four-year terms, subject to Senate confirmation.

Electrical and Elevator Board

Junior Owings, Board Sec.
503-373-7509;
Email: junior.l.owings@state.or.us

Walter E. Conner, chair

The board's 15 members are appointed by the governor, subject to Senate confirmation. Under ORS 455.138 the board assists in administering the Electrical Safety Law and advises and approves electrical rules and codes, as well as revocations or suspensions of electrical licenses.

The board advises on rules governing elevator safety and hears appeals. The board also approves related division fees and training programs, hears code appeals, and makes scientific and technical findings related to code interpretations.

Manufactured Structures and Parks Advisory Board

Patrick Lewis, Board Sec.
503-373-1266; Email: pat.d.lewis@state.or.us

John W. Eames III, chair

ORS 446.280 established this board to advise the DCBS director on adopting, administering and enforcing the standards for the national manufactured housing, manufactured dwelling

park, recreational vehicle, recreation park, and an organizational camp and picnic park programs.

The board approves related division fees and training programs, hears code appeals, and makes scientific and technical findings related to code interpretations. The DCBS director appoints the board's 12 members to four-year terms.

Plumbing Board, State

Terry Swisher, Board Sec.
503-373-7488;
Email: terry.l.swisher@state.or.us

Arthur Atchison, chair

The governor appoints the board's seven members to four-year terms, subject to Senate confirmation. Under ORS 693.115, the board advises on plumbing code formulation and approves plumbing products as described in ORS chapter 447. The board also approves related division fees and training programs, hears code appeals, and makes scientific and technical findings related to code interpretations. Under ORS chapters 670 and 693, the board also examines plumbers and issues licenses.

Business Administration Division

Joan Hader, Admin.
Labor & Industries Bldg.
350 Winter St. NE, Salem 97310; 503-378-3305;
Fax: 503-378-3134;
Email: joan.k.hader@state.or.us;
Web: www.cbs.state.or.us

The Business Administration Division provides central support to the Department of Consumer and Business Services, including financial management, accounting, payroll, collections, budgeting, purchasing and mail delivery services.

Minority, Women and Emerging Small Business, Office of

Cheri Tebeau-Harrell, Certification Mgr.
350 Winter St. NE, Salem 97310; 503-378-5651;
Fax: 503-373-7041;
Email: cheri.tebeau-harrell@state.or.us;
Web: www.cbs.state.or.us

The Office of Minority, Women and Emerging Small Business (OMWESB) administers the Disadvantaged, Minority and Women, and Emerging Small Business Enterprise certification program. These programs are designed to promote targeted economic opportunities to small businesses in the state.

The office provides certification to disadvantaged, minority and women-owned businesses, and emerging small businesses who meet the eligibility requirements. It publishes a directory of certified firms, and distributes it to public agencies, prime contractors and private corporations. The office links interested disadvantaged, minority and women-owned businesses with buyers, contract managers, and project managers who need products and services that the businesses can provide.

Finance and Corporate Securities, Division of

Cecil R. Monroe, Admin.
350 Winter St. NE, Room 21, Salem 97310;
Finance Section: 503-378-4140;
Corporate Securities Section: 503-378-4387;
Fax: 503-378-4178; Email: dfcsmail@state.or.us;
Web: www.cbs.state.or.us

The Division of Finance and Corporate Securities regulates Oregon's state-chartered financial institutions, including banks, trust companies, savings and loan associations, credit unions, consumer finance companies, mortgage bankers and brokers, and credit service organizations. It also regulates and registers public offerings of securities, and licenses securities broker-dealers, and investment advisors and salespersons. Check and money-order sellers, debt collection agencies, debt consolidating agencies, pawnbrokers and special qualifications corporations are also regulated by the division. The division answers questions regarding laws, rules and licensing requirements and provides consumers and businesses with public records about financial institutions, registered securities offerings, and the employment and discipline record of investment advisors and salespersons, and securities dealers.

Information Management Division

Dan Adelman, Admin.
350 Winter St. NE, Room 300, Salem 97310;
503-378-8254; Fax: 503-378-3134;
Email: dan.a.adelman@state.or.us;
Web: www.cbs.state.or.us

The Information Management Division gathers, stores, analyzes, processes and reports data and information related to workers' compensation, occupational safety and health, insurance, building codes, securities, finance and other department programs. Its functions include systems development, information products, computer operations, research, data analysis and an information center.

Insurance Division

Charles Nicoloff, Deputy Admin.
350 Winter St. NE, Room 440, Salem 97310;
503-378-4271 ext. 640; Fax: 503-378-4351;
Email: dcbs.insmail@state.or.us; Web:
www.cbs.state.or.us/external/ins/docs/divdes.htm

The Insurance Division protects the insurance-buying public through regulation of insurance companies and agents, makes financial and market conduct evaluations of insurance companies and health area service contractors, tests and licenses insurance agents, and assures that insurance premiums are adequate and reasonable. Individuals who have complaints about insurance companies and their agents can contact the Consumer Protection Section of the division at 503-378-4271, ext. 600. The section will investigate complaints or take appropriate action against violators of Oregon's insurance laws.

Insurance Consumer Advocacy

Marcia Martin, Consumer Advocate
350 Winter St. NE, Room 440, Salem 97310;
503-378-4271; Fax: 503-378-4351;
Email: dcbs.insmail@state.or.us; Web:
www.cbs.state.or.us/external/ins/docs/divdes.htm

Oregon Insurance Consumer Advocacy is an insurance division program that protects the interests of the insurance-buying public through public education, policy analysis, and advocacy. Consumer Advocacy publishes consumer guides and sponsors out-reach programs, monitors industry practices and analyzes their impact on consumers and facilitates consumer participation in advisory committees and other agency decision-making. Consumer Advocacy also identifies and advocates for administrative and legislative reforms that would benefit Oregon consumers.

Insurance Guaranty Association

Ken Kennell, Admin.
10700 SW Beaverton Hwy., Suite 426, Beaverton 97005; 503-641-7132; Fax: 503-641-7127

This association guarantees that covered property and casualty insurance claims on policies such as homeowners, auto and liability insurance will be paid if a licensed insurance company becomes insolvent. This association is funded through assessments on all property and casualty insurance companies doing business in Oregon.

Life and Health Insurance Guaranty Association

James B. Kleen, Admin.
PO Box 4520, Salem 97302-8520;
503-588-1974; Fax: 503-588-2029

John W. Mangen, chair
The association guarantees that covered life and health insurance claims will be paid when a company becomes insolvent. The association is funded through assessments on all life and health insurance companies doing business in Oregon.

Health Insurance Reform Advisory Committee (HIRAC)

Maxi McKibben, Coord.
350 Winter St. NE, Room 440, Salem 97310;
503-378-8105; toll-free: 1-800-438-0842;
Fax: 503-378-4351;
Email: maxine.a.mckibben@state.or.us

The Health Insurance Reform Advisory Committee (HIRAC) was authorized by the 1995 Legislature in Senate Bill 152. The bill amends and expands small employer health reform and establishes common definitions and marketing reform for general group and individual health contracts. Subject to approval by the director, the committee makes recommendations on the level of benefits for the new portability plan and implementation requirements of Senate Bill 152. Members are appointed by the director.

Medical Insurance Pool

Howard "Rocky" King, Admin.
1225 Ferry St. SE, Salem 97310; 503-373-1692 (voice/TDD); toll-free: 1-800-542-3104;
Fax: 503-373-7704; Email: omip.mail@state.or.us
Web: www.cbs.state.or.us/external/omip/index.html

Tom Hedford, Pacific Heritage Assurance, chair
The Oregon Medical Insurance Pool (OMIP) is a component of the Oregon Health Plan. OMIP was established by the Legislature to provide health insurance for Oregonians who have been turned down for individual health

insurance because of current or former medical problems.

Insurance Pool Governing Board

Howard "Rocky" King, Admin.
1225 Ferry St. SE, Salem 97310; 503-373-1692;
toll-free: 1-800-542-3104; Fax: 503-373-7704;
Email: ipgb.mail@state.or.us

Glen Knickerbocker, chair
This voluntary component of the Oregon Health Plan makes health insurance more affordable for the self-employed and employers with up to 25 workers who have not purchased group health insurance for any employee within the last two years. The IPGB provides businesses with a choice of insurance carriers and affordable insurance plan options.

Senior Health Insurance Benefits Assistance

Marcia Martin, Mgr.
503-378-4484; toll-free: 1-800-722-4134;
Email: dcbs.insmail@state.or.us; Web:
www.cbs.state.or.us/external/ins/docs/divdes.htm

Senior Health Insurance Benefits Assistance (SHIBA) is a program of the Insurance Division that assists Medicare beneficiaries in making informed health insurance decisions. SHIBA program staff train and support the statewide network of volunteers who provide one-on-one assistance in comparing insurance policies, filing claims and making appeals. Program staff also conduct public outreach, produce printed materials and answer general questions for Medicare beneficiaries on the toll-free line.

Occupational Safety and Health Division

Peter De Luca, Admin.
350 Winter St. NE, Room 430,
Salem 97310-0220; 503-378-3272;
toll-free: 1-800-922-2689 (message only);
Fax: 503-378-5729;
Email: admin.web@state.or.us;
Web: www.cbs.state.or.us/external/osha

The Oregon Occupational Safety and Health Division (OR-OSHA) administers the Oregon Safe Employment Act (OSEAct) and enforces the Oregon Occupational Safety and Health Rules, which establish minimum safety and health standards for all industries. The division's enforcement staff inspects workplaces for occupational safety and health hazards, investigates complaints about safety and health issues on the job, and investigates all fatal accidents and catastrophes to determine if the Oregon Safe Employment Act has been violated.

The division has four major programs: Consultative Services; Standards, Training and Technical Resources; Enforcement; and Administration. The programs provide technical, education, consultative and resource services to employers and workers. They programs provide a basis for employers to implement state-of-the-art occupational safety and health injury and illness prevention plans.

Safe Employment Education and Training Advisory Committee

Phyllis Straight-Millan, Coord.
503-378-3272; Email: ed.web@state.or.us

Created by the 1989 Legislature, this committee is made up of seven members: one representing DCBS, three representing labor and three representing employers. Members are responsible for advising the DCBS director in the administration of the Occupational Safety and Health Grant Program. The committee reviews training grant applications and recommends grant awards. $200,000 is available to be awarded each year.

The committee is also responsible for choosing recipients for the Workers' Memorial Scholarship Program. This program uses interest from monies placed in a special account set up by the 1991 Legislature to help educate children or spouses of workers killed or permanently disabled in workplace accidents.

Small Business Ombudsman

John Booton, Ombudsman
165 Labor and Industries Bldg., Salem 97310;
503-378-4209; Fax: 503-373-7639;
Email: john.r.booton@state.or.us;
Web: www.cbs.state.or.us/external/sbo/index.html

The Small Business Ombudsman for Workers' Compensation, established by the 1990 Special Legislative Session, advises the DCBS director on all aspects of the workers' compensation system. The ombudsman is responsible for developing education programs and materials for small business operators, identifying trends in consumer complaints and proposing solutions. The

ombudsman is the small business advocate at workers' compensation ratemaking and rulemaking hearings.

Workers' Compensation Ombudsman

Maria Carraher, Ombudsman
350 Winter St. NE, Room 160, Salem 97310;
503-378-3351; toll-free: 1-800-927-1271;
Fax: 503-373-7639;
Email: maria.a.carraher@state.or.us;
Web: www.cbs.state.or.us

The Workers' Compensation Ombudsman, established by the 1987 Legislature, reports to the DCBS director and serves as an independent advocate for injured workers in their dealings with the workers' compensation system.

The ombudsman's office informs and educates injured workers of their rights within the workers' compensation system. The ombudsman assists with negotiation and mediation of settlements and resolves disputes between the parties. Information about the office is included in every workers' compensation claim closure notice sent out to injured workers.

Workers' Compensation Board

Joan Fraser, Admin.
2250 McGilchrist SE, Salem 97310;
503-373-1660; Fax: 503-373-7742;
Email: margie.l.stice@state.or.us;
Web: www.cbs.state.or.us

Nelson Hall, chair
The Workers' Compensation Board is an independent adjudicatory agency within the Department of Consumer and Business Services. The board's mission is to provide timely and impartial resolution of disputes arising under the Workers' Compensation Law and the Oregon Safe Employment Act. The five-member, full-time board consists of one public member and two members each representing business and labor. Members are appointed by the governor to four-year terms.

The board oversees the work of the Hearings Division whose Administrative Law Judges conduct contested case hearings and provide mediation on cases within the board's jurisdiction. The board also functions as the review body for appeals of workers' compensation Orders. In addition, the board approves alternative settlements such as claim disposition agreements and hears appeals under the Oregon Crime Victim Assistance program.

Workers' Compensation Division

Mary Neidig, Admin.
350 Winter St. NE, Salem 97310; 503-945-7881;
Fax: 503-945-7514;
Email: dcbs.wcdmail@state.or.us;
Web: www.cbs.state.or.us

The Workers' Compensation Division administers, supervises and enforces the Workers' Compensation Law to ensure that employers provide coverage for their workers, that workers with occupational injuries or diseases receive their entitled benefits, and that parties are provided with resources and procedures for fair resolution of disputes.

The division monitors, supervises and regulates various service providers and the claims management of insurers and self-insured employers.

This regulatory responsibility is balanced with fair and consistent policies that encourage a healthy business climate for companies regulated by the division. The division also administers the Workers Benefit Fund. One use of the fund provides incentives to employers in the form of reduced workers' compensation and operation costs for employing or reemploying injured workers.

Medical Care, Advisory Committee on

350 Winter St. NE, Room 200, Salem 97310;
503-945-7724; Fax: 503-378-6444;
Web: www.cbs.state.or.us

Mark A. Melgard, M.D., chair
This committee, appointed by the director, provides advice concerning medical care provided to injured workers by private insurers and self-insured employers. It prepares and submits, or reviews and recommends, appropriate rules and regulations governing such care to the director for consideration, and reviews proposed standards for medical evaluation of disabilities.

Workers' Compensation Management-Labor Advisory Committee

Bill Braly, Admin.
350 Winter St. NE, Salem 97310; 503-378-4268;
Fax: 503-378-6444; Email: bill.braly@state.or.us

Bob Shiprack, Tim Pope, co-chairs
The Workers' Compensation Management-Labor Advisory Committee (MLAC) was created by Senate Bill 1197 in the May 1990 Special Legislative Session. Members of the committee are appointed by the governor and subject to Senate confirmation. Members equally represent management and labor and are responsible for reviewing and making recommendations to the director and Legislature on issues involving workers' compensation. The committee is also responsible for reviewing the standards of permanent disability adopted under ORS 656.726.

Corrections, Department of

David S. Cook, Dir.
Benjamin de Haan, Deputy Dir.
2575 Center St. NE, Salem 97310-0470;
503-945-0920; Fax: 503-373-1173;
Web: www.doc.state.or.us

The Department of Corrections was created by the 64th Legislative Assembly in June 1987 and operates under ORS chapter 423. The department's mission is to reduce the risk of criminal conduct, in partnership with communities, by employing a continuum of community supervision, incarceration, sanctions and services to manage offender behavior. The department's overarching direction originates in the Oregon Constitution, which was amended in November 1996, to say, "Laws for the punishment of crimes shall be founded on these principles: protection of society, personal responsibility, accountability for one's actions and reformation."

The department has custody of offenders sentenced to prison for more than 12 months. Oregon currently houses offenders in 12 state prisons. More than 1,000 inmates are housed in out-of-state rental beds to prevent overcrowding. Due to a prediction that the prison population will more than double by 2006, the state has embarked on an ambitious prison construction program. Construction is slated to begin on seven new prisons between 1997 and 2005. The department will also expand several existing prisons.

The Department of Corrections provides administrative oversight and funding for the community corrections activities of Oregon's 36 counties, but as of January 1, 1997, Oregon counties manage their own offenders who are subject to jail, parole, post-prison supervision and/or probation. The department continues to provide interstate compact administration and jail inspections. The department also provides central information and data services regarding felons statewide and is responsible for evaluating the performance of community corrections.

The Oregon Department of Corrections is recognized nationally among correctional agencies for providing inmates with the cognitive, behavioral and job skills they need to become productive citizens. Oregon has one of the lowest recidivism rates in the nation: more than two-thirds of its former offenders remain out of prison for more than three years.

Business and Finance Division

Sue Acuff, Asst. Dir.
2575 Center St. NE, Salem 97310-0470;
503-945-9007; Fax: 503-373-1173

The Business and Finance Division encompasses the budget, fiscal services, research and facilities management activities of the agency. The Budget Section provides budget development and monitoring, and financial analysis. Fiscal Services manages accounting, central trust, payroll, purchasing and central warehouse operations for the entire department.

The Research Unit provides regular management information reports and performs review, evaluation and outcome studies regarding department programs. Facilities Management oversees planning and implementation of new prison siting and construction, as well as maintenance of current institutions.

Community Corrections Division

Scott Taylor, Asst. Dir.
2575 Center St. NE, Salem 97310-0470;
503-945-9050; Fax: 503-373-7810

The Community Corrections Division, through intergovernmental agreements with the counties, provides supervision, services and sanctions to felony offenders in the community who the courts

sentence to probation, who are on parole or post-prison supervision after completion of a prison sentence, or who are sentenced or revoked to incarceration periods of 12 months or less.

Probation/parole officers monitor the behavior of more than 30,000 felony offenders living in the communities of Oregon at an average cost of $2.36 per offender per day.

Community corrections funding supports both the supervision of offenders and the development of community-based sanctions and correctional programs.

Counties plan a system of sanctions and programs to hold offenders accountable for their behavior including electronic surveillance, community work crews, day reporting centers, intensive supervision, sex offender supervision and treatment, alcohol and drug treatment and employment assistance.

Correctional Programs Division

Steven J. Ickes, Asst. Dir.
2575 Center St. NE, Salem 97310-0470;
503-945-8876; Fax: 503-373-1173

Work, and eliminating the barriers to work through education and treatment, have become the core purpose of inmate program services. During the 1995-97 biennium, the Correctional Programs Division was reorganized into a division of its own. This reorganization has made it possible to focus on issues dealing with inmate assessment, accountability and responsibility. Automated systems are being developed to assist with decision making and inmate work initiatives.

Basic department programs provided to offenders while in secure custody include: inmate assessment; religious services; health services; workforce development, education and training; cognitive programming; counseling and treatment services; inmate work programs; and job placement at the point of transition back into the community.

The goal of Correctional Programs is to reduce the rate of recidivism by providing inmates with work, education and job skills that will assist them in finding employment upon release. These foundations help individuals make a successful transition back into the community.

Corrections Education Advisory Board

Shannon DeLateur, Workforce Development Education and Training Admin.
*2575 Center St. NE, Salem 97310-0470;
503-378-2449, ext. 254; Fax: 503-378-5592*

**Sharlene Walker, Team Leader,
Human Resources Partnerships**
*Office of Community College Services, Public
Service Bldg., 255 Capitol St. NE, Salem 97310;
503-378-8648; Fax: 503-378-8434*

The five-member advisory board is drawn from the Department of Education, Office of Community College Services, the Board of Parole and Post-Prison Supervision, and a member-at-large. The committee chair is authorized under ORS 423.085 and serves as the administrator of correctional education.

Human Resources Division

Karen Roach, Asst. Dir.
*2575 Center St. NE, Salem 97310-0470;
503-945-9028; Fax: 503-373-6427*

The Human Resources Division is composed of the personnel-related services of recruitment; affirmative action; employee development and training; employee safety and risk management; organization and leadership development; and consultation and assistance in administering the department's classification, compensation, human resources' policies and labor contracts. The division is responsible for developing and implementing a comprehensive, full-service human resources program that will enable the department to effectively recruit, develop and retain a highly qualified and rapidly growing workforce of several thousand employees, volunteers and contractors.

Information Systems and Services Division

Jean Hill, Asst. Dir.
*2575 Center St. NE, Salem 97310-0470;
503-945-0965; Fax: 503-945-9000*

The Information Systems and Services Division provides leadership in and support of the department's use of technology. The department's Central Records Unit is located within this division. The focus of this division is to provide high quality and accessible systems and technology solutions that support the department's mission. In addition to the Department of Corrections' staff, daily users of the department's automated systems include law enforcement agencies (city police departments, sheriffs' departments, Oregon State Police); county corrections

*A normally dry pasture lies under water at Turner Farm in Marion County during the 1996 flood.
Photo by Beth Buglione.*

Executive

Executive

agencies; Oregon Board of Parole and Post-Prison Supervision; district attorneys and courts.

The critical nature of the Information Systems and Services Division is evidenced by the breadth and depth of the services it provides, as well as the necessity of accessibility to automated systems 24-hours each day. These automated systems include: a comprehensive and integrated offender database and tracking system; the Corrections Information System (CIS); integrated fiscal services and prison manufacturing system, the Automated Fiscal and Manufacturing Information System (AFAMIS); and automated office systems, e-mail, calendaring, word processing, bulletin boards, etc.

The system operates 24-hours per day, seven days per week and is comprised of a high speed statewide network with 16 mini-computers and several UNIX and PC servers. There are approximately 2,500 workstations connected directly to the network; however, users number well over 3,000. The system and data are available to other public safety agency personnel via the Department of Administrative Services (DAS) computer network backbone.

The division is composed of the following units: Operations and User Support, Applications Development and Maintenance, East Region Support and Central Records.

The Information Systems and Services Division provides the automated tools and processes which supply information for decision making in the operation of the state's 12 prisons and its probation and parole supervision functions in 36 counties. In addition, these tools are essential for budget and planning purposes, policy development, prison population projections, research and program evaluation.

The Central Records Unit is the repository for nearly all legal files pertaining to offenders who have been, or currently are, under the custody or supervision of the department. The unit is responsible for the maintenance of the department's official offender records and, as necessary, for the appropriate distribution, sealing, expunging, exemplifying and archiving of these records.

Inspections Division

Mrs. Les S. Dolecal, Inspector General
2575 Center St. NE, Salem 97310-0470; 503-945-0931; Fax: 503-373-7092

The Inspections Division provides an oversight function on behalf of the director and deputy director of the department. The division comprises three units—Internal Audits, Investigations and Rules/Compliance/Hearings.

The Internal Audits Unit reviews department programs and units to assess procedures, identify areas of concern and ensure appropriate use of agency monies. The unit has two auditors.

The Investigations Unit is responsible for investigating allegations of employee, inmate and visitor misconduct. It also collects evidence of criminal behavior for referral to the State Police, investigates conspiracies to introduce contraband in the institutions, monitors inmate communications and performs other functions as requested by the director, deputy director and inspector general. Two supervisors, seven investigators and five canine teams (drug detection dogs) are assigned to the Investigations Unit.

The Rules/Compliance/Hearings Unit is responsible for preparing and distributing agency rules and procedures throughout the department. This unit is the department's liaison with the Department of Justice and provides an archival function for the Department of Corrections. The eight hearings officers assigned to adjudicate inmate misconduct are also managed by this unit.

Inmate Work Programs

Michael Taaffe, Admin.
2585 State St., Salem 97310; 503-378-2449; Fax: 503-378-5592

Inmate Work Programs comprises Industries, Private Partnerships, and Inmate Work Crews. These three programs—as directed by the constitutional amendment of 1994's Ballot Measure 17—employ inmates to reduce idleness and to lower the costs of operating government or achieve a net profit in private-sector activities.

Eligible inmates are required to participate in work and training assignments a total of 40 hours each week. Inmates' compensation is garnished for such purposes as paying room and board, taxes, court costs, fines, victim restitution and family support.

An additional benefit is that inmates participate in meaningful work experiences, which may help them find gainful employment upon release, potentially reducing repeat offenses and lowering recidivism rates.

Industries

Farm/Dairy Operation: Located at the Mill Creek Correctional Facility east of Salem, the farm produces milk, dairy products and meat for Oregon's correctional facilities and for sale to public and private institutions and businesses throughout the state.

Furniture Factory: Inmates at the Oregon State Penitentiary in Salem manufacture high-quality stock and custom furniture, upholstered office furniture, modular panel systems, mattresses and pillows.

Garment Factory: Located at the Eastern Oregon Correctional Institution in Pendleton, inmates produce the Prison Blues line of denim jeans and clothing. Jeans, jackets, t-shirts, sweatshirts, work shirts and hats are manufactured and sold throughout the U.S. and internationally. All Department of Corrections inmates wear Prison Blues jeans stamped in orange with the word "INMATE."

Laundry: Commercial laundry operations located at Oregon State Penitentiary in Salem and Eastern Oregon Correctional Institution in Pendleton provide quality hand labor and cleaning services (including pick-up and delivery) to public and private institutions and businesses throughout the state.

Metal Shop: Metal items are fabricated by inmates at Oregon State Penitentiary in a cooperative program between OSP and Industries. Products include gates, doors, tables, bed frames, lockers/secure storage, and custom work (including sculpture, such as the decorative overpass fencing at the Chenowith interchange near The Dalles).

Services: Inmates inside Oregon's correctional institutions are interviewed, hired and trained to provide public- and private-sector customers with services such as telecommunications, computer-aided design and mapping (CAD/CAM), mailing, desktop publishing and general office services.

Private Partnerships

Inmate Work Programs can partner with private-sector businesses to employ inmate labor and develop industries both inside and outside of correctional facilities. Inmate Work Programs may provide industrial space and other related incentives to businesses to encourage the development and growth of successful partnerships.

Inmate Work Crews

Crews of supervised inmates provide skilled and unskilled labor for work such as park maintenance, construction, flood control and cleanup, wildfire fighting, repetitive assembly, litter maintenance, grounds keeping, farm labor, painting, and janitorial services. Crews are available for contracted deployment at sites around the state.

Prison Industries Board

Nancy Towslee, Exec. Dir.
2575 Center St. NE, Salem 97310-0470; 503-945-0956; Fax: 503-373-1173

The Prison Industries Board comprises the governor, secretary of state and state treasurer. The board is required to meet quarterly and set policy and approve expenditures from the state prison work programs account and agreements with private enterprises. It provides any other regulatory oversight prescribed by rule or statute. The board also has a nine-member advisory committee.

Prison Industries Board Advisory Committee

Nancy Towslee, Exec. Dir.
2575 Center St. NE, Salem 97310-0470; 503-945-0956; Fax: 503-373-1173

Eric Blackledge, chair; Dennis O'Donnell, vice-chair.

The Prison Industries Board Advisory Committee has nine members appointed by the governor. The director of the Department of Corrections is the executive secretary of the advisory committee and the department staffs the committee. The purpose of the committee is to provide advice and assistance to the Prison Industries Board in developing and implementing public and private inmate work opportunities.

Institutions Division

Al Chandler, Asst. Dir.

2575 Center St. NE, Salem 97310-0470;
503-945-0950; Fax: 503-373-1173

Oregon's adult correctional institutions are centrally managed by the assistant director of institutions. Responsibilities include 12 correctional facilities, administration of inmate classification and transfer, out-of-state contract housing, inmate transportation, the fugitive apprehension unit, gang management and emergency preparedness.

Columbia River Correctional Institution

Michael A. McGee, Supt.

9111 NE Sunderland Ave., Portland 97211-1799;
503-280-6646; Fax: 503-280-6012

Columbia River Correctional Institution is a 500-bed minimum security prison located in Northeast Portland. The institution opened in September 1990, and houses 260 female and 240 male inmates in separate dormitory-style housing units.

Major program activities for 400 general population inmates consist of community service work projects supervised by correctional staff, institution support and maintenance work, and educational and cognitive skills classes.

One hundred inmates (50 men; 50 women) are housed in a separate living area designed specifically for use as a residential alcohol and drug treatment center. Inmates voluntarily participate in a therapeutic community program designed to address serious addiction and substance abuse problems.

Eastern Oregon Correctional Institution

George H. Baldwin Jr., Supt.

2500 Westgate, Pendleton 97801-9699;
541-276-0700; Fax: 541-276-1841

Eastern Oregon Correctional Institution (EOCI) was authorized in 1983 by the 62nd Legislative Assembly as the first medium-security adult male correctional facility established outside Marion County. Until its conversion to a prison, EOCI had been a state mental hospital with most of the buildings constructed in 1912–13. The first inmates were received on June 24, 1985. The 1,600-bed facility is Pendleton's second largest employer.

EOCI is the state's only facility where the internationally-recognized "Prison Blues" line of blue denim clothing is manufactured. The garment factory is one of two prison industries programs operating at the facility. The laundry cleans clothing and other items for EOCI and Snake River Correctional Institution, and other local organizations. Other work opportunities for inmates include: food service, clerical, and facility maintenance.

EOCI contracts with Blue Mountain Community College to provide education services at the institution. Approximately 1,000 inmates have received either a GED certificate or an adult high school diploma since the education program began in 1986. Inmate cognitive skills programs include: The Cognitive Restructuring Program, Steps to Freedom alcohol and drug program, Breaking Barriers, parenting skills, the 12-Step AA/NA programs, the Pathfinders Program and the Franklin Reality Model. Other counseling/treatment services available are: HIV education/pre-post counseling, mental health direct treatment services, crisis intervention, mental health counseling groups and outpatient alcohol and drug treatment.

Mill Creek Correctional Facility

Robert Schiedler, Supt.

5465 Turner Rd. SE, Salem 97301-9400;
503-378-5807; Fax: 503-378-8235

Mill Creek Correctional Facility (MCCF) is located five miles southeast of Salem, and houses 312 minimum custody inmates. It is a 2,089-acre working farm, complete with dairy buildings and barns, including a complete milk-processing plant and a modern slaughterhouse facility. In addition to offering work and training opportunities for inmates in the community, the farm produces milk and beef used to offset inmate food costs at the Salem-based and other correctional institutions.

Oregon Corrections Intake Center

Larry Daniels, Mgr.

2206-B Kaen Rd., Oregon City 97045-4090;
503-655-8420; Fax: 503-655-8450

Under an intergovernmental agreement between the state of Oregon and Clackamas County, the Department of Corrections constructed the 200-bed Oregon Corrections Intake Center (OCIC) adjacent to the Clackamas County Jail in Oregon City. It was completed in 1991.

The intake center is the first such center in the state. It facilitates the induction of male inmates into the Department of Corrections penal system by centrally housing them until the classification process, as well as an assessment of educational, vocational, mental and physical health needs, is completed. Upon completion of the process, which takes 7 to 14 days, inmates are assigned and transported to an appropriate institution.

Oregon State Correctional Institution

Nick Armenakis, Supt.

3405 Deer Park Dr. SE, Salem 97310-9385; 503-373-0100; Fax: 503-378-8919

Oregon State Correctional Institution (OSCI), a medium security facility located three miles east of Salem on North Santiam Highway 22, was established by action of the 1955 Legislature and became fully operational June 1, 1959.

The 840-bed facility provides housing and confinement for males serving sentences for felony convictions from all counties of Oregon. The facility provides useful work and self-improvement programs to enhance inmates' ability to reintegrate into the community.

Oregon State Penitentiary

S. Frank Thompson, Supt.

2605 State St., Salem 97310-0505; 503-378-2445; Fax: 503-378-3897

Oregon State Penitentiary (OSP), Oregon's first state prison, was originally located in Portland in 1851. In 1866 it was moved to a 26-acre site in Salem and enclosed by a reinforced concrete wall averaging 25 feet in height. OSP is the state's only maximum security prison.

The penitentiary houses up to 2,100 inmates. It has special housing units for maximum custody inmates; disciplinary segregation; offenders with psychiatric problems; and inmates sentenced to death. The 196-bed, self-contained Intensive Management Unit provides housing and control for those male inmates who disrupt or pose a substantial threat to the general population in all department facilities.

Oregon Women's Correctional Center

Sonia Hoyt, Supt.

2809 State St., Salem 97310-0500; 503-373-1907; Fax: 503-378-6392

Oregon Women's Correctional Center (OWCC) opened in January 1965. OWCC had an original design capacity of 76 beds. Remodeling projects and double bunking have expanded the capacity to 190 beds in cells and dormitories.

OWCC is the only medium custody adult female prison in the state and is the only full-service prison in the Oregon Department of Corrections. It operates as an intake and release center for women with all custody and program levels. It maintains a segregation unit, maximum custody housing and a substance abuse transitional treatment program (INFOCUS).

Other inmate programs include mental health treatment, self help classes and educational/professional technical programs. In addition, OWCC has work opportunities for all eligible inmates.

Powder River Correctional Facility

Debra Slater, Supt.

3600 13th St., Baker City 97814-1346; 541-523-6680; Fax: 541-523-6678

The Powder River Correctional Facility (PRCF) was opened on November 9, 1989. The facility was established to provide minimum security inmates with the opportunity to participate in a residential alcohol and drug treatment program or labor camp program prior to their release. The facility houses 178 adult male inmates: 128 labor inmates and 50 alcohol and drug treatment inmates. Inmates enrolled in the alcohol and drug treatment program follow a strict regimen of work, education, individual and group counseling, family therapy, recreation and other program activities for 10 to 12 hours daily. Labor inmates perform community service in and around Baker City and serve on fire crews in conjunction with the Department of Forestry.

Santiam Correctional Institution

Robert Schiedler, Supt..

4005 Aumsville Hwy. SE, Salem 97301-9112; 503-378-5807; Fax: 503-378-8235

Santiam Correctional Institution (SCI) is a 510-bed minimum security facility located in southeast Salem. Community reintegration programs are developed and coordinated for inmates prior to release from prison. While waiting for release, inmates are assigned to supervised work activities in the community and participate in alcohol and drug, sex offender, and cognitive and educational programs.

Shutter Creek Correctional Institution
Bill Beers, Supt.
2000 Shutters Landing Rd., North Bend 97459-0303; 541-756-6666; Fax: 541-756-6888

Acquired from the U.S. General Services Administration at no cost to Oregon taxpayers in January 1990, this former Air National Guard Radar Station has been converted into a 216-bed minimum security prison.

The Shutter Creek Correctional Institution (SCCI) consists of 56 acres containing 20 buildings surrounded by forest land. Existing barracks were converted to provide four 50-bed dormitories for men, as well as a small women's dorm.

The facility currently houses 50 male inmates who perform public service in forests, parks, highways and beaches, as well as approximately 166 male and female inmates who are voluntary participants in the Oregon SUMMIT boot camp program, which was implemented in March 1994. The SUMMIT program is an intense, 16-hour-a-day, 7-day-a-week program, including military dress, bearing, physical training, cognitive change, education, substance abuse education and treatment, and community living.

Snake River Correctional Institution
Daniel P. Johnson, Supt.
777 Stanton Blvd., Ontario 97914-0595; 541-881-5000; Fax: 541-881-5460

Snake River Correctional Institution (SRCI) is a multi-security facility which opened in August 1991. Although sited for 3,000 beds, only 576 medium security and 72 minimum security beds were constructed in Phase I. In 1994, the Oregon Legislature approved construction of the remaining 2,352 beds at a cost of $175 million, representing the largest general-funded public works project in state history.

When completed, the institution will be the largest prison in Oregon with 2,336 medium security beds,

154 minimum security beds and 510 special housing beds (administrative segregation, disciplinary segregation, intensive management, infirmary and special management units). The expanded institution has several unique features such as decentralization of inmate services which provides for the separation of various offenders. It also has a comprehensive corridor system, connecting housing, program and work areas so inmates can move from one area to another at all times of day under all types of weather conditions. Upon completion in mid-1998, the institution's operating budget will be more than $100 million and employ 1,150 corrections professionals.

South Fork Forest Camp
Michael A. McGee, Supt.
48300 Wilson River Hwy., Tillamook 97141-9799; 503-842-2811; Fax: 503-842-6572

South Fork Forest Camp is located 28 miles east of Tillamook, two miles off Highway 6. Since 1951, the camp's inmates have performed reforestation projects under the Forest Rehabilitation Act. One hundred fifty minimum security inmates are housed at the camp and work under the direction of the Department of Forestry.

Counselors and Therapists, Board of Licensed Professional

Carol F. Fleming, Admin.
3218 Pringle Rd. SE, Suite 160, Salem 97302-6312; 503-378-5499; Email: lpc.lmft@state.or.us

Donna M. Ford, LPC, chair, Portland, 1997; John P. Deihl, LMFT, Aloha, 1998; Martin E. Henner, Eugene, 1997; Linda J. James, LPC, Salem, 1997; John M. Kimmel, LMFT, Medford, 1998; Rory F. Richardson, PhD, LPC, Tillamook, 1998; Carol F. Sisson, PhD, LPC, Bend, 1998.

Authorized in 1989 by ORS chapter 675, the State Board of Licensed Professional Counselors and Therapists consists of seven members appointed for three-year terms by the governor: three licensed professional counselors, two licensed marriage and family therapists, a faculty member, and a public representative.

The board determines professional qualifications and examines and issues licenses to counselors and marriage and family therapists; sets standards for and regulates the practice of licensees; sets and enforces continuing education requirements; publishes an annual directory; and investigates alleged violations and complaints against licensees.

Criminal Justice Commission

Phillip Lemman, Exec. Dir.
155 Cottage St. NE, Salem 97310; 503-378-2053; Fax: 503-378-8666

William F. Gary, attorney, Eugene; J. Eduardo Lopez, developer, Salem; Linda Moore, community volunteer, Bend; Charles Moose, Portland police chief; Dale Penn, Marion County District Attorney, Salem; Ann Rupe, title company owner, Ontario; one vacancy.

The Oregon Criminal Justice Commission was created by the 1995 Legislature to fulfill two new functions and continue other duties from its predecessor agency, the Criminal Justice Council.

The commission serves as the focal point for state public safety policy development and agency coordination. Its primary responsibility is to develop a state criminal justice policy and a long-range, public safety plan for Oregon. The plan will make recommendations to the governor and Legislature regarding capacity and use of state prisons and local jails, implementation of community corrections programs, programs to use in addition to or in lieu of incarceration, whether new facilities or alternative programs are needed, and methods to reduce risk of future criminal conduct.

The commission also will provide technical assistance to Local Public Safety Coordinating Councils created under 1995 Senate Bill 1145. That legislation strengthens the state and local public safety partnership by giving counties responsibility and funding for incarceration and services for felony offenders sentenced to less than one year incarceration, and for parole and probation violators. The commission will continue responsibility for adopting sentencing guidelines and serve as an information resource and clearinghouse for local, state and federal agencies.

Dentistry, Oregon Board of

JoAnn L. Bones, Exec. Dir.
1515 SW 5th Ave., Suite 602, Portland 97201; 503-229-5520; Fax: 503-229-6606

Lewis E. Blue, D.M.D., president, Eugene, 2000; H. Clayton Stearns, D.M.D., vice-president, Salem, 1997; Lynda Ciri, R.D.H., Portland, 1997; Ben Curtis, D.D.S., Portland, 1998; Herbert W. Goodman, D.D.S., Portland, 1997; Kristine M. Hudson, Portland, 1998; Eugene O. Kelley, D.M.D., Beaverton, 1999; Pamela J. Philips, R.D.H., Medford, 1998; Edward Straka, D.D.S., Bend, 2000.

The governor appoints nine board members: five dentists, one dentist specialist, two dental hygienists and one public member. Members serve for four years.

The Oregon Board of Dentistry, created in 1887, administers the Dental Practice Act (ORS chapter 679 and 680.010–680.170 and OAR 818-01-000 through 818-41-100). The board examines and licenses dentists, seven dental specialties and dental hygienists. It issues anesthesia permits and certifies dental assistants in radiologic proficiency and expanded functions. The board investigates alleged violations of the Dental Practice Act and may discipline violators, including revoking or suspending a license. The board also provides education and information regarding the Dental Practice Act.

The board adopts rules necessary for examination and regulation of the practice of dentistry, dental hygiene and auxiliary personnel. The board's revenues include license, permit and certification fees.

Dietitians, Board of Examiners of Licensed

Ann Aalund, Exec. Dir.
800 NE Oregon St., #21, Suite 407, Portland 97232; 503-731-4085; Fax: 503-731-4207

Professional members: Susan Greathouse, L.D., chair, Portland, 1998; Sabine Artaud-Wild, L.D., Portland, 1998; Kathleen Ellis, L.D., Tillamook, 1999; Mary Cluskey, L.D., Albany, 1998; Physician member: Bart Duell, Portland, 1998; Public members:

Patricia Lewis, South Beach, 1999; Caroline Smith, Salem, 1998. Members are appointed by the Health Division administrator.

The Board of Examiners of Licensed Dietitians was created by the 1989 Legislative Assembly. Operating under ORS chapter 691, it oversees the practice of licensed dietitians by determining qualifications of applicants for licensure, setting standards of practice and investigating complaints of alleged violations of practice.

Disabilities Commission

Eugene Organ, Exec. Dir.
1257 Ferry St. SE, Salem 97310; 503-378-3142 (voice/TTY); toll-free: 1-800-358-3117, Oregon only; Fax: 503-378-3599

Jan Campbell, chair, Portland; Mary Byrkit, Portland; Kenneth Crowley, Wilsonville; Donn DeBernardi, Portland; Janine DeLaunay, Portland; JoAnna Gaumond, Salem; Alicia Hays, Eugene; Diane Imel, Wilsonville; George McCart, Prineville; Kristine Merlich, Bend; Robert Pike, Portland; Henry Stack, Portland. The commission is authorized by ORS chapter 185. Commissioners are appointed by the governor and confirmed by the Senate for not more than two consecutive three-year terms.

The Disabilities Commission identifies and publicizes the needs and rights of individuals with disabilities; advises the legislature, the governor, state agencies and other public and private agencies on disability issues; coordinates interagency efforts in the delivery of disability-related services, and promotes the rehabilitation and employment of the disabled.

The commission conducts Oregon's **Client Assistance Program**, which helps clients in federally-funded rehabilitation programs by explaining rules and procedures, client rights and responsibilities, and mediating conflicts.

The **Deaf and Hearing Impaired Access Program** assists state agencies in ensuring that programs and services are accessible to deaf and hearing impaired persons.

The commission has been designated the coordinating agency for implementing the Americans With Disabilities Act in Oregon.

The Oregon Disabilities Commission also administers Technology Access for Life Needs (TALN). TALN provides information and advocacy on assistive technology for people with disabilities.

Dispute Resolution Commission

Alice B. Phalan, Exec. Dir.
1174 Chemeketa St. NE, Salem 97310; 503-378-2877; Fax: 503-373-0794; Email: odrc@open.org

The Dispute Resolution Commission, established in 1989, is responsible for administering the Dispute Resolution Act (ORS 36.100–36.210). Commissioners are appointed by the governor and confirmed by the Senate for four-year terms. The commission supports community dispute resolution programs approved by county commissions for funding.

The commission establishes program standards, qualifications and training for mediators in state-funded programs and methods of evaluating dispute resolution programs. It recommends operation rules and procedures of court mediation. The commission operates the **Public Policy Program** to encourage use of dispute resolution in disputes that affect public interest and/or involve public decision-making at local, state and federal levels.

Economic Development, Department of

William C. Scott, Dir.
775 Summer St. NE, Salem 97310; 503-986-0123; Fax: 503-581-5115; Web: www.econ.state.or.us

The Oregon Economic Development Department was created in 1973 by ORS chapter 285 as a cabinet-level agency directly accountable to the governor. The agency invests lottery, federal and other funds to help communities and businesses create better jobs and improve their economic opportunities and quality of life.

The five-member Oregon Economic Development Commission, appointed by the governor, helps the agency develop policies and strategies to implement its vision of "More and Better Jobs for Oregonians." The agency is focusing its efforts on creating more jobs in areas that have yet to achieve economic prosperity and on creating better, higher-paying jobs in areas that have already attained economic stability.

The department works with local and regional partners to diversify and strengthen local economies and to coordinate job creation with growth management. It works with industry partners to expand markets, improve know-how and skills, attract capital and increase margins, so that Oregon workers will have jobs that pay better and are more secure.

Regional development officers provide continual agency outreach to communities and businesses throughout Oregon. The officers represent all agency programs and act as liaisons to other state and federal agencies. They serve as key local contacts for the 12 regions of the state. They can be contacted at:

Baker, Malheur counties:
541-523-7463, Baker City

Benton, Lane, Lincoln, Linn counties:
541-757-4230, Corvallis

Clackamas, Hood River counties:
503-650-3768, Oregon City

Clatsop, Columbia, Tillamook counties:
503-842-4045, Tillamook

Coos, Curry, Douglas counties:
541-267-4651, Coos Bay

Crook, Deschutes, Jefferson counties:
541-388-6266, Bend

Gilliam, Grant, Morrow, Sherman, Wasco, Wheeler counties: 541-298-4140, The Dalles

Harney, Klamath, Lake counties:
541-947-4240, Lakeview

Jackson, Josephine counties:
541-776-6234, Medford

Marion, Polk, Yamhill counties:
503-588-6236, Salem

Multnomah, Washington counties:
503-229-5625, Portland

Umatilla, Union, Wallowa counties:
541-963-8676, La Grande

Central and Field Operations

503-986-0104

Central and Field Operations directs, supports and provides outreach and fiscal accountability for the department's service delivery efforts. Central Operations includes the Office of the Director, the Regional Development officers and Central Services Division.

Industry Development Division

503-986-0200

The Industry Development Division focuses its business growth efforts on rural and distressed areas of the state. The division works to maintain long-term economic vitality by anchoring key businesses to the state through two specific efforts: Business Outreach and Services, and Business Finance.

Through **Business Outreach and Services**, the division helps small businesses expand and larger businesses compete, and it supports development of targeted industries key to Oregon's diversification. Staff work with businesses, associations and other state agencies to ensure that state policy keeps a strong business climate intact. They help companies and associations build training programs in partnership with local community colleges. They enable Oregon's home-grown businesses to grow and thrive by improving access to capital, transfer of technology, strategic planning and management practices. Staff also coordinate information on the state, areas within the state and the readiness of industrial sites to help companies that want to move into the state.

Business Finance administers programs that bridge the gap between lenders and small companies, support jobs and new company creation, and focus on small business management consulting, business networking and business retention services.

International Division

503-229-5625

The International Division helps Oregon companies gain access to and

> *Since the Oregon Economic Development Department was founded in 1973, it has had one overriding task—to diversify the state's economy. A major part of this task has been to attract large, high technology investments from outside Oregon because the state's base of non-resource industry was so small. For a detailed description of Oregon's economy, see the Economy chapter on page 213.*

compete in international markets. International Market Development staff help firms find distribution channels in foreign markets and compete globally. Local staff work hand-in-hand with Oregon's overseas offices, which are located in Tokyo, Taipei and Seoul.

Companies find assistance researching a market, developing a marketing strategy, visiting a market to establish initial contacts, localizing products and following up on leads. Through International Awareness initiatives, the division supports missions abroad by the governor, and hosts foreign official and educational delegations, including those from Oregon's "sister states."

Regional Development Division

503-986-0120

The Regional Development Division helps local jurisdictions maintain healthy communities. Communities with strong leadership, up-to-date infrastructure and the ability to care for disadvantaged residents are best able to support businesses which create the jobs and revenues that make community upkeep possible. The division focuses on three efforts: Regional Strategies/Rural Development, Infrastructure, and Housing and Community Facilities.

Regional boards—comprised of private sector volunteers— develop six-year plans focused on strengthening and diversifying regions, which are made up of contiguous counties. The boards also develop plans for responding to the priorities of rural communities within their region.

Regional Strategies/Rural Development funds support implementation of these plans. Staff also provide support to the president's Northwest Economic Adjustment Initiative, designed to help natural resource-dependent communities diversify their economies, and administer the enterprise zone program, which enables communities to give incentives to companies that want to expand or locate in the area. Regional Strategies/Rural Development contracts with Rural Development Initiatives, Inc., and Livable Oregon to build local leadership skills and revitalize downtowns.

Through Infrastructure efforts, division staff provide loans and grants to cities, counties and special districts to finance water and wastewater

improvements. The division administers both state and federal funds, and it works with other state and federal agencies to improve delivery of government financing for infrastructure projects.

Housing and Community Facilities supports the construction and refurbishment of senior centers, emergency shelters, facilities for disabled residents and day care facilities. These programs also support establishment of revolving loan funds for rehabilitation of single-family homes and farmworker housing.

Oregon Ports Division

503-986-0243

The Oregon Ports Division provides technical, financial and intergovernmental coordination assistance to ports to help them develop facilities that aid the efficient shipping of products and improve the local economy. It manages three financial assistance programs to finance port infrastructure development and port-related business development projects, planning for business operation and facilities development, marketing port facilities and services, and navigation projects. Ports staff also provide technical assistance for ports seeking permits, developing business and operational plans and putting together project financing packages. The Ports Division coordinates its efforts with transportation and natural resource agencies, and acts as liaison between Oregon ports and the federal government to best serve port needs.

For a list of Oregon ports, see page 334 in the Local Government chapter.

Boards and Commissions
Oregon Tourism Commission

503-986-0000

The Oregon Tourism Commission promotes Oregon as a visitor destination and encourages increased visitor expenditures in the state. Staff work closely with Oregon's regions and communities, providing expertise and assistance in the marketing, development and evaluation of tourism resources. The commission is responding increasingly to environmental, developmental and long-range planning issues, and staff are immersed in rural development planning and strategy development. The Tourism Commission provides statewide leadership in addressing the needs of the tourism industry, and plays an "umbrella" role in marketing the state.

Oregon Arts Commission

503-986-0088

The Oregon Arts Commission works with a variety of customers to promote the arts in Oregon. From the individual artist to organizations and educational institutions, the commission acts as an adviser and catalyst. Commission staff help build local ability to improve community involvement in the arts, and annually undertakes specific projects serving Oregon's cultural community. The commission provides grants to non-profit arts organizations and individual artists, information about arts resources in Oregon, and support for lifelong arts education experiences. The commission works in partnership with 11 regional program providers.

For detailed descriptions of Oregon's arts organizations and opportunities, see the Arts and Sciences chapter on page 199.

Film and Video Office

503-229-5832

The Film and Video Office serves as a liaison between production companies and Oregon businesses, citizens and government. The office markets film locations and the film and television workforce within Oregon. Through the Oregon Multimedia Initiative, the office promotes Oregon companies and workers in the emerging area of multimedia. The office also recruits film and video related businesses to relocate to Oregon on a permanent basis. Approximately 250 films have been made in Oregon.

Oregon Progress Board

503-986-0033

The mission of the Oregon Progress Board is to oversee implementation of *Oregon Shines*, the state's strategic plan. The core tool the board uses is the Oregon Benchmarks, which measure how well Oregon is doing as a people, place and economy. Developing and monitoring the Oregon Benchmarks are the core activities of the Progress Board. The board also supports efforts by local governments and citizen groups to develop outcome-based strategic plans at the city, county and regional level.

ED-NET

Raymond J. Lewis, Dir.
7140 SW Macadam Ave., Portland 97219; 503-293-1992; Fax: 503-293-1989; Web: www.orednet.org/ednet.html

Tom Bruggere, chair; David Gilbert, vice-chair.

Oregon ED-NET is a statewide telecommunications network created in 1989 (ORS 354.505–354.550) to enhance economic development opportunities by providing improved access to education, training and information for all Oregonians. ED-NET uses a combination of satellite, microwave, telephone

A flood of the Willamette River in 1953 caused a washout of Highway 58 between Oakridge and Eugene.

Photo courtesy of the Oregon Historical Society. Negative number OrHi 67888.

and cable technologies to transmit live, interactive courses, staff development, data sharing, conferencing and meetings to citizens in virtually any community. The agency also operates COMPASS, a statewide online computer conferencing and information dial-up network. It serves organizations in the education, business, government and non-profit sectors.

Education Commission of the States

Dr. Frank Newman, Pres.
707 17th St., Suite 2700, Denver, CO 80202-3427; 303-299-3600; Fax: 303-296-8332; Email: ecs@ecs.org; Web: www.ecs.org

Gov. John Kitzhaber; Roger Bassett; Sen. Lenn Hannon; Sen. Tom Hartung; Rep. Carolyn Oakley; State Supt. of Public Instruction Norma Paulus; Rep. Larry Sowa.

The Education Commission of the States (ECS) is a nonprofit, nationwide compact of states and territories formed in 1965 to help governors, state legislators, state education officials and others develop policies to improve the quality of education. The commission undertakes major studies in areas such as school finance, legal issues, governance and improved quality of education.

The commission is funded by state dues and other grants and contracts. ORS 348.950 authorizes Oregon's participation.

Employment Department

Virlena Crosley, Dir.
875 Union St. NE, Salem 97311; 503-378-3208; Fax: 503-373-7298; Web: www.emp.state.or.us

The Oregon Employment Department serves citizens by helping workers find suitable jobs; providing qualified applicants for employers; supplying statewide and local labor-market information; providing unemployment insurance benefits, other job placement and career development services; and promoting and regulating child care. Its mission is to promote the employment of Oregonians by maintaining a diversified, multi-skilled workforce, promoting quality child care and providing support during periods of unemployment.

Established by the Legislature in 1993, the department offers a number of services. It serves employers through timely recruitment of a qualified workforce, customizing labor market information for use as a business planning tool, and by offering different levels of job-matching services (self-referral, self-selection and job matching) based on the needs of each employer. Labor market economists and research analysts identify major workforce policy areas that require additional research and then bring their findings and ideas for solutions to decision makers. Statewide and local/regional economic information is prepared for use by employers, community leaders and policy makers.

The Employment Department helps job seekers find jobs that make optimum match between their skills and the employer's needs, providing them with up-to-date information about trends in occupations and skills for them to successfully compete in the job market, and by working with other agencies to direct them to appropriate training, skill building programs and job experiences.

Twenty-eight full-service and 16 outreach offices serve Oregonians statewide, providing a range of services for both employers and job applicants.

Oregon Employers Council

Zel Flanagan, State Coord.
875 Union St. NE, Salem 97311; 503-378-1642; Fax: 503-373-7401

Gwen Harvey, chair
The Oregon Employers Council is made up of employers statewide who advise the department on policy, procedural and law changes as well as providing low-cost seminars for Oregon employers.

Unemployment Insurance Advisory Council

Virlena Crosley, Dir., Employment Dept.
875 Union St. NE, Salem 97311; 503-378-3208; Fax: 503-373-7298

Pat Maberry, chair
The Unemployment Insurance Advisory Council includes representatives of the public, business and labor. The council advises the director of the Employment Department on employment service, unemployment insurance matters and child-care issues.

Employment Appeals Board

875 Union St. NE, Salem 97311; 503-378-4462; Fax: 503-378-5023

Renee Bryant, chair; Nita Brueggeman, Mary T. Feldbruegge.

Three members are appointed to the Employment Appeals Board by the governor to review hearing decisions in contested unemployment insurance claims cases.

Occupational Information Committee

Dave Allen, Acting Exec. Dir.
875 Union St. NE, Salem 97311; 503-378-5747; Fax: 503-373-7515

The Occupational Information Committee (OIC) is one of two major committees of the Oregon Workforce Quality Council (see Office of Educational Policy and Planning). The committee coordinates and oversees the development, delivery and use of occupational and educational information. This information is used for educational program planning and evaluation, economic development and individual career decision-making.

The Occupational Information Committee, mandated by federal legislation, is funded by the National Occupational Information Coordinating Committee.

Child Care Division

Janis Elliot, Admin.
875 Union St. NE, Salem 97311; 503-373-7282; Fax: 503-378-6484

The Child Care Division is responsible for child care regulations, child care resource and referral (CCR&R) and child care coordination. The Child Care Division also administers the child care and development block grant. These funds provide subsidies for low-income working and student parents, grants to develop community-based child care programs, and training and technical assistance to child care providers.

Child Care, Commission for

Wendy Willet, Exec. Officer
875 Union St. NE, Salem 97311; 503-378-3509; Fax: 503-378-5417

The Commission for Child Care was first established in 1985. In 1993, the Legislature moved the commission to the newly-created Employment Department, "to address the issues, problems and alternative solutions that are critical to the development of accessible, affordable and quality day care services." This change reflects the recognition that child care is a fundamental issue for the productivity of Oregon's diverse workforce and economy.

The commission sponsors and supports legislation to address child care issues, including regulation, the statewide resource and referral program, parental leave and dependent care assistance options and tax credits for employers. In addition, commission members collaborate with other agencies, programs and organizations within the child care community, participating in advisory groups and conferences.

The commission is comprised of 15 members, three of whom are representatives of the Legislative Assembly, appointed to two-year terms and serving as non-voting members. The twelve voting members represent specific areas of interest and are appointed to three-year terms. Appoint authorities are the governor, the speaker of the House and the president of the Senate. The commission chair is designated by the governor to serve for a term of one year.

Employment Relations Board

Old Garfield School Bldg., 528 Cottage St. NE, Salem 97310; 503-378-3807

Daniel C. Ellis, chair, Portland, 1997; Allen M. Hein, Portland, 1996; David W. Stiteler, Salem, 1999. The board consists of three members appointed by the governor for four-year terms.

The Employment Relations Board was established in 1977 and operates under ORS chapter 240, ORS 243.650–243.782, ORS 662.405–662.445 and ORS 663.005–663.325. The board determines appropriate bargaining units for state and local governments and private companies not involved in interstate commerce. The board also conducts elections to determine which labor organization, if any, the employees want to represent them in collective-bargaining. It resolves unfair labor practice complaints and determines whether strikes are lawful.

The board's Conciliation Service Division provides mediation services for resolving collective-bargaining disputes in public and private employment and provides lists of fact-finders and arbitrators for the resolution of labor disputes.

The board reviews personnel actions alleged to be arbitrary, contrary to law or rule, or taken for political reasons that affect unrepresented, classified state employees.

Engineering and Land Surveying, State Board of Examiners for

Edward B. Graham, Exec. Sec.
750 Front St. NE, Suite 240, Salem 97310; 503-378-4180; Fax: 503-373-1243

Steven T. Schenk, president, Lake Oswego, 1997; Keith R. Battleson, Bend, 1999; Larry M. Carson, Portland, 1998; Suzanne T. Crane, Clackamas, 1997; Charles L. Crump, Salem, 1999; Colin H. Handforth, Portland, 1997; Ron A. Hoffine, Coos Bay, 2000; R. Charles Pearson, Lake Oswego, 1999; Joel G. Smith, Redmond, 1999; Robert A. Walker, Beaverton, 2000; Richard H. Zbinden, Klamath Falls, 1997.

The Board of Examiners for Engineering and Land Surveying's objective is to assure that engineers and land surveyors registered to practice in Oregon demonstrate and maintain suitable standards of technical and professional knowledge and the ability and performance required for the public's safety, health and welfare.

ORS chapter 672 grants authority for the board to establish and maintain standards, examine applicants, register qualified practitioners, and enforce the laws, rules and regulations governing engineering and land surveying, using investigations, hearings and penalties when warranted. The board was established in 1919.

Environmental Quality, Department of

Langdon Marsh, Dir.
811 SW 6th Ave., Portland 97204; 503-229-5696; TDD: 503-229-6993; toll-free (Oregon only): 1-800-452-4011; Fax: 503-229-6124; Web: www.deq.state.or.us

The Department of Environmental Quality (DEQ) was created in 1969 when the State Sanitary Authority was dissolved. The Sanitary Authority was created in 1938 when outraged citizens overwhelmingly supported an initiative petition to clean up the Willamette River. Today, operating under ORS chapters 454, 459, 466, 467 and 468, DEQ is responsible for protecting and enhancing Oregon's water and air quality and for managing the proper disposal of solid and hazardous wastes.

The DEQ consists of 675 scientists, engineers, technicians, administrators, clerks and environmental specialists. The agency's headquarters are in Portland with regional administrative offices in Bend, Eugene, and Portland; and field offices in Baker City, Coos Bay, Grants Pass, Medford, Pendleton, Roseburg, Salem, and The Dalles. A modern pollution-control laboratory operates on the Portland State University campus.

The agency completed a major reorganization during the 1995–97 budget period that transferred about 50 percent of the Portland headquarters staff to positions in the field. This move toward putting more people "on the ground" reversed the previous two-to-one ratio of headquarters-based personnel to staff at work in communities. Oregon's communities and regulated users now have more direct access to DEQ staff for consultation and technical assistance.

The DEQ director has the authority to issue civil penalties (fines) for violation of pollution laws and standards. The DEQ relies on several advisory committees of citizens and government officials to help guide its decision-making.

Environmental Quality Commission

The commission, DEQ's policy and rule-making board, adopts administrative rules, issues orders and judges appeals of fines or other department actions and hires the DEQ director. Appointed to four-year terms by the governor, commission members are: Henry Lorenzen, chair, Pendleton; Melinda Eden, Milton-Freewater; Linda McMahan, Portland; Tony Van Vliet, Corvallis; Carol Whipple, Elkton.

The **Air Quality Program** regulates some 1,000 sources of industrial air pollution through permits. DEQ operates a vehicle inspection program in the Portland area and in the Rogue Valley; develops control strategies to reduce pollutants in cities that do not meet clean air standards; and protects the public from asbestos in buildings that are being demolished or remodeled.

The **Environmental Cleanup Program** maintains an inventory of all sites in the state with a confirmed release of hazardous material into the environment. The department assesses these sites for potential threats to human health and the environment, and, where appropriate, supervises development and implementation of cleanup strategies.

Through its **Hazardous and Solid Waste Program**, DEQ oversees Oregon's only hazardous waste landfill located at Arlington and regulates hazardous waste disposal from the point of origin until final disposal. The department emphasizes pollution prevention techniques and offers technical assistance to businesses to minimize the amount of hazardous waste generated. A special section regulates underground storage tanks, a major threat to the environment because of the potential for tank contents to leak and pollute groundwater. Solid waste landfills are regulated by DEQ permits, which set requirements for design, operation and monitoring.

DEQ promotes solid waste reduction education and implements a statewide recycling law that requires cities to provide curbside recycling collection and reduce garbage volume going into landfills.

The **Water Quality Program** sets and enforces water quality standards and monitors 19 river basins for water quality. DEQ also monitors and assesses groundwater and implements strategies to protect this valuable resource. Oregon law prohibits discharging pollution into Oregon water without a DEQ permit. More than 360 waste discharges from city sewage treatment plants and industrial facilities are regulated by permits. DEQ develops strategies to reduce pollution carried by stormwater runoff from urban areas, agriculture, forest practices and construction. The program provides loans to local governments for sewage treatment systems.

Fish and Wildlife, Department of

Rudy Rosen, Dir.
2501 SW 1st Ave.; PO Box 59, Portland 97207;
503-872-5272; Fax: 503-872-5276

Commercial Fishery Permit Boards

The Fishery Permit Boards were established as part of the 1979 law placing a moratorium on new entries into certain Oregon commercial fisheries. The roe herring permit limitations were adopted by Legislature in 1983. Members serve as an appeals and review board to revoke, authorize issuance of or reinstate permits. Members of the individual boards are also commercial fishermen. Two public representatives serve on all boards.

Fish and Wildlife Commission

Web: www.dfw.state.or.us

Jeff Feldner, Logsden, 1999; Susan Foster, Gresham, 2000; Jim Habberstad, The Dalles, 1997; Paul N. McCracken, Portland, 1999; Janet Mclennan, Portland, 1999; John L. Perry, Junction City, 1999; Phillip W. Schneider, Portland (Commissioner Emeritus at large); Katy O'Toole Spencer, La Grande, 1997.

The commission consists of seven voting members appointed by the governor for staggered four-year terms. One commissioner must be from each congressional district, one from east of the Cascades and one from the west. The commission was formed in 1975 as a result of merging the formerly separate fish and wildlife commissions.

The department consists of the commission, the director (who is appointed by the commission) and a statewide staff of 800 permanent employees. It operates under ORS chapters 496–513.

The commission formulates general state programs and policies concerning management and conservation of fish and wildlife resources and establishes seasons, methods and bag limits for recreational and commercial take.

The department's biennial budget is about $173 million. This includes nearly $13 million transferred to the State Police to fund enforcement of fish and wildlife laws. Three-fourths of landings, license and other fees collected from commercial fisheries go into the state general fund. One-fourth is deposited in the Commercial Fisheries Fund for use by the department. Sport license and tag fees are deposited in the Fish and Wildlife Fund for department use. In 1996, about 2.4 million sport licenses and tags and 8,500 commercial-fishing licenses and permits were issued.

The department is headquartered in Portland with regional offices in Bend, Clackamas, Corvallis, La Grande, Newport and Roseburg. Twenty-one district offices are also strategically located statewide. The department operates a variety of facilities designed to enhance fish and wildlife resources, including 34 fish hatcheries, one game farm, numerous wildlife areas, public shooting grounds, hunting and fishing access sites and several research stations.

Forestry, Department of

James E. Brown, State Forester
2600 State St., Salem 97310; 503-945-7211;
503-945-7422; Fax: 503-945-7212;
Email: james.e.brown@state.or.us;
brian.r.ballou@state.or.us;
Web: www.odf.state.or.us

Forestry, Board of

David E. Gilbert, chair, La Grande, 1997; Dick Baldwin, Eugene, 1998; Sam Johnson, Portland, 2000; Wayne Krieger, Gold Beach, 1998; Y. Sherry Sheng, Portland, 1998; Howard Sohn, Roseburg, 2000; Brad Witt, Salem, 2000.

The seven-member board, appointed by the governor, makes policy and provides vision to the overall management and protection of the state's 11 million acres of state-owned and private forest land. No more than three members of the board may receive any significant portion of their income from the forest products industry.

The board operates under ORS chapter 526 in setting forest policy for the state. It authorizes a forestry program for Oregon, designated to assure an adequate future wood supply with favorable effects on society, the economy and the environment.

The Department of Forestry, authorized by ORS 526.008 and established in 1911, is under the direction of the state forester, who is appointed by the Board of Forestry. The statutes direct the state forester to act on all matters pertaining to forestry, the protection of forest lands and the conservation of forest resources.

These activities include: fire protection for 16 million acres of private, state and federal forests; the detection and control of harmful forest insect pests and forest tree diseases on 12 million acres of state and private lands; the management of 786,276 acres of state-owned forest lands; and the operation of a 15-million-tree forest nursery. The department also administers the Oregon Forest Practices Act, Log Brands Act, Small Tract Optional Tax Law, forest land classification, forestry assistance to Oregon's 24,000 non-industrial private woodland owners, forest resource planning and community and urban forestry assistance.

County Forest Land Classification Committees

James E. Brown, State Forester
2600 State St., Salem 97310; 503-945-7211

Under ORS 526.305—526.370, each county may establish a county classification committee of five persons, one appointed by the state forester, one by the director of Oregon Agricultural Experiment Station and three by the county governing body. At least one must be an owner of forest land and at least one an owner of grazing land. These committees are charged with investigating forest lands to determine how the lands are to be classified. Class 1 includes all forest land primarily suitable for timber production, Class 2 includes all forest land suitable for joint timber and livestock grazing, and Class 3 includes all forest land suitable primarily for grazing and other agricultural uses.

These classifications are used by the Board of Forestry and the state forester in administering all of Oregon's forest and fire laws, promoting the primary use for which that land is classified.

The committee must hold public hearing before final classifications and reclassification. Appeals by landowners may be taken to the circuit court. When no classification of forest land is made by a committee, the state forester may make this determination.

Emergency Fire Cost Committee

Tom Lane, Admin.
2600 State St., Salem 97310; 503-945-7449

The committee supervises and controls the distribution of monies from the Oregon Forest Land Protection Fund established under ORS 477.750 for emergency fire fighting expenditures in controlling forest fires.

Four members are appointed to the committee by the State Board of Forestry to serve four-year terms.

Forest Trust Land Advisory Committee

This committee, established under ORS 527.735 by the 1987 Legislature, advises the Oregon Board of Forestry and the state forester on the management of state forests and on matters in which counties have responsibility pertaining to forest land management.

Forest Resource Trust Advisory Committee

This committee was established under ORS 526.700 by the 1993 Legislature. The Trust provides funds for financial, technical and related assistance to private non-industrial forest landowners for timber stand establishment and improved management of forest lands for timber production as well as wildlife, water quality and other environmental purposes. The Oregon Board of Forestry has overall responsibility for management of the Forest Resource Trust. The committee assists the board in setting policy, investing funds and otherwise assisting Board members in carrying out trustee duties. The State Forester is responsible for implementing Board policies and Trust programs.

Regional Forest Practices Committees

James E. Brown, State Forester
2600 State St., Salem 97310; 503-945-7211

The Northwest Oregon, Southwest Oregon and Eastern Oregon Regional Forest Practice Committees are authorized under ORS 527.650. Nine members are appointed to each committee by the Board of Forestry to serve three-year terms. Each committee makes recommendations to the Board of Forestry on forest practice rules appropriate to the forest conditions in its regions. Charlie Stone, Forest Practices Act Director for the Department of Forestry, is the secretary for all committees

Geologist Examiners, State Board of

Edward B. Graham, Admin.
750 Front St. NE, Suite 240, Salem 97310; 503-378-4180; Fax: 503-373-1243

Michael T. Long, chair, Eugene, 1996; L. Carl Brandhorst, Monmouth, 1998; Audrey Eldridge, Jacksonville, 1998; Lanny H. Fisk, Bend, 1999; Donald A.

Hull, state geologist, Portland; Dorian Kuper, Tualatin, 1999.

The purpose of the Board of Geologist Examiners, established in 1977, is to safeguard the health, welfare and property of Oregonians affected by the geologic fields of ground water, land-use planning, mineral exploration and development, geologic hazards and the further development of the science of geology through the regulation of professional practice.

ORS 672.505–672.991 authorizes the board to determine qualifications, examine and register geologists, certify those with engineering specialty, grant reciprocity for comparable requirements in other states, and suspend, revoke or refuse to renew registration or certification and assess civil penalties when warranted.

Geology and Mineral Industries, Department of

Donald A. Hull, State Geologist
John D. Beaulieu, Deputy State Geologist
800 NE Oregon St. #28, Suite 965, Portland 97232; 503-731-4100; Fax: 503-731-4066

The Department of Geology and Mineral Industries was formed July 1, 1937, and operates under ORS chapters 516, 517, 520 and 522. It is the state's centralized source of geologic information that can be used by the public and by government to reduce future loss of life and property due to earthquakes, tsunamis, coastal erosion and other geologic hazards. The department produces geologic maps to help Oregonians understand and prepare for earthquakes. It serves as a cost effective steward of mineral production, focusing on environmental, reclamation, conservation, and related economic, engineering, and technical issues. It is the lead regulator for geologic resources (oil; gas; geothermal energy; metallic and industrial minerals; and sand, gravel, and crushed stone).

The department's **Mined Land Reclamation Program**, located at 1536 Queen Ave. SE, Albany (503-967-2039), is the lead coordinating agency for state mining regulation, operating through an interagency team-permit process. In Oregon, exploration and operating permits and bonds are required to ensure reclamation of land disturbed by mining.

The department provides geologic data to assist in policy development through publications and release of electronic data and through department participation in and coordination with state, federal, and local governmental natural resource agencies as well as with industry and other private sector groups. The department's geologic library is a specialized central repository for both published and unpublished state geologic information. Technical and non-technical publications are available at the Nature of the Northwest Information Center in Portland and at the department's field offices in Baker City and Grants Pass.

Geology and Mineral Industries Governing Board

Jacqueline Haggerty, chair, Enterprise, 1999; Don Christensen, Depoe Bay, 2000; John W. Stephens, Portland, 1997. The governor appoints members to four-year terms. The State Geologist is appointed by the governing board.

Nature of the Northwest Information Center

800 NE Oregon St., #5, Suite 177, Portland 97232; 503-731-4444; Fax: 503-731-4066; Web: www.naturenw.org

The information center is operated by the Department of Geology and Mineral Industries on behalf of other state natural resource agencies in partnership with the USDA Forest Service. The center provides one-stop shopping for natural resource, natural science, and outdoor recreation maps, books, and brochures (some for sale, some free), produced primarily by state, federal and local government natural resource agencies.

Government Standards and Practices Commission

L. Patrick Hearn, Exec. Dir.
100 High St. SE, Suite 220, Salem 97310; 503-378-5105; Fax: 503-373-1456

Ilo Bonyhadi, Portland, 1998; Mary McCauley Burrows, Eugene, 1999; Rachel Gerber, Beaverton, 2000; Don Reiling, Albany, 1999; Fred Thompson, Salem, 1999; vacant, 2001; vacant, 2001.

The Government Standards and Practices Commission (GSPC), established by vote of the people in 1974, is a seven-member citizen commission charged with enforcing government standards and practices (ethics) laws. Government standards and practices laws are intended to assure that public officials do not violate public trust. The GSPC also enforces lobbying laws and some provisions of public meeting laws. Prior to 1993, the agency was known as the Oregon Government Ethics Commission.

Health Division Licensing Programs

Susan K. Wilson, Admin.
700 Summer St. NE, Suite 100, Salem 97310-1351; 503-378-8667; Fax: 503-585-9114; Email: hdlp.mail@state.or.us; Web: www.hdlp.hr.state.or.us

The Health Division Licensing Programs are an administrative consolidated service delivery model located within the Department of Human Resources, Health Division Licensing Office.

Athletic Trainer Registration Program

The 1993 Legislature enacted a voluntary registration program for athletic trainers, created within the Health Division. The program has registered approximately 98 athletic trainers based on training and certification by the National Athletic Trainer Association. The law requires review of qualifications for registration, issuing a certificate of registration, and maintaining a roster of registered athletic trainers.

The 1995 Legislature granted authority to establish a fee structure to fund costs associated with administering the program, and established a registration period and renewal cycle for the program. There is no board, council or advisory group established for the program. The Health Division licensing staff provides service. Statutory authority is ORS 688.700 (temporarily numbered).

Barbers and Hairdressers, Board of

Jacqueline J. Backus, Gresham, 1999; Clyde E. Casto, Salem, 1997; Carol

Henigan, Pendleton, 1997; Brenda Hoxsey, Portland, 1999; Dianna Martin-Peterson, Portland, 1999; Richard Schmidt, Salem, 1999; Carleen Spencer, Portland, 1998.

The professional licensing board was established in 1977 by merging the Board of Barber Examiners (created in 1897) and the Board of Cosmetic Therapy (created in 1927). It became a health-related licensing board in 1987 (authorized by ORS 690.005–690.235; 690.992 and 690.995). This policy board certifies and licenses approximately 25,000 practitioners providing barbering, hair design, facial and nail technology services; 4,400 independent contractors; 3,800 barbering/beauty facilities; and maintains records for approximately 7,000 individuals who are in an "inactive" status.

The board prepares and administers a written certification examination, conducts daily walk-in on-site computerized testing; prescribes safety and sanitation standards for facilities; records consumer complaints; investigates law and rule violations; and has the authority to revoke or suspend certificates and licenses or issue civil penalties.

The board's primary purpose is to protect the health and safety of 1.2 million consumers purchasing services. Oregon consumers are assured that technical expertise and safety standards exist in handling dangerous tools and chemical compounds in the workplace through routine inspection of businesses and vocational schools.

The assistant director for health, administrator of the Health Division, appoints the seven-member board and provides an administrator and staff to carry out the board's duties. Board operations are supported by certificate, license, examination fees, civil fines and monies from other licensing programs that use board facilities and services.

Body Piercing Program

The 1995 Legislature enacted licensing of business facilities offering body piercing services and registration of technicians performing body piercing. The law requires licensed facilities to meet prescribed safety, sanitation, and sterilization standards; establishes disclosure of risk factors for posting to the public, and provides for a consumer

The Board of Barbers and Hairdressers implemented a system of walk-in examinations in 1996 with computerized testing to minimize delay in issuing certification to qualified applicants. It also donated $900,000 to the Oregon Scholarship Commission Grant Program as "seed" money in awarding scholarships to individuals entering the industry as barbers, hairdressers, facial or nail technologists.

complaint process and routine inspections of facilities. The Health Division has the authority to suspend or revoke licensure, or issue civil penalties.

Registration of technicians establishes an entry-level framework to assure consumers are served in a licensed facility where prescribed sterilization procedures are observed. Routine inspections ensure disclosure of risk factors are provided to clients receiving services. Due to the cross-over within jewelry stores, beauty establishments and tattoo facilities, the program was established with an emphasis on consumer protection.

Approximately 107 body piercing facilities have been licensed and 215 body piercing technicians have been registered. The program is supported by application and license/registration fees and civil fines. There is no board, council or advisory group established for the program. The program is administered by the Health Division licensing staff within the consolidated model of Health Division Licensing Programs office. Program operations are supported by facility and registration fees. Statutory authority is ORS chapter 562.

Denture Technology, Board of

Marilyn E. Grannell, Salem, 1998; Jean Hardnett, Portland, 1997; Kenneth Holden, Eugene, 2000; Darcy C. Kerr, Roseburg, 1997; Shawn M. Murray, Florence, 1997; two vacancies.

The program was created by Ballot Measure 5 in 1979 and licenses approximately 132 denturists who construct, fit and repair full dentures. The program establishes policies and criteria for quality assessment in the practice of denture technology and reviews clinical competence for license reinstatement. Enforcement staff investigates consumer complaints and law and rule violations, and has authority to suspend or revoke licenses and issue civil penalties for violations.

The 1993 Legislature established requirements for special training and examination for oral pathology endorsement. Statutory authority is ORS 680.500–680.575.

Board operations are supported by application, examination and license fees and civil fines. The seven-member policy board is appointed by the assistant director for Health, administrator of the Health Division.

Direct Entry Midwifery, Board of

Laura Arce, Dayton, 1999; Kate Davidson, Silverton, 1998; Anne Frye, Portland, 1999; Lisa Gladden, La Pine, 1998; Gail M. Hart, Portland, 1998; Mark Nichols, M.D., Portland, 1999; Marion Toepke, Dexter, 1999.

Voluntary licensing of direct entry midwives was enacted by the 1993 Legislature to provide a mechanism of 84obtaining financial reimbursement through medical assistance programs (third party reimbursements) to "qualified" direct entry midwives. The board prescribes standards for licensure qualifications, and training and experience; prescribes and administers written and oral examinations; monitors continuing education and participation in peer review; develops practice standards; investigates complaints and law and rule violations; has the authority to suspend, place on probation or revoke licensure; and issue civil penalties.

The program has licensed approximately 50 midwives, and is supported by examination and license fees and civil fines.

The law created a seven-member policy board, with members appointed by the assistant director of Human Resources, Health Division administrator. The board is not created within the Health Division but is a board operating within the umbrella of the Health Division. The relationship between the board and Health Division is distinguished from that of other "health-related boards" by the line of authority to the administrator residing with the assistant director of Human Resources, Health Division administrator, rather than within the

board's authority. Statutory authority is ORS 676.230 (temporary due to sunset provision contained within the law).

Electrologists, Permanent Color Technicians and Tattoo Artists, Council for

Thomas A. Holeman, M.D., Clackamas, 1997; Tera Lum, Salem, 1997; Paul Richards, Pendleton, 1997; Trudy Ude, Portland, 1997; one vacancy.

The five-member advisory council is appointed by the governor without Senate confirmation and members serve two-year terms. Statutory authority is ORS 690.350–690.420, 690.992 and 690.997.

The electrology licensing program was established in 1987 and licenses approximately 176 electrologists who provide "permanent" hair removal by inserting a needle/conductor into the hair follicles and directing energy to the hair cell.

The 1993 Legislature enacted regulation of the practice of tattooing through license of permanent color technicians and tattoo artists. Legislation attached licensure, enforcement and regulation to the existing electrology governing body.

Tattooing marks or colors the skin by insertion of nontoxic dyes or pigments under the dermis of the skin with a "needle" so as to form indelible marks for cosmetic, medical or figuration purposes. Approximately 81 tattoo artists and 60 facilities or small businesses have been licensed.

The council advises in the administration and enforcement of licensed electrologists, permanent color technicians and tattoo artists. The law requires training and experience for examination as an electrologist, instructor of electrolysis, permanent color technician and tattoo artist, and trainers; prescribes written and practical examinations; continuing education; curricula and registration of schools of electrolysis; and safety, sanitation/sterilization and practice standards. The Health Division conducts routine inspection of electrologists and tattoo business facilities and investigates complaints, law and rule violations, and has the authority to suspend or revoke licensure or issue civil penalties.

Hearing Aid Dealers, Advisory Council for

Joe R. Boatmun, Lebanon, 1999; Loyal D. Ediger, Eugene, 1998; Christopher Gustafson, Salem, 1998; Gayle M. Jacobson, The Dalles, 1999; Sean McMenomey, M.D., 1999; Norman Rose, Woodburn, 1998; Lois B. Witherspoon, Salem, 1998.

The program, established in 1960, licenses approximately 349 hearing aid dealers and 17 trainees. The seven-member advisory council, created within the Health Division, advises the division on training and experience requirements for examination; issues temporary licenses; administers a national written examination and state-prepared practical examination; monitors continuing education; prescribes forms and content of consumer statements and medical release forms; conducts periodic inspections of audiometric testing equipment and facilities; investigates complaints, law and rule violations; has the authority to suspend or revoke licensure and issue civil penalties.

The 1995 Legislature revised the composition of the council specifying one member to be a user of hearing aid devices. In addition, exemption from examination was implemented for audiologists who completed prescribed training and testing in their field. The program is supported by license and examination fees and civil fines.

Members are appointed to three-year terms by the governor without Senate confirmation. Statutory authority is ORS 694.015–694.185.

Sanitarians Registration Board

Ronald E. Baker, Roseburg, 1997; Roger W. Everett, Bend, 1998; Diane G. Hall, Portland, 1997; Charles Herrick, Tualatin, 1998; Karen A. Landers, Salem, 1999; Susan Schwendiman, Brownsville, 1999; one vacancy.

The registration program was created in 1967 and registers approximately 350 sanitarians and trainees who perform duties in environmental sanitation, including but not limited to scientific investigation and education, and counseling in environmental sanitation. The 1995 Legislature added a specialized classification of registration for "waste water" sanitarians and trainees. The board prescribes standards for

registration qualification, training and experience; prescribes and administers written and oral examinations, using a national written examination via a professional testing service; prescribes, approves and monitors continuing education; and reviews complaints.

The 1995 Legislature revised the board's structure from an autonomous board to a policy-making board within the Health Division, transferring administrative and staffing duties pertaining to laws, rules, budget, personnel, and enforcement to the division. The law grants authority to investigate complaints and issue civil penalties for violations of laws and rules. The board is supported from application, examination and registration fees, and civil fines.

The seven-member board is appointed by the governor and is subject to confirmation by the Senate. Statutory authority is ORS 700.005–700.310 and 700.990.

Hispanic Affairs, Commission on

Celia Nuñez-Brewster, Exec. Dir.
Public Service Bldg., 255 Capitol St. NE, Fourth Floor, Salem 97310; 503-378-3725, ext. 4184; Fax: 503-378-8282

Liliana Olberding, chair, Hillsboro, 1999; Emilio Hernandez, vice-chair, Springfield, 1998; Diego Castellanos, Nyssa, 1999; Manuel A. Castaneda, Aloha, 1999; Lynda Jasso-Thomas, Florence, 1999; Henry Montes, Medford, 1999; Trinidad T. Ortiz, Madras, 1997; Nancy Padilla, Hermiston, 1997; one vacancy.

The Commission on Hispanic Affairs was created by the 1983 Legislature (ORS 185.310) to work for the implementation of economic, social, legal and political equality of Hispanics in Oregon. Nine commission members are appointed by the governor; the president of the Senate and speaker of the House each appoint one member.

The commission monitors existing programs and legislation to ensure that the needs of Hispanics are met. Other duties are to identify and research problem areas and recommend appropriate action; to maintain a liaison between the Hispanic community and government entities; and to encourage Hispanic representation on state boards and commissions.

Housing and Community Services Department

Baruti L. Artharee, Dir.

1600 State St., Salem 97310-0302;
503-986-2000; TTY: 503-986-2100;
Fax: 503-986-2020; Email: info@hcs.state.or.us;
Web: www.hcs.state.or.us

The Oregon Housing and Community Services Department (OHCSD) is the state's housing finance and human investment department. Its mission is to work in partnership with community based organizations to build affordable housing and to provide services to alleviate the causes of poverty and to empower Oregonians.

The department's purpose is to increase housing opportunities for lower-income Oregonians and provide services to alleviate the causes of poverty. The department is a central source of housing information, planning, educational services and technical assistance to state agencies. The director is appointed by the governor and receives Senate confirmation.

The Oregon Housing Division of the Department of Commerce was established in 1971. This organization became the Oregon Housing Agency in 1987 and in 1991 the Legislature merged the Housing Agency with the State Community Services Program to form the Oregon Housing and Community Services Department, under the authority of ORS chapters 317, 446 and 456.

The department provides financing for its housing programs primarily by issuing bonds. It has revenue bonding authority of $1.03 billion and general obligation bonding authority of approximately $854.7 million (equal to one-half of 1 percent of Oregon's taxable property true cash value). Bond proceeds enable the agency to provide mortgage financing at below-market interest rates and operate programs focusing primarily on first-time home buyers, federally subsidized rental units for lower-income households, and housing to meet the special needs of elderly and disabled persons. Federal funds are used for homeless shelters, weatherization and programs to promote self-reliance.

Director, Office of the
Baruti L. Artharee, Dir.

The director's office provides the direction and focus of programs and operations.

Housing Council, State

Peter Tarzian, chair, 1997; Daniel C. Robertson, vice-chair, 1998; Russell E. Dale, 2000; Bertha M. Ferran, 1999; Ruby Mason, 1999; Margaret S. Van Vliet, 1998; Kenneth Wilson, 1997.

The State Housing Council was created in 1971 as an advisory board. The 1989 Legislature changed its structure to make it a policy-making board. The council is a seven-member governing body appointed by the governor to four-year terms, upon Senate confirmation. The council develops policies to stimulate and increase the supply of housing for persons and families of lower income; reviews loans or grants in excess of $100,000 which are presented by the Housing and Community Services Department director; advises the governor, the Legislative Assembly, state agencies and local governments on public and private actions at all levels that may affect the cost or supply of housing; and adopts rules necessary for the administration and enforcement of department statutes.

Bond Finance Division
Lynn Schoessler, Deputy Dir.

Asset and Property Management Section
Pauline Phillips, Mgr.

The Asset and Property Management Section is responsible for multi-family and elderly program loans after they are closed and the developments are in operation. The section ensures, through project financial review and inspections, the department's financial security and that the investment (the property) is maintained in decent, safe and sanitary condition. The section also ensures that federal regulations, state statutes, bond indenture provisions and the provisions of loan documents are complied with by borrowers and management agents.

Housing Finance Section
Victor Smeltz, Mgr.

The Housing Finance Section manages multi-family and single-family programs which provide affordable housing for moderate-, low- and very-low-income Oregonians. The section is responsible for underwriting loan applications to determine whether housing developments are financially feasible and program guidelines are met. Once projects are selected for funding, the section continues to work with project owners and developers to ensure compliance with program regulations.

Human Resources Unit
Jo Anne Nathan, Human Resources Mgr.

Human Resources provides all human resource management services for the Housing and Community Services Department. The unit and Human Resources Management Team oversees such issues as ensuring compliance with human resource management-related governing rules, regulations and policies, and jointly administers such programs as recruitment, training, career development, benefits, employee relations, safety, workers' compensation, ADA, affirmative action, position development and maintenance, and performance management.

Community Services and Grant Programs Division
Gustavo Wilson, Admin.

The Community Services and Grant Programs Division links the federal government, state government and private developers with local community-based organizations to provide services and housing to assist low-income Oregonians achieve self-reliance.

Community Services Section
Dan Van Otten, Mgr.

The Community Services Section serves as a link between the federal and state funders and local community action agencies to support community development through agency delivery of services to low-income individuals. The intent of the services is to help design and operate such programs as crisis intervention case management services, resource development, housing rehabilitation and self-sufficiency programs which help clients by interrupting the incidence of poverty to become self-reliant. The section is also responsible for setting standards, monitoring compliance and performance evaluation, as well as providing training and technical assistance to each of its providers and vendors.

Housing Resource Section
Robert Gillespie, Mgr.

The Housing Resource Section manages affordable housing grant funds to bridge the difference between private and public financing to ensure feasibility through restricted affordable rents and total project costs. Funds are made available on a competitive basis twice annually through a Consolidated Funding Cycle (CFC) and subsidies are provided through either direct grants or tax incentives. The section's purpose is to create long-term affordable housing developments with services to enhance the lives and capabilities of lower-income Oregonians.

Community Action Directors of Oregon
Carmel Bentley, Exec. Dir.

Community Action Directors of Oregon (CADO) is a nonprofit organization consisting of directors of Oregon community action agencies, the Oregon Human Development Corporation and associate members. It serves as the advisory body to the Housing and Community Services Department on anti-poverty planning and program initiatives.

Financial Management Division
Jack Kenny, Chief Financial Officer

The Financial Management Division provides financial management and internal control support functions.

Debt Management Unit
Robert Larson, Debt Mgr.

This unit directly supports the department's mission to create affordable housing through the issuance of bonded debt to acquire mortgage loans at below market interest rates for Oregonians at or below median income. This unit is responsible for all administrative functions relating to bonded debt of the department's three bond programs.

Financial Operations Section
Nancy Cain, Mgr.

The Financial Operations Section coordinates the department's financial activities relating to disbursements, budget preparation and tracking, federal grant monitoring and reporting, federal cash management and cost allocation rates. It also provides for the allocation of federal and state grant

The area around Jefferson and Crabtree in Marion County was untravelled for days during the 1996 floods due to agricultural dikes breaking and high water in Thomas Creek and the Santiam River. Photo by Marti Cheek.

awards between the department and its subgrantees, develops and maintains personal and professional services contracts, and evaluates and improves the department's internal control structures.

Financial Services Section
Susan Gahlsdorf, Mgr.

The Financial Services Section maintains the department's accounting records and is responsible for financial reporting both internally for management purposes, and externally to bond trustees, the state of Oregon, the federal government, and the finance community. The section conducts financial analyses, investment analyses, management decision analyses, and internal operational control assessments as well as managing the department's investment portfolio, payroll and benefit functions, cashiering functions, and mail distribution.

Planning and Development Division
Ross Cornelius, Admin.

The Planning and Development Division administers and ties together internal and external planning and initiatives of the department to anticipate future trends and needs affecting the sponsor,

developer and recipients of affordable housing in Oregon; communicates the department's activities and resources, spearheads community development and partnership outreach, and applies appropriate technology to the evolving data needs of the department's stakeholders and staff.

Communications Unit
Sandy McDonnell, Mgr.

The unit and communications team provides leadership and technical assistance in the implementation of the department communications plan. This includes communicating with stakeholders and customers to increase their awareness and build stronger partnerships as well as the planning and design of publications including newsletters, press releases, brochures and other marketing materials which promote department programs or activities.

Community Development Team

The team provides technical financial expertise and assistance to community-based sponsors and organizations who are developing needs-based affordable housing throughout the state. Four Community Development Officers (CDOs) assist community-based sponsors in the identification of development funding resources and financial packaging of affordable housing developments.

Management Information Systems Section
Maury Johnson, Mgr.

The Management Information Systems Section develops and maintains the department's evolving information, computer, network, telecommunication resources and capabilities, and supports the growing exchange of data and information with the department's financial and recipient partners.

Planning and Development "A" Team
David Foster, Community Housing Planner/ Team Leader

The section helps Oregon communities make informed decisions and prioritize activities related to community development and services. It assists in obtaining resources for the department's housing and service programs, mediating conflicts between mobile home park tenants and landlords, tracking legislation and rule development, and managing the Community Development Corporation and Community Housing Development Opportunity Grant programs and Consolidated Plan program.

Human Resources, Department of

Gary K. Weeks, Dir.
Human Resources Bldg., 500 Summer St. NE, Salem 97310-1012; 503-945-5944; TTY: 503-945-5928; Fax: 503-378-2897; Email: dhr.info@state.or.us; Web: www.hr.state.or.us

The Department of Human Resources (DHR) is the state's health and social services agency, delivering nationally recognized services that benefit the lives of every Oregonian. It was established in 1971 under ORS 409.101.

The department's mission is to help people be independent, healthy and safe. To achieve its objectives, DHR manages more than 200 programs through six divisions and three program offices.

The department's programs include assistance to the poor; job-finding and job-training services; vocational rehabilitation; and help to children, families, the elderly and people with physical disabilities, mental illness and developmental disabilities. Health services include public health, Medicaid, alcohol and drug-abuse treatment, and mental health treatment. Phone numbers for many services are listed in local phone directories under State of Oregon, Department of Human Resources.

The department administers numerous programs, both federally and state financed, serving Oregonians both directly and through county governments, hospitals and other providers. Nearly 80 percent of the department's budget goes in direct payments to foster parents, county health and mental health departments, physicians and hospitals, private and non-profit treatment and service providers, general assistance, and other services.

DHR has based its planning and service delivery on the Oregon Benchmarks, and a series of goals, strategies, and measurable outcomes to meet citizen expectations. The department has formed three budget and planning clusters that work across division lines to take a comprehensive approach to defining and meeting common objectives and integrating service delivery.

To achieve its goals, DHR has a number of department-wide strategies: outcome-oriented management, investments in prevention, integrated service delivery, community partnerships, skilled workforce and administrative efficiencies.

Director, Office of the

The Office of the Director provides department leadership and manages program services while integrating the work of the divisions. Department-wide services provided through the director's office include personnel, communications, contracts, accounting, budgeting and information systems.

Major program functions in the Office of the Director are:

Alcohol and Drug Abuse Programs, Office of
Toni Phipps, Interim Dir.
500 Summer St. NE, Salem 97310-1016; 503-945-5763; Fax: 503-378-8467; Email: oadap.info@state.or.us; Web: www.oadap.hr.state.or.us

The Office of Alcohol and Drug Abuse Programs (OADAP) is the lead state agency for Oregon's alcohol and drug abuse prevention, intervention and treatment services. OADAP was established in 1973 as an office within the Mental Health Division. In 1985, it was made a part of the Office of the Director. It operates under ORS 409.410 and 409.420.

Alcohol and Drug Abuse Programs, Governor's Council on
Toni Phipps, Interim Dir.
500 Summer St. NE, Salem 97310-1016; 503-945-5763; Fax: 503-378-8467

Cynthia Carlson, chair
This council assesses the economic and social impact of alcohol and drug abuse in Oregon; and recommends, monitors, and evaluates the statewide plan for prevention, intervention and treatment encompassing 16 agencies.

Community Partnership Team
Chuck Dimond, Dir.
500 Summer St. NE, Salem 97310; 503-945-6131; Fax: 503-378-2897

The Community Partnership Team (CPT) strengthens DHR's collaboration

with communities. Using the Oregon
Benchmark planning structure, the CPT
brings state and local partners together
to define desired human services outcomes and develop strategies to achieve
them. The CPT works with public, private and not-for-profit entities across
Oregon to achieve results.

The CPT includes specialists in planning, communications, evaluation and
service integration. The DHR Volunteer
Program helps the team reach out to
communities; and the Oregon Option
leverages help from federal partners in
reducing administrative barriers to
delivering services. The CPT also staffs
the department's Policy Council, which
works toward integrating department
policy with what is learned from the
community-based initiatives.

DHR Volunteer Program
Georgena Carrow, State Dir.
500 Summer St. NE, Salem 97310;
503-945-5759; Fax: 503-378-2897

The Volunteer Program helps the
department provide human services in
the most cost-effective way by recruiting,
training and placing volunteers. The
program focuses its efforts in three
areas: 1) helping clients in most of the
DHR agencies find work experience
opportunities; 2) finding citizen volunteers to help DHR clients access the
services they need, such as providing
transportation to medical appointments;
and 3) helping communities identify
human service needs, and coordinating
volunteer efforts to meet those needs.
During 1995, the Volunteer Program
was placed in the newly formed Community Partnership Team.

Medical Assistance Programs, Office of
Hersh Crawford, Dir.
500 Summer St. NE, Salem 97310-1014;
503-945-5772; Fax: 503-373-7689

The Office of Medical Assistance Programs (OMAP) administers the Medicaid
component of the Oregon Health Plan
(OHP), a blueprint for universal access
to basic and affordable health coverage
that was created by the Oregon Legislature in a series of laws from 1989-1993.
OMAP is now operating a five-year Medicaid reform and expansion demonstration project under the OHP, in which
380,000 Oregonians are enrolled statewide. This project was implemented
under a waiver from the federal government in February 1994. The plan is
legislatively mandated to improve the
health of Oregonians by expanding
access to health coverage, prioritizing
services and delivering them in a cost-
effective manner through a managed
care system.

Medicaid Advisory Committee
Hersh Crawford, Dir.
500 Summer St. NE, Salem 97310-1014;
503-945-5772

Michael Biermann, DMD, and Michael
Garland, co-chairs

The committee advises OMAP on health
and medical-care issues. The 15 members
are appointed by the governor from health
professionals, providers of medical care
and services, welfare recipients and the
public.

Adult and Family Services Division
Sandie Hoback, Admin.
500 Summer St. NE, Salem 97310-1013;
503-945-5601; Fax: 503-373-7492;
Email: afs.info@state.or.us;
Web: www.afs.hr.state.or.us

The Adult and Family Services Division (AFS) helps low-income families
become self-sufficient and provides
temporary cash, food stamps and child
care benefits to meet their basic needs.
It helps clients enter the workforce
through the welfare reform program
"JOBS for Oregon's Future," which offers
education and employment training.
The division also helps families obtain
child support payments.

AFS operates 51 field offices that
serve approximately 32,000 single- and

two-parent families. About half of the money for welfare benefits and all of the money for food stamp coupons comes from the federal government, with the remainder of the division's budget coming from state and specialized funds.

Recognized as a national leader in innovative, effective welfare reform, AFS is committed to helping families leave welfare and remain self-sufficient through employment, or avoid coming on welfare altogether.

Public Welfare Review Commission

Sandra J. Harms, Exec. Asst.
500 Summer St. NE, Salem 97310-1013;
503-945-5601; Fax: 503-373-7492

Debra F.J. Lee, chair
The commission, composed of 16 members appointed by the governor, advises on public assistance programs for AFS clients and receives information from other organizations and the public.

Health Division

Elinor C. Hall, Admin.
800 NE Oregon St., #21, Suite 925,
Portland 97232; 503-731-4000; Vital Records
requests: 503-731-4095; Fax: 503-731-4078;
Email: ohd.info@state.or.us;
Web: www.ohd.hr.state.or.us

The Health Division works in partnership with 34 local health departments to assure that public health systems are in place, to identify community activities and environmental factors that put the health of Oregonians at risk, and to follow up to see that corrections have been made.

Public health professionals develop and recommend ways to prevent health hazards and to promote good health. Public health focuses on the community rather than the individual. Emphasis is on prevention, not restoration or cure.

One of the most effective ways to protect community health is to assure that systems affecting health are safeguarded. These systems, such as hospitals, radiation sources, drinking water and ambulances, are monitored by the Health Division. The division also works to prevent the spread of communicable disease and assures that various preventive services are in place to protect the health of mothers and children through immunization, family planning, teen pregnancy prevention and prenatal care.

The division collects, analyzes and makes available health-related data for policy development and planning. The Vital Records Unit (503-731-4095) provides birth, death, marriage and divorce certificates to the public.

Public health in Oregon was organized into a State Board of Health by the 1903 Legislature. This statewide department of public health was merged, along with other human service agencies, into the Department of Human Resources by the 1971 Legislature.

The following groups advise the Health Division:

Conference of Local Health Officials

Malinda Schofield, Health Div. staff
800 NE Oregon St., Portland 97232;
503-731-4000; Fax: 503-731-4078

Tom Engle, chair
Including all local health officers, public health administrators and other health professionals, the Conference of Local Health Officials provides advice on implementing Oregon's public-health laws and Health Division rules.

Drinking Water Advisory Committee

Dave LeLand, Health Div. staff
800 NE Oregon St., Portland 97232;
503-731-4010; Fax: 503-731-4077

Doug Wise, chair
The Drinking Water Advisory Committee provides advice and recommendations on matters relating to the Safe Drinking Water Quality Act.

Emergency Medical Services Committee

Greg Lander, Health Div. staff
800 NE Oregon St., Portland 97232;
503-731-4011; Fax: 503-731-4077

John Jui, M.D., F.A.C.E.P., chair
The Emergency Medical Services Committee advises on all issues relating to emergency medical services and standards, including: EMT certification, training, testing, and professional discipline; and ambulance service and vehicle licensing.

Public Health Advisory Board

Malinda Schofield, Health Div. staff
800 NE Oregon St., Portland 97232;
503-731-4000; Fax: 503-731-4078

Sheila Dale, chair
Fifteen members of the Public Health Advisory Board appointed by the

governor advise on statewide health issues and participate in public health policy development.

Radiation Advisory Committee

Ray Paris, Health Div. staff

800 NE Oregon St., Portland 97232; 503-731-4014; Fax: 503-731-4077

Mathews B. Fish, M.D., chair

The Radiation Advisory Committee provides guidance on radiation matters including review of regulations and standards for the safe use, handling, disposal and control of all radiation sources within the state.

Trauma Advisory Board, State

Lisa Irwin, Health Div. staff

800 NE Oregon St., Portland 97232; 503-731-4011; Fax: 503-731-4077

Bill Long, M.D., chair

Members of the State Trauma Advisory Board advise on standards, policies and procedures for the trauma-care system.

Mental Health and Developmental Disability Services Division

Barry S. Kast, M.S.W., Admin.

2575 Bittern St. NE, Salem 97310; 503-945-9499; Fax: 503-378-3796; Email: mhdds.dinfo@state.or.us; Web: www.mhddsd.hr.state.or.us

The mission of the Mental Health and Developmental Disability Services Division is to prevent or reduce the negative and disabling effects of mental illness and developmental disabilities. This includes people who are involuntarily committed to the division for care.

A team of nearly 3,400 employees across the state provides an interlocking, complex system of services in a variety of areas: medicine, therapy, social work and administrative support.

The division has two programs: mental health services and developmental disability services, and operates the major facilities described below. It also oversees 33 community mental health programs. Whenever possible, people receive services in their home community. The division was established in 1961 by ORS 430.021.

Eastern Oregon Training and Psychiatric Centers

Steve Shambaugh, Supt.

2525 Westgate, Pendleton 97801; 541-276-0991; Fax: 541-276-1147

The Eastern Oregon Psychiatric Center and the Eastern Oregon Training Center serve adults who are mentally ill and adults with developmental disabilities in central and eastern Oregon.

Fairview Training Center

Charles Farnham, Supt.

2250 Strong Rd. SE, Salem 97310; 503-986-5090; Fax: 503-986-5091

This residential facility serves adults with developmental disabilities. Fairview has transitioned many residents into community-based services.

Oregon State Hospital

Stan F. Mazur-Hart, Ph.D., Supt.

2600 Center St. NE, Salem 97310; 503-945-2870; Fax: 503-945-2867

The Oregon State Hospital is a specialty hospital serving the entire state from facilities in Salem and Portland. Five clinical programs provide treatment services for specific populations. They are Adult Treatment Services; Child, Adolescent and Geropsychiatric Treatment Services; Forensic/Hospital Treatment Services; Forensic Residential Treatment Services; and Correctional Treatment Services.

Boards and Councils

Three advisory boards and councils advise the division or carry out statutory responsibilities related to mental health and developmental disability services.

Developmental Disabilities Council

Charlotte Duncan, Exec. Dir.

540 24th Place NE, Salem 97310; 503-945-9941; Fax: 503-945-9947

Kathryn Richards, chair

The governor-appointed Developmental Disabilities Council advocates for the independence, productivity, community integration and inclusion of Oregonians with developmental disabilities. It receives an annual federal grant to engage in individual and community capacity-building activities and systems advocacy to promote a comprehensive system of services that are consumer- and family-centered.

Mental Health Advisory Board

Barry S. Kast, M.S.W., Admin.
2575 Bittern St. NE, Salem 97310; 503-945-9499

Irvine R. Smith, chair
The Mental Health Advisory Board studies the problems of mental health and developmental disabilities and recommends policies and procedures for state mental health programs.

Mental Health Planning and Management Advisory Council

Madeline Olson, Asst. Admin., MHS Programs
2575 Bittern St. NE, Salem 97310; 503-945-9700

Chris Johnson, chair
The Mental Health Planning and Management Advisory Council reviews plans for services for people who are mentally and emotionally disturbed and helps set policy and program priorities.

State Office for Services to Children and Families

Kay Dean Toran, Dir.
500 Summer St. NE, Salem 97310-1017;
503-945-5651; Fax: 503-581-6198;
Email: scf.info@state.or.us;
Web: www.scf.hr.state.or.us

The mission of the State Office for Services to Children and Families (SCF) is to protect Oregon's abused and neglected children and provide them with safe and permanent families. SCF is responsible for providing a safety net for children. The agency works to increase involvement of families and communities in the needs of children so that more children remain safe in their own homes, or if that is not possible, in other permanent families. The agency also provides treatment for children who require residential services to meet their treatment needs.

Forty-one branch offices statewide provide a variety of direct services with additional services provided by local community resources. SCF provides protective services, including foster care, adoptions and purchased residential treatment. Family preservation and remedial services to families are provided jointly by SCF, local contractors and private local providers. These include services such as parent training, family counseling, respite care, family sex abuse treatment and adoption planning.

Children with special needs such as those with developmental disabilities, mental, or severe emotional disabilities, receive additional services. SCF also regulates residential treatment facilities, adoption agencies and foster homes.

Senior and Disabled Services Division

Roger Auerbach, Admin.
500 Summer St. NE, Second Floor, Salem 97310-1015; 503-945-5811 (voice/TTY); Fax: 503-373-7823;
Email: sdsd.info@state.or.us;
Web: www.sdsd.hr.state.or.us

The Senior and Disabled Services Division (SDSD) serves seniors and people with disabilities through programs that encourage independence, dignity and quality of life. Meeting the individual needs of older and disabled citizens occurs through advocacy, planning and coordination. The service delivery system, using Area Agencies on Aging and state offices, places emphasis on local planning, decision making and service delivery.

The Senior Services Division was created by ORS 410.070 in 1981, and was designated the State Unit on Aging, responsible for administering the federal Older Americans Act and the state-funded Oregon Project Independence. In 1990, the programs for adults without children in the Adult and Family Services Division (Medicaid, General Assistance, and Food Stamps) were transferred to the renamed Senior and Disabled Services Division.

SDSD provides assistance to individuals who are severely disabled or elderly and at risk of institutionalization. Services include cash assistance, medical care, assistance with activities of daily living in an individual's own home or in some other care setting, nursing facility care and food stamps.

As the federally designated State Unit on Aging, SDSD is responsible for advocacy, planning, budgeting, fund disbursement, management information, training, monitoring of area agency activity and providing technical assistance for the state's aging programs.

SDSD relies on consumer and advocate input for decision making. It receives advice from Disability Services Advisory Councils throughout the state, the Oregon Disabilities Commission and the Governor's Commission on Senior Services.

Senior Services, Governor's Commission on
Pat List, Senior Advocacy Coord.
500 Summer St. NE, Second Floor, Salem 97310-1015; 503-945-5811 (voice/TTY); Fax: 503-373-7823

Phyllis Rand, chair
The 24-member Governor's Commission on Senior Services is the official advisory body on senior citizen issues for the governor, Legislature, and Senior and Disabled Services Division. The commission provides advice, identifies and recommends actions to meet the needs of seniors, and acts as an advocate for the elderly.

Vocational Rehabilitation Division
Joil A. Southwell, Admin.
500 Summer St. NE, Salem 97310; 503-945-5880; Fax: 503-378-3318; Email: vrd.info@state.or.us; Web: www.vrd.hr.state.or.us

The mission of the Vocational Rehabilitation Division (VRD) is to help Oregonians with disabilities achieve and maintain employment and independence. VRD administers Disability Determination Services and Rehabilitation Services.

Disability Determination Services (DDS) is a federally funded program regulated by the Social Security Administration. DDS is responsible for ensuring that Oregon claimants, who are eligible under the Social Security Disability laws for Supplemental Security Income (SSI) or Social Security Disability Insurance (SSDI) promptly obtain benefits.

Rehabilitation Services is a federal/state funded program providing vocational rehabilitation assistance to eligible persons with disabilities who are vocationally disabled under terms of the Rehabilitation Act of 1973, as amended. VRD offers rehabilitation services in collaboration and partnership with other state agencies, local private non-profit rehabilitation organizations, independent living service providers and employers.

VRD uses voluntary advisory groups that help provide input about policy, program, planning and service delivery.

VRD's local offices often establish ad hoc and ongoing advisory groups.

Independent Living Council, State
Tim Holmes, chair
The purpose of the State Independent Living Council (SILC) is to provide direction and consumer input on matters of policy and program development to the agency's statewide Independent Living Rehabilitation Services program.

Rehabilitation Advisory Council, State
Ruthanne Cox-Carothers, chair
The mission of the Rehabilitiation Advisory Council is to provide advice and guidance on the development, implementation and review of the division's rehabilitation services for Oregonians with disabilities through consumer and business input.

Land Conservation and Development, Department of
Richard P. Benner, Dir.
1175 Court St. NE, Salem 97310-0590; 503-373-0050; Fax: 503-362-6705

Land Conservation and Development Commission
Richard P. Benner, Dir.
1175 Court St. NE, Salem 97310-0590; 503-373-0050; Fax: 503-362-6705; Web: www.lcd.state.or.us

William R. Blosser, chair, Dayton, 1998; Randall Franke, Salem, 2000; Gary Harris, Madras, 2000; Hector Macpherson, Albany, 1998; Gussie McRobert, Gresham, 2000; Steven L. Pfeiffer, Portland, 1997; R. Charles Vars Jr., Corvallis, 1999.

The Department of Land Conservation and Development administers the Regional Problem Solving (RPS) Program created by Senate Bill 1156 in 1995. This pilot program enables cities and counties to work together more effectively when dealing with land-use issues that transcend local boundaries. In 1996 projects were started in Clatsop, Deschutes, Josephine and Polk counties to address regional issues.

Oregon's Land Conservation and Development Commission (LCDC) has seven members who are appointed by the governor and confirmed by the Senate.

LCDC's administrative arm is the Department of Land Conservation and Development (DLCD). The department administers Oregon's statewide land-use planning program and Oregon's federally approved coastal-management program. The agency's director is appointed by LCDC.

Oregon's statewide planning program was created in 1973 when the Legislature passed the Oregon Land Use Act (popularly known as Senate Bill 100). Under that program, authorized by ORS chapter 197, all cities and counties have adopted comprehensive plans that meet mandatory state standards. The standards are 19 statewide planning goals that deal with land use, development, housing and conservation of natural resources. The program also requires the coordination of land-use plans and programs adopted by local governments and state and federal agencies.

Oregon's innovative and extensive program for land-use planning is widely acclaimed and has served as a model for other state programs. It was named the Outstanding Land Use Program in the Nation in 1982 by the American Planning Association. The national conservation organization, Renew America, rated Oregon's growth-management efforts as the best in the country in 1988, 1989 and 1990.

Oregon's planning program continues this state's century-long efforts to protect resources and provide for orderly development. Such planning has produced some important results: a lessening of urban sprawl; better conservation of farm and forest land; a faster and more efficient development process; and more protection for resources like beaches, wetlands and wildlife habitat.

Citizen Involvement Advisory Committee

Mitch Rohse, Committee staff

Patricia Combes, Joseph; Harold Haynes, Forest Grove; Robert Moldenhauer, Roseburg; Mary Palmer, Portland; Barbara Wiggin, Gresham; two vacancies.

The state's Citizen Involvement Advisory Committee (CIAC) advises the Land Conservation and Development Commission (LCDC) and local governments on citizen involvement in land-use planning. CIAC is a permanent committee, established by ORS 197.160 to "assure widespread involvement in all phases of the planning process."

CIAC has seven members, one from each congressional district and two at large. CIAC meets quarterly in Salem. The state's Department of Land Conservation and Development provides support staff for the committee.

Land Use Board of Appeals

Hearings Referees: Virginia L. Gustafson, Corvallis, 1999; Suzanne C. Hanna, Harrisburg, 1999; Peter Livingston, Portland, 1999.
306 State Library Bldg., 250 Winter St. NE, Salem 97310; 503-373-1265

The governor appoints the three-member board to serve four-year terms with confirmation by the Senate. The referees serving on the Land Use Board of Appeals (LUBA) must be members of the Oregon State Bar.

LUBA was created by legislation in 1979 (ORS chapter 197) and has exclusive jurisdiction to review all governmental land-use decisions, whether legislative or quasi-judicial in nature. The Legislature stated "... it is the policy of the Legislative Assembly that time is of the essence in reaching final decisions in matters involving land use, and that those decisions be made consistently with sound principles governing judicial review."

Prior to LUBA's creation, land-use appeals were heard by the Land Conservation and Development Commission and the circuit courts. LUBA was created to simplify the appeal process, speed resolution of land-use disputes and provide consistent interpretation of state and local land-use laws. The tribunal is the first of its kind in the United States.

Landscape Architect Board

Gil Bellamy, Admin.
750 Front St. NE, Suite 260, Salem 97310; 503-378-4270; Fax: 503-378-6091

Jim Figurski, chair, Lake Oswego, 1997; Hal Beighley, Beaverton, 1999; Gladys Biglor, Bend, 1997; Paul Kyllo, Sutherlin, 1997; Andy Leisinger, Salem, 2000.

The governor appoints the board members consisting of three registered landscape architects and two public members to serve three-year terms which expire on June 30 of the year indicated.

Since 1981 the Oregon Landscape Architect Board has operated under ORS 671.310–671.459 and OAR chapter 804. The board registers landscape architects either by examination or by reciprocity.

More than 250 landscape architects are registered in Oregon.

Landscape Contractors Board

Kenneth K. Keudell, Admin.
700 Summer St. NE, Suite 300, PO Box 14140, Salem 97309-5052; 503-378-4621; Fax: 503-373-2213

Daniel L. Fahndrich, chair, Salem, 1997; Kim B. Jones, vice-chair, Bend, 1997; Jeffrey J. Bennett, Portland, 1998; Audrey Castile, Tigard, 1997; John Galbraith, Medford, 1998; Marilyn S. Oliver, Tigard, 1997; Michael A. Snyder, Oregon City, 1997.

The governor appoints the seven-member board to serve three-year terms. Five members are from the landscape industry and two are public members.

Operating under ORS 671.510–671.990 since 1972, the Landscape Contractors Board licenses landscaping businesses and landscape contractors. Individual landscape contractors must meet experience and/or education requirements and pass competency exams. Landscaping businesses must post security bonds, submit evidence of liability insurance and employ a licensed landscape contractor.

The board receives and investigates consumer complaints, answers consumer and contractor questions and enforces compliance with the licensing law.

Approximately 1,100 landscape contractors and 900 landscaping businesses are licensed in Oregon.

Library, Oregon State

Jim Scheppke, State Librarian
State Library Bldg., 250 Winter St. NE, Salem 97310-0640; 503-378-4243; TTY: 503-378-4276; Fax: 503-588-7119; Web: www.osl.state.or.us/oslhome.html

State Library, Board of Trustees

Sheila Burns, chair, Ashland, 1997; Gerald Young, vice-chair, La Grande, 1998; Evelyn Crowell, Portland, 1997; Phyllis Lichenstein, Salem, 1998; Peggy Mangis, Salem, 2000; Colleen Mitchell, Portland, 1999; DeAnna Noriega, Grants Pass, 2000.

Members of the board of trustees are appointed by the governor; all terms expire June 30 of respective years.

The mission of the State Library is to provide quality information services to Oregon state government, provide reading materials to blind and print-disabled Oregonians, and provide leadership, grants and other assistance to improve local library service for all Oregonians.

The State Library was founded in 1905 and is authorized by ORS chapter 357.

Information Services (Phone: 503-378-4277). The State Library provides direct research and reference assistance to state agencies and to persons on official state business or involved in public decision making. Among its more than 1 million items are in-depth collections in public administration, environmental science, political science, and the social sciences. Specialized collections include state and federal government publications, and a comprehensive collection of books and other materials about Oregon.

The **Genealogical Resource Center** is a service provided in cooperation with the Willamette Valley Genealogy Society. Volunteers are available to assist persons with family history research.

Talking Book and Braille Services (Salem phone: 503-378-3849; Portland: 503-224-0610; toll-free: 1-800-452-0292). This unit makes books and other library materials available to approximately 43,000 Oregonians with visual or other disabilities. The Library of Congress has designated the Oregon State Library as a regional library in their national network of libraries serving print-disabled persons. The Library of Congress provides the State Library with a large collection of books on cassette and record, and in braille, as well as reading equipment. All materials and equipment are available through the mail and are postage free.

The TBABS Advisory Council is a seven-member council assisting the State Library Board in planning for the improvement of talking book and braille services. Its members represent consumer groups, state agencies, libraries and patrons.

Library Development Services
(Phone: 503-378-2112). This unit of the State Library plans for statewide library development, provides consultation and continuing education services to local library staff and trustees, and administers all state and federal library grant programs. The Oregon Intellectual Freedom Clearinghouse, a special project of the unit, provides assistance to libraries facing challenges to intellectual freedom and publishes an annual report documenting challenges that were reported by local libraries during the year.

The Library Services and Technology Act (LSTA) Advisory Council is a 14-member council mandated under the federal Library Services and Technology Act to advise the State Library Board on the use of federal library development funds. Its members represent public, academic, school, special and institutional libraries, and library users, including disabled and disadvantaged persons.

Liquor Control Commission, Oregon

Pamela S. Erickson, Admin.
9079 SE McLoughlin Blvd., Portland 97222-7355; 503-872-5000; toll-free: 1-800-452-6522; Fax: 503-872-5266

W. Eugene Hallman, chair, Pendleton, 1998 (541-276-3857); Marc Kelley, Portland, 1998; Kaye Kennett, Elmira, 2000; Robert Puentes, Salem, 1999; Amoy Williamson, Portland, 2000.

The five citizen commissioners are appointed by the governor to four-year terms, subject to Senate confirmation. They provide the policy direction of the Oregon Liquor Control Commission (OLCC). Each commissioner represents a state congressional district, and one is from the food and beverage industry. Together they appoint the administrator.

The Liquor Control Commission operates under ORS chapters 471, 472 and 473. Its mission is to effectively regulate the sale, distribution, and responsible use of alcoholic beverages in order to protect Oregon's public health, safety and community livability.

The OLCC was created in 1933 by a special session of the Legislature after national prohibition ended. Oregon chose a "control" state system, giving the state the exclusive right to sell packaged hard liquor. Hard liquor is sold through 235 retail liquor stores operated by contracted agents.

It was also authorized to license private businesses that sell beer and wine by the drink or in the package. The Liquor Control Act passed in 1953 permits the sale of hard liquor by the drink in restaurants and private clubs. These "dispenser" licenses are issued by the OLCC. In addition, the OLCC administers the mandatory Alcohol Server Education Program, which focuses on responsible alcohol service. All alcohol servers must complete the course every five years. The OLCC also enforces the Bottle Bill law. Under this law, any malt or carbonated beverage sold in Oregon must have a refund value of not less than 5 cents. If the container is reusable by more than one manufacturer, the refund value is 2 cents.

Liquor store sales in fiscal year 1995–96 were $184 million. Another $13.7 million was collected in liquor license fees, privilege taxes on beer and wine, and in fines paid for liquor law violations. Of the net revenue generated by the OLCC, 56 percent goes to the state's general fund; cities receive 20 percent, counties 10 percent, and City Revenue Sharing gets 14 percent. Half of the privilege taxes collected go to the Mental Health Alcoholism and Drug Services account. The Wine Advisory Board receives a special 2-cent tax on all wines to promote the development and marketing of Oregon wines. Allocations from liquor revenues for the 1995–96 fiscal year totalled $72.4 million.

The OLCC has regional offices in Bend, Eugene and Medford, as well as its headquarters in Portland.

Long Term Care Ombudsman, Office of the

Meredith A. Cote, Ombudsman
3855 Wolverine St. NE, Suite 6, Salem 97310; 503-378-6533; toll-free: 1-800-522-2602; TTY: 503-378-5847; Fax: 503-373-0852

The mission of the Office of the Long Term Care Ombudsman is to enhance the quality of life, improve the level of care, protect the individual rights and promote the dignity of each Oregon citizen housed in a nursing facility, adult foster care home, residential care facility or assisted living facility. Specifically, the office is charged with investigating and resolving complaints made by or on behalf of long term care facility residents. This objective is achieved by trained volunteers who are a routine presence in long term care facilities throughout the state. The office is authorized by ORS 441.100–441.153 and the federal Older Americans Act. The Ombudsman Program was formed in 1981.

Long Term Care Ombudsman Advisory Committee

The Long Term Care Ombudsman Advisory Committee is charged with monitoring the Long Term Care Ombudsman Program and advising the governor and the Legislature about the program. The seven committee members are appointed as follows: one each by the governor, president of the Senate, speaker of the House, and the House and Senate minority leaders, and two members representing senior organizations selected by the governor.

Lottery, Oregon State

Chris Lyons, Dir.
500 Airport Rd. SE, Salem 97301; 503-540-1000; Fax: 503-540-1009; Web: www.das.state.or.us/lottery/

Lottery Commission

Gregory A. Aitchison, M.D., Bandon, 2000; Keith Lewis, Heppner, 1996; Eugene D. "Debbs" Potts, Grants Pass, 1997; Donald Scarborough, Salem, 2000; Janet C. Towle, Beaverton, 1999.

Citizen initiatives resulted in two ballot measures approved by Oregon voters in November 1984. The measures, which became ORS chapter 461, the Oregon State Lottery Act, required the establishment of the Oregon State Lottery under the direction of a lottery commission. The five members and the director are appointed by the governor and confirmed by the Senate.

The Lottery's first instant tickets went on sale April 25, 1985. Megabucks, its first on-line computer-operated game,

was introduced November 20, 1985. In 1989, the Legislature authorized America's first sports lottery based on the outcome of professional sporting events. Sports Action, which began in the fall of 1989, raises funds for intercollegiate athletics and academic scholarships. Other games include Keno, Powerball, Daily 4 and breakopens.

In April 1992, the Oregon Lottery began operating a video game system, the first in the nation to be on-line to a central computer system 24 hours a day.

The Oregon Constitution dedicates lottery earnings for economic development, job creation and public education. Every two years, the Legislature meets and decides which state and local government agencies will receive lottery funds. Those agencies manage the use of those funds for specific programs and projects. The Lottery transferred more than $1.2 billion in earnings to the Economic Development Fund from 1985 to June 30, 1996. In addition, counties receive 2.5 percent of video net receipts for local economic development projects.

At least 84 percent of the Lottery's total annual revenue is returned to the public in the form of prizes and net proceeds benefitting the public purpose. No more than 16 percent of its total annual revenues may be spent on operating expenses.

Marine Board, State

Paul E. Donheffner, Dir.
435 Commercial St. NE, #400, Salem 97310; 503-378-8587; Fax: 503-378-4597

Court Boice, Gold Beach, 2000; Nancy J. Hungerford, Oregon City, 1997; Tom Keel, Umpqua, 1997; Tom O'Connor, Lake Oswego, 1999; Rick Wren, Bend, 1999. The governor appoints the five members for four-year terms.

The Marine Board is Oregon's boating agency, dedicated to safety, education and access in an enhanced environment. The Marine Board returns user fees (marine fuel tax and title and registration fees) to boaters in the form of educational programs, law enforcement and improved boating facilities.

Established in 1959 and authorized under ORS 830.105, the board titles and registers recreational vessels, currently numbering about 195,000. It establishes statewide boating regulations and advises and assists county sheriffs and the State Police in marine law enforcement.

To promote safe boating, the board publishes brochures and provides boating-education courses; the board also sponsors water-safety programs for youth. The Marine Board provides grants to develop and maintain accessible boating facilities and protect water quality. The board also registers guides, outfitters and charterboat operators.

Massage Technicians, State Board of

Vicky A. Williams, Exec. Dir.
800 NE Oregon St., #21, Suite 407, Portland 97232; 503-731-4064; Fax: 503-731-4207

Chauncey Farrell, L.M.T., chair, Klamath Falls, 1998; Ivan Fernandez, L.M.T., Salem, 1998; Lindy Ferrigno, L.M.T., Portland, 1998; Linda Glenn, public member, Portland, 1997; Glenath Moyle, L.M.T., Portland, 1997. The governor appoints five members, one of whom is licensed in a health-related field, for terms of four years.

The board is authorized under ORS 687.115 to protect the public through the administration and establishment of rules pertaining to the practice of massage. The board certifies classes, conducts examinations and issues licenses; enforces hygienic habits and sanitary conditions for the practice of massage; imposes fines and suspends or revokes licenses of rule violators. Requirements are 330 hours of education: 100 hours of anatomy/physiology, 45 hours of kinesiology, 50 hours of pathology, 135 hours of massage practice and theory.

The board was first established in the early 1950s as an independent board and then placed under the auspices of the Oregon State Health Division from 1971 to 1975 when it again became independent.

Medical Examiners, State of Oregon Board of

Kathleen Haley, Exec. Dir.
620 Crown Plaza, 1500 SW 1st Ave., Portland 97201-5826; 503-229-5770; Fax: 503-229-6543

James H. Sampson, M.D., chair, Portland, 1998; J. Bruce Williams, M.D., vice-chair, Corvallis, 1997; Sarah

Hendrickson, M.D., secretary, Eugene, 1998; Terry L. Connor, D.O., West Linn, 1997; H. Eric Dolson, public member, Sisters, 2000; Edward A. Heusch, D.O., Portland, 1999; Catherine M. Mater, public member, Corvallis, 1998; Erik Nielsen, M.D., Portland, 2000; George A. Porter, M.D., Portland, 1998; Rosemary C. Lee Selinger, M.D., Grants Pass, 1999; Fred R. Stark, M.D., Ontario, 1998. All terms expire February 28 of the years indicated.

The 11-member Board of Medical Examiners is appointed by the governor and confirmed by the Senate. It includes seven M.D. members, two D.O. members, and two public members. The Board of Medical Examiners, created in 1889 and authorized under ORS chapter 677, has responsibility for administering the Medical Practice Act, and establishing the rules and regulations pertaining to the practice of medicine in Oregon.

The board licenses and registers graduates of medical and osteopathic schools and investigates and disciplines violators of its rules and regulations and those complaints of known violations of the Medical Practice Act.

In addition to licensing doctors of medicine and doctors of osteopathy, the board is also responsible for licensing

Bighorn sheep were reintroduced to Hart Mountain National Wildlife Refuge in the early 1950s, and the herd now numbers almost 400.

Photo courtesy of the Hart Mountain National Wildlife Refuge.

and disciplining podiatrists, physician assistants, acupuncturists and respiratory care practitioners. The board also is responsible for developing and implementing a diversion program for chemically dependent licensees regulated under ORS chapter 677.

Board staff most frequently answer questions on the requirements for licensure of the medical professionals whom it licenses, questions from applicants regarding the status of their application file, requests from hospitals, medical associations, and the public for verification of licensure, interpretation of the board's statutes and rules and regulations, and when and how to file a complaint against a licensee of the board.

As of October 1996 there are 10,793 Oregon licensed physicians (M.D./D.O.).

Acupuncture Committee

*620 Crown Plaza, 1500 SW 1st Ave.,
Portland 97201-5826; 503-229-5770;
Fax: 503-229-6543*

Joel L. Seres, M.D., chair, Portland, 1999; Malvin Finkelstein, acupuncturist, Eugene, 1998; Lowell E. Kobrin, M.D., Coos Bay, 1998; Sheila Moran, acupuncturist, Portland, 1997; Louisa M. Silva, M.D., Salem, 1997; Joseph Soprani, acupuncturist, Portland, 1999; Erik Nielsen, M.D., board liaison, Portland, 1997.

The Acupuncture Committee members are appointed by the board, and the committee presently consists of three acupuncturists, three physicians and a physician board member as board liaison.

Since 1975 the Board of Medical Examiners has been authorized by ORS chapter 677 to determine the qualifications of a person authorized to practice acupuncture. The board has adopted rules and regulations regarding the standards for education, training and licensure of acupuncturists.

As of October 1996 there are 259 Oregon licensed acupuncturists.

Diversion Program Supervisory Council

Susan V. McCall, M.D., M.P.H., Medical Dir.
*6950 SW Hampton, Suite 220, Tigard 97223-8331;
503-620-9117; Fax: 503-684-5512;
Information: 503-968-1205*

Ernest H. Price, M.D., chair, Portland, 1998; Donald E. Girard, M.D., Portland, 1998; Susan E. Polchert, M.D., Eugene,

1997; William H. Stenstrom, M.D., Leaburg, 1997.

A supervisory council of five members is appointed by the State Board of Medical Examiners to serve a two-year term of office, and each is eligible for reappointment. No current board member or staff shall serve on the council. In the event of a vacancy, the board shall make an appointment for the unexpired term.

Effective July 1989, ORS chapter 705 established the Diversion Program Supervisory Council to develop and implement a diversion program for chemically dependent licensees regulated under ORS chapter 677. Operation of the program includes participation in and administration of assessments, interventions, recovery monitoring, relapse management, education and research, and being a consulting resource for licensees, Oregon hospitals, medical staffs and medical societies.

Physician Assistant Committee

*620 Crown Plaza, 1500 SW 1st Ave.,
Portland 97201-5826; 503-229-5770;
Fax: 503-229-6543*

Dana Gray, P.A., chair, Hillsboro, 1997; Bruce D. Carlson, M.D., Hermiston, 1999; Robert Davis, P.A., Vale, 1999; Darrel R. Purkerson, R.Ph., St. Helens, 1997; Sarah Hendrickson, M.D., board liaison, Eugene, 1997.

The Board of Medical Examiners appoints one of its members and one additional physician, one of whom must supervise a physician assistant; the Oregon Society of Physician Assistants appoints two members, and the Oregon State Board of Pharmacy appoints one pharmacist as a member. Terms are for three years and expire June 30 of year listed.

Pursuant to legislative authority provided by ORS 677.540 effective June 22, 1981, a Physician Assistant Committee was created under the Board of Medical Examiners. Its duties, under ORS 677.545, are to make recommendations to the board in the approval of applications for licensure, for practice description changes of licensed physician assistants and for prescribing and dispensing privileges.

As of October 1996 there are 248 Oregon licensed physician assistants.

Podiatry, Advisory Council on

620 Crown Plaza, 1500 SW 1st Ave.,
Portland 97201-5826; 503-229-5770;
Fax: 503-229-6543

M. Thomas Robertson, D.P.M., chair, Salem, 1998; Vernia Huffman, public member, St. Helens, 1997; Lisa M. Lipe, D.P.M., Newberg, 1996; John D. Mozena, D.P.M., Portland, 1997; Rosemary Selinger, M.D., board liaison, Grants Pass, 1997.

Four members, three licensed podiatrists and one public member, are appointed by the governor for three-year terms. The Board of Medical Examiners appoints as the fifth council member a member of the board who is also a physician.

Pursuant to chapter 339, Oregon Laws 1981, the State Board of Podiatry Examiners was abolished and all of its duties and powers were transferred to the Board of Medical Examiners.

These duties are to issue licenses on the basis of national board endorsement for the practice of podiatry within the state; revoke licenses for violations of ORS chapter 677; and make and enforce reasonable rules and regulations for the procedure of the board. An Advisory Council on Podiatry was created in 1981 under ORS 677.855 to advise the board in carrying out these duties and enforcing the provisions of ORS chapter 677.

As of October 1996 there are 143 Oregon licensed podiatrists.

Respiratory Care Practitioners Committee

620 Crown Plaza, 1500 SW 1st Ave.,
Portland 97201-5826; 503-229-5770;
Fax: 503-229-6543

Pete Mardesich, R.C.P., chair, Portland, 1998; Marie Keyes, R.C.P., Portland, 1999; Richard J. Maunder, M.D., Portland, 1999; Valerie R. P. Robinson, M.D., Portland, 1998; Gary Russell, R.C.P., Eugene, 1999; J. Bruce Williams, M.D., board liaison, Corvallis, 1997.

ORS 677.873 specifies the membership of the Respiratory Care Practitioners Committee as being three respiratory care practitioners, and two physicians. A liaison member from the Board of Medical Examiners is also a committee member. Terms are for three years.

Senate Bill 672 was signed into law by the governor on August 5, 1991, and the Board of Medical Examiners became responsible for the licensure of respiratory care practitioners in the state. Since they had not previously been state licensed, administrative rules have been written stating the requirements for initial licensure, describing the biennial registration renewal process, and the number of hours and kinds of continuing education required every two years.

As of October 1996 there are 966 Oregon licensed respiratory care practitioners.

Military Department, State of Oregon

Major General Raymond F. Rees,
The Adjutant General, Oregon National Guard
1776 Militia Way SE., PO Box 14350, Salem
97309-5047; 503-945-3991

The Oregon National Guard is commanded by Major General Raymond F. Rees, the adjutant general. The Assistant General (Army) position is held by Brig. Gen. Norman Hoffman and Brig. Gen. William H. Doctor is the assistant adjutant general (Air). The 142nd Fighter Wing in Portland Air Base is commanded by Col. Bruce Marshall while the 114th Fighter Squadron in Kingsley Field, Klamath Falls, is commanded by Col. Billy J. Cox. Brigadier General James V. Torgerson commands the 82nd Troop Command Brigade with headquarters in Lake Oswego and Brig. Gen. Alexander H. Burgin commands the 41st Enhanced Infantry Brigade with headquarters in Tigard.

Members of the Military Council are appointed under ORS 396.145 and serve at the pleasure of the governor. The department is authorized under ORS 396.305.

Members of the Military Council are: Maj. Gen. Raymond F. Rees, chair; Brig. Gen. Alexander Burgin; Brig. Gen. William Doctor; Brig. Gen. Norman Hoffman; Col. Gary R. Allen; Col. Lynn E. Ashcroft; Col. Carol A. Brown; Col. Douglas A. Pitt; Col. Charles L. Rosenfield and Brig. Gen. James Torgerson.

Originally authorized with the formation of Oregon's Provisional Government, the Oregon National Guard has grown from a single mounted rifle company in 1844 to a highly trained military force of more than 9,000 men and women who serve as citizen soldiers.

The first official militia unit was formed in 1847.

In peacetime, the Guard serves the governor with its active command and administration vested in the adjutant general. As part of the Total Force, Oregon National Guard is also available to the federal government upon receipt of orders from the president in accordance with Section 102, Title 32 of the United States Code.

Members of the Oregon Army and Air National Guard have been activated in support of peacekeeping missions such as Operation Joint Endeavor and are serving in federal duty status in various locations throughout Europe.

Like their predecessors, members of the Oregon National Guard are volunteers. They serve in one of 100 federally recognized Army Guard units or one of 18 Air Guard units. Every type of military occupational skill can be found in the Oregon National Guard.

Unlike other reserve forces, the National Guard has another important function in addition to the defense of our nation. It is the only military organization trained and equipped to aid in state emergencies upon order of the governor. Guard members also support many community activities with volunteer help and equipment. All activities are performed within the framework of training required by the National Guard's state and federal missions.

The Oregon National Guard is involved in many programs working directly with at-risk youth in drug demand reduction programs. In addition, the guard performs more than 100,000 hours a year on projects like the Make A Wish Foundation, Camp Rosenbaum, the Oregon Food Bank and clean-up projects.

The Oregon Military Department is the headquarters for the Army and Air National Guard. The Military Department supervises in all matters pertaining to personnel administration, supply and logistical support of the Oregon National Guard, State Defense Force and all state-owned or leased armories, posts, camps, military reservations and rifle ranges.

The Oregon National Guard operates under two budgets: a federal appropriation and the state of Oregon provides 3 percent of the total operational budget. The value of federal equipment used by both the Army and Air Guard exceeds $1.1 billion. This is largely due to the value of the air assets.

The Oregon State Defense Force (OSDF), a non-paid 700-plus member volunteer state-militia force commanded by Brig. Gen. Colin Ackerson, is the only sizable civil-defense organization in the state. If the National Guard were mobilized for war, the OSDF would assume the mission of the National Guard as a state force.

Mortuary and Cemetery Board, State

Lucinda Potter, Exec. Dir.

Portland State Office Bldg., 800 NE Oregon St., #21, Suite 430, Portland 97232-2109; 503-731-4040; Fax: 503-731-4494

Gene Bateman, Newport, 1997; Margaret Bowen, Yamhill, 2000; James Caldwell, Astoria, 1999; Patrick Dunham, Pendleton, 2000; Samuel J. Duplessis, Portland, 2000; Michael Garcia, Salem, 2000; Roderic Grosz, Portland, 1998; Bill Loomis, Keizer, 1997; Don Masaoy, Portland, 1999; Alex Thurber, Portland, 1998; Judy Waggle, Albany, 1999. All terms expire on December 31 of the year indicated. All board members are appointed by the governor. Public board members excepted, members must have had five consecutive years of experience immediately preceding their appointment.

The State Mortuary and Cemetery Board was established in 1921 as the Funeral Directors and Embalmers Board and operates under ORS 692.010–692.990. The board's programs include education and impartial oversight through regular inspections of licensed facilities, testing, licensing of funeral service practitioners, embalmers, limited funeral service practitioners, funeral establishments, cemeteries, crematoriums and immediate disposition companies, and registration of pre-need salespersons; investigation of complaints, holding hearings, and imposing sanctions when necessary. The board also monitors and administers an apprenticeship program for practitioners entering the profession.

The board is self-supporting and derives its financing from licensing, examination and death registration fees.

Naturopathic Examiners, Board of

Kathleen Soderberg, Exec. Officer
407-B State Office Bldg., 800 NE Oregon St., #21, Portland 97232; 503-731-4045; Fax: 503-731-4207

Kathleen Germain, N.D., chair, Lake Oswego, 1997; Richard Barrett, N.D., Portland, 1998; Joseph Kassel, N.D., Veneta, 1997; Linda Meloche, N.D., Carlton, 1999; Priscilla M. Taylor, public member, Lake Oswego, 1997. All terms expire June 30 of the year indicated.

The Board of Naturopathic Examiners consists of five members appointed by the governor for three-year terms. In 1926, ORS 685.160 authorized the board to examine, register and license naturopathic physicians. The board enforces compliance with the naturopathic statute through administrative procedures, revocation of licenses and court actions. The board also certifies doctors qualified to practice natural childbirth.

Northwest Power Planning Council

John Brogoitti, Oregon Council Member (1999)
Joyce Cohen, Oregon Council Member (1998)
620 SW 5th Ave., Suite 1025, Portland 97204-1424; 503-229-5171; Fax: 503-229-5173

Regional Office: 851 SW 6th Ave., Suite 1100, Portland 97204-1348; 503-222-5161 or toll-free:1-800-222-3355; Fax: 503-795-3370; Web: www.nwppc.org

Through the Northwest Power Act of 1980 (PL 96-502), the U.S. Congress authorized Idaho, Montana, Washington and Oregon to create the Northwest Electric Power and Conservation Planning Council (commonly known as the Northwest Power Planning Council), a planning and policy-making body. The four state governors each appoint two members to the council. Oregon representation is mandated by ORS 469.805. Oregon council members serve three-year terms.

Congress charged the council with developing a program to protect, mitigate and enhance fish and wildlife affected by the development, operation, and management of hydroelectric facilities in the Columbia River Basin while assuring the Pacific Northwest an adequate, efficient, economical, and reliable power supply; developing a power plan that included a 20-year demand forecast, an energy conservation program, and the fish and wildlife program; and involving the public extensively in the decision-making process.

Nursing, State Board of

Joan C. Bouchard, R.N., M.N., Exec. Dir.
800 NE Oregon St., Suite 465, Portland 97232-2162; 503-731-4745; Fax: 503-731-4755; Email: Oregon.bn.info@state.or.us

Katrina D. Susi, RN, president, Pendleton, 1997; Julia Fontanilla, RN, secretary, Pacific City, 1997; Channa Commanday, RN, Portland, 1998; Madelon M. Cook, LPN, North Bend, 1997; Ila J. Cronen, LPN, Bend, 1997; John W. Hakanson, Milwaukie, 1996; Patricia C. Krumm, RN, Oregon City, 1996; Linda L. Manous, RN, Coos Bay, 1998; Pamela L. Ross, RN, Salem, 1998. Terms expire December 31 of years indicated. Members are appointed by the governor to serve no more than two consecutive three-year terms.

The Oregon State Board of Nursing was established in 1911 (ORS chapter 678) to regulate nursing practice and

Ice Lake as viewed from Craig Mountain in the Wallowas offers an idyllic alpine vista. Photo by Gary Fletcher.

education for the purpose of protecting the public's health, safety and well-being. The board examines, licenses and renews licenses of qualified registered professional nurses and licensed practical nurses; certifies all nursing assistants and establishes standards for their training and certification; certifies nurse practitioners and grants prescriptive authority to qualified nurse practitioners; prescribes essential curricula and standards for nursing education programs preparing persons for licensure; surveys and approves nursing education programs which meet board standards; and investigates complaints about nurses and nursing assistants to determine whether there have been violations of the law or administrative rules governing nurses and nursing assistants. With the exception of the Nursing Assistant Program, all activities of the board are financed by license fees.

Nursing Home Administrators, Board of Examiners of

Barbara Orazio, Exec. Officer
800 NE Oregon St., Suite 407, Portland 97232; 503-731-4046; Fax: 503-731-4207

Richard Herington, NHA, chair, Portland, 1997; Jeanette Bremer, public member, Portland, 1999; Nancy Findholt, NHA, Union, 1999; Hamilton Jackson, public member, 1999; Maurice Reece, NHA, Keizer, 1998; James Scarborough, public member, 1997; William Simonson, pharmacist, Portland, 1997; Joy Smith, R.N., Hubbard, 1999; physician member vacant. Members are appointed by the governor for three-year terms that expire June 30. At the pleasure of the governor, a member is eligible for reappointment but cannot serve more than two consecutive terms.

Created in 1971 and authorized by ORS 678.800, the duties of the Board of Examiners of Nursing Home Administrators are to develop and enforce standards; to formulate appropriate examinations; and to issue, revoke or suspend licenses. The board investigates complaints charging that any nursing home administrator has failed to comply with required standards; studies nursing homes and their administrations to improve licensing standards; evaluates and approves continuing education

courses to meet training requirements; controls an ongoing trainee program for prospective nursing home administrators; and maintains a register of all licensed nursing home administrators and trainees.

Occupational Therapy Licensing Board

Peggy G. Smith, Exec. Officer
800 NE Oregon St., #21, Suite 407, Portland 97232-2162; 503-731-4048; Fax: 503-731-4207

Susan Nelson, OTR/L, chair, Portland, 1997; Tony Jacobs, public member, Corbett, 1997; Karen Kennard, public member, Lyons, 1997; Judy Meredith, OTR/L, Bend, 1998; Loni Shapiro, OTR/L, Eugene, 2000. The board is composed of five members appointed by the governor to four-year terms. Three are licensed occupational therapists and two are public members. Terms expire on October 1 of the year indicated.

The Occupational Therapy Licensing Board was created in 1977 and is authorized by ORS chapter 675 to regulate occupational therapy practice by determining qualifications for licensure; to grant, suspend, revoke licenses according to statute and rules; and to investigate alleged violations of the Occupational Therapy Practice Act.

Oil Heat Commission

Terrie J. Heer, Admin.
1300 SE Gideon, Portland 97202-2419; 503-731-3002; Fax: 503-731-3003; Email: ohc@teleport.com; Web: www.teleport.com/~ohc/

Jeff Abbott, chair, Bend, 1997; Mary Ellen Farr, Portland, 1999; Doug Gaynor, Gladstone, 1998; Lila Leathers-Fitz, Portland, 1997; Bill Parker, Eugene, 1999; Charlie Porcelli, Portland, 1998; Ted Spence, Portland, 1997.

Established in 1989 under ORS chapter 926, the Oil Heat Commission is charged with promoting the long-term, efficient use of oil heat and protecting public health and safety by ensuring environmental cleanup of heating oil tank releases.

This landmark legislation established a national precedent. Through the commission, whose members are appointed by the governor, the industry will strive to maintain residential market share.

Through the innovative environmental protection program, property owners will receive financial assistance for heating oil tank cleanup, which must meet the Department of Environmental Quality's high standards.

The commission is financed by monthly assessments of heating oil dealers based on 3 percent of gross revenues derived from the retail sale of heating oil in Oregon.

Optometry, Board of

David W. Plunkett, Admin.
3218 Pringle Rd. SE, Suite 100, Salem 97302-6306; 503-373-7721; Fax: 503-378-3616; Email: oregon.obo@state.or.us

Ann A. Easly, O.D., president, Ontario, 1997; Joan Miller, O.D., Hillsboro, 1997; Mitzi M. Naucler, Salem, 1997; John P. Reslock, O.D., Myrtle Point, 1999; Douglas Smith, O.D., Medford, 1998.

The five-member Board of Optometry, created in 1905, consists of four doctors of optometry and one public member, appointed by the governor for three-year terms. The board is authorized by ORS chapter 683. Duties are to examine applicants for licensure; suspend, revoke or impose probation; and limit the practice or impose a civil penalty for violation of the statutes. The board makes rules and enforces professional standards for the practice of optometry in Oregon. Activities are supported by fees assessed applicants and licensed optometrists.

Parks and Recreation Department

Robert Meinen, Dir.
1115 Commercial St. NE, Salem 97310-1001; 503-378-6305; Fax: 503-378-6447; general state park information: 1-800-551-6949; state park reservations: 1-800-452-5687

The mission of the Oregon Parks and Recreation Department is to "provide and protect outstanding natural, scenic, cultural, historic and recreational sites for the enjoyment and education of present and future generations."

The department accomplishes the mission primarily by operating Oregon's

state park system under the provisions of ORS chapter 390. The state parks director administers the system through a headquarters staff in Salem. The department was created initially as a branch of the Highway Department in 1921. The 1989 Legislature created a separate Parks and Recreation Department effective January 1, 1990.

Oregon's state parks are among the most popular in the U.S.; combined day-use and camping attendance of nearly 40 million visitors consistently ranks the system among the 10 most visited in the nation.

Special programs also protect outstanding resources—the Ocean Shores Recreation Area, Recreation Trails, the State Historic Preservation Office, Scenic Waterways and the Willamette River Greenway. Department activities are funded primarily by park user fees and recreation vehicle license fees.

Parks and Recreation Commission

Brian Booth, chair, Portland, 1997

The commission sets policy for the department and has specific authority to purchase and sell property and set fees for use of parks facilities. Members serve rotating four-year terms and are appointed by the governor, with Senate confirmation. The seven-member commission represents citizens from each of Oregon's five congressional districts, plus one represents citizens on the east side of the Cascade Mountains and one represents citizens west of the summit of the Coastal Mountains.

Historic Preservation, Advisory Committee on

James Hamrick, Deputy State Historic Preservation Officer
503-378-6508 ext. 231

Dr. Ward Tonsfeldt, chair, Bend, 1997

The committee consists of nine members appointed by the governor, including recognized professionals in the fields of history, architecture, archaeology and architectural history. It reviews nominations to the National Register of Historic Places pursuant to the National Historic Preservation Act of 1966 and the Statewide Comprehensive Historic Preservation Plan as authorized by ORS chapter 358.

Heritage Commission

Hugh Davidson, Coord.
503-378-6508 ext. 299

Daniel Robertson, chair, Yoncalla, 1999

The Oregon Heritage Commission consists of nine citizen members appointed by the governor and six ex officio members. Commissioners represent the cultural and geographic diversity of the state and heritage interests, including archaeology, historic preservation, museums, cultural-heritage tourism and heritage-related business owners. Ex officio commissioners represent the Oregon Historical Society and various state agencies.

ORS chapter 358 charges the commission with broad responsibilities to assure the conservation and development of Oregon's heritage. The commission is designated the primary agency for coordination of statewide heritage activities.

Recreational Trails Advisory Council

Peter D. Bond, Coord.
503-378-6378 ext. 246

Ernie Drapela, chair, Gresham, 1997

The council consists of seven members appointed by the Oregon Parks and Recreation Commission to advise the commission regarding the Oregon Recreational Trails System.

Parole and Post-Prison Supervision, Board of

Jim Eckland, Exec. Dir.
2575 Center St. NE, Salem 97310-0470; 503-945-0900; Fax: 503-373-7558

Dianne L. Middle, chair, Salem, 1998; Michael R. Washington, Portland, 1997; Michael G. Weatherby, Fairview, 1999.

The governor appoints the members for four-year terms (ORS 144.005) and also appoints the chair and vice-chair. The full-time Board of Parole and Post-Prison Supervision was authorized in 1969 by the 55th Legislative Assembly. During 1975, the 58th Legislative Assembly enlarged the board to five members, specifying that at least one member must be a woman. The membership has since been reduced to three. During 1989, the 65th Legislative Assembly changed the name of the board to reflect the implementation of sentencing guidelines.

The board's mission is to work in partnership with the Department of Corrections and local supervisory authorities to protect the public and reduce the risk of repeat criminal behavior through incarceration and community supervision decisions based on applicable laws, victims' interests, public safety and recognized principles of offender behavioral change.

The board imposes prison terms and makes release decisions only on offenders whose criminal conduct occurred prior to November 1, 1989. The board sets conditions of supervision for all offenders being released from prison; imposes sanctions for violations of supervision; and determines whether discharge from parole supervision is compatible with public safety. Discharge from supervision for offenders sentenced under sentencing guidelines occurs automatically upon expiration of the statutory period of post-prison supervision.

Prison Terms and Parole Standards, Advisory Commission on

Jim Eckland, Exec. Sec.
2575 Center St. NE, Salem 97310; 503-945-0900; Fax: 503-373-7558

The Advisory Commission on Prison Terms and Parole Standards is made up of the three members of the Board of Parole and Post-Prison Supervision, three circuit court judges appointed by the chief justice of the Supreme Court, and the legal adviser to the governor.

Current commission members include Parole Board members Dianne L. Middle, Salem; Michael R. Washington, Portland; Michael G. Weatherby, Fairview. In addition, the governor's legal counsel and Circuit Court Judges Richard C. Beesley, Klamath County;

Frank Knight, Benton County; and Robert Redding, Multnomah County, round out the commission. The director of the Department of Corrections is an ex officio, non-voting member.

The commission is required to meet at least annually and was authorized in 1977 under ORS 144.775. It proposes rules to the State Board of Parole and Post-Prison Supervision establishing ranges of duration of imprisonment and variations from the ranges for persons committing crimes prior to November 1989.

Pharmacy, State Board of

Ruth Vandever, R.Ph., Exec. Dir.
State Office Bldg., 800 NE Oregon St., #9, Suite 425, Portland 97232; 503-731-4032; Fax: 503-731-4067

Joseph Schnabel, president, Salem, 1997; John Block, Corvallis, 1998; Allan Dulwick, Aloha, 2000; Helen Noonan-Harnsberger, Klamath Falls, 2000; Mike Patrick, Redmond, 1999; Lenolia Z. Talton, Portland, 1997; Marie Williams, Portland, 1998.

The State Board of Pharmacy consists of seven members appointed by the governor to four-year terms. Five members must be practicing pharmacists, licensed in Oregon for at least five years; two members represent the general public.

Created in 1891 and authorized under ORS 689.115, the board regulates pharmacy practices to assure that only qualified individuals practice pharmacy in this state. The board regulates the quality and distribution of controlled substance, prescription and over-the-counter drugs within the state. It licenses pharmacists by examination or through reciprocity with other states. It registers and inspects hospital and retail pharmacies, drug wholesalers, manufacturers and over-the-counter drug outlets, and investigates violations of its rules. Compliance is enforced by administrative procedures and court action. Board activities are financed by license fees.

The board enforces ORS chapter 689. It serves as a source of information about drugs and drug law for the public and Legislature. It handles all license and certificate renewals on an annual basis; conducts investigations; holds meetings and hearings to discuss complaints and proposed legislation; approves continuing education seminars; and proposes administrative rules and statutory amendments when necessary.

Physical Fitness and Sports, Governor's Council on

4840 SW Western Ave., Suite 900, Beaverton 97005; 503-520-1319; Fax: 503-520-9747

The Governor's Council on Physical Fitness and Sports is a volunteer organization established by Executive Order EO-94-05 to actively promote the preventive and life-long benefits associated with physical fitness and proper nutrition.

In 1996 Tiger Woods won his third U.S. Amateur title at Pumpkin Ridge Golf Glub in North Plains. The U.S. Women's Open will be staged here in July 1997. Photo courtesy of Pumpkin Ridge Golf Club.

The council's objectives are to raise the awareness of the values and benefits of fitness, nutrition and sports programs; encourage the involvement of every Oregonian in physical activities, proper nutrition and sports programs; and establish the council as a primary resource for health and fitness information. Specific projects designed to help achieve these objectives include Fitness Leadership Awards; Fitness Day in Oregon, a statewide event set for May 21, 1997; Shape Up Across Oregon, a set of goals for Oregonians to strive for in their quest to become physically fit; and The Fitness Break Program, a tool to help teachers integrate fitness into their daily classroom routines.

Physical Therapist Licensing Board

Georgia A. Spence, Exec. Officer
800 NE Oregon St., Suite 407, Portland 97232;
503-731-4047

Barbara Beardsley, PT, chair, Corvallis, 1997; Linda Barbee, PT, Portland, 1998; Rose Dusan-Speck, PT, Bend, 1998; Eric Fogel, PT, Ashland, 1997; Patricia Moffit, PTA, Corvallis, 1998; Dorthea Petersen, public member, Gold Beach, 1997; physician member (to be appointed).

The Physical Therapist Licensing Board was created in 1971 and authorized under ORS 688.160. Board members are appointed by the governor to serve four-year terms. The board regulates the practice of physical therapy through enforcement of statute and rules, which includes investigation of complaints, licensure of physical therapists and physical therapist assistants, administration of licensing exams and promulgation of administrative rules.

Police, Department of Oregon State

LeRon R. Howland, Supt.
Dennis J. O'Donnell, Deputy Supt.
400 Public Service Bldg., Salem 97310;
503-378-3720; Fax: 503-378-8282 and
503-363-5475

The Department of State Police was created in 1931 under ORS 101.020. The department merged several state-level law enforcement functions into a single agency. The primary purpose of the department was to serve as a rural patrol and to assist local city police and sheriffs' departments.

The current mission of the Oregon State Police is to develop, promote and maintain the protection of Oregon's residents, property and natural resources and to enhance safety and livability by servicing and protecting its citizens and visitors through leadership, action and coordination of Oregon's public safety resources.

The Department of State Police has experienced many modifications during the past six decades in providing the most effective and efficient public safety services and in responding to the state's needs.

In 1939 Oregon law authorized a support unit, the Crime Laboratory, located at the University of Oregon Medical School. Today, the Forensics Services Division consists of regional laboratories located in Bend, Coos Bay, Medford, Ontario, Pendleton, Portland and Springfield to more efficiently serve local law enforcement needs.

After nearly a decade of service the original Bureau of Criminal Identification expanded its duties to include all fingerprint records and photographs that were transferred from the state penitentiary, and implementation of the Automated Fingerprint Identification System (AFIS) that allows for automated fingerprint searches of all Oregon fingerprint records and those held by western states.

In 1993 the legislature expanded the department's role in public safety with the consolidation of Oregon Emergency Management, Office of State Fire Marshal, Law Enforcement Data System and the Boxing and Wrestling Commission into the agency. This consolidation centralized many of the state's emergency response and regulatory responsibilities.

In 1995 the legislature incorporated the State Medical Examiners Office into the Department of State Police. Also in that year the Criminal Justice Services Division was transferred from the Department of Administrative Services to the State Police.

The agency accomplishes its mission by providing law enforcement services that are fair and impartial while providing direct services that benefit citizens; preserving the peace; preventing and detecting crime; maintaining emergency service systems by planning, preparing and providing for mitigation and/or management of emergencies or disaster; providing and coordinating programs that protect life and property from fire, hazardous materials, and other perils; maintaining a statewide law enforcement data system that ensures access to criminal justice information services; and coordinating with public safety entities at the national, state and local level to maximize public safety resources. The department operates under a service-oriented public safety philosophy that relies on problem-solving with all levels of communities and also seeks prevention strategies.

The department is organized into three bureaus: Operations Services, Support Services and Intergovernmental Services which are served by 13 divisions. Some of the agency's specialized programs and services include: transportation safety; major crime investigation; forensic services including DNA identification, automated fingerprint identification, and computerized criminal history files; drug investigation; fish and wildlife enforcement; gambling enforcement and regulation; state emergency response coordination; state Fire Marshal Service and Conflagration Act coordination; statewide Law Enforcement Data System; coordination of federal grants to law enforcement; medical examiner services; and Special Weapons and Tactics (SWAT).

Boxing and Wrestling Commission

Bruce Anderson, Exec. Dir.
9450 SW Commerce Circle, Suite 315, Wilsonville 97070; 503-682-0582; Fax: 503-682-2751

Lloyd Davis, chair, Eugene, 1997; Adofo Akil, Portland, 1998; Jack E. Battalia, M.D., Portland, 1997; F. Louis Rios, M.D., Dallas, 2000; Greg Smith, Pendleton, 2000. Members are appointed by the superintendent of state police.

Created by the 1987 Legislative Assembly and operating under ORS chapter 463, the commission became part of the Oregon State Police by decision of the 1993 Legislature. It is responsible for the supervision, licensing and control of all professional boxing contests and wrestling matches or exhibitions conducted within the state. Its purpose is to protect the participants

and the public interest by: enforcing the laws and rules, providing licensing standards, enforcing contracts and financial obligations of promoters, establishing medical safety standards, qualifying officials, certifying ringside physicians, investigating alleged violations of statutes and rules applying to boxing and wrestling, and preventing the exploitation of participants.

Emergency Management Division

Myra Thompson Lee, Admin.
503-378-2911; Fax: 503-588-1378

Established by ORS chapter 401, the Emergency Management Division's purpose is to assure overall coordination of emergency disaster planning, preparedness, response and recovery efforts among state and local agencies statewide.

The division manages the governor's Emergency Operations Center; is liaison with local, federal and private agencies and organizations; conducts training for public officials and agency heads, emergency program managers, emergency response personnel and support services; coordinates ground search-and-rescue plans; and serves as the central coordinating point for the Oregon Emergency Response System (OERS).

The administrator chairs the OERS Council, which includes representation from every state agency with a primary role in the preparedness for or management of a major emergency or disaster. The division ensures the statewide implementation of 911 emergency telephone service statewide, administers the 911 telephone tax, and implements the provisions of ORS chapter 401 pertaining to local 911 systems.

Fire Marshal, Office of State

Robert T. Panuccio, State Fire Marshal
4760 Portland Rd. NE, Salem 97305; 503-373-1540; Fax: 503-373-1825

Created in 1917, the Office of State Fire Marshal is charged with reducing the loss of life and property from fire, explosion and hazardous materials; and minimizing the fire and life-safety hazards of structures, equipment and materials exposed to fire risks. Program areas include fire prevention and investigation, training, Community Right-To-Know, public education and firesetter intervention, industry licensing and permits, non-retail gasoline dispensing, managing

Executive

the Regional Hazardous Materials Emergency Response Team system, and directing the statewide structural firefighting agencies in times of emergency.

In 1993 this office was consolidated into the Oregon State Police under the Public Safety umbrella. It is one of OSP's 13 divisions.

Law Enforcement Data System Division

Lloyd A. Smith, Dir.
400 Public Service Bldg., Salem 97310; 503-378-3054; Fax: 503-363-8249

The 1993 Legislature transferred the Law Enforcement Data System (LEDS) from the Executive Department to the Department of State Police. LEDS became a division within the Intergovernmental Services Bureau.

The LEDS Division is the focal point and "control agency" for access by law enforcement and criminal justice agencies in Oregon to online information in the FBI National Crime Information Center (NCIC) and the interstate law enforcement switching network, the National Law Enforcement Telecommunications System (NLETS), which is operated by a consortium of states. The central LEDS message switching system processes between 11 and 12 million messages a month, serving more than 5,400 user devices in Oregon. LEDS also operates the Oregon Uniform Crime Reporting (OUCR) program, which processes and distributes Oregon crime and arrest statistics and provides Oregon data to the FBI for the national crime statistics program.

The central LEDS online files contain a large variety of information entered and accessed by user agencies throughout the Oregon law enforcement and criminal justice community. This information includes arrest warrants, corrections offenders, criminal histories, sex offender registrants, restraining/stalking orders, missing persons, and stolen vehicles/property.

Medical Examiner Division

Larry V. Lewman, M.D., State Medical Examiner
301 NE Knott, Portland 97212; 503-280-6061; Fax: 503-280-6041

The 1995 Legislature incorporated the State Medical Examiner Office into the Intergovernmental Services Bureau of the Oregon State Police. The office was renamed the Medical Examiner Division.

The Medical Examiner Division provides direction and support to the state death investigation program. The medical examiner manages all aspects of the state medical examiner program and is responsible for supervising county offices in each of the 36 counties. The division is staffed by four full-time forensic pathologists, supported by two staff personnel.

The main activity of the division is to certify the cause and manner of a death requiring investigation within the authority of ORS chapter 146. This activity includes post mortem examination and alcohol and drug analyses. The division also maintains appropriate records and provides lectures and training on legal medicine and death investigation. This training is provided to medical school physicians and students, law students, police officers, emergency medical technicians, and other persons associated with the death investigation system.

Criminal Justice Services Division

Gregory J. Peden, Dir.
400 Public Service Bldg., Salem 97310; 503-378-3720; Fax: 503-378-6993

The Criminal Justice Services Division was transferred from the Department of Administrative Services to the Oregon State Police in 1995. The division is responsible for administering approximately $34 million in federal grants each biennium through several federal grant programs. The division is also responsible for the Criminal Justice Information Systems project for the state. The division develops the governor's drug and violent crime strategy each year and funds programs under juvenile crime prevention, law enforcement, domestic violence, adult corrections and information systems.

Medical Examiner Advisory Board

Diana Stephan
State Medical Examiner Program
301 NE Knott St., Portland 97212; 503-280-6061; Fax: 503-280-6041

Donald C. Houghton, chair

The Medical Examiner Advisory Board develops policy for administration of the state death-investigation program.

Psychiatric Security Review Board

Mary Claire Buckley, J.D., Exec. Dir.
Suite 907, 620 SW 5th Ave., Portland 97204;
503-229-5596; Fax: 503-229-5085

Kim Drake, P.P.O., chair, 2000; Vern Faatz, 1997; Hilda Galaviz-Stoller, J.D., 1997; George Saslow, M.D., 2000; Stephen Scherr, Ph.D., 1999. All terms expire on June 30 of indicated years. The five board members are appointed by the governor.

The Psychiatric Security Review Board, created in 1978 and operating under ORS chapter 161, has jurisdiction over persons in Oregon found by a court to be "guilty except for insanity." The board's jurisdiction is not to exceed the maximum period of time the person could have been incarcerated had he or she been found responsible.

The board has the authority to: commit a person to a state hospital designated by the Mental Health Division; conditionally release a person from a state hospital to a community-based program; discharge a person from the board's jurisdiction; and, where appropriate, revoke the conditional release of a person under its jurisdiction and order the return to a state hospital pending a full hearing before the board.

Psychologist Examiners, State Board of

Bonnie Wilson, Admin.
3218 Pringle Rd. SE, Suite 130, Salem 97302-6309; 503-378-4154; Fax: 503-378-3575

Brad Avakian, chair, Portland, 1997; Kenneth Ihli, Ph.D., vice-chair, Portland, 1998; Maria Beals, Ph.D., Corvallis, 1997; Ralph Bramucci, Ph.D., Portland, 1999; Rochelle Silver, Ph.D., Salem, 1997; Martin Waechter, Ph.D., Eugene, 1998; William Willey, Dundee, 1997.

The Board of Psychologist Examiners, created in 1973 as a licensing body, consists of seven members appointed by the governor: five must have doctoral degrees and be licensed psychologists; two are public members.

Regulated under ORS 675.010–675.150, the board's duties are to determine qualifications, examine and license individuals to practice psychology in Oregon.

The board has the authority to deny, suspend, revoke or restore licenses. In its disciplinary role, it investigates alleged violations of the statutes and imposes appropriate sanctions. It adopts a code of ethics and enforces continuing education requirements.

Public Employes Retirement System (PERS)

Fred J. McDonnal, Exec. Dir.
200 SW Market St., Suite 700; PO Box 73, Portland 97207-0073; 503-229-5824

After June 1, 1997
11410 SW 68th Parkway, Tigard 97223; 503-598-7377

The PERS mission is to provide the highest quality services so each member has the opportunity for a successful retirement.

The system was established in 1946 and is authorized by Oregon Revised Statutes chapter 238. PERS provides service and disability retirement income and death benefits. Benefits are pre-funded through contributions from participating employers, their employes and income from investments.

PERS serves more than 146,000 active members, 30,024 inactive members and 66,000 retirees and beneficiaries. At the end of 1995, there were 927 employer members.

Public Employes Retirement Board

Pat Riggs-Henson, chair, Eugene, 1997; Emile Holeman, vice-chair, Pendleton, 1998; Len Anderson, Portland, 1999; Patricia Brown, Portland, 1998; I.S. "Bud" Hakanson, Roseburg, 1997; Russell Joki, Tualatin, 1997; Pamela Lesh, Portland, 1998; Jim Loewen, Sublimity, 1998; Peter Ozanne, Portland, 1999; Lester Von Flue, Silverton, 1998; Gary Weeks, Salem, 1999.

The PERS Board is made up of 11 members. All are appointed by the governor and confirmed by the Senate. Terms are for three years.

Eight of the trustees must represent the public sector. Three must represent the private sector. Of the eight public-sector members, four must be from management and four from collective-bargaining units. One must be retired.

Public Safety Standards and Training, Board on

Steve Bennett, Exec. Dir.
*550 N Monmouth Ave., Monmouth 97361-1330;
503-378-2100; Fax: 503-378-3330*

Tim Thompson, chair, Grants Pass, 1999; George Dunkel, vice-chair, Aloha, 1999; Jack Carriger, Salem, 1998; Dave Cook, Salem, 1998; John Courtney, La Grande, 1999; Elizabeth Cruthers, Portland, 1999; Manuel Fagundes, Portland, 1998; Ron Goodpaster, Tigard, 1998; Garry Gross, Portland, 1999; James Hicks, La Grande, 1998; LeRon Howland, Salem, 1999; Dale Kamrath, Veneta, 1999; James Keller, Klamath Falls, 1999; Louis Lampreht, Albany, 1998; Kathleen McChesney, Portland, 1999; Robert McManus, Eugene, 1998; Charles Moose, Portland, 1999; Marilyn Nelson, Eugene, 1999; Robert Panuccio, Salem, 1999; Clark Seely, Salem, 1998; James Spinden, Hillsboro, 1999; John Velke, Portland, 1999; Bob Wall, Portland, 1999. The 23-member board is appointed by the governor under ORS chapter 181.

Formed in 1961 under ORS 181.610–181.690, the board establishes minimum standards for recruitment and training of city, county and state police officers; corrections officers; parole and probation officers; and emergency telecommunicators. In 1993 the board was combined with the Fire Standards and Accreditation Board by legislative action and went from 14 to 23 members. The board's function now includes the training and accreditation of fire personnel and agencies and recommending standards for fire protection equipment.

The board examines and licenses all polygraph examiners; determines eligibility of candidates for the office of sheriff; conducts training programs; operates the public safety training facility at Western Oregon State College; certifies qualified officers in various levels of career competence; and inspects and certifies instructors and training programs. Management services provide research assistance to any police, sheriff, corrections, parole and probation, telecommunication or fire agency in the state.

The board's name changed in 1991 from Board on Police Standards and Training to reflect the agency's expanded role.

Public Utility Commission

*550 Capitol St. NE, Salem 97310-1380;
503-378-6611; Fax: 503-378-5505;
Web: www.puc.state.or.us*

Roger Hamilton, chair; Ron Eachus, Joan Smith, commissioners.

The primary responsibility of the Public Utility Commission is to ensure that customers of the state's utility industries receive safe, reliable service at reasonable rates. At the same time, the PUC is required by law to allow the regulated companies an opportunity to earn a fair return on their investments.

Operating under ORS chapters 756 through 759, and 772, the PUC regulates customer rates and services of the state's investor-owned electric, natural gas and telephone utilities; and certain water companies. The commission does not regulate people's utility districts, cooperatives or municipally-owned utilities except in matters of safety.

The PUC operates through an open decision-making process and encourages public involvement in those decisions. In addition to holding public hearings on specific issues, the commission conducts its business in public meetings scheduled every two weeks at PUC headquarters in Salem. The

At nearly 10,000', the Matterhorn is the highest peak in the Wallowa Mountains.

Photo by Gary Fletcher.

commission's regulatory responsibilities are carried out by a staff of approximately 109 employees.

Each year, the PUC issues a variety of reports that are available to the public, including statistical reports on utility companies.

Racing Commission

Steven W. Barham, Exec. Dir.
800 NE Oregon St., #11, Suite 310, Portland 97232; 503-731-4052; Fax: 503-731-4053

Stephen S. Walters, chair, 1999; Laura A. Fine, vice-chair, 1997; George Rankins, 1999; Richard D. Reid, DVM, 2000; Tom Towslee, 1999.

The Racing Commission was established by legislative action in 1933 to regulate the pari-mutuel racing industry for the protection of public safety, health and welfare. Members are appointed by the governor and confirmed by the Senate. The commission currently regulates all horse and greyhound racing if pari-mutuel wagering is conducted. Regulation occurs both on track and at off-track wagering facilities and covers all aspects of the operation.

Proceeds from pari-mutuel racing not used for the operation of the agency are transferred to the general fund for state use. The executive director, supervisor of horse racing, supervisor of greyhound racing, supervisor of pari-mutuels, chief of security/investigations and other officials appointed by the commission currently administer 11 horse and one greyhound pari-mutuel race meets, which are conducted annually at various locations throughout the state.

Radiologic Technology, Board of

Lianne Thompson, Exec. Officer
407 State Office Bldg., 800 NE Oregon St., Portland 97232-2162; 503-731-4088; Fax: 503-731-4207; Email: lianne.g.thompson@state.or.us

Glen Plam, LRTT, chair, Portland, 1997; Kim Ashbeck, LRT, Vancouver, 1998; Kenneth Faulkner, Ph.D., West Linn, 1998; Lee Flanders, LRT, Portland, 1999; Betty Palmer, LRT, Portland, 1999; Kenneth Stevens Jr., M.D., Portland, 1997; David Taylor, LRT, Salem,

1998; Darrell Hocken, RT, advisory. The Board of Radiologic Technology consists of seven members appointed by the governor to serve three-year terms that expire June 30 of the year indicated.

The board, founded in 1977, operates under ORS 688.405–688.990 and OAR chapter 337 to protect the public by administering Oregon licensing requirements for persons who use ionizing radiation on human beings in the practice of medicine for diagnostic or therapeutic purposes, including radiation therapy, fluoroscopy, CT scans, mammography, bone densitometry, radiography and other means of medical imaging.

Real Estate Agency

Scott W. Taylor, Commiss.
1177 Center St. NE, Salem 97310-2503; Licensing and Information: 503-378-4170; Regulation and Enforcement: 503-378-8414; Fax: 503-373-7153

The Real Estate Agency is a multipurpose agency with programs centered on the commodity of real property. It was established in 1919 for the purpose of creating a healthy real estate marketplace and to assure that licensees conduct their services with high fiduciary standards. It is a consumer protection agency with regulatory authority based on a standard of trustworthiness, which must also be met by all new applicants for licensing. The agency is administered by the Real Estate Commissioner who is appointed by the governor.

The agency is responsible for the licensing, education and enforcement of Oregon's real estate laws applicable to brokers, salespersons, property managers, real estate marketing organizations; licensing and regulation of escrow agents (ORS chapter 696); and subdivision (ORS chapter 92), condominium (ORS chapter 100), timeshare and campground (ORS chapter 94) registration/public report issuance.

Each year the agency processes and tests more than 5,000 license applicants and monitors regulated activities in over 4,700 escrow and real estate offices. Land developers with offerings to Oregon citizens have thousands of disclosure filings with the agency.

The agency provides educational material and seminars for real estate professionals. The agency also conducts investigations and hearings when complaints are filed against licensees, registrants and real property developers.

Real Estate Board

1177 Center St. NE, Salem 97310-2503;
503-378-4170

Doris E. Andersen, Medford, 1998; Ann G. Elgin, Pendleton, 1999; Victor Y. Kee, Astoria, 1998; Joyce L. Plymer, Bandon, 1998; James Sibbald, Roseburg, 1999; Dan J. Volkmer, Portland, 2000; Fred Wenger III, Salem, 1999; James L. Whitney, Pendleton, 1997; Donna B. Wilkerson, Eugene, 1998. The governor appoints the nine-member advisory board consisting of seven industry members and two public members.

Board members serve four-year terms and through the chair advise the governor when appropriate. They meet bi-monthly to review experience and education waivers of real estate licensing applicants.

Resource and Technology Development Fund

John A. Beaulieu, Pres.

Cascadia Pacific Management, 4370 NE Halsey St., Suite 233, Portland 97213-1566;
503-282-4462; Fax: 503-282-2976;
Email: info@cpmllc.com; Web: www.cpmllc.com

Stanley Timmermann, chair, Pendleton, 1997; Lesley M. Hallick, Portland, 1997; James M. Hurd, Beaverton, 1997; Mary F. Olson, Oregon City, 1997; John Owen, Philomath, 1997; John D. Webber, Portland, 1997.

Oregon Resource and Technology Development Fund (ORTDF) board members are appointed by the governor. The ORTDF is chartered to invest in early-stage businesses and applied research projects. From its founding in 1986 to October 1995, the fund has received $12.3 million in lottery funds.

With these funds and investment returns, ORTDF invested in 50 ventures and four entrepreneurial support organizations. Returns from ORTDF investments are used for operating expenses and reinvestment in new businesses.

Revenue, Department of

Jim Brown, Deputy Dir.
457 Revenue Bldg., 955 Center St. NE, Salem 97310-2501; 503-945-8214; Fax: 503-945-8738; Web: www.dor.state.or.us

Most Oregonians think of the Department of Revenue only when they send in their personal income tax returns. Actually the department also administers more than 30 other tax programs. These include corporation, income and excise taxes, gift and inheritance taxes, tobacco taxes and amusement device taxes.

Also included are revenues the department collects and distributes for some local governments, including Tri-Met and the Lane Transit District. In fiscal year 1994-95, nearly $2.4 billion was raised through the personal income tax. The department processes about 1.4 million income tax returns each year. In all, the department processes about 4 million documents a year.

The department collects delinquent accounts for about 150 other state agencies and community colleges, including the Department of Human Resources, Justice Department, Department of Higher Education and the circuit and district courts of Oregon. Collections for these other agencies totaled more than $16 million in fiscal year 1995-96.

Though the department collects no property taxes, it is responsible for seeing that property tax laws are applied fairly and equitably throughout the state. It also provides training and assistance for county assessors, tax collectors, treasurers and local government budget officials. The department appraises utility property, timberland and most large industrial property, providing valuations for county tax rolls. It collects timber severance taxes for distribution to local districts.

Charitable Checkoff Commission

Rick Main, Adviser
Revenue Bldg., 955 Center St. NE, Salem 97310-2501; 503-945-8288; Fax: 503-945-8737

Sen. Lenn Hannon; Sue Martino; Ruth McFarland; David Paradine; Richard Paul; Rep. Lonnie Roberts; Beverly Vonfeld; and Rick Main, ex officio.

The Oregon Charitable Checkoff Commission was established during the

1989 legislative session to determine if organizations qualify for listing on the individual income tax return to receive contributions by means of a checkoff. The commission consists of five voting members appointed by the governor; two non-voting legislative members; and an ex officio member appointed by the director of the Department of Revenue.

SAIF Corporation

Katherine L. Keene, Pres. and CEO
400 High St. SE, Salem 97312-1000;
503-373-8000; Fax: 503-373-8181;
Web: www.saif.com

Board: Marjorie May Cross, Bend, 1997; Jon Egge, Milwaukie, 1999; Howard Shapiro, Portland, 1997; William D. Thorndike Jr., Medford, 1998; one vacancy.

SAIF is a self-supporting, not-for-profit publicly owned workers' compensation insurance carrier which returns all funds in excess of expenses, claims and required surplus to its eligible policy-holders through dividends, rate reductions and improved services.
It competes with private insurance companies and is the largest workers' compensation insurer in Oregon.

SAIF Corporation was created by the Legislature in 1979 as a successor to the State Accident Insurance Fund, a state agency, to be a competitive force in the marketplace to keep rates low and service high. Its statutory mission is to "make insurance available to as many Oregon employers as inexpensively as may be consistent with the overall integrity of the Industrial Accident Fund ... and sound business principles."

SAIF is governed by a five-member board of directors appointed by the governor to four-year terms and confirmed by the Senate. It is not tax supported, but derives its income from premiums paid by policyholders and returns on investments made by the State Treasurer. It is audited by the Secretary of State's office and receives legal advice from the state Department of Justice. Along with all other insurance carriers doing business in Oregon, it is regulated by the Department of Consumer and Business Services.

SAIF's corporate headquarters are in Salem. It has local offices in Baker City, Bend, Corvallis, Eugene, Medford, North Bend, Pendleton, Portland, Roseburg and Salem.

Scholarship Commission

Douglas L. Collins, Exec. Dir.
1500 Valley River Dr., Suite 100, Eugene 97401;
541-687-7400; toll-free: 1-800-452-8807;
Fax: 541-687-7419; Web: www.teleport.com/~ossc

David Mesirow, chair, Portland, 1997; George Bell, Salem, 2000; Saji Prelis, Corvallis, 1998; Stacey Standley, Portland, 1997; Nathelle Togni, Salem, 1998; Diane Tsukamaki, Tualatin, 1999; Nancy Wakefield, Tillamook, 2000.

The Scholarship Commission was created in 1959 and operates under ORS chapter 348. The duties of the agency are to administer a variety of state-funded, U.S. federal government and privately funded student financial aid programs for the benefit of Oregonians attending postsecondary institutions.

The major state-funded program is the Need Grant, which provided $12.3 million in 1995–96 to 14,350 students. The agency's largest programs are the Oregon Federal Family Education Loan Programs, which are administered cooperatively by the State of Oregon, the U.S. Department of Education, and private lenders such as banks and credit unions. In 1995–96, the Scholarship Commission guaranteed 25,300 loans for a total of $80 million.

The Scholarship Commission helps administer more than 130 privately funded scholarship programs which provided 1,300 students with $2.3 million in 1995–96. In addition, the commission offers information about student financial aid to the public, to high school counselors, to college financial aid officers and to other state agencies.

Speech-Language Pathology and Audiology, State Board of Examiners for

Brenda Felber, Exec. Officer
800 NE Oregon St., Suite 407, Portland 97232;
503-731-4050; Fax: 503-731-4207;
Email: brenda.felber@state.or.us

Laurene L. Howell, M.D., chair, Portland, 1999; Joanna R. Burk, Milton-Freewater, 1999; Michele R. Ecker, Albany, 1999; Howard R. Hickam,

Albany, 1999; Allen Mehr, Salem, 1998; Lezlie Pearce-Hopper, Creswell, 1999; Susan Evans Peterson, Albany, 1998. The Board of Examiners for Speech-Language Pathology and Audiology consists of seven members appointed by the governor to serve three-year terms.

The board was established in 1973 and is authorized under ORS chapter 681. Duties are to adopt rules governing standards of practice; investigate alleged violations; and to grant, suspend, deny or revoke licenses.

State Fair and Exposition Center

Robert R. Vernon, Dir.
2330 17th St. NE, Salem 97310-0140;
503-378-3247; Fax: 503-373-1788;
Web: www.fair.state.or.us/fair.html

State Fair Advisory Commission

Darlene Turner, chair, Joseph, 1997.

The State Fair Advisory Commission was established by ORS 565.020 in 1977. The governor appoints the director and the five members of the commission to four-year terms.

The first state fair was held near Oregon City in 1861 and moved to Salem the following year. It has grown steadily since with more than 700,000 attending the last 12-day extravaganza, making it one of the largest events of its kind in the nation.

Key to the fair's popularity are the 14 open-class competitive divisions, national and regional livestock shows, the state's biggest and longest-running horse show, and some of the largest 4-H and FFA exhibitions in the country.

Big-name entertainment takes place daily at the 8,700-seat L.B. Day Amphitheatre. Attractions can be enjoyed at Fountain Plaza stage, Cultural Arts stage, and Artisans' Village stage.

As summer and the annual fair approach, its permanent staff of 32 swells to approximately 800 with the addition of seasonal staff. Included on the 185-acre fairgrounds are two exhibition halls totaling 48,000 and 36,000 square feet respectively; 4-H dormitory, auditorium and barn; FFA and livestock pavilions; a beef barn; indoor horse show stadium; show horse barns, racetrack and stables. Many of these facilities are available year-round for rental.

State Lands, Division of

Paul Cleary, Dir.
775 Summer St. NE, Salem 97310-1337;
503-378-3805; Fax: 503-378-4844

State Land Board

The State Land Board is composed of the governor, who serves as chair, the secretary of state and the state treasurer. Under constitutional and statutory guidelines, the board is responsible for managing the assets of the Common School Fund (land and money) as well as for additional functions assigned by the Legislature.

The Common School Fund was established as a constitutional trust when Oregon was admitted to the union on February 14, 1859. At that time, the federal government granted to the state the 16th and 36th sections of every township, or other lands "in lieu" of these sections, to support the public schools.

The fund's land base now includes more than 650,000 acres of grazing and agricultural land; 132,000 acres of forest land, including the Elliott State Forest in Coos and Douglas counties; 800,000 acres of off-shore land and estuarine tidelands; and submerged and submersible lands of the state's extensive navigable waterway system.

The **Division of State Lands**, created by the Legislature in 1967 (ORS chapter 273), manages these lands. The division's director is appointed by the State Land Board. The division currently has 65 employees and a 1995–97 operating budget of $11.2 million. Proceeds from management of lands and waterways and other activities of the division and the Land Board become part of Common School Fund principal.

The fund now exceeds $420 million. Interest from fund investments is distributed semi-annually to counties for school support, based on the school-age population of each county. In the 1993-95 biennium, an estimated $20 million in Common School Fund investment earnings were distributed to Oregon counties.

In addition to its land and fiscal management functions, the division provides other public services. It is responsible for administering the state's removal-fill law, which protects Oregon's waterways from uncontrolled alteration.

Under the Unclaimed Property Act, the division director also acts as trust agent for "abandoned funds" such as bank accounts and uncashed checks. Additionally, Oregon's probate law designates the director of the Division of State Lands as the personal representative in the probate of an estate of a deceased person who has left neither a will nor known heirs.

Other division responsibilities include: leasing state-owned mineral rights for exploration and production of oil, gas, hard minerals and geothermal energy; management of the Tongue Point Marine Industrial Site in Astoria; providing opportunities to lease or buy state land; maintenance of historical records related to early land transactions, including deeds, leases and plats; performance of administrative functions for the Natural Heritage Advisory Council; management oversight and performance of administrative services for the South Slough National Estuarine Reserve; lead state agency for the protection and maintenance of Oregon's unique wetlands resources; and management of coastal resources seaward of the mean high tide line.

Natural Heritage Advisory Council

775 Summer St. NE, Salem 97310;
503-378-3805; Fax: 503-378-4844

Stephen Anderson, chair

The Natural Heritage Advisory Council (NHAC), created by the 1979

Legislature, is a nine-member body of scientists and other citizens. Ex officio members include the directors of the Departments of Fish and Wildlife, Parks and Recreation, and Agriculture; the state highway engineer; the chancellor of the state system of higher education; the director of the Division of State Lands; and the Oregon state forester.

The council's charge is to identify areas in Oregon that contain native or rare plant, animal and aquatic species as well as rare geologic features. In cooperation with the State Land Board, NHAC seeks to protect these resources by enlisting voluntary cooperation of public and private landowners. To carry out these objectives, NHAC developed the Natural Heritage Plan, approved by the Legislature in 1981 and updated in 1988.

South Slough National Estuarine Reserve

Michael Graybill, Mgr.
PO Box 5417, Charleston 97420; 541-888-5558;
Fax: 541-888-5559

Established in 1974, South Slough National Estuarine Reserve was the first reserve created under the 1972 federal Coastal Zone Management Act.

Under policy guidance from the State Land Board, the reserve is managed through a cooperative agreement between the state and federal governments. An eight-member commission, appointed by the governor, provides management oversight. In conformance with Oregon statutes, the director of the Division of State Lands chairs the commission.

Malheur Bird Refuge in Harney County is a migratory stop for hundreds of thousands of ducks, geese and other waterfowl each year. More than 250 species have been identified in the refuge and surrounding area.

Photo by Eric W. Valentine.

Tax Supervising and Conservation Commission

Courtney Wilton, Admin. Officer
724 Mead Bldg., 421 SW 5th Ave., #724,
Portland 97204-2189; 503-248-3054;
Fax: 503-248-3053; Email: tscc@aol.com;
Web: www.multnomah.lib.or.us/tscc/

Richard Anderson; Anthony Jankans; Roger McDowell; Charles Rosenthal; Ann Sherman. Members are appointed by the governor for four-year terms. The Tax Supervising and Conservation Commission is authorized under ORS 294.610 and was established in 1919.

The commission is an independent, impartial panel of five citizen volunteers established to encourage the efficiency and economy of local governments operating in Multnomah County. Jurisdiction is exercised over 36 municipal corporations that are subject to Local Budget Law. The commission certifies the legality of budgets and tax levies; conducts public hearings on budgets, tax levies and bonding proposals; provides advisory services; and collects and reports financial data from the local units. Activities are funded by appropriations from the Multnomah County general fund.

Teacher Standards and Practices Commission

David V. Myton, Exec. Sec.
255 Capitol St. NE, Suite 105, Salem
97310-1332; 503-378-6813; Fax: 503-378-4448

Charles W. Bugge, Hood River, 1997; Teresa Ferrer Carter, Salem, 1996; Toby Clauson, Lebanon, 1998; Karen Famous, Roseburg, 1996; Robert Goerke, Medford, 1997; LeRoy Gornick, Baker City, 1997; Jennifer Heiss, Eugene, 1998; Jonathan Hill, Lakeview, 1998; David Krug, Portland, 1996; Paul R. Meyer, Portland, 1997; Martin Morris, Monmouth, 1998; Patrick Pullam, Corvallis, 1998; Richard Steiner, Beaverton, 1996; Susan Tarrant-Berg, Lake Oswego, 1996; Patricia Walker, Lake Oswego, 1997; Sue Wetzel, Portland, 1998; Susan Wilcoxen, Seaside, 1998.

Three-year terms expire on December 31 of the years indicated. Commissioners are appointed by the governor and may serve two terms. Membership consists of four elementary teachers, four secondary teachers, four school administrators, two teacher educators, one school-board member and two members from the general public.

Established by ORS 342.359 in 1965, TSPC maintains and improves performance of the education profession through: approving teacher preparation programs offered by Oregon colleges and universities; licensing teachers, administrators and other personnel employed in Oregon schools; and taking disciplinary actions when educators commit crimes or violate Standards for Competent and Ethical Performance. Approximately 75,000 Oregonians hold licenses as educators.

Transportation, Oregon Department of (ODOT)

Grace Crunican, Dir.
135 Transportation Bldg., Salem 97310-1354;
503-986-3200; Fax: 503-986-3432;
Web: www.odot.state.or.us

The Oregon Department of Transportation (ODOT) works to develop and maintain an integrated, balanced, statewide transportation system that moves people, goods and services safely and efficiently throughout the state.

ODOT is actively involved in developing Oregon's system of highways, roads and bridges; its aviation system; public transportation services; rail passenger and freight systems; bicycle and pedestrian paths; ports and marine transportation; and pipelines. Equally important are transportation safety programs, driver and vehicle licensing, and motor carrier enforcement.

The Oregon Department of Transportation was established in 1969 by ORS 184.615, and reorganized in 1973 and 1993 by legislative action.

ODOT's director is appointed by the Transportation Commission, subject to approval by the Oregon Senate. The director oversees the activities of six ODOT branches: Communications, Driver and Motor Vehicle Services, Finance and Administration, Motor Carrier Transportation, Transportation Development and Transportation Operations.

About 4,400 employees work at ODOT offices, motor carrier enforcement stations and maintenance stations statewide.

Transportation Commission, Oregon

135 Transportation Bldg., Salem 97310-1354;
503-986-3200; Fax: 503-986-3432

Henry Hewitt, chair, Portland, 1997; Susan E. Brody, vice-chair, Eugene, 2000; Steven H. Corey, Pendleton, 1997; Stuart Foster, Medford, 1997; John Russell, Portland, 2000.

The Oregon Transportation Commission meets monthly to oversee Department of Transportation activities relating to aeronautics, highways, public transportation, transportation safety, and drivers and motor vehicles. The commission establishes state transportation policy according to ORS 184.610–184.640. It also guides the planning, development and management of a statewide integrated transportation network that provides efficient access, is safe, and enhances Oregon's economy and livability.

The governor appoints five commissioners, considering different geographic regions of the state. One member must live east of the Cascade Range; no more than three can belong to one political party.

Communications

John Elliott, Mgr.

135 Transportation Bldg., Salem 97310-1354;
503-986-3455; Fax: 503-986-3432

The Communications Branch coordinates the department's overall outreach efforts including public involvement, governmental relations, media relations, community and employee communications and support for the director.

Driver and Motor Vehicle Services

Jan Curry, Mgr.

1905 Lana Ave. NE, Salem 97314-2250;
503-945-5000; Fax: 503-945-5254

ODOT's Driver and Motor Vehicle Services (DMV) contributes to public safety by licensing only qualified persons and vehicles to drive on streets and highways.

There are 2.8 million drivers and 3.3 million vehicles registered in Oregon. Each year, DMV processes 750,000 driver licenses, 1.5 million vehicle licenses and 1 million vehicle titles.

DMV is one of the largest revenue-collecting agencies in the state. More than $223 million will be collected by DMV during the 1995-97 biennium through vehicle registrations and driver license fees. These revenues are dedicated to highway improvements and safety programs.

DMV actively promotes highway safety by verifying that drivers are insured and by keeping bad drivers off the road. Each day, DMV records about 1,900 driving convictions and issues about 1,500 license suspensions.

DMV's driver and vehicle computer records are used by police agencies about 30,000 times daily and by insurance companies, banks, lawyers and others more than 11,000 times daily.

DMV licenses commercial driving schools and instructors, all-terrain vehicle and snowmobile dealers and instructors, and vehicle dealers and wreckers. DMV investigators regularly inspect dealer and wrecker businesses and check tow vehicles for proper equipment.

Daily, about 12,000 customers are served at more than 60 local DMV offices statewide, including DMV Express offices open evenings and Saturdays at major shopping malls. Half of DMV's work force is centrally located in Salem, processing mail-in transactions and supporting field office services.

Altogether, DMV computers process about 40 million transactions annually.

DMV introduced a new digital photo license design in late 1996. The new "credit-card" style has many features that make it hard to duplicate or falsify. The most notable feature of the new license is the digitized photo which is stored on DMV's database for quick retrieval and identification by the agency and law enforcement personnel. It will take about eight years, or until sometime in 2004, before all current Oregon licenses and identification cards will be renewed to the new credit-card style.

> *The 1995 Legislature mandated the transfer of the Public Utility Commission's Transportation Program into the Department of Transportation. In 1996 ODOT formed a Motor Carrier Transportation Branch to regulate the commercial operations of motor carriers using Oregon's roads and highways.*

Finance and Administration

Finance and Administration oversees the following support functions:

Financial Services

Ben Wallace, Chief Financial Officer

434 Transportation Bldg., Salem 97310-1354;
503-986-3900; Fax: 503-986-3907

Human Resources/Organization Development

Sandy DeLuna, Mgr.

102 Transportation Bldg., Salem 97310-1354;
503-986-3861; Fax: 503-986-3862

Information Systems

Dave White, Mgr.

555 13th St. NE, Salem 97310-1333;
503-986-3500; Fax: 503-986-3242

Support Services

Tom Luther, Mgr.

2800 State St. NE, Salem 97310-1344;
503-986-2726; Fax: 503-986-2717

Motor Carrier Transportation

Gregg Dal Ponte, Mgr.

550 Capitol St. NE, Salem 97310-1380;
503-378-6699; Fax: 503-378-6880

A law passed by the 1995 Oregon Legislature mandated the transfer of the Public Utility Commission's Transportation Program into the Oregon Department of Transportation, effective January 1, 1996. On February 16, 1996, ODOT formed a Motor Carrier Transportation Branch to regulate the commercial operations of motor carriers using Oregon's roads and highways. The branch is responsible for issuing operating authority, collecting highway use tax, registering heavy vehicles and enforcing motor carrier safety and size and weight laws.

On July 31, 1996 there were 32,957 carriers registered with the Motor Carrier Transportation Branch and 262,620 active plates. Total revenues collected from highway use tax and registration fees amount to approximately $215 million annually.

Transportation Development

Ron Schaadt, Interim Mgr.

555 13th St. NE, Salem 97310-1333;
503-986-3420; Fax: 503-986-3423

Transportation Development Branch is ODOT's strategic planning and policy group. The branch guides overall statewide transportation development through the long-range Oregon Transportation Plan, individual modal plans, corridor plans, transportation policy analysis and research. The top goal is to provide Oregonians with a safe, balanced, interconnected statewide transportation system that uses all modes effectively and efficiently to support economic development and livability.

Transportation Development also includes efforts to develop high-speed rail, intercity bus services, freight rail, aviation, public transit and to actively promote transportation safety.

Aeronautics Section

Betsy Johnson, Mgr.

3040 25th St. SE, Salem 97310-0100;
503-378-4880; Fax: 503-373-1688

Aeronautics was founded in 1921 as the first government aviation agency in the United States. Agency goals include: developing aviation as an integral part of Oregon's transportation network; creating and implementing strategies to protect and improve Oregon's aviation system; encouraging aviation-related economic development; supporting aviation safety and education; and increasing commercial air service and general aviation in Oregon.

Aeronautics owns or operates 34 Oregon airports and annually licenses or registers more than 400 other public and private airports, heliports and landing areas. The agency also registers all pilots and non-military aircraft based in Oregon; oversees statewide aviation system planning and helps with community airport planning; and conducts aviation safety and public education programs.

Aeronautics activities are funded mainly by user fees. Pilot registration fees are used solely for air search and rescue missions. State aviation fuel taxes, aircraft registrations, airport licensing fees, and leases and agreements on state-owned airports support other Aeronautics programs. Additional funds come from projects sponsored by the Federal Aviation Administration Airport Improvement Program. No state general fund revenue is used by Aeronautics.

Public Transit Section

Joni Reid, Mgr.
555 13th St. NE, Salem 97310-1333;
503-986-3300; TDD: 503-986-3416;
Fax: 503-986-4189

Public Transit helps develop the use of transit, ridesharing, walking, bicycling, telecommuting and other alternatives to driving alone. Top goals include planning, developing and encouraging use of the most appropriate modes of transportation, and providing mobility and access for people unable to drive. Public Transit coordinates, plans, researches and funds public passenger transportation systems in Oregon. It also supports local programs and provides facilities to encourage the use of travel modes that reduce traffic congestion and maintain our quality of life.

Public Transit administers state and federal funds to help urban areas develop mass transit systems; provides funding and training to small city and rural transit agencies; and develops and supports intercity bus and passenger rail services. It administers programs to provide transportation for elderly and disabled Oregonians; coordinates a statewide demand-management/ rideshare program to promote using alternatives to driving alone; and provides transit planning and technical help to Oregon communities.

Transportation Safety Section

Ed Marges, Mgr.
555 13th St. NE, Salem 97310-1333;
503-986-3490; toll-free: 1-800-922-2022;
Fax: 503-986-4189

Transportation Safety and the Oregon Transportation Safety Committee are responsible for administering a statewide safety program. Transportation Safety plans and coordinates the implementation of prevention programs designed to reduce traffic accidents and injuries, encourage and support local traffic safety organizations, and improve data systems. It also awards grants to state and local agencies and non-profit groups.

Transportation Safety carries out a comprehensive public information program; encourages communities, state agencies and private organizations to implement safety programs for youth and general audiences; coordinates motorcycle safety training; encourages bicycle safety training; plans training programs for transportation safety professionals; and completes special studies.

Transportation Operations

Kenneth Husby, P.E., Deputy Dir./
State Highway Engineer

135 Transportation Bldg., Salem 97310-1354;
503-986-3200; Fax: 503-986-3432

The ODOT deputy director manages Transportation Operations which includes five ODOT region offices; all design, engineering and maintenance activities; and civil rights.

Transportation Operations designs, maintains, operates and oversees construction of Oregon's 7,450 miles of state highways. These activities include: identifying highway needs; maintaining state highway routes; acquiring rights of way; designing highways, bridges and related structures; awarding highway construction and modernization contracts; supervising contractors; obtaining federal highway funds; helping counties and cities improve roads and streets; testing materials; evaluating environmental impacts of proposed projects; and conducting traffic studies and other research projects.

ODOT's five regional offices are responsible for transportation operations in their area. Each region has several district offices responsible for transportation system maintenance.

Region 1: 123 NW Flanders, Portland 97209-4037; 503-731-8200; Fax: 503-731-8259

Region 2: 2960 State St., Bldg. 1, Salem 97310-1344; 503-986-2600; Fax: 503-986-2630

Region 3: 3500 Stewart Parkway, Roseburg 97470-1687; 541-957-3500; Fax: 541-957-3547

Region 4: 63055 N Hwy. 97, Bend 97708-5309; 541-388-6180; Fax: 541-388-6231

Region 5: 3012 Island Ave., La Grande 97850; 541-963-3177; Fax: 541-963-9079

Boards and Advisory Committees

Aviation Advisory Committee

Betsy Johnson, Aeronautics Mgr.
3040 25th St. SE, Salem 97310-0100;
503-378-4880; Fax: 503-373-1688

The nine-member Aviation Advisory Committee advises the Aeronautics manager of the ODOT Commission on aviation policy matters. The committee helps develop strategies to support aviation-related business and economic development throughout the state.

Transportation Safety Committee

Ed Marges,
ODOT Transportation Safety Section
555 13th St. NE, Salem 97310-1333;
503-986-4190; toll-free: 1-800-922-2022;
Fax: 503-986-4189

Walter Pendergrass, chair, Portland, 2000.

The Transportation Safety Committee advises the department and the commission on transportation safety matters. Committee members are appointed by the governor to four-year terms.

DUII, Governor's Advisory Committee on

ODOT Transportation Safety Section
555 13th St. NE, Salem 97310-1333;
503-986-4190; toll-free: 1-800-922-2022;
Fax: 503-986-4189

Peter Glazer, chair, Lake Oswego, 1999
The Advisory Committee on DUII develops administrative and legislative objectives to reduce driving under the influence of intoxicants (DUII) and monitors their implementation; heightens public awareness of the DUII problem; and educates the public on the dangers of driving while impaired by alcohol or other drugs.

Motorcycle Safety Advisory Committee, Governor's

ODOT Transportation Safety Section
555 13th St. NE, Salem 97310-1333;
503-986-4190; toll-free: 1-800-922-2022;
Fax: 503-986-4189

Wayne Schumacher, chair, Oregon City, 1999.

The eight-member Motorcycle Safety Advisory Committee meets with and advises ODOT's Transportation Safety Section on all aspects of motorcycling safety in Oregon. The committee is appointed by the governor.

Winter Recreation Advisory Committee

Karen Morrison, Prog. Coord.
800 Airport Rd., Salem 97310; 503-986-3000;
Fax: 503-986-3032

Glenn Menzie, chair, Ashland, 1998

The seven-member Winter Recreation Advisory Committee advises the Oregon Transportation Commission on designating winter recreation parking locations statewide. The committee represents ski area operators, the Pacific Northwest Ski Association, Oregon State Snowmobile Association and the general public.

The Transportation Commission appoints committee members to serve four-year terms.

All-Terrain Vehicle Account Allocation Committee

Karen Morrison, Prog. Coord.
800 Airport Rd., Salem 97310; 503-986-3000;
Fax: 503-986-3032

Pat Harris, chair, Klamath Falls, 1997
This committee advises the Transportation Commission on the use of

Hart Lake as seen from the top of the Stockade Creek Trail.

Photo courtesy of the Hart Mountain National Wildlife Refuge.

special funds to acquire, develop and maintain ATV facilities; and to provide ATV safety and education programs, and first aid and police services. Funds for the program come from ATV fuel taxes, title, registration and permit fees.

Seven voting and four non-voting committee members are appointed to four-year terms by the Transportation Commission.

Bicycle and Pedestrian Advisory Committee

Michael Ronkin, Bicycle/Pedestrian Prog. Mgr.

210 Transportation Bldg., Salem 97310; 503-986-3555; Fax: 503-986-3896

John Deagen, chair, Corvallis, 1998
The Bicycle and Pedestrian Advisory Committee advises ODOT on regulating bicycle and pedestrian traffic and establishing bikeways and walkways. ODOT, cities and counties are required by law to provide walkways and bikeways. Committee members are appointed by the governor to four-year terms.

Covered Bridge Advisory Committee

Terry J. Shike, Bridge Engineer

329 Transportation Bldg., Salem 97310-1333; 503-986-4200; Fax: 503-986-3407

Sen. Mae Yih, chair, 1997
The Covered Bridge Program was established to restore and maintain Oregon's covered bridges. The advisory committee is a liaison advocate to counties, elected officials and covered bridge owners. ODOT has an annual covered bridge inspection program and makes grants to public or private entities that own public-access bridges.

Historic Columbia River Highway Advisory Committee

Jeanette Kloos, Scenic Area Coord.

123 NW Flanders, Portland 97209-4037; 503-731-8234; Fax: 503-731-8259

Lewis L. McArthur, chair, Portland, 1998.
The Historic Columbia River Highway Advisory Committee advises ODOT and the Parks and Recreation Department in developing programs to preserve, restore and manage the scenic highway in the Columbia River Gorge.

Maritime Pilots, Oregon Board of

Susan Johnson, Admin.

800 NE Oregon St., Suite 507, Portland 97232; 503-731-4044; Fax: 503-731-4043

George Miller, chair, Portland, 2000
Since 1846, the Board of Maritime Pilots has promoted public safety by providing for competent pilot services on the Columbia and Willamette rivers, Columbia River Bar, Coos Bay and Yaquina Bay. The board establishes requirements for maritime pilots; administers exams; and licenses and regulates maritime pilots.

The nine-member board, appointed by the governor to four-year terms, includes three private citizens, three professional maritime pilots, and three maritime shipping industry members.

Rural Transit Assistance Program Advisory Committee

Jean Palmateer, RTAP Coord.

PO Box 1124, The Dalles 97058; 541-296-2602; Fax: 541-298-7139

Bernadette Barrett, chair, Corvallis, 1996
The Rural Transit Assistance Program helps provide training statewide for local transportation agencies, offers training program scholarships, provides technical help for specific problems and helps coordinate local transportation services and resources.

Committee members are appointed by the ODOT Public Transit Manager to three-year terms.

Uniform State Laws, Commission on

520 SW Yamhill St., Suite 800, Portland 97204-1383; 503-226-6151

Oglesby H. Young, chair, Lake Oswego, 1998; Martha Lee Walters, Eugene, 2000; Donald Joe Willis, Portland, 1997. Each commissioner is appointed by the governor for a four-year term.

The Commission on Uniform State Laws works with the National Conference of Commissioners on Uniform State Laws to promote uniformity in laws among states where uniformity is desirable. One of the best examples of the work of the commission is the Uniform Commercial Code which has been adopted in all 50 states and forms the backbone of the commercial law in this country. Each commissioner works on drafting committees and attends the annual meetings of the National Conference where each proposed act is studied and debated by the entire conference.

Statutory authority for the formation of the commission was adopted by the 1949 Legislature (ORS 172.010 and 172.020). However, Oregon has been represented at the National Conference of Commissioners on Uniform State Laws by governor-appointed commissioners under general executive authority since 1908.

Veterans' Affairs, Department of

Jon A. Mangis, Dir.
Frank Wallis, Deputy Dir.
700 Summer St. NE, Salem 97310-1201;
503-373-2000; Fax: 503-373-2362;
TDD: 503-373-2217

The department has been serving Oregon's military veterans since 1945. The Legislature created the department in answer to the citizens' mandate to provide for Oregon soldiers, sailors and airmen returning from duty in World War II. Since then, benefits managed by the department have been extended to include veterans of later eras.

In addition to providing counseling and claims service to veterans, their dependents and survivors, the department administers the Veterans' Home and Farm Loan Program. The program was designed to answer a need for equity for returning war veterans. Oregon Senate Concurrent Resolution Number 2, passed in 1943, said, in part, "... it would not be fitting that those who remained at home should by reason thereof gain economic advantage over our patriotic defenders." The resolution continued, "Let it be in the declared policy of the State of Oregon to place our returning military and naval forces as nearly as possible on the same economic equality as those who remained at home."

That policy, resulting in the program to provide below-market home loans to qualified veterans, has not changed, although the program itself has been revised and expanded.

Veterans' Affairs, Advisory Committee to the Director of
700 Summer St. NE, Salem 97310; 503-373-2383

Bill Ward, chair, The Dalles
The committee consists of nine members appointed by the governor. It is required by Oregon statute to act in an advisory capacity to the director.

Veterans' Services Division
Robert B. Brown, Admin.

Claims Program
1220 SW 3rd Ave., Suite 1509, Portland 97204;
503-326-2611; Fax: 503-497-1053

In addition to providing benefit counseling services, the claims office represents veterans in the presentation of claims and appeals before the U.S. Department of Veterans Affairs.

Conservatorship Program
700 Summer St. NE, Salem 97310-1270;
503-373-2085; toll-free: 1-800-692-9666;
Fax: 503-373-2392

The Conservatorship Program manages the estates of veterans and their dependents who are considered "protected persons" by various Oregon probate courts and who are unable to manage their own financial affairs.

Counseling Program
700 Summer St. NE, Salem 97310-1270;
503-373-2085; toll-free: 1-800-692-9666;
Fax: 503-373-2392

Veterans' Benefit Counselors provide assistance to veterans, dependents, and survivors who wish to apply for state and federal benefits. Counselors provide this assistance both in the Salem, and Portland offices and through outreach efforts to nursing homes, correctional facilities, other state institutions and private residences.

Veterans' Loan Division
Tom Cowan Jr., Admin.
700 Summer St. NE, Salem 97310-1201;
503-373-2000; toll-free: 1-800-828-8801

Since 1945, the department has made nearly 300,000 home and farm loans, with the principal amount of slightly more than $7 billion. The loan program is financed through sale of tax-exempt, self-liquidating, general obligation bonds.

Oregon Veterans' Home

Lyall Fraser, Project Dir.
700 Summer St. NE, Salem 97310-1201;
503-373-2016

The 1993 Legislative Assembly authorized the Director of Veterans' Affairs to establish and administer a State Veterans' Home—a long-term-care facility for needy, disabled veterans. The home is anticipated to open by fall 1997, and will provide nursing care and Alzheimer's disease care in the 151-bed facility.

Veterinary Medical Examining Board

Molly Emmons, Exec. Officer
800 NE Oregon St., Suite 407, Portland 97232;
503-731-4051; Fax: 503-731-4207

Robert J. Anderson, DVM, Portland, 1998; Stanley Blinkhorn, DVM, Eugene, 1997; Kris Kash, Beaverton, 1997; Thomas Keck, DVM, Dallas, 1997; Mark McFarland, DVM, Madras, 1999; Fraser Pierson, Medford, 1996; Vera Rogers, DVM, Days Creek, 1997. All members are appointed by the governor and confirmed by the Senate. The Veterinary Medical Examining Board was established in 1903 by ORS chapter 686. The Veterinary Medical Examining Board seeks to protect animal health, public health and consumers of veterinary services through the regulation of veterinary professions in Oregon. The board examines and licenses veterinarians, veterinary technicians and animal euthanasia technicians; handles complaints of veterinary services; and imposes disciplinary proceedings against those who violate the laws and rules of the Veterinary Practice Act.

Water Resources Department

Martha O. Pagel, Dir.
Commerce Bldg., 158 12th St. NE, Salem 97310;
503-378-8455; toll-free: 1-800-624-3199;
Fax: 503-378-8130;
Email: webmaster@wrd.state.or.us;
Web: www.wrd.state.or.us

The Water Resources Department was established in 1909 and is authorized by the Water Act, ORS 537.010. By law, all surface and groundwater in Oregon belongs to the public. It is the job of the Water Resources Department (WRD) to manage Oregon's public water to ensure a sufficient supply to sustain its growing economy, quality of life and natural heritage. That means preserving an equitable balance between public and private uses of water. The department strives to protect existing uses of water while maintaining adequate levels in waterways to support fish, wildlife, water quality and recreation. The agency promotes water conservation and coordinates water planning activities with other agencies and citizen groups. The agency also manages information about streamflows, water rights and well-log files for public review.

As administrative chief of the Water Resources Department, the director is charged with carrying out the water management policies set by the Water Resources Commission and with overseeing the enforcement of Oregon's water laws. The director is appointed by the governor for a four-year term, subject to confirmation by the Senate.

WRD employs a wide variety of experts, including hydrologists, engineers, geologists, technicians, planners and administrative specialists. Agency staff monitor water levels at hundreds of gaging stations, map and study underground aquifers and help design long-term water plans for Oregon's river basins. They supply local governments and citizen groups with information and technical assistance to make and carry out their own water programs.

The agency is organized into five divisions: Field and Technical Services, Resource Management, Water Rights and Adjudications, Director's Office, and Administrative Services. Agency headquarters and the Northwest Regional office are in Salem.

The department is represented throughout the state by a network of five regional and 12 field offices from which watermasters carry out their responsibilities. Among a variety of other duties, regional managers meet with user groups to explain current water law and how local practices fit in and develop working agreements with other agencies for data collection. Watermasters, under the direction of regional managers, enforce water laws and measure the waters of the state.

Boats bob on the tide at the mouth of the Siuslaw River in Florence. Photo by Bill Cigler.

Water Resources Commission

Nancy Leonard, chair, Newport, 1997; Michael Jewett, vice-chair, Ashland, 1995; John L. Frewing, Portland, 1998; Tyler Hansell, Hermiston, 1998; Ron Nelson, Redmond, 1999; two vacancies.

This seven-member citizen board oversees the activities of the Water Resources Department. Consistent with state law, the commission sets water policy for the state and determines how unallocated water will be used in the development of basin programs in each of Oregon's 18 river basins.

Through the department, the commission authorizes diversions and appropriations of surface and ground water; issues and records permits, licenses and certificates allowing use of water; establishes instream water rights; and determines critical ground water areas.

Commission members are appointed by the governor for four-year terms, subject to confirmation by the Senate.

Groundwater Advisory Committee

Donn Miller, Dept. Liaison
503-378-8455, ext. 205

Ralph Christensen, chair, Eugene; Barry Beyeler, The Dalles; Gene Clemens, Dallas; Jim Graham, Portland; Gayle Killam, Portland; Greg McInnis, Portland;

Alan Parks, Silver Lake; Chuck Stadeli, Mt. Angel. One vacancy.

Nine members are appointed by the Water Resources Commission to advise on matters relating to the management and protection of ground water resources, the licensing of well constructors and the expenditure of well construction fees.

Klamath River Basin Compact

Richard Fairclo, Commission Consultant
280 Main St., Klamath Falls 97601;
541-882-4436;
Web: www.water.ca.gov/nd/oregon/index.html

Alice Kilham, chair, Klamath Falls, appointed by President Clinton to represent the federal government; Martha O. Pagel, representative for Oregon; and William J. Bennett, representative for California.

Members facilitate and promote intergovernmental cooperation to assist in the development and proper use of the water resources of the Klamath River Basin.

Watershed Enhancement Board, Governor's

Governor's Natural Resources Offices, Public Service Bldg., Salem 97310; 503-378-3589; Fax: 503-378-3225

Voting board members are: Joe Brumbach, Soil and Water Conservation

Commission; Wayne Krieger, Oregon Board of Forestry; Nancy Leonard, Oregon Water Resources Commission; Phil Schneider, Fish and Wildlife Commission; Carol Whipple, Environmental Quality Commission.

Non-voting board members are: Hugh Barrett, USDI Bureau of Land Management; Dave Caraher, USDA Forest Service; Bob Graham, Natural Resources Conservation Service; Lyla Houglum, Oregon Cooperative Extension Service; and John Mellot, Oregon Department of Agriculture. Louise Billheimer, Governor's Watershed Policy Adviser, is the non-voting chair of the board.

The Governor's Watershed Enhancement Board (GWEB) program is aimed at helping Oregonians improve the state's watersheds. The program was created by the Legislature in 1987. Its primary functions are to provide technical assistance, administer a grant program, promote education and public awareness about watershed enhancement benefits, concepts and techniques, and support the work of local watershed councils. The 1995 Legislature combined the Watershed Health Program with GWEB and made watershed councils subject to local government recognition. It directed GWEB to administer approximately $5.5 million in Watershed Health Grants, and provided $2.6 million in lottery revenues for program administration and new watershed enhancement and education grants.

Water Development Loan Program

Roelin Smith, Finance Business Officer

Water Resources Department, Commerce Bldg., 158 12th St. NE, Salem 97310; 503-378-8455, ext. 250

The loan program was enacted by the 1977 Legislature to finance low-interest loans for irrigation and drainage projects in Oregon. Since that time, the constitution has been amended to allow the funding of loans for community water-supply projects, fish protection and watershed enhancement. Since 1977, the loan program has issued $43,511,000 in bonds and funded 180 loans for various projects.

Western States Water Council

Craig Bell, Dir.
Creekview Plaza, #A-201, 942 E, 7145 South, Midvale, UT 84047; 801-561-5300; Web: www.westgov.org/wswc

Established by the Western Governors' Conference, the council is a cooperative effort by western states to integrate development of their water resources. Member states are Alaska, Arizona, California, Colorado, Idaho, Montana, Nevada, New Mexico, North Dakota, Oregon, South Dakota, Texas, Utah, Washington and Wyoming. Delegates to the council are appointed by and serve at the discretion of the governors. Oregon's delegate is Martha O. Pagel, Salem.

Women, Oregon Commission for

Jennifer A. Webber, Exec. Dir.
*PSU Smith Center, Rm. M315
PO Box 751-CW, Portland 97207;
503-725-5889; Fax: 503-725-8152*

Diane Rosenbaum, chair, Portland, 1999; Marie Calica, Warm Springs, 1999; Jan Marie Dielschneider, Bend, 1999; Sandy Ellis, Albany, 1997; Mary Ann Gray, Gresham, 1997; Addie Jean Haynes, Portland, 1998; Gloria Roy, Eugene, 1999; Karen Rutan, Eugene, 1999; Sen. Marylin Shannon, 1997; Jacqueline Taylor, Astoria, 1997; one vacancy.

The Oregon Commission for Women (CFW) was legislatively established in 1983 to work for women's equality through advocacy and legislation. CFW assesses women's status in Oregon and publishes reports on their issues and needs. It also holds an annual "Women of Achievement" dinner to honor outstanding female role models. The commission's "Women & The Law" booklet was revised in 1996.

Youth Authority, Oregon

Rick Hill, Dir.
*530 Center St. NE, Suite 200, Salem 97301-3740;
503-373-7205; Fax: 503-373-7622*

The Oregon Youth Authority, established as a department of state government in 1995 under ORS 420A.010, is responsible for supervising the management and administration of youth correctional facilities, parole and probation services, community out-of-home placement for youth offenders, and other functions related to state programs for youth offenders between the ages of 12 and 25 years who have been committed to the Oregon Youth Authority by county juvenile courts. These programs hold youth offenders responsible for their actions and offer youth offenders opportunities to reform and become productive and responsible members of their communities.

Facilities include Hillcrest Youth Correctional Facility in Salem and MacLaren Youth Correctional Facility in Woodburn. There are Youth Offender Work/Study Camps in Corvallis, Florence, La Grande and Tillamook. New youth correctional facilities are being constructed in Albany, Burns, Grants Pass, Prineville and Warrenton with targeted completion dates in late 1997. In addition, a Youth Offender Accountability Camp ("boot" camp) is being constructed in Tillamook, with a completion date projected for Spring 1997.

OYA parole and probation services are available to all Oregon counties. In 1996, approximately 2,000 youth offenders were under state parole or probation supervision. Approximately 1,000 of these youth are placed in out-of-home youth offender foster care, shelter and group care, and residential treatment. OYA is responsible for developing, maintaining and monitoring statewide contracts for out-of-home placement resources, as well as the certification of youth offender foster homes.

JUDICIAL

One of Oregon's most familiar coastal landmarks, 235-foot Haystack Rock, stands out in this view of Cannon Beach from the south. Photo by Mitch Ward.

OREGON'S judicial system dates back to the days of provisional government, when Willamette Valley residents elected Dr. Ira L. Babcock to be supreme judge. Since that day in 1841, Oregon's judicial institutions have been enduring, stable and highly respected. Today, judges from the municipal courts to the Supreme Court deliberate on a complex array of civil, criminal and governance issues. As the third branch of government, judges review the actions of state agencies and the Legislature in light of the state Constitution.

Oregon Supreme Court

Supreme Court Bldg., 1163 State St., Salem 97310;
Records and Case Information: 503-986-5555;
TTY: 503-986-5561; Fax: 503-986-5560

The Supreme Court of Oregon is composed of seven justices elected by non-partisan statewide ballot to serve six-year terms. Justices elected to the Supreme Court must be United States citizens and members of the Oregon State Bar and must have resided in the state three years. The court has its offices and courtroom in the Supreme Court Building just east of the Oregon State Capitol in Salem. The members of the court elect one of their number to serve as chief justice for a six-year term.

Powers and Authority

The Supreme Court is created and its role is defined by Amended Article VII of the Oregon Constitution. It is primarily a court of review; that is, it reviews the decisions of the Court of Appeals in selected cases. The Supreme Court decides which cases to review, usually selecting those with significant legal issues calling for interpretation of laws or legal principles affecting many citizens and institutions of society. When the Supreme Court decides not to review a case, the Court of Appeals' decision becomes final. In addition to its review function, the Supreme Court hears direct appeals in death penalty cases and tax court cases, and may accept original jurisdiction in mandamus, quo warranto and habeas corpus proceedings.

Administrative Authority

The chief justice is the administrative head of the judicial department and, as such, exercises administrative authority over and supervises the appellate, circuit, district and tax courts. The chief justice makes rules and issues orders to carry out necessary duties and requires appropriate reports from judges and other officers and employees of the courts. As head of the judicial department, the chief justice appoints the chief judge of the Court of Appeals and the presiding judges of all local courts from the judges elected to those courts. The chief justice adopts rules and regulations establishing procedures for all courts in the state. The chief justice is also charged with supervising a statewide plan for budgeting, accounting and fiscal management of the judicial department.

The chief justice and the Supreme Court have the authority to appoint elected judges and retired judges to serve in temporary judicial assignments.

Admission, Discipline of Lawyers and Judges

The Supreme Court has the responsibility for the admission of lawyers to practice law in Oregon and the power to reprimand, suspend, or disbar lawyers upon investigation and trial by the Oregon State Bar. In admitting lawyers, the Supreme Court acts on the recommendation of the Board of Bar Examiners, which conducts examinations for lawyer applicants each February and July and screens applicants for character and fitness to practice law. The 14 members of the Board of Bar Examiners are appointed by the Supreme Court; the board includes two "public" members who are not lawyers. The Supreme Court also has the power to censure, suspend, or remove judges upon investigation and recommendation by the Commission on Judicial Fitness and Disability.

Oregon Court of Appeals

Supreme Court Bldg., 1163 State St., Salem 97310;
Records and Case Information: 503-986-5555;
TTY: 503-986-5561; Fax: 503-986-5560

The Court of Appeals, created in 1969 as a five-judge court, was expanded to six judges in 1973 and to 10 in 1977. Its judges, elected on a statewide, nonpartisan basis for six-year terms, must be United States citizens, members of the Oregon State Bar and qualified electors of their county of residence. The chief justice of the Supreme Court appoints a chief judge from among the judges of the Court of Appeals.

Court of Appeals judges have their offices in the Justice Building in Salem and usually hear cases in the courtroom of the Supreme Court Building. The court ordinarily sits in departments of three judges. The Supreme Court has authority to appoint a Supreme Court judge, a circuit court judge or a tax court judge to serve as a judge pro tempore of the Court of Appeals.

Supreme Court

Carson, Wallace P. Jr.
Chief Justice
Position 6
Served since 1982
Term expires 1/2001

Durham, Robert D.
Associate Justice
Position 3
Served since 1994
Term expires 1/2001

Fadeley, Edward N.
Associate Justice
Position 4
Served since 1989
Term expires 1/2001

Gillette, W. Michael
Associate Justice
Position 5
Served since 1986
Term expires 1/1999

Graber, Susan P.
Associate Justice
Position 7
Served since 1990
Term expires 1/1999

Kulongoski, Theodore R.
Associate Justice
Position 1
Served since 1997
Term expires 1/2003

Van Hoomissen, George A.
Associate Justice
Position 2
Served since 1988
Term expires 1/2001

Judicial

Jurisdiction

The Court of Appeals has jurisdiction of all civil and criminal appeals, except death-penalty cases and appeals from the Tax Court, and for review of most state administrative agency actions.

Reviews and Decisions

A party aggrieved by a decision of the Court of Appeals may petition the Supreme Court for review within 35 days after the Court of Appeals decision is issued. The Supreme Court determines whether to review the case. A petition for review is allowed whenever three or more Supreme Court judges vote to allow it.

Oregon Tax Court

Supreme Court Bldg., 1163 State St., Salem 97310;
503-986-5645; TTY: 503-986-5651;
Fax: 503-986-5507

The Oregon Tax Court has exclusive, statewide jurisdiction in all questions of law or fact arising under state tax laws, i.e., income taxes, corporate excise taxes, property taxes, timber taxes, cigarette taxes, local budget law, and property tax limitations.

Magistrate Division

As of September 1, 1997, the Tax Court will consist of two divisions: the Magistrate Division and the Regular Division (ORS chapter 650, Or Laws 1995). The judge of the Tax Court appoints one presiding magistrate and one or more individuals to sit as magistrates of the Magistrate Division.

Trials in the Magistrate Division are informal proceedings. Statutory rules of evidence do not apply and the trials are not reported. The proceedings may be conducted by telephone or in person. A taxpayer may be represented by a lawyer, public accountant, real estate broker or appraiser.

The filing fee is $25, unless a taxpayer elects to file as a small claims procedure for $10. The decision of magistrates in small claims procedures are final and may not be appealed. All other decisions of the magistrates may be appealed to the Regular Division of the Tax Court.

Regular Division

Appeals from the Magistrate Division are made directly to the Regular Division of the Tax Court. The judge of the Tax Court presides over trials in the Regular Division. The Regular Division is comparable to a circuit court and exercises equivalent powers. All trials are before the judge only (no jury) and are reported. The parties must either represent themselves or be represented by an attorney. Appeals from the judge's decision are made directly to the Oregon Supreme Court.

The judge serves a six-year term and is elected on the statewide, nonpartisan judicial ballot.

Court of Appeals

Richardson, William L.
Chief Judge
Position 4
Served since 1976
Term expires 1/2001

Armstrong, Rex
Associate Judge
Position 10
Served since 1995
Term expires 1/2001

Deits, Mary J.
Associate Judge
Position 9
Served since 1986
Term expires 1/1999

De Muniz, Paul J.
Associate Judge
Position 1
Served since 1990
Term expires 1/2003

Edmonds, Walter I. Jr.
Associate Judge
Position 2
Served since 1989
Term expires 1/2003

Haselton, Rick T.
Associate Judge
Position 5
Served since 1994
Term expires 1/2001

Landau, Jack L.
Associate Judge
Position 8
Served since 1993
Term expires 1/2001

Leeson, Susan M.
Associate Judge
Position 7
Served since 1993
Term expires 1/2001

Riggs, R. William
Associate Judge
Position 3
Served since 1988
Term expires 1/2001

Judicial

Warren, Edward H.
Associate Judge
Position 6
Served since 1980
Term expires 1/1999

Tax Court

Byers, Carl N.
Tax Judge
Served since 1985
Term expires 1/1999

Cases Filed in Oregon Courts 1990-95

	1990	1991	1992	1993	1994	1995
Oregon Supreme Court	263	287	344	263	409	424
Oregon Court of Appeals	4,588	5,124	5,102	4,410	4,441	4,426
Tax Court	422	139	578	464	408	370
Circuit Courts						
without juvenile	122,053	124,275	130,617	136,257	162,746	148,940
with juvenile	141,776	141,625	149,286	155,233	181,226	168,917
District Courts	518,062	508,904	490,075	436,858	387,463	407,092

Circuit Courts

The circuit courts are the state trial courts of general jurisdiction. The circuit courts have adoption and juvenile jurisdiction in all counties except Gilliam, Harney, Morrow, Sherman and Wheeler, where the county court exercises juvenile jurisdiction except for termination of parental rights proceedings, over which the circuit court has exclusive jurisdiction. The circuit courts also exercise jurisdiction in probate, guardianship and conservatorship cases in all counties except Gilliam, Grant, Harney, Malheur, Sherman and Wheeler.

Circuit court judges are elected on a nonpartisan ballot for a term of six years. They must be citizens of the United States, members of the Oregon State Bar, residents of Oregon at least three years and residents of their judicial district at least one year (except Multnomah County judges, who may reside within 10 miles of the county). As of January 1, 1997, there are 94 circuit judges serving the 36 Oregon counties. The circuit judges are grouped in 23 geographic areas called judicial districts. Multnomah County district has 22 circuit judges; Lane, 10; Washington, 8; Marion, 7; Clackamas, 6. One district has four judges, seven have three judges each, six have two judges each, and four have one judge each. Effective June 30, 1997, one additional circuit court judge will be appointed by the governor to each of the following courts: Jackson, Deschutes and Clackamas counties (ORS chapter 658, Or Laws 1995).

To expedite judicial business, the chief justice of the Supreme Court may assign any circuit judge to sit in any judicial district in the state, and he may appoint members of the Oregon State Bar as circuit judges pro tempore.

Abernethy, Pamela L.
Marion
Dist. 3—Pos. 5

Ahern, Daniel J.
Jefferson, Crook
Dist. 22—Pos. 2

Aiken, Ann
Lane
Dist. 2—Pos. 7

Alexander, Timothy P.
Washington
Dist. 20—Pos. 7

Amiton, Marshall L.
Multnomah
Dist. 4—Dept. 22

Bagley, Raymond
Clackamas (P)
Dist. 5—Pos. 4

Barber, Richard D.
Marion
Dist. 3—Pos. 4

Barron, Richard L.
Coos, Curry (P)
Dist. 15—Pos. 2

Bearden, Frank L.
Multnomah
Dist. 4—Dept. 9

Beesley, Richard C.
Klamath, Lake
Dist. 13—Pos. 3

Bergman, Linda L.
Multnomah
Dist. 4—Dept. 11

Billings, Jack
Lane
Dist. 2—Pos. 8

Judicial

Bonebrake, Alan C.
Washington
Dist. 20—Pos. 2

Brady, Alta J.
Deschutes
Dist. 11—Pos. 1

Brown, Anna J.
Multnomah
Dist. 4—Dept. 7

Brownhill, Paula J.
Clatsop, Columbia,
Tillamook
Dist. 19—Pos. 1

Ceniceros, Joseph F.
Multnomah
Dist. 4—Dept. 21

Collins, John L.
Yamhill, Polk
Dist. 12—Pos. 1

Coon, Allan H.
Josephine
Dist. 14—Pos. 2

Cramer, William D. Jr.
Grant, Harney (P)
Dist. 24

Davis, Ross G.
Jackson (P)
Dist. 1—Pos. 1

Downer, Hugh C. Jr.
Curry, Coos
Dist. 15—Pos. 3

Ellis, James R.
Multnomah
Dist. 4—Dept. 1

Foote, Gregory G.
Lane
Dist. 2—Pos. 9

Frankel, Kimberly C.
Multnomah
Dist. 4—Dept. 3

Frantz, Julie
Multnomah
Dist. 4—Dept. 10

Frost, Jackson L.
Linn
Dist. 23—Pos. 1

Gallagher, Stephen L. Jr.
Multnomah
Dist. 4—Dept. 5

Gardner, Robert S.
Benton (P)
Dist. 21—Pos. 1

Gilroy, Patrick D.
Clackamas
Dist. 5—Pos. 1

Judicial

Grove, Ted
Tillamook, Columbia,
Clatsop
Dist. 19—Pos. 4

Haas, Harl H.
Multnomah
Dist. 4—Dept. 14

Hantke, David W.
Tillamook, Columbia,
Clatsop
Dist. 19—Pos. 2

Herrell, Stephen B.
Multnomah
Dist. 4—Dept. 16

Hitchcock, John W.
Polk, Yamhill
Dist. 12—Pos. 3

Huckleberry, Robert J.
Lincoln (P)
Dist. 17—Pos. 1

Hull, Donald W.
Hood River, Wasco,
Sherman, Gilliam, Wheeler
Dist. 7—Pos. 1

Johnson, Nely L.
Multnomah
Dist. 4—Dept. 6

Jones, Robert P.
Multnomah
Dist. 4—Dept. 2

Karaman, Mitchell A.
Jackson
Dist. 1—Pos. 3

Kelly, John V.
Wasco, Hood River,
Sherman, Gilliam, Wheeler
Dist. 7—Pos. 2

Keys, William
Multnomah
Dist. 4—Dept. 19

Knight, Frank D.
Benton
Dist. 21—Pos. 2

Kolberg, Thomas W.
Douglas (P)
Dist. 16—Pos. 3

LaMar, Kristena A.
Multnomah
Dist. 4—Dept. 17

Larson, Darryl
Lane
Dist. 2—Pos. 4

Leonard, Kip W.
Lane (P)
Dist. 2—Pos. 5

Letourneau, Donald R.
Washington
Dist. 20—Pos. 3

Lipscomb, Paul J.
Marion (P)
Dist. 3—Pos. 2

Littlehales, Charles
Lincoln
Dist. 17—Pos. 2

Londer, Donald H.
Multnomah (P)
Dist. 4—Dept. 4

Lowe, John K.
Clackamas
Dist. 5—Pos. 6

Lund, Jon B.
Washington
Dist. 20—Pos. 5

Luukinen, Charles
Polk, Yamhill (P)
Dist. 12—Pos. 2

Mattison, Jack L.
Lane
Dist. 2—Pos. 2

McCormick, Rick J.
Linn (P)
Dist. 23—Pos. 2

McElligott, Michael J.
Washington
Dist. 20—Pos. 6

Mendiguren, Phillip A.
Union, Wallowa
Dist. 10

Miller, Rodney W.
Marion
Dist. 3—Pos. 7

Morgan, Robert J.
Clackamas
Dist. 5—Pos. 3

Murphy, Daniel R.
Linn
Dist. 23—Pos. 3

Nachtigal, Gayle A.
Washington (P)
Dist. 20—Pos. 8

Neilson, George W.
Jefferson, Crook (P)
Dist. 22—Pos. 1

Neufeld, Gerald C.
Josephine (P)
Dist. 14—Pos. 1

Olsen, Jack F.
Umatilla, Morrow (P)
Dist. 6—Pos. 2

Osborne, Roxanne Burgett
Klamath, Lake (P)
Dist. 13—Pos. 2

Judicial

Poole, Ronald
Douglas
Dist. 16—Pos. 1

Pope, Milo
Baker (P)
Dist. 8

Redding, Robert W.
Multnomah
Dist. 4—Dept. 20

Reed, Steven B.
Columbia, Tillamook,
Clatsop
Dist. 19—Pos. 3

Reynolds, Garry L.
Umatilla, Morrow
Dist. 6—Pos. 1

Rhoades, Jamese L.
Marion
Dist. 3—Pos. 1

Robinson, Roosevelt
Multnomah
Dist. 4—Dept. 15

Rosenblum, Ellen F.
Multnomah
Dist. 4—Dept. 8

Sawyer, Loren L.
Jackson
Dist. 1—Pos. 2

Seitz, Joan G.
Douglas
Dist. 16—Pos. 2

Selander, Robert
Clackamas
Dist. 5—Pos. 5

Snouffer, William C.
Multnomah
Dist. 4—Dept. 13

Sullivan, Michael C.
Deschutes
Dist. 11—Pos. 2

Tiktin, Stephen N.
Deschutes (P)
Dist. 11—Pos. 3

Van Rysselberghe, Pierre
Lane
Dist. 2—Pos. 10

Velure, Lyle C.
Lane
Dist. 2—Pos. 3

Welch, Elizabeth
Multnomah
Dist. 4—Dept. 18

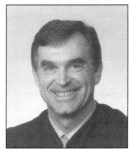

West, Greg
Marion
Dist. 3—Pos. 6

Judicial

Photos not submitted
Brewer, David V.
Isaacson, Rodger J.
Merten, Maurice K.
Milnes, Gregory E.
Norblad, Albin W.
Walberg, Robert F.

Wilson, Janice R.
Multnomah
Dist. 4—Dept. 12

Yraguen, Frank J.
Malheur (P)
Dist. 9

Circuit Court Judges by District

Dist. 1—Jackson
Justice Bldg., 100 S Oakdale, Medford 97501
Davis, Ross G. (P)
Pos. 1, Exp. 1-1-01, 541-776-7171 (169)
Karaman, Mitchell A.
Pos. 3, Exp. 1-4-99, 541-776-7171 (168)
Sawyer, Loren L.
Pos. 2, Exp. 1-4-99, 541-776-7171 (173)

Dist. 2—Lane
Lane County Courthouse, Eugene 97401
Leonard, Kip W. (P)
Pos. 5, Exp. 1-6-03, 541-682-4254
Aiken, Ann
Pos. 7, Exp. 1-1-01, 541-341-4753
Billings, Jack
Pos. 8, Exp. 1-6-03, 541-682-4250
Brewer, David V.
Pos. 1, Exp. 1-1-01, 541-682-4253
Foote, Gregory G.
Pos. 9, Exp. 1-1-01, 541-682-4427
Larson, Darryl
Pos. 4, Exp. 1-6-03, 541-682-4259
Mattison, Jack L.
Pos. 2, Exp. 1-4-99, 541-682-4257
Merten, Maurice K.
Pos. 6, Exp. 1-4-99, 541-682-4258
Van Rysselberghe, Pierre
Pos. 10, Exp. 1-1-01, 541-682-3601
Velure, Lyle C.
Pos. 3, Exp. 1-1-01, 541-682-4256

Dist. 3—Marion
PO Box 12869, Salem 97309-0869
Lipscomb, Paul J. (P)
Pos. 2, Exp. 1-1-01, 503-588-5024

Abernethy, Pamela L.
Pos. 5, Exp.1-6-03, 503-588-5051
Barber, Richard D.
Pos. 4, Exp. 1-4-99, 503-588-5033
Miller, Rodney W.
Pos. 7, Exp. 1-1-01, 503-588-5497
Norblad, Albin W.
Pos. 3, Exp. 1-1-01, 503-588-5028
Rhoades, Jamese L.
Pos. 1, Exp. 1-1-01, 503-588-7950
West, Greg
Pos. 6, Exp. 1-4-99, 503-588-5135

Dist. 4—Multnomah
Multnomah County Courthouse, Portland 97204
Londer, Donald H. (P)
Dept. 4, Exp. 1-6-03, 503-248-3846
Amiton, Marshall L.
Dept. 22, Exp. 1-1-01, 503-248-3068
Bearden, Frank L.
Dept. 9, Exp. 1-1-01, 503-248-3803
Bergman, Linda L.
Dept. 11, Exp. 1-6-03, 503-248-3041
Brown, Anna J.
Dept. 7, Exp. 1-1-01, 503-248-3348
Ceniceros, Joseph F.
Dept. 21, Exp. 1-4-99, 503-248-3546
Ellis, James R.
Dept. 1, Exp. 1-6-03, 503-248-3078
Frankel, Kimberly C.
Dept. 3, Exp. 1-1-01, 503-248-5101
Frantz, Julie
Dept. 10, Exp. 1-6-03, 503-248-3045
Gallagher, Stephen L. Jr.
Dept. 5, Exp. 1-6-03, 503-248-3274

Haas, Harl H.
Dept. 14, Exp. 1-6-03, 503-248-3052

Herrell, Stephen B.
Dept. 16, Exp. 1-1-01, 503-248-3060

Johnson, Nely L.
Dept. 6, Exp. 1-6-03, 503-248-3404

Jones, Robert P.
Dept. 2, Exp. 1-4-99, 503-248-3038

Keys, William
Dept. 19, Exp. 1-6-03, 503-248-3214

LaMar, Kristena A.
Dept. 17, Exp. 1-6-03, 503-248-3204

Redding, Robert W.
Dept. 20, Exp. 1-1-01, 503-248-3954

Robinson, Roosevelt
Dept. 15, Exp. 1-6-03, 503-248-3731

Rosenblum, Ellen F.
Dept. 8, Exp. 1-1-01, 503-248-5039

Snouffer, William C.
Dept. 13, Exp. 1-6-03, 503-248-3986

Welch, Elizabeth
Dept. 18, Exp. 1-1-01, 503-248-3008

Wilson, Janice R.
Dept. 12, Exp. 1-1-01, 503-248-3069

Dist. 5—Clackamas

Clackamas County Courthouse, Oregon City 97045

Bagley, Raymond (P)
Pos. 4, Exp. 1-1-01, 503-655-8688

Gilroy, Patrick D.
Pos. 1, Exp. 1-1-01, 503-655-8687

Lowe, John K.
Pos. 6, Exp. 1-1-01, 503-655-8678

Morgan, Robert J.
Pos. 3, Exp. 1-1-01, 503-655-8685

Selander, Robert
Pos. 5, Exp. 1-6-03, 503-655-8623

Pos. 2 vacant

Dist. 6—Morrow, Umatilla

Olsen, Jack F. (P)
Pos. 2, Exp. 1-1-01, 541-278-0341
PO Box 1307, Pendleton 97801

Reynolds, Garry L.
Pos. 1, Exp. 1-6-03, 541-278-0341 (222)
PO Box 1307, Pendleton 97801
Heppner 97836; 541-676-5264

Dist. 7—Wasco, Hood River, Sherman, Gilliam, Wheeler

Kelly, John V.
Pos. 2, Exp. 1-4-99, 541-296-3196
Wasco County Courthouse,
The Dalles 97058

Hull, Donald W.
Pos. 1, Exp. 1-4-99, 541-386-2676
Hood River County Courthouse
Hood River 97031
Moro 97039, 541-565-3650

Dist. 8—Baker

Pope, Milo (P)
Exp. 1-1-01, 541-523-6303; Baker
County Courthouse, Baker City 97814

Dist. 9—Malheur

Yraguen, Frank J. (P)
Exp. 1-1-01, 541-473-5178; 251 B
St. W, Box 3, Vale 97918

Dist. 10—Union, Wallowa

Phillip A. Mendiguren
Exp. 1-6-03, 541-962-9500, ext. 231;
Joseph Bldg., 1108 K Ave.,
La Grande 97850
Enterprise 97828, 541-426-4991

Dist. 11—Deschutes

Justice Bldg., Bend 97701

Tiktin, Stephen N. (P)
Pos. 3, Exp. 1-6-03, 541-388-5300

Brady, Alta J.
Pos. 1, Exp. 1-1-01, 541-388-5300

Sullivan, Michael C.
Pos. 2, Exp. 1-1-01, 541-388-5300

Dist. 12—Polk, Yamhill

Luukinen, Charles (P)
Pos. 2, Exp. 1-1-01, 623-9245; Polk
County Courthouse, Dallas 97338

Collins, John L.
Pos. 1, Exp. 1-4-99, 472-9371;
Yamhill County Courthouse,
McMinnville 97128

Hitchcock, John W.
Pos. 3, Exp. 1-6-03, 472-9371;
Yamhill County Courthouse,
McMinnville 97128

Dist. 13—Klamath, Lake

Klamath County Courthouse, Klamath Falls 97601

Osborne, Roxannc Burgett (P)
Pos. 2, Exp. 1-4-99, 541-883-5503 (46)
Klamath Falls 97601

Isaacson, Rodger J.
Pos. 1, Exp. 1-6-03, 541-883-5503 (35)

Beesley, Richard C.
Pos. 3, Exp. 1-6-03, 541-883-5503 (49)
Lakeview 97630, 541-947-6051

Dist. 14—Josephine

Josephine County Courthouse, Rm. 252, Grants Pass 97526

Neufeld, Gerald C. (P)
Pos. 1, Exp. 1-1-01, 541-476-2309

Coon, Allan H.
Pos. 2, Exp. 1-6-03, 541-476-2309

Dist. 15—Coos, Curry

Coos County Courthouse, Coquille 97423

Barron, Richard L. (P)
Pos. 2, Exp. 1-4-99, 541-396-3121 (244)

Walberg, Robert F.
Pos. 1, Exp. 1-1-01, 541-396-3121 (238)

Downer, Hugh C. Jr.
Pos. 3, Exp. 1-4-99, 541-247-2742;
PO Box H, Gold Beach 97444

Dist. 16—Douglas

Justice Bldg., Rm. 201, Roseburg 97470

Kolberg, Thomas W. (P)
Pos. 3, Exp. 1-4-99, 541-440-4430

Poole, Ronald
Pos. 1, Exp. 1-6-03, 541-440-4427

Seitz, Joan G.
Pos. 2, Exp. 1-4-99, 541-440-4433

Dist. 17—Lincoln

PO Box 100, Newport 97365

Huckleberry, Robert J. (P)
Pos. 1, Exp. 1-1-01, 541-265-4236 (252)

Littlehales, Charles
Pos. 2, Exp. 1-1-01, 541-265-4236 (251)

Dist. 19—Tillamook, Columbia, Clatsop

Hantke, David W. (P)
Pos. 2, Exp. 1-4-99, 503-842-7914
(114); Tillamook County Courthouse,
Tillamook 97141

Brownhill, Paula J.
Pos. 1, Exp. 1-6-03, 503-325-8555
(304); Clatsop County Courthouse,
Astoria 97103

Grove, Ted
Pos. 4, Exp. 1-6-03, 503-397-2327
(314); Columbia County Courthouse,
St. Helens 97051

Reed, Steven B.
Pos. 3, Exp. 1-6-03; 503-397-2327
(313); Columbia County Courthouse,
St. Helens 97051

Dist. 20—Washington

Washington County Courthouse, Hillsboro 97124

Nachtigal, Gayle A. (P)
Pos. 8, Exp. 1-4-99, 503-693-4562

Alexander, Timothy P.
Pos. 7, Exp. 1-6-03, 503-648-8772

Bonebrake, Alan C.
Pos. 2, Exp. 1-1-01, 503-648-8872

Letourneau, Donald R.
Pos. 3, Exp. 1-1-01, 503-640-3418

Lund, Jon B.
Pos. 5, Exp. 1-4-99, 503-640-3457

McElligott, Michael J.
Pos. 6, Exp. 1-1-01, 503-648-8675

Milnes, Gregory E.
Pos. 4, Exp. 1-4-99, 503-640-3503

Pos. 1 vacant

Dist. 21—Benton

Benton County Courthouse, Corvallis 97330

Gardner, Robert S. (P)
Pos. 1, Exp. 1-1-01, 541-757-6827

Knight, Frank D.
Pos. 2, Exp. 1-4-99, 541-757-6843

Dist. 22—Jefferson, Crook

Neilson, George W. (P)
Pos. 1, Exp. 1-6-03, 541-475-3317;
County Courthouse, 75 SE "C" St.,
Madras 97741-1794
Prineville 97754, 541-447-6541

Ahern, Daniel J.
Pos. 2, Exp. 1-6-03, 541-475-3317;
County Courthouse, 75 SE "C" St.,
Madras 97741-1794
Prineville 97754, 541-447-6541

Dist. 23—Linn

PO Box 1749, Albany 97321

McCormick, Rick J. (P)
Pos. 2, Exp. 1-1-01, 541-967-3848

Frost, Jackson L.
Pos. 1, Exp. 1-1-01, 541-967-3848

Murphy, Daniel R.
Pos. 3, Exp. 1-1-01, 541-967-3848

Dist. 24—Grant, Harney

Grant County Courthouse, Canyon City 97820
Harney County Courthouse, Burns 97720

Cramer, William D. Jr. (P)
Exp. 1-1-03, 541-573-5207

(P) – Presiding Judge

Circuit Judges Association:

President—C. Gregory West
Vice President—Julie Frantz
Secretary—Darryl Larson
Treasurer—John Collins

District Courts

The district courts are trial courts with jurisdiction limited to $10,000 in civil cases and to misdemeanor criminal cases, including traffic offenses, where conviction is punishable by a fine of up to $3,000, imprisonment of one year or less, or both. District courts may conduct preliminary hearings in felony matters, but may not try cases involving title to real property. The district courts have small claims departments which have jurisdiction for recovery of money or damages where the amount claimed does not exceed $2,500.

District court geographical jurisdiction is by county, with 63 judges sitting in 30 of Oregon's 36 counties as of January 1, 1997. Four of the judges serve in a two-county district court (Union-Wallowa; Crook-Jefferson; Morrow-Umatilla). Multnomah County has 14 district judges: Lane, Marion and Washington, five; Clackamas and Jackson, three; Coos, Deschutes, Douglas, Josephine, Klamath and Linn, two; Benton, Clatsop, Columbia, Curry, Hood River, Lake, Lincoln, Malheur, Polk, Tillamook, Wasco and Yamhill, one each.

District judges are elected on a nonpartisan ballot in the individual county for a term of six years. They must be citizens of the United States, residents of or have a principal office in the county in which the court is located at least one year prior to their election, and must be active members of the Oregon State Bar. District court judges may be assigned to serve temporarily as circuit court judges. Effective January 15, 1998, district court jurisdiction, authority, powers, functions and duties are transferred to circuit court (ORS chapter 658, Or Laws 1995).

Baisinger, Glen D.
Linn—Dept. 2

Bechtold, Paula M.
Coos—Dept. 2

Beckman, Douglas G.
Multnomah—Dept. 5

Branford, Thomas O.
Lincoln

Carlson, Cynthia
Lane—Dept. 3

Carp, Ted
Lane—Dept. 2

Crowley, Paul G.
Hood River (P)

Dickerson, Henry R. Jr.
Benton

Dickey, Don A.
Marion—Dept. 5

Freeman, Clifford
Multnomah—Dept. 6

Freerksen, Karl W. Jr.
Washington—Dept. 2

Gernant, David
Multnomah—Dept. 9

Gillespie, Michael J.
Coos—Dept. 1

Guimond, Joseph C.
Marion—Dept. 1

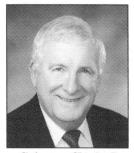

Guinasso, Charles B.
Multnomah—Dept. 1

Harris, Wayne R.
Yamhill

Haslinger, Barbara
Deschutes—Dept. 1

Hernandez, Marco A.
Washington—Dept. 3

Hodges, Bryan T.
Lane—Dept. 4

Holland, Lauren S.
Lane—Dept. 1

Jack, Alan R.
Clackamas—Dept. 3

Kantor, Henry
Multnomah—Dept. 8

Koch, Dale R.
Multnomah—Dept. 4

Kurshner, Paula J.
Multnomah—Dept. 13

Lasswell, William L.
Douglas—Dept. 1

Leggert, Terry A.
Marion—Dept. 2

Lewis, John B.
Washington—Dept. 5

Loy, Michael S.
Multnomah—Dept. 11

Mackay, William J.
Josephine—Dept. 1

Marcus, Michael H.
Multnomah—Dept. 12

Judicial

Maurer, Jean Kerr
Multnomah—Dept. 2

Maurer, Steven L.
Clackamas—Dept. 1

McCormick, John A.
Linn—Dept. 1

Mickelson, Richard K.
Curry

Millikan, Robert C.
Douglas—Dept. 2

Moultrie, Thomas L.
Multnomah—Dept. 7

Murgo, Rudy M.
Umatilla, Morrow—Dept. 1

Nelson, Phillip
Clatsop

O'Neal, Loyd
Josephine—Dept. 2

Ochoa, Joseph V.
Marion—Dept. 4

Orf, Rebecca G.
Jackson—Dept. 2

Perkins, Edward L.
Deschutes—Dept. 2

Pratt, J. Burdette
Malheur—Dept. 1

Price, Steven L.
Washington—Dept. 1

Rambo, Richard B.
Klamath—Dept. 2

Schiveley, Mark
Jackson—Dept. 3

Simpson, Lane W.
Lake—Dept. 1

Smith, Berkeley A.
Columbia

Thompson, Gary S.
Crook, Jefferson

Valentine, Eric W.
Union, Wallowa (P)

Wallace, Jeffrey M.
Umatilla, Morrow—Dept. 2

White, Raymond B.
Jackson—Dept. 1

Wilson, John B.
Marion—Dept. 3

Wittmayer, John
Multnomah—Dept. 14

Judicial

Wogan, Cameron F.
Klamath—Dept. 1

Wyatt, Merri Souther
Multnomah—Dept. 10

District Court Judges by County

Benton
Benton County Courthouse, Corvallis 97330
Dickerson, Henry R. Jr.
Exp. 1-1-01, 541-757-6830

Clackamas
Clackamas County Courthouse,
Oregon City 97045
Darling, Deanne
Dept. 2, Exp. 1-6-03, 503-655-8643
Jack, Alan R.
Dept. 3, Exp. 1-1-01, 503-655-8643
Maurer, Steven L.
Dept. 1, Exp. 1-1-01, 503-655-8643

Clatsop
Clatsop County Courthouse, Astoria 97103
Nelson, Philip L.
Exp. 1-4-99, 503-325-8536 (303)

Columbia
Columbia County Courthouse, St. Helens 97051
Smith, Berkeley A.
Exp. 1-4-99, 503-397-1660 (317)

Coos
Coos County Courthouse, Coquille 97423
Gillespie, Michael J.
Dept. 1, Exp. 1-4-99,
541-396-3121 (261)
Bechtold, Paula M.
Dept. 2, Exp. 1-1-01, PO Box 324,
North Bend 97459, 541-756-2020

Crook
Crook County Courthouse, Prineville 97754
Thompson, Gary S.
Dept. 1, Exp. 1-6-03, 541-447-6541

Curry
Curry County Courthouse, PO Box H,
Gold Beach 97444
Mickelson, Richard K.
Exp. 1-4-99, 541-247-2812

Deschutes
Justice Bldg., Bend 97701
Haslinger, Barbara
Dept. 1, Exp. 1-6-03, 541-388-5300
Perkins, Edward L.
Dept. 2, Exp. 1-4-99, 541-388-5300

Douglas
Justice Bldg., Rm. 201, Roseburg 97470
Lasswell, William L.
Dept. 1, Exp. 1-1-01, 541-440-4397
Millikan, Robert C.
Dept. 2, Exp. 1-6-03, 541-440-4400

Hood River
Hood River County Courthouse,
Hood River 97031
Crowley, Paul G. (P)
Exp. 1-4-99, 503-386-1862

Jackson

Justice Bldg., 100 S Oakdale, Medford 97501

Orf, Rebecca G.
Dept. 2, Exp. 1-6-03,
541-776-7171 (172)

Schiveley, Mark
Dept. 3, Exp. 1-6-03,
541-776-7171 (164)

White, Raymond B.
Dept. 1, Exp. 1-1-01,
541-776-7171 (163)

Jefferson

Jefferson County Courthouse, Madras 97741

Thompson, Gary S.
Dept. 1, Exp. 1-6-03, 541-475-3317

Josephine

Josephine County Courthouse, Grants Pass 97526

Mackay, William J.
Dept. 1, Exp. 1-6-03, 541-476-2309

O'Neal, Loyd
Dept. 2, Exp. 1-1-01, 541-476-2309

Klamath

Klamath County Courthouse, Klamath Falls 97601

Rambo, Richard B.
Dept. 2, Exp. 1-1-01, 541-883-5503 (38)

Wogan, Cameron F.
Dept. 1, Exp. 1-4-99, 541-883-5503 (43)

Lake

Lake County Courthouse, Lakeview 97630

Simpson, Lane W.
Dept. 1, Exp. 1-6-03, 541-947-6051

Lane

Lane County Courthouse, Eugene 97401

Carlson, Cynthia
Dept. 3, Exp. 1-1-01, 541-682-4218

Carp, Ted
Dept. 2, Exp. 1-6-03, 541-682-4497

Henry, Eveleen
Dept. 5, Exp. 1-6-03, 541-682-4300

Hodges, Bryan T.
Dept. 4, Exp. 1-1-01, 541-682-4027

Holland, Lauren S.
Dept. 1, Exp. 1-4-99, 541-682-4415

Lincoln

PO Box 100, Newport 97365

Branford, Thomas O.
Exp. 1-1-01, 541-265-4236 (246)

Linn

PO Box 1749, Albany 97321

Baisinger, Glen D.
Dept. 2, Exp. 1-1-01, 541-967-3844

McCormick, John A.
Dept. 1, Exp. 1-1-01, 541-967-3844

Malheur

251 B Street W, Box 3, Vale 97918

Pratt, J. Burdette
Dept. 1, Exp. 1-6-03, 541-473-5194

Marion

PO Box 12869, Salem 97309-0869

Dickey. Don A.
Dept. 5, Exp. 1-6-03, 503-373-4445

Guimond, Joseph C.
Dept. 1, Exp. 1-6-03, 503-588-5160

Leggert, Terry A.
Dept. 2, Exp. 1-1-01, 503-588-5492

Ochoa, Joseph V.
Dept. 4, Exp. 1-1-01, 503-373-4361

Wilson, John B.
Dept. 3, Exp. 1-4-99, 503-588-5030

Morrow

Morrow County Courthouse, Heppner 97836

Murgo, Rudy M.
Dept. 1, Exp. 1-4-99, 541-278-0341

Wallace, Jeffrey M.
Dept. 2, Exp. 1-4-99, 541-676-5264

Multnomah

Multnomah County Courthouse, Portland 97204

Baker, Dorothy
Dept. 3, Exp. 1-1-01, 503-248-3062

Beckman, Douglas G.
Dept. 5, Exp. 1-1-01, 503-248-3201

Freeman, Clifford
Dept. 6, Exp. 1-6-03, 503-248-3227

Gernant, David
Dept. 9, Exp. 1-1-01, 503-248-3835

Guinasso, Charles B.
Dept. 1, Exp. 1-1-01, 503-248-3540

Kantor, Henry
Dept. 8, Exp. 1-6-03, 503-248-3972

Koch, Dale R.
Dept. 4, Exp. 1-1-01, 503-248-5008

Kurshner, Paula J.
Dept. 13, Exp. 1-1-01, 503-248-5010

Loy, Michael S.
Dept. 11, Exp. 1-6-03, 503-248-3813

Marcus, Michael H.
Dept. 12, Exp. 1-6-03, 503-248-3250

Maurer, Jean Kerr
Dept. 2, Exp. 1-6-03, 503-248-3804

Moultrie, Thomas L.
Dept. 7, Exp. 1-1-01, 503-248-3985

Wittmayer, John
Dept. 14, Exp. 1-6-03, 503-248-3165

Wyatt, Merri Souther
Dept. 10, Exp. 1-1-01, 503-248-3029

Polk

Polk County Courthouse, Dallas 97338

Horner, William
Exp. 1-1-01, 503-623-9266

Tillamook

Tillamook County Courthouse, Tillamook 97141

Roll, Rick W.
Exp. 1-4-99, 503-842-2598

Umatilla

Murgo, Rudy M.
Dept. 1, Exp. 1-4-99, 541-278-0341
PO Box 1307, Pendleton 97801

Wallace, Jeffrey M.
Dept. 2, Exp. 1-4-99, 541-567-5225
PO Box 173, Hermiston 97838

Union

1007 Fourth St., La Grande 97850

Valentine, Eric W. (P)
Exp. 1-6-03, 541-963-9789

Wallowa

Wallowa County Courthouse, Enterprise 97828

Valentine, Eric W. (P)
Exp. 1-6-03, 541-426-4991

Wasco

Wasco County Courthouse, The Dalles 97058

Donnell, James C.
Exp. 1-4-99, 541-296-2209

Washington

Washington County Courthouse, Hillsboro 97124

Campbell, Nancy W.
Dept. 4, Exp. 1-1-01, 503-640-3443

Freerksen, Karl W. Jr.
Dept. 2, Exp. 1-1-01, 503-640-3590

Hernandez, Marco A.
Dept. 3, Exp. 1-6-03, 503-681-3851

Lewis, John B.
Dept. 5, Exp. 1-1-01, 503-693-4403

Price, Steven L.
Dept. 1, Exp. 1-6-03, 503-693-4999

Yamhill

Yamhill County Courthouse, McMinnville 97128

Harris, Wayne R.
Exp. 1-1-01, 503-472-9371

(P) = Presiding Judge

District Judges Association:

President—Rudy Murgo
President Elect—Merri Souther Wyatt
Secretary/Treasurer—Gary Thompson
Delegate—Terry Leggert

Senior Judges

Under Oregon law, a judge who retires from the district court, circuit court, Oregon Tax Court, Court of Appeals or Supreme Court, except a judge retired under the provisions of ORS 1.310, may be designated a senior judge of the state by the Supreme Court, eligible for temporary assignment by the Supreme Court to any state court at or below the level in which he or she last served as a full-time judge. The current roster of senior judges follows:

From Supreme Court—Ralph M. Holman, Berkeley Lent, Hans Linde, Kenneth J. O'Connell, Edwin Peterson, Betty Roberts, Gordon W. Sloan, Richard L. Unis.

From Court of Appeals—Edward Branchfield, John H. Buttler, Robert H. Foley, George M. Joseph, Virgil Langtry, Kurt C. Rossman, Herbert M. Schwab, Robert Y. Thornton, John Warden.

From Circuit Court—Philip T. Abraham, Ted Abram, Edwin E. Allen, John C. Beatty, William A. Beckett, Winston L. Bradshaw, Sid Brockley, Clarke C. Brown, W.F. Brownton, John M. Copenhaver, Charles Crookham, L.A. Cushing, Mercedes F. Deiz, H.W. Devlin, William L. Dickson, Pat Dooley, Jeff Dorroh, Thomas E. Edison, Duane R.

Ertsgaard, Charles H. Foster, James C. Goode, P.K. Hammond, Glen Hieber, William Jackson, Dale Jacobs, Lee Johnson, Donald Kalberer, Harlow F. Lenon, William O. Lewis, James M. Main, James A. Mason, Robert B. McConville, William McLennan, A.R. McMullen, Richard Mengler, L.A. Merryman, Thomas M. Mosgrove, John J. Murchison, Albert R. Musick, Kathleen B. Nachtigal, Clifford Olsen, Hollie M. Pihl, Donald A.W. Piper, Phillip J. Roth, Charles A. Sams, Donald H. Sanders, Douglas R. Spencer, Robert M. Stults, Alfred T. Sulmonetti, Wendell H. Tompkins, Stephen S. Walker, William W. Wells, Darrell J. Williams, Lyle R. Wolff, George J. Woodrich.

From District Court—Frank R. Alderson, Robert H. Anderson, H. William Barlow, Wayne H. Blair, Aaron Brown Jr., Anthony L. Casciato, George F. Cole, Richard J. Courson, Walter W. Foster, Robert L. Gilliland, Robert E. Jones, Winfrid K. Liepe, Robert L. Mills, Charles H. Reeves, Carl G. Stanley, Joseph J. Thalhofer.

Judicial Conference

The Judicial Conference, created under ORS 1.810, is composed of all judges of the Supreme Court, Court of Appeals, Tax Court, circuit courts, district courts and all senior judges certified under ORS 1.300. The chief justice of the Supreme Court is chair of the conference, and the state court administrator acts as executive secretary. The conference is directed to make a continuous survey and study of the organization, jurisdiction, procedure, practice and methods of administration and operation of the various courts within the state.

Under the direction of an executive committee, the conference usually works under a committee structure in such subject areas as judicial administration, judicial education, judicial conduct and special courts.

The Judicial Conference meets yearly to conduct educational seminars, issue committee reports and adopt recommendations. It reports annually to the governor with recommendations for legislation and other matters conference members wish to bring to the attention of the governor or the Legislature.

State Court Administrator

Kingsley W. Click, State Court Admin.
510 Justice Bldg., (mail: Supreme Court Bldg., 1163 State St.) Salem 97310; 503-986-5500; TTY: 503-986-5504; Fax: 503-986-5503

The state court administrator, a statutory position created by the 1971 Legislature, assists the chief justice in exercising administrative authority and supervision over the courts of the state. Among the specific duties are: supervision of the personnel plan for nonjudge staff of the state courts; supervision of the accounting system for the state courts; preparation of the consolidated budget for the state courts and management of that budget; management of the legislative program for the judicial department; maintenance of the inventory of state property in the control of the courts; collection and compilation of statistics relating to the courts in Oregon; establishment and supervision of a statewide automated information system; supervision and management of the indigent defense services program budget; establishment and supervision of education programs for judges and nonjudge staff; continuing evaluation of the administrative methods and activities, records, business and facilities of the courts; development of statewide administrative, personnel, fiscal and records policies and procedures concerning the courts; and preparing and maintaining a continuing long-range plan for the future needs of the courts.

In addition, the state court administrator supervises staff responsible for daily management of the records of all cases on appeal to the Court of Appeals and Supreme Court, publication of the Oregon Reports, Oregon Reports Court of Appeals and the Tax Court opinions, as well as advance sheets for the opinions of all three courts. The administrator also has responsibility for administrative management of the Supreme Court, Court of Appeals, Tax Court, Office of the State Court Administrator and the State Citizen Review Board program.

The state court administrator is secretary to the Oregon Judicial Conference and is responsible for maintaining the roster of attorneys authorized to practice law in Oregon and for coordinating with the Oregon State Bar for admission of new attorneys.

Supreme Court Library

Joe K. Stephens, Law Librarian
Supreme Court Bldg., Salem 97310;
503-986-5640; TTY: 503-986-5561;
Fax: 503-986-5560

The Supreme Court Library traces its history to the organization of the territorial government of Oregon. The Territorial Act of 1848 provided for the establishment of a library "to be kept at the seat of government for the use of the governor, legislative assembly, judges of the Supreme Court, secretary, marshall, and attorney of said territory, and such other persons, and under such regulations, as shall be prescribed by law."

Today, the library's primary mission is to support the research of Oregon's appellate courts, but the library continues to serve other branches of government and state agencies. The library is open to practicing lawyers and to the general public.

The library collection encompasses primary legal material from all U.S. jurisdictions, both historical and current, including statutes and case law from all 50 states and the federal government. The collection also includes secondary material in virtually all areas of law and a large number of legal periodicals.

The library operates under the supervision of the state court administrator.

Related Organizations

Board of Bar Examiners

Marlyce A. Gholston, Admissions Dir.
5200 SW Meadows Rd., PO Box 1689,
Lake Oswego 97035-0889; 503-620-0222;
Fax: 503-684-1366

Jas Adams, chair, Salem, 1997; Thomas W. Sondag, vice-chair, Portland, 1997; Jane Angus, Portland, 1999; Jonathan Alan Bennett, Portland, 1999; William J. Blitz, Eugene, 1999; George A. Cabrera, Monmouth, 1997; Emily S. Cohen, Portland, 1998; Mitchell E. Hornccker, Portland, 1997; Doris R. Jewett, Lake Oswego, 1997; Karla J. Knieps, Klamath Falls, 1998; Richard A. Lee, Portland, 1998; Lynne Morgan, Portland, 1998; Loren D. Podwill, Portland, 1997; D. Michael Wells, Eugene, 1999.

The Board of Bar Examiners acts for the Supreme Court in evaluating an applicant's qualifications to practice law in Oregon. Board activities in determining an applicant's qualifications for admission to the Bar include preparation, grading and evaluation of a bar examination; and investigation and evaluation of the character and fitness of each applicant.

Oregon State Bar

Karen L. Garst, Exec. Dir. (ext. 312)
George A. Riemer, Deputy Dir. and General Counsel (ext. 405)
5200 Meadows Road, PO Box 1689,
Lake Oswego 97035-0889; 503-620-0222;
toll-free: 1-800-452-8260; Fax: 503-684-1366;
Email: kgarst@osbar.org; griemer@osbar.org
Web: www.osbar.org

Jeff J. Carter, president, Salem, 1997; Richard D. Baldwin, Portland, 2000; Joyce E. Cohen (public member), Portland, 2000; Isaac Dixon (public member), Tualatin, 1997; Sidney A. Galton, Portland, 1997; John Paul (Toby) Graff, Portland, 1998; Barrie J. Herbold, Portland, 1997; Mark A. Johnson, Portland, 1999; Edward Jones, Portland, 1998; Kevin T. Lafky, Salem, 1998; Evelyn C. Minor-Lawrence (public member), Beaverton, 1999; David M. Orf, Medford, 2000; Michael V. Phillips, Eugene, 1997; Frances Portillo (public member), Portland, 1998; Lawrence B. Rew, Pendleton, 2000; Kevin K. Strever, Newport, 1998.

The Oregon State Bar was established in 1935 to license and discipline lawyers. The bar organization is a large public corporation with diverse program responsibilities for the benefit of the public, lawyers, government and the courts. The state bar plays a key role in the admission and discipline of lawyers in Oregon. It also operates a lawyer referral service and Tel-law program, conducts continuing legal education programs and publishes a wide variety of legal and public service material, sponsors a legislative program to improve the laws and judicial system of Oregon, provides malpractice coverage for lawyers in private practice and funds and supports numerous law-related and public service programs through Oregon Law Foundation.

The Oregon State Bar is a full-service professional organization having not only regulatory, but significant public service and law improvement responsibilities.

Council on Court Procedures

Maury Holland, Exec. Dir.
University of Oregon School of Law, Eugene 97403; 541-346-3990; Fax: 541-346-1564

The council, established in 1977 by ORS 1.725–1.750, promulgates rules governing pleading, practice and procedure in all civil proceedings in all courts of the state. The rules are submitted to the Legislature and go into effect on January 1 of the following year unless amended, repealed or supplemented by the Legislature. The following is a list of members, term-expiration dates and the statutory appointing authority:

William A. Gaylord, chair, Portland, 1997; Bruce C. Hamlin, vice-chair, Portland, 1999; John H. McMillan, treasurer, Salem, 1999 (public member chosen by the Supreme Court); Robert D. Durham, Salem, 1999 (one justice chosen from the Supreme Court); Mary J. Deits, Salem, 1997 (one judge chosen from the Court of Appeals); David V. Brewer, Eugene, 1999; Sid Brockley, Oregon City, 1997; Stephen L. Gallagher Jr., Portland, 1997; Rodger J. Isaacson, Klamath Falls, 1999; Nely L. Johnson, Portland, 1997; Milo Pope, Canyon City, 1997 (six circuit court judges chosen by the Executive Committee of the Circuit Judges Association); Don A. Dickey, Salem, 1999; Michael H. Marcus, Portland, 1997 (two district court judges chosen by the Executive Committee of the District Judges Association); J. Michael Alexander, Salem, 1997; Patricia Crain, Medford, 1997; Diana L. Craine, Lake Oswego, 1999; John E. Hart, Portland, 1997; Stephen Kanter, Portland, 1999; Rudy R. Lachenmeier, Portland, 1997; David B. Paradis, Medford, 1999; Karsten Hans Rasmussen, Eugene, 1999; Stephen J.R. Shepard, Eugene, 1997; Nancy S. Tauman, Oregon City, 1997 (12 members of the Oregon State Bar, at least two of whom shall be from each of the congressional districts of the state, appointed by the board of governors of the Oregon State Bar).

Commission on Judicial Fitness and Disability

Pamela Knowles, Exec. Dir.
PO Box 9035, Portland 97207; 503-222-4314

Maryalys E. Urey, chair, Baker City, 2001; Edward Alcantar, Grants Pass, 2000; Donald N. Atchison, Bend, 1998; Charles Davis, Portland, 2000; Hon. Barbara Haslinger, Bend, 2001; Hon. Robert P. Jones, Portland, 2000; Richard T. Kropp, Albany, 1999; Hon. Donald Londer, Portland, 2000; Agnes M. Petersen, St. Helens, 2000.

Commission members, serving four-year terms, are three judges appointed by the Supreme Court, three lawyers appointed by the Oregon State Bar and three citizens appointed by the governor subject to Senate confirmation.

The purpose of the commission, operating under ORS 1.410–1.480, is to investigate complaints against judges and to recommend to the Oregon Supreme Court whether disciplinary action is necessary. A judge of any court may be removed or suspended from judicial office or censured by the Supreme Court under the Oregon Constitution, Article VII, section 8.

County Courts

At one time, county courts existed in all 36 Oregon counties. The title "county judge" is retained in some counties as the title of the chair of the board of county commissioners. There is no requirement that county judges be members of the bar.

Where a county judge's judicial function still exists, it is limited to juvenile and probate matters and occupies only a portion of the judge's time, which is primarily devoted to nonjudicial administrative responsibilities as a member of the county board.

Only seven counties, all east of the Cascades, now have county judges who retain any judicial authority: Gilliam, Harney, Sherman and Wheeler (both juvenile and probate jurisdiction); Grant and Malheur (probate only); and Morrow (juvenile only).

Justice Court

Justice court is held by a justice of the peace within the district for which he or she is elected, except in those cities where district courts have been established. The county commissioners have power to establish justice court district boundaries. The justice of the peace is a remnant of territorial days when each precinct of the state was entitled to a justice court. Thirty justice courts currently administer justice in 19 counties.

Justice courts have jurisdiction within their county concurrent with the circuit court in all criminal prosecutions except felony trials. Actions at law in justice courts are conducted using the mode of proceeding and rules of evidence similar to those used in the circuit courts, except where otherwise specifically provided.

Justice courts have jurisdiction over traffic, boating, wildlife, and other violations occurring in their county. Justices of the peace also perform weddings at no charge if performed at their offices during regular business hours.

The justice court has small claims/civil jurisdiction nonexclusive where the money or damages claimed does not exceed $2,500, except in actions involving title to real property, false imprisonment, libel, slander or malicious prosecution.

A justice of the peace must be a citizen of the United States, a resident of Oregon three years, and a resident of the justice court district one year prior to becoming a nonpartisan candidate for election to that office. The names of the Oregon justices of the peace can be found in the Local Government chapter in the section titled "County Government."

Municipal Court

Most incorporated cities in Oregon have a municipal court, as authorized by state law.

Municipal courts have jurisdiction over violations of the city's municipal ordinances and concurrent jurisdiction with district courts over criminal cases occurring within the city limits or on city-owned or controlled property. The usual types of cases adjudicated by municipal courts are criminal misdemeanors, including misdemeanor traffic crimes where the maximum penalty does not exceed a $2,500 fine or one year in jail, or both; other minor traffic infractions; certain minor liquor and drug violations; parking violations; and municipal code violations such as animal and fire violations. Municipal judges can perform weddings within their jurisdiction.

Although municipal courts are not courts of record, the procedures in such courts are controlled to a large extent by state statute and are similar to the procedures in district courts, particularly as to the introduction of evidence and the conduct of jury trials. Some cases can be removed on motion from municipal court to district court if there is a district court in the county. Appeals from municipal court are to the district court if the county has a district court.

Municipal judges are appointed by the city council in most instances except for a few judges who are elected by the city's voters. The qualifications of a municipal judge are determined by the city council or the city charter. A municipal judge need not be an attorney. The names of the municipal judge for each city in Oregon can be found in the Local Government chapter in the section titled "Incorporated Cities and Towns."

Public Defender

Sally L. Avera

603 Chemeketa St. NE, Salem 97310;
503-378-3349

The Public Defender is appointed by the Public Defender Committee, which in turn is appointed by the Supreme Court. Her duty is to represent indigent defendants on appeals to the Court of Appeals and the Supreme Court, which includes direct felony, misdemeanor and parole appeals.

The Public Defender Committee consists of at least five members appointed to four-year terms. Present members are: Robert C. Cannon, 2000; Benjamin Lombard Jr., Ashland, 1996; Shaun McCrea, Eugene, 1997; George Rives, Newberg, 1996; Dr. John Thompson, Portland, 1997; Michael Wise, 2000. The committee was created in 1963 and is authorized by ORS 151.210–151.290.

LEGISLATIVE

Saddle Mountain, near Seaside, is one of the tallest peaks in the northern Coast Range with an elevation of 3,283 feet. Photo by Ray Propst.

O **REGON'S** Legislature convened first in 1860. Since that time, sessions have grown many months longer, the number of bills during a session has multiplied, and issues have become more complicated and more difficult. What has not changed is the willingness of men and women from throughout the state to come to Salem, facing long hours and time away from jobs and family, to debate the issues confronting Oregon. The following pages introduce those individuals and describe the institution of the Oregon Legislature.

Oregon's Legislative Assembly

Source: Legislative Administration
140 State Capitol, Salem 97310; 503-986-1848

Senate President

Brady Adams, Senate President
S-203 State Capitol, Salem 97310; 503-986-1600

The Senate president is elected by the members of the Senate to select committee chairs and membership, preside over its daily sessions and coordinate its administrative operations. Subject to the rules of the Senate, the president refers measures to committees, directs Senate personnel, and mediates questions on internal operation.

The Senate president has a small permanent staff to assist in carrying out responsibilities of the office between sessions. The office helps coordinate Senate operations and provides a variety of public information services. In cooperation with the speaker of the House, the president coordinates and supervises the work product of the legislative branch of Oregon state government and represents that branch in contacts with the executive branch. The president's office works closely with both parties to ensure session goals are met.

Senator Bob Kintigh of Springfield is currently serving as Senate president pro tem, by election of the members.

Secretary of the Senate

Judy Hall, Secretary of the Senate
232 State Capitol, Salem 97310; 503-986-1851

The secretary, an elected officer of the Senate, is responsible for and supervises Senate employees engaged in keeping measures, papers and records of proceedings and actions of the Senate; supervises preparation of the daily agenda, all measures, histories, journals and related publications and is in charge of publication of documents related to the Senate; has custody of all measures and official papers and records of the Senate except when released to authorized persons by signed receipt; serves as parliamentary consultant to the Senate and advises officers of the Senate and the Rules Committee on parliamentary procedure.

During the interim, the secretary receives messages from the governor announcing executive appointments requiring Senate confirmation; prepares the agenda for the convening of the Senate, and supervises publication of the official record of proceedings.

Speaker of the House of Representatives

Lynn Lundquist, Speaker of the House
269 State Capitol, Salem 97310; 503-986-1200

The Speaker of the House of Representatives is elected by House members to preside over the House daily sessions and to administer daily operations. The speaker appoints chairs and members to each committee and refers bills to appropriate committees, subject to the rules of the House.

The House speaker has a small permanent staff to assist in conducting duties of the office. The office coordinates interim operations between the House and Senate and provides information to the public on House operations. The speaker's office coordinates and supervises joint statutory committees and joint interim committees and task forces.

Representative Bill Markham of Riddle is currently serving as House speaker pro tem, by election of the members.

Chief Clerk of the House of Representatives

Ramona Kenady, Chief Clerk
H271 State Capitol, Salem 97310; 503-986-1870

The chief clerk, elected by the members of the House of Representatives, has the following general duties: to supervise the keeping of a correct journal and to be official custodian of all other records of the proceedings of the House; to notify the Senate of all acts of the House and to certify to and transmit all bills, resolutions and papers requiring Senate concurrence immediately upon their passage or adoption; to secure proper authentication of bills that have passed both houses and transmit them to the governor.

Under the Oregon system the chief clerk also prepares the agenda and coordinates the details for the opening organization of the House; acts as parliamentarian as directed by House Rules; supervises and authenticates the revision and printing of the House

Journal at the end of the legislative session; and, at the end of session, prepares for custody of the state archivist all legislative records that are to be permanently filed.

Caucus Offices

Gene Derfler, Senate Majority Leader
S223 State Capitol, Salem 97310; 503-986-1950

Cliff Trow, Senate Democratic Leader
S323 State Capitol, Salem 97310; 503-986-1700

Lynn Snodgrass, House Majority Leader
H295 State Capitol, Salem 97310; 503-986-1400

Peter Courtney, House Democratic Leader
H395 State Capitol, Salem 97310; 503-986-1900

Caucus offices provide many services to their members during both session and interim periods. Each office is directed by a leader chosen by the respective political party. The operations of the four offices are not identical, but typical services include conducting research; writing speeches and press releases and providing other public information services; serving as liaison to state and federal agencies to help solve constituent problems; organizing caucus activities; and circulating information about legislative business among caucus members during both session and interim periods.

Organization

Oregon's Legislative Assembly is composed of two houses—the Senate and House of Representatives. The Senate consists of 30 members elected for four-year terms. Half of the Senate seats are filled every two years. The House consists of 60 representatives elected for two-year terms. Except in cases of persons selected to fill vacancies, legislators are elected in even-numbered years from single-member districts. Election by single-member district means that each Oregonian is represented by one senator and one representative.

To qualify for a seat in the Legislature, one must be 21 years of age, a U.S. citizen and reside in the legislative district for at least one year prior to election.

As the result of an initiative ballot measure passed by Oregon voters in November, 1992, the Constitution was amended to limit terms for the Legislature, statewide offices and congressional offices. Oregon Legislature limits are six years in the House of Representatives, eight years in the Senate, 12 total. The limit is eight years for each statewide elected office. Oregon members of the U.S. Congress are limited to six years in the House of Representatives, 12 in the Senate. There are no limits for judicial offices. Candidacy is barred if new term would exceed limits. Appointment or election to fill a vacancy counts as a full term.

Each house elects a presiding officer to preside over daily sessions, oversee operations and perform other duties set by rule, custom and law. These officers are known as president of the Senate and speaker of the House.

Functions

The primary functions of the Legislature are to enact laws, finance state government and furnish an arena for discussion of public issues. The latter function is frequently performed without enactment of formal legislation.

The Legislature reviews and revises the governor's proposed budget and passes tax laws to provide needed revenue. The Oregon Constitution provides that the state must not spend money in excess of revenue.

The Legislature also influences executive branch decisions. Laws enacted by the Legislature, along with adoption of the budget, establish state policy that directs all state agency activity. The Senate confirms gubernatorial appointments to certain offices. To ensure that legislative intent is followed, the Legislative Counsel Committee reviews administrative rules of state agencies.

Committee Process

During the 1995 regular session, 2,727 measures were introduced in the Legislature. Nearly one-third of these became law. Most of the discussion and revision of bills and other measures is done in committees. The process begins when a measure is introduced and referred to a committee. The committee may hear testimony on the measure, frequently from members of the public, and may amend the measure if necessary and send it to the floor of its house for debate. The committee can also table the measure and end its consideration. Unlike many state legislatures, Oregon does not amend measures during floor debate.

Legislative

Chronology of Legislative Sessions in Oregon

Ses.	Year	Date	Length in Days	Ses.	Year	Date	Length in Days
1	1860	Sept. 10-Oct. 19	40	37	1933	Jan. 9-Mar. 9	60
2	1862	Sept. 8-Oct. 17	40	38	1935	Jan. 14-Mar. 13	59
3	1864	Sept. 12-Oct. 22	41	39	1937	Jan. 11-Mar. 8	57
4	1866	Sept. 10-Oct. 20	41	40	1939	Jan. 9-Mar. 15	66
5	1868	Sept. 14-Oct. 28	44	41	1941	Jan. 13-Mar. 15	62
6	1870	Sept. 12-Oct. 20	39	42	1943	Jan. 11-Mar. 10	59
7	1872	Sept. 9-Oct. 23	45	43	1945	Jan. 8-Mar. 17	69
8	1874	Sept. 14-Oct. 21	38	44	1947	Jan. 13-Apr. 5	83
9	1876	Sept. 11-Oct. 20	40	45	1949	Jan. 10-Apr. 16	100
10	1878	Sept. 9-Oct. 18	40	46	1951	Jan. 8-May 3	116
11	1880	Sept. 13-Oct. 23	41	47	1953	Jan. 12-Apr. 21	100
12	1882	Sept. 11-Oct. 19	39	48	1955	Jan. 10-May 4	115
13	1885	Jan. 12-Feb. 21	40	49	1957	Jan. 14-May 21	128
14	1887	Jan. 10-Feb. 18	39	50	1959	Jan. 12-May 6	115
15	1889	Jan. 14-Feb. 22	39	51	1961	Jan. 9-May 10	124
16	1891	Jan. 12-Feb. 20	39	52	1963	Jan. 14-June 3	143
17	1893	Jan. 9-Feb. 17	39	53	1965	Jan. 11-May 14	127
18	1895	Jan. 14-Feb. 23	40	54	1967	Jan. 11-June 14	157
19	1897	Jan. 11-Mar. 2	*	55	1969	Jan. 13-May 23	131
20	1899	Jan. 9-Feb. 18	40	56	1971	Jan. 11-June 10	151
21	1901	Jan. 14-Mar. 4	50	57	1973	Jan. 8-July 6	180
22	1903	Jan. 12-Feb. 20	39	58	1975	Jan. 13-June 14	153
23	1905	Jan. 9-Feb. 17	40	59	1977	Jan. 10-July 5	177
24	1907	Jan. 14-Feb. 23	41	60	1979	Jan. 8-July 4	178
25	1909	Jan. 11-Feb. 20	41	61	1981	Jan. 13-Aug. 1	202
26	1911	Jan. 9-Feb. 18	41	62	1983	Jan. 10-July 15	187
27	1913	Jan. 13-Mar. 5	51	63	1985	Jan. 14-June 21	159
28	1915	Jan. 11-Feb. 20	41	64	1987	Jan. 12-June 28	168
29	1917	Jan. 8-Feb. 19	43	65	1989	Jan. 9-July 4	177
30	1919	Jan. 13-Feb. 27	46	66	1991	Jan. 14-June 30	168
31	1921	Jan. 10-Feb. 23	45	67	1993	Jan. 11-August 5	207
32	1923	Jan. 8-Feb. 22	46	68	1995	Jan. 9-June 10	153
33	1925	Jan. 12-Feb. 26	46				
34	1927	Jan. 10-Feb. 25	47				
35	1929	Jan. 14-Mar. 5	50				
36	1931	Jan. 12-Mar. 6	54				

The House of Representatives never formally convened as its members failed to reach agreement on organization.

After a measure has been considered by a committee and passed by the house in which it was introduced, it is sent to the other body where a similar procedure is followed.

If the bill is amended in the second house, the house of origin can concur in the amendments. If it does not concur, the presiding officers of each house appoint a conference committee to resolve differences.

If both houses pass a bill in identical form, including any amendments approved by the other chamber, it is enrolled (printed in final form) for the signatures of the presiding officers and governor. The governor may sign the bill, veto it or let it become law without signature. The governor may also veto line items of appropriation bills but may not veto an act referred for a vote of the people or an act initiated by the people.

The Oregon Constitution and state law require that deliberations of the Legislative Assembly and its committees be open to the public. The law also requires that public notice of meetings be given to interested persons and the public. These practices ensure a legislative process open to public scrutiny.

Effective Date of Laws

The effective date of a bill varies. Usually a bill becomes law 90 days after adjournment. If a bill has an emergency clause, it becomes effective as soon as the governor signs it. A bill may also specify the date the law will become effective.

The Oregon Constitution prohibits tax measures from having an emergency clause. This means that the people have the right to refer a tax measure by petition before it goes into effect.

Session Schedule

The Legislature convenes in the State Capitol at Salem the second Monday of each odd-numbered year (January 13, 1997). The constitution does not limit the length of sessions, but recent sessions have lasted approximately six months.

Special sessions may be called by the governor or by a majority of each house to deal with emergencies. Oregon governors have convened special sessions, and Gov. John Kitzhaber called one session in 1995 and one in 1996. The Legislative Assembly has never exercised its power to call itself into special session.

Contacting a Legislator and Obtaining Legislative Information

To reach your legislator or for legislative information, the following numbers are available:

• Outside Salem: 1-800-332-2313 (session only)
• Within Salem: 503-986-1187 (interim and session)

During the interim, individual legislators may be reached by calling the telephone numbers listed on pages 158–160 and 166–170.

Interim Between Sessions

After adjournment of regular sessions, the work of the Legislature continues. Legislators study issues likely to be important during future sessions, become acquainted with new issues, prepare drafts of legislation and exercise legislative oversight.

Convening of the Senate to Act on Executive Appointments

The Senate convenes at the call of the president to act on executive appoint-ments made during legislative interim periods. This procedure was adopted to assist compliance with Article III, section 4 of the Oregon Constitution. A gubernatorial appointment must be confirmed before the appointee can take office.

A statutory Committee on Executive Appointments was created by the Legislature in 1929 to act on gubernatorial appointments to the Board of Higher Education. Subsequent Legislatures added to the governor's authority to appoint but retained the Senate's authority to confirm or deny approval on most appointments. Gubernatorial appointments made during a regular session of the Legislature or at a special session are acted on by the Senate prior to adjournment *sine die.*

History

The present legislative system began when Oregon's Provisional Legislature met formally for the first time in Oregon City December 2-19, 1845. However, an earlier pre-provisional committee met in August of the same year after the formal ratification of Oregon's Organic Articles and Laws of 1843 and the inauguration of George Abernethy as governor. The first provisional Legislature, a unicameral body with autonomous powers, conducted its sessions in a rather casual manner and frequently suspended its rules to take care of unexpected situations. It met annually or more frequently until February 1849, five months before the first Territorial Legislature met, also in Oregon City, July 16-24, 1849.

The Territorial Legislature was bicameral. It had both an upper "council" of nine members and a lower house of 18 members elected from the eight existing county divisions that had regular annual meetings. Unlike the Provisional Legislature, its actions were subject to review in Washington, D.C. At the time of statehood and adoption of the constitution the present bicameral system was adopted. The Legislature then met in the fall of even-numbered years until 1885, when the sessions were moved to the early winter months of odd-numbered years to accommodate farm-oriented members.

Senate Districts

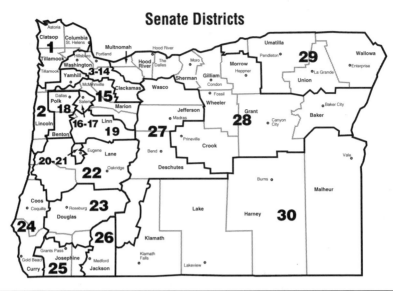

Senate-Representative Districts

Sen.	Rep. Dist.	Sen.	Rep. Dist.	Sen.	Rep. Dist.	Sen.	Rep. Dist.
1	1 and 2	9	16 and 21	17	32 and 33	25	49 and 51
2	4 and 29	10	15 and 19	18	34 and 35	26	50 and 52
3	6 and 7	11	20 and 22	19	36 and 37	27	54 and 55
4	8 and 9	12	25 and 26	20	39 and 40	28	56 and 59
5	3 and 5	13	24 and 27	21	41 and 42	29	57 and 58
6	11 and 12	14	10 and 23	22	43 and 44	30	53 and 60
7	13 and 14	15	28 and 38	23	45 and 46		
8	17 and 18	16	30 and 31	24	47 and 48		

Representative Districts

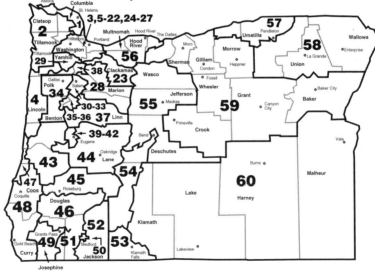

President of the Senate

Brady Adams (R, District 25), 52, is president of Evergreen Federal Savings and Loan in Grants Pass, one of the most successful financial institutions in Oregon. An Oregon native, Adams was elected to the Oregon Senate in 1992. Brady and his wife Pat live in Grants Pass and have two grown children. Adams has served on the Labor and Government Operations Committee, the Rules and Elections Committee, the Revenue and School Finance Committee, and the Oregon Health Plan Committee. A graduate of Portland State University, Adams received a degree in marketing. In 1995, as a freshman lawmaker, Adams was unanimously chosen by his Republican colleagues to serve as Senate Majority Leader, the first Republican to hold that position since 1955. In 1997, following a unanimous vote, Adams was elected President of the Senate.

Baker, Ken
R—Dist. 14

Brown, Kate
D—Dist. 7

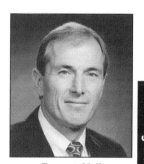

Bryant, Neil
R—Dist. 27

Burdick, Ginny
D—Dist. 6

Castillo, Susan
D—Dist. 20

Derfler, Gene
R—Dist. 16

Legislative

Dukes, Joan
D—Dist. 1

Duncan, Verne
R—Dist. 12

Dwyer, Bill
D—Dist. 21

Ferrioli, Ted
R—Dist. 28

Fisher, Bill
R—Dist. 23

George, Gary
R—Dist. 2

Gordly, Avel
D—Dist. 10

Hamby, Jeannette
R—Dist. 5

Hannon, Lenn
R—Dist. 26

Hartung, Tom
R—Dist. 3

Kintigh, Bob
R—Dist. 22

Leonard, Randy
D—Dist. 9

Lim, John
R—Dist. 11

Miller, Randy
R—Dist. 13

Nelson, David
R—Dist. 29

Qutub, Eileen
R—Dist. 4

Shannon, Marylin
R—Dist. 15

Stull, Shirley
R—Dist. 17

Tarno, Veral
R—Dist. 24

Timms, Eugene
R—Dist. 30

Trow, Cliff
D—Dist. 18

Legislative

Wilde, Thomas
D—Dist. 8

Yih, Mae
D—Dist. 19

State Senators by District

District/Counties	Name/Address/Phone	Occupation/Terms*	Birthplace/Date
1 Clatsop and portions of Tillamook, Columbia and Washington	Joan Dukes (D) S318 State Capitol Salem 97310-1347 503-986-1701	Legislator 1987/1991/1995/ 1997	Tacoma, WA 10/1947
2 Lincoln and portions of Lane, Polk, Tillamook and Yamhill	Gary George (R) 15195 NE Ribbon Ridge Newberg 97132 503-538-4122	Farmer/Small Business Owner 1997	Dos Palos, CA 10/1943
3 Portions of Columbia, Multnomah and Washington	Tom Hartung (R) 13975 NW Burton St. Portland 97229 503-629-8985	Consultant 1971/1979/1995/ 1997 (1967/1969)	Eugene, OR 6/1927
4 Portion of Washington	Eileen Qutub (R) 11135 SW Partridge Lp. Beaverton 97007 503-579-3165	Certified Real Estate Appraiser 1997 (1995)	York, NE 3/1948
5 Portion of Washington	Jeannette Hamby (R) PO Box 519 Hillsboro 97123-0519 648-7185	Small Business Owner/Legislator 1983/1987/1991/ 1995/1997 (1981)	Biwabik, MN 3/1933
6 Portion of Multnomah	Ginny Burdick (D) 4641 SW Dosch Rd. Portland 97201 503-244-1444	Communication Consultant/Legislator 1997	Portland, OR 12/1947
7 Portion of Multnomah	Kate Brown (D) PO Box 82699 Portland 97282 503-777-6274	Attorney/Adjunct Professor, Portland State University 1997 (Appt. 1991/1993/1995)	Spain 6/1960
8 Portion of Multnomah	Thomas Wilde (D) 3826 N Longview Ave. Portland 97227 503-281-5940	Author/Home Remodeler 1997	Minneapolis, MN 2/1956
9 Portion of Multnomah	Randy Leonard (D) 4530 SE 67th Ave. Portland 97206 503-771-8256	Lieutenant, Portland Fire Bureau Appt. 1993/1995/ 1997	Portland, OR 8/1952
10 Portion of Multnomah	Avel Gordly (D) 1915 NE 16th #3 Portland 97212 503-288-0837	Legislator 1997 (Appt. 1991/ 1993/1995)	Portland, OR 2/1947
11 Portion Multnomah	John Lim (R) PO Box 1616 Gresham 97030 503-239-5200	Businessman 1993/1995/1997	Yeoju, South Korea 12/1935
12 Portion of Clackamas	Verne Duncan (R) 16911 SE River Rd. Milwaukie 97267 503-659-8091	Retired Educator Appt. 1997	McMinnville, OR 4/1934

* Senate terms for four years unless appointed; (representative terms for two years).

District/Counties	Name/Address/Phone	Occupation/Terms*	Birthplace/Date
13 Portions of Clackamas and Washington	Randy Miller (R) PO Box 1795 Lake Oswego 97035 503-638-2622	Businessman 1995/1997 (1983/1985/ 1987/1989/1991)	Portland, OR 12/1946
14 Portions of Clackamas and Multnomah	Ken Baker (R) 10121 SE Sunnyside Rd. #120 Clackamas 97015 503-652-2587	Attorney/Small Business Owner 1995/1997 (1993)	Washington, DC 4/1947
15 Portions of Clackamas, Linn, Marion and Yamhill	Marylin Shannon (R) 7955 Portland Rd. NE Brooks 97305 503-463-9624	Homemaker/ Educator Appt. 1995/1997	La Grande, OR 9/1941
16 Portions of Marion and Polk	Gene Derfler (R) 1408 - 34th Ave. NW Salem 97304 503-399-8013	Associate Broker, Coldwell Banker/ Mt. West 1995/1997 (1989/ 1991/1993)	Portland, OR 5/1924
17 Portion of Marion	Shirley Stull (R) PO Box 21358 Keizer 97307-1358 503-393-7001	Real Estate Agent 1995/1997	Los Angeles, CA 10/1949
18 Portions of Benton and Polk	Cliff Trow (D) 1835 NW Juniper Pl. Corvallis 97330 541-752-5395	Professor of History 1975/1979/1983/ 1987/1991/1995/ 1997	Topeka, KN 7/1927
19 Portions of Benton and Linn	Mae Yih (D) 34465 Yih Ln. Albany 97321 541-327-2666	Homemaker/ Legislator 1983/1987/1991/ 1995/1997 (1977/ 1979/1981)	Shanghai, China 5/1928
20 Portion of Lane	Susan Castillo (D) PO Box 5309 Eugene, OR 97405 541-343-1581	Journalist Appt. 1997	Los Angeles, CA 8/1951
21 Portion of Lane	Bill Dwyer (D) 5558 Thurston Rd. Springfield 97478 541-726-0187	Legislator/Consultant Appt. 1991/1993/ 1995/1997 (1987/ 1989/1991)	Philadelphia, PA 6/1934
22 Portions of Lane and Douglas	Bob Kintigh (R) 38865 E Cedar Flat Rd. Springfield 97478 541-726-2519	Forester/Business Owner 1987/1991/1995/ 1997	Irwin, PA 1/1922
23 Portions of Douglas, Jackson and Josephine	Bill Fisher (R) 268 Akin Ln. Roseburg 97470 541-672-1908	Nursing Home Owner/Operator 1997 (1993/1995)	Artesia, CA 3/1936
24 Coos, Curry and portions of Douglas and Lane	Veral Tarno (R) PO Box 657 Coquille 97423 541-396-6965	Retired Sheriff 1997 (1993/1995)	Nashville, AR 4/1937

Legislative

District/Counties	Name/Address/Phone	Occupation/Terms*	Birthplace/Date
25 Portions of Jackson and Josephine	Brady Adams (R) S203 State Capitol Salem 97310-1347 503-986-1600	President, Evergreen Federal 1993/1995/1997	Portland, OR 2/1945
26 Portion of Jackson	Lenn Hannon (R) 240 Scenic Dr. Ashland 97520 541-482-5210	Insurance Agent 1975/1979/1983/ 1987/1991/1995/ 1997	Roseburg, OR 7/1943
27 Deschutes, Jefferson and portions of Klamath and Wasco	Neil Bryant (R) PO Box 1151 Bend 97709-1151 541-382-4331	Attorney 1993/1995/1997	Spokane, WA 7/1948
28 Baker, Crook, Gilliam, Grant, Hood River, Sherman, Wheeler and portions of Clackamas, Morrow, Multnomah and Wasco	Ted Ferrioli (R) 111 Skyline John Day 97845 541-575-2321	Natural Resource Association Director 1997	Spokane, WA 2/1951
29 Umatilla, Union, Wallowa and portion of Morrow	David Nelson (R) 1407 NW Horn Pendleton 97801 541-278-1396	Farmer 1997	Pendleton, OR 8/1941
30 Harney, Lake, Malheur and portion of Klamath	Eugene Timms (R) 1049 N Court Burns 97720 541-573-2744	Businessman Appt. 1982/1985/ 1989/1993/1995/ 1997	Burns, OR 5/1932

Members of the Oregon House of Representatives

Speaker of the House

A native Oregonian, Lynn Lundquist (R, District 59), was nominated to the Speaker's post after only one session in the Legislature. During his freshman term, Lundquist served on the Ways and Means Committee and was chair of a Commerce Subcommittee. Lundquist earned a bachelor's degree in Agricultural Economics from Oregon State University and a master's degree in Economics from the University of Connecticut. The Speaker also served in the U.S. Army in the1950s. Speaker Lundquist has served on the Newberg School Board, Yamhill County Budget Committee, Crook County Planning Commission, Oregon State Board of Agriculture and as president of the Oregon Cattleman's Association. Lynn and his wife Barb have seven children and have taken in several troubled teens. They own and operate a ranch in Powell Butte.

Adams, Ron
R—Dist. 27

Beck, Chris
D—Dist. 12

Beyer, Lee
D—Dist. 42

Beyer, Roger
R—Dist. 28

Bowman, Jo Ann
D—Dist. 19

Brian, Tom
R—Dist. 9

Carpenter, Chuck
R—Dist. 7

Carter, Margaret
D—Dist. 18

Corcoran, Tony
D—Dist. 44

Courtney, Peter
D—Dist. 33

Deckert, Ryan
D—Dist. 8

Devlin, Richard
D—Dist. 24

Edwards, Randall
D—Dist. 15

Eighmey, George
D—Dist. 14

Fahey, Mike
D—Dist. 17

Gardner, Dan
D—Dist. 13

Harper, Steve
R—Dist. 53

Hill, Jim
R—Dist. 5

Jenson, Bob
D—Dist. 57

Johnson, Eldon
R—Dist. 51

Johnston, Bryan
D—Dist. 31

Jones, Denny
R—Dist. 60

Josi, Tim
D—Dist. 2

Kruse, Jeff
R—Dist. 45

Lehman, Mike
D—Dist. 47

Lewis, Leslie
R—Dist. 29

Lokan, Jane
R—Dist. 25

Luke, Dennis
R—Dist. 54

Markham, Bill
R—Dist. 46

Messerle, Ken
R—Dist. 48

Milne, Patti
R—Dist. 38

Minnis, John
R—Dist. 20

Montgomery, Bob
R—Dist. 56

Oakley, Carolyn
R—Dist. 36

Piercy, Kitty
D—Dist. 39

Prozanski, Floyd
D—Dist. 40

Rasmussen, Anitra
D—Dist. 11

Repine, Bob
R—Dist. 49

Roberts, Lonnie
D—Dist. 21

Ross, Barbara
D—Dist. 35

Schrader, Kurt
D—Dist. 23

Shetterly, Lane
R—Dist. 34

Shields, Frank
D—Dist. 16

Simmons, Mark
R—Dist. 58

Snodgrass, Lynn
R—Dist. 10

Sowa, Larry
D—Dist. 26

Starr, Charles
R—Dist. 3

Strobeck, Ken
R—Dist. 6

Sunseri, Ron
R—Dist. 22

Taylor, Jackie
D—Dist. 1

Thompson, Terry
D—Dist. 4

Uherbelau, Judith
D—Dist. 52

VanLeeuwen, Liz
R—Dist. 37

Watt, John
R—Dist. 50

Wells, Larry
R—Dist. 30

Welsh, Jim
R—Dist. 43

Westlund, Ben
R—Dist. 55

Legislative

Whelan, Tom
D—Dist. 32

Wooten, Cynthia
D—Dist. 41

State Representatives by Districts

District/Counties	Name/Address/Phone	Occupation/Terms*	Birthplace/Date
1 Portions of Clatsop and Columbia	Jackie Taylor (D) 1324 Miller Ln. Astoria 97103 503-325-1267	Retired Drug Store Owner Appt. 1996/1997	Thomas, OK 2/1935
2 Portions of Clatsop, Columbia, Tillamook and Washington	Tim Josi (D) 6740 Base Line Rd. Bay City 97107 503-377-4040	Landscape Contractor 1991/1993/1995/ 1997	Tillamook, OR 5/1950
3 Portion of Washington	Charles Starr (R) 8330 SW River Rd. Hillsboro 97123 503-642-2024	General Contractor 1993/1995/1997	Eastland, TX 10/1932
4 Lincoln and portions of Lane, Polk, Tillamook and Yamhill	Terry Thompson (D) 5123 NW Agate Way Newport 97365 541-986-1404	Commercial Fisherman 1995/1997	Newport, OR 12/1945
5 Portion of Washington	Jim Hill (R) 434 NE Lincoln St. Hillsboro 97123 503-648-6664	Mgr., Public Affairs 1997	Portland, OR 8/1964
6 Portion of Washington	Ken Strobeck (R) PO Box 6690 Beaverton 97007 503-203-9588	Public Affairs Dir. 1995/1997	Eugene, OR 12/1951
7 Portions of Columbia, Multnomah and Washington	Chuck Carpenter (R) 3436 NW Ashland Dr. Beaverton 97006 503-645-5789	Analyst International Operations 1995/1997	Rochester, NY 1/1962
8 Portion of Washington	Ryan Deckert (D) PO Box 2247 Beaverton 97075 503-626-0940	Employment Counselor 1997	Corpus Christi, TX 3/1971
9 Portion of Washington	Tom Brian (R) 7630 SW Fir Tigard 97223 503-639-1182	Legislator, Land Use and Business Consultant 1989/1991/1993/ 1995/1997	Newberg, OR 7/1948
10 Portions of Clackamas and Multnomah	Lynn Snodgrass (R) 12995 SE Hacienda Dr. Boring 97009 503-658-4223	Small Business Owner/Homemaker 1995/1997	Salem, OR 6/1951
11 Portion of Multnomah	Anitra Rasmussen (D) 3844 SW Jerald Way Portland 97221 503-223-2374	Computer Software Instructor 1995/1997	Eugene, OR 7/1958
12 Portion of Multnomah	Chris Beck (D) 2083 NE Johnson #10 Portland 97216 503-274-1517	Project Mgr., The Trust for Public Land 1997	Portland, OR 5/1963

* Representative terms for two years unless appointed

District/Counties	Name/Address/Phone	Occupation/Terms*	Birthplace/Date
13 Portion of Multnomah	Dan Gardner (D) PO Box 82342 Portland 97282-0342 503-235-6218	Electrician 1997	Peoria, IL 11/1958
14 Portion of Multnomah	George Eighmey (D) 1423 SE Hawthorne Blvd. Portland 97214 503-231-9970	Attorney 1993/1995/1997	Chicago, IL 5/1941
15 Portion of Multnomah	Randall Edwards (D) 5616 SE Hawthorne Blvd. Portland 97215 503-236-3792	Policy and Communications Specialist 1997	Eugene, OR 8/1961
16 Portion of Multnomah	Frank Shields (D) 10932 SE Salmon St. Portland 97216 503-252-5956	Pastor/Legislator 1993/1995/1997	New Castle, PA 3/1945
17 Portion of Multnomah	Mike Fahey (D) 6809 N Armour St. Portland 97203 503-283-6998	Union Representative 1995/1997	Vanport, OR 10/1946
18 Portion of Multnomah	Margaret Carter (D) 3939 NE MLK Jr. Blvd. #106 Portland 97212 503-282-1585	College Counselor 1985/1987/1989/ 1991/1993/1995/ 1997	Shreveport, LA 12/1935
19 Portion of Multnomah	Jo Ann Bowman (D) 3145 NE 15th Portland 97212 503-284-1887	Staff Asst., Multnomah County Chair 1997	Baltimore, MD 10/1957
20 Portion of Multnomah	John Minnis (R) 23765 NE Holladay Troutdale 97060 503-666-7186	Police Detective Appt. 1985/1987/ 1989/1991/1993/ 1995/1997	Garden City, KS 12/1953
21 Portion of Multnomah	Lonnie Roberts (D) 15815 SE Mill Portland 97233 503-255-9887	Legislator 1981/1983/1985/ 1987/1989/1991/ 1993/1995/1997	Portland, OR 10/1937
22 Portion of Multnomah	Ron Sunseri (R) 4100 SE 26th Place Gresham 97080 503-663-3800	Real Estate Broker 1991/1997	Portland, OR 1/1948
23 Portion of Clackamas	Kurt Schrader (D) 2525 N Baker Dr. Canby 97013 503-266-2432	Veterinarian 1997	Bridgeport, CT 10/1951
24 Portions of Clackamas and Washington	Richard Devlin (D) 10290 SW Anderson Ct. Tualatin 97062 503-692-5240	Legal Investigator 1997	Eugene, OR 9/1952
25 Portion of Clackamas	Jane Lokan (R) 5317 SE El Centro Way Milwaukie 97267 503-654-9691	Small Businesswoman 1995/1997	Quincy, OR 9/1921

District/Counties	Name/Address/Phone	Occupation/Terms*	Birthplace/Date
26 Portion of Clackamas	Larry Sowa (D) PO Box 68720 Milwaukie 97268 503-657-4753	Veterinarian/Small Business Owner/ Farmer 1987/1989/1991/ 1993/1995/1997	Molalla, OR 8/1938
27 Portions of Clackamas and Washington	Ron Adams (R) PO Box 305 Marylhurst 97036 503-636-6194	Dir., Undergraduate Mgmt. Program, Marylhurst College 1993/1995/1997	Palmer, NE 6/1934
28 Portions of Clackamas, Linn and Marion	Roger Beyer (R) 39486 S. Cooper Rd. Molalla 97038 503-829-7421	Tree Farmer 1997	Oregon City, OR 9/1960
29 Portion of Yamhill	Leslie Lewis (R) PO Box 418 Newberg 97132 503-537-0879	Small Business Owner 1995/1997	Medford, OR 2/1954
30 Portion of Marion	Larry Wells (R) 3080 Jeff-Scio Dr. SE Jefferson 97352 541-327-2469	Farmer 1995/1997	Albany, OR 4/1936
31 Portions of Marion and Polk	Bryan Johnston (D) 2218 Treemont Ct. S Salem 97302 503-375-3361	Mediator 1995/1997	Chicago, IL 2/1949
32 Portion of Marion	Tom Whelan (D) 5314 Eastlake Ct. SE Salem 97302 503-364-7344	Firefighter 1997	Portland, OR 6/1948
33 Portion of Marion	Peter Courtney (D) 2925 Island View Dr. N Salem 97303 503-585-7449	Asst. to the Pres., Western Oregon State College 1981/1983/1989/ 1991/1993/1995/ 1997	Philadelphia, PA 6/1943
34 Portions of Benton and Polk	Lane Shetterly (R) PO Box 1025 Dallas 97338 503-623-6695	Attorney 1997	Dallas, OR 10/1955
35 Portion of Benton	Barbara Ross (D) 4175 Morning St. Corvallis 97330 541-752-3605	Human Services Admin. 1995/1997	Kerrville, TX 2/1936
36 Portions of Benton and Linn	Carolyn Oakley (R) 3197 Crest Lp. NW Albany 97321 541-928-7745	Small Business Owner/Legislator 1989/1991/1993/ 1995/1997	Portland, OR 6/1942
37 Portion of Linn	Liz VanLeeuwen (R) 27070 Irish Bend Lp. Halsey 97348 541-369-2544	Legislator/Farmer 1981/1983/1985/ 1987/1989/1991/ 1993/1995/1997	Lakeview, OR 11/1925

District/Counties	Name/Address/Phone	Occupation/Terms*	Birthplace/Date
38 Portions of Marion and Yamhill	Patti Milne (R) PO Box 627 Woodburn 97071 503-982-4156	Real Estate Appraiser 1993/1995/1997	Morristown, NJ 4/1948
39 Portion of Lane	Kitty Piercy (D) 1371 W 4th Ave. Eugene 97402 541-334-6727	Teacher 1995/1997	Tampa, FL 7/1942
40 Portion of Lane	Floyd Prozanski (D) PO Box 11511 Eugene 97440 541-342-2447	Attorney 1995/1997	Lubbock, TX 10/1954
41 Portion of Lane	Cynthia Wooten (D) PO Box 1756 Eugene 97440 541-485-3366	Public Relations/ Marketing 1993/1995/1997	Santa Monica, C 11/1946
42 Portion of Lane	Lee Beyer (D) 1439 Lawnridge Ave. Springfield 97477 541-726-2533	Legislator/Business Advisor Appt. 1991/1993/ 1995/1997	Norfolk, NE 6/1948
43 Portions of Douglas and Lane	Jim Welsh (R) PO Box 458 Elmira 97437 541-935-6503	Sawmill Management 1995/1997	Eugene, OR 10/1948
44 Portion of Lane	Tony Corcoran (D) 34475 Kizer Creek Rd. Cottage Grove 97424 541-942-1213	Union Representative 1995/1997	County Cork, Ireland 5/1949
45 Portion of Douglas	Jeff Kruse (R) 174 Burkhart Rapids Ln. Roseburg 97470 541-673-7201	Farmer/Legislator 1997	Roseburg, OR 9/1951
46 Portions of Douglas, Jackson and Josephine	Bill Markham (R) PO Box 300 Riddle 97469 541-874-2834	Small Business Owner, Timber and Logging 1969/1971/1973/ 1975/1977/1979/ 1981/1983/1985/ 1987/1989/1991/ 1993/1995/1997	Chehalis, WA 10/1922
47 Portions of Coos, Douglas and Lane	Mike Lehman (D) 320 Central Ave Suite 512 Coos Bay 97420 541-888-2150	Attorney 1995/1997	Coos Bay, OR 5/1953
48 Curry and portion of Coos	Ken Messerle (R) 1740 Coos City- Sumner Rd. Coos Bay 97420 541-269-7406	Legislator/Consultant 1997	Coos Bay, OR 5/1940
49 Portion of Josephine	Bob Repine (R) PO Box 1195 Grants Pass 97526 541-476-1081	Small Business Owner 1989/1991/1993/ 1995/1997	Long Beach, CA 10/1948

Legislative

District/Counties	Name/Address/Phone	Occupation/Terms*	Birthplace/Date
50 Portion of Jackson	John Watt (R) PO Box 4661 Medford 97501 541-773-8832	Computer Systems Consultant 1991/1993/1995/ 1997	Lebanon, OR 12/1948
51 Portions of Jackson and Josephine	Eldon Johnson (R) 3650 Ross Lane Central Point 97502 541-773-5463	Small Business Owner 1979/1981/1983/ 1985/1987/1989/ 1991/1993/1995/ 1997	West Point, NE 8/1930
52 Portion of Jackson	Judith Uherbelau (D) 69 Manzanita #2 Ashland 97520 541-488-5008	Attorney 1995/1997	Masury, OH 8/1938
53 Portion of Klamath	Steve Harper (R) 7121 Sierra Place Klamath Falls 97603 541-884-2168	Legislator 1997	Tampa, FL 10/1943
54 Portions of Deschutes and Klamath	Dennis Luke (R) PO Box 9069 Bend 97708 541-389-5877	Builder 1993/1995/1997	Salem, OR 12/1946
55 Jefferson and portions of Deschutes and Wasco	Ben Westlund (R) 20590 Arrowhead Dr. Bend 97701 541-383-4444	Agri-Business 1997	Long Beach, CA 9/1949
56 Hood River and portions of Clackamas, Multnomah and Wasco	Bob Montgomery (R) PO Box 65 Cascade Locks 97014 541-374-8690	Small Businessman/ Llama Rancher 1995/1997	Flat Rock, IL 7/1936
57 Portions of Morrow and Umatilla	Bob Jenson (D) 2126 NW 21st St. Pendleton 97801 541-276-2707	Retired Community College Teacher 1997	Omaha, NE 5/1931
58 Union, Wallowa and portion of Umatilla	Mark Simmons (R) PO Box 572 Elgin 97827 541-437-9060	Spokesman for The Northwest Timber Workers Resource Council/Heavy Equipment Mechanic 1997	Riverside, CA 1/1957
59 Baker, Crook, Gilliam, Grant, Sherman, Wheeler and portions of Morrow and Wasco	Lynn Lundquist (R) PO Box 8 Powell Butte 97753 541-548-1215	Rancher 1995/1997	Portland, OR 11/1934
60 Harney, Lake, Malheur and portion of Klamath	Denny Jones (R) 1461 NW 3rd Ave. Ontario 97914 541-889-8348	Semi-retired Cattle Rancher 1973/1975/1977/ 1979/1981/1983/ 1985/1987/1989/ 1991/1993/1995/ 1997	Ione, OR 9/1910

Statistical Summary Sixty-Eighth Legislative Assembly

Source of Information: Legislative Counsel

Regular Session

Session Length	153 Calendar Days
Convened	Jan. 9, 1995
Adjourned	June 10, 1995
Bills Introduced	2,727
Other Measures	173
Total	2,900
Constitutional Amendments	105

Senate Total Membership	30
Democrats	11
Republicans	19

President: Gordon Smith (R), Pendleton

House Total Membership	60
Democrats	26
Republicans	34

Speaker: Beverly Clarno (R), Bend

Bills	House	Senate	Total
Introduced	1,514	1,213	2,727
Passed	404	457	861
Vetoed	26	25	51
Passed Both Houses	378	432	810
Unsigned by Governor	1	1	2

Resolutions and Memorials			
Introduced	103	70	173
(Constitutional Amendments)	(66)	(39)	(105)
Adopted	24	24	48
(Constitutional Amendments)	(4)	(7)	(11)

Statutory Committees and Interim Offices

Source: Legislative Administration
140-A State Capitol, Salem 97310; 503-986-1848

Legislative Administration Committee

Dave Henderson, Legislative Admin.

The Legislative Administration Committee (LAC) provides services to the Legislative Assembly, its support staff and the public. The committee, authorized by ORS 173.710, is composed of the president of the Senate, the speaker of the House, three senators appointed by the president and four representatives appointed by the speaker. The committee appoints an administrator to serve as its executive officer. The administrator's office coordinates and oversees the oper-

ation of the following administrative units:

Capitol Use Services

Rotunda Area, State Capitol, Salem 97310;
503-986-1388

Capitol Use Services, located on the first floor of the Capitol, provides guided tours and video presentations on the legislative process and Capitol history. The unit also schedules and coordinates various Capitol special events and disseminates a wide range of information to legislators, staff, and the public. It operates the Capitol Gift Shop, which markets Oregon products, crafts and art.

Committee Records

Room 349, State Capitol, Salem 97310;
503-986-1182

Minutes, exhibits and tapes of all legislative committee proceedings from the previous two sessions and interims are filed and stored in Room 349. Records research and general bill information is available.

Employee Services

Room 140, State Capitol, Salem 97310;
503-986-1373

Employee Services processes payroll information for members and staff and provides information about health, dental, life and disability insurance, deferred compensation, flexible spending account, workers' compensation insurance, credit unions, U.S. Savings Bonds, the Public Employes Retirement System (PERS), and electronic deposit for payroll checks.

Facility Services

Room 132, State Capitol, Salem 97310;
503-986-1777

Facility Services is responsible for operational support within the State Capitol building, oversight of security and food service, risk management and historic preservation. Services are provided through two sections: Operations and Maintenance, and Legislative Publications and Distribution Services.

Legislative Publications and Distribution Services

Room 49, State Capitol, Salem 97310;
503-986-1180

In addition to serving as the Legislature's central mail and publication distribution office, Legislative Publications and Distribution Services is the site at which the public may receive copies of legislative measures and publications. This unit is also responsible for coordinating telephone services within the Capitol, distributing supplies and overseeing property management operations.

Special Legislative Sessions in Oregon[1]

Year	Date	Length in Days
1860	Oct. 1-Oct. 2	2
1865	Dec. 5-Dec. 18	14
1885	Nov. 11-Nov. 24	14
1898	Sept. 28-Oct. 15	20
1903	Dec. 21-Dec. 23	3
1909	Mar. 15-Mar. 16	2
1920	Jan. 12-Jan. 17	6
1921	Dec. 19-Dec. 24	6
1933	Jan. 3-Jan. 7	5
1933	Nov. 20-Dec. 9	20
1935	Oct. 21-Nov. 9	20
1957	Oct. 28-Nov. 15	19
1963	Nov. 11-Dec. 2	13[2]
1965	May 21-May 25	5
1967	Oct. 30-Nov. 21	23
1971	Nov. 16-Nov. 22	7
1974	Jan. 24-Feb. 24	14[3]
1975	Sept. 16-Sept. 16	1
1978	Sept. 5-Sept. 9	5
1980	Aug. 4-Aug. 8	5
1981	Oct. 24-Oct. 24	1
1982	Jan. 18-Mar. 1	37
1982	June 14-June 14	1
1982	Sept. 3-Sept. 3	1
1983	Sept. 14-Oct. 4	21
1984	July 30-July 30	1
1990	May 7-May 7	1
1992	July 1-July 3	3
1995	July 28-Aug. 4	8
1996	Feb. 1-Feb. 1	1

[1]Historical records are not consistent on actual dates.

[2]Nine-day recess, Nov. 22 to Dec. 2, due to death of President Kennedy.

[3]Does not include recess from Jan. 24 to Feb. 11.

Operations and Maintenance
Room 60H, State Capitol, Salem 97310; 503-986-1360

Operations and Maintenance provides building services in the areas of custodial, maintenance, key control, heating/cooling plant operations, and coordinates telephone services within the Capitol. In addition, this group is responsible for all major construction projects and capitol improvements within the building.

Financial Services
Room S406, State Capitol, Salem 97310; 503-986-1695

Financial Services provides budgeting, accounting and financial reporting services for the Legislative Assembly, Legislative Administration, and the Commission on Indian Services. Accounting Services are provided for the Legislative Fiscal and Revenue offices.

Information Systems/ Computer and Media Technologies
Room S424, State Capitol, Salem 97310; 503-986-1914

Information Systems/Computer and Media Technologies supports the Legislative Assembly by collecting, processing and distributing information. This unit improves internal and external communications and enhances the decision-making process by promoting awareness of what, how, when and where information is available; simplifying access to all legislative information; providing audio, video, internet, computer, and print technologies to the legislative community; and providing job-related education.

Legislative Library
Room 347, State Capitol, Salem 97310; 503-986-1668

The Legislative Library provides information services to members, staff, government agencies, other legislatures and to the public. The library contains more than 8,000 catalogued documents on legislative issues; 185 periodicals and newspaper subscriptions; measure analyses from recent sessions and interims, as well as legislative calendars, journals and laws from past sessions. These items are available primarily for use by legislators and legislative staff.

The Honorable Representative Tony Federici (1937-1995)

Tony Federici, a long-time resident of St. Helens, was first elected to the District 1 seat in the Oregon House of Representatives in 1992. He won re-election in 1994.

Federici, a Democrat, was best known at the Legislature for his insight and expertise on revenue issues. He was a strong advocate for adequate financing of public schools and a vocal supporter of small business.

Long active in civic, charitable and community affairs, Federici was selected by the St. Helens Chamber of Commerce as Citizen of the Year in 1989. He was a St. Helens Port Commissioner and two-term St. Helens City Council member. Federici also served nine years on the Portland Metropolitan Area Local Government Boundary Commission, including two years as its chair.

Federici was born in St. Helens on March 21, 1937. He served two years in the U.S. Army and graduated from the University of Oregon. He was a junior high school teacher in Salem for two years before moving to St. Helens in 1965 to open Tony's Shoes, which he operated with his wife Nancy until his death. In addition to his wife, he is survived by his son, Nick, of Olympia, Washington; and his daughter, Catherine, of Los Alamos, New Mexico.

Policy and Research Office

Room 453, State Capitol, Salem 97310; 503-986-1813

The Policy and Research Office supports the Legislative Assembly by providing professional services to legislative committees, legislators, legislative offices and staff, government agencies and the public. Staff responsibilities include administration of standing, session and interim committees, research projects, legislative library collection, public notification, measure analysis, and session staff coordination and training. The Policy and Research Office also includes Committee Records and the Legislative Library.

Legislative Counsel Committee

Thomas G. Clifford, Legislative Counsel
S101 State Capitol, Salem 97310; 503-986-1243

The Legislative Counsel Committee is a joint legislative committee authorized under ORS 173.111. The committee consists of the president of the Senate and four other members of the Senate appointed by the president and the speaker of the House of Representatives and five other members of the House appointed by the speaker. The president

and the speaker are authorized to designate an alternate from among their members to exercise his/her powers as a member of the committee.

The committee has a continuing existence and functions whether or not the Legislature is in session. The committee selects, as its full-time executive officer, the legislative counsel who employs a legal and clerical staff.

One of the principal duties of the legislative counsel and legal staff is the drafting of measures for legislators and legislative committees and, when time permits, for state agencies. Research and legal services are provided legislative committees at their request.

The committee reviews state agency rules pursuant to ORS 183.710–183.725.

During each regular legislative session, the committee is responsible for the publication and distribution of the advance sheets of the session laws. The committee staff prepares, for publication in the legislative calendars and journals, indexes and tables pertaining to all measures introduced. Immediately after a legislative session, the staff prepares and publishes a digest of acts passed and, as soon as possible after the session, publishes and distributes the official session laws. The committee, through the legislative counsel and staff, edits, indexes, annotates and publishes Oregon Revised Statutes (ORS).

Law Improvement Committee

Thomas G. Clifford, Exec. Sec.

S101 State Capitol, Salem 97310; 503-986-1243

The Law Improvement Committee, reinstated in 1981 (ORS 173.315), supervises the conduct of a continuous substantive law revision program. Its duties are to examine the law of Oregon and to recommend changes needed to modify or eliminate antiquated and inequitable rules of law and to harmonize the law with present-day conditions.

The Law Improvement Committee consists of the co-chairs of the Legislative Counsel Committee, the chair of the House and Senate Judiciary committees, one person appointed by the dean of each law school, one person from the Oregon State Bar and one person from the Department of Justice.

Asset Forfeiture Oversight Advisory Committee

State Capitol, Salem 97310; 503-986-1243

The Asset Forfeiture Oversight Advisory Committee monitors seizures made under the 1989 asset forfeiture law and the use to which proceeds are put. It is also charged with making recommendations to increase the fairness, effectiveness and efficiency of the act.

Appointments are made by the governor, attorney general, speaker of the House and president of the Senate.

Joint Legislative Audit Committee

Mike Stinson, Deputy Legislative Fiscal Officer

H178 State Capitol, Salem 97310; 503-986-1828

The Joint Legislative Audit Committee was created in 1989 pursuant to ORS 171.580-171.590. The committee reviews financial and compliance audits for the purpose of recommending changes in the agency operations or state financial and other systems. The

The Honorable Senator Bill McCoy (1921-1996)

Senator Bill McCoy was a compassionate and caring advocate for all Oregonians. He was a trailblazer in Oregon's black community and will long be remembered as a strong supporter of families, healthcare and education.

Bill McCoy was elected to the Oregon House of Representatives in 1973, becoming the first African-American to serve in the Oregon Legislature. In 1974, he was appointed to a vacant seat in the State Senate, and by 1996 was the longest-serving member of that body.

While a member of the House, he introduced a resolution ratifying the 14th Amendment to the Constitution of the United States, making former slaves citizens and giving them full civil rights—something other states had done more than a century earlier.

Bill McCoy was born in Indianola, Mississippi and served in the Navy from 1942 until 1946. He moved to Portland and graduated from the University of Portland in 1950. In 1951 he married Gladys Sims, who later served as chair of the Multnomah County Board of Commissioners until her death in 1993.

They had seven children: Krista, William, Paul, Mary, Cecelia, Peter, and Martha.

At the time of his death, McCoy was running for his 13th legislative session, and playing golf—two things he loved.

committee also sets priorities for program evaluations and performance audits and determines the type of audit, evaluation or review to be performed. Once these priorities are set, the committee assigns tasks to the Legislative Fiscal Office; Department of Administrative Services, Fiscal and Policy Analysis Division; and the Secretary of State, Audits Division. The Legislative Fiscal Office provides staff assistance to the committee.

Joint Committee on Information Management and Technology

Mike Stinson, Deputy Legislative Fiscal Officer
H178 State Capitol, Salem 97310; 503-986-1828

The Joint Committee on Information Management and Technology was created to establish statewide information systems goals and policies, to make recommendations regarding established and proposed information resource management programs and information technology acquisitions, and to conduct studies of data processing efficiency and security. The committee consists of seven members: four appointed by the speaker of the House of Representatives and three appointed by the president of the Senate.

Staff services are provided by the Legislative Fiscal Office. Committee meetings generally coincide with the meetings of the Emergency Board. The committee operates pursuant to ORS 171.852–171.855.

Emergency Board

Mike Stinson, Deputy Legislative Fiscal Officer
H178 State Capitol, Salem 97310; 503-986-1828

The Emergency Board, created under ORS 291.324, has 17 members consisting of the president of the Senate, the speaker of the House of Representatives, the co-chairs of the Joint Committee on Ways and Means, six other Senate members and seven other House members. Between sessions, the Emergency Board may allocate to any state agency, out of emergency funds appropriated to the board for that purpose, additional monies beyond the amount appropriated to the agency by the Legislature or monies to carry on an activity required by law for which an appropriation was not made. The board may authorize an agency to expend from funds dedicated or continuously appropriated for the purpose of the agency sums in excess of the amount budgeted for the agency; may approve a budget for a new activity coming into existence at a time that would preclude the submitting of a budget to the Legislature; and may revise the budgets of state agencies to the extent of authorizing transfers between expenditure classifications.

Committee on Executive Appointments

c/o Secretary of the Senate
232 State Capitol, Salem 97310; 503-986-1851

Article III, Section 4 of the Oregon Constitution provides that the Legislative Assembly, in the manner provided by law, may require that all appointments and reappointments to state public office made by the governor shall be subject to confirmation by the Senate. During the interim period between legislative sessions the Executive Appointments Committee, pursuant to ORS 171.565, reviews the governor's appointments and reappointments, which by law are subject to Senate confirmation.

The committee, consisting of nine members appointed by the Senate president, has the duty and responsibility of reviewing the background and qualifications of appointees to ensure statutory requirements are met. Each appointee appears before the committee for a personal interview unless such appearance is waived in accordance with Senate Rules. The committee submits its specific recommendations to the full Senate for its vote on confirmation.

Legislative Fiscal Office

Mike Stinson, Deputy Legislative Fiscal Officer
H178 State Capitol, Salem 97310; 503-986-1828

The Legislative Fiscal Office is a permanent, non-partisan legislative service agency created in 1959 pursuant to ORS 173.410–173.450. The Office provides research, analysis and evaluation of state expenditures, financial affairs, program administration and agency organization for legislators, legislative committees and their staffs. The staff also provides fiscal impact statements on all legislative measures and staff assistance to the Joint Committee on Information Management

Legislative   175 and Technology and the Joint Legislative Audit Committee. The Fiscal Office staff reports to the Joint Ways and Means Committee during the session and to the Emergency Board during the interim.

Commission on Indian Services

Karen Quigley, Exec. Officer

167 State Capitol, Salem 97310; 503-986-1067

The Commission on Indian Services was created in 1975 under ORS 172.100 et seq. and operates as a small agency within the legislative branch of state government.

The commission's specific statutory responsibilities include: (1) compiling information about services for Indians; (2) developing and sponsoring programs to (a) inform Indians of services available to them, and (b) make Indian needs and concerns known to public and private agencies whose activities affect Indians;

(3) encouraging and supporting agencies to expand and improve services for Indians; (4) assessing state services for Indians and recommending necessary improvements; and (5) reporting biennially to the governor and the Legislature on all matters of concern to Indians in Oregon.

Since the commission was created, it has assumed responsibility for coordinating issues of cultural resources protection.

The commission normally consists of 13 members appointed by the legislative leadership to two-year terms of office. Each of Oregon's nine federally-recognized Indian tribal groups are entitled to one member each. There is also a member from the Portland area Indian community and one from the Willamette Valley. One state senator and one state representative are also seated on the commission.

GOVERNMENT FINANCE

Revelers celebrate the Fourth of July with a fireworks display at Seaside. Photo by Ray Propst.

GOVERNMENT finance—the way government is paid for—affects every individual. The impact comes either through the tax bill or through the benefits received from state and local government services or, more frequently, from both directions. The following pages discuss state and local government revenues and the way government money is distributed. Also included is a discussion of Oregon's property tax limitation measure and its impact on revenue collections and Oregon's taxpayers.

State and Local Government Finance

Source: Department of Administrative Services
Office of Economic Analysis, 155 Cottage St. NE, Salem, OR 97310; 503-378-3106.

Overview

Oregon law requires state and local governments to balance their budgets. The following pie charts show the combined revenues collected by state and all local governments.

- The figures in the pie charts are for the 1992-93 fiscal year, the most recent Census Bureau data available. Total revenues for 1992-93 were $16.3 billion.

- Income and property taxes produce 78 percent of all tax and fee revenue. The property tax is an entirely local funding source. Property taxes have declined as a share of total revenue due to Measure 5 (described in the next section) while the income tax share has risen.

- The main federal revenues received by state and local governments are human resource grants (such as Medicaid, welfare and nursing home), education grants, forest land payments (mostly to counties) and transportation grants.

- The bulk of fees charged for service are college tuition, room, board and other charges; patient charges at public hospitals; and sewer, water and electric bills of publicly-owned utilities.

- Much of the interest revenues and costs are tied up in bonding programs. For example, the state collects interest on home loans to veterans and uses it to pay interest on the state bonds issued to finance the program.

Declining role of Property Taxes

Voters approved Measure 5, a property tax limit, in 1990. Measure 5 reduced property tax rates, especially for schools, and shifted primary responsibility for funding schools to the state. Measure 5 rate reductions have reduced property taxes for school operations from $1.6 billion in 1990–91 to $1.0 billion in 1995–96.

In November 1996, voters approved Measure 47 ("the Cut and Cap"), which cuts the 1997-98 tax on each property to its 1994-95 tax or 10 percent less than its 1995-96 tax, whichever is lower. Once set at this base level, future growth in property taxes on an individual basis is capped at 3 percent per year. This measure will accelerate the process of reducing the importance of property taxes as a revenue source for local governments.

Statewide Effect of Measure 47 on Property Taxes

Year	Property taxes (millions of $)
1995-96	$2,248
1996-97	2,486
1997-98	2,220
1998-99	2,354

Source: Legislative Revenue Office, Research Report 3-96.

1992–93 Combined State and Local Government Revenue—$16.3 Billion

Dollar figures in billions

A Federal, $2.7
B Property Taxes, $2.5
C Income Taxes, $2.6
D Other Taxes and Fees, $1.5
E Charges for Service (Ind. Utilities), $2.5
F Interest, $.8
G Insurance Trust Revenue, $2.9
H All Others, $.8

A 17%
B 16%
C 16%
D 9%
E 15%
F 5%
G 17%
H 5%

Source: U.S. Census Bureau, Oregon State and Local Government Finances by Level of Government: 1992-93

Oregon's tax burden, measured by dividing total state-local taxes by total personal income in the state, has fallen significantly over the past five years, as shown in the chart below. The state-local tax burden peaked at 12.8 percent of income in fiscal year 1977-78. It had declined to 12.1 percent by 1990-91. The percent of income paid in state-local taxes in the 1995-96 fiscal year is estimated to be 10.4 percent. Tax bills were temporarily offset that year by payment of surplus kicker refunds. Without the payment of personal and corporate 2 percent surplus kicker refunds the tax burden would have been 10.7 percent in 1995-96.

The primary reason for the state's declining tax burden over the first half of the 1990s is falling property tax revenue caused by the passage of Measure 5 in 1990. Property tax collections fell from $2,550.6 million in 1990-91 fiscal year to $2,248.0 million in 1995-96, a decline of 11.9 percent. Total personal income

rose 41.1 percent during the period. This reduced the property tax burden from 5.2 percent of income in 1990-91 to 3.3 percent in 1995-96 fiscal year.

The passage of Measure 47 will reduce the state's overall tax burden further. Property taxes will rise an estimated 10.6 percent in 1996-97 but following implementation of Measure 47, will fall a projected 10.7 percent in 1997-98 as the "cut" portion of the measure takes effect. This will leave property taxes slightly below their 1995-96 level. Property tax collections will then be limited by a 3 percent annual cap on individual tax bills. Property taxes are estimated to be 2.8 percent of personal income in the 1998-99 fiscal year.

Under current law the overall tax burden for the state in 1998-99 fiscal year is estimated to be 10.1 percent. This would represent the lowest state and local tax burden in Oregon since the 1950s. In 1992-93, only six states had a tax burden lower than 10.1 percent. The

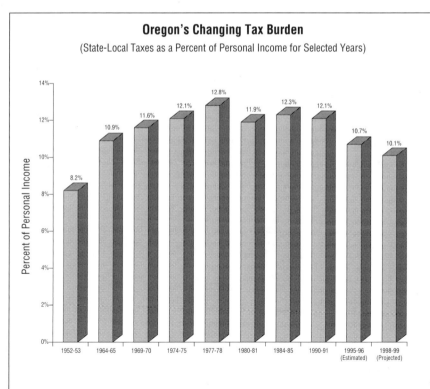

Oregon's Changing Tax Burden

(State-Local Taxes as a Percent of Personal Income for Selected Years)

The 1995-96 figure is adjusted for the temporary effects of the kicker refund paid in December 1995. If the kicker were included, Oregon's tax burden would be 10.4 percent.

Government Finance

tax burden would be even lower in 1997-98 under current law due to projected 2 percent surplus kicker refunds.

State General Fund and Lottery Expenditures

The combined effects of Measure 5, a growing state population, and higher than average increases in the prison and senior populations, as well as health care cost increases, have led to substantial increases in public safety, K-12 and community college, and human resource spending in the past eight years. Most of the increase in the K-12 and community college spending is to help make up for Measure 5's reduction of school property taxes. Increased tax collections have helped offset the increases in spending in these programs, but not enough to prevent reductions in some programs and increases in college tuition at state schools.

The table below shows how General Fund spending was distributed over the past eight years. State aid to local schools has increased to over 47 percent of general fund spending in 1995-97, up from 29 percent prior to Measure 5.

1995-97 General Fund and Lottery Budget

The pie charts at the top of page 181 show the estimated resources and expenditures for the combined General Fund and Lottery for the current biennium. The General Fund comes mainly from state income taxes and other state taxes.

State General Fund Spending (Excludes Lottery)

	1989-91	1991-93	1993-95	1995-97	Percent of 1995-97 Budget
Education					
Local General Aid	1,302	2,096	2,804	3,489	47.3%
Higher Education and Other	875	900	760	634	8.6%
Human Resources	1,202	1,440	1,692	1,873	25.4%
Public Safety and Courts	623	724	766	1,030	14.0%
Other	530	345	331	346	4.7%
Total	**$4,532**	**$5,505**	**$6,353**	**$7,372**	**100.0%**

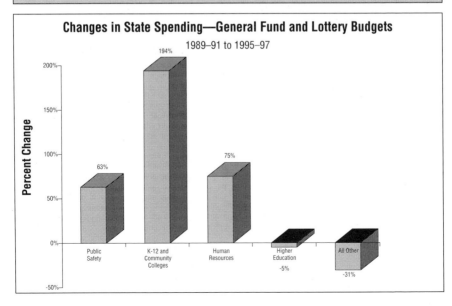

Changes in State Spending—General Fund and Lottery Budgets
1989–91 to 1995–97

1995–97 General Fund and Lottery Resources
$8.6 Billion (Estimated)

Dollar figures in billions

A   Personal Income Taxes, $6.22
B   Lottery, $.73
C   Corporate Income Tax, $.52
D   Beginning Balance, $.5
E   All Other, $.34
F   Cigarette Taxes, $.18
G   Insurance Taxes, $.14

Lottery includes beginning balance

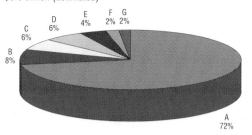

1995–97 General Fund and Lottery Expenditures
$8.1 Billion (Estimated)

Dollar figures in billions

A   K-12 Schools, $3.66
B   Community Colleges, $.33
C   Higher Education, $.53
D   All Other Education, $.14
E   Public Safety (includes judicial), $1.03
F   Human Resources, $1.92
G   All Other, $.43

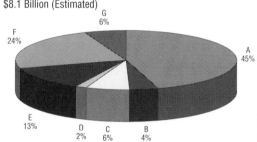

1995–97 All Funds Resources Summary
$50.2 Billion (Estimated)

Dollar figures in billions

A   Beginning Balance (includes Trust Funds such as PERS), $23.46
B   Other Funds, $13.19
C   General Fund, $7.4
D   Federal Funds, $4.33
E   Federal Funds as Other Funds, $1.04
F   Lottery, $.73

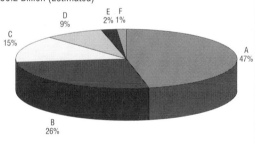

1995–97 All Funds Expenditures
$23.1 Billion (Estimated)

Dollar figures in billions

A   K-12 Schools, $4.11
B   Community Colleges, $.36
C   Higher Education, $2.07
D   All Other Education, $.21
E   Public Safety (includes judicial), $1.76
F   Human Resources, $5.25
G   Economic and Community, $3.90
H   Transportation, $1.65
I   Administration, $2.36
J   All Other, $1.40

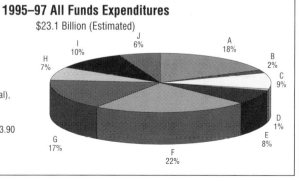

Government Finance

Income taxes account for 78 percent of the resources available in 1995-97. Education spending will account for over 57 percent of the General Fund and Lottery expenditures during 1995-97. Oregon's strong economic growth has provided rising income tax revenue, funding the spending increases without requiring an increase in tax rates. The introduction of video poker in 1992 has led to a significant increase in Lottery revenue.

1995-97 All Funds Resources and Expenditures

The charts at the bottom of page 181 display the resources and expenditures for all funds available to state government in 1995-97. The figures show all funding sources available to the state, including the General Fund, Lottery, federal funds and other funds.

The General Fund and Lottery expenditures accounted for only 32 percent of all expenditures in 1995-97, and is the only part that can be spent wherever it is needed. Federal funds make up 17.5 percent of state expenditures for 1995-97. Most federal funds come with conditions attached, such as requiring the state to maintain certain service levels or provide matching state funds. Other funds provide funding for the remaining 50.5 percent of state expenditures. Expenditures of these funds are typically limited to the purposes for which the funds were raised such as unemployment insurance payments, gas taxes for highways, or maintaining state parks with park user fees.

EDUCATION

Swans glide gracefully on a pond near the Grant County town of Prairie City with the Strawberry Mountains in the background. Photo by Sandi Rennels.

WHEN Oregonians are asked to rate what is important to them, education consistently ranks near the top of the list. From the state's earliest days, Oregonians have worked to create a rich array of programs and institutions for their children. The result has been highly rated local school districts and nationally acknowledged colleges and universities. The following pages discuss the variety of educational opportunities, including primary, secondary, community colleges, and state and private colleges, available in Oregon.

Elementary and Secondary Education in Oregon

Source: Department of Education
255 Capitol St. NE, Salem 97310-0203;
503-378-3569; TDD: 503-378-2892;
Fax: 503-373-7968

Oregon's public school system was created by the Territorial Legislature in 1849. The Oregon Constitution assigns the Legislature primary responsibility for establishing a public school system and provides for an elected state superintendent of public instruction. In 1951, the Legislature established the State Board of Education, which is responsible for setting policy for administering and operating public elementary and secondary schools and community colleges.

The Department of Education serves 220 school districts which educate 561,500 K-12 students and 21 education service districts which offer expertise and specialized resources to school districts. In addition, the department manages the Oregon School for the Blind, Oregon School for the Deaf and education programs for adjudicated youth.

Oregon Educational Act for the 21st Century

Economically and socially, Oregon is becoming more dynamic and complex every day. As students graduate from high school, they enter an increasingly demanding world. Oregon schools are raising their academic standards to help students meet the challenges they will face after high school. Traditional basics—reading, writing and arithmetic —are at the heart of Oregon's education plan, along with new basics—advanced mathematics, science and technology— necessary for college and work in the 21st century.

The Oregon Educational Act for the 21st Century—passed by an overwhelming majority of the Legislature in 1991 and clarified and strengthened through amendment in 1995—signals a concerted effort to improve the performance and accountability of Oregon schools. The law calls for:

- Rigorous academic standards;
- Classroom assignments and tests to measure student progress toward the standards;
- Annual public reports on student achievement of the standards;
- Increased parental involvement in schools; and
- Less state regulation so teachers can help students achieve the standards without government interference.

Thousands of parents and teachers from across Oregon helped draft academic content standards specifying what students should know and be able to do in six areas: English, mathematics,

Students gather outside Waller Hall at Willamette University, established in 1842 as the first collegiate institution in North America west of the Missouri River.

Photo courtesy of Oregon Historical Society. Negative number OrHi 55629.

science, the social sciences (history, civics, geography and economics), the arts and a second language. The standards, adopted by the State Board of Education in September 1996, contain requirements such as "use correct spelling, grammar, punctuation, capitalization and paragraphing" by the end of the fifth grade, "perform numeric and algebraic calculations using paper and pencil, calculators and computer programs" by the end of the tenth grade and demonstrate other learning. Student progress toward the standards will be evaluated at grades three, five, eight, 10 and 12. Students who achieve grade 10 standards will receive a Certificate of Initial Mastery. Students who achieve grade 12 standards will receive a Certificate of Advanced Mastery.

Students in eighth grade in the 1996-97 school year will be in the first class expected to achieve English and mathematics standards by grade 10. A new subject area will be added each year. Students who are in fourth grade in the 1996-97 school year will be in the first class expected to achieve the standards in all six areas. Many school districts in Oregon already are improving what and how they teach and test students to reinforce the academic standards. The Certificates of Initial and Advanced Mastery will certify that students have achieved Oregon's highest educational standards. Armed with these achievements, Oregon students will be ready for the 21st century.

Early Childhood Education

Early childhood education is the foundation of school improvement. If children receive the support they need as they begin school, they will be better able to achieve high academic standards as they continue their education. The Oregon Educational Act for the 21st Century recommends that schools develop kindergarten through grade three programs that:

• Encourage parent participation;

• Apply successful teaching practices and sound educational research;

• Acknowledge children's individual differences such as learning styles and cultural backgrounds;

• Plan children's transitions from pre-kindergarten through grade 3; and

Average Oregon SAT Results Compared Nationally

Verbal

	Oregon	National
1996	523	505
1995	525	504
1994	513	499
1993	518	500
1992	516	500

Mathematics

	Oregon	National
1996	521	508
1995	522	506
1994	515	504
1993	515	503
1992	510	501

For the sixth year in a row, Oregon's Average Scholastic Aptitude Test college entrance exam scores in 1996 were well above the national average.

• Assist families who request such assistance with obtaining health care and other social services.

The Oregon Head Start Pre-kindergarten program, modeled after the federal Head Start program, fosters the healthy development of low-income three- and four-year-olds to enhance their chances for success in school. The greatest challenge for pre-kindergarten is meeting the growing need. In 1995-96, the Oregon and federal Head Start programs together were able to serve just 29 percent of Oregon's 22,522 eligible children. Oregon also funds three "Together for Children" projects—in Bend, Eugene and Medford—encouraging communities to tailor local parent education programs to participating families' needs.

Professional Technical Education

Professional technical education helps secondary and post-secondary students achieve high academic standards and prepare for productive, rewarding careers. By offering students opportunities to explore various worlds of work, professional technical education enables students to gain knowledge and skills they can translate to careers.

Professional technical education:

- Integrates classroom and workplace instruction;
- Equips students with the knowledge and skills they need to move successfully from high school to continuing education and/or careers;
- Creates smooth transitions for students between education and employment;
- Builds partnerships among schools, businesses and industries to provide quality curriculum and instruction for students;
- Offers career preparation options; and
- Supports programs leading to high school Certificates of Initial and Advanced Mastery and college degrees.

The Department of Education works closely with high schools, community colleges, private vocational schools, apprenticeship programs and other programs and organizations to help students gain a high level of knowledge and skills to help them move successfully between education and employment. The department coordinates education and employment training through the federal Job Training Partnership Act, Oregon Department of Corrections, Oregon Department of Human Resources' vocational rehabilitation division and other organizations.

Special Education

More than 62,000 Oregon children and youth with disabilities receive special education or other special services. Most of these students (96.5 percent) attend a regular public school where they receive specialized instruction. Others receive services in a state-operated or state-supported program. The goal for these students is the same as for all students: to receive an education that prepares them for living and working in integrated community settings.

Oregon School for the Deaf
Don Lorenzen, Dir.
999 Locust St. NE, Salem 97303-5254;
503-378-3825 (Voice/TDD); Fax: 503-373-7879

Established in 1890, the Oregon School for the Deaf (OSD) enrolls students who, because of hearing impairment, need a more intense level of service and/or more intense sign language environment than can be provided through their regular public school. OSD is funded by legislative appropriation and is operated by the Oregon Department of Education. In 1996-97, about 120 students were enrolled at the school, at no cost to their families.

Teachers certified to teach the deaf use Total Communication in all instructional settings. Total Communication uses a variety of modes depending on individual student needs. Modes may include: American Sign Language, English-like signing, spoken English or print. The academic curriculum is enhanced by classes in speech, computer literacy, driver education, art and drama. OSD's high school is Oregon's only residential comprehensive secondary program designed exclusively for the deaf.

The school offers an equal opportunity for students to participate and excel. Daily socialization with deaf peers builds confidence. Student government and community activities develop leadership skills. Casco League football, basketball, track and volleyball teams anchor a strong sports program and provide opportunities for interaction with hearing peers.

Students who cannot attend OSD as day students are eligible for residential services. Specially trained counselors give 24-hour guidance, teaching practical self-help, social and leisure-time skills. Older students supervised in dorm apartments assume all household tasks and learn skills required for independent living.

A center of deaf culture for more than 100 years, OSD features successful deaf adult role models on staff and deaf studies coursework.

Oregon School for the Blind
Ann Hicks, Dir.
700 Church St. SE, Salem 97301-3714;
503-378-3820; Fax: 503-373-7537

The Oregon School for the Blind (OSB) provides intensive educational and related services for students who are visually impaired. Its mission is to encourage students to realize their potential as independent persons in accordance with their special needs.

Established in 1873, the school is operated by the Oregon Department of Education and funded by legislative appropriation. Students ages five through 21 who need a more intense level of special education than can be provided locally are served by OSB at no cost to their families. In 1996-97, about 55 students were enrolled at the school.

Academic, vocational, living and independent travel skills training are augmented by adaptive physical education and music classes. Community activities improve socialization skills and provide interaction with disabled peers. Parent counseling, physical and occupational therapy, and health care are provided.

As a statewide resource, the school shares materials and provides consultation and assessment services, including access to the statewide vision clinic on site. On-campus summer workshops extend learning beyond the regular school year. Sessions may include intensive Braille, computer education, living skills, outdoor learning, creative enrichments and work experience.

Juvenile Corrections Education Programs

John Pendergrass, Admin.

Office of Special Education, Oregon Department of Education, 255 Capitol Street NE, Salem 97310-0203; 503-378-3598, ext. 646; Fax: 503-373-7968

The Office of Special Education is responsible for educating youth housed in Oregon Youth Authority correctional facilities. Approximately 1,000 students, ages 12 to 21, are served at MacLaren, Hillcrest and six smaller facilities. Five additional regional facilities and two boot camps are expected to open in 1997.

The education program operates 220 days a year. It emphasizes general education and professional/technical education. Approximately 80 percent of students receive special education services. Art, foreign language, parenthood education, alcohol and drug education, career development and other curricula help students prepare for a successful transition back to Oregon communities.

The Oregon Youth Authority is responsible for security, treatment, recreation, medical, residential and transition services which support a safe, secure environment and provide the opportunity for rehabilitation of youth offenders.

Statewide Interagency Coordinating Council for Early Intervention Services

Jane Mulholland, Asst. Supt.

OSB/OSD and Regional Programs, Office of Special Education, Oregon Department of Education, 255 Capitol Street NE, Salem 97310-0203; 503-378-3598, ext. 642; Fax: 503-373-7968

Diana Allen, Corvallis, 1999; Michael T. Bailey, 1997; Kerry Barnett, Salem; Bonnie Braeutigam, Salem; Clark C. Campbell, Salem; Paula Epp, Sandy, 1996; Jerry Fuller, Salem; Ginger A. Gorham, Umpqua, 1996; Grant Higginson, Portland; Marcie Ingledue, Grants Pass, 1998; Steven B. Johnson, Salem; Bryan Johnston, Salem; April Lackey; Joanna Lucas, Salem, 1998; Melvin G. (Bud) Moore, Portland, 1997; Judith T. Newman, Eugene, 1997; Robert E. Nickel, M.D., Eugene; Katherine A. Palmer, Pendleton, 1998; Joyce M. Peters, Monmouth, 1997; Juanita H. Santana, Wilsonville, 1998; Marian Smith, Salem; Steve Smith, Roseburg, 1998; James D. Toews, Salem.

The Statewide Interagency Coordinating Council for Early Intervention Services was established in 1988. The council now advises the state superintendent of public instruction and the State Board of Education on the needs of preschool children with disabilities, reviews any related administrative rules proposed by the State Board, comments on the distribution of funds for early intervention and early childhood special education, and helps develop and report data and evaluations of these programs.

Oregon began implementing a state-operated program for infants and preschoolers with disabilities in 1992. Early childhood special education services are available to eligible children following all the federal special education regulations. Early intervention services are provided with federal and state funds.

Education Service Districts

In 1993, the Legislature passed Senate Bill 26, placing all of Oregon's school districts in an education service district (ESD). Education service districts provide school districts with expertise and specialized resources that few could provide on their own (ORS 334.005). In recent years, the Legislature merged education service

Students dig for bones, seeds, bugs and other artifacts from about 10,000 years ago at Mammoth Park in Woodburn. The dig was part of a class sponsored by the First Americans Archeological Field class through Oregon State University. Photo by Martha Heyen.

districts. Currently, 21 ESDs provide important links between the Department of Education and local districts.

Local districts participate in deciding what services ESDs will offer, ensuring that the services reflect local needs. Support for special education, instruction, instructional media, cooperative purchasing, graphic arts, printing and data processing are typical needs ESDs serve.

Through their strong relationship with the Department of Education, ESDs coordinate and deliver department information and materials regarding curriculum, assessment, school improvement teams, child-find, data collection and other issues. ESDs coordinate more than $200 million annually in local, state and federal resources to provide important equal educational opportunities to the children of Oregon.

Community Colleges

Source: **Roger J. Bassett, Commissioner**
Office of Community College Services,
255 Capitol St. NE, Salem 97310-1341;
503-378-8648

For the past 35 years, Oregon's community colleges have met a major share of the state's adult education needs. Today, Oregon's 17 community colleges serve more than 335,559 students a year and are an integral part of the postsecondary education system.

The community college student is generally older than the typical four-year college student, with an average age of

37 years. Many of these older students are returning to college to upgrade their job skills, with the goal of keeping current in their chosen field. Many returning students hold baccalaureate or master's degrees.

The Legislature has charged community colleges with three responsibilities:

Transfer education. Thousands of students each year take advantage of the two-year college transfer program that gives them the opportunity to stay home for the first two years of a four-year college education.

Professional technical education and training. Community colleges are responsible for providing technical job-related training to a large portion of Oregon's labor force. Developed in cooperation with local employers, community college programs are state-of-the-art. Students enrolled in a professional technical education program can work toward a one-year certificate or a two-year degree.

Developmental education. Community colleges also provide developmental education programs to help adult learners complete their high school education. Often, after earning a GED certificate or Adult High School Diploma, adults choose to continue their education in vocational or two-year transfer classes to upgrade job skills.

Every community college offers workshops, seminars and classes geared to the non-traditional student. These courses range from personal-interest classes to on-site industry training.

The community college network is a primary delivery system for education programs that are essential to Oregon's economic health. Community colleges serve as the home for Small Business Development Centers (SBDCs), which are linked as a statewide network created in 1983 by the Legislature in cooperation with the U.S. Small Business Administration. SBDCs work with local businesses to foster entrepreneurship, good management skills, economic development, joint venture capital and creation of locally-based jobs.

Community colleges respond regularly to requests from business and industry for specialized training. The college contracts directly with firms, and the training programs take place either on campus or at the business site.

Using community college training programs, companies can save a considerable amount of start-up time by providing training for workers before the business is ready to go into production.

Community colleges work within the State Board of Education, under the direction of the Commissioner of Community Colleges. They are not a part of the State System of Higher Education.

When the Legislature created community colleges in Oregon, it did not establish a series of institutions. Rather, it created a mechanism for residents of a community to form their own colleges through the initiative process.

The Legislature consistently has supported the principle that community colleges should be controlled locally through locally-elected boards. These boards are required by statute to keep in touch with the needs of the people they serve and to assure development of programs to meet those needs.

Blue Mountain Community College
Ronald L. Daniels, Pres.
2410 NW Carden Ave.; PO Box 100, Pendleton 97801-0100; 541-276-1260

1995-96 enrollment: 2,667

Central Oregon Community College
Dr. Robert L. Barber, Pres.
2600 NW College Way, Bend 97701-5998; 541-383-7700

1995-96 enrollment: 2,921

Chemeketa Community College
Dr. Gerard I. Berger, Pres.
4000 Lancaster Dr. NE; PO Box 14007, Salem 97309-7070; 503-399-5000

1995-96 enrollment: 11,023

Clackamas Community College
Dr. John S. Keyser, Pres.
19600 S Molalla Ave., Oregon City 97045-9049; 503-657-6958 ext. 2401

1995-96 enrollment: 6,160

Clatsop Community College
Dr. John Wubben, Pres.
1653 Jerome Ave., Astoria 97103-3698; 503-325-0910

1995-96 enrollment: 1,376

Columbia Gorge Community College
Dr. William E. Bell, Pres.
400 East Scenic Dr., The Dalles 97058-2282; 541-296-6182

1995-96 enrollment: 757

Klamath Community College
Dr. Rod Wright, Interim Pres.
241 Williams Ave., Klamath Falls 97601-2704; 541-882-3521

Opened Fall 1996.

Lane Community College
Dr. Jerry Moskus, Pres.
4000 E 30th Ave., Eugene 97405-0640; 541-747-4501

1995-96 enrollment: 12,147

Linn-Benton Community College
Jon Carnahan, Pres.
6500 SW Pacific Blvd., Albany 97321-3774; 541-917-4999

1995-96 enrollment: 6,042

Mt. Hood Community College
Dr. Joel E. Vela, Pres.
26000 SE Stark St., Gresham 97030-3300; 503-667-6422

1995-96 enrollment: 7,272

Oregon Coast Community College Service District
Dr. Patrick O'Connor, Pres.
332 SW Coast Hwy., Newport 97365-4928; 541-265-2283

1995-96 enrollment: 529

Portland Community College

Dr. Daniel F. Moriarty, Pres.
PO Box 19000, Portland 97280-0990;
503-244-6111

1995-96 enrollment: 18,798

Rogue Community College

Dr. Harvey O. Bennett, Pres.
3345 Redwood Hwy., Grants Pass 97527-9298;
541-471-3500

1995-96 enrollment: 3,630

Southwestern Oregon Community College

Dr. Stephen J. Kridelbaugh, Pres.
1988 Newmark, Coos Bay 97420-2912;
541-888-2525

1995-96 enrollment: 2,596

Tillamook Bay Community College Service District

Jerry Hallberg, Pres.
6385 Tillamook Ave., Bay City 97107-9641;
503-842-8222

1995-96 enrollment: 357

Treasure Valley Community College

Dr. Berton L. Glandon, Pres.
650 College Blvd., Ontario 97914-3498;
541-889-6493

1995-96 enrollment: 1,872

Umpqua Community College

Dr. James Kraby, Pres.
PO Box 967, Roseburg 97470-0226;
541-440-4600

1995-96 enrollment: 3,313

Total 1995-96 enrollment in Oregon Community Colleges was 81,460.

Higher Education in Oregon

Source: Department of Higher Education
PO Box 3175, Eugene 97403; 541-346-5700;
Fax: 541-346-5764

The Oregon State System of Higher Education (OSSHE) consists of seven colleges and universities under the control of the governor-appointed State Board of Higher Education. The chancellor is the system's chief executive officer, with three vice-chancellors having responsibilities for Academic Affairs, Finance and Administration, and Corporate and Public Affairs. The three statewide universities, three regional colleges, and one specialized institution within Oregon's State System of Higher Education include Eastern Oregon State College (La Grande), Oregon Institute of Technology (Klamath Falls), Oregon State University (Corvallis), Portland State University (Portland), Southern Oregon State College (Ashland), University of Oregon (Eugene), and Western Oregon State College (Monmouth). Oregon Health Sciences University (Portland) is an affiliated institution.

In instruction, research and service, public higher education plays a key role in furthering Oregon's economic, intellectual, and cultural growth and diversity. In addition to the institutions' principal mission—instruction—they also perform agricultural, high technology, and other research and service. Strengthening their roles in these areas is the Oregon Center for Advanced Technology Education, which delivers high technology education to Oregon companies and expanding

Enrollment at State System Institutions

Academic year 1995-96 unduplicated headcount enrollment

Eastern Oregon State College	3,896
Oregon Institute of Technology	3,186
Oregon State University	17,588
Portland State University	35,188
Southern Oregon State College	7,565
University of Oregon	22,534
Western Oregon State College	6,348
Total State System enrollment for the year 1995-96	**96,305**

Oregon Health Sciences University, an affiliated institution, had a fall 1995 enrollment of 1,434.

"centers of excellence" in Corvallis, Eugene and Portland.

Each Oregon county has access to public higher education services offered by OSSHE institutions and their 28 affiliated education centers. Total unduplicated headcount for the 1995-96 academic year was 96,305, which includes regular classes and continuing education courses. Non-credit enrollment for the 1995-96 academic year totaled 129,500.

OSSHE manages the wise investment of state dollars through consolidation of services, sharing of resources and innovative uses of technology. The State Board of Higher Education and staff actively seek the advice and support of business, industry, government, K-12 and community college leaders in finding ways to provide cost-effective delivery of services that meet the changing needs of Oregonians.

Funding for OSSHE institutions, excluding capital construction, comes from the following sources: General Fund, 27.5 percent; tuition and fees, 21.7 percent; sales and service fees, 18.4 percent; federal funds, 15.4 percent; donations and grants, 7 percent; lottery, 1.8 percent; and other, 8.2 percent.

State Board of Higher Education

Joseph W. Cox, Chancellor
PO Box 3175, Eugene 97403; 541-346-5700; Fax: 541-346-5764

Herbert Aschkenasy, president, Albany, 1997; Tom Imeson, vice-president, Portland, 1999; Diane Christopher, Medford, 1999; Gail McAllister, Burns, 1999; Esther Puentes, Portland, 2000; Les Swanson Jr., Portland, 1997; April Waddy, Portland, 1997; Jim Whittaker, Pilot Rock, 2000; Jim Willis, Salem, 1997; Phyllis Wustenberg, Bay City, 2000; John Wykoff, Portland, 1998.

The governor appoints the 11 board members, subject to Senate confirmation. Nine members are appointed for four-year terms, and two State-System students are appointed for two-year terms.

The State Board of Higher Education, operating under ORS chapter 351, appoints a chancellor as chief executive officer; establishes system-wide policy; sets institutional guidelines; approves curricular programs; reviews and approves budgets; and manages property and investments.

Western Interstate Commission for Higher Education

Oregon WICHE Commissioners
PO Box 3175, Eugene 97403; 541-346-5729

The Western Interstate Commission for Higher Education (WICHE) is a public interstate agency created in 1953 by governors and legislators of the 13 western states. It was formed to help provide high-quality, cost-effective postsecondary education programs through cooperation and collaboration among the western states and their institutions of higher education.

WICHE has three student exchange programs. The Professional Student Exchange Program (PSEP), the Western Regional Graduate Program (WRGP) and the Western Undergraduate Exchange (WUE). PSEP provides financial assistance to a limited number of students who wish to enroll in selected professional programs not available in the student's home state. WRGP provides students in participating states access to more than 100 selected master's and doctoral programs at resident tuition rates.

WUE enables undergraduates to enroll in designated institutions and programs in other participating states on a space available basis at 150 percent of resident tuition. WICHE also provides research and information services concerning higher education.

WICHE is funded by state dues, supplemented by grants and contracts and governed by 39 commissioners—three appointed by the governor of each state.

Oregon's WICHE membership is authorized by ORS 351.770, and its commissioners are Roger Bassett, Salem; Joseph W. Cox, Eugene; and George E. Richardson Jr., Portland.

Eastern Oregon State College

Dr. David Gilbert, Pres.
1410 "L" Ave., La Grande 97850-2899; 541-962-3512; 1-800-452-8639; Fax: 541-962-3493; Web: www.eosc.osshe.edu

Located 260 miles east of Portland and 174 miles west of Boise, Idaho, on Interstate 84, Eastern Oregon State College (EOSC) is the only four-year college in eastern Oregon. Established in 1929, Eastern is a multipurpose regional college, serving 10 eastern Oregon counties. It offers 21 baccalaureate degrees in the areas of teacher education, liberal arts and sciences, and business; four preprofessional programs; two associate degrees; and a master's in teacher education. The college serves as the central hub of northeast Oregon, attracting students and visitors to a wide variety of fine arts and theatrical performances.

EOSC, in cooperation with Oregon Health Sciences University, offers a nursing degree, and with Oregon State University, degrees in agricultural business management, rangeland resources, crop science and agricultural and resource economics. Eastern offers both a four-year and a fifth-year teacher undergraduate teacher education program. Both are delivered regionally over ED-NET. Through its Division of Extended Programs, Eastern delivers entire degree programs to students in the region, and operates centers in Baker City, Burns, Enterprise, John Day, La Grande, Ontario, Pendleton, Portland, and the Confederated Tribes of the Umatilla Indian Reservation.

Oregon Health Sciences University

Dr. Peter Kohler, Pres.

3181 SW Sam Jackson Park Rd., Portland 97201; 503-494-8311; Fax: 503-494-8935

Oregon Health Sciences University (OHSU) is the state's only academic institution dedicated to the education of health professionals and biomedical researchers. Located atop Portland's Marquam Hill, OHSU includes the schools of dentistry, medicine, and nursing; OHSU Hospital; Doernbecher Children's Hospital; dozens of primary care and specialty clinics; three research institutes; and several outreach and public service units.

OHSU's primary mission is to educate tomorrow's health professionals—dentists, nurses, physicians, allied health professionals, and biomedical scientists. Its three academic units have received the highest accreditation granted nationally.

With more than 8,300 employees, OHSU is Portland's largest employer. It generates about $1.7 billion a year in economic activity for the state. The majority (82 percent) of its $500 million annual budget is derived from clinical activities, and gifts, grants and contracts. OHSU receives 10 percent of its budget from state appropriations.

Oregon Institute of Technology

Dr. Lawrence J. Wolf, Pres.

3201 Campus Dr., Klamath Falls 97601-8801; 541-885-1000; Fax: 541-885-1115; Email: oit@mail.oit.osshe.edu; Web: www.oit.osshe.edu

Oregon Institute of Technology (OIT), which provides a computer-intensive, industry-responsive curricula, is the only accredited public institute of technology in the Pacific Northwest. The institute offers bachelor's degree programs in engineering and health technologies and management, and a Master of Science in Engineering Technology program. In cooperation with Oregon Health Sciences University, OIT also offers a nursing degree. OIT interacts regularly with the industries and businesses that employ its graduates. The college's successful placement rate is based on the uncommon aspects of the institute's program offerings and curricula, including extensive lab instruction, clinical experiences and senior projects.

OIT is the only campus in the nation which is totally heated and cooled geothermally. While the college is based in Klamath Falls, OIT also serves the Portland area, the heart of Oregon's high tech community, through two additional locations, one in Clackamas County and another in Washington County.

At the Portland area locations, OIT offers bachelor's degree completion (upper division classes) in electronics, software and manufacturing engineering technology and industrial management. Accelerated degree completion programs, technical classes, workshops, contract training and certification training are also available. To learn more about OIT, visit the institute's web site at *www.oit.osshe.edu.*

Oregon State University

Dr. Paul G. Risser, Pres.

Corvallis 97331; 541-737-0123; Fax: 541-737-2400; Email: ncs@ccmail.orst.edu; Web: www.orst.edu

Oregon State University (OSU) equips students to excel as working professionals and world citizens by providing a unique blend of academic programs, exemplary scholarly research and an exceptional learning environment within the secure setting of one of the most beautiful campuses in the United States.

As Oregon's oldest state-assisted institution of higher education, founded in 1868, OSU is Oregon's only Carnegie 1 comprehensive research university. The university is internationally respected for teaching, research and public service and is a Land Grant, Sea Grant and Space Grant university.

Students come to OSU from every state in the nation and more than 100 countries to pursue undergraduate and graduate degrees in more than 200 distinct academic programs. With an enrollment of more than 14,000, OSU prepares students to achieve success in agricultural sciences, business, engineering, forestry, health and human performance, home economics and education, liberal arts, oceanography and atmospheric sciences, pharmacy, science, and veterinary medicine.

A distinguished faculty of 2,000 scholars attracts more than $110 million each year in external research grants. OSU faculty are at the forefront of developments in electronic communications, biotechnology, computer and marine science, advanced materials, family studies, human and environmental health.

Research done by OSU's Agricultural Experiment Station and branch stations throughout the state adds practical values for students and society. Through Extended Education, OSU serves citizens in all of Oregon's 36 counties.

In addition, OSU is a leader in international education. The university has agreements, contracts and exchange programs with more than 75 foreign countries.

Unique programs and facilities add to OSU's reputation for academic excellence. Oregon State is the only university in the country with two national centers supported by the National Institute of Environmental Health Sciences. Three on-campus supercomputers—the largest concentration in Oregon—offer unique support for educational and research programs.

Portland State University

Dr. Judith A. Ramaley, Pres.
630 SW Mill St., PO Box 751, Portland 97207-0751; 503-725-3000; toll-free: 1-800-547-8887, ext. 5256; Fax: 503-725-4882; Web: www.pdx.edu

Nearly 15,000 students are enrolled at Portland State University (PSU), including more than 4,200 graduate students. In addition, 25,000 students are served each year through the School of Extended Studies. Academic units include the College of Liberal Arts and Science, and the Schools of Business Administration, Education, Engineering and Applied Science, Fine and Performing

The Electrical and Computer Engineering Building at Oregon State University is one of the largest projects ever developed with funds from the Oregon Lottery. The building was dedicated in 1988. Photo courtesy of Oregon State University.

Arts, Graduate School of Social Work, Urban and Public Affairs and the School of Extended Studies.

Portland State offers 61 bachelor's and 56 master's degrees as well as doctoral degrees in education, electrical and computer engineering, environmental sciences and resources, public administration and policy, social work and social research, systems science, and urban studies and planning. PSU grants one-quarter of the state's graduate degrees annually. In addition to strong academic offerings, PSU students and faculty engage in an array of research activities. In 1995-96, faculty grants and contracts from public and private sources totaled $15.5 million.

As Oregon's only urban university, PSU has an agenda that stresses innovative and collaborative programs that bring together educational institutions, government, public and private agencies and the business community. Service programs include the Center for Black Studies, Center for Science Education, Center for Population Research and Census, Center for Software Quality Research, Center for Urban Studies, Institute on Aging, Institute of Portland Metropolitan Studies, Portland Education Network, Regional Research Institute for Human Services, Speech and Hearing Clinic, and Transportation Studies Center.

PSU is a dynamic university with a national reputation for excellence. In 1996, PSU was recognized by both the W.K. Kellogg Foundation and the Pew Charitable Trust for innovations in undergraduate education.

Portland State University, a national model for the urban university, is the second largest university in the Oregon State System of Higher Education. More than 2 million people live within commuting distance of the PSU campus.

Southern Oregon State College

Stephen J. Reno, Pres.
1250 Siskiyou Blvd., Ashland 97520;
541-552-6111; Fax: 541-552-6329;
Email: admissions@wpo.sosc.osshe.edu
Web: www.sosc.osshe.edu

Southern Oregon State College (SOSC) is distinctive in the State System of Higher Education as Oregon's principal small public institution with a mission of providing a full range of excellent and thorough instruction in the liberal arts and sciences. The campus features small class sizes, teachers who know and work directly with their students, and a faculty and staff fully committed to education in and beyond the classroom.

The college serves students through 21 departments in four schools: Arts and Letters, Business, Sciences, and Social Science and Education. There are 37 baccalaureate degree offerings and selected professional and graduate programs. The Oregon Health Sciences University offers nursing degree programs at Southern.

SOSC and the city of Ashland form a cultural center that has gained national recognition. On- and off-campus music and theater groups, art galleries, the Oregon Shakespeare Festival, and other attractions bring 260,000 visitors a year to the city. SOSC is a designated center of excellence for the fine and performing arts in the Oregon State System. The Schneider Museum of Art on campus serves the southern Oregon and northern California region.

In addition to the 175-acre Ashland campus, the college operates a center in Medford and offers distance learning programs through satellite links and on-site instruction in communities throughout the southern Oregon region.

University of Oregon

David Frohnmayer, Pres.
Eugene 97403; 541-346-1000;
Fax: 541-346-3017

The University of Oregon, the state's largest comprehensive research university, is the center of liberal arts and professional education in Oregon. To serve the needs of its students and the state, the university is divided into a College of Arts and Sciences, with departments in the sciences, social sciences and humanities; a four-year Honors College; and six professional schools and colleges in business, education, architecture and allied arts, journalism and communications, law, and music.

Educating Oregon students and citizens to be informed and effective members of the global community is the top priority of the university. Its success can be measured by its inclusion as the state's sole representative—and one of only 31 public institutions nationally—

Robert Kaplan, Reed College professor of biology, was selected as 1996-97 U.S. Professor of the Year by the Carnegie Foundation for the Advancement of Teaching.

Photo courtesy of Reed College.

in the prestigious Association of American Universities.

The Eugene campus includes 42 major buildings and covers 276 acres; the Oregon Institute of Marine Biology is on the Oregon coast at Charleston; and the Pine Mountain Observatory is in central Oregon near Bend.

Western Oregon State College

Dr. Betty J. Youngblood, Pres.
Monmouth 97361; 503-838-8000;
Fax: 503-838-8474

Western Oregon State College (WOSC) —the oldest college in the Oregon State System of Higher Education—was founded in 1856 by pioneers who crossed the Oregon Trail. Today, it continues as a comprehensive liberal arts college, with more than 4,000 students, who are primarily from Oregon.

As one of four regional colleges in the state, Western is the only small, public institution serving the mid-Willamette Valley and the greater Salem metropolitan area. Western offers 30 bachelor's and three master's degrees through its two schools—the School of Liberal Arts and Sciences, and the School of Education. Western offers a four-year accredited teacher education program.

Western extends its mission beyond the classroom. Teaching Research, which is funded annually by more than $6 million in grants, is known nation-

wide for its role in education research. Western is the only college in the United States to house a Public Service Park. The Park links business and government with the college in a unique arrangement. Current Park members are the Oregon Police Academy and the Oregon Military Academy. Western also serves Polk and Marion counties as a resource center for the arts, athletic and enrichment activities.

Independent Colleges and Universities

Source: Dr. Gary Andeen, Exec. Dir.
Oregon Independent Colleges Association,
7150 SW Hampton St., #101, Portland 97223;
503-639-4541; Fax: 503-639-4851;
Email: andeen@admin.ogi.edu

Oregon's private colleges and universities fulfill an important public purpose by providing higher education to 30 percent of the state's four-year college students.

Early pioneers to the Oregon Territory established Willamette University as the first institution of higher learning west of St. Louis in 1842. Ever since, visionary Oregonians have been creating academic centers supported by families, voluntary contributions and community initiative rather than by taxes or government funding.

The diversity of Oregon's people is reflected in the diversity of these institutions, providing undergraduate liberal arts and sciences curricula, specialized two- and four-year professional and technical training, and a wide range of graduate studies.

Enrolling more than 25,000 students and employing some 5,500 tax-paying Oregonians, these institutions add a combined annual budget of more than $400 million to the state's economy. They keep thousands of Oregonians from leaving the state for specialized college experiences elsewhere, and also attract an additional 10,000 out-of-state students, making Oregon a net importer of high-quality college students.

Educating this number of additional students at our public colleges and universities would require at least $250 million more in state tax dollars per biennium. State taxpayers invest over 30 times more funds per year on an average public college student (in tuition subsidies) than they do on an average independent college student (in state student aid).

The Dividends of Independent Higher Education

Oregon's independent higher education institutions produced more than 6,000 graduates in the 1995-96 school year. This represented 30 percent of all bachelor's degrees awarded in the state, 32 percent of all master's degrees, and 65 percent of all first professional degrees.

Oregon's independent institutions:

- Convert $30-40 million of gifts per year from private capital to the public purpose of educating students.

- Attract more than $20 million per year from government contracts for research.

- Teach most classes with experienced professors, not graduate students.

- Sustain a four-year graduation rate more than twice that of public four-year institutions, saving families money in tuition and fees and giving students a head start on a career.

- Offer talented volunteer faculty and students to enrich our communities in government, schools, businesses, social services, religion, and the arts.

Affording a Private College

Independent colleges and universities generally believe the primary responsibility for funding one's higher education belongs to the student and his or her family, assisted as necessary with outside support from public and private aid.

Tuition, however, never covers all the costs of educating a student. Other support includes equipment and facilities purchased or donated by others over many years, as well as teachers supported by endowments, and field experiences donated by businesses, schools and health agencies.

Most students at independent colleges depend on a wide array of direct financial assistance to meet their tuition and other costs. Among the sources of this aid are the colleges themselves, private donors, community scholarship funds, churches, foundations, corporations, and state and federal financial aid programs.

Three-quarters of all students at Oregon's independent colleges and universities receive financial assistance totaling nearly $200 million per year. All students who desire the distinctive opportunities provided at an independent college or university are encouraged to apply to the colleges of their choice and to request financial aid at the same time. Many students accepted by a private college are surprised to find that the direct cost to them and their families is about the same as that expected at a government-owned institution.

Bassist College*
Gary Smith, Pres.
2000 SW 5th Ave., Portland 97205; 503-228-6528

Fall 1995 enrollment: 103

Cascade College
Dennis Lynn, Pres.
9101 E Burnside St., Portland 97216; 503-255-7060

Fall 1995 enrollment: 234

Concordia University*
Charles Schlimpert, Pres.
2811 NE Holman, Portland 97211; 503-288-9371

Fall 1995 enrollment: 976

Dove Bible Institute
John Dungey, Admin.
845 Alder Creek Dr., Medford 97504;
541-776-9942
Fall 1995 enrollment: 50

Eugene Bible College
Robert Whitlow, Pres.
2155 Bailey Hill Rd., Eugene 97405;
541-485-1780
Fall 1995 enrollment: 261

George Fox University*
Edward Stevens, Pres.
414 N Meridian, Newberg, 97132; 503-538-8383
Fall 1995 enrollment:1,712

ITT Technical Institute
James Horner, Dir.
6035 NE 78th Crt., Portland 97218;
503-255-6135
Fall 1995 enrollment: 588

Lewis and Clark College*
Michael Mooney, Pres.
0615 SW Palatine Hill Rd., Portland 97219;
503-768-7000
Fall 1995 enrollment: 3,188

Linfield College*
Vivian Bull, Pres.
900 SE Baker St., McMinnville 97128;
503-434-2200
Fall 1995 enrollment: 2,814

Marylhurst College*
Nancy Wilgenbusch, Pres.
PO Box 261, Marylhurst 97036; 503-636-8141
Fall 1995 enrollment: 1,286

Mount Angel Seminary*
Patrick Brennan, Pres.
St. Benedict 97373; 503-845-3951
Fall 1995 enrollment: 156

Multnomah Bible College
Joseph Aldrich, Pres.
8435 NE Glisan St., Portland 97220;
503-255-0332
Fall 1995 enrollment: 730

National College of Naturopathic Medicine
Clyde Jensen, Pres.
11231 SE Market St., Portland 97216;
503-255-4860
Fall 1995 enrollment: 250

Northwest Christian College*
James Womack, Pres.
828 11th Ave. E, Eugene 97401; 541-343-1641
Fall 1995 enrollment: 408

Oregon College of Arts and Crafts
Joseph Wedding, Pres.
8245 SW Barnes Rd., Portland 97225;
503-297-5544
Fall 1995 enrollment: 510

Oregon College of Oriental Medicine
Elizabeth Goldblatt, Pres.
10525 SE Cherry Blossom Dr., Portland 97216;
503-253-3443
Fall 1995 enrollment: 145

Oregon Graduate Institute*
Paul Bragdon, Pres.
PO Box 91000, Portland 97291-1000;
503-690-1121
Fall 1995 enrollment: 530

Pacific Northwest College of Art*
Sally Lawrence, Pres.
1219 SW Park Ave., Portland 97205;
503-226-4391
Fall 1995 enrollment: 257

Pacific University*
Faith Gabelnick, Pres.
20443 College Way, Forest Grove 97116;
503-357-6151
Fall 1995 enrollment: 1,850

Pioneer Pacific College
Raymond Gauthier, Pres.
25195 SW Parkway Ave., Wilsonville 97070;
503-682-3903
Fall 1995 enrollment: 159

Process Work Center of Portland
Joseph Goodbread, CEO
733 NW Everett, Portland 97209; 503-223-8188
Fall 1995 enrollment: 250

Reed College*
Steven Koblik, Pres.
3203 SE Woodstock Blvd., Portland 97202;
503-771-1112
Fall 1995 enrollment: 1,290

Salem Bible College
Charles E. Self, Pres.
4500 Lancaster Dr. NE, Salem 97305;
503-304-0092
Fall 1995 enrollment: 11

University of Portland*

David Tyson, Pres.

5000 N Willamette Blvd., Portland 97203; 503-283-7911

Fall 1995 enrollment: 2,630

Walla Walla College School of Nursing*

Lucy Krull, Dean

10355 SE Market, Portland 97216; 503-251-6115

Fall 1995 enrollment: 101

Warner Pacific College*

Jay Barber Jr., Pres.

2219 SE 68th Ave., Portland 97215; 503-775-4366

Fall 1995 enrollment: 670

Western Baptist College*

David Miller, Pres.

5000 Deer Park Dr. SE, Salem 97301; 503-581-8600

Fall 1995 enrollment: 694

Western Business College

Randy Rogers, Exec. Dir.

425 SW Washington, Portland 97204; 503-222-3225

Fall 1995 enrollment: 125

Western Seminary*

Ronald Hawkins, Pres.
5511 SE Hawthorne Blvd., Portland 97215; 503-233-8561

Fall 1995 enrollment: 469

Western States Chiropractic College*

William Dallas, Pres.
2900 NE 132nd Ave., Portland 97230; 503-256-3180

Fall 1995 enrollment: 458

Willamette University*

Jerry Hudson, Pres.
900 State St., Salem 97301; 503-370-6300

Fall 1995 enrollment: 2,568

Total fall 1995 enrollment: 25,473

*Independent colleges accredited by Northwest Association of Schools and Colleges.

ARTS AND SCIENCES

A little girl reaches out to touch Keiko, the orca whale who touched the hearts of thousands of Americans when he was moved to the Oregon Coast Aquarium in January 1996 for rehabilitation. Photo by Jean Moule.

OREGON communities share an appreciation for arts, culture and the state's remarkable history. People throughout the state also have a common commitment to expand our knowledge and understanding of the physical world—and the universe around us. Oregon benefits from an abundance of resources that encourage and promote education and involvement with these important elements of our society. The following pages describe some of the opportunities available to Oregonians and visitors in the area of arts, culture and the sciences.

Culture and the Arts

Source: Christine D'Arcy, Exec. Dir.
*Oregon Arts Commission, 775 Summer St. NE,
Salem 97310; 503-986-0082;
Web: www.das.state.or.us/OAC*

Oregon's tremendous natural beauty is balanced by its citizens' participation in the arts and the value they place on arts, cultural and educational assets. Throughout the state, individuals, organizations and local communities collaborate to promote cultural activities for residents and visitors.

From Ashland to Astoria, from the Wallowa Valley Arts Council to the Coos Art Museum, Oregonians have ensured that the arts receive attention in their communities. Oregon's annual Governor's Arts Awards recognize the special contributions to the arts made by individuals and others each year.

The Oregon Arts Commission oversees a network of regional and local arts councils, non-profit arts groups as well as arts education programs and services. Providing grant support, technical assistance and information, the commission works to see that access to the arts exists across Oregon. Through regional partnerships it provides local arts programs and services. The commission's Arts Education program links Oregon youth to the arts through residencies with professional artists and training for teachers. The Arts Builds Communities initiative supports community cultural collaborations with funding and resource team training. Oregon's growing population of individual artists, writers and performers are assisted through its Fellowship program.

Oregonians recognize that maintaining their quality of life goes beyond protection of the natural environment. The Legislature passed one of the first laws providing that 1 percent of funding for all new and remodeled state buildings will be used to purchase or commission works of art. Communities in Multnomah and Lane Counties have also established art in public places programs, resulting in the integration of artwork in the designs for light rail, airports, streets and other public spaces.

Oregon's arts and cultural industry has economic value. The non-profit industry alone employs more than 28,000 people and generates $64 million annually. With indirect spending included, the arts contribute more than $250 million to the state's economy, and play an even more significant role in regional economic development areas such as tourism, graphic and product design, and other creative fields.

Oregon's Largest Arts Organizations

Oregon Shakespeare Festival

Libby Appel, Artistic Dir.
Paul Nicholson, Exec. Dir.
PO Box 158, Ashland 97520; 541-482-2111

The Oregon Shakespeare Festival is one of the largest non-profit theaters in the U.S. Established in 1935, it has an annual attendance of more than 340,000. It presents 11 plays in repertory from mid-February through October

The Prairie Dog Music Company sings songs of the pioneer experiences on the Oregon Trail.

Photo courtesy of the National Historic Oregon Trail Interpretive Center in Baker City.

on its three stages. The festival also offers backstage tours, classes, lectures, concerts, play readings and the Exhibit Center, a museum of festival history.

Oregon Symphony Association
Don Roth, Pres.
711 SW Alder, Portland 97205; 503-228-1353

With James DePreist, music director, the association is a major professional orchestra performing an extensive and varied menu of musical services to an equally varied audience. Performances include the classical concert series, pops concerts, youth and educational concerts, family concerts and special performances, as well as touring concerts throughout the state.

Portland Art Museum
John E. Buchanan Jr., Exec. Dir.
1219 SW Park Ave., Portland 97205; 503-226-2811

The Portland Art Museum, founded in 1892, is the region's oldest and largest visual and media arts center, and one of the state's greatest cultural assets. The museum's treasures span 35 centuries of international art.

The museum's strengths include: the renowned Rasmussen Collection of Northwest Coast Native American art; Chinese tomb figures and archaic bronzes; Japanese ukiyo-e prints and paintings; 22,000 prints, photographs and drawings housed in the Gilkey Center for Graphic Arts; European and American paintings and sculpture; and regional contemporary art.

The museum's Northwest Film Center presents films five nights a week and is widely acclaimed for its classes and the annual Portland International Film Festival. The Museum's Eye on Art school tours for children bring more than 30,000 students to the museum annually.

Portland Opera
Robert Bailey, Gen. Dir.
1516 SW Alder, Portland 97205; 503-241-1407

International casts perform with the Portland Opera Orchestra and Chorus in a five-production season of grand opera and musical theater. Foreign language operas are easily understandable through the company's projected English translations. The company's Education and Outreach programs continue year-round, including in-school programs, student dress rehearsals, pre-performance lectures, and costume shop and backstage tours. The Resident Artists of Portland Opera tour communities throughout the state.

Portland Opera recently joined forces with Jujamcyn Theaters to establish Portland's Broadway Theater Season, through which Oregon will enjoy the very best of nationally touring Broadway productions.

Local and Regional Arts Agencies in Oregon

Baker City
Crossroads Art Center
Betty Peacock, PO Box 854, Baker City 97814-0854; 541-523-6750

Beaverton
Beaverton Arts Commission
Jayne Scott, PO Box 4755, Beaverton City Hall, Beaverton 97076-4755; 503-526-2288

Bend
Central Oregon Arts Association
Cate O'Hagan Windus, 875 NW Brooks St., Bend 97701; 541-317-9324

Regional Arts Council of Central Oregon
Ira Allen, 63085 N Hwy. 97 #103, Bend 97701-5754; 541-382-5055

Brookings
Brookings Area Arts Council
Finch Hoffer, PO Box 1737, Brookings 97415-0056; 541-469-9023

Curry County Regional Arts Council
Blanch Lombard, PO Box 1737, Brookings 97415-0056; 541-469-7460

Burns
Harney County Arts and Crafts
Willie Schumacher, PO Box 602, Burns 97720-0602; 541-573-6321

Cannon Beach
Cannon Beach Arts Association
Jim Kingwell, PO Box 684, 1064 S Hemlock, Cannon Beach 97110-0684; 503-436-2359

Oregon Coast Performing Arts Society
Miriam Webber, PO Box 546, Cannon Beach 97110-0546; 503-436-1580

Clatskanie

Clatskanie Arts Commission
Lee McDonald, PO Box 1110,
Clatskanie 97016-1110; 503-728-4497

Condon

Greater Condon Arts Association
Boyd Harris, PO Box 165, Condon 97823-0033;
541-384-4497

Coos Bay

South Coast Arts and Humanities
Lionel Youst, HC 52, Box 584,
Coos Bay 97420-9541; 541-267-3762

Coquille

Coquille Performing Arts Council
Rochelle Wiese, PO Box 53, Coquille 97423-0053;
541-396-5131; Fax: 541-396-2113

Coquille Valley Art Association
Patricia Weaver, HC 83 Box 625,
Coquille 97423-9737; 541-396-3354

Cornelius

Centro Cultural
Sabino Sardineta, PO Box 708, 1110 N Adair,
Cornelius 97113-9015; 503-357-0326

Corvallis

Corvallis Arts Guild
Bonnie Hall, 4090 NW Dale Dr.,
Corvallis 97333; 541-752-7967

Elgin

Elgin Arts Council
Janet Scoubes, PO Box 283, Elgin 97827-0283;
541-437-0842

Enterprise

Wallowa Valley Arts Council
Shelley Curtis, PO Box 306,
Enterprise 97828-0306; 541-432-7171

Florence

Florence Arts and Crafts Association
Sharon Roesch, PO Box 305,
Florence 97439-0011; 541-997-2789

Florence Performing Arts
Beverly Moore, PO Box 3287,
Florence 97439-0179; 541-997-9115

Forest Grove

Valley Art Association
Doreen Masterson, PO Box 333, 3138 22nd Ave.,
Forest Grove 97116-0333; 503-357-3703

Gearhart

Trails End Art Association and Gallery
Charlotte Mast, 656 Ave "A", Gearhart 97138;
503-368-5330

Gladstone

Gladstone Art Guild
Norma Schneider, 6968 SE Oakridge Dr.,
Gladstone 97027-1314; 503-654-1398

Gold Beach

Central Curry Council for the Arts and Humanities
Cathy Thornsberry, PO Box 374,
Gold Beach 97444-0374; 541-247-6467

Grants Pass

Grants Pass Museum of Art
Hatje Joswick, Riverside Park, PO Box 966,
Grants Pass 97526-0081; 541-479-3290

Gresham

Gresham Art Committee
Connie Otto, 1333 NW Eastman Pkwy.,
Gresham 97030-3813; 503-669-2537

Halfway

Cornucopia Arts Council
Penny Sabin, PO Box 824, Halfway 97834-0824;
541-742-6315

Harbor

Pelican Bay Arts Association
Margaret Nelson, PO Box 2568,
Harbor 97415-0319; 541-469-9378

Hermiston

Desert Arts Council
Linda Gillease, Blue Mountain Community
College, 980 SE Columbia Dr.,
Hermiston 97838-9422; 541-567-1800

Hillsboro

Hillsboro Community Arts
Susan Addy, Hillsboro Parks and Recreation,
626 SE 9th Ave., Hillsboro 97123-1026;
503-681-6420

Hood River

Columbia Gorge Regional Arts Association
Kent Smith, 207 2nd St., Hood River 97031-2003;
541-386-4512

John Day

Juniper Arts Council
Denice Lewis, PO Box 190,
John Day 97845-0190; 541-820-4331

Keizer

Keizer Art Association
Phyllis Rattray, PO Box 21154,
Keizer 97307-1154; 503-390-3010

King City

King City Artist Guild
Marianne Pfeiffer, 12765 SW Prince Albert St.,
King City 97224; 503-620-3738

Klamath Falls

Klamath Arts Council
Sue Cogley, 4035 S 6th,
Klamath Falls 97603-4730; 541-884-8699

Ross Ragland Theatre
Rebecca Sario, 218 N 7th St.,
Klamath Falls 97601-6017; 541-884-0651

La Grande

La Grande Arts Commission
Donna Betts, PO Box 670,
La Grande 97850-0670; 541-963-9649

Lake Oswego

Lake Oswego Arts Commision
Clair Siddell, PO Box 176, Lake Oswego 97034;
503-635-8985

Lake Oswego Festival of Arts
Joan Sappington, PO Box 368,
Lake Oswego 97034-0368; 503-636-3634

Lebanon

Lebanon Fine Arts and Crafts
Connie Allen, PO Box 863, 31783 Eastway St.,
Lebanon 97355-0863; 541-451-4666

Manzanita

Manzanita Creative Arts Council
Norma Seely, PO Box 85, Manzanita 97130

McMinnville

Arts Alliance of Yamhill County
Monaca Setzoil-Phillips, PO Box 898,
McMinnville 97128-0898; 503-843-3513

Medford

Rogue Valley Art Association
Nancy Jo Mullen, 40 S Bartlett,
Medford 97501-7216; 541-772-8118

Milwaukie

North Clackamas Fine Art Guild
Norma Schneider, PO Box 22676,
Milwaukie 97269-2676; 503-654-1398

Molalla

Molalla Arts Group
Jonel LaFever, 137 Shirley St., Molalla 97038

Monmouth

Monmouth-Independence Community Art
Association
Dan Cannon, PO Box 114,
Monmouth 97361-0114; 503-838-8326

The PORTLAND!
Exhibit at the Oregon
Historical Society
provides hands-on
activities including
Neighborhood Windows,
a computerized look at
Portland's diverse
neighborhoods—from
past to present.

Photo courtesy of the
Oregon Historical
Society.

Nyssa

Nyssa Fine Arts Council
Marie Wilson, PO Box 2356, Nyssa 97913-0356;
541-372-2981

Oregon City

Clackamas County Arts Council
Harriet P. Jorgensen, 19600 S Molalla Ave.,
Oregon City 97045-7998; 503-656-9543

Pendleton

Arts Council of Pendleton
Jack Lenihan, PO Box 573,
Pendleton 97801-0573; 541-276-8495

Tiimutla Art Council
Pat Walters, 233 SE 4th, Pendleton 97801-2508;
541-278-0115

Port Orford

Port Orford Arts Council
Sharon Leahy, PO Box 771,
Port Orford 97465-0771; 541-332-0045

Prineville

Juniper Art Council
Lorene Allen, 1568 Mt. View, PO Box 190,
Prineville 97754-0741; 541-575-1227

St. Helens

Columbia Arts Guild
Jeane Steigel, PO Box 621, St. Helens 97051-0621;
503-397-6762

Columbia River Cottage Arts Association
Sheri Hope-Decker, 285 N 7th, St. Helens 97051;
503-397-9716

Salem

Salem Art Association
David Cohen, Exec. Dir., 600 Mission St. SE,
Salem 97302-6203;

Saralyn Hilde, Bush Barn Art Center Gallery,
503-581-2228

Sandy

Sandy Arts Society
Meri Ealy, 37611 SE Kelso Rd., Sandy 97055;
503-668-3611

Seaside

Columbia Pacific Arts Forum
Suzan Brewer, PO Box 586, Seaside 97138-0586;
503-738-3628

Jewell Box Players
Susan Norman, Elsie Rt. Box 1220, Seaside 97138;
503-755-2404

North Coast Writers' League
Greg Kabanuk, PO Box 625, Seaside 97138-0625;
503-738-7403

Northwest Performing Arts
Kathleen Wysong, PO Box 401,
Seaside 97138-0401; 503-738-5061

Sisters

Sisters Arts Council
Betsey Williams, PO Box 106, Sisters 97759-0106;
541-549-8184

Springfield

Springfield Arts Commission
Kathleen Jensen, 225 N 5th St.,
Springfield 97477-4695; 541-726-3677

Emerald Empire Art Gallery and Association
Izzy Fletcher, 421 North A St.,
Springfield 97477-4607; 541-747-2661

Supporters of Arts and Letters in Springfield
Nan Kennedy, 1404 Centennial Blvd.,
Springfield 97477-3258; 541-747-8242

Sunriver

Sunriver Art Association
Bud Schirmer, PO Box 3117,
Sunriver 07707-0117; 541-593-5746

Tigard/Tualatin

Arts Commission of Tigard, Tualatin, Sherwood
Mary Rush, 13137 SW Pacific Hwy.,
Tigard 97223-5036; 503-684-0187

Tualatin Arts Group
Bryce Frazell, PO Box 369,
Tualatin 97062-0369; 503-692-2000

Tillamook

Tillamook Arts Association
Sherri Miller, PO Box 634, Tillamook 97141-0634

Welches

Wy'East Artisans Guild
Meri Ealy, PO Box 272, Welches 97067;
503-668-3611

West Linn

West Linn Art Commission
Cathy McNichol, 3830 Robin Creek Ln.,
West Linn 97068-1024; 503-657-0550

Wheeler

Art Ranch
Lorraine Ortiz, PO Box 694, 487 Hwy 101,
Wheeler 97147-0694; 503-368-6055

Wilsonville

Wilsonville Arts Council
Theonie Gilmore, 24242 SW Gage Rd.,
Wilsonville 97070; 503-638-6933

Woodburn

Woodburn Art Center
Eileen Wikoff, 2551 Boones Ferry Rd.,
Woodburn 97071; 503-982-3268

Woodburn Art League
Diana Ober, 14260 Wilco Hwy. NE,
Woodburn 97071

Regional Arts Councils

Arts Council of Southern Oregon

Kathie Olsen, Exec. Dir.
33 North Central, Suite 300, Medford 97501;
541-779-2820; Fax: 541-772-4945

Serving Josephine and Jackson counties.

Eastern Oregon Regional Arts Council

Sally Wiens, Exec. Dir.
#220 Loso Hall, Eastern Oregon State College,
La Grande 97850; 541-962-3624;
Fax: 541-962-3596; Email: wienss@eosc.osshe.edu

Serving Harney, Malheur, Baker, Grant, Wallowa, Union, Umatilla, Morrow, Gilliam and Wheeler counties.

Lane Arts Council

Douglas Beauchamp, Exec. Dir.
164 West Broadway, Eugene 97401; 541-485-2278;
Fax: 541-485-2478; Email: lanearts@efn.org;
Web: www.efn.org/~laneartc

Serving Lane county.

Linn-Benton Council for the Arts

Corby Stonebraker, Exec. Dir.
Corvallis Arts Center, 700 SW Madison,
Corvallis 97330; 541-754-1551;
Email: caclbca@peak.org

Serving Linn and Benton counties.

Mid-Valley Arts Council

Michael Kissinger, Exec. Dir.
170 High St. SE, in the Elsinore Theater,
Salem 97301; 503-364-7474;
Fax: 503-375-0284 (c/o STAGE)

Serving Marion, Polk and Yamhill counties.

Oregon Coast Council on the Arts

Sharon Morgan, Exec. Dir.
PO Box 1315, Newport 97365; 541-265-9231;
Fax: 541-265-9464; Email: occa@newportnet.com

Serving Columbia, Clatsop, Tillamook, Lincoln, Coos and Curry counties.

The End of the Oregon Trail Interpretive Center, with its distinctive 50-foot high wagon-shaped buildings, opened in June of 1995 in Oregon City, the true end of the Oregon Trail.
Photo by Gary Poush/ZUMA.

Regional Arts and Culture Council

Bill Bulick, Exec. Dir.
Donna Milraney, Assoc. Dir.
309 SW 6th Avenue, Suite 100, Portland 97204;
503-823-5111; Fax: 503-823-5370;
Email: info@racc.org; Web: www.racc.org/~racc

Serving Multnomah, Washington and Clackamas counties.

Umpqua Valley Arts Association

Eileen Paul, Exec. Dir.
PO Box 1105, Roseburg 97470; 541-672-2532;
Fax: 541-672-7696; Email: uvaa@wizzards.net

Serving Douglas county.

Oregon History

Oregonians are proud of their state's history. Whether our ancestors lived here before Lewis and Clark arrived or migrated to Oregon in recent years, we share an interest in the people and stories of Oregon's past. Many organizations are dedicated to various aspects of Oregon history. Some of these are listed below.

Oregon's Major Heritage and History Organizations

End of the Oregon Trail Interpretive Center

David M. Porter, Exec. Dir.
1726 Washington St., Oregon City 97045;
503-657-9336; Fax: 503-657-3076;
Web: www.teleport.com/~eotic

At the End of the Oregon Trail Interpretive Center, visitors step back in time 150 years to those days when "Oregon Fever" swept the country like wildfire. More than 300,000 people crossed this land on the Oregon Trail in search of a dream, in search of a new life, in search of the "land at Eden's Gate."

Visitors first enter the Missouri Provisioners Depot. Trail guides dressed in period clothing present the story about the struggles of the times and how pioneers were lured by tales of the bountiful Oregon Territory. Supplies and provisions were carefully selected for the long arduous journey.

The westward trip is recreated in the Cascade Theater. A 25-minute state-of-the-art mixed media show with surround-sound and special effects provides the backdrop. Daily life along the trail comes alive as fictitious characters recount the adventures, emotions and stories of their own journeys.

Arrival in Oregon City is the final stop. The Oregon City Gallery features a fine collection of artifacts such as a Barlow Road toll book, clothing, tools and household items. The George Abernethy Store offers a variety of Oregon products and heritage items. Living history interpreters engage visitors in "hands on" demonstrations and exhibits of daily life in pioneer times.

The Center site offers several outdoor historic displays. The Heritage Gardens flourish with authentic heirloom vegetation such as flax, pioneer Cosmos, antique roses, vegetables, fruits and herbs. "Trail guides" describe how early settlers planted, cultivated and harvested these plants for cooking, dyeing and home remedies. Also in the gardens are two historic markers acknowledging the End of the Oregon Trail. The Willamette Chapter of the Daughters of the American Revolution erected a marker in 1917 and Clackamas County Historical Society recognized the western terminus of the trail in 1976.

The End of the Oregon Trail Interpretive Center is open daily, except Thanksgiving, Christmas and New Year's Day, and is located in Oregon City.

The Museum at Warm Springs

Michael Hammond, Exec. Dir.
2189 Highway 26, Warm Springs 97761;
541-553-3331; Fax: 541-553-3338

Completed in early 1993, The Museum at Warm Springs was created by the Confederated Tribes of the Warm Springs Reservation of Oregon to preserve the traditions of the Warm Springs, Wasco and Paiute tribes and to keep alive their legacy. The museum's celebrated permanent collection includes treasured artifacts, historic photographs, narratives, graphics, murals and rare documents.

Traditional dwellings, a tule mat lodge, wickiup and plankhouse have been meticulously constructed to show life as it was long ago.

The changing exhibit gallery explores all dimensions of the Native American experience, past and present: exhibitions, programs and lectures by prominent Native American scholars, artists and poets are perfectly framed. The summer months feature live demonstrations of

drumming, dancing, storytelling, beadworking and hide-tanning. A gift shop offers an impressive array of books and tapes on Native American cultures as well as traditional beadwork, silver jewelry, baskets and other Native American crafts.

Museum hours are 10 a.m. to 5 p.m. The museum is open every day except Christmas, New Year's and Thanksgiving.

National Historic Oregon Trail Interpretive Center

David B. Hunsaker, Dir.
PO Box 987, Baker City 97814; 541-523-1843; Fax: 541-523-1834

Operated by the U.S. Department of Interior's Bureau of Land Management, the National Historic Oregon Trail Interpretive Center is located at Flagstaff Hill on Highway 86, five miles east of Baker City. The 509-acre site features a 23,000 square-foot facility with permanent exhibits offering audio, video, dioramas and artifacts to recreate the experiences of Oregon Trail emigrants. The Interpretive Center also includes exhibits on Native American culture, mining and history of the BLM. A 150-seat theater hosts an active schedule of lectures and performances.

From atop Flagstaff Hill, visitors see more than 13 miles of the Oregon Trail route. Visitors may also view close-up trail ruts at the base of Flagstaff Hill. During the summer, living history characters interpret pioneer life at a wagon encampment.

The center is open daily from 9 a.m. to 6 p.m., April 1 to October 31 and 9 a.m. to 4 p.m., November 1 to March 31. It is closed Christmas and New Year's Day.

Oregon Geographic Names Board

Thomas McAllister, Pres.
Chet Orloff, Sec.
1200 SW Park Ave., Portland 97205; 503-306-5200; Fax: 503-221-2035

The board is an affiliate of the U.S. Board on Geographic Names. It is associated with the Oregon Historical Society, which maintains the board's correspondence and records.

The board supervises naming of all geographic features within the state. Recommendations are considered by the local board and then sent to the U.S. board in Washington, D.C. for final action, to prevent confusion and duplication in naming geographic features and to correct previous naming errors.

Oregon Historical Society

Chet Orloff, Exec. Dir.
1200 SW Park Ave., Portland 97205; 503-306-5200, TDD: 503-306-5194; Fax: 503-221-2035; Email: orhis@ohs.org; Web: www.ohs.org

Judge Owen M. Panner, Pres.

For more than 120 years, the Oregon Historical Society (OHS) has provided a place for history—a home for our

The Alvord Desert, in Harney County, is one of the driest places in North America. Photo courtesy of Malheur Field Station.

heritage, our culture, our beginnings and our future.

The society has expanded far beyond its original mission of collecting, preserving, publishing and sharing Oregon's rich history. Today, OHS offers a broad array of educational, interpretive, technical assistance and field services programs.

Attractions include exhibits covering a wide range of historical topics; lectures and special events; a museum store; and the research library with its wealth of books, maps, documents, oral histories, photographs and film footage.

OHS also publishes books about the history of Oregon and the Pacific Northwest; operates educational programs for children and adults; provides outreach services to other historical societies and every five years presents Century Farm awards. The society provides an interpretive program at the James F. Bybee pioneer homestead on Sauvie Island, northwest of Portland. Restored by OHS, but owned by Multnomah County, the 1857 house, grounds and pioneer orchard are open from June 1 through Labor Day.

The Oregon Historical Society Museum and the Museum Store are open Tuesday through Saturday from 10 a.m. to 5 p.m. and on Sunday from noon to 5 p.m. The Research Library is open Wednesday through Saturday from 11:30 a.m. to 5 p.m. Admission is charged for the museum.

Oregon Lewis and Clark Trail Committee

James M. Hamrick, Deputy State Historic Preservation Officer
1115 Commercial St. NE, Salem 97310-1001; 503-378-6508, ext. 231

The Oregon Lewis and Clark Trail Committee was established in 1970 by Executive Order 79-07. The committee was directed to promote awareness of the historic significance of the Lewis and Clark Expedition, and encourage development and protection of historical sites and outdoor recreation sources along the Lewis and Clark Trail.

Oregon Trail Advisory Council

Karen Bassett, Communications Specialist
1115 Commercial St. NE, Salem 97310; 503-399-9243; Fax: 503-378-6447

The Oregon Trail Advisory Council (OTAC) was established by Executive Order 84-10 to promote, develop and protect the historic Oregon Trail.

OTAC formed the Oregon Trail Coordinating Council (OTCC) to oversee the 150th anniversary of the Oregon Trail in 1993 and to coordinate educational and heritage tourism opportunities along the Oregon Trail.

The OTCC coordinates the development of Oregon's historic trails, as designated under ORS 358.057, as heritage tourism resources resulting in positive cultural and economic impacts for the state. Both organizations can be contacted at the above address. OTAC members are appointed by the governor.

Oregon Council for the Humanities

*812 SW Washington, Suite 225, Portland 97205;
503-241-0543; toll-free: 1-800-735-0543;
Fax: 503-241-0024; Email: och@teleport.com*

The Oregon Council for the Humanities
(OCH) was established as a state-based
affiliate of the National Endowment
for the Humanities (NEH) in 1971 to
stimulate public appreciation for, and
participation in, the humanities. The
humanities include fields of study such
as history, philosophy, literature, languages, archaeology, jurisprudence and
the history and criticism of the arts.
Since it began, OCH has helped plan and
fund more than 2,000 public programs
in communities throughout Oregon.
Competitive grants are available to public and non-profit organizations to
develop and carry out these programs.

In addition, OCH offers the "Oregon
Chautauqua," an annual catalog of
lectures, exhibits and films available for
use by community groups; publishes a
semi-annual magazine, Oregon Humanities; and carries out a variety of special
initiatives such as an exhibit and video
on Columbia Villa, a public housing
project in Portland.

NEH provides the organization's principal funding, with support from corporations, foundations and individuals
throughout Oregon.

Natural Sciences and Technology

Oregon has a varied set of facilities
designed to help children and adults
learn about a changing world. Along
with the many visitors centers available
in state and national parks and forest
areas, other independent centers teach
us about the world in which we live and
encourage us to speculate about those
things yet to be learned.

The following is a list of major public
facilities in Oregon that provide the
public with information about science,
industry and technology.

The High Desert Museum

Jerry N. Moore, Acting Pres.
*59800 S Hwy. 97, Bend 97702; 541-382-4754;
Fax: 541-382-5256; Web: www.highdesert.org*

The High Desert Museum is a private,
non-profit institution located four miles

south of Bend and 10 miles north of
Sunriver. A living museum, its emphasis
is on the natural and cultural history of
the arid Northwest, including two-thirds
of Oregon, and on the management of
arid land resources.

The main facility is highlighted by the
28,000 square-foot Earle A. Chiles Center on the Spirit of the West. Its Hall of
Exploration and Settlement depicts eight
time periods in the West's development.
The Desertarium, also part of the main
facility, features small and seldom-seen
animals of the region in naturalistic
habitats.

Outside exhibits include an extensive
stream and interpretive pond system
with wildlife viewing stations; a birds-
of-prey demonstration area; vivid historical exhibits; and live porcupines
and otters.

The museum produces a variety of
programs and hands-on learning opportunities. It is open every day except
Thanksgiving, Christmas and New Year's.

Malheur Field Station

*HC 72 Box 260, Princeton 97721; 541-493-2629;
Web: www.eosc.osshe.edu/~dkerley/malheur.htm*

Malheur Field Station is a private,
non-profit natural science institute
located in remote eastern Oregon, 160
miles southeast of Bend. It educates the
public on the natural science and natural history of the Great Basin region
of Oregon through school field trips,
science camp for kids, family weekends
and in-service teacher education.

The station leases its land from the
Malheur National Wildlife Refuge, a
major rest area for hundreds of Pacific
Flyway bird species. Malheur is a mecca
for birders, K-12 school groups, university classes, Elderhostelers, corporate
retreats and travelers from throughout
the Northwest.

Researchers and college students have
been using the station's labs and collections for 25 years, resulting in greater
understanding of Great Basin Desert
ecology. Because of its location at the
center of a vast desert region, the field
station has over the years been host
to photographers, novelists, artists,
botanists, entomologists, herpetologists,
ichthyologists, mammologists, anthro-
pologists, archaeologists, geologists,
astronomers, survivalists and wilderness
advocates.

Mongoose lemurs, native to northwestern Madagascar and a few nearby islands, are one of the most endangered of all lemur species; this one resides at the Center for Species Survival (CSS) at Metro Washington Park Zoo.

Photo courtesy of Metro Washington Park Zoo.

Lodging and food service are available to the public between March 14 and October 15, 1997. Conference rooms, classrooms and darkrooms are available for nominal fees. The Great Basin Natural History Museum, the field station's centerpiece, has a large collection of desert flora and fauna specimens, a natural science library and museum exhibits curated by the Portland Audubon Society.

Malheur Field Station is a quiet place, but frequently caters to visiting groups of 25 to 100 people. Desert Conference, held annually at the station, sleeps and feeds up to 250 guests. The dining hall serves healthy breakfasts and dinners, and provides sack lunches for field trips. Lodging is basic but clean, ranging from bunk houses to private rooms and trailers. Guests provide their own sleeping bag, pillow and towel. Most facilities are handicap accessible.

Metro Washington Park Zoo

Y. Sherry Sheng, Dir.
4001 SW Canyon Rd., Portland 97221;
503-226-1561; Fax: 503-226-6836

Nestled on 65 acres in the forested hills of Washington Park, Metro Washington Park Zoo is just a five minute drive from downtown Portland. It is the perfect place to explore the native habitats and lifestyles of animals from around the globe. Exhibits are designed to replicate the natural geographic region of each species. Humboldt penguins from Peru live in a penguinarium with rocky shores and gentle surf; ponds, streams and marshes house creatures native to the western Cascades; polar bear exhibits simulate Arctic habitats; African savanna and rain forest areas feature hippos, rhinos, giraffes, crocodiles, bats and naked mole-rats.

In addition to being Oregon's most popular paid attraction, the zoo is committed to conservation, research and education. It is home to 26 endangered and 43 threatened species, and it participates in 13 species survival plans. The zoo recently completed construction of the Center for Species Survival, an off-site breeding and research facility. Metro Washington Park Zoo is recognized around the world for its Asian elephant breeding program and its innovative approach to environmental enrichment. More than 80,000 students annually supplement their classroom learning with field trips to the zoo, and 70,000 students participate in community outreach programs.

Oregon Coast Aquarium, Inc.

Phyllis A. Bell, Pres.
2820 SE Ferry Slip Rd., Newport 97365;
541-867-3474; Fax: 541-867-6846;
Web: www.aquarium.org

Nancy Dennis, board chair
The Oregon Coast Aquarium, located in Newport, is a non-profit institution occupying a 32-acre site on Yaquina Bay, adjacent to the Oregon State University Mark O. Hatfield Marine Science Center. Aquarium exhibits are housed in a 40,000 square-foot building and on six acres of elaborately rocked pools, caves, cliffs and bluffs.

Indoor exhibits include four galleries replicating habitats found in coastal wetlands, sandy and rocky shores, and off Oregon's coast in deeper waters. Also indoors are a demonstration lab, US WEST Whale Theater, changing exhibit area, full-service cafe and gift shop. Outdoor exhibits include Keiko, the killer whale; sea otters; harbor seals and sea lions; wave-pummeled tide pools; a coastal cave featuring a giant Pacific octopus; the largest walk-through seabird aviary in North America; a nature trail and a children's play area. The aquarium is open every day except Christmas and is handicap accessible.

Oregon Museum of Science and Industry (OMSI)

Patrick LaCrosse, Pres.

1945 SE Water Ave., Portland 97214-3354; 503-797-4000; Web: www.omsi.edu

Harry Demorest and Robert L. Harrison, board co-chairs

Established in 1944, the Oregon Museum of Science and Industry (OMSI) is an independent, non-tax based educational and cultural resource center with an international reputation for excellence in science exhibitry and informal science education. It is dedicated to improving the public's understanding of science and technology through a wide variety of innovative science programming.

In 1992 OMSI moved to an 18.5 acre campus on the east bank of the Willamette River in downtown Portland. The complex includes six exhibit halls, seven interactive science labs and a planetarium. In addition to the museum, OMSI houses a 300-seat, five-story domed OMNIMAX=AE Theater, a riverside cafe, science store and the 219-foot *USS Blueback* submarine moored just outside in the river. Free parking accommodates 800 vehicles.

In addition to the exhibits on permanent display in the museum, OMSI designs, creates and builds science exhibits for travel to other science centers nationwide. Currently OMSI has more than 25 exhibits in circulation.

OMSI also boasts the most extensive science education program in the world. OUTREACH brings a unique brand of traveling science education to more than 350,000 students in seven western states. OMSI Teacher Education programs provide 60 hours of programming to more than 700 teachers each year, and OMSI camps serve 9,800 kids

in 32,000 student days of science instruction annually.

The museum is open seven days a week from 9:30 a.m. to 7 p.m. from Memorial Day through Labor Day; and Tuesday through Sunday from 9:30 a.m. to 5:30 p.m. from Labor Day through Memorial Day. It is open until 8 p.m. on Thursdays throughout the year, and is always open on Portland Public School holidays. OMSI is closed on Christmas Day.

Oregon State University Hatfield Marine Science Center

Dr. Lavern J. Weber, Dir.

2030 S Marine Science Dr., Newport 97365; 541-867-0100; Fax: 541-867-0138

The Hatfield Marine Science Center (HMSC) is a field station of Oregon State University located on the south side of the Yaquina Bay estuary, adjacent to the Oregon Coast Aquarium. The public wing with its beloved touch pool and octopus tank was completely remodeled and redesigned in 1996 with the theme "Searching for Patterns in a Complex World." The totally new interactive exhibits and computer simulations enable visitors to play the role of scientific explorers using some of the current research underway at the center. Core exhibits highlight how people discover patterns at the global, bird's eye, eye level and microscopic scale.

The bookstore is stocked with marine, nearshore and estuarine books, posters, science kits and tools for all ages. Informal education programs are offered in the auditorium, along the estuary nature trail, beside the docks and in workshops. Hands-on laboratories are available for school and organized groups with prior reservations, and a dedicated corps of volunteers assists visitors with their individual explorations. The public wing accommodates those with special needs.

Behind the scenes, undergraduate and graduate courses are offered and the center serves as a coastal research park for scientists with a number of state and federal agencies as well as with OSU. It is served by the Guin Library, the branch of the OSU Library that specializes in marine resource materials. The Coastal Oregon Marine Experiment Station is also located at the center.

Pacific Northwest Museum of Natural History

Phil Lamb, Exec. Dir.
1500 E Main St., Ashland 97520; 541-488-1084;
Fax: 541-482-1115;
Web: www.projecta.com/nwmuseum

The Pacific Northwest Museum of Natural History, opened July 1, 1994, is the most comprehensive natural history museum between Vancouver, B.C. and San Francisco, California. The 30,000 square-foot museum is in the forefront of new museums that are concept-based, rather than collection-based. It is devoted to informal education in the natural sciences and offers multi-sensory natural exhibits, interactive video adventures, hands-on games and experiments.

A museum tour transports visitors to the Oregon coast, the high desert, and the Cascades and marshes of the Pacific Northwest through computer-generated, interactive exhibits. An interactive computer "passport" system allows visitors to use what they learn to make decisions about the use of timber, rangeland and water resources. Understanding how nature works, how humans interact with nature and our responsibility to steward resources for the future is the goal of this concept-based edu-tainment center.

University of Oregon Museum of Natural History

C. Melvin Aikens, Dir.
Patricia Krier, Program Dir.
1680 E 15th Ave., Eugene 97403-1224;
541-346-3024; Fax: 541-346-5122

The University of Oregon Museum of Natural History, founded in 1936, maintains collections and produces exhibits and programs of lectures and workshops relating to anthropology (including archaeology), zoology and geology.

The Oregon State Museum of Anthropology, created by the Oregon Legislature in 1935, is now part of the Museum of Natural History, and has ultimate responsibility for curating anthropological materials belonging to the state. Where conditions permit, these collections are available for loan to public museums and are used for research, teaching and display at the Museum of Natural History. The archaeological research section of the Oregon State Museum of Anthropology conducts research on contract for federal and state agencies.

World Forestry Center

John L. Blackwell, Pres.
4033 SW Canyon Rd., Portland 97221;
503-228-1367; Fax: 503-228-3624;
Email: mail@worldforest.org;
Web: www.worldforest.org/~wfc

Young Ju Park, board chair

The World Forestry Center, located in Portland's Washington Park near the zoo, is a private, non-profit forestry-education organization. Through classes, tours, exhibits and demonstrations, it illustrates and interprets benefits of the forest environment and promotes appreciation and understanding of forests and forest resources worldwide.

The center also operates the Magness Tree Farm, an 80-acre demonstration forest near Wilsonville, with a visitors' center and log bunkhouse used for summer camps. The area is also a wildlife sanctuary. Individuals and groups of all ages are welcome to visit and take advantage of the farm's varied educational activities, many of which are free of charge.

Merlo Hall, added to the center's campus in 1989, houses the World Forest Institute. This facility was designed as an international forest information clearinghouse.

ECONOMY AND NATURAL RESOURCES

The 4.1-mile-long Astoria Bridge connects Oregon and Washington with what is believed to be the longest continuous through truss series of any bridge in the world. Photo by Ray Propst.

OREGON'S bountiful natural resources have long attracted people to the state—for jobs, for recreation and for the sheer joy of living in a beautiful land. Although high technology jobs now out-number wood products-related jobs in Oregon, natural resources still play a central role in Oregon's economy. The following section describes the interconnection between resources and economic health, the changes occurring in the state, and the present and projected status of Oregon's economy.

Economic Performance

In 1996, Oregon enjoyed its fifth year of solid economic growth, setting new population and employment records, with low unemployment and inflation rates. During that period, and indeed for the past 10 years, Oregon's economy has moved from one dominated by forest products to one more oriented toward high technology and services.

This structural shift has been accompanied by fast population growth and a change in the goods derived from Oregon's abundant natural resources. Many people who value the quality of life afforded by clean air and water, outdoor activities and open spaces are moving to Oregon. Sustaining the environment and managing the impacts of a quickly growing population have become an integral part of Oregon's economic future.

Employment

Oregon's 1996 rate of job creation—about 4 percent—ranked among the nation's best. Job growth spanned most industries, with exceptions in forest products, nondurable goods manufacturing, government and a few other industries.

Employment gains in Oregon far outpaced gains across the nation in high technology manufacturing, construction, trade and private sector service industries. Between 1990 and 1995, employment increased by 13.6 percent in Oregon, twice as fast as the national increase in employment during the same period.

Oregon's performance improved most rapidly in the past few years. Between August 1995 and August 1996, total non-agricultural employment in Oregon grew at the fifth highest rate in the nation. Construction and service employment grew at the fourth fastest rate in the nation.

Income

During the 1980s, Oregon's per capita income lost ground relative to the nation. The sharp economic downturn in the early 1980s reduced Oregon's per capita income to only 91 percent of the national average. However, strong growth in wage and salary income since 1990 pushed total per capita income up to an estimated 96 percent of the national average in 1996. Oregon's per capita income adjusted for inflation grew at the fourth fastest rate among the western states between 1990 and 1995, increasing 7.1 percent, compared to 4.8 percent growth for the nation as a whole.

Unemployment

Oregon's economy is operating at high capacity in the Portland metro area and the Willamette Valley region. In 1996, the statewide average unemployment rate was 5.2 percent. There is some surplus in the labor markets of the southern part of the state, with many counties having unemployment rates above 7 percent.

Housing markets are strong, and population continues to grow, mostly due to in-migration at about 1.7 percent annually—twice the national rate.

Economic Forces

Oregon's strong performance in the past 10 years is due to a favorable combination of internal and external forces.

The long period of national economic expansion has supported Oregon's economy. At the same time, California's weak economy has led to in-migration of labor and capital, and California's recent recovery means an improved market for Oregon's products. California's unemployment rate remains higher than Oregon's, encouraging continued migration to Oregon. The shift in federal budget priorities reflected in the declining role of national defense expenditures has also helped Oregon.

Internally, a restructuring of Oregon's economy from timber to high technology has positioned the state to take advantage of the shift from consumer to capital goods that has characterized the national economy in the 1990s. Tight labor markets have increased wages and per capita income relative to the nation, making Oregon an attractive job market for residents of other states and stimulating demand for retail goods and services within Oregon. Oregon's perceived high quality of life has also encouraged in-migrants. In addition, relatively low housing and labor costs in the early 1990s made Oregon attractive to relocating business.

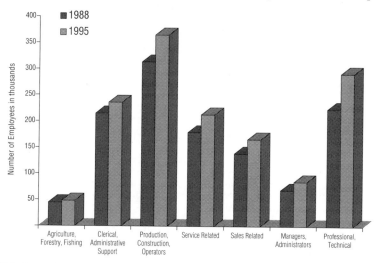

Employment Comparisons by Occupational Group

■ 1988
■ 1995

Number of Employees in thousands

Occupational groups (left to right): Agriculture, Forestry, Fishing · Clerical, Administrative Support · Production, Construction, Operators · Service Related · Sales Related · Managers, Administrators · Professional, Technical

While the number of employees in agriculture and forestry-related fields has grown only slightly in the past eight years, numbers of employees in other areas of the economy have grown much more rapidly. Source: Office of Economic Analysis.

Outlook

Oregon's economy is expected to continue its growth, though at a slower pace. Employment, total personal and per capita income, and population growth rates are all expected to exceed the national average. Oregon's unemployment level and jobless rate are expected to move a little higher and continue to vary widely throughout the state.

Continuation of the nation's economic expansion, implementation of the semiconductor industry's aggressive investment plans in Oregon, strong export activity, and continued population growth at nearly double the national rate are the key factors expected to keep Oregon's economy growing.

Population Growth

Oregon's population grew by 290,000 people between 1990 and 1995. Seventy percent of that growth came from people moving into the state.

Many people move to Oregon to enjoy the quality of life—the clean air and water, recreational opportunities and land. As the population continues to grow, pressures on the very environment that supports the quality of life in the state increase.

Today, many parts of Oregon are experiencing problems with congested roads and overburdened infrastructure. Development threatens the open spaces valued by residents and necessary for the agriculture industry. Industrial and residental waste tests the carrying capacity of air and water—assets that attract both residents and today's high technology industries.

Oregon's Strategy

Oregon's first strategic plan, "Oregon Shines," produced in 1989, emphasized economic growth. The Oregon Progress Board and Governor Kitzhaber's "Oregon Shines" Task Force reviewed the plan in 1996. The group revised the plan to address concerns that the improved economy has not reduced some of Oregon's social problems as much as had been expected and that Oregon's high quality of life may be eroding.

"Oregon Shines II," released in January 1997, sets the goals of achieving:
• Quality jobs for all Oregonians;

- Safe, caring and engaged communities; and
- Healthy, sustainable surroundings.

The plan includes a list of "Benchmarks," measurable indicators Oregon uses to track progress toward its strategic goals.

Manufacturing

Oregon's economy has moved from one dominated by forest products to one oriented toward high technology and services. Manufacturing's share of total payroll in Oregon fell by 5 percent between 1985 and 1995 to 21 percent. At the same time, the service industry's share increased from 17 to 22 percent.

Within the manufacturing sector, the shift between timber and high technology has been pronounced. High technology increased from 24 percent of

manufacturing payroll in 1985 to 32 percent in 1995. Timber declined from 39 percent of manufacturing payroll in 1985 to 27 percent in 1995. All other manufacturing industries remained relatively unchanged in their share of total manufacturing payroll.

The state gained an estimated 3,400 manufacturing jobs overall from 1995 to 1996 and 52,000 non-agricultural jobs in total.

Oregon has never been more diversified. There are several ways to measure a state's level of diversification. On each of them, Oregon fares well, at least above average compared to other states. By one measure, Oregon's economy rose from 11th to 4th most diversified state economy between 1985 and 1994. Forest products used to make up more than 60 percent of manufacturing jobs and more than 15 percent of all jobs. Today no manufacturing industry employs

Top 25 Private Sector Employers in Oregon—June 1995

Primary Name	Headquarters	Avg. No.
Fred Meyer, Inc.	Portland	11,500
Safeway Stores, Inc.	Clackamas	9,286
Sisters of Providence in Oregon State	Portland	7,676
The US National Bank of Oregon	Portland	7,466
Intel Corporation	Hillsboro	6,723
Barrett Business Services, Inc.	Portland	4,862
Kaiser Foundation Health Plan of NW	Portland	4,553
Tektronix, Inc.	Beaverton	4,520
Albertsons, Inc.	Boise, ID	4,363
First Interstate Bank of Oregon, NA	Phoenix, AZ	4,305
US West Communications, Inc.	Denver, CO	4,102
Hewlett-Packard Co.	Corvallis	4,000
Freightliner Corporation	Portland	3,961
Peace Health	Bellevue, WA	3,697
WalMart Stores	Bentonville, AR	3,696
Willamette Industries, Inc.	Portland	3,650
Meier & Frank	Portland	3,448
Roseburg Forest Products Co.	Roseburg	3,445
PayLess Drug Stores Northwest, Inc.	Wilsonville	3,361
Boise Cascade Corporation	Boise, ID	3,300
Legacy Emanuel Hospital & Health	Portland	3,282
United Parcel Service	Portland	3,248
Weyerhaeuser Company	Tacoma, WA	3,135
Nordstrom-Best, Inc.	Seattle, WA	2,826
Nike, Inc.	Beaverton	2,778

Compiled by Marketing Section, Oregon Economic Development Department.

Tektronix, Oregon's first high technology company, was founded in 1946 by Howard Vollum (right) and Jack Murdock. It is now a $1.8 billion company and employs 7,900 people worldwide.

Photo courtesy of Tektronix.

more than 4 percent of Oregon's workforce. This bodes well for sustaining Oregon's economic strength. The more kinds of businesses that find a home in the state, the less susceptible the economy will be to downturns in any one sector.

Oregon's high technology industry is particularly strong, thanks in part to its diversity. The industry produces a wide variety of goods, including software, semiconductors, computers, instruments and other capital equipment.

The industry started five decades ago with the founding of Tektronix, a manufacturer of electronic measuring devices. Since then, companies have spun off from Tektronix, grown from other sources of entrepreneurship in the state, and from other states and countries. Intel, Hewlett-Packard, Sony and other big-name companies are in Oregon, along with many small, mid-size and other large companies.

Oregon's high technology companies are located primarily in the Portland metropolitan area, but they are gradually spreading to other parts of the state. The Interstate 5 corridor from Portland to Corvallis and Eugene, parts of southern Oregon and Bend are all home to high technology today.

Industry profits are growing rapidly, with total revenue in 1996 estimated at $16 billion by the American Electronics Association. Revenues increased by almost 60 percent between 1993 and 1995. The industry today employs about 54,000 workers, has a median wage of $43,700, and will add an estimated 15,000 jobs by 1998.

Forestry

Forests have long defined Oregon's natural, economic and cultural landscape. Oregonians look to their forests as a source of timber, recreation, clean air and water, and wildlife habitat. Healthy forests ensure a vigorous forest landbase, both economically and ecologically.

Oregon's Forest Practices Act assures that Oregon's forests will continue to be important to the state's economy and influence quality-of-life. For example, forest practice rules today provide strong protection for all streams, rivers and bodies of water. Reforestation standards have become stricter. Rules governing road building, chemical use on forest land, and wildlife habitat protection have been broadened and better defined.

As Oregon becomes more populated, as its economic base changes and as its cultural values shift, the relationship Oregonians have with their forests becomes increasingly complex. Seeing through that complexity to a more complete understanding of issues and the condition of the forests is critical to making informed choices about the future of Oregon's forest landscape.

Oregon's Forest Landbase

Oregon's total land area is 61.4 million acres. Almost half of this, 27.5 million acres, is forested. Oregon's forests are divided into two major geographic regions: eastern Oregon and western Oregon, which are separated by the Cascade Range. Douglas-fir and western hemlock are the primary conifer species in western Oregon. In eastern Oregon, ponderosa pine and lodgepole pine are the primary conifers. Several species of true fir and larch also grow east of the Cascades. Non-commercial forests are found along the crest of the Cascade Range and in the high-desert country of eastern Oregon. Species in these forests include alpine fir, mountain hemlock and western juniper.

Sixty-one percent of Oregon's forests is publicly owned, and almost 57 percent of Oregon's forests is federal land. Sixty-seven percent of the state's forest land, or 18.3 million acres, is capable of producing timber for commercial harvest; 14 percent, or 3.8 million acres, is capable of producing commercial timber but is withdrawn from commercial production; 19 percent, or 5.4 million acres, contains less-suitable commercial forest.

Forest land available for commercial timber management has decreased significantly over the past 25 years. For example, 9 billion board feet were harvested from Oregon forest lands in 1971. In 1995, this figure declined to 4.3 billion board feet. Much of this is due to dramatic decreases in timber harvesting from federal land, which plummeted from 5.5 billion board feet harvested in 1972 to just over 650 million board feet in 1995. Timber harvesting on privately owned commercial forest lands has declined as well, but not as dramatically, dropping from 3.1 billion board feet in 1971 to 2.7 billion board feet in 1995. The only increase in timber harvesting by land ownership occurred among private nonindustrial forest landowners. In 1996, private nonindustrial landowners harvested 450 million board feet; in 1995, this same group harvested over 700 million board feet of commercial timber.

Estimates show that Oregon's commercial landbase has decreased by more than 24 percent since 1945. Private forest land has been lost due to urban expansion and other non-timber uses. Changes in designated uses for public land have also reduced the number of acres available for commercial management.

Forestry Issues

Private Forest Lands

Private forest lands represent a larger portion of Oregon's timber supply due to harvest limitations placed on federal forest land. Timber harvest levels on non-industrial forest lands—parcels typically smaller than 5,000 acres and owned by individuals, not corporations—have more than doubled since 1981, and harvest levels on industry-owned forest lands have also increased during the same period. The relative percentage of overall harvest, however, emphasizes the importance of Oregon's private forest lands.

Nearly all of the timber harvested from private forest lands is second-growth. Since private forest lands are being reforested, they will play a major role in sustaining Oregon's long-term timber supply.

The increasing importance of Oregon's private forest landbase has raised some interesting challenges, many of them related to regulation. The Board of Forestry and the Department of Forestry administer the Oregon Forest Practices Act to assure the continuous harvest of timber on private lands, consistent with the sound management of soil, air, water, and fish and wildlife resources. In recent years, the Forest Practices Act has undergone several legislative amendments that have increased protection for important forest resource sites.

Due to the unpredictability of federal forest management direction—and a steady demand for wood products in domestic and export markets—private forest lands will remain an important part of Oregon's forest landbase.

Federal Forest Lands

The management direction of Oregon's federal forests has undergone a major shift in recent years. A combination of factors—including protection measures for the northern spotted owl, increased

Workers at Parks Bronze in Enterprise put the finishing touches on Bugs Bunny and Daffy Duck monuments for Warner Brothers. Fine arts foundries have grown to employ dozens of displaced lumber workers in Wallowa County.

Photo by Gary Fletcher.

public involvement, changing public values and a declining forest products economy—have made for challenging times.

Federal timber harvest levels have declined as timber sales have been appealed and forest set-asides for habitat protection have increased. Reduced revenues have affected local services and infrastructure—where a percentage of harvest tax dollars are reinvested—and the overall structure and funding of federal agencies.

At the same time, the United States Department of the Interior (USDI) Bureau of Land Management (BLM) and the US Department of Agriculture Forest Service—Oregon's largest federal forestry agencies—are in the process of changing their overall management strategies for federal forest lands. The preferred approach is known as ecosystem management, where all planned actions are considered and made in a large-scale geographic context.

Another major management shift for federal agencies involves providing habitat for threatened or endangered species. Species currently listed, or candidates for listing, are the northern spotted owl, the marbled murrelet, and various populations, stocks and species of anadromous fish (four species of salmon and one of steelhead trout).

These listings have a profound effect on the management of all forest lands, but particularly public lands managed by the federal government. Federal land management actions cannot be taken without intense consultation and plan-

ning. The agencies must prove that proposed actions either have no adverse effect on a listed species or its habitats, or that expected actions having positive effects elsewhere will offset the locally negative ones.

State Forest Lands

The Department of Forestry manages about 789,000 acres of forest land that are held in reserve for the benefit of counties, schools and local taxing districts. Nearly 657,000 acres are Board of Forestry lands, which are managed by the department for the counties. More than 132,000 acres of Common School Lands are managed by the department for the State Land Board. These state forest lands are not managed with the same "multiple-use" strategy as lands managed by the USDA Forest Service. According to statute, state forest lands are managed to produce sustainable revenue for counties, schools and local taxing districts.

Despite the fact that these state forest lands make up only 3 percent of Oregon's commercial forest landbase, the state has become a major supplier of timber due to restrictions placed on harvest activity in federal forests.

Oregon has five major state forests—Clatsop, Elliott, Santiam, Sun Pass and Tillamook—together with a number of small tracts scattered across the state. Unlike federal lands, which contain the majority of mature forests, state forests generally contain younger trees. For example, the Tillamook State Forest was burned in a series of disastrous fires in

Steam-driven equipment, such as this log skidder, was used to drag heavy logs out of the woods in the early days of forestry in Oregon.

Photo courtesy of Oregon Department of Forestry.

the 1930s, 1940s and 1950s, and much of the Elliott State Forest burned in 1868.

Although state forests are composed of younger trees, department foresters have found both northern spotted owl and marbled murrelet nest sites and activity centers. Both birds are typically considered species that nest in mature forests. The state has responsibility under both the state and federal endangered species acts to protect listed species. To do this and meet financial commitments to the Common School Fund and counties, the Department of Forestry developed a Habitat Conservation Plan for the Elliott State Forest, which was approved by the U.S. Fish and Wildlife Service in October 1995. This plan protects the habitat of sensitive species concurrent with timber harvesting. It is a comprehensive approach that looks at the long-term management and health of the forest.

A second Habitat Conservation Plan is being written as part of a revised long-range management plan for the Northwest Oregon state forests—a plan that encompasses the Clatsop, Santiam and Tillamook state forests, along with scattered tracts of state-owned forest land

in northwest Oregon. The plan, a multi-year process involving several state agencies, also includes a revolutionary silvicultural plan for managing the forests—structure-based management. This concept prescribes a mix of active forest management techniques and practices that produce an array of forest stand structures across the landscape, from open areas where new trees are being established, to older forest structures featuring "old growth" characteristics—numerous large trees, multi-layered canopies, and substantial numbers of down logs and large snags. Individual stands would constantly, but the range of stand types and their relative abundance across the landbase would be reasonably stable. Because the structures are in a dynamic balance across the landscape, the forest provides a steady flow of timber volume, jobs, habitats and recreational opportunities.

A further challenge facing state land managers is to provide recreational opportunities. Increasingly, Oregonians look to state lands for a variety of activities. The Department of Forestry has a recreation plan for the Tillamook State Forest, implemented in 1993, that provides a range of activities and educational opportunities within a working forest.

Reforestation

The forest products industry is one of the state's largest, and Oregon is among the nation's leading timber producers. These same forests attract both residents and out-of-state visitors to hunt, fish, camp and travel through the great variety of forested areas and enjoy the scenic beauty of the state. Forests are also key contributors to clean air and water, fish and wildlife habitat and stable soils. For all these reasons, Oregon law has required reforestation following timber harvesting since 1941. About 100 million seedlings are planted in Oregon each year.

Oregon's Forest Practices Act requires reforestation to begin at the completion of a timber harvest, or one year after tree stocking has been reduced, whichever comes first. Replanting must be completed within another year. By the end of the sixth year, a free-to-grow stand must be established that meets or exceeds the minimum stocking requirements for that site class, up to 200 seedlings per acre. To ensure compliance with the state's forest practice rules, Oregon Department of Forestry personnel monitor harvested areas to determine seedling survival and stocking density.

The Department of Forestry helps non-industrial landowners with reforestation by offering advice through its Service Forestry Program. Service foresters help landowners develop plans for long-term forest land management, and key components of this plan are forest rotation and replanting. Landowners may also seek advice from the Oregon State University Extension Service or from private consulting foresters.

The department also administers the Forest Resource Trust, a tree-planting program with the focus of converting underproducing forest land into healthy, productive forest land. The trust was created by the 1993 Legislature, and provides financial and technical assistance to nonindustrial private forest landowners. Funding is provided as an investment in a landowner's forest. Trust funds are repaid when the landowner harvests the forest.

Forest Protection

Forest Health

The damage caused to Oregon's forests from insects and disease annually exceeds the damage caused by wildfire. Each year, approximately 1.6 billion board feet of timber are killed by the Douglas-fir tussock moth, the western spruce budworm, the mountain pine beetle and the fir engraver beetle, and diseases such as laminated root rot and mistletoe.

This proliferation of insects and diseases has left many valuable forest stands vulnerable to catastrophic wildfire. Options being considered for reducing this wildfire risk include salvage logging and the strategic burning of heavily damaged areas. Both methods would interrupt the existing pathways a wildfire could use and thus help keep future fires small.

Protecting damaged forests from wildfire is only part of regaining forest health. Rebuilding the forests so they will have natural resistance to fire and insect and disease damage, and provide wildlife habitat are the long-term goals.

For example, ponderosa pine will likely replace many of the damaged stands of Douglas-fir and true fir in northeastern Oregon because ponderosa pine is more resistant to frequent, low-intensity fires, which have occurred naturally in this area, and it is less susceptible to many of the insect and disease outbreaks that have plagued the region. Management plans will also focus on forest characteristics found to be linked to long-term forest health: structural diversity of a stand, protection of valuable water sources and enhancement of wildlife habitat.

A key component in rebuilding these forests is education. To help provide answers to the many questions about forest health, the Oregon Department of Forestry has a full-time forest health management staff. Its members constantly monitor the state's forests for signs of insect and disease outbreaks, and they provide information about combating current problems as well as managing a forest for disease and insect prevention.

Forest Fire Protection

Oregon is coming to the end of a decade-long period of below-normal precipitation, which depleted ground moisture and allowed forest and brush lands to become extremely dry. During the 1996 fire season, major fires burned hundreds of thousands of acres of forest land, much of it in Oregon's national forests. Recent budget constraints at the federal level have put more pressure on state and regional fire-fighting resources to cope with the increased risk. Limited fire-fighting resources coupled with a higher-than-normal number of wildfires have emphasized the importance of the initial attack—controlling a fire while it is still small enough to be manageable—and of maintaining healthy, fire-resistant forests.

In many areas east of the Cascade Range, insect and disease epidemics have killed large acreages of standing trees. The extended drought has turned these dead trees into easily ignited fuel. The vast areas of dead and dying forests often include another significant problem: homes and other structures.

Thousands of homes and other buildings have been built in areas known as the wildland/urban interface, where populated regions blend with the wooded natural environment. People living in these high-risk areas stand a good chance of facing a destructive—and potentially lethal—wildfire. Many structures in these areas lack minimum fire safety precautions or fire resistant building materials. Fires starting in these areas are often devastating; and the presence of homes and other structures intermingled with forest land makes fighting a wildfire much more difficult and costly, posing serious safety concerns for firefighters.

Wildfire agencies are working closely with insurance companies, local land use planning offices and the Oregon Building Codes Agency to require fire-safe building practices and materials. A major public education effort is underway to help homeowners understand their responsibilities for fire safety and the risk of living in interface areas.

Another problem facing wildland fire managers is the unprotected lands issue. There are areas within Oregon that are vulnerable to wildfire but are without publicly funded protection. When fires occur on these lands they often threaten public and private lands that are eligible for protection and, in more dramatic situations, place homes and lives at risk. State fire-fighting actions on these lands are made possible only after the governor invokes the Conflagration Act, which authorizes the use of fire protection resources outside of normal protection boundaries.

The unprotected lands issue is being brought before the 1997 Legislature. The Department of Forestry and other wildland fire management agencies believe it would help stabilize wildland fire protection in Oregon if there were fewer unprotected lands in the state. A revenue source, such as a per-acre wildland fire protection tax, would enable state fire managers to allocate resources for the protection of these lands.

Resource Protection and Diversity

The Oregon Forest Practices Act, passed in 1971, was the first of its kind in the nation to require resource protection during logging operations. Nine other states have since adopted forest practice regulations. The act specifically requires that all operators notify the Department of Forestry when they are planning any forest operation—from road building and maintenance to tim-

ber harvesting. Each year, Department of Forestry offices receive about 20,000 notifications. The notification process provides information on the location and type of planned activity. Department foresters then follow up on operations that require special care, typically operations near streams or sensitive wildlife sites.

A Board of Forestry committee recommended in 1996 non-regulatory incentives that will help nonindustrial private landowners to better manage their forest lands. The challenge is to have support systems in place that both increase landowner awareness of forest investment opportunities and provide incentives that encourage and enable landowners to make needed enhancements to their lands. The incentives approach is not intended to replace forest practice rules or the enforcement of forest protection laws; rather, incentives are intended to encourage enlightened forest management practices through education and cooperation instead of through rule-making and enforcement.

As incentives and other non-regulatory forest protection strategies evolve, the Forest Practices Act continues its focus on balancing forest resource protection and timber harvest activities. Clearly, this is a difficult balance to achieve and the act has evolved over the years in response to changing public values and emerging science. In 1987, the Department of Forestry began an inventory of thousands of sensitive resource sites that require protection during forest operations. In 1991, amendments to the act increased levels of stream protection, required retention of trees for wildlife habitat and scenic purposes, and limited the size and spacing of clearcuts.

Special consideration for species on federal and state threatened and endangered species lists have always been a part of the Forest Practices Act. Private forest landowners are also required to follow the federal Endangered Species Act and avoid "taking" any protected species.

Studies are now underway at regional, state, and local levels to provide useful information about how to restore anadromous fish populations in western Oregon, and to examine cumulative effects from timber harvesting and other human activities.

Protecting sensitive habitat areas is an important part of maintaining diversity. Other efforts underway on state, federal and private lands seek to further enhance ecosystem diversity. Federal forest managers are experimenting with approaches that mimic natural processes through harvest techniques that leave many standing trees—producing an uneven, layered canopy of trees, which is attractive to many bird and wildlife species—and by leaving large logs and branches on the forest floor to support a variety of plant and animal communities.

Foresters on all ownerships are using a wider selection of native tree species during reforestation to mimic a more natural forest, composed not only of Douglas-fir but of hemlock, cedar, pine and other native species. In some areas plagued by a natural root disease, foresters are using red alder—a fast-growing hardwood tree—that replenishes nitrogen in the soils of diseased sites.

A partnership program, known as the Stream Enhancement Initiative (SEI), is bringing together private landowners, the Department of Forestry and the Department of Fish and Wildlife to help revitalize important fish-bearing streams. Under this voluntary program, forest operators, foresters and biologists meet to plan enhancement work, such as placing boulders and large logs in streams. Adding such structures improves fish habitat.

A forest smoke management program administered by the Department of Forestry protects air quality. Planned forest burning is carefully conducted according to detailed weather forecasts and daily burning instructions.

The science and application of forest management has changed dramatically during the past 10 years. Some forest planners are now developing management plans on an ecosystem approach that views a planned harvest unit in the context of the larger ecosystem. This new approach may hold the key to even greater species diversity in Oregon's forests.

Urban Forestry

Many people take trees for granted, especially the trees in their own communities. Too often, people only notice their community trees when they are affected by them. The windstorm of December 12, 1995, showed Oregonians this fact in stark detail. Large Douglas-fir trees that shaded many a home in the Portland area came crashing down under the 80-mph winds. Root systems that had been cut or otherwise damaged by home-building or other construction projects gave up their fight for survival, and people and property suffered. Anyone wondering why communities should manage their trees need only look to the effects of what was the most devastating windstorm since Columbus Day 1962.

The Department of Forestry's Urban and Community Forestry Assistance

A fleet of forest fire-fighting trucks await dispatch from the Oregon Department of Forestry's Salem headquarters. Photo courtesy of the Oregon Department of Forestry.

Program provides the leadership and technical services necessary to support the stewardship of Oregon's urban and community forests. Through this program, technical assistance is available to Oregon cities, counties, colleges and universities, volunteer planting groups, state agencies, and other entities. This assistance is provided through on-site visits, technology transfer, grants program management, and educational programming. Since 1991, the Department of Forestry has made more than 1,700 technical assists to local units of government and community groups. In this same period, the program distributed $1 million in federal matching grants. which leveraged $2 million in local in-kind and cash expenditures.

Other Forest Benefits

Millions of people visit forest recreation areas to hike trails, visit waterfalls, swim in lakes, fish in rivers and climb mountains. The forests hold vast riches, both natural and cultural. Mushrooms, for example, have become a major "secondary" forest product in several regions of the state.

While secondary forest products will continue to influence forest management plans, recreation has emerged as perhaps the highest non-timber priority in long-term forest management for all landowners. An example of this trend can be found in one of the Pacific Northwest's best known forests, the Tillamook State Forest in northwest Oregon.

While the Tillamook State Forest was being restored after the Tillamook Burn, families and individuals began looking to the area as a source of enjoyment and recreation. Over the years, motorcycle riders began riding the logging roads. Hikers and horseback riders began using the old wagon routes as trails. Anglers scouted the rivers for salmon and trout. And underlying the entire recreational experience of the Tillamook was a historical record of the forest's past occupants and users.

Today, a foundation has been laid for organized, improved recreation in the Tillamook State Forest. The area's primary use is for timber production, but management plans are being developed for preserving and developing important cultural history sites, separate trails for motorized and non-motorized users, and the development of campsites and other recreation areas.

This example of developing managed, non-timber forest uses is being repeated in other areas of the state.

Agriculture

Agriculture is a leading Oregon industry, with 1995-96 farm and ranch sales of $3.4 billion. Producers purchase more than $3 billion of inputs, including seed, feed, supplies and services from local companies, which make up a big portion of business in rural and urban parts of the state. As commodities move from farm to consumer, another $2 billion in value is added through processing. Add in transportation, marketing, warehousing and storage, and related services, and nearly 18 percent of the economy is related to agriculture. Approximately 140,000 jobs are tied to agriculture, with about 60,000 of these on the farm.

Roughly 80 percent of Oregon's agriculture production goes out of the state, with half of it marketed overseas. More than 60 percent of the volume of exports through the Port of Portland are agricultural products.

Products

Oregon leads the nation in the production of Christmas trees, grass seed, hazelnuts, peppermint, raspberries, blackberries, loganberries and other berry crops. Oregon is a major producer of hops, strawberries, prunes, plums, onions, cauliflower, pears and nursery products.

Greenhouse and nursery products rank as the state's number one commodity, bringing in annual sales of $419 million. Hay is number two with sales of $304 million. Cattle and calves, a historic leader in farm sales that has recently suffered from low prices, is now ranked number three with $295 million in sales. Wheat, at $287 million, and grass seed, at $236 million, complete the top five commodities.

Oregon is a major exporter of soft white wheat, frozen French fries, grass seed, hay and processed corn. Major customers include Japan, South Korea, Pakistan, the Philippines and Saudi Arabia. With more than 200 commodities, ranging from azaleas to wheat,

Oregon's agricultural base is tremendously diversified.

Agricultural Regions

The state has several distinct agricultural regions. The Willamette Valley is the most diversified. Specialty crops include vegetables, berries, hazelnuts, hops and nursery products. Regional strengths include proximity to processing, abundant rainfall and a long growing season.

Tree fruits, potatoes and livestock dominate southern Oregon's agricultural industry. Strengths of this region include high quality products, excellent marketing programs and proximity to California markets. Constraints include limited water and lack of diversity among commodities.

Fisheries and dairy farms are abundant in the coastal region. Increasing consumption of dairy products and seafood, as well as new ways to process under-used species of fish, present growth opportunities. Wastewater treatment from dairies and declining salmon stocks present major challenges.

The Columbia Basin is noted for its large dryland wheat farms. Hood River and Wasco counties are famous for cherries, apples and pears. Surrounding counties in northeastern Oregon produce a number of irrigated field crops in addition to wheat and livestock. Access to Columbia River ports and irrigation development have enhanced the region's capabilities, but increased instream water priorities and drawdown of the Columbia River for fish needs will present ongoing difficulties. Malheur County in eastern Oregon produces seed crops, onions, potatoes, sugar beets and other specialty crops. Excellent growing conditions and cooperative efforts with Idaho enhance the area's production and processing abilities. Workforce issues and water availability remain key problems for eastern Oregon. Harney and Lake counties in southeastern Oregon, where livestock and hay production dominate, share the water issue. Grazing on public lands also affects this area.

Jefferson County and other central Oregon areas grow a wide range of crops, including seed, peppermint and grains. Livestock and hay are the predominant

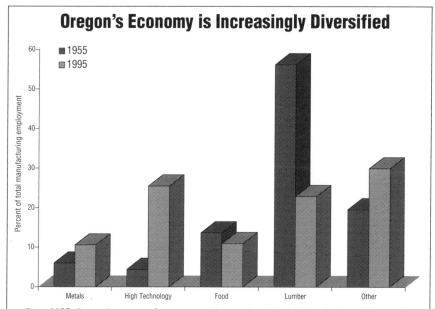

Oregon's Economy is Increasingly Diversified

Y-axis: Percent of total manufacturing employment (0–60)

Legend: ■ 1955 ■ 1995

Categories: Metals, High Technology, Food, Lumber, Other

Since 1955, Oregon's economy has come to rely more heavily on high technology industries for employment and less on lumber. A key to Oregon's strong economy, however, is the increase in diversity of employers. Source: Office of Economic Analysis.

A Jefferson County field at harvest time with the Haystack River Recreation Area in the background. Photo by Merritt E. Williams.

commodities in other central Oregon counties. Price swings in hay and livestock, as well as water constraints and public grazing issues will continue to be concerns for the region.

Issues in Agriculture

Access to the fundamental components of production agriculture—water and land—are the biggest issues facing the industry.

Oregon agriculture relies heavily on irrigation—47 percent of all Oregon farms do some irrigation and 70-80 percent of the total value of Oregon's harvested crops are produced with irrigation. Growth in population and industry are increasing demand for water; instream needs to support fish populations also create competition for water. The Oregon Department of Agriculture is working to maintain adequate supplies of water for farmers and ranchers, focusing on development of new water storage capacity rather than continuing to divide up the existing sources into smaller and smaller chunks.

Land in Oregon is also facing competitive pressures. Oregon has 17.6 million acres in farm use, of which 16 million are zoned as Exclusive Farm Use (EFU). Of this total, 4.5 million are high-value farm soils and 1.9 million acres are prime farmland, of which 70 percent is

in the Willamette Valley, which is experiencing tremendous population growth and development.

Between 1982 and 1992, about 89,000 acres of agricultural land were converted to urban and "built-up" uses. In the past 10 years, nearly 4,800 acres were brought into urban growth boundaries. Another 18,000 acres were rezoned from agricultural lands to commercial, industrial, or residential zones over this same period.

From 1940 to 1970, the population of the Portland urban region doubled while the amount of land occupied by that population quadrupled.

The loss of agricultural land as the primary resource of the agriculture industry is a major concern as population growth continues. The Department of Agriculture is working closely with other state agencies to assure preservation of this valuable asset, which not only serves as the natural resource base for production but also adds natural beauty, open space, and wildlife habitat.

An aging farm population facing retirement and increasing costs for young people entering farming or ranching are challenges facing the transition to a new generation. Oregon farmers and ranchers average nearly 54 years of age, and within the next decade more than 75 percent of the farmland will change hands. Oregon has traditionally been dominated by small operations and family ownership. However, costs of ownership could force consolidation and concentration, potentially affecting availability of products and prices paid by local consumers, as well as the profile of Oregon's farm and ranch owners.

Consumer concern over the use of pesticides in food production and producer concern over the declining availability of pesticides are other major issues. To address them, the Department of Agriculture started the Center for Applied Agricultural Research, which channels money into applied research designed to find solutions to real-life problems. As a result, researchers are discovering ways to produce food with fewer chemicals, and growers are finding how to make better use of the chemicals still available.

The Department of Agriculture works to assist the industry and the state by ensuring: consumer protection in accurate weights and measures of food and non-food products sold in the state; food safety and superb quality of food for consumers; protection of Oregon's natural resource base; and expanded markets for agricultural products and processed foods.

The department is currently working on ways to boost food processing components of Oregon agriculture. Added processing capabilities will create more jobs and give farmers alternative marketing avenues. Much of Oregon's agricultural production currently leaves the state in bulk form. By increasing the amount processed in the state from 35 percent to more than 50 percent, about 15,000 new jobs could be created.

Fish and Wildlife

Recreational and commercial uses of fish and wildlife are major Oregon industries. Combined, all such uses generate more than $1 billion of personal income for Oregonians each year. These activities are major contributors to small businesses, ranging from individual commercial fishers and charter boat owners to food processing companies and tourism-related operations.

These uses, and the businesses they support, are important because much of the financial benefit goes to regions and communities that may be otherwise economically depressed. Sport and commercial fishing generate a sizable portion of the personal income along the coast, while hunting provides seasonal income to eastern Oregon communities.

Sport fishing has the greatest economic impact generated by fish and wildlife users. The remainder is divided among commercial fishing, sport hunting and wildlife viewing. This latter category is a relatively new but rapidly expanding area of interest. Development of viewing areas as tourist attractions is just beginning, yet already shows tremendous potential for boosting local economies.

Sport Fishing

Few states can match Oregon's variety of sport fishing opportunities. More than 62,000 miles of fishing streams and 1,600 lakes and reservoirs provide some kind of angling year round. The businesses serving the hundreds of thousands of sport anglers depend heavily on these fisheries for their income. Over 700,000 residents and out-of-state visitors purchase angling licenses annually.

Trout species found in the state are rainbow, cutthroat, brown, brook and, in the same family, Atlantic salmon. The steelhead is a migratory form of the rainbow, and both summer and winter runs of these popular sport fish thrive in Oregon streams. In some waters, land-locked sockeye salmon, called kokanee, have been introduced and provide much sport fishing.

Warmer bodies of water contain a variety of imported species, including bass, crappie, bluegill and catfish. Sport fishing is also on the increase for sturgeon and walleye on the Columbia River.

Though five species of Pacific salmon occur in Oregon, the Chinook and Coho have historically been the major catch for sport anglers. By fall, the salmon are moving into fresh water and inland fishing begins.

Coastal bays provide excellent fishing for other saltwater fish species as well as for crab. Clamming also draws thousands of people to the beaches and bays.

The Department of Fish and Wildlife operates 34 fish hatcheries that produce millions of fish annually. Several million trout are released at six to 10 inches in length, while most salmon and steelhead are released when they are about one year old and ready to migrate to the ocean.

The reflections of boats sparkle in the waters of Salmon Harbor near Reedsport in Douglas County. Photo by Gordon Coons, courtesy of the Douglas County Commissioners.

Commercial Fishing

One of Oregon's first industries was the commercial fishing trade. Rich ocean and river harvests played an important role in the development of Oregon's economy and the establishment of various cities and ports.

Commercial fishing is still an important part of the state economy. In 1995, commercial fishing operations landed almost 240 million pounds of commercial products, worth over $77 million at harvest level. In 1995, commercial fish harvesting and processing generated personal income of $135 million for residents of coastal communities and $174 million statewide.

Chinook and Coho have historically made up the bulk of the commercial salmon catch. These fish are taken by ocean trollers and gillnetters working in the Columbia River.

In 1994, a fishery resource disaster was declared in the west coast salmon fisheries because of extremely low salmon stock abundances. Ocean landings of Chinook salmon rebounded in 1995 and 1996, but Oregon coastal Coho salmon remain at historically low levels and are being considered for listing under the federal Endangered Species Act. Harvest level prices for Oregon-caught salmon are depressed because of fish farm production of salmon, particularly in Norway and Chile, and because of record harvest levels for salmon in Alaska.

While salmon hatcheries receive a great deal of attention, the harvest of various ocean groundfish actually exceeds the salmon catch in both poundage and value. Groundfish include various species of rockfish (snapper), sole, sablefish and Pacific Whiting. In 1996, landings of groundfish exceeded 213 million pounds. Harvest level revenues amounted to about $35 million.

The groundfish industry for Pacific Whiting has experienced a remarkable surge. Increased allocations for domestic processing in 1990 and 1991 caused rapid industry development. Harvest rose from an annual average of less than 1 million pounds to 5 million pounds in 1990 and 155 million in 1996.

Other species, such as Dungeness crab, pink shrimp and albacore tuna are also commercially valuable commodities contributing to the coastal economies.

Wildlife and Hunting

Hunting is a popular activity in Oregon among residents as well as visitors, contributing to the economy of communities throughout the state. Over 300,000 hunters purchase licenses annually.

Nine mammal species found in Oregon are classed as big game. Ten species of resident birds are classed as upland game and eight mammals are classed as fur bearers. More than 500 species of nongame animals and birds are found in Oregon.

Mule deer are east of the Cascades, and blacktail deer are located in the western part of the state. Roosevelt elk dwell on the west side of the mountains, while Rocky Mountain elk inhabit eastern Oregon. In the high-desert region of the southeast, pronghorn antelope are found.

Several areas in eastern Oregon now have bighorn sheep as a result of reintroductions that began in the 1950s. As these bighorn populations have grown, trapping and transplanting programs within the state have helped disperse these animals to suitable habitats. Cougar and bear are found statewide. Classed as big game, they are given protection during much of the year.

The Department of Fish and Wildlife operates 16 wildlife areas, some primarily for waterfowl or big game. In management of these areas, the department considers nongame as well as all game species present within a wildlife area.

Fish and Wildlife Issues

Work with threatened or endangered fish and wildlife has taken on added importance in recent years as attention has turned to the needs of species that are not coping well with human competition for water and land. The most publicized cases have concerned the spotted owl and salmon runs to coastal Oregon and the upper Columbia and Snake rivers.

Many other animal populations also face uncertain futures. The Department of Fish and Wildlife is required by state law to determine the status of these troubled species and, where possible, provide management strategies for their recovery. The department has joined other state natural resource and economic development agencies to integrate state efforts to protect Oregon's fish and wildlife resources as well as the communities whose economies rely on the health of these resources.

Tourism/Recreation

As Oregon's economy continues to diversify, tourism plays a vital role in creating new job opportunities and strengthening local and regional economies. In 1996, an estimated $4.5 billion was generated in Oregon by visitor expenditures—a 36 percent increase since 1991. This significant growth in Oregon's visitor industry confirms that tourism is a key component of the state's economy.

In addition to direct impacts, employment and revenue in support sectors such as business services, utilities and personal services are significant. In 1995, the total of direct and indirect sales was approximately $8.8 billion. The sectors of Oregon's economy that received the highest levels of indirect and induced impacts from tourism expenditures were the finance, insurance, real estate, medical, legal, retail sales, manufacturing and other services classifications.

Oregon's visitor industry provides important entry-level jobs as well as increasing opportunities in managerial and professional positions. It also provides important transferable skills and employment for women and minorities entering the job market. Interestingly, tourism employment has grown at a slower rate than payroll and travel spending, which in part reflects rising average wage rates in the industry. As the Oregon visitor industry matures, so do the quantity and quality of jobs.

Between 1991 and 1996, employment in the tourism industry grew 21 percent, from 57,580 people to an estimated 69,680. The industry provides entrepreneurial opportunities—nearly 75 percent of Oregon's visitor-industry businesses have a "working proprietor" whose average family income is $43,917 per year.

Tourism Resources

Tourism and the environment in Oregon are irrevocably linked. The clean, pristine natural environment is Oregon's greatest draw. Much of the economic impact from the industry is generated by visitors recreating, sightseeing and relaxing in our mountains, meadows, rivers, deserts and oceans.

These resources are the result of dynamic geologic processes. The state's geologic history created Basin and Range fault block mountains such as Steens and Hart Mountains in southeast Oregon; the various "exotic terrains" that are the foundations of Hells Canyon and the Wallowa and Blue mountains in the northeastern part of the state and the Klamath Mountains in southwest Oregon; volcanic features such as Fort Rock and Smith Rock in the High Lava Plains near Bend; the Columbia River basalt flows that solidified into cliffs over which Multnomah and other waterfalls flow in the Columbia River Gorge; the spectacular High Cascade volcanoes such as Mount Hood and Crater Lake; the sediment-filled basin known as the fertile Willamette Valley; and the volcanic island chain that forms the Coast Range.

Oregon also boasts an increasing number of man-made attractions. Since 1992, several major new attractions have opened, including the Oregon Coast Aquarium in Newport, the National Historic Oregon Trail Interpretive Center at Flagstaff Hill near Baker City, the new Oregon Museum of Science and Industry in Portland, the Museum at Warm Springs in central Oregon, the Pacific Northwest Museum of Natural History in Ashland, the End of the Oregon Trail Interpretive Center in Oregon City and others.

State Government-Operated Attractions

The Parks and Recreation Department manages about 92,000 acres of the state's most scenic natural resources and historically important public lands. In addition, the department manages the Pacific Ocean shoreline as a 362-mile-long recreation area, a scenic waterway system of 19 rivers and one lake, and the 200-mile-long Willamette River Greenway.

Expenditures by state park visitors and employees contributed nearly $550 million to local economies in 1995. Most of these estimated expenditures resulted from more than 39 million visits to 178 state park day-use areas. Another 2 million-plus campground

Rockclimbing is a popular recreational activity in many parts of Oregon. Kerry Searles of Enterprise practices his rock climbing in the Wallowas. Photo by Gary Fletcher.

visits boosted local economies and stimulated tourism activity of particular importance to Oregon's rural areas.

State government, through the Marine Board, supports boating through facility improvements, marine law enforcement, safety education and boat registration. Oregon's world-famous white water rivers, pristine lakes and spectacular Pacific coastline make water recreation very popular—about a fourth of the state's residents are boaters. The state's diverse waters also attract boaters living outside Oregon and play a major role in the tourism industry.

The coastal zone features 296 miles of coast line, 14 major bays with direct access to the Pacific Ocean along with 21 major estuaries with 133,000 acres of tide lands. Inland waters provide 50 major navigable rivers, more than 10,000 river miles of navigable streams, with 6,619 lakes and reservoirs providing 587,870 surface water acres.

Boating is big business in Oregon. Boat sales and recreational activities such as motor boating, fishing, white water rafting, charter boat fishing, windsurfing and river excursions are associ-

ated with more than $1 billion in sales and 29,200 jobs annually.

Federal Government-Operated Attractions

The USDA Forest Service manages Oregon's 14 national forests, including the Columbia River Gorge National Scenic Area, which covers more than 15.5 million acres. Besides managing for water, forage, wildlife, fish and timber products, the national forests also provide recreation opportunities. More than 270 campgrounds, 12 winter sports areas, over 11,000 miles of trails, and 1,200 miles of wild and scenic rivers offer fun and sport for all ages.

Two National Recreation Areas, one National Scenic Area and one National Volcanic Monument provide exceptional opportunities. The Oregon Dunes National Recreation Area boasts some of the most beautiful coastline and best beach-oriented recreation on the west coast. The famous Snake River and ruggedly beautiful Hells Canyon National Recreation Area are found in the far northeast corner of the state. Minutes from Portland, the Columbia River Gorge National Scenic Area is home to fabulous waterfalls and the Historic Columbia River Highway. Newberry National Volcanic Monument protects the wealth of geological wonders found within the five-mile-wide caldera of the Newberry Volcano. Forest Service interpretive centers at Cape Perpetua on the central Oregon coast, Lava Lands south of Bend, Timberline Lodge on Mt. Hood, Multnomah Falls in the Columbia River Gorge, and the Wallowa Valley Visitors Center in Enterprise help forest visitors better understand complex social and environmental processes affecting the landscape.

The USDI National Park Service administers four of Oregon's most spectacular areas: Crater Lake National Park, Oregon Caves National Monument, the John Day Fossil Beds National Monument and Fort Clatsop National Memorial.

The BLM's western Oregon forests provide recreation for the state's major population centers, as well as for smaller towns and rural areas of western Oregon. Hunting and fishing on the land and in its streams are popular activities.

The agency supports white water rafting, which is turning into an important recreational industry, through its management of critical parts of the Deschutes, John Day, Owyhee and Rogue rivers.

A total of 58 BLM recreation areas in Oregon provide 1,379 campsites and 708 picnic spots surrounded by fishing, hiking, swimming and other recreational pursuits.

Tourism Issues

Tourism presents both challenges and opportunities for Oregon's environment and public land managers. The industry faces many issues: conflicting uses— for instance, snowmobilers and cross-country skiers, power water crafts and rafters; over-use and endangerment of plant and wildlife in some areas; under-used capacity in more remote areas; and others.

Tourism can help enhance the environment, restore fish and wildlife habitat and provide opportunities to educate visitors on environmental needs. An emerging niche market in "nature-based tourism" has created new businesses that are concerned with the quality of the environment, managing and designing tours that balance the needs of the visitor and the environment.

Too many visitors could adversely affect the very environment they seek to enjoy, however. It will be the challenge of public and private tourism and natural resource managers to maintain and even enhance Oregon's pristine environment, while still providing a satisfying and memorable experience that meets or exceeds visitors' expectations.

Resource and Infrastructure Fundamentals

The resource and economic infrastructure in Oregon are fundamental to determining how stable both the environment and the economy will be as the state continues to grow. Given the structures created by nature in Oregon, the state has created systems to manage the land and water, and it has developed energy and transportation infrastructure to meet basic economic needs.

As discussed in the forestry, agriculture, and fish and wildlife sections, increases in the human population are putting pressure on many of the natural systems in Oregon. As a result, the state is working to resolve issues of land and water management and seeking to improve the way Oregon uses its energy and transportation resources.

Oregon's Geology

Oregon is located on the "Ring of Fire" circling the Pacific Rim, making the state vulnerable to dynamic geologic processes that influence the health, safety and welfare of Oregonians. Recent scientific investigations reveal that large earthquakes and related hazards—such as tsunamis, landslides and volcanic eruptions—have affected Oregon in the past and will again.

Minerals

Minerals are a source of new wealth and necessary raw materials in Oregon. In recent years, the annual output value of Oregon's mines and natural gas wells averaged more than $240 million. The bright spots in Oregon's mineral resources are continuing natural gas production and the expansion of industrial minerals production. New mines and processing plants may offer year-round employment and stable tax bases in parts of rural Oregon that historically have depended on seasonal and cyclical industries such as agriculture, tourism and forestry. Changing market patterns in the western United States and other Pacific Rim nations, coupled with Oregon's favorable geology, suggest major opportunities for rural economic diversification and development.

Every Oregon community benefits directly from indispensable supplies of sand and gravel, crushed rock and other building materials. Development of local sources of industrial minerals can assist existing Oregon businesses and give them a competitive advantage. Industrial mineral production can stimulate port activity as Oregon products penetrate foreign markets and imports sustain the local metals industry. Industrial minerals are used in countless ways, including many for environmental protection, and they provide a rural economic growth opportunity.

Minerals exploration and production are regulated by the Mined Land Reclamation Program of the Department of Geology and Mineral Industries in cooperation with other state, federal and local agencies to ensure the protection of the environment and future beneficial use of mined lands.

Mineral Fuels

Emerging concerns over energy supplies have prompted efforts to identify and develop traditional resources such as natural gas. Private concerns continue to lease lands and explore for natural gas in Oregon. The Mist Gas Field in Columbia County in northwestern Oregon is the only producing natural gas field in the Pacific Northwest. Total natural gas production from the field to date has exceeded $110 million. Also, two depleted gas reservoirs at the Mist Gas Field store 10 billion cubic feet of imported pipeline gas during the summer to meet peak demands during the following winter.

Oregon exhibits excellent potential for geothermal energy, and thousands of acres of public domain and state land have been leased for exploration. In relatively recent geologic time, volcanism occurred across much of Oregon, and the earth is still hot in many places at depth.

Land Ownership and Management

Of the more than 61 million acres of land within Oregon's borders, almost 53 percent is owned by the federal government, mainly under the control of the USDA Forest Service and the BLM. Another 3 percent is owned by state and local governments.

State-owned lands are managed by several agencies. The Department of Administrative Services manages most state land dedicated to office buildings and like uses. The Division of State Lands manages lands granted to Oregon at statehood for the benefit of schools, about 650,000 acres of grazing lands, two-thirds of which are located in Malheur and Harney counties. The Division of State Lands also manages state-owned lands beneath Oregon's navigable waterways, including the territorial sea. The Land Board has assigned management of 132,000 acres of forest lands, approximately 90,000 of which are included in the Elliott State Forest in Coos and Douglas counties, to the

Department of Forestry. State law provides for the protection and the public's right to the use of Oregon's beaches. State parks include more than 90,000 acres of land.

Several counties have assumed management of tax-foreclosed properties. Additional public holdings include city-owned areas, reclamation and dam projects, highway rights of way, wildlife reserves and other miscellaneous areas.

USDA Forest Service Lands

The USDA Forest Service administers 15.6 million acres of land in Oregon's 13 national forests—the Deschutes, Fremont, Malheur, Mt. Hood, Ochoco, Rogue River, Siskiyou, Siuslaw, Umatilla, Umpqua, Wallowa-Whitman, Willamette and Winema. They cover the Coast Range, most of the Cascades and the highlands of northeastern Oregon.

National forest lands are managed under Forest Land and Resource Management plans, which were developed in close coordination with other federal agencies and state and local governments. These plans, which are updated to reflect changing conditions and values, provide for multiple-use management of these lands, emphasizing the principles of ecosystem management, resource sustainability, forest products and forest health.

USDI Bureau of Land Management Lands

The BLM manages 15.7 million acres in Oregon. The land ranges from some of the west's best-watered, most highly productive forest land bordering the Pacific Ocean to arid, but scenic, dry lake beds in the southeastern part of the state.

BLM manages ranges, forests, minerals/wildlife habitat, water, recreation and other resources to encourage multiple uses wherever possible without sacrificing other values, like the preservation of wilderness. The bulk of BLM's ownership is in southeastern Oregon rangelands, but the agency also manages the 2.2 million acres of timber-rich Oregon and California Railroad lands in western Oregon (O&C lands).

The O&C lands are remnants of a land grant to the O&C Railroad in the last century when federal subsidies encouraged railroad construction to open the country to trade and travel. After the railroad defaulted on its agreement, the land came back to federal ownership. These high-value, publicly-owned timberlands have provided important raw material for the region's wood products industry. County governments in which O&C timberlands are located receive half the incomes from the harvested timber, helping them finance schools, roads, and other important services for their residents.

Sweeping, wide-open eastern Oregon vistas provide much more than scenery. They provide important habitat for wildlife, including wild horses. More than 200,000 cattle graze these ranges, contributing to the state's agricultural economy while ranchers pay the federal government for the grazing privileges.

Land Use Planning

Oregon has a long tradition of carefully managing its bountiful natural resources. That tradition is based on environmental and economic considerations. In a state with an economy tied closely to forestry, agriculture and tourism, conservation of farmland, forests and water resources is essential.

Oregon's statewide planning program emphasizes both conservation and development. The program aims to limit development on rural farm and forest lands, while encouraging development in appropriate places. Oregon's planning program is based on the idea that conservation and development are not conflicting forces—that they must, in fact, be complementary. Oregon has broken new ground by treating planning as a comprehensive design for living, a design unified by statewide goals.

Today, many communities are faced with problems associated with rapid growth and sprawl. Oregon's Department of Land Conservation and Development, which administers the state's land use planning laws, and the Department of Transportation are providing joint consultation to communities to help them cope with those problems. Teams of experts in planning and urban design work with local officials as they review and respond to development proposals and update land use ordinances.

Efforts are also underway to focus land use planning at a regional level.

Although still in the experimental stage, the intent is to bring local governments and state agencies together to address issues that transcend the boundaries of any one community.

Oregon's Water Resources

Oregon's water resources are fundamental to all of the state's ecosystems and industries. Water is also at the center of much of the scenic and recreational values that attract visitors. Resource-based economies like agriculture, fisheries, forestry and mining all rely on water and a healthy ecosystem for their long-term success.

Oregon has a network of 112,000 miles of rivers and streams and over 6,000 lakes and reservoirs. The state's largest river, the Willamette, has more runoff per square mile than any other major river in the United States. Oregon is bounded on the north by the Columbia and on the east by the Snake. Other major stream systems in the state include the Deschutes, John Day, Klamath, Owyhee, Rogue and Umpqua rivers. Oregon has an estimated annual surface-water run-off of over 66 million acre-feet—roughly enough water to cover the entire state one foot deep.

However, belying its popular reputation, Oregon can be surprisingly dry. The eastern two-thirds of the state is largely high desert, with rainfall often dropping below 12 inches per year. Even in wetter western Oregon, the summers are usually marked by little or no precipitation. Annual water shortages are common in many areas of the state. In part, this is because most of Oregon's water supply comes from winter rains and mountain snow packs. The peak demands for agriculture and cities come during the summer—the time of lowest streamflow. How to meet existing and future water demands—and achieve balance between protecting Oregon's natural heritage and promoting its economy—is a challenge currently being faced by Oregon's citizens.

To meet these growing demands, the state is increasingly turning toward its groundwater resource. Although the state monitors wells to prevent overdrafting of aquifers, total groundwater supply has not been quantified because of Oregon's complex geology. Currently, the Oregon Water Resources Department and the U.S. Geological Survey are studying the groundwater resources in the Deschutes and the Willamette Basins. These two basins have been selected for study due to the increasing demands on the resources as the Willamette Valley and Central Oregon continue to grow in population.

The program includes a set of statewide water policies and specific rules for most of the state's 18 major river basins. The statewide policies address a range of water issues from water allocation to hydro-electric development. These policies are then implemented through a series of basin plans set by administrative rules. These plans determine the kinds of allowable water uses and identify areas of water shortage or surplus.

Energy

Energy is a large part of Oregon's economy. In 1993, Oregon households, businesses and manufacturing firms spent more than $5 billion on oil products, electricity and natural gas.

Around 35 percent of the energy used in Oregon comes from petroleum products. Electricity accounts for nearly 15 percent of total use. Natural gas, wood and other energy sources account for the rest.

Electricity

In 1994, Oregonians purchased nearly 45 million kilowatt-hours of electricity. Industrial manufacturing firms used about 34 percent and households used 37 percent of the electricity purchased.

The electrical system in Oregon is part of a regional network in which a mix of public and private utilities and the Bonneville Power Administration sell electricity. Portland General Electric, Pacific Power and Idaho Power are the privately-owned electric utilities that serve Oregon. Oregon's 36 publicly owned utilities include 11 municipal utilities, 19 cooperatives and six people's utility districts. Most of their power comes from Bonneville, the federal agency that markets electricity from the region's federal dams and Washington Nuclear Plant 2. Manufacturing firms produced about 2 percent of their own power.

Until the 1970s, Oregon's major source of electricity was hydropower. Hydro still dominates the generation mix today, but coal, natural gas and nuclear have been added to the resource base.

The Northwest experienced an electricity surplus during the 1980s. Electricity demand has been growing rapidly since 1986. However, at the same time demand has been growing, the electric transmission system has, to an ever greater extent, linked the entire west coast. One effect of this has been availability of surplus power from other areas of the west. Another is increased pressure to deliver power over wider distances. Abundant hydropower from Canada was shipped to California to meet warm weather loads in 1996. Unanticipated events took small transmission lines out of service in July and August of that year. As a result of these events, large parts of the west coast found themselves without power in the resultant cascade of transmission line failures.

The closing of the Trojan Nuclear Plant in 1993 eliminated about 700 average megawatts. Actions to save endangered fish could reduce hydropower production by 400 or more average megawatts. Over the next 10 years, largely due to expected population growth, the region may need new electricity supplies equivalent to about four times the power that Trojan would have generated. Much of this can come from available power in other areas of the region. But, in times of high demand, transmission capacity may not be sufficient to meet the need.

Two new gas-fired combustion turbines have been built in north central Oregon. These plants are near available transmission and gas pipelines, but far from population centers where most of the power is used. This forces increased reliance on the transmission system.

Even with available power from elsewhere on the west coast, utilities and independent developers are planning to build new power plants. The electricity supply is becoming more competitive. Changes in the marketplace and new technologies will have a big impact on how the power system operates and, eventually, on how consumers buy their power.

Oil

Oregon uses more oil than any other energy source. In 1994, Oregonians purchased more than 2.7 billion gallons of oil products—gasoline, distillate and residual oils, liquefied petroleum gases, kerosene and jet fuels. Most oil products, more than 81 percent, are used for transportation. The rest goes to manufacture goods, power farm machinery, and heat homes and buildings.

Oregon has no oil resources, although some may exist off its coast. It also has no refineries other than an asphalt refinery in Portland. Most of Oregon's oil products come from Puget Sound refineries through the Olympic pipeline. The remainder comes from California by tanker, truck, and rail and from Salt Lake City through the Chevron pipeline. The refineries serving Oregon rely on a mix of foreign and domestic oil.

Natural Gas

Natural gas supplies more than 14 percent of Oregon's total energy. In 1994, more than 1.2 billion therms of natural gas were sold in Oregon. About 43 percent was used by manufacturers. Households claimed nearly 20 percent for space and water heating. About 20 percent was used by commercial firms, schools and governments for space and water heating and cooking. The use of natural gas for generating electricity has and will continue to boost the quantity of natural gas sold.

Most of Oregon's natural gas comes from Canada and the San Juan Basin in the Rocky Mountain states. Oregon's only producing natural gas field is near Mist in Columbia County, although the Department of Geology and Mineral Industries has recently identified a similar geological formation in the Tyee basin near Roseburg. These may be the subject of exploratory drilling in the future. In 1991, the Mist fields provided 2 percent of total natural gas sales.

Three natural gas utilities serve Oregon: Northwest Natural Gas, Cascade Natural Gas, and WP Natural Gas, a division of Washington Water Power Company. Northwest Natural accounts for nearly 81 percent of Oregon's natural gas sales. Many large industrial customers buy natural gas directly from natural gas producers.

Renewable Resources

Oregon relies on renewable resources more than any other state. Hydro and wood together provide nearly a quarter of Oregon's total energy use. Today, geothermal, solar, and wind are used primarily for home and business heating, but utilities are planning to increase their use for generating electricity as well.

Biomass technology, which uses energy sources such as animal waste and wood residues, produces about 105 billion Btus per year in Oregon. This is about 16 percent of the non-transportation energy consumed in the state.

Bonneville and the electric utilities have stepped up efforts to look at renewable resources for electricity generation. Results have been mixed. A 30-megawatt geothermal plant planned for the Newberry volcano in central Oregon has been abandoned by the developer. A 25-megawatt wind project in Umatilla County is planned, and a biogas plant in Benton County is currently producing power.

Conservation

Oregon is known nationally for its emphasis on conservation. Oregon's new homes, office buildings and other structures are among the most energy-efficient in the nation. Every Oregon household and business has access to incentives for conserving energy. Nearly all of Oregon's households have installed at least one efficiency measure in their homes.

The conservation efforts of the state and electric utilities have, in effect, eliminated the need for a coal fired power plant. Conservation has reduced natural gas and oil use as well, particularly in industrial processing and in heating homes, schools and offices.

The future of conservation with the electricity market moving toward more competition is somewhat uncertain. PGE, Pacific and Bonneville had been counting on conservation in their least-cost plans to supply more than 1,000 average megawatts of electricity. The biggest opportunities for more conservation will come from reducing hot water use, weatherizing homes and improving the efficiency of home appliances, commercial lighting, industrial processes,

Economy

and electrical generation, transmission and distribution systems.

Under a deregulated electric industry, new ways will need to be found to capture cost-effective opportunities for conservation. Utilities cannot compete with independent power producers in a wholesale market and fund conservation activities. This was the subject of much discussion in a recent regional review of the electric industry brought together by the governors of Oregon, Washington, Idaho and Montana. Legislative proposals at both the state and federal level will shape the future of electricity conservation.

Most of the conservation potential from oil is in the more efficient use of gasoline. Just how much we save will depend on gas prices, federal vehicle efficiency standards, the competitiveness of alternative fuels, residential land-use patterns, and the availability and convenience of alternative modes of travel. Meeting the state transportation goal for cutting travel 20 percent per capita in Eugene, Medford, Portland and Salem during the next 30 years could reduce gasoline use 15 percent by 2015.

Over the next decade, nearly 80 million therms of natural gas could be saved through more efficient space and water heating systems, boilers, ovens, cookers, dryers and furnaces, and appropriate operation and maintenance of steam systems.

Transportation

Highways and other transportation facilities play an essential role in developing and maintaining a strong economy. Transportation and economic development are directly linked—a healthy economy depends on moving goods and people quickly, efficiently and cost-effectively. Even a small transportation disruption can affect the population and economy. Failing to maintain existing highways and other transportation facilities results in productivity losses and poor economic growth.

Roads and Highways

When the Oregon Highway Department was created in 1913, vehicles registered in Oregon numbered 13,957; and the state highway system consisted of 1,070 miles of primary roads and 1,830 miles of secondary roads.

By 1940, Oregon's highway system had grown to 7,131 total miles. Today, the Oregon Department of Transportation operates and maintains about 7,500 total road miles. These highways have more than 18,000 lane-miles of pavement. The total road mileage in Oregon—including state, city, county and other agency-owned roads—is 97,275 miles. To construct a road system of this size today would cost more than $60 billion for the pavement alone.

State Highway Fund

The State Highway Fund comprises revenues collected from vehicle fuel taxes, commercial carrier weight-mile taxes and vehicle registrations. Oregon uses these revenues for construction and maintenance of public highways, roads, streets and roadside rest areas.

Counties receive about one quarter of the State Highway Fund, distributed based on the number of registered

Portland's light rail, MAX, celebrated its 10th birthday in 1996 by providing nearly 9 million rides on its 15-mile route from Portland to Gresham. The Westside MAX, an 18-mile route from Portland to Hillsboro, is scheduled to open in Fall 1998.

Photo courtesy of the City of Gresham.

vehicles; cities receive about 16 percent, distributed based on population; and the Department of Transportation uses the balance on state highways.

Commercial Trucking

Oregon's transportation network and trucking industry are important partners in maintaining a growing economy.

The Portland metropolitan area is the second largest warehousing and distribution center on the west coast. One in 11 Oregonians—110,042 people—worked in the trucking industry in 1995. During 1994, trucks moved 287,568 tons of outbound freight each business day, and carried 82.4 percent of all freight moved in the state—almost 170 million tons. As important as commercial trucks are to the Northwest today, they will continue to expand their role.

Public Transit

Oregon's population is expected to increase by 1.2 million people in the next 20 years. The Willamette Valley population will grow by 700,000 people. Many road construction projects become obsolete soon after they are finished because of the growing traffic.

Reducing reliance on new highway construction supports the state's land use goals by preserving valuable land for housing, businesses, agriculture and other essential uses. The state is working on a long-range public transportation plan to promote alternatives to single occupant auto use. The plan will be completed in 1997.

Public transit is already important to a large segment of Oregon's population. About 17 private and public providers connect Oregon communities with at least weekly intercity bus service. About 92 percent of Oregonians live within 10 miles of scheduled intercity buses.

In Oregon communities with populations of 50,000 or less, 25 small city and rural-area systems provide fixed-route, dial-a-ride or subsidized taxi services. Special transportation services exist statewide, providing mobility for people who are elderly or who have disabilities.

Annually, demand-management programs (ridesharing, telecommuting, etc.) in Bend, Corvallis, Eugene, Medford, Portland and Salem reduce driving by 19.1 million miles, pollutant emissions by 762,000 pounds and gasoline use by 962,000 gallons.

In 1990, more than 70 percent of Oregonians commuted to and from work alone. The Oregon Benchmarks program seeks to reduce that number to 50 percent by the year 2000. (Transit districts now listed in Local Government section on page 336.)

Rail Service

Oregon, which owes much of its agricultural, industrial and economic growth to railroad lines, continues to be well served by freight and passenger trains. The system includes 2,600 route-miles, operated by 21 different railroads carrying both freight and passengers.

Although the rail system is 300 miles shorter today than in 1986, it carries more rail traffic, with an increase of 28 percent between 1986 and 1992. However, during that same period, rail traffic originating in Oregon decreased. The Oregon Department of Transportation expects another 27 percent increase in rail traffic by the year 2000.

In 1995, rail freight traffic in and out of Oregon totaled 53.8 million tons. Most freight originating in Oregon (8 million of the 14 million tons sent annually) is shipped to California and Washington.

Farm products represent the state's single largest commodity shipped by rail in Oregon. Annually, terminating and through movements of farm products exceed 5 million tons each. Lumber and wood products represent the next largest commodity shipped by rail—primarily originating within the state.

The passenger rail line from Eugene to Portland is part of the federally designated Pacific Northwest High Speed Rail Corridor that extends to Vancouver, Canada. This means preference for Federal Railroad Administration funding to develop advanced passenger train service in the corridor. The Oregon Department of Transportation is developing Oregon's portion of the corridor with the long-range goal of providing service at speeds of more than 100 miles per hour in rural areas.

Today, Oregon is served by five Amtrak scheduled trains running on tracks owned by the Burlington Northern, Santa Fe and Union Pacific railroads. State-sponsored service improvements in the Eugene-Vancouver, Canada Pacific Northwest High Speed

Economy

Rail Corridor have boosted ridership since 1994. Some Oregon stations have shown passenger increases of more than 60 percent since the start of these new services, but patronage on the route through eastern Oregon has decreased to 20-30 percent.

Aeronautics

Oregon is served by more than 400 airports, heliports and other landing areas. The state owns and operates 34 general aviation airports located to serve important recreational, agricultural and forestry areas, or as a safe haven for pilots in emergencies.

Scheduled passenger airline service is available to seven Oregon communities: Eugene, Klamath Falls, Medford, North Bend, Pendleton, Portland and Redmond. Portland International Airport (PDX) is the largest commercial airport in Oregon. It is also one of the west coast's fastest growing airports.

Nearly 3.1 million visitors arrived in Oregon in 1996 via the state's commercial and general aviation airports. Spending by these visitors and the associated spin-off impacts accounted for a total of $5.6 billion in Oregon's economy. Aviation-related tenants at Oregon's airports support 24,700 jobs statewide, and the annual output or spending related to tenants is estimated at $5.9 billion.

Ports

Since 1792, when Captain Robert Gray became the first Yankee sailor to navigate the Columbia River in his search for beaver pelts, Oregon's history has been deeply rooted in a tradition of trade. Waterways have been and continue to be Oregon's link to lucrative world markets.

The 1891 Legislature created the Port of Portland and empowered it to dredge and maintain a 25-foot channel along the Columbia River between Portland and the sea. Other deep draft ports followed: Coos Bay in 1909, Newport in 1910 and Astoria in 1914. The coastal ports of Bandon, Bay City (now Garibaldi), Coquille River, Nehalem, Port Orford, Siuslaw, Toledo and Umpqua also were formed in the early 1900s.

Many of the ports were critical to domestic trade from California; others were formed to accommodate local fishing fleets. Several additional port districts, primarily serving barge traffic in the upper Columbia River, were established in the 1930s and include Arlington, Cascade Locks, Hood River, The Dalles and Umatilla. Finally, in the 1940s and 1950s, local economic development priorities stimulated creation of the last group of Oregon ports, including Alsea, Brookings Harbor, Gold Beach, Morrow, St. Helens and Tillamook Bay.

Today, 23 Oregon port districts serve the state. A list of these is found in the Local Government section on page 334.

Oregon ports support water-borne-cargo transportation, air passenger and freight services, ship repair, fisheries, recreation and tourism. Ports also engage in industrial development. Altogether, Oregon ports make available nearly 14,000 acres of land for industrial development and more than 800 acres for commercial purposes.

Second in the world in grain exports, the Columbia-Snake River system provides the state's major commercial transportation route. The U.S. Army Corps of Engineers and the Port of Portland work cooperatively in a local/federal partnership to maintain the river channel. To accommodate Oregon product growth, efforts are underway to deepen the lower Columbia channel from 40 to 43 feet.

The Port of Portland, located on the Columbia River 110 miles from the Pacific coast, is Oregon's largest and most diversified port, exporting the second largest volume of goods of any other west coast port in 1995.

In addition to five marine terminals served by three major rail lines and two interstate highway systems, the port

Growth in Exports to Top Five Countries

Country	Percent increase 1989–95	Dollar value in millions 1995
Japan	47%	2,139
Canada	74%	1,168
Korea	147%	839
Singapore	468%	510
Germany	117%	454

Source: Office of Economic Analysis

The "Portland," last of the steam tugs operating on the Willamette River, steams under the Burnside Bridge in Portland. The boat, a permanent exhibit at the Oregon Maritime Museum, celebrates its 50th birthday in 1997. Photo by Elizabeth Thomson-Becker.

manages the Portland Ship Repair Yard, Portland International Airport and general aviation airports in Troutdale, Hillsboro and Mulino.

The 125-acre Portland Ship Repair Yard handles more than 45 percent of all commercial repair work done on the west coast. It is the only publicly-owned, privately-operated major shipyard in the U.S.

Oregon ports located on the upper portion of the Columbia are key to the successful functioning of the river system. Grain, forest products and containerized goods produced inland are trucked or carried by rail to these destinations, where they are transferred to river barges and carried to the Lower Columbia. On upriver return trips, barges generally carry petroleum products. Because of cost-efficient transportation with payload both directions, the upriver ports have enabled Oregon producers to put goods on the world market at competitive prices.

In recent years, the ports have spearheaded activities that contribute to more economic diversity for the state. Tourism and recreation services are a growing priority at many ports. Most coastal ports maintain marinas to serve commercial and recreational fishing interests and encourage development of charter fishing services. The Port of Hood River has been involved in development of a nationally-recognized facility for windsurfers; and the Port of Cascade Locks manages a successful sternwheeler tourboat.

Sources of Information

Information for this chapter was compiled by the Economic Development Department. This information was gathered from the following agencies which can be contacted directly with questions.

Office of Economic Analysis, Department of Administrative Services

155 Cottage St. NE, Salem 97310-0310; 503-373-7643; Web: www.oea.das.state.or.us

Oregon Employment Department

875 Union St. NE, Salem 97311; 503-378-2736; Web: www.emp.state.or.us

Oregon Progress Board

775 Summer St. NE, Salem 97310
503-986-0033; Web: www.econ.state.or.us/opb

Oregon Economic Development Department

775 Summer St. NE, Salem 97310;
503-986-0123; Web: www.econ.state.or.us

Oregon Department of Forestry

2600 State Street, Salem 97310; 503-945-7200;
Web: www.odf.state.or.us

Oregon Department of Agriculture

635 Capitol St. NE, Salem 97310-0110;
503-986-4550; Web: www.oda.state.or.us/oda.html

Department of Fish and Wildlife

2501 SW 1st Ave., Portland 97297;
503-872-5268; Web: www.dfw.state.or.us

Oregon Tourism Commission

775 Summer St. NE, Salem 97310; 503-986-0000

Oregon Parks and Recreation Department

1115 Commercial St. NE, Salem 97310-1001;
Park information: 1-800-551-6949;
Park reservations: 1-800-452-5687;
Web: www.ohwy.com/or/o/oprd.htm

Oregon State Marine Board

435 Commercial St. NE, #400, Salem 97310;
503-378-8587;
Web: www.marinebd.osmb.state.or.us

USDA Forest Service

333 SW 1st Ave., PO Box 3623, Portland
97208-3623; 503-872-2750;
Web: www.naturenw.org

USDI Bureau of Land Management

1515 SW 5th Ave., PO Box 2965, Portland
97208; 503-952-6002; Web: www.or.blm.gov

Department of Geology and Mineral Industries

800 NE Oregon St. #28, Suite 965,
Portland 97232; 503-731-4100;
Web: sarvis.dogami.state.or.us

1831 First St., Baker City 97814; 541-523-3133

5375 Monument Dr., Grants Pass 97526;
541-476-2496

Nature of the Northwest Information Center

800 NE Oregon Street #5, Suite 177, Portland
97232; 503-872-2750; Web: www.naturenw.org

Division of State Lands

775 Summer St. NE, Salem 97310; 503-378-3805

Pacific Northwest Research Station, USDA Forest Service

PO Box 3890, Portland 97208-3890;
503-326-7132; Web: www.fs.fed.us/pnw

Department of Land Conservation and Development

1175 Court St. NE, Salem 97310-0590;
503-373-0050; Web: www.lcd.state.or.us

Water Resources Department

158 12th St. NE, Salem 97310; 800-624-3199,
503-378-8130; Web: www.wrd.state.or.us

Oregon Department of Energy

625 Marion St. NE, Salem 97310; 503-378-4040

Oregon Department of Transportation

135 Transportation Bldg., Salem 97310;
503-986-3200; Web: www.odot.state.or.us

Ports Division, Oregon Economic Development Department

775 Summer St. NE, Salem 97310; 503-986-0243;
Web: www.econ.state.or.us/ports.htm

Oregon Public Ports Association

727 Center St. NE, Suite 208, Salem 97301;
503-585-1250

MEDIA DIRECTORIES

The reflection of South Sister in Green Lake is almost as vivid as the real thing. Photo by Eric W. Valentine.

OREGONIANS have long valued access to accurate information. In the 1970s, Oregon became one of the first states to adopt sunshine legislation—assuring open meetings and public notice. A statewide vote overwhelmingly approved financial disclosure requirements for public officials. The media play a critical role in making sure that accurate information reaches Oregonians in a timely, reliable way. While advances in communications are imminent, today, newspapers, magazines, broadcast and cable television and radio are Oregonians' principal ways of keeping informed. The following pages list today's media resources.

Newspapers Published in Oregon

Source: Oregon Newspaper Publishers Association, J. LeRoy Yorgason, Exec. Dir.
7150 SW Hampton St., Suite 111, Portland 97223-8395; 503-624-6397; Fax: 503-639-9009

Albany

Albany Democrat-Herald, PO Box 130, Albany 97321-0041; 541-926-2211; Fax: 541-926-7209; Mon.–Sat. p.m.; John E. Buchner (P); Hasso Hering (E); Circ.: 21,744; Estab.: 1865.

Ashland

Ashland Daily Tidings, PO Box 7, Ashland 97520; 541-482-3456; Fax: 541-482-3688; Mon.–Sat. p.m.; J. Michael O'Brien (P); Jeff Keating (E); Circ.: 5,688; Estab.: 1876.

Astoria

The Daily Astorian, PO Box 210, Astoria 97103; 503-325-3211; Fax: 503-325-6573; Mon.–Fri. p.m.; George Potter (General Mgr.); Steve Forrester (E); Circ.: 9,438; Estab.: 1873.

Baker City

Baker City Herald, PO Box 807, Baker City 97814; 541-523-3673; Fax: 541-523-6426; Mon.–Fri. p.m.; Jack R. Turner (P); Dean Brickey (E); Circ.: 3,273; Estab.: 1870.

The Record-Courier, PO Box 70, Baker City 97814; 541-523-5353; Fax: 541-523-5353; Thurs.; Byron C. Brinton (P); Ron Brinton (E); Circ.: 4,800; Estab.: 1901.

Bandon

Western World, PO Box 248, Bandon 97411; 541-347-2423; Fax: 541-347-2424; Wed.; Greg McNair (P&E); Circ.: 2,590; Estab.: 1902.

Beaverton

Beaverton Valley Times, PO Box 370, Beaverton 97075; 503-684-0360; Fax: 503-620-3433; Thurs.; Steven J. Clark (P); Mikel Kelly (E); Circ.: 4,830; Estab.: 1921.

Bend

Cascade Business News, 330 NE Marshall Ave., 97701; 541-388-5665; Fax: 541-388-6927; Pamela Hulse Andrews

The Bulletin, 1526 NW Hill St., Bend 97701; 541-382-1811; Fax: 541-385-5802; Mon.–Fri. p.m., Sun. a.m.; Gordon Black (P); Rick Attig (E); Circ.: 27,196; Estab.: 1903.

Brookings

Curry Coastal Pilot, PO Box 700, Brookings 97415; 541-469-3123; Fax: 541-469-4679; Wed. and Sat.; Charles R. Kocher (P); Jerry Teague (E); Circ.: 6,974; Estab.: 1946.

Brownsville

The Times, PO Box 278, Brownsville 97327; 541-466-5311; Fax: 541-466-5312; Wed.; Don and Wannell Ware (P); Don Ware (E); Circ.: 1,104; Estab.: 1887.

Burns

Burns Times-Herald, 355 N Broadway, Burns 97720; 541-573-2022; Fax: 541-573-3915; Wed.; Donna Clark (P); Pauline Braymen (E); Circ.: 3,245; Estab.: 1887.

Canby

Canby Herald, PO Box 1108, Canby 97013; 503-266-6831; Fax: 503-266-6836; Wed.; William D. Cassel (P); Cam Sivesind (E); Circ.: 4,555; Estab.: 1906.

Cave Junction

Illinois Valley News, PO Box M, Cave Junction 97523; 541-592-2541; Wed.; Robert R. "Bob" Rodriguez (P&E); Circ.: 3,302; Estab.: 1937.

Clackamas

Clackamas Review, 7007 SE Lake Rd., Milwaukie 97267; 503-786-1996; Fax: 503-786-6977; Fri.; William R. Swindells (P); Tom Gauntt (E); Circ.: 3,300; Estab.: 1916.

Clatskanie

The Clatskanie Chief, PO Box 8, Clatskanie 97016; 1-800-340-3350; Fax: 503-728-3350; Wed.; Deborah Steele Hazen (P&E); Circ.: 2,328; Estab.: 1891.

Condon

The Times-Journal, PO Box 746, Condon 97823; 541-384-2421; Fax: 541-384-2411; Thurs.; McLaren and Janet Stinchfield (P); McLaren Stinchfield (E); Circ.: 1,640; Estab.: 1886.

Pittock Mansion was built overlooking the city of Portland in 1914 by Henry and Georgiana Pittock who came west on the Oregon Trail in the 1850s.

Photo courtesy Oregon Historical Society. Negative number OrHi 51681.

Coos Bay
The World, PO Box 1840, Coos Bay 97420; 541-269-1222; Fax: 541-267-0294; Mon.–Fri. p.m., Sat. a.m.; Don Brown (P&E); Circ.: 15,777; Estab.: 1878.

Coquille
The Coquille Valley Sentinel, PO Box 400, Coquille 97423; 541-396-3191; Fax: 541-396-3624; Wed.; Frederick Taylor (P); Corey Albert (E); Circ.: 2,094; Estab.: 1882.

Corvallis
Corvallis Gazette-Times, PO Box 368, Corvallis 97339; 541-753-2641; Fax: 541-758-9505; Mon.–Sun. a.m.; Beth C. Clark (P); Michael Gast (E); Circ.: 13,620 (M-F), 15,253 (Sun.); Estab.: 1862.

Cottage Grove
Cottage Grove Sentinel, PO Box 35, Cottage Grove 97424; 541-942-3325; Fax: 541-942-3328; Wed.; Jody Rolnick (P); Mark Bowder (E); Circ.: 5,092; Estab.: 1886.

Creswell
The Chronicle, PO Box 428, Creswell 97426; 541-895-2197; Fax: 541-895-2361; Wed.; Gerri O'Rourke (P&E); Circ.: 875; Estab.: 1965.

Dallas
The Polk County Itemizer Observer, PO Box 108, Dallas 97338; 503-623-2373; Fax: 503-623-2395; Wed.; Nancy J. Adams (P); Virginia Henderson (E); Circ.: 6,242; Estab.: 1875.

Dayton
Dayton Tribune, PO Box 69, Dayton 97114; 503-864-2310; Thurs.; George and Edwina Meitzen (P&E); Circ.: 440; Estab.: 1912.

Drain
The Drain Enterprise, PO Box 26, Drain 97435; 541-836-2241; Thurs.; Betty Anderson (P); Sue Anderson (E); Circ.: 1,225; Estab.: 1951.

Eagle Point
Upper Rogue Independent, PO Box 900, Eagle Point 97524; 541-826-7700; Fax: 541-826-1340; Tues.; Nancy Leonard (P&E); Circ.: 2,300; Estab.: 1976.

Enterprise
Wallowa County Chieftain, PO Box 338, Enterprise 97828; 541-426-4567; Fax: 541-426-3921; Thurs.; Donald L. Swart (P); Richard W. Swart (E); Circ.: 4,172; Estab.: 1884.

Estacada
Clackamas County News, PO Box 549, Estacada 97023; 503-630-3241; Fax: 503-630-5840; Wed.; William H. "Bill" and Pat James (P); Keppie Keplinger (E); Circ.: 1,748; Estab.: 1904.

Eugene
Eugene Weekly, 1251 Lincoln, 97401; 541-484-0519; Fax: 541-484-4044; Sonja Snyder (P); Debra Gwartney (E); *The Register-Guard*, PO Box 10188, Eugene 97440-2188; 541-485-1234; Fax: 541-984-4699; Mon.–Sun. a.m.; Alton "Tony" F. Baker III (P&E); Circ.: 75,301 (M-F), 83,561 (Sat.), 78,636 (Sun.); Estab.: 1862.

Media Directories

Florence

The Siuslaw News, PO Box 10, Florence 97439; 541-997-3441; Fax: 541-997-7979; Wed.; Paul R. Holman (P); Robert Serra (E); Circ.: 6,181; Estab.: 1890.

Forest Grove

News-Times, PO Box 408, Forest Grove 97116; 503-357-3181; Fax: 503-359-8456; Wed.; J. Brian Monihan (P); Jim Hart (E); Circ.: 3,825; Estab.: 1886.

Noticias en Espanol, PO Box 408, 97116; 503-357-3181; 3rd Wed.

Gold Beach

Curry County Reporter, PO Box 766, Gold Beach 97444; 541-247-6643; Fax: 541-247-6644; Wed.; Robert and Betty Van Leer (P); Betty Van Leer (E); Circ.: 3,329; Estab.: 1914.

Grants Pass

Grants Pass Daily Courier, PO Box 1468, Grants Pass 97526; 541-474-3700; Fax: 541-474-3814; Mon.–Sat. p.m.; Dennis Mack (P); Dennis Roler (E); Circ.: 18,205; Estab.: 1885.

Gresham

The Outlook, PO Box 747, Gresham 97030; 503-665-2181; Fax: 503-665-2187; Wed. and Sat.; William R. Hunter (P); David Magnuson (E); Circ.: 8,826; Estab.: 1911.

Halfway

Hells Canyon Journal, PO Box 646, Halfway 97834; 541-742-7900; Fax: 541-742-7933; Wed.; Steve Backstrom (P); Pat Garrigus (E); Circ.: 1,473; Estab.: 1984.

Heppner

Heppner Gazette-Times, PO Box 337, Heppner 97836; 541-676-9228; Wed.; David Sykes and April Hilton Sykes (P); April Hilton Sykes (E); Circ.: 1,422; Estab.: 1883.

Hermiston

The Hermiston Herald, PO Box 46, Hermiston 97838; 541-567-6457; Fax: 541-567-4125; Tues.; Claudia L. Stewart (P); Michael Kane (E); Circ.: 4,058; Estab.: 1906.

Hillsboro

Hillsboro Argus, PO Box 588, Hillsboro 97123; 503-648-1131; Fax: 503-648-9191; Tues. and Thurs.; Walter V. McKinney (P); Val Hess (E); Circ.: 14,313; Estab.: 1873.

Hood River

Hood River News, PO Box 390, Hood River 97031; 541-386-1234; Fax: 541-386-6796; Wed. and Sat.; James Kelly (P); Keith Fredrickson (E); Circ.: 5,271; Estab.: 1905.

Jefferson

Jefferson Review, PO Box 330, Jefferson 97352; 541-327-2241; Thurs.; Jack Gillespie (P&E); Circ.: 792; Estab.: 1890.

John Day

Grant County Press, PO Box 820, John Day 97845; 541-575-0035; Fax: 541-575-2265; Wed.; Beverly Higley (Gen. Mgr. & E); Circ.: 1,408; Estab.: 1994.

The Blue Mountain Eagle, PO Box 69, John Day 97845; 541-575-0710; Fax: 541-575-1244; Thurs.; Karla Averett (Gen. Mgr.); Dean Rhodes (E); Circ.: 3,576; Estab.: 1868.

Junction City

Tri-County News, PO Box 395, Junction City 97448; 541-998-3877; Fax: 541-998-3878; Thurs.; Edward Hawley (P); Judy Hunt (E); Circ.: 2,010; Estab.: 1977.

Keizer

Keizertimes, PO Box 20025, Keizer 97307; 503-390-1051; Fax: 503-390-8023; Thurs.; Leslie Zaitz (P&E) and Scotta Callister (P); Circ.: 3,500; Estab.: 1979.

Klamath Falls

Herald and News, PO Box 788, Klamath Falls 97601; 541-885-4410; Fax: 541-885-4456; Mon.–Fri. p.m., Sun. a.m.; Dwight Tracy (P); Patrick Bushey (E); Circ.: 17,210 (M-F), 17,745 (Sun.); Estab.: 1906.

La Grande

The Observer, PO Box 3170, La Grande 97850; 541-963-3161; Fax: 541-963-7804; Mon.–Sat. p.m.; Robert K. Moody (P); Ted Kramer (E); Circ.: 7,704; Estab.: 1896.

Lake Oswego

Lake Oswego Review, PO Box 548, Lake Oswego 97034; 503-635-8811; Fax: 503-635-8817; Thurs.; Robert D. Bigelow (P); Dana Haynes (E); Circ.: 7,103; Estab.: 1920.

Lakeview

Lake County Examiner, PO Box 271, Lakeview 97630; 541-947-3378; Fax: 541-947-4359; Thurs.; Matilda Flynn (Gen. Mgr.); Erik Hogstrom (E); Circ.: 2,551; Estab.: 1880.

Lebanon

Lebanon Express, PO Box 459, Lebanon 97355; 541-258-3151; Fax: 541-259-3569; Wed.; Mary Jo Parker (P); Rob Oster (E); Circ.: 3,468; Estab.: 1887.

Lincoln City

The News Guard, PO Box 848, Lincoln City 97367; 541-994-2178; Fax: 541-994-7613; Wed.; David Price (P); Steve Mims (E); Circ.: 5,302; Estab.: 1927.

Madras

The Madras Pioneer, 241 SE 6th St., Madras 97741; 541-475-2275; Fax: 541-475-3710; Wed.; Tony Ahern (P); Susan Matheny (E); Circ.: 3,635; Estab.: 1904.

McKenzie Bridge

McKenzie River Reflections, 59059 Old McKenzie Hwy., McKenzie Bridge 97413; 541-822-3358; Tues.; Ken Engelman (P); Louise Engelman (E); Circ.: 997; Estab.: 1978.

McMinnville

News-Register, PO Box 727, McMinnville 97128; 503-472-5114; Fax: 503-472-9151; Tues., Thurs. and Sat.; Jeb Bladine (P&E); Circ.: 10,018; Estab.: 1866.

Medford

Mail Tribune, PO Box 1108, Medford 97501; 541-776-4411; Fax: 541-776-4415; Mon.–Sun. a.m.; Gregory H. Taylor (P); Robert L. Hunter (E); Circ.: 27,106 (M-Th, Sat.); 35,398 (Fri.); 32,198 (Sun.); Estab.: 1906.

Mill City

The Mill City Enterprise, PO Box 348, Mill City 97360; 503-897-2772; Fax: 503-897-2335; Thurs.; Gale A. Hann (P&E); Circ.: 1,234; Estab.: 1927.

Milton-Freewater

Milton-Freewater Valley Times, PO Box 170, Milton-Freewater 97862; 541-938-0702; Fax: 541-938-0691; Tues.; Terry M. Hager (P); Nick Peterson (E); Circ.: 1,701; Estab.: 1994.

Molalla

Molalla Pioneer, PO Box 168, Molalla 97038; 503-829-2301; Fax: 503-829-2317; Wed.; William D. Cassel (P); Bob Hawley (E); Circ.: 2,979; Estab.: 1911.

Moro

Sherman County Journal, PO Box 284, Moro 97039; 541-565-3515; Thurs.; Dan C. Bartlett (P&E); Circ.: 843; Estab.: 1888.

Myrtle Creek

Umpqua Free Press, PO Box 729, Myrtle Creek 97457; 541-863-5233; Fax: 541-863-5234; Wed.; Robert F. and Sharon W. Scherer (P); Robert F. Scherer (E); Circ.: 2,512; Estab.: 1902.

Myrtle Point

Myrtle Point Herald, PO Box 606, Myrtle Point 97458; 541-572-2717; Fax: 541-572-2828; Wed.; Laura Isenhart (P); Scott Balius (E); Circ.: 1,904; Estab.: 1889.

Newberg

The Graphic, PO Box 700, Newberg 97132; 503-538-2181; Fax: 503-538-1632; Wed. and Sat.; David Thouvenel (P&E); Circ.: 5,405; Estab.: 1888.

Newport

News-Times, PO Box 965, Newport 97365; 541-265-8571; Fax: 541-265-3103; Wed. and Fri.; Mary Jo Parker (P); Leslie O'Donnell (E); Circ.: 8,914; Estab.: 1882.

Oakridge

Dead Mountain Echo, PO Box 900, Oakridge 97463; 541-782-4241; Fax: 541-782-3323; Thurs.; Larry and Debra Roberts (P); John Warner (E); Circ.: 1,002; Estab.: 1973.

Ontario

Argus Observer, PO Box 130, Ontario 97914; 541-889-5387; Fax: 541-889-3347; Mon.–Fri. p.m., Sun. a.m.; Francis R. McLean (P); Larry Hurrle (E); Circ.: 7,777 (M-F), 8,558 (Sun.); Estab.: 1896.

Oregon City

Oregon City News, PO Box 1016, Oregon City 97045; 503-557-1819; Fax: 503-557-0940; Jim MacKenzie (P)

The Oregon Spectator, PO Box 1508, Oregon City 97045; 503-656-3936; Fax: 503-656-2634; Rick Beasley and Ralph A. Hatley (P&E).

Pendleton

Agri-Times Northwest, PO Box 189, Pendleton 97801; 541-276-7845; Fax: 541-276-7964; 1st and 3rd Fri.; Forrest "Bill" Johnson (P); Virgil Rupp (E); Circ.: 3,033; Estab.: 1984.

*East Oregonian, PO Box 1089, Pendleton 97801; 541-276-2211; Fax: 541-276-8314; Mon.–Fri. p.m., Sat. a.m.; Clyde H. Bentley (Gen. Mgr); David Cash (E); Circ.: 12,059; Estab.: 1875.

*Pendleton Record, PO Box 69, Pendleton 97801; 541-276-2853; Thurs.; Marguerite Maznaritz (P&E); Circ.: 866; Estab.: 1911.

Philomath

*Benton Bulletin, PO Box 340, Philomath 97370; 541-929-3043; Thurs.; Edward Hawley (P); John Butterworth (E); Circ.: 885; Estab.: 1976.

Port Orford

*Port Orford News, PO Box 5, Port Orford 97465; 541-332-2361; Fax: 541-332-8101; Wed.; Louis L. Felsheim (P); Paul L. Peterson (E); Circ.: 1,047; Estab.: 1958.

Portland

Associated Press, One World Trade Center, 14th Floor, 121 SW Salmon, Suite 1450, 97204; 503-228-2169; Fax: 503-228-5514; Eva Parziale.

Business Journal, PO Box 14490, Portland 97214; 503-274-8733; Fax: 503-227-2650; Fri.; Candace Clement (P); Steve Jones (E); Circ.: 10,800; Estab.: 1984.

*Daily Journal of Commerce, PO Box 10127, Portland 97210; 503-226-1311; Fax: 503-224-7140; Mon.–Fri. a.m.; Dorothy H. Smith (P); Kevin Harden (E); Circ.: 4,607; Estab.: 1872.

El Hispanic, PO Box 306, 97205; 503-736-9878; Fax: 503-736-9947; Thurs.

N.W. Examiner, 2066 NW Irving St., Portland 97209; 503-241-2353; 3rd Sat. of month; Allan Classen (P&E); Circ.: 15,000; Estab.: 1986.

Portland Observer, 4747 NE M. L. King Blvd., Portland 97211; 503-288-0033; Fax: 503-288-0015; Wed.; Charles Washington (P&E); Circ.: 30,000; Estab.: 1970.

S.E. Examiner, PO Box 14791, Portland 97293; 503-234-1770; 1st Sat. of month; Nancy Tannler (P&E); Circ.: 20,000; Estab.: 1989.

St. Johns Review, 700 N Hayden Island Dr., Suite 210; 97217; 503-283-5086; Fax: 503-735-1446; Every other Fri.; Gayla Whitman (P); Ty Walker (E); Circ.: 2,700; Estab.: 1904.

The Asian Reporter, 3241 NE Broadway #D, 97232; 503-281-2199; Fax: 503-281-2398; Wed.

Hikers ascend 8,884-foot Ruby Peak in the Eagle Cap Wilderness on a New Year's Day Hike.

Photo by Gary Fletcher.

The Multnomah Village Post,
PO Box 80351, 97219; 503-244-6933;
Fax: 503-244-2148; Donald Snedecor
(P&E)

*The Oregonian, 1320 SW Broadway,
Portland 97201; 503-221-8327;
Fax: 503-227-5306; Mon.–Sun. a.m.;
Fred A. Stickel (P); Sandra Mims Rowe
(E); Circ.: 338,586 (M-F); 323,871 (Sat.);
439,704 (Sun.); Estab.: 1850.

The Skanner, 337 N Williams Ave.,
Portland 97227; 503-287-3562; Fax:
503-284-8200; Wed.; Bernie Foster (P);
Bobbie Foster (E); Circ.: 21,000;
Estab.: 1975.

Willamette Week, 822 SW 10th Ave.,
Portland 97205; 503-243-2122;
Fax: 503-243-1115; Wed.; Richard
Meeker (P); Mark Zusman (E);
Circ.: 71,000; Estab.: 1970.

Prineville

*Central Oregonian, 558 N Main St.,
Prineville 97754; 541-447-6205;
Fax: 541-447-1754; Tues. and Thurs.;
James O. Smith (P); Bill Sheehy (E);
Circ.: 3,813; Estab.: 1881.

Redmond

*The Redmond Spokesman, PO Box
788, Redmond 97756; 541-548-2184;
Fax: 541-548-3203; Wed.; Carl Vertrees
(P); Scott Maben (E); Circ.: 4,155;
Estab.: 1910.

Reedsport

*The Courier, PO Box 268,
Reedsport 97467; 541-271-3633;
Fax: 541-271-3138; Thurs.; Dan Olson
(P&E); Circ.: 1,955; Estab.: 1901.

Rogue River

*Rogue River Press, PO Box 1485,
Rogue River 97537; 541-582-1707;
Fax: 541-582-0201; Wed.; Dave and
Heidi Ehrhardt (P); Dave Ehrhardt (E);
Circ.: 1,819; Estab.: 1962.

Roseburg

*The News-Review, PO Box 1248,
Roseburg 97470; 541-672-3321;
Fax: 541-673-5994; Mon.–Fri. p.m.,
Sun. a.m.; Ronald J. Stewart (P); Bart
Smith (E); Circ.: 19,120 (M-F), 19,892
(Sun.); Estab.: 1868.

Salem

Capital Press, PO Box 2048, Salem
97308; 503-364-4431; Fri.; Michael
Forrester (P&E); Circ.: 35,000;
Estab.: 1928.

Salem Times, PO Box 20025,
Salem 97307; 503-390-1051; Fri.;
Leslie Zaitz (P&E); Scotta Callister (P);
Estab.: 1994.

Senior News Monthly, PO Box 229,
Salem 97308; 503-399-8478;
Fax: 503-399-1645; John Honey (P);

*Statesman Journal, PO Box 13009,
Salem 97309; 503-399-6611;
Fax: 503-399-6873; Mon.–Sun. a.m.;
Sara M. Bentley (P); Julia Wallace (E);
Circ.: 58,733(M-F); 68,807 (Sat.);
69,416 (Sun.); Estab.: 1851.

The Oregon Monitor, PO Box 662,
Salem 97308; 503-363-1794;
Fax: 503-362-7297; J.D. Cornutt (P&E);

Sandy

*Sandy Post, PO Box 68,
Sandy 97055; 503-668-5548;
Fax: 503-665-2187; Wed.; William R.
Hunter (P); Dave Magnuson (E);
Circ.: 2,251; Estab.: 1937.

Sandy Profile, PO Box 850,
Sandy 97055; 503-668-7447;
Fax: 503-668-3423; Nancy Burgess (P&E).

Scappoose

*The South County Spotlight, PO Box
C, Scappoose 97056; 503-543-6387;
Fax: 503-543-6380; Wed.; Art and Sally
Heerwagen (P); Art Heerwagen (E);
Circ.: 3,173; Estab.: 1961.

Seaside

*Seaside Signal, PO Box 848, Seaside
97138; 503-738-5561; Fax: 503-738-5672;
Thurs.; Tom Mauldin (P); Cat Mauldin
(E); Circ.: 3,096; Estab.: 1905.

Sheridan

*The Sun, PO Box 68, Sheridan 97378;
503-843-2312; Fax: 503-843-3830;
Wed.; George Robertson (P&E);
Circ.: 2,392; Estab.: 1890.

Sherwood

Sherwood Gazette, PO Box 913,
Sherwood 97140; 503-625-3536;
Chris Corrado (P).

Silverton

*Silverton Appeal Tribune, PO Box 35,
Silverton 97381; 503-873-8385;
Fax: 503-873-8064; Wed.; Joe Petshow
(Interim Gen. Mgr. & E); Circ.: 2,993;
Estab.: 1880.

Sisters

The Nugget Newspaper, PO Box 698, Sisters 97759; 541-549-9941; Fax: 541-549-9940; Wed.; Eric and Kiki Dolson (P&E); Circ.: 6,000; Estab.: 1977.

Springfield

The Springfield News, PO Box 139, Springfield 97477; 541-746-1671; Fax: 541-746-0633; Wed. and Sat.; J. Mark Garber (P); Rob Romig (E); Circ.: 10,284; Estab.: 1904.

St. Helens

The Chronicle, PO Box 1153, St. Helens 97051; 503-397-0116; Fax: 503-397-4093; Wed. and Sat.; Pamela A. Petersen (P); Greg Cohen (E); Circ.: 5,757; Estab.: 1881.

Stayton

The Stayton Mail, PO Box 400, Stayton 97383; 503-769-6338; Fax: 503-769-6207; Tues.; Joe Petshow (Interim Gen. Mgr. & E); Circ.: 2,923; Estab.: 1894.

Sutherlin

The Sun Tribune, PO Box 430, Sutherlin 97479; 541-459-2261; Fax: 541-459-1542; Thurs.; Ronald J. Stewart (P); Linda Schnell (E); Circ.: 816; Estab.: 1910.

Sweet Home

The New Era, PO Box 39, Sweet Home 97386; 541-367-2135; Fax: 541-367-2137; Wed.; Alex Paul (P&E); Circ.: 2,427; Estab.: 1929.

The Dalles

The Dalles Daily Chronicle, PO Box 902, The Dalles 97058; 541-296-2141; Fax: 541-298-1365; Mon.–Fri. p.m., Sun. a.m.; Marilyn Roth and Harold Steininger (P); Tom Stevenson (E); Circ.: 5,800 (D); 16,200 (Tues.); 8,600 (Sun.); Estab.: 1892.

Tigard

Tigard Times and *Tualatin Times*, PO Box 370, Beaverton 97075; 503-684-0360; Fax: 503-620-3433; Thurs.; Steven J. Clark (P); Mikel Kelly (E); Circ.: 5,668; Estab.: 1956.

Tillamook

Headlight-Herald, PO Box 444, Tillamook 97141; 503-842-7535; Fax: 503-842-8842; Wed.; Linda Shaffer (P); Scott Frank (E); Circ.: 7,758; Estab.: 1888.

Vale

Malheur Enterprise, PO Box 310, Vale 97918; 541-473-3377; Fax: 541-473-3268; Wed.; Peter and Barbara Schaffeld (P); Rachel Haueter (E); Circ.: 2,185; Estab.: 1909.

Veneta

West-Lane News, PO Box 188, Veneta 97487; 541-935-1882; Fax: 541-935-4082; Thurs.; Edward Hawley (P); Judy Hunt (E); Circ.: 1,785; Estab.: 1961.

Warrenton

The Columbia Press, PO Box 130, Warrenton 97146; 503-861-3331; Fri.; Gary and Julia Nevan (P); Gary Nevan (E); Circ.: 1,045; Estab.: 1922.

Welches

Mountain Times, PO Box 1031, Welches 97067; 503-622-3289; Fax: 503-622-5984; Tom and Marie Teven (P&E).

West Linn

West Linn Tidings, PO Box 548, Lake Oswego 97034; 503-635-8811; Fax: 503-635-8817; Thurs.; Bob Bigelow (P); Julie Vertrees (E); Circ.: 3,168; Estab.: 1979.

Wilsonville

The Villager of Charbonneau, PO Box 516, Wilsonville 97070; 503-694-5515; Fax: 503-694-5783; 1st week of month; K.C. Weary (E); Circ.: 1,722; Estab.: 1976.

Woodburn

Woodburn Independent, PO Box 96, Woodburn 97071; 503-981-3441; Fax: 503-981-1253; Wed.; Les Reitan (P); Nikki DeBuse (E); Circ.: 4,692; Estab.: 1888.

* Meets the statutory definition of "newspaper" under ORS chapter 193 for purposes of public notices.

Selected Periodicals Published in Oregon

Following is a representative sample of the many periodicals published in Oregon, compiled by the Oregon State Library.

Key: BM—Bi-monthly; BW—Bi-weekly; Irreg—Irregular publication schedule; M—Monthly; Q—Quarterly; SA—Semi-annual; SM—semi-monthly; W—Weekly

Acreage Magazine (M) 1978: Malheur Publishing Company, PO Box 130, Ontario 97914; 541-889-7627

Agri-Times (W) 1984: J-A Publishing Corporation, PO Box 189, Pendleton 97801; 541-276-7845

American Indian Basketry Magazine (Q) 1979: Institute for the Study of Traditional American Indian Arts, PO Box 66124, Portland 97290

Animal Law (SA) 1995. Northwestern School of Law, 10015 SW Terwilliger Blvd., Portland 97219

Automotive News of the Pacific Northwest (M) 1919: 14789 SE 82nd Dr., Clackamas 97015

Backwoods Home Magazine (BM) 1989: 1257 Siskiyou Blvd., Suite 213, Ashland 97520

Birth to Three and Beyond (BM) 1978: 3875 Kinkaid, Eugene 97405-4501; 541-484-5316

Black Sheep Newsletter (Q) 1974: Black Sheep Press, 25455 NW Dixie Mountain Rd., Scappoose 97056; 503-621-3063

Blue Stocking (Q) 1993: PO Box 4525, Portland 97208

Book Dealers World (Q) 1980: North American Bookdealers Exchange, Box 606, Cottage Grove 97424

Brown's Business Reporter (W) 1959: Comp-Graphics, Inc., PO Box 1376, Eugene 97440; 541-345-8665

Calapooya Collage (A) 1983: PO Box 309, Monmouth 97361

Calyx (SA) 1976: PO Box B, Corvallis 97339; 541-753-9384

Cascade Horseman (M): Klamath Publishing, PO Box 1390, Klamath Falls 97601

Cascades East (M) 1976: Sun Publishing Co., 716 NE 4th St., Bend 97701; 541-382-0127

Christian News Northwest (M) 1994: PO Box 974, Newberg 97132; 503-537-9220.

Christian Parenting Today (BM) 1988: Good Family Magazines, PO Box 850, Sisters 97759; 541-549-8100

Commercial Review (W) 1890: 1725 NW 24th, Portland 97210; 503-226-2758

Competitive Advantage, The (M) 1986: PO Box 10091, Portland 97210; 503-274-2953

Computer Bits (M) 1991: PO Box 329, Forest Grove 97116

Crow's Weekly Letter (W) 1900: C.C. Crow Publications, Inc., PO Box 25749, Portland 97298

Dialog (Q) 1961: Blindskills, Inc., PO Box 5181, Salem 97304; 503-581-4224

Different Drummer (Q) 1994: 14417 SW Laurie, Oak Grove 97267

Environmental Law (Q) 1970: Northwestern School of Law, Lewis and Clark College, 10015 SW Terwilliger Blvd., Portland 97219

Fireweed: Poetry of Western Oregon (Q) 1990: 1330 E 25th St., Eugene 97403

Flyfishing (BM) 1978: Frank Amato Publications, PO Box 82112, Portland 97282

Heartsong Review (SA) 1986: PO Box 5716, Eugene 97405-0710

Heritage Newsletter (M) 1987: 35145 Balboa Place SE, Albany 97321; 503-928-6809

Home Computer Magazine (10x yearly) 1981: Emerald Valley Publishing Co., PO Box 21705, Eugene 97402-0411; 541-485-8796

Home Power (BM) 1987: Home Power, Inc., PO Box 520, Ashland 97520

In Stride Magazine (M) 1980: 12675 SW 1st St., Beaverton 97005; 503-643-0271

Inkfish (M): Box 1293, Waldport 97354

Lane Electric Ruralite (M) 1953: Ruralite Services, Inc., PO Box 558, Forest Grove 97116-2333; 503-357-2105

Lariat (M) 1949: Lariat Company, 12675 SW 1st St., Beaverton 97005

Lifeprints (Q) 1983: Blindskills, Inc., PO Box 5181, Salem 97304; 503-581-4224

Media Directories

Lower Columbia Business (M) 1991: Walker & Co. Marketing Communication, PO Box 1088, Seaside 97138-1088; 503-738-3398.

Marketing (M) 1992: Marketing Magazine, PO Box 1048, Wilsonville 97070-1048; 503-682-9698

Midwifery Today and Childbirth Education (Q) 1985: PO Box 2672, Eugene 97402; 541-344-7438

Northwest Labor Press 1987: 1827 NE 44th Ave., Suite 200, PO Box 13150, Portland 97213; 503-288-3311

Northwest Palate (BM) 1987: PO Box 10860, Portland 97210; 503-224-0966

Northwest Travel (BM) 1991: Northwest Regional Magazines, 1525 12th St., Suite C, PO Box 18000, Eugene 97439

Oregon Business Magazine (M) 1981: MIF Publications, Inc., 610 SW Broadway, Suite 200, Portland 97205; 503-223-0304

Oregon Coast (BM) 1982: PO Box 18000, Florence 97439; 541-997-8401

Oregon Geology (BM) 1979: Suite 965, 800 NE Oregon St., Portland 97232; 503-872-2750

Oregon Grange Bulletin (M) 1990: Oregon State Grange, 1125 SE Madison, Suite 102, Portland 97214

Oregon Historical Quarterly (Q) 1900: Oregon Historical Society, 1200 SW Park Ave., Portland 97205

Oregon News-Leader (M) 1993: PO Box 20307, Keizer 97307; 503-463-8095

Oregon Outpost (BM) 1995: PO Box 266, Canyon City 97820-0266; 541-474-2918

Oregon Outside (BM) 1995: Educational Publications Foundation, PO Box 18000, Florence 97439-0130

Oregon Spectator (M) 1993: Masonic Building, 707 Main St., Suite 405, Oregon City 97045

Oregon Wheat (7 per year) 1962: Oregon Wheat Growers League, PO Box 400, Pendleton 97801; 541-276-7330

Over the Rainbow (Q) 1982: Mobility International USA, PO Box 3551, Eugene 97403; 541-343-1284

La Posta (BM) 1969: Post Publications, PO Box 135, Lake Oswego 97034; 503-657-5685

ProWOMAN (BM) 1990: MatriMedia Inc., PO Box 6957, Portland 97228

Pulphouse (Q) 1988: Pulphouse Publishing, Inc., PO Box 1227, Eugene 97440

QCWA News (Q) 1957: Quarter Century Wireless Association, 159 E 16th St., Eugene 97401

Rain (Q) 1974: PO Box 30097, Eugene 97403

Random Lengths (W) 1944: PO Box 867, Eugene 97440; 541-686-9925

Random Lengths Export (BW) 1968: PO Box 867, Eugene 97440

Resource Recycling (M) 1982: Resource Recycling, Inc., PO Box 10540, Portland 97210; 503-227-1319

Rubberstampmadness (BM) 1980: RSM Enterprises, Inc., 408 SW Monroe St., Suite 210, Corvallis 97333; 541-752-0075

Salmon Trout Steelheader (BM) 1967: PO Box 82112, Portland 97282

Shots (BM) 1986: PO Box 109, Joseph 97846

Silverfish Review (3 per year) 1979: PO Box 3541, Eugene 97401; 541-344-5060

Skipping Stones: a Multi-Cultural Children's Quarterly (Q) 1988: 1309 Lincoln St., Eugene 97440; 541-342-4956

Small Farmers Journal (Q) 1976: PO Box 1627, Sisters 97759; 541-549-2064

Southern Oregon Heritage (Q) 1995: Southern Oregon Historical Society, 206 N Central Ave., Medford 97501-5926; 541-773-6535

Special Events (M) 1982: 9560 SW Nimbus Ave., Beaverton 97005

Spectroscopy (9 per year) 1985: 859 Willamette St., Eugene 97401; 541-343-1200

Sproutletter (Q) 1980: PO Box 62, Ashland 97520; 541-488-2326

Stamp Collector (W) 1976: Van Dahl Publications, PO Box 706, Albany 97321; 541-928- 5156

Summit Magazine (BM) 1955: Summit Publications, Inc., 1221 May St., Hood River 97031

Tinnitus Today (Q): American Tinnitus Association, PO Box 5, Portland 97207; 503-248-9985

Traffic Manager (BM) 1925: Daily Journal of Commerce, PO Box 10127. Portland 97210; 503-226-1311

Trail Blazer Horseback Trail Riding
(BM) 1978: 18243 Rock Springs Court,
Bend 97701

Travelin' Magazine (BM) 1991: PO Box
23005, Eugene 97402; 541-485-8533

Western Places (Q) 1992: PO
Box 2093, Lake Grove 97035

Western Polled Hereford Journal (M)
1987: Klamath Publishing, PO Box 788,
Klamath Falls 97601

Wild Forest Review (M) 1994:
3758 SE Milwaukie, Portland 97202;
503-234-0093

Willamette Law Review (Q) 1978:
College of Law, Willamette University,
Salem 97301

Willamette Week (W) 1974: 2 NW 2nd
Ave., Portland 97209

Willamette Writer (M) 1965: PO
Box 2485, Portland 97205

Writer's NW (Q) 1985: Media Weavers,
Inc., 1738 NE 24th St., Portland 97212

Oregon Radio Stations

**Source: Oregon Association of Broadcasters
Bill Johnstone, Exec. Dir.**

*PO Box 449, 111 W 7th St., Eugene 97440-0449;
541-343-2101; Fax 541-343-0662*

Albany
KRKT (990), Country
KRKT-FM (99.9), Classic Country
*1207 9th St., Albany 97321; 541-926-8628;
Fax: 541-928-1359; Gary M. Grossman*

KWIL (790), Christian
KHPE-FM (107.9), Contemp. Christian
*PO Box 278, Albany 97321; 541-926-2233;
Fax: 541-926-3925; Dave Winchester*

Ashland (see Medford)
Astoria
KAST (1370), News/Talk
KAST-FM (92.9), Adult Contemp.
*1006 West Marine Dr., Astoria 97103;
503-325-2911; Fax: 503-325-5570; Jim Servino*

KKEE-FM (94.3), Pure Gold
*1490 Marine Dr., Astoria 97103; 360-642-8555;
Fax: 503-325-6145; Robert Hooper*

KVAS (1230), Hot Country
*1490 Marine Dr., Astoria 97103; 503-325-6221;
Fax: 503-325-6145; Robert Hooper*

Baker City
KBKR (1490), News/Talk
KKBC-FM (95.3), Country
*PO Box 907, La Grande 97850; 541-963-4121;
Fax: 541-963-3117; Bryan Christle*

KCMB-FM (104.7), Country
*PO Box 886, Baker City 97814; 541-523-3400;
Fax: 541-523-5481; Randy McKone*

Bandon
KBDN-FM (96.5), Classic Rock n' Roll
PO Box 250, Coquille 97423; Connie Williamson

Banks (see Portland)
Bend
KBND (1110), News/Talk
*PO Box 5037, Bend 97708; 541-382-5263;
Fax: 541-388-0456; Mike Cheney*

KICE-FM (100.7), Progressive Country
*PO Box 751, Bend 97709; 541-388-3300;
Fax: 541-388-3303; Sam Kirkaldie*

KLRR-FM (107.5), Adult
Contemp./AAA
*PO Box 5037, Bend 97708; 541-382-5263;
Fax: 541-388-0456; Mike Cheney*

KNLR-FM (97.5), Contemp. Christian
*PO Box 7408, Bend 97708; 541-389-8873;
Fax: 541-389-5291; Terry Cowan*

KQAK-FM (105.7), Oldies
*854 NE 4th, Bend 97701; 541-383-3825;
Fax: 541-383-3403; Clifton Topp*

KSJJ-FM (102.9), Country
*PO Box 5068, Bend 97708-5068; 541-382-5611;
Fax: 541-389-8486; Norm Louvau*

KTWS-FM (98.3), Classic Rock
*PO Box 5037, Bend 97708; 541-389-9500;
Fax: 541-388-0456; Mike Cheney*

KXUX (940), Nostalgia
KXIX-FM (94.1), Modern Rock
*PO Box 5068, Bend 97708-5068; 541-382-5611;
Fax: 541-389-8486; Norm Louvau, Randy Posvar*

Brookings
KURY (910), News/Talk
KURY-FM (95.3), Variety
*PO Box 1029, Brookings 97415; 541-469-2111;
Fax: 541-469-6397; Vern Garvin*

Burns
KZZR (1230), Country
*PO Box 877, Burns 97720; 541-573-2055;
Fax: 541-573-5223; Stan Swol*

Cave Junction
KCNA-FM (102.7, Grants Pass), (97.7,
Medford), Oldies
*1257 N Riverside Ave., #10, Medford 97501;
541-474-7564; Fax: 541-772-4233; Dean Flock*

Central Point (see Medford)

Coos Bay
KBBR (1340), News/Talk
KACW-FM (107.3), Adult Contemp.
PO Box 308, North Bend 97459; 541-756-5108;
Fax: 541-756-6813; Stephen Walker

KDCQ-FM (93.5), Oldies
PO Box 478, Coos Bay 97420; 541-269-0935;
Fax: 541-269-9376; Bruce Latta

KHSN (1230), Adult Standards/News/
Talk
PO Box 180, Coos Bay 97420; 541-267-2121;
Fax: 541-267-5229; Craig Finley

KOOS-FM (94.9), Country
PO Box 180, Coos Bay 97420; 541-267-2121;
Fax: 541-267-5229; Craig Finley

KYTT-FM (98.7), Contemp. Christian
KYSG-FM (106.5), Gospel
580 Kingwood, Coos Bay 97420; 541-269-2022;
Fax: 541-267-0114; Rick Stevens

Coquille
KWRO (630), News/Talk
KSHR-FM (97.3), Hot Country
PO Box 250, Coquille 97423; 541-396-2141;
Fax: 541-396-2143; Connie Williamson

Corvallis
KEJO (1240), Adult Pop Standards
KFLY-FM (101.5), Adult Contemp.
PO Box K, Corvallis 97339; 541-754-6633;
Fax: 541-754-6725; Jim Iverson

KLOO (1340), News/Talk/Sports
KLOO-FM (106.1), Oldies
PO Box 965, Corvallis 97339-0965;
541-753-4493; Fax: 541-752-0404; Lee Jamison

Cottage Grove
KNND (1400), Country
KCGR-FM (100.5), Adult Contemp.
321 Main St., Cottage Grove 97424;
541-942-2468; Fax: 541-942-5797;
Diane O'Renick

Dallas
KWIP (880), Spanish Music
PO Box 469, Dallas 97338; 503-623-0245;
Fax: 503-623-6733; Diane Burns

Eagle Point (see Medford)

Enterprise
KWVR (1340), Country/Talk
KWVR-FM (92.1), Country
220 West Main St., Enterprise 97828;
541-426-4577; Fax: 541-426-4578; Lee Perkins

Eugene
KDUK-FM (104.7), Contemp. Hits
PO Box 1120, Eugene 97440; 541-485-1120;
Fax: 541-484-5769; Dave Woodward

KEED (1600), Christian Country
83 Centennial Loop, Suite 5, Eugene 97401;
541-683-1600; Fax: 541-334-6684;
Dave Winchester

KEHK-FM (102.3), All Rock/All Hits
PO Box 2341, Eugene 97402; 541-485-5846;
Fax: 541-485-0969; Michael Atterberry

KKNU-FM (93.1), Contemp. Country
925 Country Club Rd., Suite 200, Eugene 97401;
541-484-9400; Fax: 541-344-9424; Bob Oxarart

KKNX (840), Oldies
945 Garfield St., Eugene 97402; 541-342-1012;
Fax: 541-342-6201; John S. Mielke

KKXO (1450), Adult Standards
KMGE-FM (94.5), Adult Contemp.
925 Country Club Rd., Suite 200, Eugene 97401;
541-484-9400; Fax: 541-344-9424; Bob Oxarart

KNRQ (1320), New Rock
KNRQ-FM (95.3), New Rock
2100 West 11th, Suite 200, Eugene 97402;
541-342-7096; Fax: 541-484-6397;
Rick Cavagnaro

KORE (1050), Christian/Talk
2080 Laura St., Springfield 97477-2197;
541-747-5673; Fax: 541-746-0680; Larry Knight

KPNW (1120), News/Talk/Sports
KODZ (99.1), Oldies
PO Box 1120, Eugene 97440; 541-485-1120;
Fax: 541-484-5769; Dave Woodward

KQFE-FM (88.9), Religious
5120 Franklin Blvd., #4, Eugene 97405;
541-726-9156; Carmen Brambora

KUGN (590), News/Talk
KUGN-FM (97.9), Contemp. Country
PO Box 2341, Eugene 97402; 541-485-5846;
Fax: 541-485-0969; Michael Atterberry

KZEL-FM (96.1), Classic Rock
2100 West 11th, Suite 200, Eugene 97402;
541-342-7096; Fax: 541-484-6397;
Rick Cavagnaro

Florence
KCST (1250), Soft AC/Country
KCST-FM (106.9), Soft AC/Country
PO Box 20000, Florence 97439; 541-997-9136;
Fax: 541-997-9165; Jon Thompson

Gleneden Beach (see Newport)

Gold Beach
KGBR-FM (92.7), AC/Country
PO Box 787, Gold Beach 97444-1476;
541-247-7211; Fax: 541-247-4155;
Dale St. Marie

Gold Hill

KRWQ-FM (100.3), Country
3624 Avion Dr., Medford 97504; 541-772-4170;
Fax: 541-857-0326; Duane Hill

Grants Pass

KAJO (1270), News/Adult MOR
KLDR-FM (98.3), Adult Contemp.
PO Box 230, Grants Pass 97526; 541-476-6608;
Fax: 541-476-4018; Matt Wilson; Carl Wilson

KRRM-FM (94.7), Traditional Country
225 Rogue River Hwy., Grants Pass 97527;
541-479-6497; Fax: 541-479-5726; Herb Bell

Gresham (see Portland)

Hermiston

KOHU (1360), Country
KQFM-FM (99.3), Adult Contemp.
PO Box 145, Hermiston 97838-0145;
541-567-6500; Fax: 541-567-6068;
Harmon Springer

Hillsboro (see Portland)

Hood River

KIHR (1340), Country/Talk
KCGB-FM (105.5), Adult Contemp.
PO Box 360, Hood River 97031; 541-386-1511;
Fax: 541-386-7155; Mylene Walden

Jacksonville

KAPL (1300), Contemp. Christian
PO Box 1090, Jacksonville 97530; 541-899-5275;
Fax: 541-899-8068; Chris Thompson

John Day

KJDY (1400), Country
KJDY-FM (94.5), Country
PO Box 399, John Day 97845; 541-575-1185;
Fax: 541-575-2313; Phil Gray

Klamath Falls

KAGO (1150), News/Talk
KAGO-FM (99.5), Adult Contemp.
PO Box 1150, Klamath Falls 97601;
541-882-2551; Fax: 541-883-6141; Greg Dourian

KFLS-FM (96.5), Country
PO Box 1450, Klamath Falls 97601;
541-882-4656; Fax: 541-884-2845;
Robert Wynne

KFLS (1450), Oldies
KKRB-FM (106.9), Adult Contemp.
PO Box 1450, Klamath Falls 97601;
541-882-4656; Fax: 541-884-2845;
Robert Wynne

KLAD (960), Country
KLAD-FM (92.5), Country
PO Box 339, Klamath Falls 97601;
541-882-8833; Fax: 541-882-8836; Scott Allen

La Grande

KCMB-FM (104.7), Country
1009-C Adams Ave., La Grande 97850;
541-963-3405; Fax: 541-963-5090;
Randy McKone

KLBM (1450), News/Talk
KUBQ-FM (98.7), Adult Contemp.
PO Box 907, La Grande 97850; 541-963-4121;
Fax: 541-963-3117; Bryan Christle

KWRL-FM (100.1 (Changing to 99.9
May 1997)), Adult Contemp.
PO Box 370, La Grande 97850; 541-963-7911;
Fax: 541-963-7619; Rick Freeman

Lakeview

KQIK (1230), Country
KQIK-FM (93.5), Country
PO Box 93, Lakeview 97630; 541-947-3351;
Fax: 541-947-3375; Art Collins

Bonneville Dam on the Columbia River will be 60 years old in 1997. Construction of the dam began in 1933 and took four years to complete.

Photo by Kevin G. Coulton.

Lake Oswego (see Portland)

Lebanon
KGAL (1580), News/Talk;
KHSO (920) Adult Standards
PO Box 749, Albany 97321; 541-926-8683;
Fax: 541-451-5429; Charlie Eads

KXPC-FM (103.7), Country
743 Main St., Suite 10, Lebanon 97355;
541-451-1037; Fax: 541-258-5479;
Marlene Bolen

Lincoln City
KBCH (1400), Nostalgic
KCRF-FM (96.7 & 98.3), Oldies
PO Box 820, Lincoln City 97367; 541-994-2181;
Fax: 541-994-2004; Hal D. Fowler

McMinnville
KLYC (1260), Adult Contemp.
PO Box 1099, McMinnville 97128;
503-472-1260; Fax: 503-472-3243;
Larry Bohnsack

Medford
KAKT-FM (105.1), Country
1438 Rossanley Dr., Medford 97501;
541-779-1550; Fax: 541-776-2360; Dan Gittings

KBOY-FM (97.5), Classic Rock
1438 Rossanley Dr., Medford 97501;
541-779-1550; Fax: 541-776-2360; Dan Gittings

KCMX (580), News/Talk
KCMX-FM (101.9), Adult Contemp.
1438 Rossanley Dr., Medford 97501;
541-779-1550; Fax: 541-776-2360; Dan Gittings

KDOV-FM (91.7), News/Talk/Christian
845 Alder Creek Dr., Medford 97504;
541-776-5368; Fax: 541-776-0618;
Perry Atkinson

KKJJ-FM (New) (107.5), Soft Rock
3624 Avion Dr., Medford 97504; 541-858-5423;
Fax: 541-857-0326; Sherry Hill

KMED (1440), Adult Standards
3624 Avion Dr., Medford 97504; 541-773-1440;
Fax: 541-857-0326; Duane Hill

KOPE-FM (103.5), News/Talk
744 E Pine St., Central Point 97502;
541-664-5673; Fax: 541-664-8261; Alan Corbeth

KROG-FM (96.9), Hot Adult Contemp.
1257 N Riverside Ave., #10, Medford 97501;
541-772-0322; Fax: 541-772-4233; Dean Flock

KRTA (610), Spanish
1257 N Riverside Ave., #10, Medford 97501;
541-772-0322; Fax: 541-772-4233; Dean Flock

KRVC (730), Contemp. Christian
1425 N Market Blvd., Suite 9, Sacramento, CA
95834; 916-928-1515; Fax: 916-928-0888;
Lloyd Parker

KTMT (880), Sports
KTMT-FM (93.7), Contemp. Hits Radio
1438 Rossanley Dr., Medford 97501;
541-779-1550; Fax: 541-776-2360; Dan Gittings

KZZE-FM (106.3), Rock
3624 Avion Dr., Medford 97504; 541-857-0340;
Fax: 541-857-0326; Sherry Hill

Milton-Freewater
KLKY-FM (97.9), New Country
Rt 5, Box 513, Walla Walla, WA 99362;
509-527-1000; Fax: 509-529-5534; Tom Hodgins

KTEL (1490), Classic Country
112 NE 5th, Milton-Freewater 97862;
541-938-6688; Dennis Widmer

KUJ (1420), News/Talk/Sports
KUJ-FM (99.1), Top 40 (CHR)
Rt 5, Box 513, Walla Walla, WA 99362;
509-527-1000; Fax: 509-529-5534; Tom Hodgins

Myrtle Point
KAHY-FM (94.1), Talk/Entertainment
PO Box 397, Myrtle Point 97458; 541-572-8255;
Fax: 541-572-6005; Keith Riggs

Newport
KNPT (1310), News/Talk
KYTE-FM (102.7), Adult Contemp.
PO Box 1430, Newport 97365; 541-265-2266;
Fax: 541-265-6397; Dave Miller

KSHL-FM (97.5), Country
PO Box 1180, Newport 97365; 541-265-6477;
Fax: 541-265-6478; Dick Linn

KSND-FM (95.1), Adult Contemp.
PO Box 484, Newport 97365; 541-574-1005;
Fax: 541-574-0791; Keith Miller

KZUS (1230), Country
KZUS-FM (100.7), Country
PO Box 456, Newport 97365; 541-265-5000;
Fax: 541-265-9576; Cheryl Harle

North Bend (see Coos Bay)

Ontario
KSRV (1380), Country/Talk
KSRV-FM (96.1), Country
PO Box 129, Ontario 97914; 541-889-8651;
Fax: 541-889-8733; Vicki Swain

Pendleton
KTIX (1240), News/Talk
KWHT-FM (103.5), Country
PO Box 640, Pendleton 97801; 541-278-2500;
Fax: 541-276-6842; Cheryl Harle

KUMA (1290), Adult Standards
KUMA-FM (107.7), Adult Contemp.
PO Box 340, Pendleton 97801; 541-276-1511;
Fax: 541-276-1480; Ron Hughes

Phoenix (see Medford)

Portland

KBBT-FM (107.5), Alternative Rock
2040 SW 1st Ave., Portland 97201;
503-222-1011; Fax: 503-222-2047;
Dave McDonald

KBMS (1480), Urban Contemp.
601 Main St., Suite 400, Vancouver 98660;
503-222-1491; Chris Bennett

KBNP (1410), Business/News/Talk
811 SW Front Ave., Suite 430, Portland 97204;
503-223-6769; Fax: 503-223-4305;
Keith P. Lyons

KEX (1190), Adult Contemp./Talk
4949 SW Macadam Ave., Portland 97201;
503-225-1190; Fax: 503-227-5873; Dave Milner

KEZF (1040), Contemp. Christian
1425 N Market Blvd., Suite 9, Sacramento, CA
95834; 916-928-1515; Fax: 916-928-0888;
Lloyd Parker

KFXX (1520), Sports/Talk
4614 SW Kelly Ave., Portland 97201;
503-223-1441; Fax: 503-223-6909; Tom Baker

KGON-FM (92.3), Classic Rock
4614 SW Kelly Ave., Portland 97201; Tom Baker

KKCW-FM (103.3), Adult Contemp.
5005 SW Macadam Ave., Portland 97201;
503-222-5103; Fax: 503-222-0030; Ron Saito

KKEY (1150), News/Talk
PO Box 5757, Portland 97228; 503-222-1150;
Fax: 360-735-0589; Linda Weagant

KKJZ-FM (106.7), NAC
222 SW Columbia, Suite 350, Portland 97201;
503-223-0300; Fax: 503-497-2333; Stan Mak

KKPZ (1330), Religious
4700 SW Macadam Ave., Suite 102, Portland
97201; 503-242-1950; Fax: 503-242-0155;
David Harms

KKRH-FM (105.1), Classic Rock
888 SW 5th Ave., Suite 790, Portland 97204;
503-223-0105; Fax: 503-224-3070;
Harry Williams

KKRZ-FM (100.3), Contemp. Hits
4949 SW Macadam Ave., Portland 97201;
503-226-0100; Fax: 503-295-9281; Clint Sly

KKSL (1290), Religious
4700 SW Macadam Ave., Suite 102, Portland
97201; 503-242-1950; Fax: 503-242-0155;
David Harms

KKSN (910), Adult Standards
KKSN-FM (97.1), Oldies
888 SW 5th Ave., Suite 790, Portland 97204;
503-226-9791; Fax: 503-243-3299;
Harry Williams

KMUZ (1230), Spanish
1217 NE Burnside, Suite 804, Gresham 97030;
503-492-9980; Fax: 503-665-9980; Tom Trullinger

KNRK-FM (94.7), Alternate Rock
4614 SW Kelly Ave., Portland 97201;
503-223-1441; Fax: 503-223-6909; Tom Baker

KOTK (620), Talk
KINK-FM (101.9), Adult Alternative
1501 SW Jefferson, Portland 97201;
503-226-5080; Fax: 503-226-4578; Steve Keeney

KPDQ (800), Religious Talk/Music
KPDQ-FM (93.7), Religious Talk
5110 SE Stark, Portland 97215; 503-231-7800;
Fax: 503-238-7202; Darrell Kennedy

KUFO-FM (101.1), Album Oriented Rock
2040 SW 1st Ave., Portland 97201;
503-222-1011; Fax: 503-222-2047;
Dave McDonald

KUIK (1360), Talk/Sports
PO Box 566, Hillsboro 97123; 503-640-1360;
Fax: 503-640-6108; Don McCoun

KUPL (970), Straight Country
KUPL-FM (98.5), Contemp. Country
222 SW Columbia, Suite 350, Portland 97201;
503-223-0300; Fax: 503-497-2333; Stan Mak

KWJJ (1080), Contemp. Country
KWJJ-FM (99.5), Contemp. Country
931 SW King Ave., Portland 97205;
503-228-4393; Fax: 503-227-3938; Dan Volz

KXL (750), News/Talk
KXL-FM (95.5), AC 80s and 90s
0234 SW Bancroft, Portland 97201;
503-243-7595; Fax: 503-417-7660; Ray Watson,
Tim McNamara

KXYQ (1010), Talk
6035 SE Milwaukie Ave., Portland 97202;
503-235-9942; Fax: 503-233-4045; Jeff Kafoury

Prineville

KRCO (690), Country
KIJK-FM (95.1), Hot Country
PO Box K, Prineville 97754; 541-447-6239;
Fax: 541-447-4724; Jerry Hicks

KTWI-FM (96.5), Country
PO Box K, Prineville 97754; 541-447-6239;
Fax: 541-447-4724; Jerry Hicks

Redmond (see Bend)

Reedsport

KRBZ-FM (99.5), All 70s
PO Box 599, Reedsport 97467; 541-271-3300;
Fax: 541-271-5466; Colleen Fafara

Roseburg

KKMX-FM (104.3), Adult Contemp.
PO Box 5180, Roseburg 97470; 541-672-6641;
Fax: 541-673-7598; Pat Markham

KQEN (1240), Adult Hits/Sports/Talk
KRSB-FM (103.1), Contemp. Country
PO Box 5180, Roseburg 97470; 541-672-6641;
Fax: 541-673-7598; Pat Markham

KRNR (1490), Country
782 NE Garden Valley Blvd., Roseburg 97470;
541-673-5553; Fax: 541-673-3483; John Pundt

KTBR (950), Talk/Entertainment
PO Box 1760, Roseburg 97470; 541-672-4427;
Fax: 541-672-4827; Keith and Sue Riggs

Rogue River (see Grants Pass)

Salem

**KBZY (1490), Local Service Adult
Contemp.**
PO Box 14900, Salem 97309; 503-362-1490;
Fax: 503-362-6545; Roy Dittman

KCCS (1220), Christian Worship Music
4303 Market St. NE, Salem 97301; 503-364-1000;
Fax: 503-364-1022; Earl Allbritton

KYKN (1430), News/Talk
KSLM (1390), Oldies
PO Box 1430, Salem 97308; 503-390-3014;
Fax: 503-390-3728; Michael Frith

Seaside

KCYS-FM (98.1) Hot Country
PO Box 1258, Astoria 97103; 503-717-9643;
Fax: 503-717-9578; Dave Heick

KSWB (840), Sports
120 N Roosevelt, Seaside 97138; 503-738-6002;
Ken Ulbricht

St. Helens

KOHI (1600), Country/Talk
PO Box 398, St. Helens 97051; Forrest Smith

Stayton

KCKX (1460), Real Country
PO Box 158, Woodburn 97071; 503-981-9400;
Fax: 503-981-3561; Don Coss

Sweet Home

KFIR (720), Modern/Classic Country
PO Box 720, Sweet Home 97386; 541-367-5115;
Fax: On Request; Bob Ratter

KSKD-FM (107.1), Contemp. Christian
1425 N Market Blvd., Suite 9, Sacramento, CA
95834; 916-928-1515; Fax: 916-928-0888;
Lloyd Parker

The Dalles

KACI (1300), Good Time Oldies/Talk
KACI-FM (97.7), Good Time Oldies
PO Box 516, The Dalles 97058; 541-296-2211;
Fax: 541-296-2213; Alex King

**KMCQ-FM (104.5), Adult Contemp.
Hits**
PO Box 104, The Dalles 97058; 541-298-5116;
Fax: 541-298-5119; John Huffman

KODL (1440), Country
PO Box 741, The Dalles 97058; 541-296-2101;
Fax: 541-296-3766; Al Wynn

Tillamook

KMBD (1590), News/Talk
KTIL-FM (104.1), Adult Contemp.
PO Box 40, Tillamook 97141; 503-842-4422;
Fax: 503-842-2755; Van Moe

Umatilla

KLWJ (1090), Contemp. Christian
PO Box 1410, Umatilla 97882; 541-567-2102;
Fax: 541-567-2103; John Marlow

Water lapped at the doors of businesses at Riverplace, a development outside Portland's floodwall on the Willamette River, during the February 1996 flood.

Photo by Bob Yancy, Tyee Yacht Club.

Waldport
KORC (820), Adult Standards
PO Box 1419, Waldport 97394; 541-563-5100;
Fax: 541-563-5116; Matt Jarvis

Winston
KGRV (700), Christian
PO Box 1598, Winston 97496; 541-679-8185;
Fax: 541-679-6456; Scott Welch

Woodburn
KWBY (940), Spanish
Box 158, Woodburn 97071; 503-981-9400;
Fax: 503-981-3561; Don Coss

Oregon Commercial Television Stations

Source: Oregon Association of Broadcasters
Bill Johnstone, Exec. Dir.
PO Box 449, 111 W 7th St., Eugene 97440-0449;
541-343-2101; Fax: 541-343-0662

Beaverton
KWBP-TV (32); Warner Bros.
10255 SW Arctic Dr., Beaverton 97005;
503-644-3232; Fax: 503-626-3576; Tom McCoy

Bend
KFXO-TV (39); Fox
63140 Britta St., Suite D-101, Bend 97701;
541-382-7220; Fax: 541-382-5922; Cary Jones

KTVZ (TV) (21); NBC
PO Box 149, Bend 97709; 541-383-2121;
Fax: 541-382-1616; John Larkin

Brookings
KBSC-TV (49); Warner Bros.
PO Box 7649, Brookings 97415; 541-469-4999;
Fax: 541-469-0801; Dan McGrath

Coos Bay
KCBY-TV (11); CBS
PO Box 1156, Coos Bay 97420; 541-269-1111;
Fax: 541-269-7464; Bruce Bennett

KMTZ-TV (23); NBC
PO Box 7308, Eugene 97401-0208;
541-746-1600; Fax: 541-747-0866;
Brian Benschoter

Eugene
KEVU-TV (34); UPN
888 Goodpasture Island Rd., Eugene 97401;
541-342-3435; Fax: 541-683-8016;
Mark Metzger

KEZI-TV (9); ABC
PO Box 7009, Eugene 97401; 541-485-5611;
Fax: 541-342-1568; Bruce Liljegren

KLSR-TV (25); Fox
888 Goodpasture Island Rd., Eugene 97401;
541-683-2525; Fax: 541-683-8016;
Mark Metzger

KMTR-TV (16); NBC
PO Box 7308, Eugene 97401-0208;
541-746-1600; Fax: 541-747-0866;
Brian Benschoter

KVAL-TV (13); CBS
PO Box 1313, Eugene 97440; 541-342-4961;
Fax: 541-342-2635; Jim Putney

Klamath Falls
KDKF-TV (31); ABC
4509 S 6th St., Suite 308, Klamath Falls 97603;
541-883-3131; Fax: 541-883-8931; Keith Lollis

KOTI-TV (2); NBC
PO Box 2K, Klamath Falls 97601; 541-882-2222;
Fax: 541-882-2222; Patsy Smullin

Medford
KDRV-TV (12); ABC
PO Box 4220, Medford 97501; 541-773-1212;
Fax: 541-779-9261; Keith Lollis

KMVU-TV (26); Fox
820 Crater Lake Ave., Medford 97504;
541-772-2600; Fax: 541-772-7364; Peter Rogers

KOBI-TV (5); NBC
PO Box 1489, Medford 97501; 541-779-5555;
Fax: 541-779-5564; Patsy Smullin

KTVL-TV (10); CBS
PO Box 10, Medford 97501-0202; 541-773-7373;
Fax: 541-779-0451; Kingsley Kelley

Pendleton
WatchTV, Inc. (K16DD); Telemundo
6107 Marine Dr., Suite 6, Portland 97203;
503-289-2456; Fax: 503-289-2215;
Gregory Herman

Portland
KATU-TV (2); ABC
PO Box 2, Portland 97207; 503-231-4222;
Fax: 503-231-4233; Jim Boyer

KGW-TV (8); NBC
1501 SW Jefferson St., Portland 97201;
503-226-5000; Fax: 503-226-5120;
Dennis Williamson

KNMT-TV (24); Independent
432 NE 74th Ave., Portland 97213;
503-252-0792; Fax: 503-256-4205; Marta Lewis

KOIN-TV (6); CBS
222 SW Columbia, Portland 97201;
503-464-0600; Fax: 503-464-0717;
Peter Maroney

KPDX-TV (49); Fox
910 NE M.L. King Blvd., Portland 97232;
503-239-4949; Fax: 503-239-6184; Cary Jones

KPTV-TV (12); UPN
PO Box 3401, Portland 97208; 503-230-1200;
Fax: 503-736-1290; Marty Brantley

WatchTV, Inc. (K68EI); Telemundo
6107 Marine Dr., Suite 6, Portland 97203;
503-289-2456; Fax: 503-289-2215;
Gregory Herman

Roseburg
KMTX-TV (46); NBC
PO Box 7308, Eugene 97401-0208;
541-746-1600; Fax: 541-747-0866;
Brian Benschoter

KPIC-TV (4); CBS
PO Box 1345, Roseburg 97470; 541-672-4481;
Fax: 541-672-4482; Don Clithero

KROZ-TV (36); Warner Bros.
931 NW Highland, Roseburg 97470;
541-673-3636; Fax: 541-673-1136; Ron Lee

Salem
KBSP-TV (22); HSN/Independent
4923 Indian School Rd. NE, Salem 97305;
503-390-2202; Fax: 503-390-6829;
Judith Koenig

Oregon Public/Educational Radio and Television Stations

Source: Oregon Association of Broadcasters
Bill Johnstone, Exec. Dir.
PO Box 449, 111 W 7th St., Eugene 97440-0449;
541-343-2101; Fax 541-343-0662

Ashland
KSOR-FM (90.1), KSMF-FM (89.1),
KSRG-FM (88.3)
Southern Oregon State College, 1250 Siskiyou
Blvd., Ashland 97520; 541-552-6301;
Fax: 541-482-6329; Ronald Kramer

Astoria
KMUN-FM (91.9)
PO Box 269, Astoria 97103; 503-352-0010;
Doug Sweet

Bend
KOAB-TV (3), KOAB-FM (91.3)
PO Box 509, Bend 97709; 541-389-0237;
Max Culbertson

Central Point
KCHC-FM (91.7)
School District #6, Medford; 541-664-1241;

Coos Bay
KSBA-FM (88.5)
Southern Oregon State College, 1250 Siskiyou
Blvd., Ashland 97520; 541-552-6301;
Fax: 541-482-6329; Ronald Kramer

Corvallis
KBVR-TV (11, cable)
KBVR-FM (88.7)
Oregon State University, Corvallis 97331;
541-754-3374; Frank Ragulsky

KOAC-TV (7), KOAC (550)
239 Covell Hall, Oregon State University,
Corvallis 97331; 541-737-4311;
Fax: 541-737-4314; Virginia Breen

Eagle Point
KEPO-FM (92.1)
School District #9, PO Box 97, Eagle Point
97524; 541-826-3364

Eugene
KLCC-FM (89.7)
Lane Community College, 4000 E 30th Ave.,
Eugene 97405; 541-726-2224;
Fax: 541-744-3962; Steve Barton

KRVM (1280), KRVM-FM (91.9)
Eugene School District 4J, 1574 Coburg Rd.,
Suite 237, Eugene 97401; 541-687-3370;
Fax: 541-687-3573; Carl Sundberg

KWAX-FM (91.1)
University of Oregon, 2365 Bonnie View Dr.,
Eugene 97401; 541-346-4238;
Fax: 541-343-2123; Paul Bjornstad

Florence
K211BP (90.5)
Eugene School District 4J, 1574 Coburg Rd.,
Suite 237, Eugene 97401; 541-687-3370;
Fax: 541-687-3573; Carl Sundberg

Forest Grove
KPUR-FM (94.5)
Pacific University, 2043 College Way, Forest
Grove 97116; 503-359-2255; Mike Geraci

Grants Pass
KAGI (930)
Southern Oregon State College, 1250 Siskiyou
Blvd., Ashland 97520; 541-552-6301;
Fax: 541-482-6329; Ronald Kramer

Gresham
KMHD-FM (89.1)
Mt. Hood Community College, 26000 SE Stark St., Gresham 97030; 503-661-8900; John Rice

Klamath Falls
KSKF-FM (90.9)
Southern Oregon State College, 1250 Siskiyou Blvd., Ashland 97520; 541-552-6301; Fax: 541-482-6329; Ronald Kramer

KTEC-FM (89.5, 96.9 TCI)
Oregon Institute of Technology, PO Box 2009, Klamath Falls 97601; 541-885-1840; Fax: 541-885-1857; Jason Stec

La Grande
KEOL-FM (91.7)
Eastern Oregon State College, La Grande 97850; 541-963-1389; Joe Garner

KTVR-TV (13)
PO Box R, La Grande 97850; 541-963-3900; Fax: 541-963-7742; Debbi Hinton

McMinnville
KSLC-FM (90.3)
Linfield College, McMinnville 97128; 503-472-3851; Craig Singleary

Medford
KSYS-TV (8)
34 S Fir St., Medford 97501; 541-779-0808; Fax: 541-779-2178; William Campbell

Newberg
KFOX (530)
George Fox College, Sub Box F, Newberg 97132; 503-538-8383; Deb Lacey

Newport
KLCO-FM (90.5)
Lane Community College, 4000 E 30th Ave., Eugene 97405; 541-726-2224; Fax: 541-744-3962; Steve Barton

Oakridge
KAVE-FM (92.1)
Eugene School District 4J, 1574 Coburg Rd., Suite 237, Eugene 97401; 541-687-3370; Fax: 541-687-3573; Debbie Gillespie

Ontario
KMBA-TV (Ch. 19)
Treasure Valley Community College, 650 College Blvd., Ontario 97914; 541-889-6493; Fax: 541-881-2721; Russell Strawn

Pendleton
KRBM-FM (90.9)
Blue Mt. Community College, PO Box 100, Pendleton 97801; 541-276-1260; Fax: 541-276-6119; Maynard Orme

Portland
KBOO-FM (90.7)
20 SE 8th Ave., Portland 97214; 503-231-8032; Suzanne White

KBPS (1450), KBPS-FM (89.9)
School District #1, 515 NE 15th Ave., Portland 97232; 503-280-5828; Darryl Conser

KBVM-FM (88.3)
PO Box 5888, Portland 97228; 503-283-7455; Fax: 503-283-7355; Bernie Muller

KDUP (860)
University of Portland Comm. Dept., 5000 N Willamette Blvd., Portland 97203; 503-283-7121; Sally Click

KLC-FM (93.1)
Lewis and Clark College, Portland 97219; 503-293-2700; Stuart Kaplan

KOPB-TV (10), KOPB-FM (91.5)
Oregon Public Broadcasting, 7140 SW Macadam Ave., Portland 97219; 503-244-9900; Fax: 503-293-4165; Maynard Orme

KRRC-FM (104.1)
Reed College, Portland 97202; 503-771-2180; Ana Brown

Reedsport
KSYD-FM (92.1)
Eugene School District 4J, 1574 Coburg Rd., Suite 237, Eugene 97401; 541-687-3370; Fax: 541-687-3573; Carl Sundberg

Roseburg
KSRS-FM (91.5)
Southern Oregon State College, 1250 Siskiyou Blvd., Ashland 97520; 541-552-6301; Fax: 541-482-6329; Ronald Kramer

Talent
KSJK (1230)
Southern Oregon State College, 1250 Siskiyou Blvd., Ashland 97520; 541-552-6301; Fax: 541-482-6329; Ronald Kramer

Warm Springs
KWSO-FM (91.9)
PO Box 489, Warm Springs 97761; 541-553-1968; Fax: 541-553-3348; Mike Villalobos

Media Directories

Cable TV

Source: Oregon Cable Telecommunications
Association, Michael Dewey, Exec. Dir.

*960 Liberty St. SE, Suite 200, Salem 97302-4154;
503-362-8838; Fax: 503-399-1029*

Cable television was developed in the late 1940s in communities unable to receive broadcast TV signals because of terrain or distance from broadcast stations. In fact, Astoria is believed to be the site of the first cable TV system. Cable provides broadcast signals, satellite signals and public and leased access services to its subscribers.

The large channel capacity of coaxial cable allows cable systems to deliver many channels and services. Some companies originate their own programming and/or provide access channels for use by the public, for education or government entities. Two-way communication is possible but largely limited to larger markets. Cable TV provides an array of other types of programming services, including children's programming, 24-hour news, all sports, exclusive movies, financial news and a great deal more.

The Oregon Cable Telecommunications Association (OCTA) represents it Oregon members who are cable companies. It does not regulate cable TV or cable companies.

Arlington
Arlington TV Cooperative, 184 On the Mall, 97812; 541-454-2707

Astoria
Falcon Cable, Box 60, 97103; 503-325-6114; Fax: 503-325-7421

Beaverton
TCI-Tualatin Valley, 14200 SW Brigadoon Ct., 97005; 503-605-4598; Fax: 503-646-8004

Bend
American Telecasting of Bend 20332 Empire Ave., Suite F7, 97001; 541-382-4031; Fax: 541-382-6835

Bend Cable Communications, Inc. Box 5067, 97708; 541-382-5551; Fax: 541-385-3271

Brookings
Falcon Cable, 01 Railroad St., 97415; 541-626-1700

Burns
TCI Cablevision, 85 E B St., 97720; 541-573-2941

Canby
North Willamette Telecom, Box 850, 97013; 503-263-8080; Fax: 503-266-8297

Cascade Locks
City of Cascade Locks, Box 308, 97014; 541-374-8484; Fax: 541-374-8752

Cheshire
Country Vision Cable, PO Box 199, 97419; 541-726-0315; Fax: 541-726-4933

Clackamas
Cable America Corp., 19950 SE Hwy. 212, 97015; 503-658-3052

Clatskanie
TCI Cablevision, PO Box 388, 97016; 503-728-3511

Colton
Colton Cable TV, PO Box 68, 97017; 541-824-3211; Fax: 541-824-9944

Condon
Condon TV Systems, Inc., PO Box 366, 97823; 541-384-2261

Coos Bay
Falcon Cable, 1400 Newmark Ave., 97420; 541-888-5561; Fax: 541-888-9292

SAH Systems 485 Shorepines Vista, 97420; 541-888-9841; Fax: 541-888-5271

Corvallis
TCI Cablevision, 820 NW Cornell St., 97330; 541-758-8808; Fax: 541-758-8818

Cottage Grove
Falcon Cable, Box 1089, 97424; 541-942-1336

Dallas
Falcon Cable, PO Box 86, 97338; 623-3241; Fax: 503-623-9446

Depoe Bay
Summit Cablevision, PO Box 367, 97341; 541-765-2139; Fax: 541-765-2137

Dufur
SB Northstate Cablevision, PO Box 297, 97021; 541-467-2409

Elgin
Elgin TV Association, Inc., Box 246, 97827; 541-437-4575

Enterprise
Crestview Cable TV, 103 Hwy. 82,
Suite 1A, 97828; 541-426-3636

Estacada
Mastertech, Inc., 355 Broadway,
97023; 503-630-2565

Eugene
Chambers Communications Corp.,
PO Box 7009, 97401; 541-485-5611;
Fax: 541-342-1568

TCI Cablevision, PO Box 2500, 97402;
541-431-3500; Fax: 541-431-3655

Florence
Falcon Cable, Box S, 97439;
541-997-8404; Fax: 541-997-8408

Fossil
Fossil Community TV, Box 209,
97830; 763-2698; Fax: 541-763-2124

Glide
Glide Cablevision, PO Box 609, 97443;
541-496-0515

Gold Beach
Falcon Cable, 125 6th St., 97444;
541-247-7952

Grants Pass
TCI Cablevision, Box 1129, 97526;
541-476-6606; Fax: 541-474-1570

Halsey
RTI Cable Television, Box 227, 97348;
541-369-2211; Fax: 541-369-2233

Heppner
Heppner TV, 162 N Main St., 97836;
541-676-9663; Fax: 541-676-5442

Hood River
Falcon Cablevision, 1215 12th St.,
97031; 541-386-3100;
Fax: 541-386-6015

Ione
Ione City TV Co-Op, PO Box 254,
97843; 541-422-7171

Jacksonville
Sunnyside Cable TV, 5361 Hwy. 238,
97530; 541-899-1341

Klamath Falls
Bly Cable Co., 2809 Montelius St.,
97601; 541-884-9880

TCI Cablevision, PO Box 8, 97601;
541-882-5533; Fax: 541-884-4270

La Grande
TCI Cablevision, PO Box 1401, 97850;
541-963-4189; Fax: 541-963-6743

Lakeview
TCI Cablevision, PO Box 1338, 97630;
541-947-3772; Fax: 541-947-3635

Lebanon
TCI Cablevision, 148 W Grant St.,
97355; 541-258-6090;
Fax: 541-259-3202

Lincoln City
Falcon Cable, 1344 NE Hwy. 101,
97367; 541-994-3111;
Fax: 541-994-7438

Lyons
People's Telephone Co., PO Box 69,
97358; 503-859-2136

Madras
Crestview Cable TV, 527 C St. #E,
97741; 541-475-2969

McMinnville
TCI Cablevision, 4025 Nimbus Loop,
97128; 503-472-1121;
Fax: 503-472-0230

Medford
American Telecasting of Medford,
3971 Crater Lake Hwy., 97504;
541-772-9707; Fax: 541-773-1574

TCI Cablevision, Box 399, 97501;
541-779-1814; Fax: 541-776-2278

Milton-Freewater
TCI Cablevision, 303 N Columbia,
97862; 541-938-5859

Milwaukie
Jones Intercable, Inc., PO Box 22367,
97222; 503-654-2266;
Fax: 503-652-0464

Monroe
Monroe Area Communications,
PO Box 198, 97456; 541-847-5135;
Fax: 541-847-9997

Mount Vernon
Blue Mountain Cable TV Co.,
Box 267, 97865; 541-932-4613

North-State Cablevision Co.,
One Telephone Dr., 97865;
541-467-2211

Myrtle Creek
Jones Intercable, PO Box 1700,
97457; 541-863-4914;
Fax: 541-863-6832

Nehalem
Falcon Cable, 13990 Tideland Rd.,
97131; 503-623-3241;
Fax: 503-623-9446

Netarts
Falcon Cable, 4970 Grab Ave., 97143;
503-842-6682

Netarts Cable TV, Inc., PO Box 196,
97143; 503-842-4943

Newberg
Tele-Communications, Inc.,
2502 Portland Rd., 97132;
503-538-7480

Newport
TCI Cablevision, PO Box 950, 97365;
541-265-2263; Fax: 541-265-5064

Ontario
Chambers Communications, PO Box
398, 97914; 541-889-3173;
Fax: 541-889-4453

Parkdale
Valley TV, 4949 Baseline Rd., 97041;
541-352-6760

Pendleton
TCI of NE Oregon, Box 248, 97801;
276-2821; Fax: 276-0134

Portland
Paragon Cable, 3075 NE Sandy Blvd.,
97232; 503-230-2099;
Fax: 503-230-2218

TCI Cablevision, 3500 SW Bond, 97201;
503-243-7426; Fax: 503-243-7413

Prineville
Crestview Cable, 390 N Beaver St.,
97754; 541-447-4342;
Fax: 541-447-5987

Redmond
Falcon Cable, 741 SW 17th St., 97756;
541-923-2263; Fax: 541-923-0241

Roseburg
Falcon Cable, 988 W Harvard, 97470;
541-673-1267; Fax: 541-672-5193

Salem
Country Cablevision, Ltd., PO Box
12038, 97309-0038; 503-588-8247;
Fax: 503-588-0544

Mill Creek Cable TV, Inc., 3100 Turner
Rd. SE, 97302; 503-363-7717

TCI-Salem, 1710 Salem Industrial Dr.
NE, 97303; 503-370-2770;
Fax: 503-370-2751

Scio
Scio Cablevision, Box 26, 97374-0026;
503-394-3366; Fax: 503-394-3999

Shady Cove
Phoenix Cablevision, PO Box 828,
97539; 541-878-3247;
Fax: 541-878-2458

Sheridan
Stuck Electric, 147 W Main St.,
97378-1849; 503-843-2322;
Fax: 503-843-2321

Silverton
Falcon Cable, 204 W Main St., 97381;
503-623-3241; Fax: 503-623-9446

Springfield
Cableview, Inc., 1860 N 42nd St.,
97478; 541-726-0315

Falcon Cable, PO Box 808, 97477;
541-746-4132; Fax: 541-746-8665

St. Helens
TCI Cablevision, PO Box 308, 97051;
503-397-5804; Fax: 503-397-5686

Stayton
North Santiam Communications,
Box 314, 97383; 503-769-7898;
Fax: 503-769-4216

Sunriver
North Santiam Communications,
PO Box 3275, 97707; 541-593-1296;
Fax: 541-593-1001

Talent
Sera Enterprises, 1027 S Pacific Hwy.,
97540; 541-535-7760

Tangent
Tangent TV Cable Co., 33004 Garden
Ln., 97389; 541-976-9000

The Dalles
Cascade Cable, Box 397, 97058;
541-298-4983

Falcon Cable, 409 Union St., 97058;
541-296-1146; Fax: 541-298-5213

Tillamook
Falcon Cable, 1014 Pacific Ave.,
97141; 503-623-3241;
Fax: 503-623-9446

Umatilla
Columbia Basin Cable, 611 6th St.,
97882; 541-922-5759

Waldport
Alsea River Cable TV, 320 Hemlock,
97394; 541-563-4807

TCI Cablevision, 820 Mill St., 97394;
541-563-4456

Warm Springs
Warm Springs Cable Co., PO Box 520,
97761; 541-553-1597

Woodburn
Monitor Telecommunication System,
PO Box 588, 97071; 503-634-2100;
Fax: 503-634-2900

Northland Cable Television, 635 Glatt
Circle, 97071; 503-982-4085;
Fax: 503-982-4804

NATIONAL AND INTERNATIONAL

A swallow perched on a bird house looks over Ladd Marsh in Union County.
Photo by Eric W. Valentine.

THE federal government owns more than 50 percent of all land within Oregon's borders, so the state has always had a unique relationship with Washington, D.C. As congress considers such critical areas as international trade and natural resource concerns, that relationship becomes increasingly important. Also, Oregonians increasingly view themselves as members of a world society, with stronger links to cultures within Oregon and outside the nation. This chapter provides key information about the federal government, Native American people in Oregon and international connections.

Gordon H. Smith

Republican. Born in Pendleton, May 25, 1952. Brigham Young University, B.A., 1976; Southwestern University, law degree, 1979. Purchased Smith Frozen Foods in 1980, now one of the largest private label packers of frozen vegetables in the U.S. He and his wife, Sharon, have three children.

Elected to the State Senate, 1992; became Senate President in 1994. Elected to the U.S. Senate, 1996. Member, Budget, Energy and Natural Resources, and Foreign Relations Committees; member, Water and Power, Forests and Public Land Management, and Energy Research, Development, Production and Regulation Subcommittees; chair of the Subcommittee on European Affairs; member, Subcommittee on Near Eastern and South Asian Affairs, and International Operations Subcommittee. Term expires: 2003.

Washington, D.C. Office: SD B-34, Washington, D.C. 20510; 202-224-4209; Fax: 202-228-3997.

District Office: 1220 SW 3rd Ave., Suite 618, Portland 97204; 503-326-3386.

Ron Wyden

Democrat. Born in Wichita, Kansas, May 3, 1949. Stanford University, A.B. in Political Science, 1971; University of Oregon School of Law, J.D., 1974. He and his wife, Laurie Oseran, have two children. Co-director, Oregon Gray Panthers, 1974–80; director, Oregon Legal Services for the Elderly, 1977–79; public member, Oregon Board of Examiners of Nursing Home Administrators, 1978–79.

Elected to Congress, 1980; reelected 1982, 1984, 1986, 1988, 1990, 1992, 1994. Elected to the U.S. Senate, 1996. Member, Commerce, Environmental and Public Works, Budget, and Aging Committees. Term expires 1999.

Washington, D.C. Office: 259 Russell, Senate Office Bldg., Washington, D.C. 20510; 202-224-5244; Email: senator@wyden.senate.gov; Web: www.senate.gov/~wyden.

District Offices: Bend—The Jamison Bldg., 131 NW Hawthorne Ave., Suite 107, Bend 97701; 541-330-9142; Fax: 541-330-6266. **Eugene**—The Center Court Bldg., 151 W 7th Ave., Suite 435, Eugene 97401; 541-431-0229; Fax: 541-431-0610. **La Grande**—Sac Annex Bldg., 105 Fir St., Suite 210, La Grande 97850; 541-962-7691; Fax: 541-963-0885. **Medford**—The Federal Courthouse, 310 W 6th St., Room 118, Medford 97501; 541-858-5122; Fax: 541-858-5126. **Portland**—500 NE Multnomah St., Suite 320, 97232; 503-326-7525; Fax: 503-326-7528. **Salem**—707 13th St. SE, Suite 110, Salem 97301; 503-589-4555; Fax: 503-589-4749.

U.S. Representatives

Elizabeth Furse—First District

Counties: Clatsop, Columbia, Washington, Yamhill and small parts of southwestern Multnomah and northwestern Clackamas.

Elizabeth Furse, Democrat. Born in Nairobi, Kenya, October 13, 1936. Attended Rhodes University in South Africa, 1952; Evergreen State College, B.A., 1972. Director, Western Washington Indian Program, American Friends Service Committee, 1974–77; Attended Northwestern School of Law, Lewis and Clark College, 1978–79; Tribal Restoration Coordinator, Native American Program, Oregon Legal Services, 1980–86. She and her husband, John C. Platt, have two children and one grandchild. Co-owner of Helvetia Vineyards with husband.

Elected to Congress, 1992; reelected in 1994 and 1996. Member, Commerce Committee; member, Subcommittees on Energy and Power; Health and Environment; Finance; and Hazardous Materials. Term expires 1999.

Washington, D.C. Office: 316 Cannon Office Bldg., Washington, D.C. 20515; 202-225-0855; Fax: 202-225-9497

District Office: 2701 NW Vaughn, Suite 860, Portland 97210; 503-326-2901; toll-free: 800-422-4003; Fax: 503-225-9497; Email: furseori@hr.house.gov.

Bob Smith—Second District

Counties: All counties east of the Cascades, all of Jackson and most of Josephine.

Robert F. Smith, Republican. Born in Portland, June 16, 1931. Willamette University, B.A., 1953. Rancher and businessman. Director, First State Bank of Oregon; director, Key Bank; director, Farmers Insurance Exchange Board; director, Board of Trustees of Willamette University. He and his wife, Kaye, have three children and own homes in Medford and Burns.

Elected to Oregon House of Representatives, 1960; served as House Speaker, 1969–73; elected to the State Senate, 1973; served as Senate Republican Leader, 1977–82. Elected to Congress, 1982; reelected, 1984, 1986, 1988, 1990, 1992 and 1996. Chair, Committee on Agriculture; member, Committee on Resources. Term expires 1999.

Washington, D.C Office: 1126 Longworth House Office Bldg., Washington, D.C. 20515; 202-225-6730.

District Office: 843 E Main St., Suite 400, Medford 97504; 541-776-4646.

National/International

U.S. Representatives

Earl Blumenauer—Third District

Counties: Most of Multnomah and northern part of Clackamas.

Earl Blumenauer, Democrat. Born in Portland, August 18, 1948. Attended Lewis and Clark College, Portland State University, University of Colorado at Denver and Kennedy School of Government at Harvard. Received B.A., political science, 1970; law degree, 1976.

Elected to State House of Representatives, 1972; reelected, 1974 and 1976. Elected to Multnomah County Board of Commissioners, 1978; reelected, 1982. Elected to Portland City Council, 1986; reelected 1990 and 1994.

Elected to Congress in 1996. Member, Economic and Educational Opportunities Committees. Term expires 1999.

Washington, D.C. Office: 113 Longworth House Office Bldg., Washington, D.C. 20515; 202-225-4811; Email: write.earl@mail.house.gov.

District Office: 516 SE Morrison St., Suite 250, Portland 97214; 503-231-2300; Fax: 503-230-5413.

Peter DeFazio—Fourth District

Counties: Coos, Curry, Douglas, Lane, Linn, northern part of Josephine and most of Benton.

Peter DeFazio, Democrat. Born in Needham, Massachusetts, May 27, 1947. Tufts University, B.A., 1969; University of Oregon, M.A., 1977. Honorable discharge U.S. Air Force Reserve, 1971. He and his wife Myrnie L. Daut, own a home and live in Springfield. Aide to Congressman Jim Weaver, 1977–82; elected to Lane County Board of Commissioners, 1982.

Elected to U.S. Congress 1986, reelected 1988, 1990, 1992, 1994 and 1996. Member, House Transportation and Infrastructure Committees, House Resources Committee; Aviation and Surface Transportation Subcommittees; ranking Democrat on Water and Power Subcommittee. Term expires 1999.

Washington, D.C. Office: 2134 Rayburn House Office Bldg., Washington, D.C. 20515; 202-225-6416; Fax: 202-225-0373; Email: pdefazio@hr.house.gov; Web: www.house.gov/defazio/inaex.htm

District Offices: Coos Bay—PO Box 1557, Coos Bay 97420; 541-269-2609. **Eugene**—151 W 7th Ave., Suite 400, Eugene 97401; 541-465-6732; toll-free: 800-944-9603.

Roseburg—PO Box 2460, Roseburg 97470; 541-440-3523.

Darlene Hooley—Fifth District

Counties: Lincoln, Marion, Polk, Tillamook, northern Benton, most of Clackamas.

Darlene Hooley, Democrat. Born in Williston, North Dakota, April 4, 1939. Oregon State University, B.S., 1961. Health and PE teacher at Woodburn and Gervais schools, 1962–65; Portland Public Schools, 1965–67; St. Mary's Academy, 1967–69. Served on West Linn City Council, 1976–80; Oregon State Legislature, 1980–87; Clackamas County Commission, 1987–96. Member of the Oregon Trail Foundation Board. Former member of Oregon Progress Board and Area Agencies on Aging, and former co-chair of Commission on Children and Families. Married to John with two children.

Elected to Congress in 1996. Member of House Banking Committee. Second Committee and Subcommittees not assigned as of January 31, 1997. Term expires 1999.

Washington, D.C. Office: 1419 Longworth House Office Bldg., Washington, D.C. 20515; 202-225-5711; Fax: 202-225-5699.

District Office: 315 Mission St. SE, Suite 101, Salem 97302; 503-588-9100.

Congressional Districts

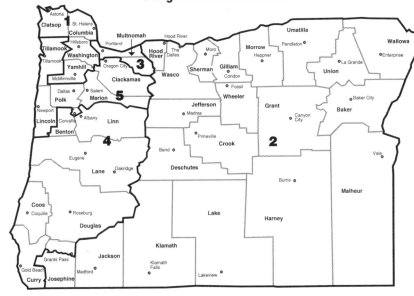

National/International

U.S. Government Officials

President of the United States

William Jefferson Clinton
The White House, 1600 Pennsylvania Ave.,
Washington, D.C. 20500; 202-456-1414;
Email: president@whitehouse.gov;
Web: www.whitehouse.gov

Educational Background: Georgetown University, Bachelor of Arts, 1968; Rhodes Scholar, University College, Oxford; Yale University, Juris Doctoris, 1973. **Governmental Experience**: Attorney General of Arkansas, 1976-78; Governor of Arkansas, 1978-80, 1982-1993. Elected President, 1992; reelected, 1996.

Vice-President of the United States

Albert Arnold Gore Jr.
Old Executive Office Bldg., Washington, D.C. 20501; 202-456-1414;
Email: vicepresident@whitehouse.gov;
Web: www.whitehouse.gov

Occupational Background: Journalist; Home Builder. **Educational Background**: Harvard University, A.B.; Vanderbilt School of Religion; Vanderbilt Law School. **Governmental Experience**: U.S. House of Representatives 1977-85; U.S. Senate 1985-93; Elected Vice-President, 1992; reelected, 1996.

The Cabinet

Chief of Staff
Erskine Bowles
The White House, 1600 Pennsylvania Ave. NW, Washington, D.C. 20500; 202-456-1414;
Web: www.whitehouse.com

Department of Agriculture
Dan Glickman, Secretary
14th and Independence Ave. SW, Washington, D.C. 20250; 202-720-3631; Web: www.usda.gov

Department of Commerce
William Daley, Secretary (Nominee)
14th and Constitution Ave. NW, Washington, D.C. 20506; 202-482-2112; Fax: 202-482-6007;
Web: www.doc.gov

Department of Defense
William Cohen, Secretary
The Pentagon, Washington, D.C. 20301; 703-695-5261; Fax: 703-697-9080;
Web: www.dtic.dla.mil/defenselink

Department of Education
Richard W. Riley, Secretary
600 Independence Ave. SW, Washington, D.C. 20202; 202-401-3000; Fax: 202-401-0596;
Web: www.ed.gov

Department of Energy
Federico Pena, Secretary (Nominee)
1000 Independence Ave. SW, Washington, D.C. 20585; 202-586-4940; Fax: 202-586-5049;
Web: www.doe.gov

Department of Health and Human Services
Donna E. Shalala, Secretary
200 Independence Ave. SW, Washington, D.C. 20201; 202-690-6343; Fax: 202-690-7203;
Web: www.us.dhhs.gov

Department of Housing and Urban Development
Andrew M. Cuomo, Secretary (Nominee)
451 7th St. SW, Washington, D.C. 20410; 202-708-0417; Fax: 202-619-8365;
Web: www.hud.gov

Department of Interior
Bruce Babbitt, Secretary
1849 C St. NW, Washington, D.C. 20240; 202-208-7351; Fax: 202-208-5048;
Web: www.doi.gov

Department of Justice
Janet Reno, Attorney General
950 Pennsylvania Ave. NW, Washington, D.C. 20530; 202-514-2001; Fax: 202-514-4371;
Web: www.usdoj.gov

Department of Labor
Alexis M. Herman, Secretary (Nominee)
200 Constitution Ave. NW, Washington, D.C. 20210; 202-219-7316; Fax: 202-219-8822;
Web: www.dol.gov

Department of State
Madeline K. Albright, Secretary
2201 C St. NW, Washington, D.C. 20520; 202-647-6575; Fax: 202-647-7120;
Web: www.state.gov

Department of Transportation
Rodney E. Slater, Secretary (Nominee)
400 7th St. SW, Washington, D.C. 20590; 202-366-5580; Web: www.dot.gov

Mt. Hood serves as a beautiful backdrop to Willamette Falls and Oregon City. Photo by Sherry Rohrer.

Department of the Treasury
Robert E. Rubin, Secretary
1500 Pennsylvania Ave. NW, Washington, D.C.
20220; 202-622-2000; Fax: 202-622-0073;
Web:www.ustreas.gov

Department of Veterans Affairs
Jesse Brown, Secretary
810 Vermont Ave. NW, Washington, D.C. 20420;
202-273-4800; Fax: 202-273-4877;
Web:www.va.gov

Environmental Protection Agency
Carol M. Browner, Secretary
401 M St. SW, Washington, D.C. 20460;
202-260-4700; Fax: 202-260-0279

Office of Management and Budget
Franklin E. Raines, Dir.
1600 Pennsylvania Ave. NW, Washington, D.C.
20503; 202-395-3080

United Nations Ambassador
Bill Richardson, Nominee
799 United Nations Plaza, New York, NY 10017;
212-415-4000

United States Trade Representative
Charlene Barshefsky (Nominee)
600 17th St. NW, Washington, D.C. 20506;
202-395-3230; Fax: 202-395-7226;
Web: www.ustr.gov

National Drug Control Policy Director
Barry R. McCaffrey, Dir.
Office of National Drug Control Policy,
Washington, D.C. 20500; 202-395-6700;
Fax: 202-395-6708.

U.S. Government in Oregon

For further information contact the Federal
Information Center, 1-800-688-9889

Action

Corporation for National Service
2010 Lloyd Center, Portland 97207;
503-231-2103

Agriculture, Department of

Office of the General Counsel
1220 SW 3rd Ave., Room 1734,
Portland 97204; 503-326-3115

Agricultural Marketing Service
Fruit and Vegetable Division:
NW Marketing Field Office; 1220 SW
3rd Ave., Room 369, Portland 97204;
503-326-2724
Market News Branch: Livestock and
Grain Market News; 1220 SW 3rd
Ave., Room 1772, Portland 97204;
503-326-2237
Processed Products Branch: 340 High
St. NE, Salem 97301; 503-399-5761

Agricultural Research Service
3320 NW Orchard Ave., Corvallis 97330;
541-750-8700
Columbia Plateau Conservation
Research Center, PO Box 370,
Pendleton 97801, 541-278-3292

National/International

Eastern Oregon Agricultural Research Center, HC71, 451 Hwy 205, Burns 97720, 541-373-3042

Horticultural Crops Research Laboratory, 3420 NW Orchard Ave., Corvallis 97330; 541-757-8760

National Clonal Germplasm Repository, 33447 Peoria Rd., Corvallis 97333; 541-750-8712

National Forage Seed Production Research Center, 3450 SW Campus Way, Corvallis 97331; 541-750-8722

Agricultural Statistics Service

1220 SW 3rd, Room 1735, Portland 97204; 503-326-2131

Animal and Plant Health Inspection Service

Plant Protection and Quarantine, 6135 NE 80th Ave., Suite A-5, Portland 97218; 503-326-2814

Veterinary Services, 530 Center St. NE, Suite 335, Salem 97301; 503-399-5871

Extension Service

Oregon State University, Ballard Hall 101, Corvallis 97331-3606; 541-737-2716

Farm Service Agency

Formerly the Agricultural Stabilization and Conservation Service

PO Box 1300, Tualatin 97062-1300; 503-692-6830

Federal Grain Inspection Service

PO Box 3837, Portland 97208; 503-326-7887

Food and Consumer Service

Field Office, 2029 Lloyd Center, Portland 97232-1314

Food Safety and Inspection Service

530 Center St. NE, Room 403, Salem 97301; 503-399-5831

Forest Service

Pacific Northwest Region, PO Box 3623, Portland 97208-3623; 503-326-3625

Pacific NW Forest Research Station, PO Box 3890, Portland 97208-3890; 503-326-5640

Corvallis Forestry Sciences Lab, 3200 SW Jefferson Way, Corvallis 97331; 541-750-7365

Portland Forestry Sciences Lab, PO Box 3890, Portland 97208-3890; 503-321-5802

Columbia River Gorge National Scenic Area, 902 Wasco Ave., Suite 200, Hood River 97031; 541-386-2333

Deschutes National Forest, 1645 Hwy. 20 East, Bend 97701-4864; 541-383-5531

Fremont National Forest, 524 North G St., Lakeview 97630-0058; 541-947-2151

Malheur National Forest, PO Box 909, John Day 97845; 541-575-1731

Mt. Hood National Forest, 2955 NW Division St., Gresham 97030; 503-666-0700

Ochoco National Forest, 3160 NE 3rd St., Prineville 97754-0490; 541-416-6500

Rogue River National Forest, 333 W 8th St., PO Box 520, Medford 97501; 541-858-2200

Siskiyou National Forest, 200 NE Greenfield Rd., PO Box 440, Grants Pass 97526; 541-471-6509

Siuslaw National Forest, Box 1148, Corvallis 97339; 541-750-7000

Umatilla National Forest, 2517 SW Hailey, Pendleton 97801-3942; 541-278-3760

Umpqua National Forest, PO Box 1008, Roseburg 97470; 541-957-3200

Wallowa-Whitman National Forest, PO Box 907, Baker City 97814; 541-523-6391

Willamette National Forest, PO Box 10607, Eugene 97440; 541-465-6533

Winema National Forest, 2819 Dahlia St., Klamath Falls 97601; 541-883-6714

Natural Resources Conservation Service

Formerly Soil Conservation Service

101 SW Main St., Room 1300, Portland 97204; 503-326-2751; 503-414-3200; Web: www.ncg.nrcs.usda.gov

Water and Climate Center

101 SW Main St., Portland 97204-3225; 503-414-3107

Rural Economic and Community Development Service

Formerly Farmers Home Administration

101 SW Main St., Suite 1410, Portland 97204-3222; 503-414-3300

Rural Utilities Service

2828 NE 10th Ave., Portland 97212; 503-282-4588

Telephone Program

PO Box 23726, Tigard 97281;
503-590-9859

Commerce, Department of

Economic Development Administration

121 Salmon St., Suite 244,
Portland 97204; 503-326-3078; Web:
www.doc.gov/resources/EDA_info.html

International Trade Administration

One World Trade Center, 121 SW Salmon
St., Suite 242, Portland 97204;
503-326-3001; Web: www.ita.doc.gov

National Oceanic and Atmospheric Administration

Web: www.noaa.gov

National Marine Fisheries Services

525 NE Oregon St., Suite 500, Portland
97232-2737

Columbia Basin Fish and Wildlife
Authority, 2501 SW 1st Ave., Suite 200,
Portland 97201; 503-326-7031

Pacific States Marine Fisheries Comm.,
45 SE 82nd Dr., Suite 100, Gladstone
97027; 503-650-5400

Pacific Fishery Management Council,
2130 SW 5th Ave., Suite 224,
Portland 97201; 503-326-6352

National Weather Service Offices

Web: www.nws.noaagov

Water and Weather Forecast Office,
5241 NE 122nd Ave., Portland
97230-1089; 503-326-2340

Medford Office: 4003 Cirrus Dr.,
Medford 97504-4187; 541-776-4326

Pendleton Office: 2001 NW 56th Dr.,
Pendleton 97801-4532; 541-276-8134

Consumer Product Safety Commission

Consumer Hotline (24 hours/day):
1-800-638-2772; TTY: 1-800-638-8270

Defense, Department of

Air Force, Department of

Kingsley Field (ANG), 222 Arnold Ave.,
#11, Klamath Falls 97603-1925;
541-885-6350

A young boy enjoys a peaceful afternoon of fishing in Chimney Lake, Eagle Cap Wilderness. Photo by Eric W. Valentine.

Portland International Airport (ANG),
6801 NE Cornfoot Rd., Portland
97218-2797; 503-335-4104

Army, Department of

Camp Rilea, Oregon National Guard
Training Site (ARNG), Rt. 2, Box 497 E,
Warrenton 97146-9711; 503-861-4000

Umatilla Army Depot, SDSTE-UA-CO,
Hermiston 97838-9544; 541-564-5200

Army Corps of Engineers

North Pacific Division, PO Box 2870,
Portland 97208-2870; 503-326-3700

Portland District, PO Box 2946, Portland
97208-2946; 503-326-6000

Navy, Department of

Marine Corps Recruiting Office,
1220 SW 3rd Ave., Room 519,
Portland 97204; 503-326-3022

Navy Recruiting Office, 437 SW 4th Ave.,
Portland 97204; 503-222-1867

Naval and Marine Corps Reserve Ctr.,
1015 Airport Rd. SE, Salem 97301;
503-399-5886

Education, Department of

Web: www.ed.gov

ERIC Clearinghouse on Education
Management, 5207 University of
Oregon, Eugene 97403-5207;
541-346-5044; toll-free: 800-438-8841

National/International

Energy, Department of

Bonneville Power Administration

Eugene District, 1600 Valley River Dr., Suite 230, Eugene 97401; 541-465-6958

Portland District, PO Box 3621-A, Portland 97208; 503-230-5000

Portland Field Office, 525 NE Oregon St., Suite 210, 97232; 503-872-2853

Federal Energy Regulatory Commission

101 SW Main St., Suite 905, Portland 97204; 503-326-5840

Environmental Protection Agency

Western Ecology Division, 200 SW 35th St., Corvallis 97333; 541-754-4601

Oregon Operations Office, 811 SW 6th Ave., 3rd Flr., Portland 97204; 503-326-3250

Western Fish Toxicology, 1350 SE Goodnight Ave., Corvallis 97330; 541-754-4708

Federal Communications Commission

Portland, 1220 SW 3rd Ave., 97204; 503-326-4114

Federal Mediation and Conciliation Service

1220 SW 3rd Ave., 16th Fl., 97204; Commissioners: Thomas Drew, 503-326-2177; Paul F. Stuckenschneider, 503-326-2178; Constance M. Weimer, 503-326-2176

General Services Administration

Federal Information Center: 1-800-688-9889

Health and Human Services, Department of

Office of Inspector General

Office of Audit Services, 530 Center St. NE, Suite 500, Salem 97301; 503-399-5727

Office of Investigations, 700 NE Multnomah, Suite 256, Portland 97201; 503-231-2299

Public Health Service

Food and Drug Administration, 9780 SW Nimbus Ave., Beaverton 97008; 503-671-9332

Indian Health Service

1220 SW 3rd Ave., Room 476, Portland 97204-2892; 503-326-3288

Chemawa Indian Health Center, 3750 Chemawa Rd. NE, Salem 97305; 503-399-5941

Housing and Urban Development, Department of

520 SW 6th Ave., Portland 97204-1596; 503-326-2561

Interior, Department of

Office of the Solicitor

500 NE Multnomah St., Suite 607, Portland 97232; 503-231-2126

Office of the Secretary of the Interior

Office of Environmental Policy and Compliance, 500 NE Multnomah St., Suite 600, Portland 97232-2036; 503-231-6157

Bureau of Indian Affairs

Chemawa Indian School, 3700 Chemawa Rd. NE, Salem 97305-1199; 503-399-5721

Portland Area Office, 911 NE 11th Ave., 97232; 503-231-6702

Bureau of Land Management

Oregon State Office, PO Box 2965, Portland 97208; 503-952-6002

District Offices

Burns, HC74-12533, Hwy. 20W, Hines 97738; 541-573-4465

Coos Bay, 1300 Airport Ln., North Bend 97459-2000; 541-756-0100

Eugene, 2890 Chad Dr., Eugene 97408; 541-683-6600

Lakeview, PO Box 151, Lakeview 97630; 541-947-2177

Medford, 3040 Biddle Rd., Medford 97504; 541-770-2200

Prineville, 185 E 4th St., PO Box 550, Prineville 97754; 541-447-4115

Roseburg, 777 NW Garden Valley Blvd., Roseburg 97470; 541-440-4930

Salem, 1717 Fabry Rd. SE, Salem 97306; 503-375-5646

Vale, 100 Oregon St., Vale 97918;
541-473-3144

Bureau of Reclamation

Klamath Basin Area Office, 6600
Washburn Way, Klamath Falls 97603;
541-883-6935

Columbia River Inter-Tribal Fish Commission

Portland, 729 NE Oregon St., Suite 200,
97232; 503-238-0667

Fish and Wildlife Service

Web: www.fws.gov

Pacific Region, 911 NE 11th Ave.,
Portland 97232-4181; 503-231-6118

Law Enforcement Division

Portland, 911 NE 11th Ave.,
97232-4181; 503-231-6125
Wilsonville, 9025 SW Hillman Ct.,
Suite 3134, 97070; 503-682-6131

National Wildlife Refuge Division

Western Oregon Refuge Complex, 26208
Finley Refuge Rd., Corvallis 97333;
541-757-4730

Geological Survey

Biological Resource Division

Forest and Rangeland Ecosystems
Science Center, 3030 SE Clearwater
Dr., Corvallis 97333; 541-757-4840

Water Resources Division

Medford, 910 S Central, Suite E,
Medford 97501; 541-776-4256
Portland, 10615 SE Cherry Blossom Dr.,
97216; 503-251-3265

National Park Service

Web: www.nps.gov

Crater Lake National Park, PO Box 7,
Crater Lake 97604; 541-594-2211
Fort Clatsop National Monument, Rt. 3,
Box 604-FC, Astoria 97103;
503-861-2585
John Day Fossil Beds Monument,
HC 82, Box 126, Kimberly
97848-9701; 541-987-2333
Oregon Caves National Monument, 19000
Caves Hwy., Cave Junction 97523

Justice, Department of

Office of the U.S. Trustee

Portland, 851 SW 6th Ave., Room 1300,
97204-1350; 503-326-4004

Drug Enforcement Administration

Eugene, Res. Office, 211 E 7th,
Room 230, 97401; 541-465-6861
Medford, Res. Office, 310 W 6th St.,
Room B6, 97501; 541-776-4260
Portland, Res. Office, 1220 SW 3rd Ave.,
#1565, 97204; 326-3371

Federal Bureau of Investigation

Portland Field Office, Crown Plaza,
1500 SW 1st Ave., Portland 97201;
503-224-4181

Immigration and Naturalization Service

Portland, 511 NW Broadway, Room 414,
97209; 503-326-3006

U.S. Attorney's Office

Eugene Branch Office, 701 High St.,
97401; 541-465-6771
Portland, 888 SW 5th Ave., Suite 1000,
97204-2024; 503-727-1000

U.S. Marshals Service

Eugene, 211 E 7th, Room 149, 97401;
541-465-6701
Portland, 620 SW Main, Room 420,
97205-2025; 503-326-5177

Labor, Department of

Bureau of Labor Statistics

71 Stevenson St., Sixth Floor, San
Francisco, CA 94119; 415-975-4350;
Web: www.stats.bls.gov

Employment Standards Administration

Office of Federal Contract Compliance
Programs, 111 SW Columbia St.,
#1020, Portland 97201; 503-326-4112

Wage and Hour Division

Eugene, 211 E 7th, Room 102, 97401;
541-465-6447
Medford, 310 W 6th St., Room 207,
97501; 541-776-4272
Portland, 111 SW Columbia, Suite 1010,
97204; 503-326-3057

National/International

Employment and Training Administration

Bureau of Apprenticeship and Training
Portland, 1220 SW 3rd Ave., Room 629, 97204; 503-326-3157

Occupational Safety and Health Administration
Portland, 1220 SW 3rd Ave., Room 640, 97204; 503-326-2251

Veterans Employment and Training Services
Salem, 875 Union St. NE, Room 108, 97311; 503-378-3338

National Labor Relations Board
Portland, 222 SW Columbia St., Room 401, 97201-6604; 503-326-3085

Office of Personnel Management
Portland, Federal Job Information Testing Center, 1220 SW 3rd Ave., Room 376, 97204; 24-Hr. Info. Record: 503-326-3141

Railroad Retirement Board
Portland, 1220 SW 3rd, Room 377, 97204; 503-326-2143

Small Business Administration
District Office, 222 SW Columbia St., Suite 500, Portland 97201-6605; 503-326-5221; TTY: 503-326-2501; toll-free: 800-827-5722

Social Security Administration
General Information and Services: 1-800-772-1213

Transportation, Department of

Coast Guard
Portland, Recruiting Office, 321 SW Salmon St., 97204-1142; toll-free: 800-438-8724

Federal Aviation Administration
Eugene Airport, Mahlon Sweet Field, 28833 Douglas Dr., Eugene 97402; Air Traffic Control Tower, 541-465-6441; Airways Facil. System Support Center RAD/COM, 541-465-6728; Airways Facil. System Support Center NAV/COM, 541-465-6440

Eugene Airport, Mahlon Sweet Field, 28829 Lockheed Dr., Eugene 97402; Airways Facil. System Support Center II, 541-465-6412.

Medford Jackson Co. Airport, 3650 Biddle Rd., 97504; Southern Oregon SSC, 541-776-4307; Air Traffic Control Tower, 541-776-4312

Portland Air Traffic Control Tower/ TRACON, 7000 NE Airport Way, 97218; 503-326-3058

Portland Airway Facil. Sect., 7303 NE Alderwood Rd., 97218; 503-326-6850

Portland Flight Stand. Dist. Office, 1800 NE 25th, Suite 15, Hillsboro 97124; 503-681-5500

Salem Air Traffic Control Tower, 3000 25th St. SE, 97302; 503-581-3323

Federal Highway Administration
Portland, 222 SW Columbia St., Suite 600, 97201; 503-326-4902

Oregon Division, 530 Center St. NE, Suite 100, Salem 97301; 503-399-5749

Office of Motor Carrier Safety, 530 Center St. NE, Suite 100, Salem 97301; 503-399-5775

Federal Railroad Administration
703 Broadway, Room 703, Vancouver, WA 98660; 360-696-7536

Maritime Administration
Portland, 1220 SW 3rd, Room 1624, 97204; 503-326-5021

Treasury, Department of

Bureau of Alcohol, Tobacco and Firearms
Compliance Operation, Portland, 9828 E Burnside, Suite 200, 97218; 503-231-2331

Law Enforcement, Portland, 1500 SW 1st Ave., Room 350, 97201; 503-326-2171

Customs Service, U.S.
North Pacific Customs Management Center, 511 NW Broadway, Room 198, 97209; 503-326-7625

Portland, Regulatory Audit, 511 NW Broadway, Room 394, 97209; 503-326-5728

Internal Revenue Service
Federal Tax Information, toll-free: 800-829-1040

Portland, 1220 SW 3rd, Room 1126,
97204; 503-221-3960
Office of District Counsel, 222 SW
Columbia St., Room 450, 97201;
503-326-3185

Field Offices

Eugene, 2512 Oakmont Way, 97401;
541-465-6465
Medford, 960 Ellendale, Suite A, 97501
Salem, 530 Center St. NE, Suite 400,
97301; 503-399-5621

Savings Bonds Division

Portland, 1220 SW 3rd, Room 525,
97204; 503-326-3008

Secret Service

Portland, 121 SW Salmon, Suite 1330,
97204; 503-326-2162

United States Courts

Court of Appeals, Ninth Circuit

Portland, 555 SW Yamhill, 97204; Circuit
Judges: Edward Leavy, 503-326-5665;
Diarmuid O'Scannlain, 503-326-2187;
Otto R. Skopil Jr., 503-326-3543;
Library 503-326-5129

Bankruptcy Court

Portland, 1001 SW 5th, 7th Floor, 97204;
Judge Polly S. Higdon, 503-326-4961
Judge Elizabeth L. Perris, 503-326-4173;
Judge Donald D. Sullivan 503-326-4175
Eugene, Div. Office, 151 W 7th,
Suite 300, 97401; Judges:
Frank Alley, 541-465-6767;
Albert E. Radcliffe, 541-465-6802

District Courts

Eugene, 211 E 7th Ave., 100 Federal
Bldg./U.S. Courthouse 97401;
Clerk's Office, 541-465-6423
Medford, 310 W 6th St., 97501;
541-776-3926
Portland, 620 SW Main, Room 516,
97205; Clerk's Office, 503-326-2202

District Judges

Robert C. Belloni, 503-326-2242
James M. Burns, 503-326-3908
Helen J. Frye, 503-326-3060
Ancer L. Haggerty, 503-326-5092
Robert E. Jones, 503-326-6390
Malcolm F. Marsh, 503-326-5350
Owen M. Panner, 503-326-4190
James A. Redden, 503-326-6389

District Court Magistrates

Eugene, 211 E 7th Ave., Room 240,
97401; 541-465-6476
Portland, 620 SW Main St., 97205-3090;
Donald C. Ashmanskas, 503-326-5410;
John Jelderks, 503-326-2994;
Janice M. Stewart, 503-326-5468

Federal Public Defender

Eugene Branch Office, 44 W Broadway,
Suite 400, 97401; 541-465-6937
Portland, 101 SW Main, 17th Floor,
97204; 503-326-2123

Pretrial Services

Eugene, 211 E 7th Ave., Room 239,
97401; 541-465-6926
Portland, 620 SW Main St., Room 201,
97205; 503-326-3560

United States Probation Office

Eugene, 211 E 7th Ave., 97401;
541-465-6747
Medford, 6th and Holly St., 97501;
541-776-4235
Portland, 620 SW Main, Room 433,
97205; 503-326-2117
Salem, 530 Center St. NE, 97301;
503-399-5715

Veterans Administration

Benefits Information and Assistance,
toll-free: 800-827-1000
Veterans Outreach Center, 8383 NE
Sandy Blvd., Suite 110, Portland
97201; 503-273-5370
Veterans Outreach Program, Salem,
Vet. Ctr., 318 Church St. NE, 97301;
503-362-9911
Vietnam Vet Outreach Center,
1966 Garden Ave., Eugene 97403;
541-465-6918

Veterans Administration Medical Centers

Portland, 3710 SW U.S. Veterans
Hospital Rd. 97207; 503-220-8262
Roseburg, 913 N Garden Valley Blvd.,
97470; 541-440-1000

Major Political Parties in Oregon

Democratic National Committee

430 S Capitol St. SE, Washington, D.C. 20003;
202-863-8000; Email:dnc@democrats.org;
Web: www.democrats.org

Democratic State Central Committee of Oregon

711 SW Alder, Suite 306, Portland 97205; 503-224-8200

Marc Abrams, chair, Portland; Arlene Collins, first vice-chair, Portland; Mark Gardiner, second vice-chair, Portland; Wayne Kinney, secretary, La Grande; Alex Thurber, treasurer, Portland.

National committee persons: Mike Bohan, Beaverton; Mary Botkin, Portland.

Executive Director: Margaret Surguine, Portland.

Republican National Committee

310 1st St. SE, Washington, D.C. 20003; 202-863-8500; Email: info@rnc.org; Web: www.rnc.org

Republican State Central Committee of Oregon

8196 SW Hall Blvd., Suite 101, Beaverton 97008; Mailing address: PO Box 1450, Beaverton 97075-1450; 503-520-1996; Fax: 503-644-0210

Deanna Smith, chair, Salem; Perry Atkinson, vice-chair, Phoenix; Patricia Stallings, secretary, Portland; Teresa May, treasurer, Salem.

National committee persons: June Hartley, Nyssa; Dennis A. Smith, Salem.

Executive Director: Marge Hughes, Oregon City.

Indian Tribes in Oregon

Source: Commission on Indian Services
167 State Capitol, Salem 97310; 503-986-1067; Fax: 503-986-1021

Indian tribes represent unique legal entities in the United States and are distinct political communities with extensive powers of self-government. Tribal sovereignty predates the U.S. government. Treaties, federal statutes and executive agreements over the past 200 years have established a special trust relationship between tribes and the federal government. The federal Bureau of Indian Affairs has been designated by the secretary of the interior as the primary agency to protect tribal interests and administer trust responsibilities.

During the 1950s, in a move to assimilate Indians into mainstream white America, the U.S. government ended federal trusteeship of roughly 3 percent of the country's Indian population

through a process called termination. Of the 109 tribes and bands terminated, 62 are native to Oregon. Even though the tone of the termination legislation was emancipation, the net effect of the policy on terminated tribes was cultural, political and economic devastation.

In recent years, however, vigorous efforts have been mounted by terminated tribes to reestablish or restore the trust relationship. In 1977, the Confederated Tribes of Siletz won restoration; followed by the Cow Creek Band of Umpqua Indians in 1982; the Confederated Tribes of Grand Ronde in 1983; the Confederated Tribes of Coos, Lower Umpqua and Siuslaw Indians in 1984; the Klamath Tribes in 1986 and the Coquille Tribe in 1989.

Oregon now has nine federally recognized tribes: the Burns Paiute Tribe, the Confederated Tribes of Coos, Lower Umpqua and Siuslaw Indians, the Confederated Tribes of Grand Ronde, the Confederated Tribes of Siletz, the Confederated Tribes of Warm Springs, the Confederated Tribes of Umatilla Indian Reservation, the Cow Creek Band of Umpqua Indians, the Klamath Tribe and the Coquille Tribe. On May 22, 1996 Governor John A. Kitzhaber signed Executive Order No. EO-96-30 which officially recognized state/tribal government-to-government relations.

Oregon's Native American population is estimated at 38,496 according to the 1990 census. It is diverse in that each tribe and organization has its own particular history, value system, government, language and ties. Many historically rural and reservation Indians have moved to urban centers, and this transition has resulted in continually evolving values and needs. Oregon Indians can be divided into three distinct groups:

Urban/Rural: Urban Indians comprise roughly 89 percent of Oregon's Indian population. Rural Indians live in nonmetropolitan areas, either on or off the reservation.

Reservation/Nonreservation: Reservation Indians live on or near Oregon's six reservations: Burns Paiute, Siletz, Warm Springs, Umatilla, Grand Ronde and Coquille. A reservation community includes enrolled members of the tribe or tribes for whom the reservation was established, as well as Indians from other tribes living on the reservation. The reservations are strikingly different in many aspects. Size is one example.

Indian drummers and representatives of several Indian Tribes attended a ceremony with Gov. Kitzhaber in May 1996 to mark the signing of an executive order officially recognizing state/tribal government-to-government relations.

Photo courtesy of the Commission on Indian Services.

Siletz is situated on 3,987 acres; Burns Paiute on 11,700 acres; Umatilla on 157,982 acres; Grand Ronde on 10,051 acres; and Warm Springs on more than 641,035 acres. By Act of Congress in 1996, the Coquille Tribe now has reservation acreage totalling 6,317 acres.

Enrollment figures also vary widely. Burns Paiute has the smallest enrollment with 283; Warm Springs has 3,585; Siletz, 3,003; Umatilla, 1,986 and Grand Ronde is the largest with 3,531 members. Reservations differ markedly in other ways as well, including governing structure, resource base, range of available services and treaty provisions.

Nonreservation Indians are either from nonrecognized tribes or are members of recognized tribes not having a land base. Reservations are in various stages of planning for the Klamath Tribes, the Cow Creek Band of Umpqua Indians and the Confederated Tribes of Coos, Lower Umpqua and Siuslaw.

Recognized/Unrecognized: Recognized Indians are those who are enrolled members of tribes from whom the federal government has acknowledged treaty or statutory obligations. Recognized Indians can include urban/rural or reservation/nonreservation Indians.

Unrecognized Indians include those from tribes with whom federal relations have been severed by congressional action (termination) and those whose tribe has never been recognized by the federal government. Tribal diversity notwithstanding, all Indians share common concerns. On the regional level, for example, the Columbia River Intertribal

Fish Commission represents tribes in Washington, Oregon and Idaho on matters concerning fisheries management. On the statewide level, many intertribal organizations have been formed to deal with specific issues such as education, health, legal matters, aging, alcoholism and adoption.

One economic development tool available to tribes since passage of a 1988 federal law (The National Indian Gaming Regulatory Act (NIGRA) is operation of gaming centers on trust land. Six of the nine tribes in Oregon currently have gaming facilities, and one more tribe will have a facility soon. The gaming centers operate in accordance with the NIGRA and negotiated state compacts. Besides providing employment opportunities for tribal members and citizens of surrounding Oregon communities, revenues from this tribal enterprise go towards health clinics, education scholarships, housing and other services.

The Commission on Indian Services has developed *Oregon Directory of American Indian Resources,* a resource guide for Indians to provide information about and for Oregon's Indian population. Copies of this directory are available at public libraries or from the commission.

Oregon Consular Corps

Source: Oregon Consular Corps
One World Trade Center, Suite 1100,
Portland 97204; 503-464-8482; Fax: 503-464-2299

Arthur A. Riedel, Consul, Netherlands, dean; Rolf Fasth, Consul, Sweden, vice-dean; Serge D'Rovencourt, Consul, France, secretary-treasurer.

A number of foreign nations maintain consulates in Oregon. A consul is an official appointed by a government to live in a foreign city to look after the business and other interests of the home country and to assist and protect its nationals within the consular territory.

A consular representative: promotes a country's trade within the assigned area; assists and protects a country's shipping interests, legalizes ships' papers, assists native seamen in distress and adjudicates on some shipping matters; administers oaths, legalizes foreign documents as required by a country's laws, issues passports and visas; and explains a country's policies, cultural achievements and its attractions for tourism.

A complete listing of consuls is available from the Consular Corps dean.

Barbados

H. Desmond Johnson, M.D., Honorary Consul
10202 SE 32nd Ave., Suite 601, Milwaukie 97222; 503-659-0283; Fax: 503-653-4959

Belgium

John H. Herman, Honorary Consul
1870 NW 173rd, Beaverton 97006; 503-228-0465; Fax: 503-629-5517

Cyprus, Republic of

Alex Christy, Honorary Consul
1130 SW Morrison St., Suite 510, Mayer Bldg., Portland 97205; 503-227-1411; Fax: 503-227-2086

Czech Republic

Marie Amicci, Honorary Consul
10200 SW Greenburg Rd., Suite 350, Portland 97223; 503-293-9545; Fax: 503-293-9546

Denmark

Ingolf Noto, Honorary Consul
900 SW 5th Ave., Suite 2300, Portland 97204 1268; 503-294-9307; Fax: 503-220-2480

Finland

Paul M. Niskanen, Honorary Consul
2648 SW Cedar Hills Blvd., Beaverton 97005; 503-526-0391; Fax: 503-526-0902

France

Serge D'Rovencourt, Honorary Consul
The Portland Hilton, 921 SW 6th Ave., Portland 97204; 503-498-4200; Fax: 503-225-1471

Germany, Federal Republic of

Gunther H. Hoffman, Honorary Consul
200 SW Market St., Suite 1695, Portland 97201; 503-222-0490; Fax: 503-248-0138

Great Britain, United Kingdom of

Andrew M. Hay, Honorary Consul
PO Box 8134, University Station, Portland 97207; 503-227-5669; Fax: 503-227-5669

Ivory Coast

Elizabeth Hamilton-McFaddin, Honorary Consul
6316 SW Peyton Rd., Portland 97219; 503-244-2293

Japan

Takehisa Nogami, Consul General
2400 First Interstate Bank Tower, 300 SW 5th Ave., Portland 97201; 503-221-1811; Fax: 503-224-8936

Korea, Republic of

Robert W. Donaldson, Consular Asst.
1414 Bank of California Tower, 707 SW Washington, Portland 97205; 503-248-1941

Malaysia

Jay A. Killeen, Honarary Consul General
6144 SW 37th Ave., Portland 97221; 503-658-3633; Fax: 503-658-2210

Mexico

Appointment pending
545 NE 47th Ave., Suite 317, Portland 97213; 503-233-5661

Netherlands

Arthur A. Riedel, Honorary Consul
4511 N Channel Ave., Portland 97217; 503-285-9111; Fax: 503-240-2256

Norway

Larry K. Bruun, Honorary Consul
5441 SW Macadam, Suite 300, Portland 97201; 503-221-0870; Fax: 503-221-0515

Sweden

Rolf Fasth, Honorary Consul
One World Trade Center, 121 SW Salmon St., Suite 1600, Portland 97204-2988; 503-221-7017; Fax: 503-636-7321

LOCAL GOVERNMENT

A waterfall on Big Butte Creek in Jackson County inspired nearby residents to name their community Butte Falls. Photo by George Stanley.

THE individual quality and vitality of cities, towns and counties throughout Oregon create a rich fabric of cultures and identities. From Ashland to Portland and from Port Orford to Ontario, Oregon communities boast distinctive histories and unique characteristics. This section provides an overview of local and regional governments, with details on each city and county in Oregon. Demographic information illustrates population changes throughout the state.

State Capitol

Source: Legislative Administration
State Capitol, Salem 97310

Oregon's Capitol is in Salem, in the Willamette Valley on the 45th parallel, halfway between the equator and the north pole.

One of the most beautiful capitols in the nation, the four-story building is of modern Greek architecture. It was designed by Francis Keally of New York and constructed of white Vermont marble and bronze from 1935-38 at a cost of approximately $2.5 million.

In tribute to the spirit of Oregon's settlers and their westward march, a statue of the "Oregon Pioneer" stands proudly atop the capitol tower overlooking a beautifully landscaped mall. The statue, a work of Ulric H. Ellerhusen, is bronze-enameled with gold leaf. It stands nearly 23 feet high and weighs eight and one-half tons. The tower offers a panoramic view of the surrounding city, the valley and the mountains of the Cascade Range. Located on the west side of the mall are the State Library and the Labor and Industries Building; on the east side are the Public Service and Transportation buildings.

Dedicated in 1938, the State Capitol, constructed of white Vermont marble, is topped by the gold "Oregon Pioneer" statue.

Photo by Nomeca Hartwell.

Interior

The main entrance of the building leads into a rotunda 106 feet in height. Surrounding the rotunda are large murals depicting colorful events in Oregon's history, bronze reliefs and smaller murals symbolic of Oregon's industries. The murals, outstanding examples of Depression-period art, were painted by Barry Faulkner and Frank Schwarz. Centered and embedded in the marble floor is an eight-foot bronze replica of the Seal of Oregon.

Above the steps leading to the House of Representatives from the rotunda is a painting of the territorial seal. Above the steps to the Senate Chamber is a painting of the provisional seal. The names of 157 men and women who helped fashion Oregon's history are painted on the friezes near the ceiling in both of the two-story legislative chambers. Each chamber has a mural painted by Faulkner and Schwarz behind the rostrum.

The governor's suite (second floor, center) and also the Senate Chamber (second floor, east wing) are paneled in walnut. Walls in the House of Representatives (second floor, west wing) are paneled in golden oak.

History

Oregon's first Capitol, erected in 1854 at a cost of $40,000, was destroyed December 31, 1855. The complete loss of the statehouse and its contents occurred when fire broke out in the unfinished and unoccupied northeast corner of the building. The Legislature, in session at the time, was forced to seek temporary quarters in Salem's business section. Oregon's Capitol then became the Holman Building, built by Joseph Holman on the corner of Ferry and Commercial Streets in Salem, where the Legislature met for subsequent sessions until completion of a new Capitol in 1876. The Governor's Office and the State Supreme Court during this time were located in the Statesman Building, just across Ferry Street from the Holman Building. The offices for both Secretary of State and State Treasurer were maintained in the Holman Building from 1857 until 1876.

Authorized by the Legislature in 1872 at an approximate cost of $325,000, another Capitol was erected. Ground was broken in May, and the cornerstone was laid on October 8, 1873. The new structure, which faced west toward the heart of Salem, was patterned somewhat after the Capitol at Washington, D.C. It had hollow metal girders supporting a massive copper dome, two-story porticoes faced with Corinthian columns and mullion-windowed wings.

On April 25, 1935, it, too, was destroyed by fire, which started in the basement of the east wing. The strong draft created by stair and elevator wells, the rotunda and the dome-supporting girders caused the flames to spread rapidly. Only furniture, records, equipment and files were salvaged from the first floor; the rapid advance of the fire prevented the removal of anything but a few records and articles from the other floors.

State leaders began planning immediately to rebuild the statehouse. This time, they held a national competition to produce a design unique to Oregon.

From more than 100 entries, judges unanimously chose the design submitted by Francis Keally and George Jacoby. These men were affiliated with the leading New York architectural firm Trowbridge and Livington, creators of San Francisco's Palace Hotel. Completed in 1938, the current Capitol was erected on the 10-acre site of the original territorial building.

Capitol Wings Addition

A Capitol Wings construction project, completed in 1976, added 189,199 square feet to the building and consists of legislative offices, hearing rooms, legislative support services, a first floor galleria and underground parking.

The addition was the first construction project to benefit from the 1975 law requiring that one percent of all state building construction and renovation budgets be set aside for the acquisition of visual art. As a consequence, an outstanding collection of approximately 150 works of art, including 69 photographs spanning the 20th century, has now been installed.

The Capitol Gift Shop featuring Oregon products, changing exhibits of Oregon art, and a visitor services office providing information and guided Capitol tours are located in the galleria area.

Grounds

Capitol Park, to the east, contains a 7,000-pound bronze statue, "The Circuit Rider," sculpted by A. Phimister Proctor and presented to the state as a gift in 1924. The statue honors Oregon's pioneer circuit-riding ministers. Other statues in the park include those of the Reverend Jason Lee, the first missionary and colonizer in Oregon, and Dr. John McLoughlin, head of Hudson's Bay Company and first to govern the Oregon Country. These statues were created by Gifford Proctor Sr. and G.M. Proctor.

Recently added to the park are fragments of columns from the Capitol destroyed by fire in 1935. Nearly 60 citizens assisted the Historical Properties Commission in placing the column fragments on the Capitol grounds.

Willson Park, adjacent to the Capitol on the west, was formerly a Salem city park, part of the land given to the city by William Willson and his wife in 1853. It officially became part of the Capitol grounds in 1965 and is the setting of Waite fountain.

On December 15, 1982, Gov. Vic Atiyeh dedicated a new gazebo on the State Street side of Willson Park. The structure was funded by donations from a number of Salem community organizations. Labor was provided by inmates of the Oregon State Correctional Institution. The gazebo replaces a similar one which stood in the park until shortly after the old Capitol burned in 1935. It is used for band and choir concerts, speeches, and small gatherings.

Capitol Statistics

Dedicated: Oct. 1, 1938

Occupied: July 2, 1938

Capitol Wings Addition: Occupied Jan. 5, 1977

Length: 633 feet

Width: 240 feet

Usable Square Footage: 275,000

Cubic Footage: 3.2 million

Height, Original Building: 57 ft. 2 in.

Height, Wings Addition: 68 ft. 8 in.

Cost, Original Building: $2.5 million

Cost, Wings Addition: $12.5 million

In the center of the Capitol Mall directly to the north of the Capitol is the Sprague (or Capitol) Fountain, given to the people of Oregon in 1980. This fabricated bronze piece was sculpted by Tom Morandi and William Blix.

Salem—Oregon's Capital

Salem, the state capital city, is Oregon's third largest with a population of 120,835. Salem is also the county seat of Marion County, but a small portion contained within its corporate limits of 44 square miles lies across the river in Polk County. Salem is situated in the center of the Willamette Valley—one of the most fertile and agriculturally productive regions in the world—47 miles south of Portland and 64 miles north of Eugene.

Salem serves as the hub of both state government and the surrounding farming communities. State government is the largest employer, with approximately 13,000 full-time employees, 38 of the largest state agencies and over 20 smaller ones located in the immediate area. Salem is also one of the largest food processing centers in the United States.

In addition, Salem is one of Oregon's oldest cities. The Indian name for the locality was Chemeketa, said to mean "meeting or resting place." It may also have been the name of one of the bands of Calapooya Indians. In 1840-41, the Jason Lee Mission was moved from the Willamette River upstream to a site on Mill Creek. In 1842, the missionaries established the Oregon Institute. When the mission was dissolved in 1844, it was decided to lay out a townsite on the Institute lands. Either David Leslie, one of the trustees who came to Oregon from Salem, Mass., or W.H. Willson, who filed plats for what is now the main part of the city in 1850-51, selected the name "Salem." Salem is the anglicized form of the hebrew word Shalom, meaning peace.*

The location of the Oregon capital caused a spirited contest that lasted nearly 15 years. By an act of 1851, the provisional government moved the capital to Salem from Oregon City; in 1855 it was moved to Corvallis, only to move back to Salem the same year. Destruction of the Capitol at Salem on December 31, 1855, was considered an incendiary part of this controversy.

The close proximity of government provides Salem citizens with a distinct opportunity to be involved in the decision-making processes of the state. The citizens of Salem also have a long history of commitment to community improvement—a commitment recognized nationally through presentation of two All-America City Awards, one for 1960-61 and more recently for 1982-83.

*Early Salem history from **Oregon Geographic Names**, by Lewis A. McArthur.

State Buildings

Agriculture Building (1966)
635 Capitol St. NE, Salem 97310

Archives Building (1991)
800 Summer St. NE, Salem 97310

Capitol Mall Parking Structure (1991)
900 Chemeketa St. NE, Salem 97310

Commerce Building (1931)
158 12th St. NE, Salem 97310

Commission for the Blind (1977)
535 SE 12th Ave., Portland 97204

Employment Building (1974)
875 Union St. NE, Salem 97311

Executive Building (1979)
155 Cottage St. NE, Salem 97310

Forestry Buildings (1938)
2600 State St., Salem 97310

General Services Building (1954)
1225 Ferry St. SE, Salem 97310

General Services Building Annex (1967)
1257 Ferry St. SE, Salem 97310

Human Resources Building (1992)
550 Summer St. NE, Salem 97310

Justice Building (1930)
1162 Court St. NE, Salem 97310

Labor and Industries Building (1961)
350 Winter St. NE, Salem 97310

Mahonia Hall (1924)
533 Lincoln St. S, Salem 97310

Oregon Liquor Control Commission Building (1955)
9201 SE McLoughlin Blvd., Milwaukie 97222

Public Service Building (1949)
255 Capitol St. NE, Salem 97310

Public Utility Commission Building (1992)
550 Capitol St. NE, Salem 97310

Real Estate Building (1990)
1177 Center St. NE, Salem 97310

Revenue Building (1981)
955 Center St. NE, Salem 97310

SAIF Building (1974)
400 High St. SE, Salem 97312

State Fair Buildings, State Fairgrounds
2330 17th St. NE, Salem 97310

State Lands Building (1990)
775 Summer St. NE, Salem 97310

State Library (1939)
250 Winter St. NE, Salem 97310

State Lottery Building (1996)
500 Airport Rd. SE, Salem 97310

State Office Building, Eugene (1961)
165 7th St. E, Eugene 97401

State Office Building, Pendleton (1963)
700 SE Emigrant St., Pendleton 97801

State Office Building, Portland (1992)
800 NE Oregon, Portland 97232

State Printing Plant (1980)
550 Airport Rd. SE, Salem 97310

Supreme Court Building (1914)
1163 State St., Salem 97310

Transportation Building (1951)
355 Capitol St. NE, Salem 97310

Veterans' Building (1984)
700 Summer St. NE, Salem 97310

* Year is date building constructed or purchased by state.

Incorporated Cities and Towns

Source: Richard C. Townsend, Exec. Dir., League of Oregon Cities
1201 Court St. NE, Suite 200, Salem 97301; PO Box 928, Salem 97308; 503-588-6550; Fax: 503-399-4863

In the 240 cities throughout Oregon, the city councils serve as the highest authority within city governments in deciding issues of public policy. In open public forums, city councils pass laws (ordinances), adopt resolutions and generally direct discussions involving the governance of their communities and the welfare of their citizens.

Oregon cities have councils of fewer than 10 members serving either four-year terms or, in a few cities, two-year terms. Councilors are elected to the council by district, ward or at-large.

Four forms of city government determine the administrative role of any city council. Most Oregon cities over 2,500 have the council/manager or council/administrator form, in which the council hires a chief executive officer to be responsible for the daily supervision of city affairs. Portland is the only city in the state with the commission form of government, where the elected commissioners function collectively as the city council and serve as administrators of city departments. Smaller Oregon cities

The Columbia River Gorge is internationally known for its superb windsurfing conditions. Windsurfers from all over the world bring their sailboards to towns along the river.

Photo by A. Paige Baker.

typically have the mayor/council form, in which the legislative and policy-making body is a popularly elected council. A few cities have the strong-mayor form, in which the mayor, serving as the chief executive officer, has the authority to appoint administrative personnel, is responsible for city administration, and serves as the presiding officer at council meetings.

City administrators and other city employees often participate in the policy development process but are primarily responsible for effective delivery of municipal services and programs. Many local government activities and programs are directly related to federal or state madates.

City governments typically provide such services as: fire and police protection; streets and street maintenance; sewer and water treatment and collection systems; building permit activities; libraries, parks and recreation activities; other numerous social service responsibilities. Cities also have considerable responsibilities for land-use planning within their city limits and urban growth boundaries.

Regardless of the type of government, cities find their strength in a relationship between the citizens, city officials, the private sector and other government entities. Cities recognize the positive impact of working together, both regionally and on a statewide basis, to enhance community livability.

Key: In the following list, the name of each city is followed by the name of the county, address and telephone number, fax number, email address, web site, population, elevation, date of incorporation, name origin, sister city (SC) if applicable and names of city officials. City name origins from **Oregon Geographic Names,** *by Lewis A. McArthur.*

* County seat

Adair Village, Benton, 6030 NE Wm. R. Carr Ave., 97330; 541-745-5507; Fax: 541-745-5508; 565, 328', 1976. Named for Camp Adair, honoring Lt. Henry Rodney Adair.

Mayor Stephen Craig Bartlett; Council: Larry Harris, Steven McDonald, Lynn O'Bryan, Robert Schroeder; Admin./Rcdr. Wanda Tobiassen.

Adams, Umatilla, PO Box 20, 97810; 541-566-9380; Fax: 541-566-2298; 260, 1,526', 1893. Named for John F. Adams.

Mayor Jim Rohde; Council: Betty Jane Bugbee, Bruce Bugbee, Linda Bunch, Rene Corley, Ruth Easley; Rcdr./Fin. Dir. Sally Geissel-Fairley.

Adrian, Malheur, PO Box 226, 97901; 541-724-5014; 135, 2,220', 1972. Name suggested by Reuben McCeary for James Adrian, a sheepman.

Mayor Clarence E. Webb; Council: Vince Bingham, Dealda F. Linville, G. George Martin Jr., Shawn L. Snyder; Rcdr. Adele Dockter; Sewer Supt. Richard Davis.

*Albany, Linn/Benton, PO Box 490, 97321-0144; 541-917-7500; Fax: 541-917-7511; 37,095, 210', 1864. Named by Thomas and Walter Monteith for their former home, Albany, N.Y. SC: Albany, Australia.

Mayor Chuck McLaran; Council: Wayne Fisk, Kent Hickam, Doug Killin, Sharon Konopa, Jim Linhart III, Ralph Reid Jr.; Mgr. Steve Bryant; Fin. Dir./ Rcdr. Gary Holliday.

Amity, Yamhill, PO Box 159, 97101; 503-835-3711; Fax: 503-835-3780; 1,195, 161', 1880. Named for the amicable settlement of a local school dispute.

Mayor Gary Fink; Council: Brian Becker, Dagmar Biel, Janet Martin, James McDonald, Kerri Stepisnik, Laura Westfall; Rcdr. Karin Johnson.

Antelope, Wasco, PO Box 105, 97001; 541-489-3239; 65, 2,631', 1901. Named for the many antelope located here in pioneer days.

Mayor Dora Harris; Council: David Haner, Howard McMichael, Jeannie Opray, John Stewart.

Arlington, Gilliam, PO Box 68, 97812; 541-454-2743; 485, 285', 1885. Named for Nathaniel Arlington Cornish.

Mayor Fred Ericksen; Council: Jeffery Bufton, Mark Davidson, Jonathan Grady, Jerry Hanan, John Moffit, Ruben T. Wetherell; Rcdr. Kay F. West.

Ashland, Jackson, 20 E Main St., 97520; 541-482-3211; Fax: 541-488-5311; Web: www.ashland.or.us; 18,360, 1,895', 1874. Named by Abel Helman and Eber Emery, both from Ashland, Ohio. SC: Guanajuato, Mexico.

Mayor Catherine M. Golden; Council: Ken Hagen, Steve Hauck, Don Laws, Susan Reid, Brent Thompson, Carol Wheeldon; Admin. Brian L. Almquist; Fin. Dir. Jill Turner; Rcdr./Treas. Barbara Christensen; Muni. Judge Allen Drescher.

*Astoria, Clatsop, 1095 Duane St., 97103; 503-325-5821; Fax: 503-325-2017; 10,130, 19', 1856. Named for John Jacob Astor, founder and fur trader. SC: Walldorf, Germany.

Mayor Willis L. Van Dusen; Council: Donald B. Morden, Tom Potter, Douglas C. Thompson, Jim Wilkins; Mgr. Robert DeLong; Fin. Dir. John Snyder; Muni. Judge Neal Lemery.

Athena, Umatilla, PO Box 686, 97813; 541-566-3862; Fax: 541-566-2781; 1,105, 1,710', 1905. Named by school principal D.W. Jarvis for the Greek goddess.

Mayor Mark Seltman; Council: Tim Albert, Ed Boatright, Matt Evans-Koch, Raymond Miller, Jim Smith; Rcdr./Treas./Muni. Judge Katherine Dale Shafer.

Aumsville, Marion, PO Box 227, 97325; 503-749-2030; Fax: 503-749-1852; 2,585, 363', 1911. Named first by Henry Turner for his son-in-law, Aumus (Amos) Davis.

Mayor Harold L. White; Council: Chester Bridges, Craig Chadwick, Gary Delaney, Darlene Loyd; Admin. Maryann Hills; Muni. Judge: Ira Feitelson.

Aurora, Marion, PO Box 100, 97002; 503-678-1283; Fax: 503-678-2758; 675, 132', 1893. Named in honor of Dr. William Keil's daughter, Aurora.

Mayor Loretta Scott; Council: Ray Lambert, Scott Mills, Alan Southwell, Vergie Taylor, Heather Wechter; Treas./Rcdr. Melody Thompson; Muni. Judge Janice Zyryanoff.

*Baker City, Baker, PO Box 650, 97814; 541-523-6541; Fax: 541-523-2603; 9,870, 3,449', 1874. Named for Col. Edward Dickinson Baker, Oregon's first U.S. Senator.

Mayor Lawrence Griffith; Council: Bill Gwilliam, Julie Huntington, Mark Johnson, Larry Pearson, Karen Yeakley, Paul York; Mgr. Karen Woolard; Fin. Dir. Roger Dexter.

Bandon, Coos, 555 U.S. Highway 101; PO Box 67, 97411; 541-347-2437; Fax: 541-347-1415; Email: bandon@mail.coos.or.us; 2,760, 0', 1891. Named by George Bennett for Bandon, on Bandon River, County Cork, Ireland.

Mayor Judy Densmore; Council: Barbara Dodrill, Don Lynam, Gerry Procetto, Blythe Tiffany, Brian Vick, Lisa Wampole; Mgr. Matthew Winkel; Fin. Dir. Chele Gamble; Rcdr/Muni. Judge Denise M. Skillman.

Banks, Washington, PO Box 428, 97106; 503-324-5112; Fax: 503-324-6674; 570, 250', 1921. Named for Robert Banks and his father John Banks.

Mayor Michael Crippen; Council: Judy Clifford, Evelyn Maller, Bob Orkowski, Norma Stewart, Timothy Weaver, Kay Wolff; Rcdr. Bob Prickett.

Barlow, Clackamas, 106 N Main St., 97013-9191; 503-266-1330; 125, 101', 1903. Named for William Barlow, son of Samuel K. Barlow.

Mayor Doris Voutrin; Council: Michael Barnett, Patrick Madden, Hurshell Walls; Rcdr. Kathy Wagner; Treas. Millie Stegmeier.

Aumsville residents salt and butter hundreds of corn cobs during the city's annual Corn Festival.

Photo courtesy of the city of Aumsville.

Bay City, Tillamook, PO Box 3309, 97107; 503-377-2288; Fax: 503-377-4044; 1,130, 17', 1910. Named by Winfried Cone, who arrived from Bay City, Mich.

Mayor Al Griffin; Council: Art Anderson, Jim Cole, Bill Fisher, Dick Russell, Billy Schreiber, Bill Ziegler; Rcdr./Treas. Linda Wheeler.

Beaverton, Washington, PO Box 4755, 97076; 503-526-2222; 63,145, 189', 1893. Named for its location amid a large network of beaver dams. SC: Gotemba, Japan; Cheon-an, Korea; Hsinchu, Taiwan; Birobidzhan, Russia; Trossingen, Germany.

Mayor Rob Drake; Council: Evelyn Brzezinski, Dennis Doyle, Forrest Soth, Cathy Stanton, Wes Yuen; Fin. Dir. Patrick O'Claire; Rcdr. Darleen Cogburn; Muni. Judge Allen Reel.

*Bend, Deschutes, 710 NW Wall St., 97701; 541-388-5505; Fax: 541-388-5519; Email: cityofbend@bend-or.com; Web: www.bend-or.com/~cityofbend; 32,220, 3,623', 1905. Named from Farewell Bend on the Deschutes River, last view point of the river.

Mayor Bob Woodward; Council: Bryan Chitwood, Kathie W. Eckman, Benji Gilchrist, Suzanne Johannsen, Oran Teater, Jim Young; Mgr. Larry G. Patterson; Rcdr. Patricia Stell; Fin. Dir. A. Andrew Parks; Muni. Judge Lisa Bertalan.

Boardman, Morrow, PO Box 229, 97818; 541-481-9252; Fax: 541-481-3244; 2,580, 298.5', 1927. Named for Samuel Herbert Boardman, Oregon's first state parks superintendent.

Mayor Terry K. Tallman; Council: David Hirai, Dean Kegler, Thomas D. Meyers, Raymond D. Michael, Everett Moore, Jay Robinson; Mgr. Jack Palmer; Rcdr. Ernabel Mittelsdorf; Clerk/Fin. Dir. Kathy Moore.

Bonanza, Klamath, PO Box 297, 97623; 541-545-6566; 370, 4,200', 1901. Named from the Spanish word meaning prosperity and applied to good water in the area.

Mayor Betty Tyree; Council: Steve Casebeer, Rex Hunt, Lillian Slayter, Bud Stevenson, Bob Young; Treas. Madaline Depuy; Rcdr. Danise Mockridge.

Brookings, Curry, 898 Elk Dr., 97415; 541-469-2163; Fax: 541-469-3650; 5,400, 129', 1951. Named for Robert S. Brookings, lumber stockholder.

Mayor Nancy Brendlinger; Council: Julie Cartwright, Larry Curry, Bob

Hagbom, C. David Ham; Mgr. Tom Weldon; Fin. Dir./Rcdr. Beverly Adams.

Brownsville, Linn, PO Box 188, 97327; 541-466-5666; Fax: 541-466-5118; 1,415, 354', 1876. Named for Hugh L. Brown who started the first store around 1850.

Mayor Joe DeZurney; Council: Ray Bubak, Dave Heagy, Laura Nielsen, Bill Sattler, Charline Shipley-Kalupa, Don Ware; Admin. Diane J. Rinks; Muni. Judge Jad Lemhouse.

*Burns, Harney, 242 S Broadway, 97720; 541-573-5255; Fax: 541-573-5622; 2,935, 4,148', 1891. Named by George McGowen in admiration of poet Robert Burns.

Mayor Roger Reason; Council: Curt Blackburn, Dick Denstedt, Ken Pruett, Bob Raleigh, Laura Van Cleave, Ron Zuercher; Mgr. James A. Aho; Rcdr./Treas. Mary Ann Robinson.

Butte Falls, Jackson, PO Box 268, 97522; 541-865-3262; Fax: 541-865-3777; 415, 2,534', 1911. Named from the natural feature at the falls on Big Butte Creek.

Mayor Sara Beck; Council: Steve Harvey, Ethel Hoppe, Ray Macy, Alvin Thompson, Scott Waddell, Mary Wright; Rcdr. Roberta McClanahan; Muni. Judge Robert King.

Canby, Clackamas, PO Box 930, 97013; 503-266-4021; Fax: 503-266-1574; 11,430, 153', 1893. Named for Gen. Edward R.S. Canby. SC: Kurisawa, Japan.

Mayor Scott Taylor; Council: Walter Daniels, Brad Gerber, Roger Harris, Barry Lucas, Dennis Nolder, Shirley Strong; Admin. Michael J. Jordan; Rcdr. Marilyn K. Perkett; Treas. Virginia Biddle; Muni. Judge Jon Henricksen.

Cannon Beach, Clatsop, PO Box 368, 97110; 503-436-1581; Fax: 503-436-2050; 1,395, 0', 1956. Named from a small iron cannon that drifted ashore from the wrecked "Shark."

Mayor Kirk Anderson; Council: Karolyn Adamson, Laurel Hood, Bud Kramer, Frank Little; Mgr. John Williams; Muni. Judge Neal Lemery.

*Canyon City, Grant, PO Box 276, 97820; 541-575-0509; Fax: 541-575-0515; 705, 3,194', 1891. Named for its location in a canyon.

Mayor Scott Myers; Council: Greg Bremner, Dorman Gregory, Don Jones, Don Mooney, Nancy Nickel, Peggy Salisbury; Rcdr./Mgr. Tamra M. Day.

Canyonville, Douglas, PO Box 765, 97417; 541-839-4258; Fax: 541-839-4680; 1,265, 747', 1901. Named for its location in a canyon at the foot of Canyon Mountain.

Mayor Gloria McGinnis; Council: Robert Deaton, Kathleen Hammond, Ray Hanks, Fred Harder, Ralph Johannessen, Alberta Pritchett; Admin. Larry Andrew.

Carlton, Yamhill, PO Box 458, 97111; 503-852-7575; Fax: 503-852-7761; 1,470, 198', 1899. Named for John Carl Sr. and Wilson Carl.

Mayor Steve Sampson; Council: Jesse Berry, Steve Brodrick, Lester Burnham, Kathie Oriet, Bob Strahle; Clk. Tami Barker; Mgr. David Carl; Muni. Judge Joan Williams.

Cascade Locks, Hood River, PO Box 308, 97014; 541-374-8484; Fax: 541-374-8752; 1,050, 103', 1935. Named for the series of locks built in 1896.

Mayor Debra Smith; Council: Larry Cramblett, Nancy Evers, Ralph Hesgard, Gail Lewis, Rogers Wheatley, Caroline White; Admin. George R. Lewis; Fin. Dir./Rcdr. Kate Mast.

Cave Junction, Josephine, PO Box F, 97523; 541-592-2156; Fax: 541-592-6694; 1,300, 1,350', 1948. Name is from the community developed at the junction resulting from traffic going to the Oregon Caves.

Mayor James "Sully" Sullivan; Council: Timothy Block, Carl Carlisle, Greg Gutierrez, Bill Hickerson; Rcdr. Charles "Jim" Polk.

Central Point, Jackson, 155 S 2nd, 97502; 541-664-3321; Fax: 541-664-6384; 10,295, 1,272', 1889. Named by Isaac Constant for the crossing of two important pioneer wagon roads.

Mayor Rusty McGrath; Council: Duane Christensen, Garth Ellard, Carol Fischer, Barry Fronek, John LeGros, Mae McDowell; Admin. James Bennett; Fin. Dir. vacant; Muni. Judge James Mueller.

Chiloquin, Klamath, PO Box 196, 97624; 541-783-2717 or 783-2278; Fax: 541-783-2035; 755, 4,200', 1926. Named from the Klamath Indian family name, Chaloquin.

Mayor Dorothy Witcraft; Council: Edison Chiloquin, Bruce Engle, Cherie Harty, Joyce Smith, Curtis Stanton, Harry Williams; Rcdr. Jennifer Wampler.

Clatskanie, Columbia, PO Box 9, 97016-0009; 503-728-2622; Fax: 503-728-3297; 1,875, 15', 1891. Named from the Tlats-Kani, a small tribe of Indians once inhabiting the region.

Mayor Addison Harrison; Council: Linda Cooper, Larry Garlock, Robert Keyser, Jim Morgan, Ron Puzey, Gaile Steele; Mgr. Larry D. Cole; Rcdr./Treas. Arlene F. Long; Muni. Judge Rod McLean.

Coburg, Lane, PO Box 8316, 97408; 541-485-6266; Fax: 541-485-0655; 775, 400', 1893. Named by blacksmith Charles Payne for a locally owned stallion from Coburg, Germany.

Mayor Chuck Solin; Council: Virginia Beebe, Tony Chilton, Geegann Koehler, Margaret Norman, Donald Schuessler, Kathryn Ulm; Rcdr./Treas. Diane Williams; Muni. Judge Thomas C. Thetford.

Columbia City, Columbia 1840 Second St., PO Box 189, 97018; 503-397-4010; Fax: 503-366-0616; 1,465, 24', 1926. Named for the Columbia River, which was named for Capt. Robert Gray's ship "Columbia Rediviva." SC: Columbia City, Indiana.

Mayor Cheryl A. Young; Council: William Guy, Bridgett Harkins, Gary Hudson, Robert Schmor; Admin./Rcdr. Jean M. LeMont; Muni. Judge Diana Shera Taylor.

*Condon, Gilliam, PO Box 445, 97823; 541-384-2711; Fax: 541-384-2700; 790, 2,844', 1893. Named for Harvey C. Condon.

Mayor Melanie Wise; Council: Priscilla Cathcart, John E. Combs, Thomas Fatland, Hollie Harrison, David Messenger; Rcdr./Treas. Lori Anderson.

Coos Bay, Coos, 500 Central Ave., 97420-1895; 541-269-1181; Fax: 541-267-5615; Email: bgrile@ucinet.com; Web: www.presys.com/ps-home/pub-ser /coos_bay; 15,520, 10', 1874. Named for the native tribe of the Kusan family and the natural feature of the bay. SC: Choshi, Japan.

Mayor Joanne Verger; Council: Joe Benetti, Jeff McKeown, Cindi Miller, Don Spangler, Kevin Stufflebean, Judy Weeks; Mgr. Bill Elliott; Fin. Dir./ Rcdr. Gail George.

*Coquille, Coos, 99 E 2nd, 97423; 541-396-2115; Fax: 541-396-2113; Email: cityhall@mail.coos.or.us; 4,225,

40', 1885. Name origin unknown; probably American Indian but with French spelling.

Mayor Mike Swindall; Council: Mollie Anderson, E.N. Daniels, Phil Greenway, Darlene Kelley, Joseph Thurman, Loran Wiese; Mgr. Joseph G. Wolf; Rcdr./Fin. Dir. Shirley Patterson.

Cornelius, Washington, PO Box 607, 97113; 541-357-9112; Fax: 503-357-7775; Web: www.cyber-launch.com/corneliusoregon; 7,475, 175', 1893. Named for Col. Thomas R. Cornelius, pioneer.

Mayor Ralph Brown; Council: Dave Ashcraft, Neil Clough, Steve Heinrich, Scott Rice; Mgr. John Greiner; Rcdr. Mildred Otto.

*Corvallis, Benton, PO Box 1083, 97339; 541-757-6901; Fax: 541-757-6780; Web: www.ci.corvallis.or.us; 49,275, 224', 1857. Name from Latin meaning "heart of the valley." SC: Uzhgorod, Ukraine.

Mayor Helen Berg; Council: Ed Barlow-Pieterick, Mary Christian, Betty Griffiths, Guy Hendrix, Tony Howell, Todd Jay Lewis, Patrick Peters, Bruce Sorte, Tom Wogaman; Mgr. Jon S. Nelson; Fin. Dir. Nancy Brewer; Muni. Judge Mark Donahue.

Cottage Grove, Lane, 400 E Main St., 97424; 541-942-5501; Fax: 541-942-1267; Email: jtowery@aol.com; Web: www.efn.org/ncglib/lib_tbl.html; 7,870, 641', 1887. Named by G.C. Pearce, who had his home in an oak grove.

Mayor Darrel Williams; Council: Robert Baysinger, Cindy Choat, John Patterson, Doug Perkey, Kevin Stephens, Gary L. Williams; Mgr. Jeff Towery; Rcdr. Joan Hoehn; Fin. Dir. Janice Riessbeck.

Cove, Union, 504 Alder, PO Box 8, 97824; 541-568-4566; 600, 2,893', 1904. Name originally Forest Cove, referring to a natural pocket where Mill Creek flows from the Wallowa Mountains; shortened to avoid confusion with Forest Grove.

Mayor Richard Thew; Council: Wayne Bristow, Merton D. Cline, H.E. Evans, William Oliver, Donald Ott, Wallace Rudd; Rcdr./Treas. Alice Alexander.

Creswell, Lane, PO Box 276, 97426; 541-895-2531; Fax: 541-895-3647; 2,715, 535', 1909. Named by Ben Holladay for John A. Creswell, postmaster general.

Mayor Eddie McCluskey; Council: Jean Beck, Michael Dubick, Martin Heymann, Loren Levings, Sharlene Neff, Kristine Parente; Admin. Ronald L. Hanson; Rcdr./Fin. Dir. Connie Dersham; Muni. Judges R. Scott Palmer and Charles M. Zennaché.

Culver, Jefferson, PO Box 256, 97734; 541-546-6494; Fax: 541-546-3624; 795, 2,640', 1946. Name is the ancestral name of O.G. Collver.

Mayor Joanne Heare; Council: Michael Alley, Dan Harnden, Teena Hubbard, Jack Jones; Rcdr./Treas. Jeralyn Jones.

*Dallas, Polk, PO Box 67, 97338; 503-623-2338; Fax: 503-623-2339; 11,360, 325', 1874. Named for George Mifflin Dallas, vice-president under James Polk.

Mayor Gwen VanDenBosch; Council: Eldon Bevens, Warren Lamb, Kevin Marshall, Alice Propes, Glen Scatterday, Wes Scroggin, Doris Stefani, LaVonne Wilson, Ken Woods Jr.; Mgr./Rcdr. Roger Jordan; Fin. Dir. Del Funk; Muni. Judge Mark Bliven.

Dayton, Yamhill, PO Box 339, 97114-0339; 503-864-2221; Fax: 503-864-2221; 1,745, 160', 1880. Named by Andrew Smith for Dayton, Ohio.

Mayor Georgia Windish; Council: Ed Couch, John Haney, Pamela McBride, Linda McGrew, Nan Mileo, Harry Neal Webb; Admin./Rcdr. Sue Hollis; Muni. Judge Larry Gray.

Dayville, Grant, PO Box 321, 97825; 541-987-2188; Fax: 541-987-2187; 185, 2,348', 1914. Named for John Day, a member of the Astor expedition.

Mayor Peggy J. Adams; Council: Millie Grindstaff, Skip Inscore, Debbie Kowalski, Harold Maier, Merle Metcalf; Rcdr./Treas. Ruth Moore.

Depoe Bay, Lincoln, PO Box 8, 97341; 541-765-2361; Fax: 541-765-2129; 1,045, 58', 1973. Named for Willie Depoe, a Siletz Indian.

Mayor Bob Jackson; Council: Russ Hunter, Deno Martineau, Ron Nowark, Maryella Ockfen, Jan "Pogo" Robison, Naomi Wamacks; Supt. Stacey Halstead; Rcdr. Kate Becker.

Detroit, Marion, PO Box 589, 97342; 503-854-3496; 370, 1,564', 1952. Named after Detroit, Mich.

Mayor Graydon Broms; Council: Harold Hills, Mike LaMont, Tom Mask, Michelle Warden; Rcdr. Susan Crowder; Muni. Judge Steve Summers.

Donald, Marion, PO Box 388, 97020; 541-678-5543; Fax: 503-678-2750; 580, 195', 1912. Named for R.L. Donald, an official of the Oregon Electric Railway.

Mayor Naomi Parker; Council: Lynn Ahern, John Brandt, Pamela Brandt, Dave Caldwell, Frank Vanderwood, Elaine Yoder; Mgr. Janet Lane.

Drain, Douglas, PO Box 158, 97435; 541-836-2417; Fax: 541-836-7330; 1,115, 291', 1887. Named for pioneer settler Charles J. Drain.

Mayor Margrette Sparks; Council: Jim Hickson, Bill Johnson, Rance O. Pilley Jr., Ivan Sparks; Admin. Carl A. Patenode.

Dufur, Wasco, PO Box 145, 97021; 541-467-2349; Fax: 541-467-2353; 605, 1,350', 1893. Named for Andrew J. and E. Burnham Dufur.

Mayor Jalan Van Nice; Council: Virginia Albrecht, Keith Fagerberg, Howard Green, Michele Hammel, Reba Lloyd, Darrel Wolff; Rcdr. Maryln C. Sawyer.

Dundee, Yamhill, PO Box 220, 97115; 503-538-3922; Fax: 503-538-1958; 2,500, 189', 1895. Named for William Reid's home in Dundee, Scotland.

Mayor Jerry Koch; Council: Jeannette Adlong, Julie Bussanich, Roger Clark, Mona Harper, Arnie Heimbach, Ivon Miller; Rcdr. Pat Auld; Muni. Judge Carmella Ettinger.

Dunes City, Lane, PO Box 97, Westlake 97493; 541-997-3338; Fax: 541-997-5751; 1,240, 44', 1963. Named for the topographical presence of the dunes within city limits.

Mayor Rob Ward; Council: Josephine Buehler, Art Henrikson, David Jackson, Richard Micklewright, Dick Parent, Robert Petersdorf; Rcdr. Joyce Phillips.

Durham, Washington, PO Box 23483, 97281-3483; 503-639-6851; Fax: 503-598-8595; Email: durhamcity@aol.com; 1,575, 197', 1966. Named for Albert Alonzo Durham, sawmill builder.

Mayor Robert Tydeman; Council: Patrick Carroll, William Gilham, Christopher Hadfield, Gery Schirado; Admin./Rcdr. Steven Feldman.

Eagle Point, Jackson, PO Box 779, 97524; 541-826-4212; Fax: 541-826-6155; 3,605, 1,310', 1911. Named for a favorite nesting place for eagles just east of the city.

Mayor David McFall; Council: Walter Barker, Bob Bauer, Wayne Brown, Jim

The Ritner Creek Covered Bridge, completed in 1927, is the only remaining example of the State Highway Department's standardized design for a 75-foot Howe truss bridge.

Photo courtesy of Polk County Commissioners.

Goan, Kenneth Lemke, Shannon Sanders; Admin./Rcdr. John Luthy.

Echo, Umatilla, PO Box 9, 97826; 541-376-8411; Fax: 541-376-8218; 530, 638', 1904. Named for Echo Koontz, daughter of J.H. Koontz.

Mayor David McAuslan; Council: Jeannette Bell, Jerry Gaunt, Lynn Rainsberry, three vacancies to be appointed; Admin./Rcdr. Diane Berry; Muni. Judge Robert Shannon.

Elgin, Union, PO Box 128, 97827; 541-437-2253; Fax: 541-437-2253; 1,715, 2,670', 1891. Named for the wreck of the steamer "Lady Elgin."

Mayor Rick Smith; Council: Misty Bennett, Berta Churchill, Kevin Cooper, Pat McMullen, Leroy Short, John Stover; Rcdr./Admin. Joe Garlitz.

Elkton, Douglas, PO Box 508, 97436; 541-584-2547; Fax: 541-584-2547; 180, 148', 1948. Named for its location at the junction of Elk Creek and the Umpqua River.

Mayor Alfred Tyson; Council: Nancy Harbaugh, Ariel Hubbard, Charlotte McNeil, Greg Miller; Clk. Linda Higgins.

*Enterprise, Wallowa, 108 NE First, 97828; 541-426-4196; Fax: 541-426-3395; 2,020, 3,757', 1889. Named by R.F. Stubblefield at a meeting held in a tent.

Mayor Susan Roberts; Council: Bret Bane, Jeff Courtney, Linda Eddy, Irv Nuss, Brian Perren, Everett Roberts; Admin./Rcdr. Michele R. Young.

Estacada, Clackamas, PO Box 958, 97023; 503-630-8270; Fax: 503-630-8280; 2,065, 465', 1905. Named by George J. Kelly for Llano Estacado, Texas.

Mayor Allen Cameron; Council: Dennis Anderson, Pam Butcher, Richard Hartwig, John Mullins, Thomas Sager, Jane Troeh; Mgr. Greg Ellis; Rcdr. Denise Carey; Muni. Judge Dave Kushner.

*Eugene, Lane, 777 Pearl St., Rm. 105, 97401-2793; 541-687-5010; Fax: 541-687-5414; Web: www.ci.eugene.or.us; 126,325, 411', 1862. Named for Eugene F. Skinner. SC: Kakegawa, Japan; Chinju, Korea; Kathmandu, Nepal; Irkutsk, Russia.

Mayor James Torrey; Council: Pat Farr, Laurie Swanson Gribskov, Tim Laue, Bobby Lee, Scott Meisner, Nancy Nathanson, Betty Taylor; Mgr. Vicki Elmer; Rcdr./Treas. Warren Wong.

Fairview, Multnomah, PO Box 337, 97024; 503-665-7929; Fax: 503-666-0888; Email: fairview@teleport.com; Web: www.teleport.com/~fairview; 4,670, 114', 1908. Named after a Methodist church that was named after a nearby pioneer lookout.

Mayor Roger Vonderharr; Council: Len Edwards, Sherry Lillard, David McCutcheon, James R. Raze, Peter Tuomala, Mike Weatherby; Admin. Marilyn Holstrom; Rcdr. Caren Huson; Muni. Judge James Jennings.

Falls City, Polk, PO Box 10, 97344; 503-787-3631; Fax: 503-787-3023; 935, 365', 1891. Named for the falls in Little Luckiamute River, located at the west end of town.

Mayor Kirby Frink; Council: Ole Bergman, Ruth Bowman, Nancy Hibbs, Lucille Kalpakoff, Merlyn Newland, Barbara Poe; Admin. Bill Ewing.

Florence, Lane, PO Box 340, 97439; 541-997-3436; Fax: 541-997-6814; 6,400, 11', 1893. Named for a lumber ship that wrecked in 1875. SC: Ijira-mura, Japan.

Mayor Roger W. McCorkle; Council: Dave Braley, Alan Burns, Eileen Gray, Eileen McGregor; Mgr. Kenneth D. Hobson; Rcdr./Fin. Dir. Jon E. Taylor; Muni. Judge Donald A. Loomis.

Forest Grove, Washington, PO Box 326, 97116; 503-359-3200; Fax: 503-359-3207; 15,370, 210', 1872. Named for the white oak and fir forests surrounding it. SC: Nyuzen, Japan.

Mayor Michael O'Brien; Council: Meredith Bliss, James Draznin, Rod Fuiten, Victoria Johnson, Richard G. Kidd, John R. Minor; Mgr. Ivan Burnett; Rcdr. Catherine L. Jansen; Fin. Dir. Jeff Hecksel.

*Fossil, Wheeler, PO Box 467, 97830; 541-763-2698; Fax: 541-763-2124; 515, 2,654', 1891. Named by Thomas B. Hoover who discovered fossil remains on his ranch.

Mayor John Kautenberg; Council: Steve Conlee, Michael Craig, Duane Monette, Kris Poole; Rcdr./Fin. Dir. Jeanne E. Burch.

Garibaldi, Tillamook, PO Box 708, 97118; 503-322-3327; Fax: 503-322-3737; 960, 10', 1946. Named for the Italian patriot, Giuseppe Garibaldi. SC: Sparks, Nev.

Mayor Joel I. Johnson; Council: Fran Blomberg, C. Joanne Dalziel, Doug Davis, David Duffey; Rcdr./Treas./Muni. Judge Saundra L. Jones.

Gaston, Washington, PO Box 129, 97119; 503-985-3340; Fax: 503-985-3340; 620, 300', 1914. Named for Joseph Gaston, historian and railroad promoter.

Mayor Brett Costelloe; Council: Marilyn Begert, Laurie Hoodenpyl, James Prince, Jeff Rasmussen, Tory Vobora, one vacancy; Rcdr. Margaret E. Bell; Muni. Judge Robert A. Browning.

Gates, Marion/Linn, PO Box 577, 97346; 503-897-2669; Fax: 503-897-5046; 530, 941', 1950. Named for settler Mary Ann Gates.

Mayor Richard Knakal; Council: Alan Hussey, Philip Kerbs, Jerry Stevens, two vacancies; Rcdr. Laura Brandt.

Gearhart, Clatsop, PO Box 2510, 97138; 503-738-5501; Fax: 503-738-9385; 1,205, 16', 1918. Named for pioneer Philip Gearhart.

Mayor Kent Smith; Council: Geraldine Gideon, Edward Tice, Robert Whitman, Dianne Widdop; Admin. Dennis McNally; Fin. Dir. Joan Beneke.

Gervais, Marion, PO Box 348, 97026; 503-792-4222; Fax: 503-792-3791; 1,080, 184', 1878. Named for pioneer Joseph Gervais.

Mayor Robert Hawkins; Council: Ronald Foote, Fay Ladd, Tony Miller, Dave Owings, Dianna Workman; Rcdr./Mgr. M.J. Davis.

Gladstone, Clackamas, 525 Portland Ave., 97027; 541-656-5225; Fax: 541-650-8938; 11,605, 57', 1911. Named for British statesman Sir William Ewart Gladstone.

Mayor Wade Byers; Council: Judith Ervin, Carl Gardner, Brent Graham, Ray Jaren, Mark Pagano, Thomas Pagh; Admin. Ronald J. Partch; Rcdr. Helen M. Parent; Muni. Judge Philip Ringle.

Glendale, Douglas, PO Box 361, 97442; 541-832-2106; Fax: 541-832-3221; 730, 1,418', 1901. Named for the Scottish glens, or for Glendale, Mass. or Glendale, Scotland.

Mayor David J. Malinoff Jr.; Council: Ken Graven, Richard Johnstone, Robert Morford, Edward Niemiec, Brandon Shepard, Ron Snelling; Rcdr./Treas. Lynnette M. Evens; Muni. Judge Candace Hissong.

*Gold Beach, Curry, 29592 Ellensburg Ave., 97444; 541-247-7029; Fax: 541-247-2212; 2,115, 60', 1948. Named for the discovery of gold in the sands.

Mayor Marlyn Schafer; Council: Marv Hinz, Tamie Kaufman, Mike Luzmore, Pete Peters, Terry Timeus; Admin. Bill Curtis.

Gold Hill, Jackson, 420 6th Ave., PO Box 308, 97525; 541-855-1525; Fax: 541-855-4501; 1,240, 1,085', 1895. Named for the hills, the scene of an early gold discovery.

Mayor Michael Stanley; Council: Dorothy Edler, Hy Klaus, Laura Liddell, Patrick Pillon, Don Purdy; Rcdr./Treas. vacant; City Clk. Betsy Hettum; Muni. Clk. Susie Tressel.

Granite, Grant, HCR 87, Box 1, Sumpter, 97877; 541-379-3517 (cellular); 25, 4,700', 1901. Named for the prevalence of granite rocks in the area.

Mayor Jim Ruth; Council: Bill Dobell, Mitchel Fielding, Patricia Fielding, Paul Schnitzer; Rcdr./Treas. Mike Hammer.

*Grants Pass, Josephine, 101 NW "A" St., 97526; 541-474-6360; Fax: 541-479-0812; 20,255, 960', 1887. Named as a result of Gen. U.S. Grant's capture of Vicksburg. SC: Rubtsovsk, Siberia (Russia).

Mayor Gordon Anderson; Council: Lynne Attebury, Len Holzinger, Claudell King, Amy Machado, Leon Oliver, Jim Riddle, H.L. "Jack" Rollins, Douglas Smith; Mgr. William Peterson; Fin. Dir. Joanne M. Stumpf.

Grass Valley, Sherman, PO Box 191, 97029; 541-333-2434; 180, 2,269', 1901. Named for the tall rye grass.

Mayor Carsten von Borstel; Council: Joann Duarte, Kevin King, Helen Olds, Joe Sharp, Margaret Snider, John R. Weber; Rcdr. Brenda J. Padget.

Greenhorn, Baker, 911 Laurel Ln., Oregon City 97045; 503-656-7945; 3, 6,270', 1912. Named in the days of the mining fever of the 1860s.

Mayor George Massinger; Council: Joseph Gray, Lauren Hartman, Arne D. Olsen, Wayne Rofinot, Rusty Wright; Rcdr. Brad Poyser; Treas. Scott Poyser; Trustee for City Lands Larry Pearson.

Gresham, Multnomah, 1333 NW Eastman Pkwy., 97030-3813; 503-661-3000; Fax: 503-665-4553; 79,350, 301', 1905. Named for Walter Quinton Gresham, soldier and statesman. SC: Ebetsu, Japan; Sok-Cho, S. Korea; Owerri, Nigeria.

Mayor Gussie McRobert; Council: Jack Gallagher, John Leuthauser, Glenn McIntire, Bob Moore, Debbie Noah, David Widmark; Mgr. Bonnie R. Kraft; Rcdr. Phyllis R. Brough; Fin. Dir. Terry McCall.

Haines, Baker, PO Box 208, 97833; 541-856-3366; Fax: 541-856-3812; 440, 3,333', 1909. Named for Judge I.D. Haines of Baker.

Mayor Gary Hale; Council: Rick Broadie, Larry Curry, Vance Dix, Tommy Duncan, Stephen Hart, Sandra Wood; Rcdr. Jennifer Schoenfeld.

Halfway, Baker, PO Box 738, 97834; 541-742-4741; 355, 2,663', 1909. Named for its location midway between Robinette (now under water) and Cornucopia, a once-booming mining town.

Mayor Dick Crow; Council: Verdell Davis, Sheila Farwell, Tim Moore, David Romine, Herman Thompson, Veryl Waldron; Rcdr./Treas. Diana Glynn.

Halsey, Linn, 773 W 1st St., 97348; 541-369-2522; Fax: 541-369-2521; 730, 280', 1876. Named for William L. Halsey of the Willamette Valley Railroad Co.

Mayor Frank Zellner; Council: Robert Canaday, Vince Emge, Jim Long, Kraig Ohling, Casey Stutz, Allan Ward; Rcdr. Marvella Gibbs; Muni. Judge Joy Chase.

Happy Valley, Clackamas, 12915 SE King Rd., 97236; 541-760-3325; Fax: 503-760-9397; 2,825, 497', 1965. Legend has it that young men drinking hard cider to keep warm while walking to a church meeting were known as "the boys from Happy Holler."

Mayor Randy Nicolay; Council: James Olsen, Michael Schaufler, Verne Scholz, Barbara Smith; Admin. William Brandon; Rcdr. Carol Peters.

Harrisburg, Linn, 354 Smith St., 97446; 541-995-6655; Fax: 541-995-9244; 2,205, 309', 1866. Named for Harrisburg, Pa.

Mayor Walter Dickson; Council: Steve Coppi, Paul Dieterle, Lee Heckart, John Jensen, Stephen McDermott, Ann Smith; Admin. Dan Eckles; Rcdr. Grayce Coffey; Muni. Judge Jad Lemhouse.

Helix, Umatilla, PO Box 323, 97835; 541-457-2521; 185, 1,754', 1919. Named for a painful infection in the helix of a local resident's ear.

Mayor Jim Coles; Council: Mike Clayton, Stan Flerchinger, Lorin Kubishta, Maria Sallee, Henry Schuening; Rcdr. Julie Fowler.

*Heppner, Morrow, 188 W Willow, PO Box 756, 97836; 541-676-9618; Fax: 541-676-9650; 1,480, 1,955', 1887. Named for storekeeper Henry Heppner.

Mayor Robert H. Jepsen; Council: Ronald H. "Skip" Matthews, Michael McGuire, Loretta Nairns, Kathryn Robinson, Jerri Sly, Tim Van Cleave; Mgr. Gary B. Marks; Treas. Claytha René Devin.

Hermiston, Umatilla, 180 NE 2nd St., 97838; 541-567-5521; Fax: 541-567-5530; Email: hermcity@eonet.com; 11,050, 450', 1907. Named for Robert Louis Stevenson's unfinished novel, *Weir of Hermiston.*

Mayor Frank J. Harkenrider; Council: Walter E. Achuff, Kraig A. Cutsforth, Rodney S. Hardin, Jackie C. Myers, Donna K. Prewitt, Robert E. Severson, Christine F. Smalley, DuWayne F. White; Mgr. Edward Brookshier; Rcdr./Fin. Dir./ Treas. Robert D. Irby; Muni. Judge John W. Smallmon.

*Hillsboro, Washington, 123 W Main St., 97123; 503-681-6100; Fax: 503-681-6213; Web: www.ci.hillsboro.or.us; 52,105, 196', 1876. Named for David Hill, pioneer and a member of the first executive committee of three acting as governor.

Mayor Gordon Faber; Council: John Godsey, Darlene Greene, Karen McKinney, Bruce Starr, Jerry Willey, one vacancy; Mgr. Tim Erwert; Rcdr. Gail Waibel; Dir. Fin. and Sup. Svs. Robert Massar; Muni. Judge Robert Harris.

Hines, Harney, PO Box 336, 97738; 541-573-2251; 541-573-2244; Fax: 541-573-5827; 1,525, 4,155', 1930. Named for Edward Hines, railroad and lumber businessman.

Mayor Richard Everhart; Council: Chris Billings, Christina Hill, John H. Hinton, Douglas Larson, Ben Stimmel, Kevin Taylor; Rcdr./Muni. Judge Pamela Mather; Treas. Cynthia Terry.

*Hood River, Hood River, PO Box 27, 97031; 541-386-1488; Fax: 541-387-5289; 5,110, 154', 1895. Named for Mt. Hood and the river, named for Lord Hood by British explorer Lt. W.R. Broughton. SC: Tsuruta, Japan.

Mayor Paul Cummings; Council: Bill Griffith, Robert Hastings, Barbara Hughes, Andrea Klaas, Bill Nelson, Tom Turck; Mgr. Lynn Guenther; Rcdr. Jay Reynolds; Fin. Dir. Steve Everroad; Muni. Judge Wilford Carey.

Hubbard, Marion, PO Box 380, 97032; 503-981-9633; Fax: 503-981-8743; 2,185, 182', 1891. Named for early settler Charles Hubbard.

Mayor Janet LeBlanc; Council: Jerry Huddleston, Hildred Huyssoon, Clara Karstens, Don Thwing; Rcdr. Paulette David.

Huntington, Baker, PO Box 369, 97907; 541-869-2202; Fax: 541-869-2550; 575, 2,108', 1891. Named for early settlers J.B. and J.M. Huntington.

Mayor Richard L. Gasser; Council: Linda Dixon, Victor L. Graham, James Kenick, Sarita G. Raney, Robert Wilcox, Shirleen R. Woodcock; Rcdr./Muni. Judge Donna J. Rush.

Idanha, Marion/Linn, PO Box 430, 97350; 541-854-3313; 315, 1,718', 1949. Idaho legend has "Idanha" as the Indian name used on bottle labels for the spirit of the healing waters.

Mayor Karen Clark; Council: Judith Gregory, Kelly Lucas, Darrlene Mann, Paul Smith; Rcdr. Rosemary Wilson.

Imbler, Union, PO Box 40, 97841-0040; 541-534-6095; Fax: 541-534-2343; 310, 2,732', 1922. Named for the Imbler family, pioneer settlers.

Mayor Angie Johnson; Council: Chuck Anderson, Julia Bennett, Thomas E.

Deal, James McDonald, Richard Nelson, Clay Todd; Rcdr. Ruth Zemke.

Independence, Polk, PO Box 7, 97351; 503-838-1212; Fax: 503-838-5548; 4,985, 168', 1874. Named after Independence, Mo.

Mayor Tom Ritchey; Council: John Bruning, Marcelina Cedillo, Charles Grell, Melaine Pfaff, June Powers, Elaine Stuart; Mgr. Stephani Johnson; Fin. Dir. Martha Wildfang; Rcdr. Ann Buck.

Ione, Morrow, PO Box 361, 97843; 541-422-7437 or 541-422-7414; 250, 1,080', 1903. Named for Ione Arthur, a girl from Brownsville.

Mayor vacant; Council: Bob Ball, Joel Barnett, Harvey Childers, Betty Gray, Dennis Stefani, Dennis Thompson; Rcdr. Sharon Rietmann; Treas. Nancy Ekstrom.

Irrigon, Morrow, PO Box 428, 97844; 541-922-3047; Fax: 541-922-9322; 1,090, 297', 1957. Named from the words "Oregon" and "irrigation."

Mayor Donald V. Eppenbach; Council: William H. Cooley, Don Hurd, Scott Johnson, Ray Shade, Christine Sorenson, Kelly Wright.

Island City, Union, 10605 Island Ave., 97851; 541-963-5017; Fax: 541-963-3482; 865, 2,743', 1904. Located on an island formed by a slough.

Mayor Dale DeLong; Council: Joyce Beeman, Sandy Donnelly, Kevin Hampton, Kenneth Hanson, Harry Thomas, Andy Younggren; Rcdr. Judy A. Rygg.

Jacksonville, Jackson, PO Box 7, 97530; 541-899-1231; 2,025, 1,569', 1860. Named for Andrew Jackson, seventh U.S. President.

Mayor James Lewis; Council: Joyce Coleman, John Dodero, Lynn MacBeth, Jack Pfeifer, Don Wendt; Rcdr. Doris Crofoot.

Jefferson, Marion, PO Box 83, 97352-0083; 541-327-2768; Fax: 541-327-3120; 2,145, 235', 1870. Named for Jefferson Institute and third U.S. President Thomas Jefferson.

Mayor Edna Campau; Council: Christine Cason, Michael Myers, Scott Partridge, Monte Rice, Jo Robertson, Gilberto Yzaguirre; Rcdr. Bonnie J. Bell; Muni. Judge Joy Chase.

John Day, Grant, 450 E Main, 97845; 541-575-0028; Fax: 541-575-1721; 1,940, 3,083', 1901. Named for John Day, member of the Astor Expedition.

Mayor Chris Labhart; Council: Jack Grubbs, Ron Lundbom, Alfred Meyer, James A. Sheets, Roger Simonsen,

Leonard Trafton; Mgr. William H. Deist; Rcdr. Robert L. Lerud.

Johnson City, Clackamas, 8021 SE Posey St., Milwaukie 97267; 503-655-9710; 625, 60', 1970. Named for mobile park developer Delbert Johnson.

Mayor Alice Sedgwick; Council: Naoma Lee, Lela McCulloch, Georgia Ramirez, Tim Schofield; Rcdr./Clk. Marlee Erickson; Muni. Judge Phil Ringle.

Jordan Valley, Malheur, PO Box 187, 97910; 541-586-2460; 385, 4,389', 1911. Named for Michael M. Jordan, leader of a party that discovered gold.

Mayor Norman B. Pruitt; Council: Marvin D. Bowers, Barrett L. Cupp, Mitzi Elordi, Ken Freese, Paige McMichael, Maxine Telleria; Treas./Rcdr./Clk. Ila J. Harnar.

Joseph, Wallowa, PO Box 15, 97846; 541-432-3832; 1,255, 4,191', 1887. Named for Chief Joseph (1837-1904).

Mayor Shelley S. Curtiss; Council: Richelle Chitwood, Malcolm W. Dawson, Matthew Gross, Paul Morehead, Kevin Warnock, Robert Williams; Rcdr. Noma McDaniel.

Water churns through a narrow section of the North Umpqua River in Douglas County.

Photo by Gordon Coons, courtesy of the Douglas County commissioners.

Junction City, Lane, PO Box 250, 97448; 541-998-2153; Fax: 541-998-3140; 4,115, 322', 1872. Where the west- and east-side railroad lines were to come together.

Mayor John W. Peterson, III; Council: Bill Barrong, Herb Christensen, Shirley Kaping, Robert Stott, Winn Wendell, Clarke Wilde; Admin. Roberta L. Likens; Rcdr. Barbara Scott; Muni. Judge James W. Spickerman.

Keizer, Marion, PO Box 21000, 97307; 503-390-3700; Fax: 503-393-9437; 27,450, 135', 1982. Named for pioneers J.B. and T.D. Keizer.

Mayor Dennis Koho; Council: Carl Beach, Jim Keller, Jerry McGee, Dawn Meier, Al Miller, Garry Whalen; Mgr. Dorothy Tryk; Rcdr. Tracy L. Davis; Muni. Judge Erik Larson.

King City, Washington, 15300 SW 116th Ave., 97224; 503-639-4082; Fax: 503-639-3771; 2,155, 213', 1966. Name used as a royalty theme by R.B. Sorenson, president of a development company.

Mayor Jack Kloster; Council: Jan Drangsholt, pres., Jason Broeckel; Al Deschenes, Ed Otte, James "Bud" Wilkinson, Chet Zakrzewski; Mgr./Rcdr. Jane Aamold.

***Klamath Falls**, Klamath, 500 Klamath Ave., 97601; 541-883-5316; Fax: 541-883-5399; 18,765, 4,120', 1905. Named for the tribe of Indians and the natural falls. SC: Rotorua, New Zealand.

Mayor Todd Kellstrom; Council: Betty Dickson, Neil Drew, Irving H. Hart, Cheri Howard, David A. Maxwell; Mgr. James R. Keller; Rcdr. Elisa D. Fritz; Fin. Dir. George Jacobs.

***La Grande**, Union, PO Box 670, 97850; 541-962-1302; Fax: 541-963-3333; 12,415, 2,788', 1865. Name suggested by Henry Dause, a young Frenchman who often referred to the beauty of the Grande Ronde Valley and its scenery.

Mayor Mark D. Davidson; Mayor Pro Tem Di Lyn Larsen-Hill; Council: Kirk Achilles, Gary O. Hathaway, Steven J. Joseph; Mgr. R. Wes Hare II; Rcdr. Alexandra Norgan Lund.

Lafayette, Yamhill, PO Box 55, 97127; 503-864-2451; Fax: 503-864-4501; 1,795, 160', 1878. Named for Lafayette, Ind.

Mayor Ron Ross; Council: Ron Harris, Tim Jensen, John Miller, Kenny Schweiger, Alex Stolk, Theresa Syphers; Admin./Treas. Mark Gervasi.

Lake Oswego, Clackamas, PO Box 369, 97034; 503-635-0270; Fax: 503-635-0269; Web: www.ci.oswego.or.us; 34,005, 100', 1910. Named for Oswego, N.Y. and changed to Lake Oswego in a 1960 election. SC: Pucon, Chile; Yoshikawa, Japan.

Mayor Bill Klammer; Council: Bill Atherton, Bob Chizum, Heather Chrisman, Tom Lowrey, Craig Prosser, Karl Rohde; Mgr. Douglas J. Schmitz; Fin. Dir. Bob Kincaid; Rcdr. Kristi Hitchcock; Muni. Judge Tom Rastetter.

Lakeside, Coos, 915 North Lake Rd., 97459; 541-759-3011; Fax: 541-759-4752; 1,630, 28', 1974. Named for location near shores of Ten Mile and North Tenmile Lakes.

Mayor Peter Schoonover; Council: Julie Anderson, Jim Brown, Tim Crockett, Bert Guin, Terry Minard, Don Rudd; Rcdr. David Hagood.

***Lakeview**, Lake, 525 N 1st St., 97630; 541-947-2029; Fax: 541-947-2952; 2,655, 4,800', 1889. Named for the town's location, which was nearer to Goose Lake in the 1870s.

Mayor Donald R. Alger; Council: Rod Harlan, Orval Layton, Jim Rosetti, Jerald Steward; Fin. Dir./Rcdr. Ann Echavarria.

Lebanon, Linn, 925 Main St., 97355; 541-451-7421; Fax: 541-451-1260; 11,995, 347', 1878. Named for Jeremiah Ralston's birth place, Lebanon, Tenn. SC: Nagawa Machi, Japan.

Mayor Robert G. Smith; Council: Floyd Fisher, Ron Miller Jr., John Richard, Wayne Rieskamp, Ken Toombs, one vacancy; Admin. Joseph A. Windell; Fin. Dir. Judy Wendland.

Lexington, Morrow, Main St., PO Box 587, 97839; 541-989-8508; 295, 1,454', 1903. Named by William Penland, a native of Lexington, Ky.

Lincoln City, Lincoln, PO Box 50, 97367; 541-996-2152; Fax: 541-994-7232; 6,665, 11', 1965. Named for Abraham Lincoln, 16th President of the United States.

Mayor Foster Aschenbrenner; Council: Hal Caywood, Robert Derr, Lori Hollingsworth, Dave Humphrey, Ed Johann, Randy Nelson; Mgr. Robert Mack; Rcdr. Oneita McCalman; Fin. Dir. Ron Tierney.

Lonerock, Gilliam, Lonerock Rte., Condon, 97823; 541-384-3196; 25, 2,800', 1901. Named for prominent landmark, a rock about 100' high and some 60' in diameter.

Mayor Floyd Parrott; Council: Alletta Clark, Linda Davis, Lavelle Stephens; Clk./Rcdr./ Treas. Jane Campbell.

Long Creek, Grant, PO Box 489, 97856; 541-421-3601; Fax: 541-421-3075; 240, 3,754', 1891. Named for the community's close proximity to the stream.

Mayor Hal Arbogast; Council: Aliene Adams, Kelly Brown, George Hixson, Amy Kreiger; Treas./Rcdr. Sandra Leasy.

Lostine, Wallowa, PO Box 181, 97857; 541-569-2415; 235, 3,200', 1903. Named by a pioneer settler for Lostine, Kan.

Mayor Ken Arthur; Council: Glenda Neal, Krag Norton, Ken Spidell, one vacancy; Rcdr. Jane Robinson.

Lowell, Lane, PO Box 490, 97452; 541-937-2157; Fax: 541-937-2936; 955, 741', 1954. Named by Amos D. Hyland, a native of Lowell, Maine.

Mayor Warren Weathers; Council: Mike Cobiskey, Chris Moffitt, Sandy Summers; Rcdr. Dee Blacklaw; Muni. Judge Gary Darnielle, Mike Walch, pro tem.

Lyons, Linn, PO Box 10, 97358; 503-859-2167; Fax: 503-859-2602; 1,010, 661', 1958. Named for the family that established the community.

Mayor Rosalie Ader; Council: Tom Basey, Pat Kaufman, Doug Mentze, George Nydegger; Rcdr. Monika Hennings.

*Madras, Jefferson, 71 SE "D" St., 97741; 541-475-2344; Fax: 541-475-7061; 4,770, 2,242', 1911. Named for the city in India. SC: Kitimimaki, Japan.

Mayor Joe Krenowicz; Council: James DeWhitt, Rosie B. Leal, Bob McConnell, Robert Osborn, Carl Richardson, Marjean Whitehouse; Admin. Patrick Sorensen; Fin. Dir. Brenda Black; Rcdr. Karen Coleman; Clk. Wanda Johnson; Muni. Judge Edwin D. Harris.

Malin, Klamath, PO Box 61, 97632; 541-723-2021; Fax: 541-723-2021; 750, 4,058', 1922. Named for a town in Bohemia, Czechoslovakia.

Mayor Jeff Williamson; Council: Phil Beasley, John Browning, Sheldon Buller, Stan Pence, Charles Stewart, Gary Zieg; Rcdr./Treas./Clk. Kay Neumeyer.

Manzanita, Tillamook, PO Box 129, 97130-0129; 503-368-5343; Fax: 503-368-4145; 755, 31', 1946. Named from the Spanish, meaning "little apple."

Mayor James Bond; Council: Avis Brennan, Walt Pendergrass, Joyce Raker, Walt Stickel; Mgr./Rcdr. Jerald P. Taylor.

Maupin, Wasco, PO Box 308, 97037; 541-395-2698; Fax: 541-395-2499; 495, 1,041', 1922. Named for pioneer Howard Maupin. SC: The Dalles, Shaniko and communites of Pine Grove, Tygh Valley, Wamic.

Mayor Sherry Holliday; Council: Beth Ashley, Ted Kuhnhausen, Hal Laur, John Smeraglio, Paulette Tolentino, Clinton Windom; Rcdr. DeOra Patton.

Maywood Park, Multnomah, 4510 NE 102nd Ave., Annex #1, Portland 97220; 541-255-9805; 795, 77', 1967. Named by the mother of developer E.F. Taylor, who remembered what a lovely spot the woods were in May.

Mayor Jeff Steffen; Council: Ben Harrison, John Medak, Garr Nielsen, David Snodgrass; Rcdr. Jean Farrell; Fin. Dir. Gary Pomeroy.

*McMinnville, Yamhill, 230 NE 2nd St., 97128; 503-434-7301; Fax: 503-472-4101; Email: taylork@ci.mcminnville.or.us; Web: www.ci.mcminnville.or.us/mcminnville; 22,880, 157', 1882. Named by William T. Newby who was born in McMinnville, Tenn.

Mayor Edward J. Gormley; Council: Tino Aleman, Dave Hughes, Mary Massey, Robert A. Payne, Rod Tomcho, Richard Windle; Mgr. Kent L. Taylor; Rcdr./Fin. Dir. Carole M. Benedict; Muni. Judge Robert Thompson.

*Medford, Jackson, 411 W 8th St., 97501; 541-770-4432; Fax: 541-770-4444; Email: cmomed@ci.medford.or.us; Web: www.ci.medford.or.us; 57,155, 1,382', 1885. Named for its location at the middle ford on Bear Creek, and for Medford, Mass. SC: Alba, Italy.

Mayor Jerry Lausmann; Council: Curt Bennett, Linda Casey, Sal Esquivel, Lee Ferguson, Jim Key, Skip Knight, Bill Moore, Rob Patridge; Mgr. Harold A. Anderson; Rcdr. Kathleen Ishiara; Fin. Dir. Jon Jalali; Muni. Judge William Haberlach.

Merrill, Klamath, PO Box 487, 97633; 541-798-5808; Fax: 541-798-0145; 835, 4,064', 1903. Named for settler Nathan S. Merrill.

Mayor Joan Loper; Council: Richard Bement, Greg Matthews, Denise Woohouse; Rcdr./Treas. Cindy Slaton.

Metolius, Jefferson, 636 Jefferson Ave., 97742; 541-546-5533; Fax: 541-546-8809; 640, 2,530', 1913. An Indian word meaning either "white fish" or "stinking fish."

Mayor Douglas Dunlap; Council: Kay Call, Ray Dulaney, Glenn Eidemiller, Carol Harden, Kathie Rohde, Henrietta Spees; Rcdr./Treas./Muni. Judge Deanna L. Olin.

Mill City, Linn/Marion, PO Box 256, 97360; 503-897-2302; Fax: 503-897-3499; 1,640, 829', 1947. Named, when founded, for the mill located in the community.

Mayor Mary L. Smith; Council: Tom Burns, Billie Foster, Ann Holaday, Bill Sanderson, one vacancy; Rcdr. Roel Lundquist.

Millersburg, Linn, 4222 NE Old Salem Rd., 97321; 541-928-4523; Fax: 541-928-8945; 740, 222', 1974. Named for Isaac Miller, early pioneer.

Mayor Clayton Wood; Council: Skip Harris, Sharon Henschel, Barry Holsworth (also Fin. Dir.), Dennis Sadowsky; Rcdr. Barbara Castillo.

Milton-Freewater, Umatilla, PO Box 6, 97862; 541-938-5531; Fax: 541-938-3924; 6,055, 1,071', 1950. Named by the merger of two communities: Milton, named by pioneer W.J. Frazier for poet, Milton; Freewater, named for the offering of free water by city fathers.

Mayor Mary Nicholson; Council: Bob Bloch, Roy Curtis, Debra Hawes, Darrell Key, Ruth Quinn, Ralph van Deurs; Mgr. William B. Elliott; Admin. Svcs. Dir. Kathleen Zaragoza; Muni. Judge Sam Tucker.

Milwaukie, Clackamas, 10722 SE Main St., 97222; 503-786-7555; Fax: 503-652-4433; 20,065, 39', 1903. Named for Milwaukee, Wis., and means "meeting place of the waters."

Mayor Craig J. Lomnicki; Council: Rob Kappa, Jean Schreiber, Carolyn Tomei, Don Trotter; Mgr. Dan R. Bartlett; Rcdr. Pat DuVal; Fin. Dir. Angus Anderson; Muni. Judge Ron Gray.

Mitchell, Wheeler, PO Box 97, 97750; 541-462-3366; Fax: 541-462-3366; 180, 2,777', 1891. Named for John Hipple Mitchell, former U.S. Senator from Oregon.

Mayor Kyle Sweet; Council: Becky Denfeld, Curtis Holt, Dan Hopper, Bob Hubbard, Bob Hudsbeth, Penny Tuter; Clk. Annette Wornell.

Molalla, Clackamas, PO Box 248, 97038; 503-829-6855; Fax: 503-829-3676; 4,505, 371', 1913. Named for the Molalla River and the Indian Tribe.

Mayor Mike Clarke; Council: Maurice Aho, Tom Foster, Mark Haqq, Ronda Jones, Richard Lefever, Kathleen Powers;

Admin. Harvey Barnes; Rcdr./Acctg. Clk. Melanie Helmig; Muni. Judge Rodney H. Grafe.

Monmouth, Polk, 151 W Main, 97361; 503-838-0722; Fax: 503-838-0725; 7,385, 213', 1880. Named for Monmouth, Ill.

Mayor Marc Nelson; Council: Larry Dalton, Beverly Davis, Tom Hall, Jim Herzog, Jack Scheirman, John Sparks; Mgr. Stanley J. Kenyon; Fin. Dir./Rcdr. Joan E. Howard; Muni. Judge Mark Bliven.

Monroe, Benton, PO Box 486, 97456-0486; 541-847-5176; Fax: 541-847-5177; 495, 288', 1914. Named for the 5th President, James Monroe.

Mayor Dale LaRue; Council: Floyd Billings, Larry Payne, Marilyn Seitzinger, Kenneth Skinner, Terry Thompson, Luane Waytenick; Rcdr. L. Paul Dykstra; Muni. Judge G.V. McFarland.

Monument, Grant, PO Box 426, 97864; 541-934-2025; Fax: 541-934-2025; 185, 2,000', 1947. Named for a nearby rock or mountain that resembles a pulpit or rostrum.

Mayor Ron Ford; Council: Joe Duncan, Betty (B.J.) Ford, Paul Humphreys, Ellen L. Kellogg, Jim Mael, Betty Richards; Mgr. Jacqueline Oakley.

*Moro, Sherman, PO Box 231, 97039; 541-565-3535; 295, 1,807', 1899. Named for Moro, Ill.

Mayor Eileen Moreau; Council: Cindy Ellis, Gary Lane, Ernie Moore, Marc Thompson; Admin./Rcdr./Treas. Denise Scoggins.

Mosier, Wasco, PO Box 456, 97040; 541-478-3505; Fax: 541-478-3810; 290, 112', 1914. Named for settler, Jonah H. Mosier.

Mayor Stan Hendrickson; Council: Bill Akin, Herman G. Bagge, Iva Harmon, Herbert V. Morris, Andrea Rogers, William Ward; Rcdr./Treas. Jeanne Reeves.

Mt. Angel, Marion, PO Box 960, 97362; 503-845-9291; Fax: 503-845-6261; 3,010, 168', 1893. Named by the Reverend Father Adelhelm Odermatt, O.S.B., for Engelberg, Switzerland.

Mayor Tom Bolton; Council: Michael Donohue, Gerald Lauzon, Lee Layman, Gerry Moore, Mike Unger, Deanna Verboort; Admin./Rcdr. Richard Van Orman; Muni. Judge Janice Zyryanoff.

Mt. Vernon, Grant, PO Box 647, 97865; 541-932-4688; Fax: 541-932-4688; 645, 2,871', 1948. Named for a prized black stallion.

Mayor Susan Newstetter; Council: Shirley Andrews, Duane Davey, Gene Emery, Jeanie Ganty; Rcdr. Judi Driskell; Clk. Jan Lowry.

Myrtle Creek, Douglas, PO Box 940, 97457; 541-863-3171; Fax: 541-863-6690; 3,410, 640', 1893. Named for the groves of Oregon myrtle in the vicinity.

Mayor Bob Cotterell; Council: Jeredith Bartley, Kenneth Brouillard, Daniel Jocoy, Greg Leming, Ronald March; Admin. Joseph Wolf; Rcdr. Charity Hays; Muni. Judge Kenneth Madison.

Myrtle Point, Coos, 424 5th St., 97458; 541-572-2626; Fax: 541-572-3838; 2,730, 90', 1887. Named for the abundance of myrtle trees and the geographical location.

Mayor Ranelle Allen-Morris; Council: David Brunsman, Marty Klier, Christopher Long, Anthony Mattoon, Carolyn Prola, Bob Thomas; Mgr. Richard Meyers.

Nehalem, Tillamook, PO Box 143, 97131; 503-368-5627; Fax: 503-368-4175; 235, 8', 1899. Named for the Nehalem Indians.

Mayor William Lee Dillard; Council: Shirley Kalkhoven, Vern Scovell, Christopher Shepherd, Dale Stockton; Admin. Asst. Margaret Stoltenberg; Mgr./Rcdr. C. Merlin Brown.

Newberg, Yamhill, 414 E First St., 97132; 503-538-9421; Fax: 503-537-5013; Web: www.gfc.edu/newberg/newberg.html; 16,160, 175', 1889. Named by Sebastian Brutscher, for Newburgh, Germany. SC: Wadayama, Japan.

Mayor Donna Proctor; Council: Roger Currier, Alfred Howe, Donna McCain, Deborah Sumner, Lisa Thomas, Robert Weaver; Mgr. Duane R. Cole; Fin. Dir. Katherine Tri; Muni. Judge Robert Thompson.

*Newport, Lincoln, 810 SW Alder St., 97365; 541-265-5331; Fax: 541-574-0609; 9,785, 134', 1882. Named for Newport, R.I. SC: Mombetsu, Japan.

Mayor Mark Jones; Council: Dene Bateman, Rich Belloni, Mark McConnell, Dave Miller, Peggy Sabanskas, Doug Updenkelder; Mgr. Sam I. Sasaki Jr.; Rcdr./Fin. Dir. Patricia P. Bearden.

North Bend, Coos, PO Box B, 97459; 541-756-8500; Fax: 541-756-8527; Web: www.coos.or.us/~nbend; 9,885, 41', 1903. Named by Capt. Asa Simpson, founder, and son, L.J. Simpson, for its location on the "north bend" of Coos Bay.

Mayor Timm Slater; Council: Dale Bishop, Mike Erbele, Lee Golder, Doug Inman, Clair Jones, Rick Wetherell; Admin. Leroy Blodgett; Rcdr. Terri Turi; Fin. Dir. Carol Bender.

North Plains, Washington, PO Box 537, 31360 NW Commercial St., 97133; 503-647-5555; Fax: 503-647-2031; 1,470, 176', 1963. Named for the plains located in the northern part of the Tualatin Valley.

Mayor Robert Kindel; Council: Henry Drexel, Herbert Hirst, Robert King, Sandra McCuen, Cheri Olson, Ann Stearns; Rcdr. Vickie L. Seavey; Fin. Dir. Karen-Lee Stolte.

A lone windmill stands watch over fields in Gilliam County with a beautiful sunset as a backdrop.

Photo by Rena Kennedy.

North Powder, Union, PO Box 309, 97867; 541-898-2185; Fax: 541-898-2647; 555, 3,256', 1903. Named for the North Powder River and the sandy, or powdery ground used to describe the soil along the stream.

Mayor Shad Moe; Council: Joe Baltz, Iran Cheshire, Chris Colton, Alan Hack, two vacancies; Admin./Rcdr. Roberta Huddleston.

Nyssa, Malheur, 14 S 3rd St., 97913; 541-372-2264; Fax: 541-372-2377; 2,970, 2,178', 1903. Probably named for the Greek town Messene in Messenia, which was once known as Nissi, or possibly for early sheep farming—New York Stock Shipping Association (NYSSA).

Mayor J. Robert Shuster; Council: Richard Adams, Pat Brewer, Dave Hixson, Charles Kitamura, Alicia Shell, Terry Thompson; Mgr. Gordon Zimmerman; Clk. Hilda Contreras.

Oakland, Douglas, PO Box 117, 97462; 541-459-4531; Fax: 541-459-4472; 870, 430', 1878. Named for the oak trees that were so plentiful in the area.

Mayor Jack Smith; Council: Rae Bratton, Roberta Carson, Richard Fuller, Mary Jo Smith; Rcdr. Dan Altman.

Oakridge, Lane, PO Box 385, 97463; 541-782-2258; Fax: 541-782-2250; 3,200, 1,209', 1935. Name describes topography and surrounding timber cover.

Mayor Richard W. Culbertson; Council: Sue Bond, Terry Callahan, Cheryl Dyer, Frank Fay, Don Hampton, Kathy Trenery; Rcdr./Fin. Dir. Sharon S. O'Brien; Admin. Mike McAlvage; Muni. Judge Robert Peterson.

Ontario, Malheur, 444 SW 4th St., 97914; 541-889-7684; Fax: 541-889-7121; Email: ontario@cyberhighway.net; 10,290, 2,140', 1899. Named for Ontario, Canada, at the request of James Virtue. SC: Sayama, Japan.

Mayor Robert Switzer; Council: Nancy Biechler, Don Forsyth, Pat McCoshum, Joe Mollahan, Bill Peterson, David Sullivan; Mgr. Hal Schilling; Rcdr./Treas./Fin. Dir. Janice Victoria.

*Oregon City, Clackamas, 320 Warner Milne Rd., PO Box 351, 97045; 503-657-0891; Fax: 503-657-3339; 20,410, 55', 1844. Named by Dr. John McLoughlin, chief factor of the Hudson's Bay Co. SC: Tateshina, Japan.

Mayor Daniel W. Fowler; Commissioners: Edward Allick, Jack Lynch, Douglas L. Neeley, Timothy J. Powell; Mgr.

Charles Leeson; Rcdr. Jean K. Elliott; Fin. Off. David Wimmer.

Paisley, Lake, PO Box 100, 97636; 541-943-3173; 345, 4,369', 1911. Named by Charles Mitchell Innes after his home town of Paisley, Scotland.

Mayor Dwayne Kemry; Council: Bob Davis, Addie Moore, Dennis O'Leary, Ron Ropp; Rcdr./Treas. Theresa Vickerman.

*Pendleton, Umatilla, PO Box 190, 97801; 541-276-1811; Fax: 541-276-1811; Email: llehman@orednet.org; 15,900, 1,068', 1880. Named for George Hunt Pendleton, Democratic candidate for Vice President in 1864. SC: Haramachi City, Japan.

Mayor Robert E. Ramig; Council: Carolyn Anderson, John Brenne, Bob Ehmann, Phillip Houk, Marilyn Howell, Allan Pinkerton, Steve Taylor, Connie Wright; Mgr. Larry Lehman; Rcdr. Judi Zoske; Muni. Judge Robert Ridgway.

Philomath, Benton, 980 Applegate St., 97370; 541-929-6148; Fax: 541-929-3044; 3,300, 279', 1882. Named for Philomath College and Greek meaning "a lover of learning."

Mayor Van Hunsaker; Council: Mike Crocker, Marv Durham, Guy March, Dan McCabe, Juanita Ross, Marilyn Slizeski; Mgr. Randy Kugler; Rcdr. Terri Phillips; Fin. Dir. Joan Swanson; Muni. Judge Mark Donahue.

Phoenix, Jackson, PO Box 666, 97535; 541-535-1955; Fax: 541-535-5769; 3,730, 1,520', 1911. Named by Sylvester Wait, owner of a flour mill and agent for the Phoenix Insurance Co. of Hartford, Conn.

Mayor Larry Parducci; Council: Pat Burton, Dale Draper, J. Allen Harris, Mary Jane Koelle, Diana Rasmussen, one vacancy; Rcdr./Treas. Betty S. Smith; Muni. Judge James Wickre.

Pilot Rock, Umatilla, PO Box 130, 97868; 541-443-2811; Fax: 541-443-2253; 1,570, 1,637', 1912. Named for a large bluff of basalt near the community.

Mayor John R. Standley; Council: Virginia Carnes, Bob Deno, W.E. Prosser, Scott Sager, Bill Sanders, Dan Schademan; Rcdr. Jackie I. Carey; Muni. Judge Ron Pahl.

Port Orford, Curry, PO Box 310, 97465; 503-332-3681; Fax: 541-332-3830; 1,050, 59', 1935. Named for George, Earl of Orford, by Capt. George Vancouver.

Mayor Delaine Kennedy; Council: Martha W. Weaver Britell, Ralph Donaldson, Carl Eskelson, George

Kennedy, Tim Sparks, Bob Warring; Mgr. Dotti Myers; Rcdr. Norma House.

*Portland, Multnomah/Washington/ Clackamas, 1220 SW 5th Ave., 97204; 503-823-4000; Fax: 503-823-3588; Email: mayorkatz@ci.portland.or.us; Web: www.ci.portland.or.us; 503,000, 77', 1851. Named for Portland, Maine, by Francis W. Pettygrove. SC: Ashkelon, Israel; Corinto, Nicaragua; Guadalajara, Mexico; Kaohsiung, Taiwan; Khabarovsk, Russia; Sapporo, Japan; Suzhou, China; Ulsan, Korea; Mutare, Zimbabwe.

Mayor Vera Katz; Commissioners: Jim Francesconi, Charlie Hales, Gretchen Kafoury, Erik Sten; Aud. Barbara Clark; Fin. Dir./Admin. Tim Grewe.

Powers, Coos, PO Box 250, 97466; 541-439-3331; Fax: 541-439-5555; 695, 286', 1945. Named for Albert H. Powers, lumberman.

Mayor Mearl McDaniels Jr.; Council: Thea Blondell, Joann Brown, Mike Byrd, Bill Holland, Ken Mueller, Dick Wallace; Rcdr. Susan Chauncey.

Prairie City, Grant, PO Box 370, 97869; 541-820-3605; 1,180, 3,539', 1891. A descriptive name that quite accurately portrays the community.

Mayor Donald R. Welch; Council: Marvin Casebeer, Roger McKinley, Paul N. McPherren, Kevin Purnell, Kellie Reid, Paul Woodworth; Rcdr. Zelma Woods.

Prescott, Columbia, 72742 Blakely St., Rainier 97048; 503-556-8440; Fax: 503-556-4139; 60, 26', 1947. Named for Prescott machinery in the mill.

Mayor Rebecca Partlow; Council: Dan Carter, Alex Hill, James Larson, Earl Partlow; Rcdr. Donna Balcun; Fin. Dir. Terry Allen.

*Prineville, Crook, 400 E 3rd St., 97754; 541-447-5627; Fax: 541-447-5628; 6,230, 2,868', 1880. Named for merchant Barney Prine.

Mayor Paul Capell; Council: Gerald Blank, Scott Cooper, Hugh Dragich, Ann Graf, Dorless Reid, Karole Stockton; Mgr. Henry Hartley.

Rainier, Columbia, PO Box 100, 97048; 503-556-7301; Fax: 503-556-2839; 1,755, 23', 1885. Named for Mt. Rainier, which was named for Rear Adm. Peter Rainier of the Royal Navy.

Mayor Chuck Eddings; Council: Mike Avent, Cathi Erickson, Cher Fillman, Fred Forrest, Bette Lang, Steve Martin, Kenneth Worthington; Admin. Chad Olsen; Rcdr. Randy Reed; Muni. Judge Charles A. Wardle.

Redmond, Deschutes, PO Box 726, 716 SW Evergreen, 97756; 541-923-7710; Fax: 541-548-0706; Email: redmond@bendnet.com; 11,175, 2,996', 1910. Named for settler Frank T. Redmond.

Mayor Jerry Thackery; Council: Jan Anderson, Duane Gilbert, Bob Green, Michael Newell, Randy Povey, Elaine Young; Mgr. Joe Hannan; Fin. Dir. David Reeves; Rcdr. Nancy Blankenship.

Reedsport, Douglas, 451 Winchester Ave., 97467; 541-271-3603; Fax: 541-271-2809; Email: reedsport@presys.com; 4,860, 10', 1919. Named for pioneer Alfred W. Reed.

Mayor Ted Walters; Council: Bob Cline, Dennis Conger, Dale Harris, M.D., Tom Hedgepeth, Cal Henry, Jim Wells; Interim Mgr./Muni. Judge John D. Cable.

Richland, Baker, PO Box 266, 97870; 541-893-6141; 185, 2,213', 1917. Named by W.R. Usher, for the character of the soil.

Mayor Dreyfus D. Graven; Council: Ed Edwards, Nancy Gover, Dee Large, Pat Lattin, Fred Riggs, Marvin Schaber Jr.; Rcdr. Geraldine Stevens; Muni. Judge Teresa Stelting.

Riddle, Douglas, PO Box 143, 97469; 541-874-2571; Fax: 541-874-2625; 1,170, 706', 1893. Named for settler William H. Riddle.

Mayor William G. Duckett; Council: Roger Beebe, Leroy R. Broggi, Jackie Nelson, Brian Parret, Paul Parret, Greg Stratton; Rcdr. Darlene Weakley.

Rivergrove, Clackamas/Washington, PO Box 1104, Lake Oswego 97035; 503-639-6919; Fax: 503-639-6919; 300, 132', 1971. Named for the Tualatin River on the south, and the old Lake Grove area on the north.

Mayor Sue Salch; Council: Billie Cottingham, Andrew Klossner, Rosalie Morrison, Vivian Scheans; Rcdr. Tami Morrison.

Rockaway Beach, Tillamook, PO Box 5, 97136; 503-355-2291; Fax: 503-355-8221; Email: rockawaybeach@oregoncoast.com; 1,195, 17', 1942. Named for Rockaway, Long Island, N.Y.

Mayor Terry Watts; Council: Sunny Burr, Toni Hatfield, David May, Keith Ware; Mgr./Muni. Judge Don L. Mason; Rcdr. Joanne L. Dickinson.

Rogue River, Jackson, PO Box 1137, 97537; 541-582-4401; Fax: 541-582-0937; 1,965, 1,001', 1911. Named for the Rogue River.

A goose surveys the pastoral scenery in a quiet spot along the Rogue River. Photo by Rex Eipper.

Mayor Dick Handbury; Council: Ron Breshears, Bill Evans, Leigh Lucas, Glenn Martin, Earl Shamblin, Paul Thompson; Admin./Rcdr./Treas. Leahnette M. York; Muni. Judge Jim Hall.

*Roseburg, Douglas, 900 SE Douglas Ave., 97470; 541-672-7701; Fax: 541-673-2856; 19,720, 479', 1872. Named for settler Aaron Rose. SC: Shobu, Japan.

Mayor Jeri Kimmel; Council: Phil Gale, Randolph Garrison, Dan Hern, Susie Osborn, Tom Ryan, Russell Schilling, Diane Simas, Verna Ward; Mgr. Randy A. Wetmore; Rcdr. Sheila R. Cox; Fin. Dir. C. Lance Colley; Muni. Judge Kenneth Madison.

Rufus, Sherman, PO Box 27, 97050; 541-739-2321; 290, 180', 1965. Named for settler Rufus C. Wallis.

Mayor James Ritter; Council: Lynda Cool, Clifford Jett, Homer Mooney, Karen Wentz; Rcdr. Elaine Turney.

*Salem, Marion/Polk, 555 Liberty St. SE, 97301; 503-588-6255; Fax: 503-588-6354; 120,835, 154', 1857. Probably named for Salem, Mass. The Indian name was Chemeketa, which is said to have meant meeting or resting place. SC: Kawagoe, Japan; Salem, India; Simferopol, of the former USSR; Vaxjo, Sweden.

Mayor Mike Swaim; Council: Bill Burgess, Thomas DeSouza, David Glennie, Tim Grenz, Ann Gavin Sample,

Don Scott, Glenn Wheeler, Paul Wulf; Mgr. Larry Wacker; Rcdr. Jean Lay; Fin. Dir. George Shelley; Muni. Judge Frank Gruber.

Sandy, Clackamas, 39250 Pioneer Blvd., 97055; 503-668-5533; Fax: 503-668-8714; Email: 103022.57@compuserve.com; Web: www.teleport.com/~lene; 4,895, 1,000', 1913. Named for the Sandy River.

Mayor Linda Malone; Council: Don Allen, Art Blaisdell, Verne Buhler, Mike Hammons, Margaret Holman, Caren Topliff; Mgr. Scott Lazenby; Rcdr./Fin. Dir. Carol James; Muni. Judge Karen Brisbin.

Scappoose, Columbia, PO Box P, 97056; 503-543-7146; Fax: 503-543-7182; 4,130, 61', 1921. Named "gravelly plains" by the Chinook Indians.

Mayor Rita Bernhard; Council: Ken Bailey, Glenn Dorschler, Jesse Exton, Dan Linhares, David Weber; Mgr. Don Otterman; Rcdr. Donna Gedlich; Fin. Dir. Sharon Romine; Muni. Judge Donald Jimerson.

Scio, Linn, PO Box 37, 97374; 503-394-3342; 665, 317', 1866. Named for Scio, Ohio.

Mayor Anthony Lagler; Council: Dean Ferguson, Roger Gaither, Michael Harbison, Carolyn Nunn, Albert Porter, George VanAgtmael; Admin./Rcdr. Joyce Morse; Muni. Judge Joanne Bilyeu.

Scotts Mills, Marion, PO Box C, 97375; 503-873-2065; 310, 420', 1916. Named for Robert and Thomas Scott, sawmill and flour mill owners.

Mayor Bruce Knutson; Council: Phaedra Dibala, Cindy Engel, Larry Martin, Phillip Martin, Michael Pinkham, Rodney Saunders; Rcdr. Katherina Martin; Treas. Margaret Doran.

Seaside, Clatsop, 989 Broadway, 97138; 503-738-5511; Fax: 503-738-5514; 5,860, 13', 1899. Named for Ben Holladay's famous hostelry and resort, the Seaside House.

Mayor Oliver Vernor; Council: Rosemary Baker-Monaghan, Marilynn Blacketer, Dan Bouchard, Janet Perkins, Doug Ray, Kathleen Wysong; Mgr. Gene Miles; Rcdr./Fin. Dir. Mark Winstanley.

Seneca, Grant, 106 A St., 97873; 541-542-2161; Fax: 541-542-2161; 230, 4,666', 1970. Named for Judge Seneca Smith of Portland.

Mayor Keith Schatz; Council: Diane Browning, Lorraine Griffith, Brad Smith, Cyndy Woodall; Rcdr. Kristin Long.

Shady Cove, Jackson, PO Box 1210, 97539; 541-878-2225; Fax: 541-878-2226; 2,135, 1,350', 1972. Name descriptive of a little nook on the river bank.

Mayor Robert T. Anderson; Council: Victor Corchero, Lois Holland, Wendell McCaleb, Lloyd Thetford; Interim Rcdr. Arlene M. Cooper; Muni. Judge Robert E. Bluth.

Shaniko, Wasco, PO Box 17, 97057; 541-489-3317; 30, 3,340', 1901. Named for pioneer settler August Sherneckau.

Mayor Jean Farrell; Council: Charolette Hedrick, Jim Hogan, Richard Roberts, Shirley Stevens; Rcdr. Marsha Hamilton.

Sheridan, Yamhill, 120 SW Mill St., 97378; 503-843-2347; Fax: 503-843-3661; 4,800, 189', 1880. Named for Philip Henry Sheridan.

Mayor Bob Jordan; Council: Ted Aaron, Les DeHart, Frank Johnson, Tonya Mishler, Bill Stemmerman, Bob White; Mgr. Michael Sauerwein; Treas. Joel Wade; Rcdr. Opal Hamilton.

Sherwood, Washington, 20 NW Park St., 97140; 503-625-5522; Fax: 503-625-5524; 6,600, 193', 1893. Named for Sherwood Forest in Nottingham, England.

Mayor Ronald Tobias; Council: Jane Aamold, William Boyle, Mark Cottle, Thomas Krause; Fin. Dir. Polly

Blankenbaker; Mgr./Rcdr. Jon Bormet; Muni. Judge Jack Morris.

Siletz, Lincoln, PO Box 318, 97380; 541-444-2521; 1,170, 130', 1946. Named for the Siletz Indians.

Mayor Daniel E. Rilatos; Council: Elizabeth Bynum, Raymond Goodell, John Meyer, Daniel Smith; Rcdr. Marie Johnson.

Silverton, Marion, 306 S Water St., 97381; 503-873-5321; Fax: 503-873-3210; Web: www.teleport.com/~cast; 6,565, 249', 1885. Named for its location on Silver Creek.

Mayor Kenneth J. Hector; Council: Joeine Barrett, Antonia Jenkins, Patrick Nelson, Lois Riopelle, Otto Stadeli, Scott Sword; Mgr./Rcdr. David Meriwether; Fin. Off. Ben Durano; Muni. Judge Janice Zyryanoff.

Sisters, Deschutes, PO Box 39, 150 N Fir, 97759; 541-549-6022; Fax: 541-549-0561; 775, 3,182', 1946. Named for the nearby peaks, the Three Sisters.

Mayor William D. Moyer; Council: Jean Cooper, Gary Miller, Kathy Pittman, Sheryl Whent; Admin. Barbara J. Warren; Rcdr. Bernadette Sorensen.

Sodaville, Linn, 30723 Sodaville Rd., 97355; 541-258-8882; Fax: 541-258-8882 (call first); 260, 125', 1880. Named for a cold mineral spring situated nearby.

Mayor Charles Mullenix; Council: Marlene Atchley, Grace Brigham, Karen Corrington, Roger Perry; Rcdr. Penny Seward.

Spray, Wheeler, PO Box 83, 97874; 541-468-3391; Fax: 541-468-2044; 160, 1,772', 1958. Named for Mary E. and John Fremont Spray.

Mayor Marvin Britt; Council: J.R. Adams, James Lee Adams, Frank Cecil, Walter Fischer; Rcdr. Candy Humphreys.

Springfield, Lane, 225 5th St., 97477; 541-726-3700; Fax: 541-726-2363; 50,140, 459', 1885. Named for a natural spring in an open field.

Mayor Bill Morrisette; Council: Anne Ballew, Terry Beyer, Stu Burge, Norm Dahlquist, Maureen Maine, Greg Shaver; Mgr. Mike Kelly; Rcdr. Eileen Stein; Fin. Dir. Bob Duey.

*St. Helens, Columbia, PO Box 278, 97051; 503-397-6272; Fax: 503-397-4016; 8,300, 42', 1889. Named for Mt. St. Helens, which was named in honor of Baron Saint Helens, ambassador to Spain.

Mayor Donald L. Kallberg; Council: Joseph Corsiglia, James Huff, Chris Iverson, Randy Peterson; Admin. Brian D. Little; Fin. Dir. Marilyn Peterson; Muni. Judge Wallace E. Thompson.

St. Paul, Marion, PO Box 7, 97137; 541-633-4971; Fax: 503-633-4972; 355, 169', 1901. Named by Archbishop Francis Norbert Blanchet for the apostle Paul.

Mayor Joe McKay; Council: Michael Bernard, Jack Boedigheimer, Sam McKillip; Rcdr. Barbara Boedigheimer; Treas. Renee Rostel.

Stanfield, Umatilla, PO Box 369, 97875; 541-449-3831; Fax: 541-449-3264; 1,755, 592', 1910. Named for Robert N. Stanfield, U.S. Senator from Oregon.

Mayor Thomas McCann; Council: Gene Jorgenson, Virginia Miller, Rudy Olbrich, Charlotte Rauch, Don Tyrrell, Val Whitehead; Clk. Kathy Davis; Admin./Rcdr. Gerald Carlson; Muni. Judge Gregory Pierce.

Stayton, Marion, 362 N 3rd Ave., 97383; 503-769-3425; Fax: 503-769-1456; 6,035, 448', 1901. Named for settler Drury S. Stayton.

Mayor Willmer Van Vleet; Council: Daniel Brammer, Daphne Girod, Lawrence Grames, L. Lee Hazelwood, Henry Porter; Admin. Thomas L. Barthel; Fin. Dir. Erna Barnett.

Sublimity, Marion, PO Box 146, 97385; 503-769-5475; Fax: 503-769-2206; 1,985, 547', 1903. Named for the sublime scenery in the hills around the town.

Mayor Charles Henry; Council: H.D. Denson, Charles Lindsey, Wayne Palmquist, Dale Rubel; Rcdr. Sue Bernt.

Summerville, Union, PO Box 92, 97876; 541-534-2035; 150, 2,705', 1885. Named for Alexander Summerville.

Mayor Cecil McDonald; Council: Ron Caswell, George Gooder, Nancy Johnson, Ron Kee; Rcdr. Louanne McDonald.

Sumpter, Baker, PO Box 68, 97877; 541-894-2314; Fax: 541-894-2314; 175, 4,424', 1901. Named for Fort Sumter, S.C.

Mayor Norm Thorton; Council: Wes Christensen, Ona Smith, Teri Strimple, Myron Woodley; Rcdr. Toni Thompson.

Sutherlin, Douglas, PO Box 459, 97479; 541-459-2856; Fax: 541-459-9363; 5,995, 518', 1911. Named for Fendel Sutherlin.

Mayor Joe Mongiovi; Council: Jeff Admire, Dan Altman, Roger Horton, Troy Johnson, Larry Lemp, Bruce Sconce; Mgr. Don Moore; Rcdr. Vicki Luther; Fin. Dir. Jim Krueger.

Sweet Home, Linn, 1140 12th Ave., 97386; 541-367-5128; Fax: 541-367-5113; 7,450, 537', 1893. Name first applied in the form of Sweet Home Valley.

Mayor Robert Whitfield; Council: Jim Bean, Robert Danielson, Craig Fentiman, Jim Gourley, Tim McQueary, Mona Waibel; Mgr./Rcdr. James D. Corl.

Talent, Jackson, PO Box 445, 97540-0445; 541-535-1566; Fax: 541-535-7423; 4,765, 1,635', 1911. Named for settler A.P. Talent.

Mayor Frank Falsarella; Council: Joi Riley, Lisa Shapiro, Don Steyskal, Marian Telerski, Bill Waugh, Tessa West; Muni. Judge James Wricker.

Tangent, Linn, PO Box 251, 97389; 541-928-1020; 850, 248', 1893. Named for the long stretch of straight railroad track to the north and south.

Mayor Steve Nofziger; Council: Rebecca Kinyon, Mondalee Lengkeek, Don Stockton, Brad Tedrow; Rcdr. Georgia Edwards.

*The Dalles, Wasco, 313 Court St., 97058; 541-296-5481; Fax: 541-296-6906; 11,460, 98', 1857. Named from the French word "dalle," meaning flagstone and was applied to the narrows of the Columbia River.

Mayor David R. Beckley; Council: Mary Ann Davis, Bill Gosiak, Dee Hill, Bob McFadden, Robb Van Cleave; Mgr. Margaret M. Renard; Fin. Dir. Robert G. Moody Jr.; Clk. Julie Krueger.

Tigard, Washington, 13125 SW Hall Blvd., 97223; 503-639-4171; Fax: 503-684-7297; Email: cathy@ci.tigard.or.us; Web: www.ci.tigard.or.us; 35,925, 169', 1961. Named for settler Wilson M. Tigard.

Mayor Jim Nicoli; Council: Paul Hunt, Brian Moore, Bob Rohlf, Ken Scheckla; Admin. William Monahan; Rcdr. Catherine Wheatley; Fin. Dir. Wayne Lowry.

*Tillamook, Tillamook, 210 Laurel Ave., 97141; 503-842-2472; Fax: 503-842-3445; 4,275, 22', 1891. Named for the tribe of Salish Indians. SC: Pendleton, Oregon.

Mayor J. Robert McPheeters; Council: Bill Beck, John Coopersmith, Sherry Duncan, Bert Gustafson, Michael Hanback, Joe Martin; Mgr. Michael Mahoney; Rcdr./Muni. Judge Joanne Boggs.

Toledo, Lincoln, PO Box 220, 97391; 541-336-2247; Fax: 541-336-3512; 3,465, 64', 1905. Named for Toledo, Ohio.

Water covered the city of Tualatin during the February 1996 flood, making roads impassable for days.

Photo by Eric VanderHouwen.

Mayor Sharon Branstiter; Council: Jim Chambers, Andrew Dobmeier, Karen Gerttula, Glen Mackenroth, Howard Richards, Bob Zimmerman; Rcdr. Renee Ballinger; Mgr. Michael G. Dowsett.

Troutdale, Multnomah, 104 SE Kibling Ave., 97060; 503-665-5175; Fax: 503-667-6403; Email: feedback@ci.troutdale.or.us; 12,750, 94', 1907. Named from the small dale with a fish pond that Capt. John Harlow stocked with trout.

Mayor Paul Thalhofer; Council: Doug Daoust, Jim Kight, Raymond Regelein, Dave Ripma, Pat Smith, Bruce Thompson; Admin. Erik V. Kvarsten; Fin. Dir. Robert Gazewood; Rcdr. George Martinez.

Tualatin, Clackamas/Washington, PO Box 369, 97062; 503-692-2000; Fax: 503-692-5421; 20,040, 123', 1913. Named for the Tualatin River.

Mayor Lou Ogden; Council: Helen Cain, Kathy Forrest, Greg Green, Richard Hager, Sue Lamb, Tony Weller; Mgr. Steve Wheeler; Fin. Dir. Nancy Gritta.

Turner, Marion, PO Box 456, 97392; 503-743-2155; Fax: 503-743-2140; 1,330, 285', 1905. Named for Henry L. Turner who platted the town.

Mayor Steve Littrell; Council: Richard Bates, Michael Dennis, Diana Maul, Robert McWherter, Glenn Pennebaker, Richard Stutheit; Admin. Charles Spies; Rcdr. Judith Cole.

Ukiah, Umatilla, PO Box 265, 97880; no phone; 280, 3,400', 1969. Named by E.B. Gambee for Ukiah, Calif.

Umatilla, Umatilla, PO Box 130, 97882; 541-922-3226; Fax: 541-922-5758; 3,310, 296', 1864. Named for the Umatilla River.

Mayor George Hash; Council: Alan Burk, Mary Dedrick, George Fenton Jr., Valerie Jorstad, Floyd Mathews, Karla Stuck; Admin. Bonnie Parker; Fin. Off. Dawn Greer; Rcdr. Linda Gettmann; Muni. Judge Pro-Tem Theresa Krogh.

Union, Union, PO Box 529, 97883; 541-562-5197; Fax: 541-562-5196; 1,955, 2,789', 1878. Named for patriotic reasons during the Civil War.

Mayor Susan Briggs; Council: Dick Alexander, James Bovard, Sam Hamilton, Barbara James, Ken Michrina, Jack Zimmerman; Admin. Leonard Almquist; Rcdr. Jennean Lowery; Muni. Judge Jane DeClue.

Unity, Baker, PO Box 7, 97884; 541-446-3544; 110, 4,029', 1972. Named for the amicable agreement in moving a post office.

Mayor Robert Bradford; Council: Danielle Bernard, Darren Bradford, Rance Dickson, Rob Otheim; Rcdr. Lea Anne Greenwood.

*Vale, Malheur, 252 B St. West, 97918; 541-473-3133; 1,510, 2,343', 1889. Named from the French word for valley.

Mayor Rhonda L. Bernard; Council: David Castleberry, Ethan Freeman, George Glerup, Marvin McNeill, Marsha Rodriquez; Coord./Rcdr. Joseph Wrabek; Muni. Judge Howard C. Ego

Veneta, Lane, PO Box 458, 97487; 541-935-2191; Fax: 541-935-1838; 2,845, 409', 1962. Named for Veneta Hunter, daughter of E.E. Hunter.

The new bridge which spans Alsea Bay at Waldport was built in 1991 to replace the historic bridge constructed in 1936. The Alsea Bridge Interpretive Center at the south end of the bridge provides an overview of transportation development along the Oregon Coast.

Photo by Dave Clem.

Mayor J.W. Smigley; Council: Tim Brooker, Galen Carpenter, Marion Esty, Fred Miler; Admin. Jan Wellman; Rcdr. Shirley M.J. Overed.

Vernonia, Columbia, 919 Bridge St., 97064; 503-429-5291; Fax: 503-429-4232; 2,180, 620', 1891. Named for Vernonia "Vernona," daughter of Ozias Cherrington.

Mayor Jim Jacobs; Council: Donald Amundson, Sharon Parrow, Gayle Shriver, Tim Williamson; Admin. Virgie Ries; Rcdr./Fin. Dir. Jana Borst.

Waldport, Lincoln, PO Box 1120, 97394; 541-563-3561; Fax: 541-563-5810; 1,750, 12', 1911. A combination of the German word "wald," meaning forest, and the English word "port," referring to Alsea Bay.

Mayor Phyllis Boehme; Council: Kim Lehmann, Gene Moore, Tom Pankey, Dan Sagettis, one vacancy; Mgr. Arthur J. "Bud" Schmidt.

Wallowa, Wallowa, PO Box 487, 97885; 541-886-2422; Fax: 541-886-4215; 755, 2,923', 1899. An Indian word to designate a tripod of poles used to support fish nets.

Mayor Leon Fisher; Council: Robert Lewis, Star Longley, Terri Skillings, Carlene Woolsey; Rcdr. Debbie McDaniel; Treas. Betty Conrad.

Warrenton, Clatsop, PO Box 250, 97146; 503-861-2233; Fax: 503-861-2351; 3,940, 5', 1899. Named for settler D.K. Warren.

Mayor Barbara Balensifer; Commissioners: Donell Keith Dyer, Scott Holman, Lisa R. Lamping, Leslie Newton; Mgr./Auditor Gilbert G. Gramson.

Wasco, Sherman, PO Box 26, 97065; 541-442-5515; Fax: 541-442-5001; 390, 1,271', 1898. Named for the Indian tribe.

Mayor Roy Talley; Council: Jerrine Belshe, Joyce Decker, Robert Girton, Velna Parker, Fran Tindall; Clk. Cassie Strege.

Waterloo, Linn, 31140 1st St., Lebanon 97355; 541-451-2245; Fax: 541-451-3133; 220, 410', 1893. Named by local wit John Ambler after a court decision gave a substantial victory to one party in a land dispute.

Mayor Earlene Little; Council: Greg France, Richard Paull, Mark Persons, Burton Rochefort, David B. Rounds, Lisa Rounds; Rcdr. Joyce Campbell.

West Linn, Clackamas, 22825 Willamette Falls Dr., 97068; 503-657-0331; Fax: 503-650-9041; Email: westlinn@teleport.com; Web: www.teleport.com/~westlinn; 19,960, 105', 1913. Named for Lewis F. Linn and Linn City.

Mayor Jill Thorn; Council: Dee Burch, John Jackley, Mike Kapigian, Tom Neff; Mgr. Scott A. Burgess; Rcdr. Mary Walsh; Fin. Dir. Willie Gin.

Westfir, Lane, PO Box 296, 97492; 541-782-3733; Fax: 541-782-3983; 280, 1,114', 1979. Named for the Western Lumber Co.

Mayor Phyllis Julian; Council: Myron Smith, Sheila Tilton, Nancy Vargas, Reggie Vargas; Rcdr. Elizabeth Murray.

Weston, Umatilla, PO Box 427, 97886; 541-566-3313; 680, 1,796', 1878. Named by T.T. Lieuallen for Weston, Mo.

Mayor Opal Barnett; Council: Tim Crampton, Virgil Peterson, Carolyn Rencken, one member to be appointed; Admin. Lesley Patching; Muni. Judge Katherine Dale Shafer.

Wheeler, Tillamook, PO Box 177, 97147; 503-368-5767; Fax: 503-368-4273; 375, 18', 1914. Named for lumberman Coleman H. Wheeler.

Mayor Don Brinkman; Council: Faith Dorothy, Sandy Douma, William Mullen, Joann Stillman; Rcdr. Gene Cox.

Willamina, Polk/Yamhill, PO Box 629, 97396; 503-876-2242; Fax: 503-876-1121; 1,790, 225', 1903. Named for Willamina Williams and the creek.

Mayor Twila D. Hill; Council: Leon Alger, Victor Branson, Francis Eddy, Dan Goff, Mary Lou Greb, Ralph Jenne; Rcdr./Fin. Dir. Charlene Brown; Muni. Judge William Jolley.

Wilsonville, Clackamas/Washington, 30000 SW Town Center Loop East, 97070; 503-682-1011; Fax: 503-682-1015; 10,600, 175', 1969. Named by R.V. Short for Charles Wilson, a local resident.

Mayor Charlotte Lehan; Council: Bruce Barton, John Helser, Lou MacDonald, one vacancy; Mgr. Arlene Loble; Rcdr. Sandra C. King; Fin. Dir. Gary Wallis; Muni. Judge J. Michael Gleeson.

Winston, Douglas, 201 NW Douglas Blvd., 97496; 541-679-6739; Fax: 541-679-0794; Email: winston@rosenet.net; Web: www.sova.org/winston.htm; 4,170, 534', 1955. Named for Elijah Winston, the first postmaster.

Mayor Jim McClellan; Council: Steve Smart, John Steinfelt, Gary Vess, Christine Whalen; Admin./Rcdr. Bruce Kelly.

Wood Village, Multnomah, 2055 NE 238th Dr., 97060; 503-667-6211; Email: woodvillage.com@worldnet.att.net; Mayor Donald L. Robertson; Council: Tim Fier, Karen A. Hunt, Steven Rodrigues, Janet VandeRiet; Admin. Sheila Ritz.

Woodburn, Marion, 270 Montgomery St., 97071; 503-982-5222; Fax: 503-982-5244; 15,780, 182', 1889. Named from a fire that destroyed brush and felled trees and standing timber.

Mayor Nancy A. Kirksey; Council: Mary Chadwick, Kathryn Figley, Donald Hagenauer, Richard Jennings,

Many cities and counties in Oregon now have a presence on the World Wide Web. For cities and counties with official web sites or Email addresses we have included this information at the top of their listing immediately after phone and fax numbers. Many other cities and counties also have web sites developed and maintained by other organizations such as chambers of commerce and visitors' information centers.

Oregon OnLine (www.state.or.us) has a "Communities" link which connects users to a list of web sites for cities, counties and other regional entities.

Another source of online information is the USA CityLink Project (www.usacitylink.com) which provides links to cities throughout the country.

Richard Pugh, Elida Sifuentez; Admin. Christopher Childs; Fin. Dir. Ben Gillespie; Rcdr. Mary Tennant.

Yachats, Lincoln, PO Box 345, 97498; 541-547-3565; Fax: 541-547-3063; 655, 23', 1966. Named for an Indian tribe whose name means "at the foot of the mountain."

Mayor Arthur Roberts; Council: Joel Evans, Martha Gleason, Don McDonald, Paul Plunk; Rcdr. Andrea Phelps.

Yamhill, Yamhill, PO Box 9, 97148-0009; 503-662-3511; Fax: 503-662-4589; 960, 182', 1891. Named for the Yamhill Indians and the river.

Mayor Michael Le Clair; Council: Jane Heinrich, Floyd Knope, Terry McKnight, Phillip Weddington; Admin. Terrylynn Bednarzyk; Muni. Judge Joan Williams.

Yoncalla, Douglas, PO Box 508, 97499; 541-849-2152; Fax: 541-849-2552; 980, 354', 1901. Named for a prominent bald mountain to the northwest meaning "Home of the Eagles."

Mayor Robert Lee; Council: Estella Myers, Bill Shaw, Kent Smith, Bob Stroehlen; Admin./Muni. Judge Kathleen Finley.

City Populations: 1960-1996

Population data provided by the Center for Population Research and Census; 503-725-3922

	City	% Change*	1996	1990	1980	1970	1960
1	PORTLAND	14.6	503,000	438,802	366,383	379,967	372,676
2	EUGENE	12.0	126,325	112,773	105,664	79,028	50,977
3	SALEM	12.1	120,835	107,793	89,091	68,725	49,142
4	GRESHAM	16.3	79,350	68,249	33,005	10,030	3,944
5	BEAVERTON	18.5	63,145	53,307	31,962	18,577	5,937
6	MEDFORD	21.6	57,155	47,021	39,746	28,454	24,425
7	HILLSBORO	38.6	52,105	37,598	27,664	14,675	8,232
8	SPRINGFIELD	12.3	50,140	44,664	41,621	26,874	19,616
9	CORVALLIS	10.1	49,275	44,757	40,960	35,056	20,669
10	ALBANY	25.6	37,095	29,540	26,511	18,181	12,926
11	Tigard	22.0	35,925	29,435	14,799	6,499	0
12	Lake Oswego	11.2	34,005	30,576	22,527	14,615	8,906
13	Bend	57.6	32,220	20,447	17,260	13,710	11,937
14	Keizer	25.4	27,450	21,884	0	0	0
15	McMinnville	27.9	22,880	17,894	14,080	10,125	7,656
16	Oregon City	38.9	20,410	14,698	14,673	9,176	7,996
17	Grants Pass	15.7	20,255	17,503	15,032	12,455	10,118
18	Milwaukie	7.5	20,065	18,670	17,931	16,444	9,099
19	Tualatin	36.7	20,040	14,664	7,483	750	359
20	West Linn	21.8	19,960	16,389	11,358	7,091	3,933
21	Roseburg	15.5	19,720	17,069	16,644	14,461	11,467
22	Klamath Falls	5.8	18,765	17,737	16,661	15,775	16,949
23	Ashland	13.0	18,360	16,252	14,943	12,342	9,119
24	Newberg	23.5	16,160	13,086	10,394	6,507	4,204
25	Pendleton	5.0	15,900	15,142	14,521	13,197	14,434
26	Woodburn	17.7	15,780	13,404	11,196	7,495	3,120
27	Coos Bay	2.9	15,520	15,076	14,424	13,466	7,084
28	Forest Grove	13.4	15,370	13,559	11,499	8,175	5,628
29	Troutdale	62.4	12,750	7,852	5,908	1,661	522
30	La Grande	5.5	12,415	11,766	11,354	9,645	9,014
31	Lebanon	9.5	11,995	10,950	10,413	7,277	5,858
32	Gladstone	14.3	11,605	10,152	9,500	6,254	3,854
33	The Dalles	4.0	11,460	11,021	10,820	10,423	10,493
34	Canby	27.1	11,430	8,990	7,659	3,813	2,168
35	Dallas	20.6	11,360	9,422	8,530	6,361	5,072
36	Redmond	56.0	11,175	7,165	6,452	3,721	3,340
37	Hermiston	10.0	11,050	10,047	8,408	4,893	4,402
38	Wilsonville	49.2	10,600	7,106	2,920	1,001	0
39	Central Point	37.0	10,295	7,512	6,357	4,004	2,289
40	Ontario	9.5	10,290	9,394	8,814	6,523	5,101
41	Astoria	0.6	10,130	10,069	9,996	10,244	11,239
42	Baker City	8.0	9,870	9,140	9,471	9,354	9,986
43	North Bend	2.5	9,885	9,614	9,779	8,553	7,512
44	Newport	16.0	9,785	8,437	7,519	5,188	5,344

	City	% Change*	1996	1990	1980	1970	1960
45	St. Helens	10.2	8,300	7,535	7,064	6,212	5,022
46	Cottage Grove	6.3	7,870	7,403	7,148	6,004	3,895
47	Cornelius	21.6	7,475	6,148	4,402	1,903	1,146
48	Sweet Home	8.8	7,450	6,850	6,921	3,799	3,353
49	Monmouth	17.4	7,385	6,288	5,594	5,237	2,229
50	Lincoln City	12.8	6,665	5,908	5,469	4,196	0
51	Sherwood	113.4	6,600	3,093	2,386	1,396	680
52	Silverton	16.5	6,565	5,635	5,168	4,301	3,081
53	Florence	23.8	6,400	5,171	4,411	2,246	1,642
54	Prineville	16.3	6,230	5,355	5,276	4,101	3,263
55	Milton-Freewater	9.4	6,055	5,533	5,086	4,105	4,110
56	Stayton	20.4	6,035	5,011	4,396	3,170	2,108
57	Sutherlin	19.4	5,995	5,020	4,560	3,070	2,452
58	Seaside	9.3	5,860	5,359	5,193	4,402	3,877
59	Brookings	22.7	5,400	4,400	3,384	2,720	2,637
60	Hood River	10.3	5,110	4,632	4,329	3,991	3,657
61	Independence	12.7	4,985	4,425	4,024	2,594	1,930
62	Sandy	17.9	4,895	4,152	2,905	1,544	1,147
63	Reedsport	1.3	4,860	4,796	4,984	4,039	2,998
64	Sheridan	20.6	4,800	3,979	2,249	1,881	1,763
65	Madras	38.5	4,770	3,443	2,235	1,689	1,515
66	Talent	45.5	4,765	3,274	2,577	1,389	868
67	Fairview	95.3	4,670	2,391	1,749	1,045	578
68	Molalla	23.4	4,505	3,651	2,992	2,005	1,501
69	Tillamook	6.8	4,275	4,001	3,991	3,968	4,244
70	Coquille	2.5	4,225	4,121	4,481	4,437	4,730
71	Winston	10.5	4,170	3,773	3,359	2,468	2,395
72	Scappoose	17.0	4,130	3,529	3,213	1,859	923
73	Junction City	12.1	4,115	3,670	3,320	2,373	1,614
74	Warrenton	47.0	3,940	2,681	2,493	1,825	1,717
75	Phoenix	15.2	3,730	3,239	2,309	1,287	769
76	Eagle Point	19.8	3,605	3,008	2,764	1,241	752
77	Toledo	9.2	3,465	3,174	3,151	2,818	3,053
78	Myrtle Creek	11.3	3,410	3,063	3,365	2,733	2,231
79	Umatilla	8.7	3,310	3,046	3,199	679	617
80	Philomath	10.6	3,300	2,983	2,673	1,688	1,359
81	Oakridge	4.5	3,200	3,063	3,680	3,422	1,973
82	Mt. Angel	8.4	3,010	2,778	2,876	1,973	1,428
83	Wood Village	6.4	2,995	2,814	2,253	1,533	822
84	Nyssa	13.0	2,970	2,629	2,862	2,620	2,611
85	Burns	0.8	2,935	2,913	3,579	3,293	3,523
86	Veneta	12.9	2,845	2,519	2,449	1,377	0
87	Happy Valley	86.0	2,825	1,519	1,499	1,392	0
88	Bandon	24.6	2,760	2,215	2,311	1,832	1,653
89	Myrtle Point	0.7	2,730	2,712	2,859	2,511	2,886
90	Creswell	11.7	2,715	2,431	1,770	1,199	760
91	Lakeview	5.1	2,655	2,526	2,770	2,705	3,260
92	Aumsville	56.7	2,585	1,650	1,432	590	300

	City	% Change*	1996	1990	1980	1970	1960
93	Boardman	86.0	2,580	1,387	1,261	192	153
94	Dundee	50.3	2,500	1,663	1,223	588	318
95	Harrisburg	13.7	2,205	1,939	1,881	1,311	939
96	Hubbard	16.2	2,185	1,881	1,640	975	526
97	Vernonia	20.6	2,180	1,808	1,785	1,643	1,089
98	King City	4.6	2,155	2,060	1,853	1,427	0
99	Jefferson	18.8	2,145	1,805	1,702	936	716
100	Shady Cove	58.0	2,135	1,351	1,097	0	0
101	Gold Beach	36.8	2,115	1,546	1,515	1,554	1,762
102	Estacada	2.4	2,065	2,016	1,419	1,164	957
103	Jacksonville	6.8	2,025	1,896	2,030	1,611	1,172
104	Enterprise	6.0	2,020	1,905	2,003	1,680	1,932
105	Sublimity	33.1	1,985	1,491	1,077	634	490
106	Rogue River	11.7	1,965	1,759	1,308	841	520
107	Union	5.8	1,955	1,847	2,062	1,531	1,490
108	John Day	5.7	1,940	1,836	2,012	1,566	1,520
109	Clatskanie	15.1	1,875	1,629	1,648	1,286	797
110	Lafayette	38.9	1,795	1,292	1,215	786	553
111	Willamina	4.3	1,790	1,717	1,749	1,193	960
112	Rainier	4.8	1,755	1,674	1,655	1,731	1,152
	Stanfield	11.9	1,755	1,568	1,568	891	745
113	Waldport	9.7	1,750	1,595	1,274	700	667
114	Dayton	14.4	1,745	1,526	1,409	949	673
115	Elgin	8.1	1,715	1,586	1,701	1,375	1,315
116	Mill City	5.5	1,640	1,555	1,565	1,451	1,289
117	Lakeside	13.4	1,630	1,437	1,453	0	0
118	Durham	110.6	1,575	748	707	410	0
119	Pilot Rock	6.2	1,570	1,478	1,630	1,612	1,695
120	Hines	5.0	1,525	1,452	1,632	1,407	1,207
121	Vale	6.4	1,510	1,419	1,558	1,448	1,491
122	Heppner	4.8	1,480	1,412	1,498	1,429	1,661
123	Carlton	14.0	1,470	1,289	1,302	1,126	951
	North Plains	47.4	1,470	997	715	690	0
124	Columbia City	46.1	1,465	1,003	678	537	423
125	Brownsville	10.5	1,415	1,281	1,261	1,034	875
126	Cannon Beach	14.3	1,395	1,221	1,187	779	495
127	Turner	9.2	1,330	1,218	1,116	846	770
128	Cave Junction	15.5	1,300	1,126	1,023	415	248
129	Canyonville	3.8	1,265	1,219	1,288	940	1,090
130	Joseph	17.0	1,255	1,073	999	839	788
131	Dunes City	14.7	1,240	1,081	1,124	976	0
	Gold Hill	28.6	1,240	964	904	603	608
132	Gearhart	17.3	1,205	1,027	967	829	725
133	Amity	1.7	1,195	1,175	1,092	708	620
	Rockaway Beach	23.2	1,195	970	906	665	771
134	Prairie City	5.6	1,180	1,117	1,106	867	801
135	Riddle	2.4	1,170	1,143	1,265	1,042	992
	Siletz	26.3	1,170	926	1,001	596	583

	City	% Change*	1996	1990	1980	1970	1960
136	Bay City	10.0	1,130	1,027	986	898	996
137	Drain	10.3	1,115	1,011	1,148	1,204	1,052
138	Athena	10.8	1,105	997	965	872	950
139	Irrigon	47.9	1,090	737	700	261	232
140	Gervais	8.9	1,080	992	799	746	438
141	Cascade Locks	12.9	1,050	930	838	574	660
	Port Orford	2.4	1,050	1,025	1,061	1,037	1,171
142	Depoe Bay	20.1	1,045	870	723	0	0
143	Lyons	7.7	1,010	938	877	645	463
144	Yoncalla	6.6	980	919	805	675	698
145	Garibaldi	9.5	960	877	999	1,083	1,163
	Yamhill	10.7	960	867	690	516	407
146	Lowell	21.7	955	785	661	567	503
147	Falls City	14.3	935	818	804	745	653
148	Oakland	3.1	870	844	886	1,010	856
149	Island City	24.3	865	696	477	202	158
150	Tangent	52.9	850	556	478	0	0
151	Merrill	-0.2	835	837	822	722	804
152	Culver	39.5	795	570	514	407	301
	Maywood Park	1.9	795	780	845	1,230	0
153	Condon	24.4	790	635	783	973	1,149
154	Coburg	1.6	775	763	699	734	754
	Sisters	14.1	775	679	696	516	602
155	Chiloquin	12.2	755	673	778	826	945
	Manzanita	47.2	755	513	443	261	363
	Wallowa	0.9	755	748	847	811	989
156	Malin	3.4	750	725	539	486	568
157	Millersburg	3.5	740	715	562	0	0
158	Glendale	3.3	730	707	712	709	748
	Halsey	9.4	730	667	693	467	404
159	Canyon City	8.8	705	648	639	600	654
160	Powers	1.9	695	682	819	842	1,366
161	Weston	12.2	680	606	719	660	783
162	Aurora	19.0	675	567	523	306	274
163	Scio	6.7	665	623	579	447	441
164	Yachats	22.9	655	533	482	441	0
165	Mt. Vernon	19.9	645	538	569	423	502
166	Metolius	42.2	640	450	451	270	270
167	Johnson City	6.7	625	586	378	0	0
168	Gaston	10.1	620	563	471	429	320
169	Dufur	14.8	605	527	560	493	488
170	Cove	18.3	600	507	451	363	311
171	Donald	83.5	580	316	267	231	201
172	Huntington	10.2	575	522	539	507	689
173	Banks	1.2	570	563	489	430	347
174	Adair Village	2.0	565	554	589	0	0
175	North Powder	23.9	555	448	430	304	399
176	Echo	6.2	530	499	624	479	456

	City	% Change*	1996	1990	1980	1970	1960
	Gates	6.2	530	499	455	250	189
177	Fossil	29.1	515	399	535	511	672
178	Maupin	8.6	495	456	495	428	381
	Monroe	10.5	495	448	412	443	374
179	Arlington	14.1	485	425	521	375	643
180	Haines	8.6	440	405	341	212	331
181	Butte Falls	64.7	415	252	428	358	384
182	Wasco	4.3	390	374	415	412	348
183	Jordan Valley	5.8	385	364	473	196	204
184	Wheeler	11.9	375	335	319	262	237
185	Bonanza	14.6	370	323	270	230	297
	Detroit	11.8	370	331	367	328	206
186	Halfway	14.1	355	311	380	317	505
	St. Paul	10.2	355	322	312	346	254
187	Paisley	-1.4	345	350	343	260	219
188	Idanha	9.0	315	289	319	382	295
189	Imbler	3.7	310	299	292	139	137
	Scotts Mills	9.5	310	283	249	208	155
190	Rivergrove	2.0	300	294	314	0	0
191	Lexington	3.1	295	286	307	230	240
	Moro	1.0	295	292	336	290	327
192	Mosier	18.9	290	244	340	217	252
	Rufus	-1.7	290	295	352	317	0
193	Ukiah	12.0	280	250	249	0	0
	Westfir	0.7	280	278	312	0	0
194	Adams	16.6	260	223	240	219	192
	Sodaville	35.4	260	192	171	125	145
195	Ione	-2.0	250	255	345	355	350
196	Long Creek	-3.6	240	249	252	196	295
197	Lostine	1.7	235	231	250	196	241
	Nehalem	1.3	235	232	258	241	233
198	Seneca	20.4	230	191	285	0	0
199	Waterloo	15.2	220	191	211	186	151
200	Dayville	28.5	185	144	199	197	234
	Helix	23.3	185	150	155	152	148
	Monument	14.2	185	162	192	161	214
	Richland	14.9	185	161	181	133	228
201	Elkton	4.7	180	172	155	176	146
	Grass Valley	12.5	180	160	164	153	234
	Mitchell	10.4	180	163	183	196	236
202	Sumpter	47.1	175	119	133	120	96
203	Spray	7.4	160	149	155	161	194
204	Summerville	35.1	150	111	143	76	76
205	Adrian	3.1	135	131	162	0	0
206	Barlow	5.9	125	118	105	105	85
207	Unity	26.4	110	87	115	0	0
208	Antelope	91.2	65	34	39	51	46
209	Prescott	-4.8	60	63	73	105	129

210	Shaniko	15.4	30	26	30	58	39
211	Granite	212.5	25	8	17	4	3
	Lonerock	127.3	25	11	26	12	31
212	Greenhorn	0.0	3	0	0	0	0

*Estimated change in population between 1990 and 1996.

County Populations: 1960-1996

County		% Change*	1996	1990	1980	1970	1960
1	Multnomah	8.9	636,000	583,887	562,647	554,668	522,813
2	Washington	20.8	376,500	311,554	245,860	157,920	92,237
3	Clackamas	12.3	313,200	278,850	241,911	166,088	113,038
4	Lane	8.1	305,800	282,912	275,226	215,401	162,890
5	Marion	15.0	262,800	228,483	204,692	151,309	120,888
6	Jackson	14.8	168,000	146,389	132,456	94,533	73,962
7	Linn	9.6	100,000	91,227	89,495	71,914	58,867
8	Douglas	4.2	98,600	94,649	93,748	71,743	68,458
9	Deschutes	30.7	98,000	74,958	62,142	30,442	23,100
10	Yamhill	18.2	77,500	65,551	55,332	40,213	32,478
11	Benton	7.3	76,000	70,811	68,211	53,776	39,165
12	Josephine	14.9	72,000	62,649	58,855	35,746	29,917
13	Umatilla	10.6	65,500	59,249	58,861	44,923	44,352
14	Coos	2.4	61,700	60,273	64,047	56,515	54,955
15	Klamath	6.8	61,600	57,702	59,117	50,021	47,475
16	Polk	13.6	56,300	49,541	45,203	35,349	26,523
17	Lincoln	8.5	42,200	38,889	35,264	25,755	24,635
18	Columbia	6.8	40,100	37,557	35,646	28,790	22,379
19	Clatsop	3.9	34,600	33,301	32,489	28,473	27,380
20	Malheur	10.2	28,700	26,038	26,896	23,169	22,764
21	Union	3.8	24,500	23,598	23,921	19,377	18,180
22	Tillamook	10.3	23,800	21,570	21,164	18,034	18,955
23	Wasco	3.8	22,500	21,683	21,732	20,133	20,205
24	Curry	13.8	22,000	19,327	16,992	13,006	13,983
25	Hood River	12.4	19,000	16,903	15,835	13,187	13,395
26	Jefferson	23.6	16,900	13,676	11,599	8,548	7,130
27	Baker	7.7	16,500	15,317	16,134	14,919	17,295
28	Crook	12.7	15,900	14,111	13,091	9,985	9,430
29	Morrow	18.0	9,000	7,625	7,519	4,465	4,871
30	Grant	3.1	8,100	7,853	8,210	6,996	7,726
31	Lake	5.1	7,550	7,186	7,532	6,343	7,158
32	Harney	6.2	7,500	7,060	8,314	7,215	6,744
33	Wallowa	4.9	7,250	6,911	7,273	6,247	7,102
34	Gilliam	10.7	1,900	1,717	2,057	2,342	3,069
35	Sherman	-0.9	1,900	1,918	2,172	2,139	2,446
36	Wheeler	14.6	1,600	1,396	1,513	1,849	2,722
	Oregon	**8.4**	**3,181,000**	**2,842,321**	**2,633,156**	**2,091,533**	**1,768,687**

*Estimated change in population between 1990 and 1996.

County Government

For more information contact individual counties

The word county is from the French word "conte," meaning the domain of a count. However, the American county, defined by Webster as "the largest territorial division for local government within a state ...," is based on the Anglo-Saxon county of England dating back to about the time of the Norman Conquest. Counties were brought to America by the colonists and were later established in the central and western parts of this country by the pioneers as they moved westward.

Early county governments in Oregon were very limited in the services they provided. Their primary responsibilities were forest and farm-to-market roads, law enforcement, courts, care for the needy and tax collections. In response to demands of a growing population and a more complex society, today's counties provide a wide range of additional important public services including: public health, mental health, community corrections, juvenile services, criminal prosecution, hospitals, nursing homes, airports, parks, libraries, land-use planning, building regulations, refuse disposal, elections, air-pollution control, veterans services, economic development, urban renewal, public housing, vector control, county fairs, museums, dog control, civil defense, senior services and many others.

Until recently, counties functioned almost exclusively as agents of the state government. Their every activity had to be either authorized or mandated by state law. However, a 1958 constitutional amendment authorized counties to adopt "home rule" charters, and a 1973 state law granted all counties power to exercise broad "home rule" authority. As a result, the national Advisory Commission on Intergovernmental Relations has identified county government in Oregon as having the highest degree of local discretionary authority of any state in the nation.

Nine counties have adopted "home rule" charters, wherein voters have the power to adopt and amend their own county government organization. Lane and Washington were the first to adopt "home rule" in 1962, followed by Hood River (1964), Multnomah (1967), Benton (1972),

Jackson (1978), Josephine (1980), Clatsop (1988) and Umatilla (1993).

Twenty-four of Oregon's 36 counties, including the nine with charters, operate under a "board of commissioners" with from three to five elected members. The remaining 12 less populated counties are governed by a "county court" consisting of a county judge and two commissioners.

Baker County

County Seat: Courthouse, 1995 3rd St., Baker City 97814; 541-523-8200; Fax: 541-523-8240

Established: Sept. 22, 1862
Elev. at Baker: 3,471'
Area: 3,089 sq. mi.
Average Temp.: January 25.2°, July 66.6°
Population: 16,500
Assessed Value: $751,988,500
Annual Precipitation: 10.63"
Principal Industries: Agriculture, Lumber, Recreation
Points of Interest: Ghost towns in Sumpter Valley, Hells Canyon, Anthony Lakes Ski and Summer Resort, Eagle Cap Wilderness Area, Old Oregon Trail, Radium Hot Springs, Sumpter Gold Dredge, Sumpter Valley Railroad, Brownlee Reservoir, historic Baker City.

Baker County was established from part of Wasco County and named after Colonel Edward D. Baker, U.S. Senator from Oregon. A Union officer and close friend of President Lincoln, Colonel Baker was the only member of Congress to die in the Civil War. He was killed at Balls Bluff.

Auburn, which no longer exists, was the first county seat. Baker City, incorporated in 1874 and the 17th oldest city in Oregon, became county seat in June 1868.

Prior to 1861, the majority of emigrants only paused in Baker County on their journey westward, unaware of the vast agricultural and mineral resources waiting to be tapped. Then the great gold rush began and Baker County became one of the Northwest's highest gold producers. Now farming, ranching, logging and recreation have become the chief economic bases for an area that enjoys spectacular scenery, including the world's deepest gorge—Hells Canyon; an outstanding museum with the famous Cavin-Walfel rock collection; and historic buildings with interesting architecture.

County Officials: Commissioners—Judge Steve M. Bogart, chair (D), 1999, Howard C. Britton (R) 1999, Paul W. York (R) 2001; Dist. Atty. Gregory L. Baxter (NP) 2001; Assess. Harry Allen Phillips (NP) 2001; Clerk Julia Woods (NP) 1999; Justices of the Peace Larry Cole, Beverly Robertson, Teresa Stelting; Sheriff Terry W. Speelman (NP) 2001; Surv. Tom Hanley (NP) 2001; Treas. Lynne Taylor (NP) 1999.

Benton County

County Seat: Courthouse, 120 NW 4th, Corvallis 97330; 541-757-6800; Fax: 541-757-6893; Web: www.peak.org/benton-county

Established: Dec. 23, 1847
Elev. at Corvallis: 224'
Area: 679 sq. mi.
Average Temp.: January 39.0°, July 65.6°
Population: 76,000
Assessed Value: $4,397,280,639
Annual Precipitation: 42.55"
Principal Industries: Agriculture, Lumber, Research and Development, Electronics, Wineries
Points of Interest: County Courthouse, Oregon State University Campus, Horner Museum (OSU), Benton County Museum (Philomath), Alsea Falls, Marys Peak, Wm. L. Finley National Wildlife Refuge, Peavy Arboretum, McDonald Forest.

Benton County was created officially from Polk County by an act of the Territorial Government of Oregon. It is one of seven counties in the United States to be named after Senator Thomas Hart Benton of Missouri, a longtime advocate of the development of the Oregon Territory.

The county was created out of an area originally inhabited by the Klickitat Indians, who rented it from the Calapooia Indians for use as hunting grounds. At that time the boundaries began at the intersection of Polk County and the Willamette River, ran as far south as the California border and as far west as the Pacific Ocean. Later, portions of Benton County were taken to form Lane, Douglas, Jackson, Lincoln, Josephine, Curry and Coos Counties, leaving it in its present form with 679 square miles of land area.

Oregon State University, agriculture, and lumber and wood products manufacturing form the basis of Benton County's economy. A substantial portion of the nation's research in forestry, agriculture, engineering, education and the sciences takes place at OSU.

County Officials: Commissioners—Orville "Bob" Adams (R) 2001, Kent Daniels (D) 1999, Bob Speaker (D) 2001; Dist. Atty. Pete Sandrock 1999; Sheriff Stan Robson 1999; Surv. James Blair.

Clackamas County

County Seat: Courthouse, 906 Main St., Oregon City 97045; 503-655-8581; Web: www.co.clackamas.or.us

Established: July 5, 1843
Elev. at Oregon City: 55'
Area: 1,879 sq. mi.
Average Temp.: January 40.2°, July 68.4°
Population: 313,200
Assessed Value: $22,600,000,000
Annual Precipitation: 48.40"
Principal Industries: Agriculture, Metals Manufacturing, Trucking and Warehousing, Nursery Stock, Retail Services, Wholesale Trade and Construction.
Points of Interest: Mt. Hood and Timberline Lodge, Willamette Falls and Locks, McLoughlin House, Canby Ferry, Molalla Buckeroo, driving tour of Old Barlow Road, Clackamas Town Center, End of the Oregon Trail Interpretive Center, Clackamas County Historical Museum, North Clackamas Aquatic Park.

Clackamas County was named for the resident Clackamas Indians and was one of the four original Oregon counties. Oregon City, the county seat, was the first incorporated city west of the Rockies, the first capital of the Territorial Government in 1848 and the site of the first legislative session.

As capital of the Oregon Territory, Oregon City was also the site of the only federal and district court west of the Rockies in 1849 when the city of San Francisco was platted. The plat was filed in 1850 in the first plat book of the first office of records on the West Coast which is still in Oregon City. Oregon City has also been officially recognized as the end of the Oregon Trail. The area's early history is featured at the End of the Oregon Trail Interpretive Center, a living history museum on an 8.5 acre site with three 50-foot high covered wagon-shaped buildings, an outdoor amphitheater and heritage garden.

From the 55-foot elevation at Oregon City, the county rises to 11,235 feet at the peak of Mt. Hood, the only year-round ski resort in the United States and the site of Timberline Lodge National Historic Landmark. The mountain, rivers and forests offer excellent outdoor recreation activities, from skiing and river rafting to fishing and camping. The Clackamas Town Center, with more retail stores than any shopping mall in Oregon, is the hub of eastside business.

County Officials: Commissioners— Judie Hammerstad (D) 1998, Bill Kennemer (R) 2000, Ed Lindquist (D) 2000; Dist. Atty. Terry Gustafson (NP) 2000; Assess. Ray Erland (NP) 2000; Clerk John Kauffman (NP) 1998; Sheriff Ris Bradshaw (NP) 2000; Surv. Tom Milne (NP) 1998; Treas. Ginny Brewster (NP) 1998.

Clatsop County

County Seat: Courthouse, 749 Commercial, Astoria 97103; 503-325-1000; Fax: 503-325-8325

Established: June 22, 1844
Elev. at Astoria: 19'
Area: 873 sq. mi.
Average Temp.: January 41.1°, July 60.1°
Population: 34,600
Assessed Value: $3,333,145,843
Annual Precipitation: 69.59"
Principal Industries: Fishing, Tourism, Lumber, Agriculture
Points of Interest: Astoria Column, Port of Astoria, Flavel Mansion Museum, Lewis and Clark Expedition Salt Cairn, Fort Clatsop, Fort Stevens, Columbia River Maritime Museum.

Clatsop County was created from the original Tuality district and named for the Clatsop Indians, one of the many Chinook tribes living in Oregon. The Journals of Lewis and Clark mention the tribe. Fort Clatsop, Lewis and Clark's winter headquarters in 1805 and now a national memorial near the mouth of the Columbia River, also took the tribe's name.

Astoria, the first American city to be settled in the West, was established as a fur trading post in 1811 and named after John Jacob Astor. The first U.S.

The Crook County Courthouse in Prineville was built in 1909 with stone from along Crooked River within the city limits.

Photo by Gary Halvorson, courtesy of State Archives.

Post Office west of the Rocky Mountains was also established in Astoria in 1847. The first courthouse was completed in 1855; the present courthouse was erected in 1904.

Records show that the now-busy summer resort of Seaside was founded by Ben Holladay, pioneer Oregon railroad builder, in the early 1870s when he constructed the Seaside House, a famous luxury hotel for which the city was finally named. The Lewis and Clark Expedition reached the Pacific Ocean at this spot.

County Officials: Commissioners— Joe Bakkensen (NP) 2001, Bob Ellsberg (NP) 1999, George Kiepke (NP) 1999, Marsha Stone (NP) 2001, Helen Westbrook (NP) 1999; Dist. Atty. Joshua Marquis (NP) 1998; Assess. Glen E. Jones; Co. Mgr. Britt E. Ferguson; Co. Clerk Lori D. Davidson; Surv. Steven Thornton; Treas./Fin. Dir. Michael L. Robison; Sheriff John P. Raichl (NP) 1998.

Columbia County

County Seat: Courthouse, St. Helens 97051-0010; 503-397-4322; Fax: 503-397-7243

Established: Jan. 16, 1854
Elev. at St. Helens: 42'
Area: 687 sq. mi.
Average Temp.: January 39.0°, July 68.4°
Population: 40,100
Assessed Value: $2,670,279,184
Annual Precipitation: 44.60"
Principal Industries: Agriculture, Lumber, Industry, Fishing, Tourism
Points of Interest: Paper mills at St. Helens, Lewis & Clark Bridge at Rainier, Lower Sauvie Island game reserve, county fairgrounds, Trojan Nuclear Plant (operation stopped 1993).

Facts regarding early history of Columbia County are few, but it is known that a New England trading vessel, the Columbia Rediviva, commanded by Captain Robert Gray arrived in the summer of 1792 with the first white men to see the county's timbered shoreline. In 1805 Lewis & Clark traveled and camped along the county's shoreline.

Carved out of Washington County in 1854, its past was tied to commercial fishing, water transportation and lumber.

Industrialization has accelerated in recent years but dairying and horticulture remain important. Natural gas fields have been identified and are producing.

The county's northern and eastern boundaries are outlined by 62 miles of Columbia River shoreline. The Columbia is a major route of ocean-going vessels and is a popular playground for fishermen, pleasure boaters and windsurfers. The county offers the only two marine parks in Oregon: Sand Island on the Columbia River and J.J. Collins Memorial Marine Park on the Multnomah Channel. In addition, Prescott Beach County Park is also located along the Columbia River, but does not currently have any boat docking facilities.

County Officials: Commissioners— Jack R. Peterson, chair (D) 2001, Anthony Hyde (R) 2001, Joel R. Yarbor (R) 1999; Dist. Atty. Martin A. Sells (NP) 2001; Assess. Tom Linhares (D) 1999; Clerk Elizabeth Huser (D) 1999; Justice of the Peace Rod McLean; Sheriff Phil Derby (NP) 2001; Treas. Paulette Kuiper (NP) 2001; Surv. Philip Dewey (D) 2001.

Coos County

County Seat: Courthouse, 250 N Baxter, Coquille 97423; 541-396-3121; Fax: 541-396-4861; Email: coosdp@mail.coos.or.us; Web: mail.coos.or.us/~coosdp

Established: Dec. 22, 1853
Elev. at Coquille: 40'
Area: 1,629 sq. mi.
Average Temp.: January 44.2°, July 60.9°
Population: 61,700
Assessed Value: $2,800,097,060
Annual Precipitation: 56.8"
Principal Industries: Lumber, Fishing, Agriculture, Shipping, Recreation
Points of Interest: Lumber port, Myrtlewood groves, state and county parks (Shore Acres State Park and Botanical Gardens), beaches, sand dunes (Oregon Dunes National Recreation Area), museums, fishing fleets, boat basins.

Coos County was created by the Territorial Legislature from parts of Umpqua and Jackson Counties and included Curry County until 1855. The county seat was Empire City until 1896 when it was moved to Coquille.

Although trappers had been in the area a quarter-century earlier, the first permanent settlement in present Coos County was at Empire City, now part of Coos Bay, by members of the Coos Bay Company in 1853. The name "Coos" derives from a native Coos Bay Indian tribe and translates to "lake" or "place of pines."

Forest products, tourism, fishing and agriculture dominate the Coos County economy. Boating, dairy farming, myrtlewood manufacturing, ship building and repair, module fabrication and agriculture specialty products including cranberries, also play an important role. The international port of Coos Bay, considered the best natural harbor between Puget Sound and San Francisco is the world's largest forest products shipping port.

County Officials: Commissioners— Beverly Owen (D) 2001, Gordon Ross (R) 1999, Jim Whitty (D) 1999; Dist. Atty. Paul R. Burgett (NP) 2001; Assess. Gayland Van Elsberg (D) 2001; Clerk Mary Ann Wilson (D) 2001; Sheriff Michael Cook (NP) 1999; Surv. Karlas Seidel (D) 2001; Treas. Mary Barton (D) 2001.

Crook County

County Seat: Courthouse, 300 E 3rd, Prineville 97754; 541-447-6555; Fax: 541-447-1051

Established: Oct. 24, 1882
Elev. at Prineville: 2,868'
Area: 2,991 sq. mi.
Average Temp.: January 31.8°, July 64.5°
Population: 15,900
Assessed Value: $782,787,985
Annual Precipitation: 10.50"
Principal Industries: Livestock, Lumber, Recreation
Points of Interest: Pine Mills, Crooked River Canyon, Ochoco Mountains, Prineville and Ochoco Reservoirs, rockhound areas, county courthouse, Steins Pillar and other geological formations.

Crook County was formed from Wasco County and named for Maj. Gen. George Crook, U.S. Army. Geographically, the county is Oregon's most centrally located. It is also unique in that it has only one incorporated population center, the city of Prineville, founded in 1868. Prineville's colorful past was the scene of Indian raids, range wars between sheepmen and cattlemen and vigilante justice. Other communities in this sparsely settled region are Powell Butte, Post and Paulina.

Forest products, agriculture, livestock raising and recreation/tourism services constitute Crook County's total economy. Thousands of hunters, fishers, boaters, sightseers and rockhounds are annual visitors to its streams, reservoirs and Ochoco Mountains. Rockhounds can dig for free agates, limb casts, jasper and thundereggs on more than 1,000 acres of mining claims provided by the Prineville Chamber of Commerce. Major annual events include the Prineville Rockhound Pow Wow, Crooked River Roundup, County Fair and the Lord's Acre Sale.

County Officials: Commissioners— Judge Fred W. Rodgers, chair (R) 2001, Mike McCabe (R) 2001, Frank Porfily (R) 1999; Dist. Atty. Gary Williams (NP) 2001; Assess. Tom Green (R) 1999; Clerk Deanna "Dee" Berman (D) 1999; Sheriff Rodd Clark (NP) 1999; Surv. David Armstrong (D) 2001; Treas. Mary Jo Johnson (R) 2001.

Curry County

County Seat: Courthouse, PO Box 746, Gold Beach 97444; 541-247-7011; Fax: 541-247-2718

Established: Dec. 18, 1855
Elev. at Gold Beach: 60'
Area: 1,648 sq. mi.
Average Temp.: January 47.0°, July 59.0°
Population: 22,000
Assessed Value: $1,532,052,740
Annual Precipitation: 82.67"
Principal Industries: Lumber, Agriculture, Commercial and Sport Fishing, Recreation, Tourism
Points of Interest: Cape Blanco Lighthouse, Cape Sebastian and Samuel H. Boardman State Parks, Rogue River Japanese Bomb Site and coastal ports.

Named after Territorial Gov. George L. Curry, the county was formerly a part of "Coose" [sic] County. Port Orford was the county seat until 1859 when it was

replaced by Ellensburg (later renamed Gold Beach).

The county contains valuable standing timber and also offers spectacular coastal scenery, clamming and crabbing, excellent fishing (freshwater and saltwater), upriver scenic boat trips, hiking trails, and gold for the fun of panning. The Port of Brookings is considered one of the safest harbors on the coast.

Agriculture includes sheep and cattle, cranberries, blueberries, Easter lilies and horticultural nursery stock. Curry County is also a prolific producer of Myrtlewood.

County Officials: Commissioners— Lloyd H. Olds (D) 2001, Bill Roberts (R) 2001, T.V. Skinner (R) 1999; Dist. Atty. Patrick R. Foley (NP) 2001; Assess. James V. Kolen (D) 2001; Clerk Reneé Kolen (D) 2001; Sheriff Charles Denney (NP) 1999; Surv. Darryl Niemi (R) 1999; Treas. Trudi June Sthen (D) 1999.

Deschutes County

County Seat: Courthouse Administration Bldg., 1130 NW Harriman, Bend 97701; 541-388-6570; Fax: 541-388-4752

Established: Dec. 13, 1916
Elev. at Bend: 3,623'
Area: 3,055 sq. mi.
Average Temp.: January 30.5°, July 62.5°
Population: 98,000
Assessed Value: $7,658,042,893
Annual Precipitation: 12.04"
Average Snowfall: 33.8"
Principal Industries: Lumber, Agriculture, Tourism
Points of Interest: Cascade Lakes Highway, Lava Lands, Lava River Caves State Park, Lava Cast Forests, Newberry Crater, Pilot Butte, Three Sisters Wilderness Area, Mt. Bachelor ski area, Central Oregon Community College, High Desert Museum, Pine Mountain Observatory.

French-Canadian fur trappers of the old Hudson's Bay Company gave the name Riviere des Chutes (River of the Falls) to one of Oregon's most scenic rivers, from which the county of Deschutes took its name. The county was created from a part of Crook County in 1916.

Located in the heart of the state, Deschutes County encompasses the snow-capped Cascades and the fertile valley, range and forest lands of the "high country" or central Oregon plateau. It has experienced the most rapid growth of any county in the state during the past 10 years, largely due to its invigorating climate, year-round recreational opportunities for both downhill and cross-country skiing, fishing, hunting, hiking, rockhounding, and its varied industries. Principal products are lumber, plywood, cattle and potatoes.

County Officials: Commissioners— Nancy Pope Schlangen, chair (R) 1999, Robert L. Nipper (R) 1999, Linda L. Swearingen (R) 2001; Dist. Atty. Mike Dugan (NP) 1999; Assess. Kim Worrell (NP) 1999; Clerk Mary Sue Penhollow (NP) 1999; Sheriff Greg Brown (NP) 2001; Surv. Jeff Kern (R) 2001; Treas. Helen Rastovich (D) 1999.

Douglas County

County Seat: Courthouse, 1036 SE Douglas, Rm. 217, Roseburg 97470; 541-672-3311; Fax: 541-440-4408

Established: Jan. 7, 1852
Elev. at Roseburg: 479'
Area: 5,071 sq. mi.
Average Temp.: January 41.2°, July 68.4°
Population: 98,600
Assessed Value: $4,602,903,791
Annual Precipitation: 33.35"
Principal Industries: Lumber, Mining, Agriculture, Fishing, Recreation
Points of Interest: Winchester Bay and Salmon Harbor, Oregon Dunes National Recreation Area, North Umpqua River, Diamond Lake, historic Oakland, Wildlife Safari, Douglas County Museum, winery tours.

Douglas County was named for United States Senator Stephen A. Douglas, candidate for the presidency against Abraham Lincoln in 1860 and ardent congressional advocate for Oregon. When created January 24, 1851, the county was part of Umpqua County. In 1852 the Territorial Legislature created new boundaries and renamed it Douglas County.

Douglas County extends from sea level at the Pacific Ocean to 9,182-foot

Mt. Thielsen in the Cascade Range. The Umpqua River marks the dividing line between northern and southern Oregon, and its entire watershed lies within the county's boundaries. The county also contains nearly 2.8 million acres of commercial forest lands and the largest stand of old growth timber in the world, which still provides the region's main livelihood. Approximately 25-30 percent of the labor force is employed in the forest products industry. Agriculture includes field crops, orchards and livestock. Over 50 percent of the land area of the county is owned by the Federal government.

County Officials: Commissioners— Joyce Morgan (D) 2001, Doug Robertson (R) 2001, Mike Winters (R) 1999; Dist. Atty. Jack Banta (D) 1999; Assess. Doris Reddekopp (D) 1999; Clerk Doyle Shaver; Justices of the Peace Candi Hissong, Stephen H. Miller, Carol Roberts, Russell Trump; Sheriff John Pardon (NP) 2001; Surv. Romey Ware (NP) 2001; Treas. Sam Huff (NP) 2001.

Gilliam County

County Seat: Courthouse, 221 S Oregon, Condon 97823; 541-384-6351

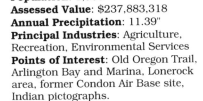

Established:
Feb. 25, 1885
Elev. at Condon: 2,844'
Area:
1,223 sq. mi.
Average Temp.:
January 31.9°, July 71.3°
Population: 1,900
Assessed Value: $237,883,318
Annual Precipitation: 11.39"
Principal Industries: Agriculture, Recreation, Environmental Services
Points of Interest: Old Oregon Trail, Arlington Bay and Marina, Lonerock area, former Condon Air Base site, Indian pictographs.

Gilliam County was established from a portion of Wasco County and was named after Colonel Cornelius Gilliam, a veteran of the Cayuse Indian War. The first county seat was at Alkali, now Arlington. At the general election of 1890, voters chose to move the county seat to Condon, known to early settlers as "Summit Springs." A brick courthouse was built in Condon in 1903 but was destroyed by fire in 1954. The present courthouse, built on the same site, was constructed in 1955.

Gilliam County is in the heart of the Columbia Basin wheat area. The economy is based mainly on agriculture, with an average farm size of about 4,200 acres. Wheat, barley and beef cattle are the principal crops. The largest individual employers in the county are two subsidiaries of Waste Management Inc.: Chemical Waste Management of the Northwest and Oregon Waste Systems, Inc., a regional state-of-the-art solid waste landfill.

With elevations of over 3,000 feet near Condon and 285 feet at Arlington, a distance of 38 miles, the county offers a variety of climates and atmosphere. Hunting, fishing and tourism are important secondary industries. Two major rivers, the John Day and Columbia, traverse the area, as well as Interstate 84. Highway 19 connects the county's major cities and serves as the gateway to the John Day Valley and other central Oregon points.

County Officials: Commissioners— Judge Laura M. Pryor, chair (D) 2001, Frank Bettencourt (R) 2001, Dennis Gronquist (D) 1999; Dist. Atty. C.S. Cutsforth (NP) 1997; Assess. Patricia Shaw (D) 1997; Clerk Rena Kennedy (D) 1999; Justice of the Peace Sharon (Chris) Nix; Sheriff Paul Barnett (NP) 1997; Surv. Bob Bagett (D), 1999; Treas. Alcenia Byrd (R) 1999.

Grant County

County Seat: Courthouse, 200 S Canyon Blvd., Canyon City 97820; 541-575-1675; Fax: 541-575-2248

Established:
Oct. 14, 1864
Elev. at Canyon City: 3,194'
Area:
4,528 sq. mi.
Average Temp.:
January 30.7°, July 68.4°
Population: 8,100
Assessed Value: $326,234,341
Annual Precipitation: 14.28"
Principal Industries: Forestry, Agriculture, Hunting, Livestock, Recreation
Points of Interest: John Day Fossil Beds National Monument, Kam Wah Chung Museum, Joaquin Miller Cabin, Grant County Historical Museum,

Sacred Totem Pole, Grant County Historical Mural, Dewitt Museum, Depot Park, Sumpter Valley Railroad, Strawberry Mountain and North Fork John Day River wilderness areas.

Grant County was created in 1864 and was named for General Ulysses S. Grant. It shares boundaries with more counties (eight) than any other county in Oregon.

Grant County contains the head waters of the John Day River, which has more miles of Wild and Scenic designation than any other river in the U.S. More than 60 percent of the land in the county is in public ownership.

County Officials: Commissioners— Judge Dennis Reynolds, chair (R) 2001, Bill Gibbs (R) 1999, Bob Kimberling (R) 2001; Dist. Atty. Ed Holpuch (NP) 2001; Assess. Lane Burton (D) 2001; Clerk Kathy McKinnon (R) 2001; Justice of the Peace Janilee Lowrance; Sheriff Fred Reusser (NP) 2001; Surv. Robert Bagett (D) 2001; Treas. Kathy Smith (R) 2001.

Harney County

County Seat: Courthouse, 450 N Buena Vista, Burns 97720; 541-573-6356

Established: Feb. 25, 1889
Elev. at Burns: 4,148'
Area: 10,228 sq. mi.
Average Temp.: January 27.5°, July 69.4°
Population: 7,500
Assessed Value: $297,450,962
Annual Precipitation: 10.13"
Principal Industries: Forestry, Manufacturing, Livestock, Agriculture
Points of Interest: Steens Mountain, Malheur Cave, Malheur Wildlife Refuge, Alvord Desert and Lake, Squaw Butte Experimental Station, "P" Ranch Round Barn, Frenchglen.

In 1826, Peter Skeene Ogden was the first white man to explore this area while leading a fur brigade for the Hudson's Bay Company. Over 50 years later Harney, the largest county in Oregon, was carved out of Grant County and named for Maj. Gen. William S. Harney, who commanded the Department of Oregon of the U.S. Army from 1858-59. He was instrumental in opening areas of eastern Oregon for settlement.

A fierce political battle, with armed night riders who spirited county records from Harney to Burns, ended with Burns as the county seat in 1890. The courthouse was constructed five years later. Burns' first newspaper was established in 1884 and its first church in 1887.

Harney County shares with Grant County the largest Ponderosa pine forest in the nation and has more than 100,000 head of beef cattle on its vast ranges. Its abundance of game, numerous campsites and excellent fishing have stimulated fast-growing recreational activities.

County Officials: Commissioners— Judge Dale White, chair (D) 1999, Kenneth J. Bentz (R) 1999, Dan Nichols (R) 2001; Dist. Atty. Tim Colahan (NP) 2001; Assess. Hunter E. De Pue (R) 1999; Clerk Maria Iturriaga (NP) 2001; Justice of the Peace Mary Ann Robinson (NP) 2003; Sheriff Greg Peterson (NP) 2001; Surv. Charles F. Palmer (NP) 2001; Treas. Ellen Franklin (R) 1999.

Hood River County

County Seat: Courthouse, 309 State St., Hood River 97031-2093; 541-386-3970; Fax: 541-386-9392

Established: June 23, 1908
Elev. at Hood River: 154'
Area: 533 sq. mi.
Average Temp.: January 33.6°, July 66.7°
Population: 19,000
Assessed Value: $1,079,480,364
Annual Precipitation: 30.85"
Principal Industries: Agriculture, Food Processing, Lumber, Recreation
Points of Interest: Bridge of the Gods, Cloud Cap Inn, Mt. Hood Recreation Area, Mt. Hood Meadows Ski Resort, Lost Lake, Panorama Point, Hood River Valley at blossom time.

The first permanent settlers in Hood River County filed a donation land claim in 1854. The first school was built in 1863 and a road from The Dalles was completed in 1867. By 1880 there were 17 families living in the valley. Hood River County was established in 1908 from Wasco County.

Agriculture, timber, lumber and recreation are the major sources of revenue and industry. Fruit grown in the fertile valley is of such exceptional quality the county leads the world in Anjou pear production. There are more than 14,000 acres of commercial orchards growing pears, apples, cherries and peaches. Hood River County also has two ports and two boat basins, with one serving local barge traffic, a steel boat manufacturing firm and Mid-Columbia yachting interests. Windsurfing on the Columbia River is a popular sport and attracts windsurfers from the United States and other countries.

County Officials: Commissioners—Beverly A. Rowland, chair (NP) 1997, Glenn Best (NP) 1997, Ken Lambert (NP) 1999, Robert Schuppe (NP) 2000, Chuck Thomsen (NP) 1999; Budget and Fin. Dir. Dan Chamness; Dist. Atty. John Sewell (NP) 1997; Justice of the Peace Roberta K. Lee (NP); Sheriff Joe Wampler (NP) 1997; Co. Admin. Jim Azumano; Rcdr. Sandy Berry; Surv. Richard J. Arnold.

Jackson County

County Seat: Courthouse, 10 S Oakdale, Medford 97501; 541-776-7248, 7231; Fax: 541-776-7118

Established: Jan. 12, 1852
Elev. at Medford: 1,382'
Area: 2,801 sq. mi.
Average Temp.: January 37.6°, July 72.5°
Population: 168,000
Assessed Value: $8,370,505,952
Annual Precipitation: 19.84"
Principal Industries: Medical, Retail, Tourism, Agriculture, Manufacturing, Lumber
Points of Interest: Mt. Ashland Ski Resort, Historic Jacksonville, Shakespearean Festival, Peter Britt Music Festival, Southern Oregon State College, pear orchards, Howard Prairie Lake, Emigrant Lake, Hyatt Lake, Fish Lake, Rogue River, Lithia Park, Lost Creek Dam, Butte Creek Mill, Crater Lake Highway, Pacific Northwest Museum of Natural History.

Named for President Andrew Jackson, Jackson County was formed in 1852 from the original Yamhill and Champoeg

districts. It included lands which now lie in Klamath, Josephine, Curry, Lake and Coos counties. The discovery of gold near Jacksonville in 1852 and completion of a wagon road, which joined the county with California to the south and Douglas County to the north, brought many pioneers.

County Officials: Commissioners—Ric Holt, chair (R), 1999, Sue Kupillas (D) 1997, Jack Walker (R) 1999; Dist. Atty. Mark D. Huddleston (NP) 1997; Co. Admin. Burke M. Raymond; Assess. Dan Ross (R) 1997; Clerk Kathy Beckett (D) 1999; Justice of the Peace Robert King Jr.; Sheriff Robert O. Kennedy (NP) 1999; Surv. Roger Roberts (R); Treas. Gary A. Cadle (D) 1997.

Jefferson County

County Seat: 75 SE "C" St., Madras 97741; 541-475-2449; Fax: 541-475-4454

Established: Dec. 12, 1914
Elev. at Madras: 2,242'
Area: 1,791 sq. mi.
Average Temp.: January 37.4°, July 70.1°
Population: 16,900
Assessed Value: $735,191,353
Annual Precipitation: 10.2"
Principal Industries: Agriculture, Forest Products, Recreation
Points of Interest: Mt. Jefferson, Warm Springs Indian Reservation, Metolius River, Black Butte, Suttle Lake, Blue Lake, Santiam Summit, Lake Billy Chinook behind Round Butte Dam, Haystack Reservoir, Priday Agate Beds.

Jefferson County was established from a portion of Crook County and named for Mount Jefferson on its western boundary. The county owes much of its agricultural prosperity to the railroad, which arrived in 1911, and to the development of irrigation projects in the late 1930s. The railroad, linking Madras with the Columbia River, was completed after constant feuds and battles between two lines working opposite sides of the Deschutes River.

Vegetable, grass and flower seeds, garlic, mint and sugar beets are cultivated on some 60,000 irrigated acres. Jefferson County also has vast acreages of range lands and a healthy industrial base related to forest products. The Warm Springs Forest Products Industry, a multi-million dollar complex owned by the Confederated Tribes of the Warm Springs Reservation—partly located in the northwestern corner of the county—is the single biggest industry. With 300 days of sunshine and a low yearly rainfall, fishing, hunting, camping, boating, water-skiing and rock hunting are popular recreations.

County Officials: Commissioners— Bill C. Bellamy (R) 2001, Janet L. Brown (D) 1999, Jodi Eagan (D) 1999; Dist. Atty. Peter L. Deuel (NP) 2001; Assess. Patsy Mault-Hurn (R) 1999; Clerk Elaine Henderson (D) 1999; Sheriff Mike Throop (NP) 2001; Surv. Gary L. DeJarnatt (R) 2001; Treas. Bonnie K. Namenuk (R) 2001.

Josephine County

County Seat: Courthouse, NW 6th & C, Grants Pass 97526; 541-474-5100; Fax: 541-474-5105; Web: www.magic.net/~jocogov

Established: Jan. 22, 1856
Elev. at Grants Pass: 948'
Area: 1,641 sq. mi.
Average Temp.: January 39.9°, July 71.6°
Population: 72,000
Assessed Value: $3,385,214,274
Annual Precipitation: 32.31"
Principal Industries: Lumber, Tourism, Agriculture, Electronics, Software
Points of Interest: Oregon Caves National Monument, Wolf Creek Tavern, Sunny Valley Covered Bridge, Redwood Highway, Rogue River fishing and boat trips, Kerbyville Museum.

Josephine County, named after Josephine Rollins, the first white woman to make this county her home, was established out of the western portion of Jackson County. The county seat was first located in Waldo, but in July of 1857 was relocated to Kerbyville, situated on the main route between the port of Crescent City, Calif. and the gold fields.

The discovery of rich placers at Sailor Diggings (later Waldo) in 1852 and the resulting gold rush brought the first settlers to this region. Several U.S. Army forts were maintained in the county and many engagements during the Rogue River Indian War (1855-1858) took place within its boundaries. In 1886, the county seat was finally located in Grants Pass, a new town built on the railroad that was completed through the state in that same year.

Grants Pass is now the departure point for most Rogue River guided fishing and boat trips. The Illinois River, one of the Rogue's tributaries, has also been designated a scenic waterway.

County Officials: Commissioners— Fred Borngasser (NP) 1999, Jim Brock (NP) 2001, Harold Haugen (NP) 2001; Dist. Atty. Tim Thompson (NP) 1999; Assess. George Trahern (NP) 2001; Clerk Georgette Brown (NP) 2001; Sheriff Dan Calvert (NP) 1999; Surv. Roger Reece (NP) 2001; Treas. John Harelson (NP) 2001.

Klamath County

County Seat: 403 Pine St., Suite 300, Klamath Falls 97601; 541-883-5100

Established: Oct. 17, 1882
Elev. at Klamath Falls: 4,105'
Area: 6,135 sq. mi.
Average Temp.: January 29.8°, July 68.0°
Population: 61,600
Assessed Value: $2,877,509,299
Annual Precipitation: 14.31"
Principal Industries: Forest Products, Agriculture, Tourism, Recreation
Points of Interest: Crater Lake National Park, Collier Memorial State Park and Logging Museum, Klamath Lake (largest lake in Oregon), seven National Wildlife Refuges, Oregon Institute of Technology (OIT), Klamath County Museums, Favell Museum of Western Art, Ross Ragland Performing Arts Theatre.

The "Clamitt" tribe of Indians, from which Klamath County was named, has had a presence for 10,000 years. White settlement began in 1846 along the Applegate Immigrant Trail, which precipitated clashes between the two cultures and caused the Modoc Indian War of 1872. The state Legislature created Klamath County by dividing Lake County in 1882. Linkville was named county seat and its name was changed to Klamath Falls in 1893.

Klamath County's present-day position as a great lumber, agriculture and distribution center was assured in the early 1900s with the coming of the railroad and the start of one of the most successful of all federal reclamation projects—the Klamath Project, which drained much of the 128 square mile Lower Klamath Lake to provide 188,000 acres of irrigable land.

Natural geothermal hot wells provide heat for many homes, businesses and the OIT campus. The full potential of this energy resource continues to be studied. Klamath is recognized for its scenic beauty, outdoor recreation, abundant waterfowl and diverse landscape.

County Officials: Commissioners—Bill Garrad (R) 1999, Al Switzer (R) 2001, Steve West (R) 2001; Dist. Atty. Edwin I. Caleb (NP) 1999; Assess. Reg LeQuieu (R) 1999; Clerk Bernetha Letsch (R) 1999; Justice of the Peace Alfred L. (Bucky) Edgar; Sheriff Carl Burkhart (NP) 2001; Surv. Francis Roberts (NP) 2001; Treas. Michael R. Long (R) 1999.

Lake County

County Seat: Courthouse, 513 Center St., Lakeview 97630; 541-947-6003; Fax: 541-947-6015

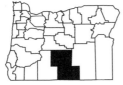

Established: Oct. 24, 1874
Elev. at Lakeview: 4,800'
Area: 8,359 sq. mi.
Average Temp.: January 28.4°, July 67.0°
Population: 7,550
Assessed Value: $346,652,599
Annual Precipitation: 15.80"
Principal Industries: Livestock, Lumber, Agriculture, Recreation, Mining
Points of Interest: Hang gliding, Hart Mountain Antelope Refuge, Fort Rock, Abert Lake and Rim, Goose Lake, Hunter's Hot Springs, Old Perpetual Geyser, Schminck Memorial Museum and Lake County Museum, Lake County Round-up Museum, Warner Canyon Ski Area, Gearhart Wilderness, Lost Forest, Crack-in-the-ground, Sheldon National Wildlife Refuge, Summer Lake Hot Springs, Hole-in-the-ground, rock hounding, Sunstones (Oregon's state gemstone) near Plush.

Lake County was created from Jackson County by the 1874 Legislature and came into being February 1, 1875. It then included the present Klamath County and all of the present Lake County except Warner Valley. In 1882 Klamath was removed and in 1885 the Warner area from Grant County was added.

Linkville, now Klamath Falls, was the first county seat. M. Bullard gave 20 acres as the Lakeview townsite. By the 1875 election a town had been started and the seat moved to Lakeview. The Hart Mountain Antelope Refuge is a 270,000 acre wildlife haven for antelope, mule deer, bighorn sheep and upland birds. A number of migratory waterfowl flyways converge on Goose Lake, south of Lakeview. And now Lakeview has been deemed the Hang Gliding Capital of the West.

County Officials: Commissioners—Kathleen J. Collins (R) 2001, Jane O'Keeffe (R) 1999, Robert M. Pardue (D) 1999; Dist. Atty. Marcus Ward (NP) 2001; Assess. Phil Israel (NP) 1999; Clerk Karen O'Connor (NP) 2001; Sheriff Charles Withers (NP) 2001; Surv. Rod Callaghan (I) 1999.

Lane County

County Seat: Courthouse, 125 E 8th, Eugene 97401; 541-682-4203; Fax: 541-682-3803

Established: Jan. 28, 1851
Elev. at Eugene: 422'
Area: 4,620 sq. mi
Average Temp.: January 40.1°, July 66.8°
Population: 305,800
Assessed Value: $16,229,908,525
Annual Precipitation: 46.04"
Principal Industries: Agriculture, Education, Fishing, Food Processing, Logging, Manufacturing of Wood Products, Recreation, Tourism
Points of Interest: Autzen Stadium, Bohemia Mines, covered bridges, dams and reservoirs, Darlingtonia Botanical Wayside, Eugene Conference Center, Eugene's Fifth Ave. Historic District, Heceta Head Lighthouse, Honeyman State Park, hot springs, Howard Buford Recreation Area, Hult Center for the Performing Arts, Lane Comm. Coll.,

McKenzie Pass, Proxy Falls, Univ. of Oregon.

Lane County was named in honor of the first territorial governor, Joseph Lane. Eighty acres of land near the Willamette River in what is now downtown Eugene were donated to the county by pioneers Eugene Skinner and Charnel Mulligan.

The Home Rule Charter became effective January 1963, enabling Lane County to enact local legislation and still comply with the Oregon statutes.

County Officials: Commissioners— Steve Cornacchia (NP) 1999, Ellie Dumdi (NP) 1999, Bobby Green Sr. (NP) 2001, Peter Sorenson (NP) 2001, Cindy Weeldreyer (NP) 1999; Dist. Atty. F. Douglass Harcleroad (NP) 1997; Assess. Jim Gangle (NP) 1999; Justices of the Peace Cindy Cable, Robert Peterson, Cindy Sinclair; Sheriff Jan Clements (NP) 2001; Co. Admin. Bill VanVactor; Elect. Admin. Annette Newingham; Surv. Bob Ezell.

Lincoln County

County Seat: Courthouse, 225 W Olive St., Newport 97365; 541-265-6611; Fax: 541-265-4176

Established: Feb. 20, 1893
Elev. at Newport: 134'
Area: 992 sq. mi.
Average Temp.: January 43.4°, July 56.9°
Population: 42,200
Assessed Value: $4,138,971,173
Annual Precipitation: 74.62"
Principal Industries: Lumber, Fishing, Agriculture, Tourism
Points of Interest: Devil's Lake, Boiler Bay State Park, Otter Crest Viewpoint, Agate Beach, Yaquina Bay State Park and Lighthouse, Seal Rock State Park, Oregon Coast Aquarium, OSU Marine Science Center, Cape Perpetua Federal Recreational Area and Museum, Yaquina Art Center.

Lincoln County was named for Abraham Lincoln, 16th president of the United States. The county was created by the state Legislature in 1893 from Benton and Polk counties and comprised the Siletz Indian Reservation, lying between Polk County and the Pacific Ocean. Forests provide the county's lumber industry with raw materials.

Newport is Oregon's oceanography research center with OSU's Marine Science Center and its fleet of ocean-going vessels. Newport is also the Dungeness crab capital of the world. Lincoln City, formed over 25 years ago by the consolidation of five small towns, is an oceanside community with numerous tourist-oriented attractions and elegant resorts.

County Officials: Commissioners— Jean Cowan (D) 2001, Nancy Leonard (D) 1999, Don Lindly (D) 1999; Dist. Atty. Daniel Glode (NP) 2001; Assess. Ed Todd (D) 1999; Clerk Dana Jenkins (D) 1999; Justice of the Peace Dan Poling; Sheriff John O'Brien (NP) 1999; Surv. Tom Hamilton (D) 2001; Treas. Linda Pitzer (D) 2001.

Linn County

County Seat: Courthouse, 300 4th Ave. SW, Albany 97321; 541-967-3825

Established: Dec. 28, 1847
Elev. at Albany: 210'
Area: 2,297 sq. mi.
Average Temp.: January 39.0°, July 65.6°
Population: 100,000
Assessed Value: $4,446,061,483
Annual Precipitation: 42.55"
Principal Industries: Agriculture and Food Products, Wood Products, Rare Metals and Manufacturing
Points of Interest: Foster and Green Peter Reservoirs, Brownsville Museum, Hoodoo Ski Bowl, Sodaville Springs (Oregon's oldest state park), South Santiam River, covered bridges, historic homes of Albany.

Linn County was named for U.S. Senator Lewis F. Linn (1795-1843) of Missouri. He was the author of the Donation Land Law which gave free land to settlers in the West.

Linn County is centrally located in the beautiful Willamette Valley, with an open-space atmosphere, but with urban attractions nearby. A mild climate with sufficient rain and sun produces one of Oregon's most diversified farming areas, leading the nation in the production of common and perennial ryegrass. Dairy farming is also important. Large corporations have selected Linn County as the location for manufacturing plants, producing mobile homes, rare metals, food processing and packaging plus many support businesses and services.

Recreational opportunities are unlimited and include fishing in the high lakes and mountain streams, picnic and camping facilities in parks and forest camps, boating and water skiing on the lakes and rivers, petrified wood and agate beds, covered bridges and historical spots.

County Officials: Commissioners—Dave Schmidt, chair (R) 2001, Larry J. Johnson (D) 1999, Catherine Skiens (D) 2001; Dist. Atty. Jason Carlile (NP) 2001; Assess. Mark Noakes (D) 2001; Clerk Steven Druckenmiller (R) 1999; Justices of the Peace Jad Lemhouse, Richard Triska; Sheriff David K. Burright (NP) 2001; Surv. Rodger N. Latham (NP) 2001; Treas. Shannon Willard (D) 2001.

Malheur County

County Seat: Courthouse, 251 B St. W, Vale 97918; 541-473-5124; Fax: 541-473-5168

Established:
Feb. 17, 1887
Elev. at Vale:
2,243'
Area:
9,926 sq. mi.
Average Temp.:
January 28.7°, July 75.6°
Population: 28,700
Assessed Value: $1,089,696,017
Annual Precipitation: 9.64"
Principal Industries: Agriculture, Livestock, Food Processing, Recreation
Points of Interest: Oregon Trail, including several miles of visible wagon ruts, Owyhee Lake, Snake River, Jordan Craters Lava Flow, Leslie Gulch, Painted Canyon, Rockhound Center (Thundereggs), hunting, fishing, Bighorn sheep and wild horses.

The county derived its name from "Riviere au Malheur" or "Unfortunate River" (later changed to "Malheur River"), named by French trappers whose property and furs were stolen from their river encampment. Malheur, located in Oregon's southeast corner, is the state's second largest county. It is 94 percent rangeland, two-thirds of which is con-

trolled by BLM. The Basques, primarily shepherds, settled in Jordan Valley in the 1890s. Today irrigated fields in the county's northeastern corner, known as Western Treasure Valley, are the center of intensive and diversified farming.

County Officials: Commissioners—Judge Russell F. Hursh, chair (R) 1999, John J. Bishop (R) 1999, R. Thomas Butler (R) 2002; Dist. Atty. Patricia Sullivan (NP) 2002; Assess. Richard Meisinger (NP) 2002; Clerk Deborah DeLong (NP) 1999; Justices of the Peace Dolores Bryant, Dick Pounds; Sheriff Andrew Bentz (NP) 2002; Treas. Janice Belnap (NP) 2002.

Marion County

County Seat: Courthouse, 100 High St. NE, Salem 97301-3670; 503-588-5212; Fax: 503-588-5237; Email: commissioners@open.org; Web: www.open.org/marion

Established:
July 5, 1843
Elev. at Salem: 154'
Area:
1,194 sq. miles
Average Temp.:
January 39.3°, July 66.3°
Population: 262,800
Assessed Value: $12,102,242,220
Annual Precipitation: 40.35"
Principal Industries: Government, Agriculture, Food Processing, Lumber, Manufacturing, Education, Tourism
Points of Interest: State Capitol, Champoeg State Park, Wheatland Ferry, Buena Vista Ferry, Silver Falls State Park, Detroit Dam and Santiam River, Breitenbush Hot Springs, Mt. Angel Abbey, food processing plants, Willamette University, Chemeketa Community College, Mission Mill Museum Village, historic Bush House, Deepwood House and Gilbert House Children's Museum.

Marion County, then called Champoick, was created by the Provisional Government Legislative Committee 16 years before Oregon gained statehood. In 1849 the name was changed to Marion honoring General Francis Marion.

The county, located in the heart of the Willamette Valley, has the Willamette River as its western boundary which was

established in 1856. Salem, the county seat, is one of the valley's oldest cities. Among its public buildings are the Courthouse, State Capitol, Capitol Mall buildings and Salem Civic Center, dedicated in 1972. The county was presided over by the Marion County Court until January 1, 1963, when the court was abolished and replaced by a Board of Commissioners.

County Officials: Commissioners—Randall Franke (R) 1999, Gary Heer (R) 2001, Mary B. Pearmine, (R) 1999; Dist. Atty. Dale Penn (NP) 2001; Assess. Doug Ebner (R) 1999; Clerk Al Davidson (R) 2001; Justices of the Peace Steven R. Summers, Janice D. Zyryanoff; Sheriff Robert Prinslow (NP) 1999; Treas. Ralph Grim (R) 2001; Admin. Off. Ken Roudybush.

Morrow County

County Seat: Courthouse, 100 Court St., Heppner 97836; 541-676-9061; Fax: 541-676-9876

Established: Feb. 16, 1885
Elev. at Heppner: 1,955'
Area: 2,049 sq. mi.
Average Temp.: January 33.1°, July 69.0°
Population: 9,000
Assessed Value: $974,947,790
Annual Precipitation: 13.59"
Principal Industries: Agriculture, Food Processing, Utilities, Lumber, Livestock, Recreation
Points of Interest: Columbia River, coal-fired generating plant, Blue Mountains, Umatilla National Forest, farming areas, hunting, fishing, Oregon Trail, Blue Mountain Scenic Byway, Morrow County Museum.

Morrow County, created from Umatilla County in 1885, is located in north-central Oregon east of the Cascades. It was named for J.L. Morrow, an early resident. In between are more than one million acres of gently rolling plains and broad plateaus. This rich agricultural land can be roughly divided into four occupational zones—increasing amounts of irrigation farming in the north; vast fields of wheat yielding to cattle and sheep ranches as you move through the center; and timber products in the south. With the advent of center

pivot irrigation technology, Morrow County became one of Oregon's fastest growing areas in terms of population, personal income, and agricultural and industrial development. The Port of Morrow serves as a gateway to Pacific Northwest and Pacific Rim markets.

County Officials: Commissioners—Judge Louis A. Carlson (R) 1999, Raymond French (R) 1999, John E. Wenholz (D) 2001; Dist. Atty. Earl Woods Jr. (NP) 1999; Assess. Gregory Sweek (NP) 2001; Clerk Barbara Bloodsworth (NP) 2001; Justice of the Peace Charlotte Gray; Sheriff Roy Drago (NP) 2001; Surv. Denny Edwards (R) 2001; Treas. Gayle Gutierrez (NP) 2001.

Multnomah County

County Seat: Courthouse, 1021 SW 4th, Portland 97204; 503-248-3511; Web: www.multnomah.lib.or.us

Established: Dec. 22, 1854
Elev. at Portland: 77'
Area: 465 sq. mi.
Average Temp.: January 38.9°, July 67.7°
Population: 636,000
Assessed Value: $38,460,937,910
Annual Precipitation: 37.39"
Principal Industries: Manufacturing, Transportation, Wholesale and Retail Trade, Tourism
Points of Interest: Oregon Historical Center, Oregon Museum of Science and Industry, Portland Art Museum, Washington Park and Zoo, Rose Test Gardens, Japanese Gardens, Columbia River Gorge, Multnomah Falls, Blue Lake Park, Oxbow Park, Pittock Mansion, Port of Portland, Memorial Coliseum, Oregon Convention Center.

Lewis and Clark recorded the Indian village of Multnomah on Sauvie Island in 1805 and applied that name to all local Indians. The name is derived from nemathlonamaq, probably meaning "downriver." Multnomah County was created from parts of Washington and Clackamas counties by the Territorial Legislature five years before the state came into existence, when citizens found it inconvenient to travel to Hillsboro to conduct county business.

The county is both the smallest in size and largest in population in Oregon. Over 50 percent of its people live in Portland, a busy metropolis dominated by rivers and greenery. The remaining area includes picturesque rural land, from pastoral farms on Sauvie Island to the rugged Columbia River Gorge and the western slopes of Mt. Hood.

County Officials: Commissioners— Beverly Stein, chair (D) 1999, Tanya Collier (D) 2001, Gary Hansen (D) 1999, Sharron Kelley (D) 2001, Dan Saltzman (D) 2001; Dist. Atty. Michael D. Schrunk (NP) 2001; Aud. Gary Blackmer (D) 1998; Sheriff Dan Noelle (NP) 1998; Dir. of Assess., Tax. and Rec. Janice Druian, appt.; Dir. of Elec. Vicki Ervin, appt.; Dir. of Fin. David Boyer, appt.; Surv. Dennis Fantz, appt.

Polk County

County Seat: Courthouse, 850 Main St., Dallas 97338; 503-623-8173; Fax: 503-623-0896

Established: Dec. 22, 1845
Elev. at Dallas: 325'
Area: 745 sq. mi.
Average Temp.: January 38.9°, July 65.6°
Population: 56,300
Assessed Value: $2,460,963,485
Annual Precipitation: 50.58"
Principal Industries: Agriculture, Forest Products, Heavy Manufacturing, Education
Points of Interest: Western Oregon State College, covered bridges, historic courthouse, Brunk House, Baskett Slough Wildlife Refuge, mountain

scenery, wineries, National Historic Trail, Confederated Tribes of Grand Ronde Headquarters and Gaming Casino.

Polk County was created by the Provisional Legislature from the original Yamhill district. It was named for then U.S. President James Knox Polk. The first county seat was Cynthia Ann. City officials later changed its name to Dallas, after Vice-President George M. Dallas, and moved the community about a mile to improve its water supply.

The first courthouse was at Cynthia Ann. The county's second courthouse burned in 1898 and was replaced with the present building built with sandstone quarried three miles west of town. A three-story office annex was completed in 1966. Polk County Human Services was consolidated in the newly acquired Academy Building in 1989.

Traveling back roads in Polk County will reveal many attractions—from covered bridges and pleasant parks to vineyards, wineries, and bed and breakfast lodgings spotting the surrounding hills. Many roads meander through beautiful, fertile valleys from the Willamette River to the timbered foothills of the Coast Range. One of Polk County's cities, Independence, was the final destination of early wagon trains to Oregon. Other cities located in Polk County are Dallas, Monmouth, Falls City and portions of Salem and Willamina.

County Officials: Commissioners— C. Ralph Blanchard (R) 1999, Ron Dodge (D) 1999, Mike Propes (R) 2001; Admin. Off. John K. Anderson; Assess. Dennis Day (R) 2001; Clerk Linda Dawson (R) 2001; Dist. Atty. Fred Avera, 2001; Sheriff Ray Steele (NP) 1999; Treas. Carolyn Wall (D) 2001.

Built in 1899, the original Sherman County Courthouse in Moro cost about $6,000.

Photo by Gary Halvorson, courtesy of State Archives.

Sherman County

County Seat: Courthouse, PO Box 365,
Moro 97039; 541-565-3606;Fax: 541-565-3312

Established:
Feb. 25, 1889
Elev. at Moro:
1,807'
Area:
831 sq. mi.
Average Temp.:
January 30.1°, July 68.3°
Population: 1,900
Assessed Value: $162,540,280
Annual Precipitation: 11.38"
Principal Industries: Tourism, Wheat, Barley and Cattle

Points of Interest: Historic county courthouse, Sherman County Museum, Gordon Ridge, John Day Dam, Sherar's Grade, Deschutes State Park, LePage Park, Giles French Park, Sherman County Fairgrounds and RV Park.

Sherman County, created in 1889 from the northeast corner of Wasco County, was named for General William Tecumseh Sherman. It was separated from Wasco County as much for its unique geological setting as for the settlers' interest in having their own political process. The rolling hills are bordered by the deep canyons of the John Day River to the east, Columbia River on the north and the Deschutes River and Buck Hollow to the west and south.

The county was settled in the 1870s by stockmen; by 1881 the homesteaders arrived, permanently changing the area by plowing and fencing the tall grass. Since that time, the county has been a wheat-growing area with miles of waving grain on rolling hills of wind-blown glacial silt.

The total absence of timber in the county exemplifies the true meaning of the "wide open spaces of the west." It has pastoral landscape with spectacular views of canyons and rivers with mountains silhouetted in the distance. Recreation abounds on the rivers, from the famous and scenic fly-fishing and white water rafting stream of the Deschutes to water-skiing, wind-surfing, boating, fishing and rafting on the John Day and Columbia rivers.

Sherman County is one of Oregon's leaders in soil and water conservation.

County Officials: Commissioners—Ken Hart (R) 2001, Judge Michael W. McArthur (R) 1999, Sharon A. Rolfe (R) 1999; Dist. Atty. Ray English (NP) 1999; Assess. Richard Stradley (R) 2001; Clerk Linda Cornie (D) 2001; Justice of the Peace Kate Martin; Sheriff Gerry Massey (NP) 2001; Surv. Daryl Ingebo (NP) 2001; Treas. Nancy McCoy (D) 1999.

Tillamook County

County Seat: Courthouse, 201 Laurel Ave.,
Tillamook 97141; 503-842-3403;
toll-free: 1-800-488-8280; Fax: 503-842-1384

Established:
Dec. 15, 1853
Elev. at Tillamook: 22'
Area:
1,125 sq. mi.
Average Temp.:
January 42.2°, July 58.2°
Population: 23,800
Assessed Value: $2,304,931,048
Annual Precipitation: 90.90"
Principal Industries: Agriculture, Lumber, Fishing, Recreation

Points of Interest: Neah-Kah-Nie Mountain, Tillamook, Nehalem, Netarts and Nestucca Bays; Oswald West State Park; Nehalem Bay State Park; Bob Straub State Park; Cape Lookout State Park; Pioneer Museum; Blue Heron Cheese Factory; Tillamook Cheese Factory; Naval Air Station Museum.

Tillamook County was formed from Yamhill and Clatsop counties. The name Tillamook comes from the Tillamook (or Killamook) Indians.

Dairy farms dominate the county's fertile valleys. It is the home of the world-famous Tillamook Cheese factory. The reforested 355,000 acre "Tillamook Burn" is rapidly maturing. Commercial thinning activity will become increasingly evident.

With 75 miles of scenic coastline, four bays and nine rivers, Tillamook County offers the finest in deep-sea and stream fishing, charter and dory boats, clamming, crabbing, beachcombing and hiking. Its forests also furnish excellent hunting.

County Officials: Commissioners—Sue Cameron (D) 2001, Jerry Dove (D) 1999, Gina (Mulford) Firman (R) 2001; Dist. Atty. William Porter (NP) 1999; Assess. Tim Lutz (D) 2001; Clerk Josephine Veltri (D) 2001; Justice of the

Peace Arlene Gahagen (NP) 2001; Sheriff Tom Dye (NP) 2001; Surv. Allan Duncan (R) 2001; Treas. Karen Richards (D) 1999.

Umatilla County

County Seat: Courthouse, 216 SE 4th St., Pendleton 97801; 541-276-7111; Fax: 541-276-4841

Established: Sept. 27, 1862

Elev. at Pendleton: 1,068'

Area: 3,231 sq. mi.

Average Temp.: January 33.5°, July 72.9°

Population: 65,500

Assessed Value: $2,612,680,700

Annual Precipitation: 12.02"

Principal Industries: Agriculture, Food Processing, Wood Products, Tourism, Manufacturing, Recreation

Points of Interest: Pendleton Round-Up, woolen mills, Old Town & County Historical Society Museum, McNary Dam, Echo Museum and historic area, Hat Rock, Battle Mountain and Emigrant Springs State Parks, Weston Historic District, Frazier Farmstead Museum in Milton-Freewater, N. Fork Umatilla Wilderness, Tollgate-Spout Springs Recreation Area, courthouse clocktower.

The county traces its creation in 1862 to regional gold rushes, which spawned the riverport of Umatilla City and brought stockraisers to the lush grasslands.

Lewis and Clark and Oregon Trail pioneers passed through, but not until the railroad arrived in 1881 and the development of dryland wheat farming did Umatilla County boom.

"Umatilla" is an Indian word meaning "water rippling over sand." Indeed, water in the form of irrigation has been key to economic diversification and growth, most recently in the Hermiston area, where the "desert now blooms." Tourism is also important in this crossroads county, and the world-famous Pendleton Round-Up draws big crowds.

County Officials: Commissioners—William S. Hansell, chair (NP) 1999, Dennis D. Doherty (NP) 2000, Emile M. Holeman (NP) 1999; Sheriff John Trumbo (NP) 2000.

Union County

County Seat: Union County Commissioners, 1106 K Ave., La Grande 97850; 541-963-1001; Fax: 541-963-1079

Established: Oct. 14, 1864

Elev. at La Grande: 2,788'

Area: 2,038 sq. mi.

Average Temp.: January 30.9°, July 70.4°

Population: 24,500

Assessed Value: $1,016,489,061

Annual Precipitation: 18.79"

Principal Industries: Agriculture, Lumber, Education

Points of Interest: Pheasant, duck, geese, elk and deer hunting, skiing at Spout Springs, Meacham and Tollgate winter sports areas, Grande Ronde Valley, Eastern Oregon State College.

Union County was named for the town of Union, which had been established two years before and named by its founders for patriotic reasons during the Civil War. It comprised a part of the northern portion of Baker County and in 1899 gave up its eastern portion to Wallowa County.

The Grande Ronde Valley in Union County is nearly table flat and is covered with the rich silt of an old lake bed. Highly diversified, with a 160-day growing season and an annual rainfall of 20 inches, the valley boasts of never having had a general crop failure. The county's 1,092 farms average 473 acres a unit.

Union County's front door opens to the rugged Wallowa Mountains. Its back door faces the Blue Mountains, attracting hikers, skiers, horseback riders, fishermen, hunters and rock climbers.

County Officials: Commissioners—John J. Howard (D) 1999, Colleen MacLeod (R) 2001, Steve McClure (R) 2001; Dist. Atty. Russell B. West (NP) 2001; Assess. Patty Gooderham (R) 2001; Clerk R. Nellie Bogue Hibbert (R) 2001; Sheriff Steve Oliver (NP) 2001; Surv. Gregory Blackman (D) 2001; Treas. Peggy Sutton (D) 2001.

Wallowa County

County Seat: Courthouse, 101 S River,
Enterprise 97828; 541-426-4543;
Fax: 541-426-0582

Established:
Feb. 11, 1887
Elev. at
Enterprise:
3,757'
Area:
3,153 sq. mi.
Average Temp.:
January 24.2°, July 63.0°
Population: 7,250
Assessed Value: $490,265,840
Annual Precipitation: 13.08"
Principal Industries: Agriculture, Art,
Livestock, Lumber, Recreation
Points of Interest: Wallowa Lake, Art
Galleries, Mount Howard gondola, Eagle
Cap Wilderness Area, Hells Canyon
National Recreation Area, Minam,
Wallowa and Grande Ronde Rivers.

This rather isolated area was claimed
by the Chief Joseph band of the Nez
Perce as their hunting and fishing
grounds. They used the word "wallowa"
to designate a tripod of poles used to
support fish nets. In 1871, the first
settlers came to Wallowa County, crossing the mountains in search of livestock
feed in the Wallowa Valley. The area
had been part of Union County since
1864 but it was carved from that county
by a legislative act in 1887.

Wallowa County is a land of rugged
mountains, gentle valleys and deep
canyons. Peaks in the Wallowa Mountains soar to almost 10,000 feet in elevation and the Snake River dips to only
about 1,000 feet above sea level. Hells
Canyon, carved by the Snake, is the
nation's deepest gorge, averaging 5,500
feet from rim to river.

The scenery in the county is spectacular and serves as a magnet for tourists.
Unrivaled opportunities for outdoor recreation create the county's reputation as a
visitors' paradise. Permanent residents
enjoy the same recreation opportunities,
adding to a high quality of life supported
by traditional farm and forest industries
as well as art and tourism.

County Officials: Commissioners—
Judge Benjamin M. Boswell (R) 2001,
Mike Hayward (R) 2001, Pat Wortman
(R) 1999; Dist. Atty. Daniel Ousley (NP)
1999; Assess. Scot Langton (NP) 2001;
Clerk Charlotte McIver (D) 2001; Sheriff

Ron Jett (NP) 2001; Surv. Jack W. Burris
(R) 2001; Treas. Ernestine Kilgore (D)
2001.

Wasco County

County Seat: Courthouse, 511 Washington,
The Dalles 97058; 541-296-2207;
Fax: 541-298-3650

Established:
Jan. 11, 1854
Elev. at The
Dalles: 98'
Area:
2,396 sq. mi.
Average
Temp.:
January 33.4°, July 73.1°
Population: 22,500
Assessed Value: $1,202,226,720
Annual Precipitation: 14.90"
Principal Industries: Agriculture
(cereal grains, cherries, apples, live-
stock), Lumber, Manufacturing, Electric
Power, Transportation, Aluminum
Points of Interest: Columbia and
Deschutes Rivers, Fort Dalles Museum,
Pulpit Rock, The Dalles Dam, Celilo
Converter Station, Indian reservation
and Kah-Nee-Ta Resort, Mt. Hood,
Sorosis Park, original Wasco County
Courthouse, St. Peter's Landmark.

When Wasco County was created from
the original Champoeg (Champooick)
district by the Territorial Legislature, it
embraced all of Oregon east of the Cascade Range, most of Idaho and parts of
Montana and Wyoming. It was named
for the Wasco (or Wascopam) Indian
tribe.

Wasco's county seat is The Dalles.
Now the trading hub of north-central
Oregon, The Dalles gained earlier fame
as the town at the end of the Oregon
Trail. Thousands of years before that,
primitive groups scratched strange
picture writings on rocks overlooking
the Columbia in this area. Later, Indian
tribes gathered for generations near
Celilo Falls to trade and fish.

The county's Indian heritage continues in evidence today. Kah-Nee-Ta, a
popular Oregon resort, is located on
the Warm Springs Indian Reservation
in its southern area.

County Officials: Commissioners—
Judge John Mabrey, chair (R) 1999,
Dan Ericksen (R) 2001, Scott McKay (D)
1999; Dist. Atty. Bernard L. Smith (NP)
2001; Assess. Herb Crook (R) 1999;

Clerk Karen LeBreton (D) 2001; Sheriff Darrell Hill (NP) 2001; Surv. C. Dennis Kramer (D) 1999; Treas. Linda L. May (R) 1999.

Washington County

County Seat: Public Services Bldg., 155 N. 1st Ave., Hillsboro 97124; 503-648-8611; Web: www.co.washington.or.us

Established: July 5, 1843
Elev. at Hillsboro: 196'
Area: 727 sq. mi.
Average Temp.: January 38.9°, July 66.6°
Population: 376,500
Assessed Value: $26,443,545,990
Annual Precipitation: 37.71"
Principal Industries: Agriculture, Lumber, Manufacturing, Food Processing, Electronics
Points of Interest: Tualatin Valley orchard lands, Pacific Univ., Wilson River and Sunset Highways to the coast, Scoggin Dam, old Scotch Church.

The original four counties of the Territory of Oregon were: Twality, Clackamas, Yamhill and Champoick. Twality was changed to Washington in honor of President George Washington by the Territorial Legislature on Sept. 3, 1849. The actual organization of Washington County government came in 1854.

Now one of the state's fastest developing areas, the fertile Tualatin Valley was once filled with beaver and a favorite hunting ground for Hudson's Fur Co. trappers. The first settlers arrived around 1840, lured by rich soil. Despite its rapid urbanization, the valley still contains prime agricultural land. Many small towns rich in history dot the area. Pacific University, founded as Tualatin Academy in 1849, is one of the oldest colleges in the West.

Washington County operates under a home rule charter approved by voters in 1962. The Northwest's largest enclosed shopping center, Washington Square, is located south of Beaverton.

County Officials: Commissioners— Linda Peters, chair (NP) 1999, Kathy Christy (NP) 1999, Andy Duyck (NP) 1999, Kim Katsion (NP) 2001, Roy Rogers (NP) 2001; Dist. Atty. Scott Upham (NP) 1999; Justice of the Peace

Jim Shartel; Sheriff Jim Spinden (NP) 2001; Aud. Alan Percell (NP) 1999; Co. Admin. Charles D. Cameron; Assess. Jerry Hanson.

Wheeler County

County Seat: Courthouse, 701 Adams St., Fossil 97830; 541-763-2911; Fax: 541-763-2026

Established: Feb. 17, 1899
Elev. at Fossil: 2,654'
Area: 1,713 sq. mi.
Average Temp.: January 35°, July 66°
Population: 1,600
Assessed Value: $78,538,547
Annual Precipitation: 14.66"
Principal Industries: Agriculture, Lumber, Tourism
Points of Interest: Painted Hills, John Day Fossil Beds, John Day River.

Wheeler County was formed by the Legislature from parts of Grant, Gilliam and Crook counties and was named for Henry H. Wheeler who operated the first mail stage line from The Dalles to Canyon City. The new county consisted of 1,656 square miles with an estimated 46 townships, population of 2,500 and taxable property of one million dollars.

Wheeler County is as rugged and uneven as any Oregon county with the terrain varying widely from sagebrush, juniper and rim rock to stands of pine and fir. Portions of two national forests lie within its boundaries with forest lands covering nearly one-third of the county. The area is probably best known as one of the most outstanding depositories of prehistoric fossils on the North American continent.

County Officials: Commissioners— Judge Jeanne E. Burch, chair (R) 2001, H. John Asher (I) 2001, Lana Jean Perry (D) 1999; Dist. Atty. Thomas W. Cutsforth (NP) 1999; Assess. Donald R. Cossitt (R) 1999; Clerk Marylin Garcia (NP) 2001; Justices of the Peace Linda Keys, Theressa Ward; Sheriff Craig Ward (NP) 2001; Treas. Nancy L. Misener (D) 1999; Surv. Bob Bagette (NP) 2001.

The Willamette River flows peacefully near Halsey, a rural Linn County community. Photo by Sig Mickelsen.

Yamhill County

County Seat: Courthouse, 535 NE 5th, McMinnville 97128; 503-472-9371; Fax: 503-434-7520

Established: July 5, 1843

Elev. at McMinnville: 157'

Area: 718 sq. mi.

Average Temp.: January 39.1°, July 65.4°

Population: 77,500

Assessed Value: $3,311,385,073

Annual Precipitation: 43.62"

Principal Industries: Agriculture, Lumber, Education, International Aviation, Dental Equipment, Manufactured Homes, Pulp and Paper, Steel

Points of Interest: Linfield College, George Fox University, Herbert Hoover House, military blockhouse, Yamhill County Historical Museum, Wheatland Ferry.

Yamhill County was one of Oregon's original four districts. The present boundaries were established in 1860. The county was named after the Yamhelas or Yamhill Indians of the Kalapooian family, who formerly lived along the Yamhill River in the western Willamette Valley.

Today, agriculture is still the county's primary industry. Wheat and barley, horticulture crops and dairy products are major agricultural products. Yamhill County ranks seventh out of Oregon's 36 counties in annual market value of its agricultural production. Yamhill County is also the heart of Oregon's wine industry. Nineteen wineries represent the largest concentration of wineries in any county and produce the greatest number of award-winning wines in the state.

A third of the county is covered with commercial timber. The mainstay of the western valley area is logging and timber products. Nonseasonal industries include a steel rolling mill, electronic and dental equipment manufacturing, an international airline and helicopter company, and a newsprint mill.

County Officials: Commissioners—Tom Bunn (R) 1999, Robert Johnstone (R) 1999; Ted Lopuszynski (D) 2001; Dist. Atty. Brad Berry (NP) 2001; Assess. Linda Stephenson (NP) 2001; Co. Clerk Charles Stern (NP) 1999; Sheriff Norm Hand (NP) 2001; Surv. Dan Linschied (NP) 1999; Treas. Harriet Miller (NP) 2001.

Regional Governments

In January 1984, the 14 regional governments in Oregon came together to form the Oregon Regional Councils Association (ORCA) to promote greater cooperation between all levels of government.

The councils are multi-jurisdictional and multi-purpose organizations. They are voluntary associations of local governments cooperating and working together on issues and problems which cross city, county, and in some cases state boundaries. The association provides a forum for information exchange and discussion of current issues of concern. For more information contact the executive director of any organization listed below.

Regional COGs in Oregon are formed under chapter 190 of the Oregon Revised Statutes.

Central Oregon Intergovernmental Council
Rick MacKay, Exec. Dir.
PO Box 575, 2363 SW Glacier Pl., Redmond 97756; 541-548-8163; Fax: 541-923-3416

Clatsop-Tillamook Intergovernmental Council
Don Ebel, Exec. Dir.
PO Box 698, Wheeler 97147; 503-368-4200; Fax: 503-368-7939

Greater Eastern Oregon Development Corporation
Dennis Newell, Exec. Dir.
PO Box 1041, Pendleton 97801; 541-276-6745; Fax: 541-276-6071

Idaho-Oregon Planning & Development Assn., Inc.
Phil Choate, Exec. Dir.
PO Box 311, Weiser, ID 83672; 208-549-2411; Fax: 208-549-0071

Lane Council Of Governments
George Kloeppel, Exec. Dir.
125 E 8th Ave., Eugene 97401; 541-682-4283; Fax: 541-682-4099

Mid-Columbia Council of Governments
Scott McKay, chair
1113 Kelly Ave., The Dalles 97058; 541-298-4101; Fax: 541-298-2084

Mid-Willamette Valley Council of Governments
David A. Galati, Exec. Dir.
105 High St. SE, Salem 97301; 503-588-6177; Fax: 503-588-6094

Northeast Oregon Economic Development District
Lisa Lang, Exec. Dir.
PO Box 3197, La Grande, 97850; 541-963-2399; Fax: 541-963-2178

101 NE 1st St., Suite 100, Enterprise, 97828; 541-426-3598; 1-800-645-9454; Fax: 541-426-9508

Oregon Cascades West Council of Governments
William Wagner, Exec. Dir.
1400 Queen Ave. SE Albany 97321; 541-967-8720; Fax: 541-967-6123

Rogue Valley Council of Governments
Mary DeLaMare-Schaefer, Exec. Dir.
PO Box 3275, Central Point 97502; 541-664-6674; Fax: 541-664-7927

Umpqua Regional Council of Governments
Stacey B. MacDonald, Exec. Dir.
1036 SE Douglas Ave., Rm 8, Roseburg 97470; 541-440-4231; Fax: 541-440-6252

Metro
600 NE Grand Ave., Portland 97232-2736; 503-797-1700; Fax: 503-797-1797; Web: www.multnomah.lib.or.us/metro

District officials: Mike Burton, executive officer, 1999; Councilors: Ruth McFarland (1) 1999; Don Morissette (2) 1999; Jon Kvistad (3) 1997; Susan McLain (4) 1999; Ed Washington (5) 1997; Lisa Naito (6) 1997; Patricia McCaig (7) 1999; Auditor Alexis Dow, 1999.

Metro covers approximately 460 square miles of the urban portions of Clackamas, Multnomah and Washington counties in northwestern Oregon. There are 24 cities in the Metro service area, including Beaverton, Gresham, Hillsboro, Lake Oswego, Milwaukie, Oregon City and Portland.

Metro, the nation's only elected regional government, is responsible for a broad range of services. According to its charter, approved by voters in 1992, Metro has primary responsibility for regional land-use and transportation planning, and is further empowered to address any other issue of "metropolitan concern." This grant of authority clearly underscores the Portland metropolitan region's commitment to maintain and enhance the livability of the region.

This commitment was again demonstrated in May 1995 when 62 percent of the citizens of the region voted to authorize $135.6 million in general obligation bonds to acquire and protect a system of regional open spaces, parks and streams.

History

Metro was formed in 1979, when voters approved the merger of a council of governments (Columbia Region Association of Governments—CRAG) that had land-use and transportation planning responsibilities with the Metropolitan Service District, which had been created to provide regional services that included the solid waste management plan and operation of a metropolitan zoo. The new Metropolitan Service District (MSD) was governed by an elected council and an elected executive officer. It had the combined authority of the two predecessor agencies and other potential additional powers.

During the years, additional responsibilities were assigned to Metro by the state Legislature with concurrence of the jurisdictions within Metro's boundaries. In 1980, Metro became responsible for regional solid waste disposal when it took over operation of the one existing publicly owned regional landfill and began construction of a transfer station. In November 1986, voters approved general obligation bond funding for the Oregon Convention Center, built and operated by Metro. In January 1990, Metro assumed management responsibility for the Portland Center for the Performing Arts, Portland Civic Stadium and Portland Memorial Coliseum (though management of the coliseum was later returned to the city, which turned it over to the new Oregon Arena Corporation). Finally, in 1994, Metro assumed management responsibility for the Multnomah County parks system and Expo Center. Ownership of these facilities was transferred to Metro on July 1, 1996.

Regional Planning Functions

Metro has long had an important coordination role in regional transportation planning. Metro is the designated metropolitan planning organization, responsible for the allocation of federal transportation funds to projects in the region. The region's success in attracting federal funding for highway and transit projects is due, in large part, to Metro's role in building and maintaining regional consensus on projects to be funded and ensuring that funding is allocated to high-priority projects.

In connection with its responsibility for transportation planning, Metro has developed a regional data center to forecast transportation and land-use needs. All local jurisdictions now rely on and contribute to this data center, eliminating duplication between governments and battles about "dueling data." This has allowed all jurisdictions in the region to focus on important policy choices rather than arguing about assumptions.

With the adoption of a state land-use planning law (SB 100), local governments were required to prepare comprehensive land-use plans. Metro (as CRAG) was the agency responsible for establishing and maintaining an urban growth boundary (UGB) for the Portland region. Through the enforcement of the UGB pursuant to Oregon's land-use laws, the region has maintained its unique character and is now a national model for urban growth management planning.

Metro's current role in regional land-use planning and growth management is an outgrowth of its role in establishing the urban growth boundary, transportation planning and data management. Local jurisdictions and the region's voters have recognized the value of a coordinated approach to land-use and livability issues, and have assigned that responsibility to Metro.

Charter Approval

The most significant development in Metro's history occurred with the approval by the voters in 1992 of a home-rule Charter. Prior to that time, Metro was organized under a grant of authority by the Oregon Legislature and the Oregon Revised Statutes. Metro's powers were limited to those expressly granted by the Legislature, and any extension of those powers had to first be approved by the Legislature.

With the growth in the region, however, and Metro's increasingly important role, the region recognized that the power and authority of the regional government should be controlled directly by the voters of the region and not by the state Legislature. Accordingly, in 1990, the Legislature referred a constitutional amendment to the voters to allow the creation of a home-rule regional government in the Portland metropolitan area. Voters approved that amendment, and a charter committee was formed shortly thereafter. In 1992, a Charter for Metro was referred to voters, who approved it. Metro thereby achieved the distinction not only of being the nation's only elected regional government (as it had been since 1979), but also the only one organized under a home-rule Charter approved by voters.

Port Districts of Oregon

Source: Oregon Public Ports Association

1288 Court Street NE - 2nd Floor, Salem 97301; 503-585-1250; Fax: 503-364-9919

Port of Alsea, 1955

PO Box 1060, Waldport 97394; 541-563-3872; Fax: 541-563-3334.

Commissioners: Bonnie Conrad; Ken Field; Charles Graham; Mel Lulay; Mark "Tom" Rowley. Port Mgr.: Maggie Rivers. Meets 2nd Wed. of the month.

Port of Arlington, 1933

PO Box 279, Arlington 97812; 541-454-2868; Fax: 541-454-2053.

Commissioners: Brad Anderson; Steve Anderson; James Morris; Richard Rende; one vacancy. Exec. Sec.: Francie Morris. Meets 1st Tues. of the month.

Port of Astoria, 1914

1 Portway, Astoria 97103; 503-325-4521; Fax: 503-325-4525.

Commissioners: Robert Filori; Warren Kan; Robert Lovell; Bill Shea; Glenn Taggart. Exec. Dir.: Jonathan Krebs. Meets 3rd Tues. of the month.

Port of Bandon, 1913

PO Box 206, Bandon 97411; 541-347-3206.

Commissioners: James Fleck; Hugh McNeil; Robert Pierce; Harry Slack; Phyllis Stinnett. Port Mgr.: Alex Linke. Meets 2nd Wed. of the month.

Port of Brookings Harbor, 1956

PO Box 848, Brookings 97415; 541-469-2218; Fax: 541-469-0672.

Commissioners: Ken Byrtus; Edmund Gray; Larry Goodman; Lloyd Whaley; John Zia. Port Mgr.: Russ Crabtree. Meets 4th Mon. of the month.

Port of Cascade Locks, 1937

PO Box 307, Cascade Locks 97014; 541-374-8619; Fax: 541-374-8428

Commissioners: Richard McCulley; Jean McLean; Ken Henning; Barbara Irving; Phil Redlock. General Mgr.: Tobin White. Meets 3rd Thurs. of the month.

Oregon International Port of Coos Bay, 1909

PO Box 1215, Coos Bay 97420; 541-267-7678; Fax: 541-269-1475.

Commissioners: Vern Brecke; Kathy Grossman; Rudy Juul; Jim Scavera; Mike Waldrup. General Mgr.: Allan Rumbaugh. Meets 3rd Wed. of the month.

Port of Coquille River, 1912

PO Box 640, Myrtle Point 97458; 503-378-1018.

Commissioners: Paul Davis; Don Gurney; Gordon Hayes; Lloyd Mast; Keith Williamson. Admin.: Scott Ashcom. Meets 3rd Wed. of the month.

Port of Garibaldi, 1906

PO Box 10, Garibaldi 97118; 503-322-3292; Fax: 503-322-0029.

Commissioners: Carol Brown; Sheri Newman; Doris Sheldon; Robert Vanderhoef; Don Wustenberg. Mgr.: Don Bacon. Meets 2nd Wed. of the month.

Port of Gold Beach, 1955

PO Box 1126, Gold Beach 97444; 541-247-6269; Fax: 541-247-6268.

Commissioners: Scott Boley; Ted Burdette; Gary Combs; Doug Danville; Ted Ferguson. Mgr.: Ron Armstrong. Meets 3rd Thurs. of the month.

Port of Hood River, 1933

PO Box 239, Hood River 97031; 541-386-1645; Fax: 541-386-1395.

Commissioners: Bill Baker; Dave Burkhart; Jean LaMaita; Robert Nickelsen; Nancy Wesche. Exec. Dir.: Greg Baker. Meets 1st and 3rd Tues. of the month.

Port of Morrow, 1958

PO Box 200, Boardman 97818; 541-481-7678; Fax: 541-481-2679.

Commissioners: Daniel Creamer; Jerry Healy; Larry Lindsay; Marv Padberg; Deane Seeger. General Mgr.: Gary Neal. Meets 2nd Wed. of the month.

Port of Nehalem, 1909

PO Box 238, Wheeler 97147; 503-368-7212.

Commissioners: Charles B. Collin; Bill Dart; Stanley A. Jud; F.E. "Shang" Knight; Dale Stockton. Admin. Sec.: Ann Morgan. Meets 4th Wed. of the month.

Port of Newport, 1910

600 SE Bay Blvd., Newport 97365; 541-265-7758; Fax: 541-265-4235.

Commissioners: Alan Brown; Rob Halverson; David Jincks; Tom Ruddiman; Ed Whelan. General Mgr.: Don Mann. Meets 4th Tues. of the month.

Port of Portland, 1891

PO Box 3529, Portland 97208; 503-231-5000; Fax: 503-731-7080.

Commissioners: Rob Cook; Alfred M. Gleason; Cheryl D. Perrin; Michael Powell; Keith Thomson; Robert Walsh; Dr. Nancy Wilgenbusch; Richard C. Wise; Junki Yoshida. Exec. Dir.: Mike Thorne. Meets 2nd Wed. of the month.

Port of Port Orford, 1919

PO Box 490, Port Orford 97465; 541-332-7121.

Commissioners: Gifford Barnes; Lynn Haller; Bill Oleson; John Spurgeon; Bruce Yocum. Port Mgr.: Gayle Paige. Meets 3rd Mon. of the month.

Port of St. Helens, 1941

PO Box 598, St. Helens 97051; 503-397-2888; Fax: 503-397-6924.

Commissioners: Eric Dahlgren; Vern Harrington; Elizabeth Johnson; Steve Salvey; Dennis Widme. General Mgr.: Peter Williamson. Meets 2nd and last Wed. of the month.

Port of Siuslaw, 1909

PO Box 1220, Florence 97439; 541-997-3426; Fax: 541-997-9407.

Commissioners: Bud Miles; Verne "Skip" Passenger; Leonard Van Curler; Lynette Wikstrom-Smith; Don Wilbur. Port Mgr.: Tom Kartrude. Meets 2nd Wed. of the month.

Port of The Dalles, 1933

3636 Klindt Dr., The Dalles 97058; 541-298-4148; Fax: 541-298-2136.

Commissioners: Myron Egbert; John Geiger; Bruce Harris; Steve Kramer; Scott Mengis. Exec. Dir.: Scott Hege. Meets 2nd Wed. of the month.

Port of Tillamook Bay, 1953

4000 Blimp Blvd., Tillamook 97141; 503-842-2413; Fax: 503-842-3680.

Commissioners: Patrick Ashby; Ken Bell; Kimber Jackson; Wayne Jackson; Jack Madison. Mgr.: Jack Crider. Meets 3rd Wed. of the month.

Port of Toledo, 1910

625 NW Bay Blvd., Toledo 97391-9720; 541-336-5207; Fax: 541-336-5160.

Commissioners: Jack Barbour; Steve Barnes; Margaret Brunett; Patricia Kaiser; Stu Strom. Port Mgr.: Penny Ryerson. Meets 3rd Tues. of the month.

Port of Umatilla, 1940

PO Box 879, Umatilla 97882; 541-922-3224; Fax: 541-922-5609.

Commissioners: Joe McLaughlin; Chester Prior; Marjorie Roff; Jerry Simpson; F.K. "Woody" Starrett. General Mgr.: Kim Puzey. Meets Tues. after 1st Wed. of the month.

Port of Umpqua, 1913

PO Box 388, Reedsport 97467; 541-271-2232; Fax: 541-271-2747.

Commissioners: Kenny Kent Jr.; Tim Lewis; Gerald Noel; Steve Reese; Keith Tymchuk. Port Mgr.: Linda Noel. Meets 1st Thurs. of the month.

Special Service Districts

Patrick J. Lynch, Exec. Dir.
*Special Districts Association of Oregon;
727 Center St. NE, Room 208, Salem 97301;
PO Box 12613, Salem 97309; 503-371-8667;
Fax: 503-371-4781*

Throughout Oregon, approximately 950 special service districts provide a broad range of community services. State statutes (ORS 198.010 and 198.335) provide for the creation of the following 28 types of districts: water control; irrigation; ports; regional air quality control authorities; fire; hospital; mass transit; sanitary districts and authorities; people's utility; domestic water supply districts and authorities; cemetery; park and recreation; metropolitan service; special road; road assessment; highway lighting; health; vector control; water improvement; weather modification; geothermal heating; transportation; county service; chemical control; weed control; emergency communications; diking; and soil and water conservation districts.

All special districts have the power to tax property inside their boundaries to finance the services they provide. All are directed by a governing body elected by the voters.

The Special Districts Association of Oregon was established in 1977 to pursue the common interests and concerns of special districts. SDAO provides a broad range of support services to member districts throughout the state in the areas of research and technical assistance, legislative representation, training programs, insurance services, information and reference materials, financing services, and employee benefits programs.

Transit Districts

Basin Transit Service Transportation District
Ernest Palmer, Gen. Mgr.
*1130 Adams, Klamath Falls 97601;
541-883-2877; Fax: 541-884-6287*

Grant County Transportation District
Donald L. Strong, chair
*PO Box 126, John Day 97845; 541-575-2370;
Fax: 541-575-1823*

Hood River County Transportation District
Linda Floyd, Exec. Dir.
720 12th St., Hood River 97031; 541-386-4202

Lane Transit District
Phyllis P. Loobey, Gen. Mgr.
*3500 E. 17th Ave., PO Box 7070, Eugene 97401;
541-741-6100; Fax: 541-741-6111*

Lincoln County Transportation District
Cynda Bruce, Gen. Mgr.
*821 SW Lee, Newport 97365; 541-265-6611;
Fax: 541-265-4106*

Rogue Valley Transportation District
Sherrin Coleman, Gen. Mgr.
*3200 Crater Lake Ave., Medford 97504;
541-779-5821; Fax: 541-773-2877*

Salem Area Mass Transit District
R.G. Anderson-Wyckoff, Gen. Mgr.
*3140 Del Webb Ave. NE, Salem 97303-4165;
503-588-2424; Fax: 503-588-0209*

South Clackamas Transportation District
Shirley Lyons, Mgr.
*PO Box 517, Molalla 97038; 503-632-7000;
Fax: 503-632-7000*

Sunset Empire Transportation District
Cindy Howe, Exec. Dir.
PO Box 179, Astoria 97103; 503-325-1000

Tri-County Metropolitan Transportation District of Oregon (Tri-Met)
Tom Walsh, Gen. Mgr.
*4012 SE 17th Ave., Portland 97202;
503-238-4915; Fax: 503-239-6451*

ELECTIONS AND RECORDS

The Historic Deepwood Estate in Salem was built in 1894 for Dr. Luke Port. The house was designed by W.C. Knighton who later designed the Oregon Supreme Court Building. The estate is now owned by the city of Salem and managed by the Friends of Deepwood.
Photo courtesy of the Oregon Historical Society. Negative number OrHi 94585.

AS developer of "The Oregon System"—the initiative, the referendum and other progressive elements of the electoral process—Oregon is nationally recognized for citizen involvement at the polls. Oregonians continue pursuing methods to increase access to the electoral process. The detailed electoral history contained here demonstrates Oregonians' commitment to citizen participation in government.

Voting and Voter Registration

Source: Secretary of State, Elections Division
*141 State Capitol, Salem 97310-0722;
503-986-1518; Web: www.sos.state.or.us*

Note: All information is subject to change by the Legislature.

Elections in Oregon

All elections in Oregon are held on one of four days, except in case of emergency. The four elections are held in March, May, September, and November of each year.

Elections are held on the:
- Second Tuesday in March;
- Third Tuesday in May;
- Third Tuesday in September; and
- First Tuesday after the first Monday in November.

Most elections are held by mail. Voters registered as of the 21st day before an election are mailed a ballot to vote and return by election day. The use of vote-by-mail was first approved on a limited basis by the Legislature in 1981 and was made a permanent feature of elections in 1987. It has been used for hundreds of local elections, several statewide measure elections, and even a special statewide election to fill a vacancy in the U.S. Senate.

The two elections held at polling sites are the primary and general elections in May and November of even-numbered years. At the primary election, voters registered in the major political parties, currently the Democratic and Republican parties, nominate candidates to run in the general election. All voters may vote on nonpartisan contests, such as judicial elections, which are also held at the primary election. Most statewide ballot measures are on the general election ballot.

Registering to Vote

Registration by mail was authorized by the 1975 Legislature and is now the method most people use to register to vote in Oregon. Forms are located in most banks and public buildings, in every county elections office and in many state agencies. They also can be obtained from the Secretary of State, Elections Division.

Date of Election	Deadline to Register*
March 11, 1997	Feb. 18, 1997
May 20, 1997	April 29, 1997
Sept. 16, 1997	Aug. 26, 1997
Nov. 4, 1997	Oct. 14, 1997
March 10, 1998	Feb. 17, 1998
May 19, 1998	April 28, 1998
Sept. 15, 1998	Aug. 25, 1998
Nov. 3, 1998	Oct. 13, 1998

*A voter registration card received in an elections office after the deadline to register, but which contains a valid postmark, will be considered to have met the registration deadline.

To register to vote, a person must be:
- A resident of Oregon;
- 18 years of age or older by election day; and
- A U.S. citizen by election day.

Oregon residents who are not U.S. citizens by the deadline to register to vote, but who will be by election day, should contact their county elections office for information about how to register to vote.

Persons who become residents of Oregon after the deadline to register for a presidential election may be eligible to vote for U.S. president and vice-president. Contact your county elections office for more information.

Important! Persons registered to vote in other states may not transfer their voter registration to Oregon. To register to vote in Oregon, a person must complete either an Oregon voter registration card or a Federal Postcard Application, which is available in most states.

How to Maintain a Current Voter Registration

Registered voters must notify their county elections office in writing if:
- Their residence or mailing address changes;
- Their name changes; or
- They wish to change political party affiliation.

A voter may notify county elections officials of changes to the above by sending a new voter registration card to the appropriate county.

A voter may update voter registration information as late as election day. However, if the voter's residence address has changed and the county elections office does not receive notice of the change prior to the seventh day before an election, the voter will be eligible to vote on only federal and statewide offices and statewide measures at that election.

If a voter has moved from one county in Oregon to another, the voter should fill out a voter registration card and send it to the new county elections office. If the voter registration card is sent after the 21st day before an election, the voter should call the county elections official to find out how to remain eligible to vote in the election.

Voting Absentee

Anyone registered to vote in Oregon may request an absentee ballot. A voter may request that the ballot be mailed, or a voter may go to the county elections office to vote the ballot. Absentee ballots are available by written request 45 days before an election.

Ballots requested by voters who are overseas or who are in the armed forces are normally mailed six to eight weeks before an election, while ballots mailed to all other persons within the United States are normally sent beginning three weeks before an election.

When a voter requests an absentee ballot, the request is honored for one election. However, if the conditions described below are met, a voter may request a ballot for more than one election. Requests must be in writing.

Permanent Absentee Voters

Any registered voter may apply to be mailed an absentee ballot for all elections.

To become a permanent absentee voter an elector can request permanent absentee status, in writing, to the appropriate county elections official, or complete a voter registration card including the permanent absentee voter portion of the card.

A ballot will be mailed for every election until the county elections official is otherwise notified or the voter is no longer a resident of the county.

Long Term Absentee Voters

Any Oregon voter who is absent from their place of residence and is:
1. Serving in the Armed Forces of the United States or who has been discharged from the Armed Forces of the United States for not more than 30 days;

2. Serving in the Merchant Marine of the United States or who has been discharged from the Merchant Marine of the United States for more than 30 days; or

3. Temporarily living outside the territorial limits of the United States and the District of Columbia

can request an absentee ballot for one or more elections. A voter must submit a written request to the appropriate county elections official to become a long term absentee voter. The request may be hand-delivered, mailed or sent by facsimile and received by the county elections official by 8:00 p.m. the day of the election.

The request must include:
1. The voter's name;

2. The voter's residence address;

3. The address to which the ballot should be mailed, if different from residence; and

4. The voter's signature.

If requesting a ballot for more than one election, the written request must also include:
1. A statement that the voter is a U.S. citizen;

2. A statement that the voter will be 18 years of age or older on the day of the election;

3. A statement that the voter's home residence has been in this state for more than 20 days preceding the election, and giving the address of last home residence;

4. A statement of the facts that qualify the voter to receive an absentee ballot for more than one election;

5. A statement that the voter is not requesting a ballot from any other state and is not voting in any other manner than by absentee ballot; and

6. A designation of political affiliation (for purposes of voting in primary elections).

Voters may request an absentee ballot using U.S. Department of Defense Standard Form 76, also known as the Federal Postcard Application (FPCA). The FPCA is available at American embassies and military installations worldwide.

Elections and Records

Voters' Pamphlet

For each primary and general election and for most special elections, the Elections Division produces and distributes to every household a pamphlet containing information about candidates and measures that will appear on the ballot at the election. Most county elections offices also produce pamphlets that contain information about local candidates and measures.

1998 Filing Deadlines

- The filing period for the 1998 primary election on May 19, 1998 begins September 11, 1997 and ends March 10, 1998. The deadline for filing voters' pamphlet material is no later than 5:00 p.m. on March 12, 1998.

- The filing period for the 1998 general election on November 3, 1998 begins June 3, 1998 and ends August 25, 1998. The deadline for filing voters' pamphlet material is no later than 5:00 p.m. on August 25, 1998.

Recent Election History

1996 Primary Election

From Official Abstract of Votes, available from the Elections Division, 141 State Capitol, Salem 97310-0722;
Web: www.sos.state.or.us/elections

Key: *Nominated; **Elected

United States Representative

U.S. Senator

Democrat	Total
Bruggere, Tom*	151,288
Dwyer, Bill	30,871
Lonsdale, Harry	76,059
Nevenich, Anna	16,827
Rust, Jerry	27,773
Miscellaneous	2,150
Republican	
Brumfield, Kirby	15,744
Fenton, Robert J.	8,958
Lewis, Jeff	13,359
Mabon, Lon	23,479
Smith, Gordon*	224,428
Miscellaneous	1,532

1st Congressional District

Democrat	Total
Furse, Elizabeth*	47,893
Miscellaneous	686
Republican	**Total**
Bordonaro, Molly Hering	13,600
Bunn, Stan	10,495
Meek, John E.	6,375
Noonan, Dick	1,573
Rutherford, Bill	10,180
Witt, Bill*	19,657
Miscellaneous	72

2nd Congressional District

Democrat	Total
Dugan, Mike*	39,366
Fuson, George E.	5,846
Miscellaneous	394
Republican	
Cooley, Wes*	31,528
Miscellaneous	6,942

3rd Congressional District

Democrat	Total
Blumenauer, Earl*	50,747
Gold, Shirley	13,812
Miscellaneous	533
Republican	
Bruun, Scott*	22,934
Miscellaneous	1,739

4th Congressional District

Democrat	Total
DeFazio, Peter A.*	63,006
Miscellaneous	309
Republican	
Cloonan, Jamie	9,685
Newkirk, John D.*	31,869
Miscellaneous	298

5th Congressional District

Democrat	Total
Collins, Loren W.	14,899
Hooley, Darlene*	27,930
Scott, Sharon	11,461
Miscellaneous	271
Republican	
Bunn, Jim*	46,318
Miller, David H.	9,480
Seeley, Clark Thomas	4,712
Miscellaneous	316

Secretary of State

Democrat	Total
Keisling, Phil*	254,477
Miscellaneous	1,574

Republican

	Total
Ash, Stan*	144,832
Wells, Paul Damian	65,271
Miscellaneous	1,804

State Treasurer

Democrat

	Total
Hill, Jim*	243,700
Miscellaneous	1,574

Republican

Clarno, Bev*	206,896
Miscellaneous	2,193

Attorney General

Democrat

	Total
Mannix, Kevin L.	97,389
Myers, Hardy*	166,031
Miscellaneous	869

Republican

Hoffer, Victor J.*	190,617
Miscellaneous	2,882

Judge of the Supreme Court

Nonpartisan

Position 1

	Total
Armstrong, Rex	120,392
Kulongoski, Ted**	359,255
Yraguen, Frank J.	81,980
Miscellaneous	1,668

Judge of the Court of Appeals

Nonpartisan

Position 1

	Total
De Muniz, Paul J.**	395,475
Miscellaneous	2,857

Position 2

Edmonds, Walter I. Jr.**	393,511
Miscellaneous	2,789

1996 General Election

From Official Abstract of Votes, available from the Elections Division, 141 State Capitol, Salem 97310-0722;
Web: www.sos.state.or.us/elections

*Elected

United States President

	Total
Browne, Harry—L	8,903
Clinton, Bill—D*	649,641
Dole, Bob—R	538,152
Hagelin, John—NL	2,798
Hollis, Mary Cal—S	1,922
Nader, Ralph—P	49,415
Perot, Ross—RF	121,221
Phillips, Howard—US	3,379
Miscellaneous	2,329

United States Senator

	Total
Bruggere, Tom—D	624,370
Hoyes, Michael L.—NL	4,425
Kutcher, Gary—P	14,193
Mohn, Paul (Stormy)—L	12,697
Phelps, Christopher—S	5,426
Smith, Gordon—R*	677,336
Thompson, Brent—RF	20,381
Miscellaneous	1,402

United States Representative

1st Congressional District

	Total
Furse, Elizabeth—D*	144,588
Johnson, Richard—L	6,310
Princ, David—S	1,146
Witt, Bill—R	126,146
Miscellaneous	414

Elections and Records

This unusual rock formation at Crater Lake National Park, called The Pinnacles, was formed during the collapse of Mt. Mazama.

Photo by Etta J. Powell.

2nd Congressional District

	Total
Dugan, Mike—D	97,195
Smith, Robert F. (Bob)—R*	164,062
Wise, Frank—L	4,581
Miscellaneous	218

3rd Congressional District

	Total
Blumenauer, Earl—D*	165,922
Bruun, Scott—R	65,259
Guillebeau, Victoria P.—S	2,449
Keating, Joe—P	9,274
Knight, Bruce Alexander—L	4,474
Miscellaneous	531

4th Congressional District

	Total
Bonville, William (Bill)—RF	3,960
DeFazio, Peter A.—D*	177,270
Duemler, David G.—S	1,373
Nathan, Tonie—L	4,919
Newkirk, John D.—R	76,649
Opus, Allan—P	1,311
Miscellaneous	4,374

5th Congressional District

	Total
Bunn, Jim—R	125,409
Duquesne, Lawrence Knight—L	5,191
Hooley, Darlene—D*	139,521
Smith, Trey—S	2,124
Miscellaneous	391

Secretary of State

	Total
Ash, Stan—R	451,576
Ashbrook, Elizabeth—NL	38,583
Furman, Mark—S	21,250
Keisling, Phil—D*	767,946
Zimmer, Jon E.—L	19,563
Miscellaneous	1,150

State Treasurer

	Total
Clarno, Bev—R	575,047
Hill, Jim—D*	676,872
Meyers, John Vincent—NL	18,565
Montchalin, Marshall—L	16,320
Perigo, Nan—S	8,387
Miscellaneous	1,108

Attorney General

	Total
Campbell, Michael Allan—NL	20,553
Cox, Thomas B.—L	33,585
Hoffer, Victor—R	517,035
Myers, Hardy—D*	658,598
Sorg, Karl—S	20,524
Miscellaneous	2,169

Judge of the Circuit Court

Nonpartisan	Total

2nd District—Position 4

Larson, Darryl L.*	77,787
Miscellaneous	29

3rd District—Position 5

Abernathy, Pamela L.*	73,327
Miscellaneous	1,388

4th District—Department 15

Robinson, Roosevelt*	141,620
Miscellaneous	4,691

4th District—Department 19

Keys, William J.*	140,249
Miscellaneous	4,499

6th District—Department 1

Reynolds, Garry L.*	11,585
Ridgway, Robert E.	10,482
Miscellaneous	8

10th District

Anderson, Bruce E.	6,095
Mendiguren, Phillip A.*	8,282
Miscellaneous	29

19th District—Position 3

Reed, Steve*	28,077
Miscellaneous	331

19th District—Position 4

Grove, Ted E.*	26,944
Miscellaneous	313

22nd District—Position 2

Ahern, Daniel J.*	7,068
Matthews, Mark B.	4,774
Miscellaneous	42

D = Democrat
I = Non-affiliated
L = Libertarian
NL = Natural Law
P = Pacific
R = Republican
RF = Reform
S = Socialist
US = US Taxpayers

Voter Participation 1970–1996

Primary Election

*Presidential election year

Year	Registered Voters	Voted	Percent
1970	1,018,017	568,551	55.8
1972*	1,158,711	734,551	63.4
1974	1,248,596	593,172	47.5
1976*	1,310,248	798,986	61.0
1978	1,390,005	603,478	43.4
1980*	1,376,573	780,649	56.7
1982	1,437,693	669,529	46.6
1984*	1,457,067	767,565	52.7
1986	1,458,300	693,821	47.6
1988*	1,366,294	753,112	55.1
1990	1,437,462	660,990	46.0
1992*	1,543,353	758,459	49.1
1994	1,730,562	661,717	38.2
1996*	1,851,499	698,990	37.8

General Election

Year	Registered Voters	Voted	Percent
1970	955,459	681,381	71.3
1972*	1,197,676	953,376	79.6
1974	1,143,073	792,557	69.3
1976*	1,420,146	1,048,561	73.8
1978	1,482,339	937,423	63.2
1980*	1,569,222	1,209,691	77.1
1982	1,516,589	1,063,913	70.2
1984*	1,608,693	1,265,824	78.7
1986	1,502,244	1,088,140	72.4
1988*	1,528,478	1,235,199	80.8
1990	1,476,500	1,133,125	76.7
1992*	1,775,416	1,498,959	84.4
1994	1,832,774	1,254,265	68.4
1996*	1,962,155	1,399,180	71.3

Windswept trees and beach grass characterize sand dunes in the Oregon Dunes National Recreation Area between Florence and Coos Bay.

Photo by George Self.

Voter Registration by County

November 5, 1996

County	Democrat	Republican	Non-affiliated*	Other	Total
Baker	3,880	4,377	1,712	203	10,172
Benton	18,213	16,504	8,333	603	43,653
Clackamas	79,809	81,025	40,593	3,986	205,413
Clatsop	9,752	6,983	4,834	586	22,155
Columbia	12,742	7,676	4,603	555	25,576
Coos	19,011	13,154	7,362	806	40,333
Crook	3,946	4,057	1,741	308	10,052
Curry	5,775	6,306	2,521	369	14,971
Deschutes	22,323	26,814	14,016	1,807	64,960
Douglas	23,823	25,485	11,400	1,102	61,810
Gilliam	533	563	204	22	1,322
Grant	1,896	2,294	921	105	5,216
Harney	1,733	2,014	759	38	4,544
Hood River	4,184	3,715	2,354	184	10,437
Jackson	37,731	43,943	23,056	2,136	106,866
Jefferson	3,372	3,530	1,770	285	8,957
Josephine	14,723	20,323	8,634	1,208	44,888
Klamath	12,593	15,579	6,401	716	35,289
Lake	1,853	2,285	662	109	4,909
Lane	87,188	63,250	42,769	4,654	197,861
Lincoln	12,669	9,495	6,423	580	29,167
Linn	24,845	22,887	12,743	1,085	61,560
Malheur	4,461	7,032	2,377	224	14,094
Marion	55,200	61,174	29,117	2,421	147,912
Morrow	1,944	1,693	894	112	4,643
Multnomah	200,565	106,323	86,723	10,487	404,098
Polk	12,839	14,790	6,456	544	34,629
Sherman	554	593	184	16	1,347
Tillamook	6,932	5,113	—	2,897	14,942
Umatilla	11,900	12,966	7,192	1,011	33,069
Union	6,049	6,541	2,729	255	15,574
Wallowa	1,851	2,369	778	36	5,034
Wasco	5,991	4,856	2,726	328	13,901
Washington	78,458	90,139	48,223	1,372	218,192
Wheeler	418	457	197	12	1,084
Yamhill	15,530	18,243	8,841	911	43,525
Totals	**805,286**	**714,548**	**400,248**	**42,073**	**1,962,155**

*A Non-affiliated voter is one who has chosen not to be a member of any political party and has indicated this on his/her voter registration card. Some counties refer to non-affiliated voters (NAV) as "Independents" or "IND."

Voter Registration for General Elections 1950–1996

Year	Democrat	Republican	Other	Total
1950	378,357	361,158	11,755	751,270
1952	416,589	421,681	13,246	851,516
1954	402,283	404,694	12,562	819,539
1956	451,179	413,659	13,114	877,952
1958	447,198	395,089	12,759	855,046
1960	480,588	405,195	14,833	900,616
1962	473,561	395,351	14,778	883,690
1964	511,973	402,336	18,152	932,461
1966	518,228	412,586	19,011	949,825
1968	530,074	420,943	20,834	971,851
1970	521,662	410,693	23,104	955,459
1972	673,710	473,907	50,059	1,197,676
1974	652,414	439,667	50,992	1,143,073
1976	794,218	497,297	128,631	1,420,146
1978	808,182	511,621	163,536	1,482,339
1980	784,129	564,771	220,322	1,569,222
1982	751,100	551,718	213,771	1,516,589
1984	792,208	594,387	222,098	1,608,693
1986	728,177	587,154	186,913	1,502,244
1988	737,489	590,648	200,341	1,528,478
1990	692,100	570,933	213,467	1,476,500
1992	792,551	642,206	340,659	1,775,416
1994	786,990	665,956	379,828	1,832,774
1996	805,286	714,548	442,321	1,962,155

Votes Cast in Oregon for U.S. President 1860-1996

Key: *Elected; **Received highest vote in Oregon but lost election nationwide

Year	Candidate	Party	Votes
1860	John Bell	Constitutional Union	212
	John C. Breckenridge	Democrat	5,074
	Stephen Douglas	Douglas Democrat	4,131
	Abraham Lincoln*	Republican	5,344
1864	Abraham Lincoln*	Republican	9,888
	George McClellan	Democrat	8,457
1868	U.S. Grant*	Republican	10,961
	Horatio Seymour**	Democrat	11,125
1872	U.S. Grant*	Republican	11,818
	Horace Greeley	Democrat-Liberal Republicans	7,742
	Charles O'Connor	National Labor Reformers	587
1876	Peter Cooper	Greenback	510
	Rutherford B. Hayes*	Republican	15,214
	Samuel Tilden	Democrat	14,157
1880	James A. Garfield*	Republican	20,619
	Winfield Hancock	Democrat	19,955
	James B. Weaver	Greenback Labor	249
1884	James G. Blaine**	Republican	26,860
	General B.F. Butler	Greenback Labor (Workingman)	726
	Grover Cleveland*	Democrat	24,604
	John P. St. John	Prohibition	492
1888	Grover Cleveland	Democrat	26,522
	Robert H. Cowdrey	United Labor	363
	Clinton B. Fisk	Prohibition	1,677
	Benjamin Harrison*	Republican	33,291

Year	Candidate	Party	Votes
1892	John Bidwell	Prohibition	2,281
	Grover Cleveland*	Democrat	14,243
	Benjamin Harrison**	Republican	35,002
	James B. Weaver[1]	Populist	26,965
1896	William J. Bryan	Democrats, People's Party and Silver Republicans	46,739
	Joshua Levering	Prohibition	919
	William McKinley*	Republican	48,779
	John M. Palmer	National (Gold) Democrats	977
1900	Wharton Barker	Regular People's	275
	William J. Bryan	Democrat People's	33,385
	Eugene V. Debs	Social-Democrats	1,494
	William McKinley*	Republican	46,526
	John G. Woolley	Prohibition	2,536
1904	Eugene V. Debs	Socialist	7,619
	Alton Parker	Democrat	17,327
	Theodore Roosevelt*	Republican	60,455
	Silas C. Swallow	Prohibition	3,806
	Thomas E. Watson	People's	753
1908	William J. Bryan	Democrat	38,049
	Eugene W. Chafin	Prohibition	2,682
	Eugene V. Debs	Socialist	7,339
	Thomas L. Hisgen	Independence	289
	William H. Taft*	Republican	62,530
1912	Eugene W. Chafin	Prohibition	4,360
	Eugene V. Debs	Socialist	13,343
	Theodore Roosevelt	Progressive	37,600
	William H. Taft	Republican	34,673
	Woodrow Wilson*	Democrat	47,064
1916	Allan L. Benson	Socialist	9,711
	J. Frank Hanley	Prohibition	4,729
	Charles Evans Hughes**	Republican	126,813
	John M. Parker[2]	Progressive	310
	Woodrow Wilson*	Democrat	120,087
1920	James M. Cox	Democrat	80,019
	William W. Cox	Industrial Labor	1,515
	Eugene V. Debs	Socialist	9,801
	Warren G. Harding*	Republican	143,592
	Aaron S. Watkins	Prohibition	3,595
1924	Calvin Coolidge*	Republican	142,579
	John W. Davis	Democrat	67,589
	Frank T. Johns	Socialist Labor	917
	Robert M. LaFollette	Independent	68,403
1928	William Z. Foster	Independent	1,094
	Herbert Hoover*	Republican	205,341
	Verne L. Reynolds	Socialist Labor	1,564
	Alfred E. Smith	Democrat	109,223
	Norman Thomas	Socialist Principles-Independent	2,720
1932	William Z. Foster	Communist	1,681
	Herbert Hoover	Republican	136,019
	Verne L. Reynolds	Socialist Labor	1,730
	Franklin D. Roosevelt*	Democrat	213,871
	Norman Thomas	Socialist	15,450
1936	John W. Aiken	Socialist Labor	500
	Alfred M. Landon	Republican	122,706
	William Lemke	Independent	21,831
	Franklin D. Roosevelt*	Democrat	266,733
	Norman Thomas	Independent	2,143

Year	Candidate	Party	Votes
1940	John W. Aiken	Socialist Labor	2,487
	Franklin D. Roosevelt*	Democrat	258,415
	Wendell L. Willkie	Republican	219,555
1944	Thomas E. Dewey	Republican	225,365
	Franklin D. Roosevelt*	Democrat	248,635
	Norman Thomas	Independent	3,785
	Claude A. Watson	Independent	2,362
1948	Thomas E. Dewey**	Republican	260,904
	Norman Thomas	Independent	5,051
	Harry S. Truman*	Democrat	243,147
	Henry A. Wallace	Progressive	14,978
1952	Dwight D. Eisenhower*	Republican	420,815
	Vincent Hallinan	Independent	3,665
	Adlai Stevenson	Democrat	270,579
1956	Dwight D. Eisenhower*	Republican	406,393
	Adlai Stevenson	Democrat	329,204
1960	John F. Kennedy*	Democrat	367,402
	Richard M. Nixon**	Republican	408,060
1964	Barry M. Goldwater	Republican	282,779
	Lyndon B. Johnson*	Democrat	501,017
1968	Hubert H. Humphrey	Democrat	358,866
	Richard M. Nixon*	Republican	408,433
	George C. Wallace	Independent	49,683
1972	George S. McGovern	Democrat	392,760
	Richard M. Nixon*	Republican	486,686
	John G. Schmitz	Independent	46,211
1976	Jimmy Carter*	Democrat	490,407
	Gerald Ford**	Republican	492,120
	Eugene J. McCarthy	Independent	40,207
1980	John Anderson	Independent	112,389
	Jimmy Carter	Democrat	456,890
	Ed Clark	Libertarian	25,838
	Barry Commoner	Independent	13,642
	Ronald Reagan*	Republican	571,044
1984	Walter F. Mondale	Democrat	536,479
	Ronald Reagan*	Republican	685,700
1988	George Bush*	Republican	560,126
	Michael S. Dukakis**	Democrat	616,206
	Lenora B. Fulani	Independent	6,487
	Ron Paul	Libertarian	14,811
1992	George Bush	Republican	475,757
	Bill Clinton*	Democrat	621,314
	Lenora Fulani	New Alliance Party	3,030
	Andre Marrou	Libertarian	4,277
	Ross Perot	Independent Initiative Party of Oregon	354,091
1996	Harry Browne	Libertarian	8,903
	Bill Clinton*	Democrat	649,641
	Bob Dole	Republican	538,152
	John Hagelin	Natural Law	2,798
	Mary Cal Hollis	Socialist	1,922
	Ralph Nader	Pacific	49,415
	Ross Perot	Reform	121,221
	Howard Phillips	US Taxpayers	3,379

[1]One Weaver elector was endorsed by the Democrats and elected as a Fusionist, receiving 35,811 votes.

[2]Vice-presidential candidate.

*Seen over Diamond Lake, Mt. Thielsen's unmis-
takable spire tops this 9,182-foot mountain in
southern Oregon.*

*Photo by Gordon Coons, courtesy of Douglas
County Commissioners.*

Initiative, Referendum and Recall

In 1902, the Oregon electorate overwhelmingly approved a ballot measure
that created the initiative and referendum, a system of direct legislation by
the people. In 1904, the electorate
enacted the direct primary and, in 1908,
the State Constitution was amended to
include recall of public officials. These
victories were the culmination of efforts
by the Direct Legislation League, a
group of political activists that progressive leader William S. U'Ren founded in
1898.

The initiative and referendum became
known nationally as the "Oregon
System," and adoption of these popular
legislative tools put Oregon in the vanguard of progressive and enlightened
politics, allowing the people to propose
new laws or change the State Constitution through a general election ballot
measure.

Since 1902, the people have passed
99 of the 288 initiative measures on the
ballot and 25 of the 61 referenda on the
ballot. During the same period, the
Legislature has referred 363 measures
to the people, of which 206 have passed.

Both houses of the Legislature must
vote to refer a statute or constitutional
amendment for a popular vote. Such
referrals cannot be vetoed by the
governor.

To place an initiative or referendum
on the ballot, supporters must obtain
a specified number of signatures from
registered voters. The number required
is determined by a fixed percentage of
the votes cast for all candidates for
governor at the general election preceding the filing of the petition. In the
1994 general election, 1,221,010 votes
were cast for governor.

- Referendum petitions require 4 percent, or 48,841 signatures.

- Initiative petitions for statutory
  enactments require 6 percent, or
  73,261 signatures.

- Initiative petitions for constitutional
  amendments require 8 percent, or
  97,681 signatures.

The constitutional amendment passed
by the people in 1902 that created the
initiative and referendum provided that
a fixed percentage of the votes cast for
justice of the Supreme Court would
determine the number of signatures
required to place an initiative or referendum on the ballot. Both a statutory
enactment and a constitutional amendment required eight percent of the votes
cast, while a referendum required five
percent of the votes cast. In 1954, the
people amended the State Constitution
to increase to ten percent the number of
signatures required for a constitutional
amendment. The current requirements
were established by a vote of the people
in 1968.

Because measures were not assigned
numbers until 1954, measures on the
ballot at previous elections are listed in
order of appearance on the ballot.

The 1993 Legislature amended state
law to require ballot measures to be
numbered 1-99 before numbering begins
again at 1.

The following list includes legislative
referrals, referenda and statewide
initiatives.

**Key: *Adopted; L-Referred by the
Legislature; I-Submitted by initiative
petition; R-Referendum by petition.**

Election Date/Measure Number/Ballot Title	Yes	No
June 2, 1902		
1. Limits Uses Initiative and Referendum—L[1]	*62,024	5,668
June 6, 1904		
1. Office of State Printer—L[1]	*45,334	14,031
2. Direct Primary Nominating Convention Law—I[2]	*56,205	16,354
3. Local Option Liquor law—I[2]	*43,316	40,198
June 4, 1906		
1. Shall act appropriating money maintaining Insane Asylum, Penitentiary, Deaf-Mute, Blind School, University, Agricultural College, and Normal Schools be approved—R	*43,918	26,758
2. Equal Suffrage Constitutional Amendment—I[1]	36,902	47,075
3. Amendment to local option law giving anti-prohibitionists and prohibitionists equal privileges—I[2]	35,297	45,144
4. Law to abolish tolls on the Mount Hood and Barlow Roadand providing for its ownership by the State—I[2]	31,525	44,527
5. Constitutional amendment providing method of amending constitution and applying the referendum to all laws affecting constitutional conventions and amendments—I[1]	*47,661	18,751
6. Constitutional amendment giving cities and towns exclusive power to enact and amend their charters—I[1]	*52,567	19,852
7. Constitutional amendment to allow the state printing, binding, and Printers' compensation to be regulated by law at any time—I[1]	*63,749	9,571
8. Constitutional amendment for the initiative and referendum on local, special, and municipal laws and parts of laws—I[1]	*47,678	16,735
9. Bill for a law prohibiting free passes and discrimination by railroad companies and other public service corporations—I[2]	*57,281	16,779
10. An act requiring sleeping car companies, refrigerator car companies, and oil companies to pay an annual license upon gross earnings—I[2]	*69,635	6,441
11. An act requiring express companies, telegraph companies, and telephone companies to pay an annual license upon gross earnings—I[2]	*70,872	6,360
June 1, 1908		
1. To Increase Compensation of Legislators from $120 to $400 Per Session—L[1]	19,691	68,892
2. Permitting Location of State Institutions at Places Other than the State Capitol—L[1]	*41,975	40,868
3. Reorganization System of Courts and Increasing the Number of Supreme Judges from Three to Five—L[1]	30,243	50,591
4. Changing Date of General Elections from June to November—L[1]	*65,728	18,590
5. Giving Sheriffs Control of County Prisoners—R	*60,443	30,033
6. Requiring Railroads to Give Public Officials Free Passes—R	28,856	59,406
7. Appropriating $100,000 for Building Armories—R	33,507	54,848
8. Increasing Annual Appropriation for University of Oregon from $47,500 to $125,000—R	*44,115	40,535
9. Equal Suffrage—I[1]	36,858	58,670
10. Fishery Law Proposed by Fishwheel Operators—I[2]	*46,582	40,720
11. Giving Cities Control of Liquor Selling, Poolrooms, Theaters, etc., subject to local option law—I[1]	39,442	52,346
12. Modified Form of Single Tax Amendment—I[1]	32,066	60,871
13. Recall Power on Public Officials—I[1]	*58,381	31,002

Election Date/Measure Number/Ballot Title	Yes	No
14. Instructing Legislature to Vote for People Choice for United States Senator—I^2	*69,668	21,162
15. Authorizing Proportional Representation Law—I^1	*48,868	34,128
16. Corrupt Practices Act Governing Elections—I^2	*54,042	31,301
17. Fishery Law Proposed by Gillnet Operators—I^2	*56,130	30,280
18. Requiring Indictment To Be By Grand Jury—I^1	*52,214	28,487
19. Creating Hood River County—I^2	*43,948	26,778

November 8, 1910

Election Date/Measure Number/Ballot Title	Yes	No
1. Permitting Female Taxpayers to Vote—I^1	35,270	59,065
2. Establishing Branch Insane Asylum in Eastern Oregon—L^2	*50,134	41,504
3. Calling Convention to Revise State Constitution—L^2	23,143	59,974
4. Providing Separate Districts for Election of Each State Senator and Representative—L^1	24,000	54,252
5. Repealing Requirements That All Taxes Shall Be Equal and Uniform—L^1	37,619	40,172
6. Permitting Organized Districts to Vote Bonds for Construction of Railroads by Such Districts—L^1	32,884	46,070
7. Authorizing Collection of State and County Taxes on Separate Classes of Property—L^1	31,629	41,692
8. Requiring Baker County to Pay $1,000 a Year to Circuit Judge in Addition to His State Salary—R	13,161	71,503
9. Creating Nesmith County From Parts of Lane and Douglas—I^2	22,866	60,951
10. To Establish a State Normal School at Monmouth—I^2	*50,191	40,044
11. Creating Otis County From Parts of Harney, Malheur and Grant—I^2	17,426	62,016
12. Annexing Part of Clackamas County to Multnomah—I^2	16,250	69,002
13. Creating Williams County From Parts of Lane and Douglas—I^2	14,508	64,090
14. Permitting People of Each County to Regulate Taxation for County Purposes and Abolishing Poll Taxes—I^1	*44,171	42,127
15. Giving Cities and Towns Exclusive Power to Regulate Liquor Traffic Within Their Limits—I^1	*53,321	50,779
16. For Protection of Laborers in Hazardous Employment, Fixing Employers' Liability, etc.—I^2	*56,258	33,943
17. Creating Orchard County From Part of Umatilla—I^2	15,664	62,712
18. Creating Clark County From Part of Grant—I^2	15,613	61,704
19. To Establish State Normal School at Weston—I^2	40,898	46,201
20. To Annex Part of Washington County to Multnomah—I^2	14,047	68,221
21. To Establish State Normal School at Ashland—I^2	38,473	48,655
22. Prohibiting Liquor Traffic—I^1	43,540	61,221
23. Prohibiting the Sale of Liquors and Regulating Shipments of Same, and Providing for Search for Liquor—I^2	42,651	63,564
24. Creating Board to Draft Employers' Liability Law for Submission to Legislature—I^2	32,224	51,719
25. Prohibiting Taking of Fish in Rogue River Except With Hook and Line—I^2	*49,712	33,397
26. Creating Deschutes County Out of Part of Crook—I^2	17,592	60,486
27. Bill for General Law Under Which New Counties May Be Created or Boundaries Changed—I^2	37,129	42,327
28. Permitting Counties to Vote Bonds for Permanent Road Improvement—I^1	*51,275	32,906
29. Permitting Voters in Direct Primaries to Express Choice for President and Vice President, to Select Delegates to National Convention and Nominate Candidates for Presidential Electors—I^2	*43,353	41,624

Election Date/Measure Number/Ballot Title	Yes	No
30. Creating Board of People's Inspectors of Government, Providing for Reports of Board in Official State Gazette to be Mailed to All Registered Voters Bi-monthly—I[2]	29,955	52,538
31. Extending Initiative and Referendum, Making Term of Members of Legislature Six Years, Increasing Salaries, Requiring Proportional Representation in Legislature, Election of President of Senate and Speaker of House Outside of Members, etc.—I[1]	37,031	44,366
32. Permitting Three-Fourths Verdict in Civil Cases—I[1]	*44,538	39,399

November 5, 1912

	Yes	No
1. Equal Suffrage Amendment—I[1]	*61,265	57,104
2. Creating Office of Lieutenant Governor—L[1]	50,562	61,644
3. Divorce of Local and State Taxation—L[1]	51,582	56,671
4. Permitting Different Tax Rates on Classes of Property—L[1]	52,045	54,483
5. Repeal of County Tax Option—L[1]	*63,881	47,150
6. Majority Rule on Constitutional Amendments—L[1]	32,934	70,325
7. Double Liability on Bank Stockholders—L[1]	*82,981	21,738
8. Statewide Public Utilities Regulation—R	*65,985	40,956
9 Creating Cascade County—I[2]	26,463	71,239
10. Millage Tax for University and Agricultural College—I[2]	48,701	57,279
11. Majority Rule on Initiated Laws—I[1]	35,721	68,861
12. County Bond and Road Construction Act—Grange Bill—I[2]	49,699	56,713
13. Creating State Highway Department—Grange Bill—I[2]	23,872	83,846
14. Changing Date State Printer Bill Becomes Effective—I[2]	34,793	69,542
15. Creating Office of Hotel Inspector—I[2]	16,910	91,995
16. Eight-hour Day on Public Works—I[2]	*64,508	48,078
17. Blue Sky Law—I[2]	48,765	57,293
18. Relating to Employment of State Prisoners—I[2]	*73,800	37,492
19. Relating to Employment of County and City Prisoners—I[2]	*71,367	37,731
20. State Road Bonding Act—I[2]	30,897	75,590
21. Limiting State Road Indebtedness—I[1]	*59,452	43,447
22. County Bonding Act—I[2]	43,611	60,210
23. Limiting County Road Indebtedness—I[1]	*57,258	43,858
24. Providing Method for Consolidating Cities and Creating New Counties—I[2]	40,199	56,992
25. Income Tax Amendment—I[1]	52,702	52,948
26. Tax Exemption on Household Effects—I[2]	*60,357	51,826
27. Tax Exemption on Moneys and Credits—I[2]	42,491	66,540
28. Revising Inheritance Tax Laws—I[2]	38,609	63,839
29. Freight Rates Act—I[2]	*58,306	45,534
30. County Road Bonding Act—I[1]	38,568	63,481
31. Abolishing Senate; Proxy Voting; U'Rren Constitution—I[1]	31,020	71,183
32. Statewide Single Tax with Graduated Tax Provision—I[1]	31,534	82,015
33. Abolishing Capital Punishment—I[2]	41,951	64,578
34. Prohibits Boycotts and Pickets—I[2]	49,826	60,560
35. Prohibits Use of Public Streets, Parks and Grounds in Cities over 5,000 Without Permit—I[2]	48,987	62,532
36. Appropriation for University of Oregon—R	29,437	78,985
37. Appropriation for University of Oregon—R	27,310	79,376

November 4, 1913 (Special Referendum Election)

	Yes	No
1. State University Building Repair Fund—R	*56,659	40,600
2. University of Oregon New Building Appropriation—R	*53,569	43,014
3. Sterilization Act—R	41,767	53,319
4. County Attorney Act—R	*54,179	38,159
5. Workmen's Compensation Act—R	*67,814	28,608

November 3, 1914

	Yes	No
1. Requiring Voters to be Citizens of the United States—L[1]	*164,879	39,847

Election Date/Measure Number/Ballot Title	Yes	No
2. Creating Office of Lieutenant Governor—L[1]	52,040	143,804
3. Permitting Certain City and County Boundaries to be Made Identical, and Governments Consolidated—L[1]	77,392	103,194
4. Permitting State to Create an Indebtedness Not to Exceed Two Percent of Assessed Valuation for Irrigation and Power Projects and Development of Untilled Lands—L[1]	49,759	135,550
5. Omitting Requirement that "All Taxation Shall Be Equal And Uniform"—L[1]	59,206	116,490
6. Changing Existing Rule of Uniformity and Equality of Taxation—Authorizing Classification of Property for Taxation Purposes—L[1]	52,362	122,704
7. To Establish State Normal School at Ashland—L[2]	84,041	109,643
8. Enabling Incorporated Municipalities to Surrender Charters and To Be Merged in Adjoining City or Town—L[1]	*96,116	77,671
9. To Establish State Normal School at Weston—L[2]	87,450	105,345
10. Providing Compensation for Members of Legislature at Five Dollars Per Day—L[1]	41,087	146,278
11. Universal Constitutional Eight Hour Day Amendment—I[1]	49,360	167,888
12. Eight-hour Day and Room-Ventilation Law for Female Workers—I[2]	88,480	120,296
13. Nonpartisan Judiciary Bill Prohibiting Party Nominations for Judicial Officers—I[2]	74,323	107,263
14. $1500 Tax Exemption Amendment—I[1]	65,495	136,193
15. Public Docks and Water Frontage Amendment—I[1]	67,128	114,564
16. Municipal Wharves and Docks Bill—I[2]	67,110	111,113
17. Prohibition Constitutional Amendment—I[1]	*136,842	100,362
18. Abolishing Death Penalty—I[1]	*100,552	100,395
19. Specific Personal Graduated Extra-tax Amendment of Article IX, Oregon Constitution—I[1]	59,186	124,943
20. Consolidating Corporation and Insurance Departments—I[2]	55,469	120,154
21. Dentistry Bill—I[2]	92,722	110,404
22. County Officers Term Amendment—I[1]	82,841	107,039
23. A Tax Code Commission Bill—I[2]	34,436	143,468
24. Abolishing Desert Land Board and Reorganizing Certain State Offices—I[2]	32,701	143,366
25. Proportional Representation Amendment to Oregon Constitution—I[1]	39,740	137,116
26. State Senate Constitutional Amendment—I[1]	62,376	123,429
27. Department of Industry and Public Works Amendment—I[1]	57,859	126,201
28. Primary Delegate Election Bill—I[2]	25,058	153,638
29. Equal Assessment and Taxation and $300 Exemption Amendment—I[1]	43,280	140,507
November 7, 1916		
1. Single Item Veto Amendment—L[1]	*141,773	53,207
2. Ship Tax Exemption Amendment—L[1]	*119,652	65,410
3. Negro and Mulatto Suffrage Amendment—L[1]	100,027	100,701
4. Full Rental Value Land Tax and Homemakers' Loan Fund Amendment—I[1]	43,390	154,980
5. For Pendleton Normal School and Ratifying Location Certain State Institutions—I[1]	96,829	109,523
6. Anti-compulsory Vaccination Bill—I[2]	99,745	100,119
7. Bill Repealing and Abolishing the Sunday Closing Law—I[2]	*125,836	93,076
8. Permitting Manufacture and Regulating Sale 4 Percent Malt Liquors—I[1]	85,973	140,599
9. Prohibition Amendment Forbidding Importation of Intoxicating Liquors for Beverage Purposes—I[1]	*114,932	109,671
10. Rural Credits Amendment—I[1]	*107,488	83,887

Election Date/Measure Number/Ballot Title	Yes	No
11. State-wide Tax and Indebtedness Limitation Amendment—I[1]	*99,536	84,031

June 4, 1917 (Special Election)

1. Authorizing Ports to Create Limited Indebtedness to Encourage Water Transportation—L[1]	*67,445	54,864
2. Limiting Number of Bills Introduced and Increasing Pay of Legislators—L[1]	22,276	103,238
3. Declaration Against Implied Repeal of Constitutional Provisions by Amendments Thereto—L[1]	37,187	72,445
4. Uniform Tax Classification Amendment—L[1]	*62,118	53,245
5. Requiring Election City, Town and State Officers at Same Time—L[1]	*83,630	42,296
6. Four Hundred Thousand Dollar Tax Levy for a New Penitentiary—L[2]	46,666	86,165
7. Six Million Dollar State Road Bond Issue and Highway Bill—L[2]	*77,316	63,803

November 5, 1918

1. Establishing and Maintaining Southern and Eastern Oregon Normal Schools—L[1]	49,935	66,070
2. Establishing Dependent, Delinquent and Defective Children's Home, Appropriating Money Therefor—L[2]	43,441	65,299
3. Prohibiting Seine and Setnet Fishing in Rogue River and Tributaries—R	45,511	50,227
4. Closing the Willamette River to Commercial Fishing South of Oswego—R	*55,555	40,908
5. Delinquent Tax Notice Bill—I[2]	*66,652	41,594
6. Fixing Compensation for Publication of Legal Notice—I[2]	*50,073	41,816
7. Authorizing Increase in Amount of Levy of State Taxes for Year 1919 (submitted by state tax commission under chapter 150, Laws 1917)	41,364	56,974

June 3, 1919 (Special Election)

1. Six Percent County Indebtedness for Permanent Roads Amendment—L[1]	*49,728	33,561
2. Industrial and Reconstruction Hospital Amendment—L[1]	38,204	40,707
3. State Bond Payment of Irrigation and Drainage District Bond Interest—L[1]	*43,010	35,948
4. Five Million Dollar Reconstruction Bonding Amendment—L[1]	39,130	40,580
5. Lieutenant Governor Constitutional Amendment—L[1]	32,653	46,861
6. The Roosevelt Coast Military Highway Bill—L[2]	*56,966	29,159
7. Reconstruction Bonding Bill—L[2]	37,294	42,792
8. Soldiers', Sailors' and Marines' Educational Financial Aid Bill—L[2]	*49,158	33,513
9. Market Roads Tax Bill—L[2]	*53,191	28,039

May 21, 1920 (Special Election)

1. Extending Eminent Domain Over Roads and Ways—L[1]	*100,256	35,655
2. Limitation of 4 Percent State Indebtedness for Permanent Roads—L[1]	*93,392	46,084
3. Restoring Capital Punishment—L[1]	*81,756	64,589
4. Crook and Curry Counties Bonding Amendment—L[1]	*72,378	36,699
5. Successor to Governor—L[1]	*78,241	56,946
6. Higher Educational Tax Act—L[2]	*102,722	46,577
7. Soldiers', Sailors' and Marines' Educational Aid Revenue Bill—L[2]	*91,294	50,482
8. State Elementary School Fund Tax—L[2]	*110,263	39,593
9. Blind School Tax Measure—L[2]	*115,337	30,739

Election Date/Measure Number/Ballot Title	Yes	No
November 2, 1920		
1. Compulsory Voting and Registration Amendment—L[1]	61,258	131,603
2. Constitutional Amendment Regulating Legislative Sessions and the Payment of Legislators—L[1]	80,342	85,524
3. Oleomargarine Bills—R	67,101	119,126
4. Single Tax Constitutional Amendment—I[1]	37,283	147,426
5. Fixing Term of Certain County Officers—I[1]	*97,854	80,983
6. Port of Portland Dock Commission Consolidation—I[2]	80,493	84,830
7. Anti-compulsory Vaccination Amendment—I[1]	63,018	127,570
8. Constitutional Amendment Fixing Legal Rate of Interest in Oregon—I[1]	28,976	158,673
9. Roosevelt Bird Refuge—I[2]	78,961	107,383
10. Divided Legislative Session Constitutional Amendment—I[1]	57,791	101,179
11. State Market Commission Act—I[2]	51,605	119,464
June 7, 1921 (Special Election)		
1. Legislative Regulation and Compensation Amendment—L[1]	42,924	72,596
2. World War Veterans' State Aid Fund, Constitutional Amendment—L[1]	*88,219	37,866
3. Emergency Clause Veto Constitutional Amendment—L[1]	*62,621	45,537
4. Hygiene Marriage Examination and License Bill—L[2]	56,858	65,793
5. Women Jurors and Revised Jury Law—L[2]	*59,882	59,265
November 7, 1922		
1. Amendment Permitting Linn County Tax Levy to Pay Outstanding Warrants—L[1]	*89,177	57,049
2. Amendment Permitting Linn and Benton Counties to Pay Outstanding Warrants—L[1]	*86,547	53,844
3. Single Tax Amendment—I[1]	39,231	132,021
4. 1925 Exposition Tax Amendment—I[2]	82,837	95,587
5. Income Tax Amendment—I[2]	54,803	112,197
6. Compulsory Education Bill—I[2]	*115,506	103,685
November 6, 1923 (Special Election)		
1. Income Tax Act—L[2]	*58,647	58,131
November 4, 1924		
1. Voters' Literacy Amendment—L[1]	*184,031	48,645
2. Public Use and Welfare Amendment—L[1]	*134,071	65,133
3. Bonus Amendment—L[1]	*131,199	92,446
4. Oleomargarine Condensed Milk Bill—R	91,597	157,324
5. Naturopath Bill—I[2]	75,159	122,839
6. Workmen's Compulsory Compensation Law for Hazardous Occupations—I[1]	73,270	151,862
7. Income Tax Repeal—I[2]	*123,799	111,055
November 2, 1926		
1. Klamath County Bonding Amendment—L[1]	*81,954	68,128
2. Six Percent Limitation Amendment—L[1]	54,624	99,125
3. Repeal of Free Negro and Mulatto Section of the Constitution—L[1]	*108,332	64,954
4. Amendment Prohibiting Inheritance and Income Taxes—L[1]	59,442	121,973
5. The Seaside Normal School Act—L[2]	47,878	124,811
6. The Eastern Oregon State Normal School Act—L[2]	*101,327	80,084
7. The Recall Amendment—L[1]	*100,324	61,307
8 Curry County Bonding or Tax Levy Amendment—L[1]	*78,823	61,472
9. Amendment Relating to Elections to Fill Vacancies in Public Offices—L[1]	*100,397	54,474
10. Klamath and Clackamas County Bonding Amendment—L[1]	*75,229	61,718

Election Date/Measure Number/Ballot Title	Yes	No
11. The Eastern Oregon Tuberculosis Hospital Act—L²	*131,296	48,490
12. Cigarette and Tobacco Tax Bill—R	62,254	123,208
13. Motor Bus and Truck Bill—R	*99,746	78,685
14. Act Appropriating Ten Percent of Self-sustaining Boards' Receipts—R	46,389	97,460
15. Income Tax Bill With Property Tax Offset—I²	50,199	122,512
16. Bus and Truck Operating License Bill—I²	76,164	94,533
17. Fish Wheel, Trap, Seine and Gillnet Bill—I²	*102,119	73,086
18. Income Tax Bill—I²	83,991	93,997
19. Oregon Water and Power Board Development Measure—I¹	35,313	147,092
20. Amendment Fixing Salaries of County Officers of Umatilla County—L²	1,988	2,646
21. To Provide Salaries for Certain Officials of Clackamas County—L²	2,826	6,199

June 28, 1927 (Special Election)

	Yes	No
1. Repeal of Negro, Chinaman and Mulatto Suffrage Section of Constitution—L¹	*69,373	41,887
2. Portland School District Tax Levy Amendment—L¹	46,784	55,817
3. Criminal Information Amendment—L¹	*64,956	38,774
4. Legislators' Pay Amendment—L¹	28,380	81,215
5. Voters' Registration Amendment—L¹	*55,802	49,682
6. State and County Officers, Salary Amendment—L¹	46,999	61,838
7. City and County Consolidation Amendment—L¹	41,309	57,613
8. Veterans' Memorial and Armory Amendment—L¹	25,180	80,476
9. State Tax Limitation Amendment—L¹	19,393	84,697
10. Income Tax Bill—L²	48,745	67,039
11. Property Assessment and Taxation Enforcement Bill—L²	31,957	70,871
12. Nestucca Bay Fish Closing Bill—R	*53,684	47,552

November 6, 1928

	Yes	No
1. Five Cent Gasoline Tax Bill—I¹	71,824	198,798
2. Bill for Reduction of Motor Vehicle License Fees—I¹	98,248	174,219
3. Income Tax Bill—I²	118,696	132,961
4. Limiting Power of Legislature Over Laws Approved by the People—I¹	108,230	124,200
5. Deschutes River Water and Fish Bill—I²	78,317	157,398
6. Rogue River Water and Fish Bill—I²	79,028	156,009
7. Umpqua River Water and Fish Bill—I²	76,108	154,345
8. McKenzie River Water and Fish Bill—I²	77,974	153,418

November 4, 1930

	Yes	No
1. Repeal of State Payment of Irrigation and Drainage District Interest—L¹	*96,061	74,892
2. State Cabinet Form of Government Constitutional Amendment—L¹	51,248	135,412
3. Bonus Loan Constitutional Amendment—L¹	92,602	101,785
4. Motor Vehicle License Tax Constitutional Amendment—L¹	71,557	115,480
5. Motor Vehicle License Tax Constitutional Amendment—L¹	63,683	111,441
6. Constitutional Amendment for Filling Vacancies in the Legislature—L¹	*85,836	76,455
7. Legislators' Compensation Constitutional Amendment—L¹	70,937	108,070
8. Two Additional Circuit Judges Bill—R	39,770	137,549
9. Income Tax Bill—R	*105,189	95,207
10. Anti-cigarette Constitutional Amendment—I¹	54,231	156,265
11. Rogue River Fishing Constitutional Amendment—I¹	96,596	99,490

Election Date/Measure Number/Ballot Title	Yes	No
12. Lieutenant Governor Constitutional Amendment—I[1]	92,707	95,277
13. People's Water and Power Utility Districts Constitutional Amendment—I[1]	*117,776	84,778
November 8, 1932		
1. Taxpayer Voting Qualification Amendment—L[1]	*189,321	124,160
2. Amendment Authorizing Criminal Trials Without Juries by Consent of Accused—L[1]	*191,042	111,872
3. Six Percent Tax Limitation Amendment—L[1]	*149,833	121,852
4. Oleomargarine Tax Bill—R	131,273	200,496
5. Bill Prohibiting Commercial Fishing on the Rogue River—R	127,445	180,527
6. Higher Education Appropriation Bill—R	58,076	237,218
7. Bill to Repeal State Prohibition Law of Oregon—I[2]	*206,619	138,775
8. The Freight Truck and Bus Bill—I[2]	151,790	180,609
9. Bill Moving University, Normal and Law Schools, Establishing Junior Colleges—I[2]	47,275	292,486
10. Tax and Debt Control Constitutional Amendment—I[1]	99,171	162,552
11. Tax Supervising and Conservation Bill—I[2]	117,940	154,206
12. Personal Income Tax Law Amendment—I[2]	144,502	162,468
13. State Water Power and Hydroelectric Constitutional Amendment—I[1]	*168,937	130,494
July 21, 1933 (Special Election)		
1. An Amendment to the Constitution of the United States of America—L[0]	*136,713	72,854
2. Soldiers and Sailors Bonus Limitation Amendment—L[1]	*113,267	75,476
3. County Manager Form of Government Constitutional Amendment—L[1]	66,425	117,148
4. Prosecution by Information and Grand Jury Modification Amendment—L[1]	67,192	110,755
5. Debt and Taxation Limitations for Municipal Corporations Constitutional Amendment—L[1]	82,996	91,671
6. State Power Fund Bonds—L[2]	73,756	106,153
7. Sales Tax Bill—L[2]	45,603	167,512
8. Repeal of Oregon Prohibition Constitutional Amendment—L[1]	*143,044	72,745
9. Oleomargarine Tax Bill—R	66,880	144,542
May 18, 1934 (Special Election)		
1. County Indebtedness and Funding Bond Constitutional Amendment—L[1]	83,424	96,629
2. Criminal Trial Without Jury and Non-unanimous Verdict Constitutional Amendment—L[1]	*117,446	83,430
3. Bill Authorizing a State Tuberculosis Hospital in Multnomah County—L[2]	*104,459	98,815
4. Bill Authorizing a State Insane Hospital in Multnomah County—L[2]	92,575	108,816
5. School Relief Sales Tax Bill—R	64,677	156,182
November 6, 1934		
1. Grange Power Bill—R	124,518	139,283
2. Limitations of Taxes on Taxable Property Constitutional Amendment—I[1]	100,565	161,644
3. Healing Arts Constitutional Amendment—I[1]	70,626	191,836
January 31, 1936 (Special Election)		
1. Bill Changing Primary Elections to September With Other Resulting Changes—L[2]	61,270	155,922

Election Date/Measure Number/Ballot Title	Ye	Elec
2. Compensation of Members of the Legislature Constitutional Amendment—L[1]	28,66	9.
3. Sales Tax Bill—L[2]	32,10	No
4. Bill Authorizing Student Activity Fees in State Higher Educational Institutions—R	50,971	
November 3, 1936		
1. Bill Amending Old Age Assistance Act of 1935—R	174,293	
2. Amendment Forbidding Prevention or Regulation of Certain Advertising If Truthful—I[1]	100,141	22.
3. Tax Limitation Constitutional Amendment for School Districts Having 100,000 Population—I[1]	112,546	203,
4. Noncompulsory Military Training Bill—I[2]	131,917	214,2
5. Amendment Limiting and Reducing Permissible Taxes on Tangible Property—I[1]	79,604	241,042
6. State Power Bill—I[2]	131,489	208,179
7. State Hydroelectric Temporary Administrative Board Constitutional Amendment—I[1]	100,356	208,741
8. State Bank Bill—I[2]	82,869	250,777
November 8, 1938		
1. Governor's 20-day Bill Consideration Amendment—L[1]	*233,384	93,752
2. Amendment Repealing the Double Liability of Stockholders in Banking Corporations—L[1]	133,525	165,797
3. Legislators Compensation Constitutional Amendments—L[1]	149,356	169,131
4. Bill Requiring Marriage License Applicants Medically Examined; Physically and Mentally—L[2]	*277,099	66,484
5. Slot Machines Seizure by Sheriffs and Destruction on Court Order—R	*204,561	126,580
6. Prohibiting Slot Machines, Pin-ball, Dart and Other Similar Games—R	*197,912	129,043
7. Townsend Plan Bill—I[3]	*183,781	149,711
8. Citizens Retirement Annuity Bill; Levying Transactions Tax to Provide Fund—I[2]	112,172	219,557
9. Bill Regulating Picketing and Boycotting by Labor Groups and Organizations—I[2]	*197,771	148,460
10. Water Purification and Prevention of Pollution Bill—I[2]	*247,685	75,295
11. Bill Regulating Sale of Alcoholic Liquor for Beverage Purposes—I[2]	118,282	222,221
12. Constitutional Amendment Legalizing Certain Lotteries and Other Forms of Gambling—I[1]	141,792	180,329
November 5, 1940		
1. Amendment Removing Office Time Limit of State Secretary and Treasurer—L[1]	163,942	213,797
2. Amendment Making Three Years' Average People's Voted Levies, Tax Base—L[1]	129,699	183,488
3. Amendment Repealing the Double Liability of Stockholders of State Banks—L[1]	157,891	191,290
4. Legislators' Compensation Constitutional Amendment—L[1]	186,830	188,031
5. Bill Changing the Primary Nominating Elections from May to September—R	156,421	221,203
6. Bill to Further Regulate Sale and Use of Alcoholic Liquor—R	158,004	235,128
7. Bill Repealing Present Liquor Law; Authorizing Private Sale, Licensed, Taxed—I[2]	90,681	309,183
8. Amendment Legalizing Certain Gambling and Gaming Devices and Certain Lotteries—I[1]	150,157	258,010

records

Election Date/Measure Number/Ballot Title	Yes	No
October 7, 1947 (Special Election)		
1. Bill Taxing Retail Sales for School, Welfare and Governmental Purposes—L[2]	67,514	180,333
2. Cigarette Tax Bill—R	103,794	140,876
November 2, 1948		
1. Constitutional Six Percent Tax Limitation Amendment—L[1]	150,032	268,155
2. Constitutional Amendment Authorizing Indebtedness for State Forestation—L[1]	*211,912	209,317
3. Bill Authorizing State Boys' Camp Near Timber, Oregon—L[2]	*227,638	219,196
4. Bill Amending Licensing and Acquisition Provisions for Hydroelectric Commission Act—R	173,004	242,100
5. Constitutional Amendment Fixing Qualifications of Voters in School Elections—I[1]	*284,776	164,025
6. Oregon Old Age Pension Act—I[2]	*313,212	172,531
7. Bill Increasing Personal Income Tax Exemptions—I[2]	*405,842	63,373
8. Oregon Liquor Dispensing Licensing Act—I[2]	210,108	273,621
9. World War II Veterans' Bonus Amendment—I[1]	198,283	265,805
10. Prohibiting Salmon Fishing in Columbia River With Fixed Appliances—I[2]	*273,140	184,834
11. Question of Authorizing Additional State Tax, to be Offset by Income Tax Funds—R	143,856	256,167
November 7, 1950		
1. Constitutional Amendment Fixing Legislators' Annual Compensation—L[1]	*243,518	205,361
2. Constitutional Amendment Lending State Tax Credit for Higher Education Buildings—L[1]	*256,895	192,573
3. Constitutional Amendment Augmenting "Oregon War Veterans' Fund"—L[1]	*268,171	183,724
4. Increasing Basic School Support Fund by Annual Tax Levy—L[2]	*234,394	231,856
5. Needy Aged Persons Public Assistance Act—R	*310,143	158,939
6. Providing Uniform Standard Time in Oregon—R	*277,633	195,319
7. World War II Veterans' Compensation Fund—I[1]	*239,553	216,958
8. Constitutional Amendment for Legislative Representation Reapportionment—I[1]	190,992	215,302
9. Making Sale of Promotively Advertised Alcoholic Beverage Unlawful—I[2]	113,524	378,732
November 4, 1952		
1. Amendment Making Superintendent of Public Instruction Appointive—L[1]	282,882	326,199
2. World War Veterans' State Aid Sinking Fund Repeal—L[1]	*454,898	147,128
3. Act Authorizing Domiciliary State Hospital for Aged Mentally Ill—L[2]	*480,479	153,402
4. Amendment Legal Voters of Taxing Unit Establish Tax Base—L[1]	*355,136	210,373
5. Amendment to Augment Oregon War Veterans' Fund—L[1]	*465,605	132,363
6. Amendment Creating Legislative Assembly Emergency Committee—L[1]	*364,739	194,492
7. Amendment Fixing Elective Terms of State Senators and Representatives—L[1]	*483,356	103,357
8. Amendatory Act Title Subject Amendment—L[1]	*315,071	121,087
9. Act Limiting State Property Tax—L[2]	*318,948	272,145
10. Motor Carrier Highway Transportation Tax Act—R	*409,588	230,240

Election Date/Measure Number/Ballot Title	Yes	
5. Authorizing Legislature to Propose Revised Constitution—L[1]	*358,367	
6. State Bonds for Higher Education Facilities—L[1]	*467,557	
7. Voter Qualification Amendment—L[1]	*508,108	1
8. Authorizing Bonds for State Building Program—L[1]	232,250	43,
9. Compulsory Retirement for Judges—L[1]	*578,471	123,
10. Elective Offices: When to Become Vacant—L[1]	*486,019	169,8
11. Financing Improvements in Home Rule Counties—L[1]	*399,210	222,73
12. Continuity of Government in Enemy Attack—L[1]	*578,266	88,998
13. War Veterans' Bonding and Loan Amendment—L[1]	*415,931	266,630
14. Personal Income Tax Bill—R	115,610	570,025
15. Billboard Control Measure—I[2]	261,735	475,290
May 18, 1962		
1. Six Percent Limitation Amendment—L[1]	141,728	262,140
2. Salaries of State Legislators—L[1]	*241,171	178,749
November 6, 1962		
1. Reorganize State Militia—L[1]	*312,680	234,440
2. Forest Rehabilitation Debt Limit Amendment—L[1]	*323,799	199,174
3. Permanent Road Debt Limit Amendment—L[1]	*319,956	200,236
4. Power Development Debt Limit Amendment—L[1]	*298,255	208,755
5. State Courts Creation and Jurisdiction—L[1]	*307,855	193,487
6. Daylight Saving Time—L[2]	*388,154	229,661
7. Constitutional Six Percent Limitation Amendment—L[1]	*270,637	219,509
8. Legislative Apportionment Constitutional Amendment—I[1]	197,322	325,182
9. Repeals School District Reorganization Law—I[2]	206,540	320,917
October 15, 1963 (Special Election)		
1. Personal and Corporation Income Tax Bill—R	103,737	362,845
May 15, 1964		
1. Authorizing Bonds for Education Building Program—L[1]	*327,220	252,372
November 3, 1964		
1. Capital Punishment Bill—L[1]	*455,654	302,105
2. Leasing Property for State Use—L[1]	*477,031	238,241
3. Amending State Workmen's Compensation Law—I[2]	205,182	549,414
4. Prohibiting Commercial Fishing for Salmon, Steelhead—I[2]	221,797	534,731
May 24, 1966		
1. Cigarette Tax Bill—L[2]	*310,743	181,957
2. Superintendent of Public Instruction Constitutional Amendment—L[1]	197,096	267,319
November 8, 1966		
1. Public Transportation System Employes Constitutional Amendment—L[1]	*468,103	123,964
2. State Bonds for Educational Facilities—L[1]	237,282	332,983
May 28, 1968		
1. Common School Fund Constitutional Amendment—L[1]	*372,915	226,191
2. Constitutional Amendment Changing Initiative—Referendum Requirements—L[1]	*321,731	244,750
3. Higher Education and Community College Bonds—L[1]	*353,383	261,014
November 5, 1968		
1. Constitutional Amendment Broadening Veterans Loan Eligibility—L[1]	*651,250	96,065
2. Constitutional Amendment for Removal of Judges—L[1]	*690,989	56,973
3. Empowering Legislature to Extend Ocean Boundaries—L[1]	*588,166	143,768

Section Date/Measure Number/Ballot Title	Yes	No
. Constitutional Amendment Broadening County Debt Limitation—L[1]	331,617	348,866
5. Government Consolidation City-County Over 300,000—L[1]	*393,789	278,483
6. Bond Issue to Acquire Ocean Beaches—I[1]	315,175	464,140
7. Constitutional Amendment Changing Property Tax Limitation—I[1]	276,451	503,443
June 3, 1969 (Special Election)		
1. Property Tax Relief and Sales Tax—L[1]	65,077	504,274
May 26, 1970		
1. Capital Construction Bonds for State Government—L[1]	190,257	300,126
2. Repeals "White Foreigner" Section of Constitution—L[1]	*326,374	168,464
3. Revised Constitution for Oregon—L[1]	182,074	322,682
4. Pollution Control Bonds—L[1]	*292,234	213,835
5. Lowers Oregon Voting Age to 19—L[1]	202,018	336,527
6. Local School Property Tax Equalization Measure—L[1]	180,602	323,189
November 3, 1970		
1. Constitutional Amendment Concerning Convening of Legislature—L[1]	261,428	340,104
2. Automatic Adoption, Federal Income Tax Amendments—L[1]	*342,138	269,467
3. Constitutional Amendment Concerning County Debt Limitation—L[1]	283,659	294,186
4. Investing Funds Donated to Higher Education—L[1]	*332,188	268,588
5. Veterans' Loan Amendment—L[1]	*481,031	133,564
6. Limits Term of Defeated Incumbents—L[1]	*436,897	158,409
7. Constitutional Amendment Authorizing Education Bonds—L[1]	269,372	318,651
8. Allows Penal Institutions Anywhere in Oregon—L[1]	*352,771	260,100
9. Scenic Waterways Bill—I[2]	*406,315	214,243
10. New Property Tax Bases for Schools—I[1]	223,735	405,437
11. Restricts Governmental Powers Over Rural Property—I[1]	272,765	342,503
January 18, 1972 (Special Election)		
1. Increases Cigarette Tax—R	*245,717	236,937
May 23, 1972		
1. Eliminates Literacy Requirement; Lowers Voting Age—L[1]	327,231	349,746
2. Repeals Requirement for Decennial State Census—L[1]	*420,568	206,436
3. Allows Legislators to Call Special Sessions—L[1]	241,371	391,698
4. Capital Construction Bonds for State Government—L[1]	232,391	364,323
5. Irrigation and Water Development Bonds—L[1]	233,175	374,295
6. Enabling County-City Vehicle Registration Tax—R	120,027	491,551
November 7, 1972		
1. Eliminates Location Requirements for State Institutions—L[1]	*594,080	232,948
2. Qualifications for Sheriff Set By Legislature—L[1]	*572,619	281,720
3. Amends County Purchase and Lease Limitations—L[1]	329,669	462,932
4. Changes State Constitution Provision Regarding Religion—L[1]	336,382	519,196
5. Minimum Jury Size of Six Members—L[1]	*591,191	265,636
6. Broadens Eligibility for Veterans' Loans—L[1]	*736,802	133,139
7. Repeals Governor's Retirement Act—I[2]	*571,959	292,561
8. Changes Succession to Office of Governor—I[1]	*697,297	151,174
9. Prohibits Property Tax for School Operations—I[1]	342,885	558,136

Election Date/Measure Number/Ballot Title	Yes	No
May 1, 1973 (Special Election)		
1. Property Tax Limitation; School Tax Revision—L^2	253,682	358,219
May 28, 1974		
1. Income, Corporate Tax, School Support Increase—L^2	136,851	410,733
2. Highway Fund Use for Mass Transit—L^1	190,899	369,038
3. New School District Tax Base Limitation—L^1	166,363	371,897
4. Authorizes Bonds for Water Development Fund—L^1	198,563	328,221
5. Increases Veterans' Loan Bonding Authority—L^1	*381,559	164,953
6. Permits Legislature to Call Special Session—L^1	246,525	298,373
November 5, 1974		
1. Liquor Licenses for Public Passenger Carriers—L^1	353,357	384,521
2. Opens All Legislative Deliberations to Public—L^1	*546,255	165,778
3. Revises Constitutional Requirements for Grand Juries—L^1	*437,557	246,902
4. Governor Vacancy Successor Age Requirement Eliminated—L^1	*381,593	331,756
5. The measure designated as Number 5 by the 1973 Legislature was moved to the May 28, 1974 primary election by the 1974 special session. On the advice of the Attorney General, this measure number was left blank.		
6. Permits Establishing Qualifications for County Assessors—L^1	*552,737	146,364
7. Tax Base Includes Revenue Sharing Money—L^1	322,023	329,858
8. Revises School District Election Voting Requirements—L^1	337,565	378,071
9. Permits State Employes to be Legislators—L^1	218,846	476,547
10. Revises Oregon Voter Qualification Requirements—L^1	*362,731	355,506
11. Right to Jury in Civil Cases—L^1	*480,631	216,853
12. Community Development Fund Bonds—L^1	277,723	376,747
13. Obscenity and Sexual Conduct Bill—R	*393,743	352,958
14. Public Officials' Financial Ethics and Reporting. This measure was also referred to all 36 counties, with 30 voting yes and 6 voting no; and all cities with governing bodies, with 153 voting yes and 90 voting no.—L^2	*498,002	177,946
15. Prohibits Purchase or Sale of Steelhead—I^2	*458,417	274,182
May 25, 1976		
1. Expands Veterans' Home-Farm Loan Eligibility—L^1	*549,553	158,997
2. Discipline of Judges—L^1	*639,977	59,774
3. Housing Bonds—L^1	*315,588	362,414
4. Authorizes Vehicle Tax Mass Transit Use—L^1	170,331	531,219
November 2, 1976		
1. Validates Inadvertently Superseded Statutory Amendments—L^1	*607,325	247,843
2. Allows Changing City, County Election Days—L^1	376,489	536,967
3. Lowers Minimum Age for Legislative Service—L^1	285,777	679,517
4. Repeals Emergency Succession Provision—L^1	*507,308	368,646
5. Permits Legislature to Call Special Session—L^1	*549,126	377,354
6. Allows Charitable, Fraternal, Religious Organizations Bingo—L^1	*682,252	281,696
7. Partial Public Funding of Election Campaigns—L^2	263,738	659,327
8. Increases Motor Fuel, Ton-Mile Taxes—R	465,143	505,124
9. Regulates Nuclear Power Plant Construction Approval—I^2	423,008	584,845
10. Repeals Land Use Planning Coordination Statutes—I^2	402,608	536,502
11. Prohibits Adding Fluorides to Water Systems—I^2	419,567	555,981

Election Date/Measure Number/Ballot Title	Yes	No
12. Repeals Intergovernmental Cooperation, Planning District Statutes—I^2	333,933	525,868
May 17, 1977 (Special Election)		
1. School Operating Levy Measure—L^1	112,570	252,061
2. Authorizes Additional Veterans' Fund Uses—L^1	*200,270	158,436
3. Increases Veterans' Loan Bonding Authority—L^1	*250,783	106,953
November 8, 1977 (Special Election)		
1. Water Development Loan Fund Created—L^1	*124,484	118,953
2. Development of Nonnuclear Energy Resources—L^1	105,219	137,693
May 23, 1978		
1. Home Rule County Initiative-Referendum Requirements—L^1	*306,506	156,623
2. Open Meetings Rules for Legislature—L^1	*435,338	80,176
3. Housing for Low Income Elderly—L^1	*291,778	250,810
4. Domestic Water Fund Created—L^1	148,822	351,843
5. Highway Repair Priority, Gas Tax Increase—L^2	190,301	365,170
6. Reorganizes Metropolitan Service District, Abolishes CRAG—L^{2,4}	*110,600	91,090
November 7, 1978		
1. Appellate Judge Selection, Running on Record—L^1	358,504	449,132
2. Authorizes Senate Confirmation of Governor's Appointments—L^1	*468,458	349,604
3. Vehicle and Fee Increase Referendum—R	208,722	673,802
4. Shortens Formation Procedures for People's Utility Districts—I^2	375,587	471,027
5. Authorizes, Regulates Practice of Denture Technology—I^2	*704,480	201,463
6. Limitations on Ad Valorem Property Taxes—I^1	424,029	453,741
7. Prohibits State Expenditures, Programs or Services for Abortion—I^1	431,577	461,542
8. Requires Death Penalty for Murder under Specified Conditions—I^2	*573,707	318,610
9. Limitations on Public Utility Rate Base—I^2	*589,361	267,132
10. Land Use Planning, Zoning Constitutional Amendment—I^1	334,523	515,138
11. Reduces Property Tax Payable by Homeowner and Renter—L^1	383,532	467,765
12. Support of Constitutional Amendment (Federal) Require Balance Budget—L^5	*641,862	134,758
May 20, 1980		
1. Constitutional Amendment Limits Uses of Gasoline and Highway User Taxes—L^1	*451,695	257,230
2. Amends Liquor by the Drink Constitutional Provision—L^1	325,030	384,346
3. State Bonds for Small Scale Local Energy Project Loan Fund—L^1	*394,466	278,125
4. Veterans' Home and Farm Loan Eligibility Changes—L^1	*574,148	130,452
5. Continues Tax Reduction Program—L^2	*636,565	64,979
6. Definition of Multifamily Low Income Elderly Housing—L^1	*536,002	138,675
November 4, 1980		
1. Repeal of Constitutional Provision Requiring Elected Superintendent of Public Instruction—L^1	291,142	820,892
2. Guarantees Mentally Handicapped Voting Rights, Unless Adjudged Incompetent to Vote—L^1	*678,573	455,020

Election Date/Measure Number/Ballot Title	Yes	No
3. Dedicates Oil, Natural Gas Taxes to Common School Fund—L[1]	*594,520	500,586
4. Increases Gas Tax from Seven to Nine Cents per Gallon—L[2]	298,421	849,745
5. Forbids Use, Sale of Snare, Leghold Traps for Most Purposes—I[2]	425,890	728,173
6. Constitutional Real Property Tax Limit Preserving 85% Districts' 1977 Revenue—I[1]	416,029	711,617
7. Nuclear Plant Licensing Requires Voter Approval, Waste Disposal Facility Existence—I[2]	*608,412	535,049
8. State Bonds for Fund to Finance Correctional Facilities—L[1]	523,955	551,383
May 18, 1982		
1. Use of State Bond Proceeds to Finance Municipal Water Projects—L[1]	*333,656	267,137
2. Multifamily Housing for Elderly and Disabled Persons—L[1]	*389,820	229,049
3. State Bonds for Fund to Finance Corrections Facilities—L[1]	281,548	333,476
4. Raises Taxes on Commercial Vehicles, Motor Vehicles Fuels for Roads—L[2]	308,574	323,268
5. Governor to Appoint Chief Justice of Oregon Supreme Court—L[2]	159,811	453,415
November 2, 1982		
1. Increases Tax Base When New Property Construction Increases District's Value—L[1]	219,034	768,150
2. Lengthens Governor's Time for Postsession Veto or Approval of Bills—L[1]	385,672	604,864
3. Constitutional Real Property Tax Limit Preserving 85% Districts' 1979 Revenue—I[1]	504,836	515,626
4. Permits Self-Service Dispensing of Motor Vehicle Fuel at Retail—I[2]	440,824	597,970
5. People of Oregon Urge Mutual Freeze on Nuclear Weapons Development—I[3]	*623,089	387,907
6. Ends State's Land Use Planning Powers, Retains Local Planning—I[2]	461,271	565,056
May 15, 1984		
1. State May Borrow and Lend Money for Public Works Projects—L[1]	332,175	365,571
2. Increases Fees for Licensing and Registration of Motor Vehicles—L[2]	234,060	487,457
November 6, 1984		
1. Changes Minimum Requirements for Recall of Public Officers—L[1]	*664,464	470,139
2. Constitutional Real Property Tax Limit—I[1]	599,424	616,252
3. Creates Citizens' Utility Board to Represent Interests of Utility Consumers—I[2]	*637,968	556,826
4. Constitutional Amendment Establishes State Lottery, Commission; Profits for Economic Development—I[1]	*794,441	412,341
5. Statutory Provisions for State Operated Lottery if Constitutionally Authorized—I[2]	*786,933	399,231
6. Exempts Death Sentences from Constitutional Guarantees Against Cruel, Vindictive Punishments—I[1]	*653,009	521,687
7. Requires by Statute Death or Mandatory Imprisonment for Aggravated Murder—I[2]	*893,818	295,988

Election Date/Measure Number/Ballot Title	Yes	No
8. Revises Numerous Criminal Laws Concerning Police Powers, Trials, Evidence, Sentencing—I²	552,410	597,964
9. Adds Requirements for Disposing Wastes Containing Naturally Occurring Radioactive Isotopes—I²	*655,973	524,214
September 17, 1985 (Special Election)		
1. Amends Constitution. Approves Limited 5% Sales Tax for Local Education—L¹	189,733	664,365
May 20, 1986		
1. Constitutional Amendment: Bans Income Tax on Social Security Benefits—L¹	*534,476	118,766
2. Constitutional Amendment: Effect on Merger of Taxing Units on Tax Base—L¹	*333,277	230,886
3. Constitutional Amendment: Verification of Signatures on Initiative and Referendum Petitions—L¹	*460,148	132,101
4. Requires Special Election for US Senator Vacancy, Removes Constitutional Provision—L¹	*343,005	269,305
5. Constitutional Amendment: $96 Million Bonds for State-County Prison Buildings—L¹	300,674	330,429
November 4, 1986		
1. Deletes Constitutional Requirement that Secretary of State Live in Salem—L¹	*771,959	265,999
2. Constitutional Amendment Revising Legislative District Reapportionment Procedures After Federal Census—L¹	*637,410	291,355
3. Constitutional Amendment Allows Charitable, Fraternal, Religious Organizations to Conduct Raffles—L¹	*736,739	302,957
4. Replaces Public Utility Commissioner with Three Member Public Utility Commission—L²	*724,577	297,973
5. Legalizes Private Possession and Growing of Marijuana for Personal Use—I²	279,479	781,922
6. Constitutional Amendment Prohibits State Funding Abortions. Exception: Prevent Mother's Death—I¹	477,920	580,163
7. Constitutional 5% Sales Tax, Funds Schools, Reduces Property Tax—I¹	234,804	816,369
8. Prohibits Mandatory Local Measured Telephone Service Except Mobile Phone Service—I²	*802,099	201,918
9. Amends Constitution. Limits Property Tax Rates and Assessed Value Increases—I¹	449,548	584,396
10. Revises Many Criminal Laws Concerning Victims' Rights, Evidence, Sentencing, Parole—I²	*774,766	251,509
11. Homeowner's, Renter's Property Tax Relief Program; Sales Tax Limitation Measure—I¹	381,727	639,034
12. State Income Tax Changes, Increased Revenue to Property Tax Relief—I²	299,551	720,034
13. Constitutional Amendment: Twenty Day Pre-election Voter Registration Cutoff—I¹	*693,460	343,450
14. Prohibits Nuclear Power Plant Operation Until Permanent Waste Site Licensed—I²	375,241	674,641
15. Supersedes "Radioactive Waste" Definition; Changes Energy Facility Study Payment Procedure—I²	424,099	558,741
16. Phases Out Nuclear Weapons Manufactured With Tax Credits, Civil Penalty—I²	400,119	590,971
May 19, 1987 (Special Election)		
1. State Role In Selection of High-Level Nuclear Waste Repository Site—L²	*299,581	100,854
2. Continues Existing Levies To Prevent School Closures: Tax Base Elections—L¹	*223,417	178,839

Election Date/Measure Number/Ballot Title	Yes	No
May 17, 1988		
1. Authorizes Water Development Fund Loans for Fish Protection, Watershed Restoration—L¹	*485,629	191,008
2. Protective Headgear for Motorcycle Operators and Passengers and Moped Riders—L²	*486,401	224,655
November 8, 1988		
1. Extends Governor's Veto Deadline After Legislature Adjourns; Requires Prior Announcement—L¹	*615,012	520,939
2. Common School Fund Investments; Using Income for State Lands Management—L¹	*621,894	510,694
3. Requires the Use of Safety Belts—L²	528,324	684,747
4. Requires Full Sentences Without Parole, Probation for Certain Repeat Felonies—I²	*947,805	252,985
5. Finances Intercollegiate Athletic Fund by Increasing Malt Beverage, Cigarette Taxes—I²	449,797	759,360
6. Indoor Clean Air Law Revisions Banning Public Smoking—I²	430,147	737,779
7. Oregon Scenic Waterway System—I²	*663,604	516,998
8. Revokes Ban on Sexual Orientation Discrimination in State Executive Branch—I²	*626,751	561,355
May 16, 1989 (Special Election)		
1. Establishes New Tax Base Limits on Schools—L¹	183,818	263,283
June 27, 1989 (Special Election)		
1. Removes Constitutional Limitation on Use of Property Forfeited To State—L¹	*340,506	141,649
2. Prohibits Selling/Exporting Timber from State Lands Unless Oregon Processed—L¹	*446,151	48,558
May 15, 1990		
1. Permits Using Local Vehicle Taxes for Transit if Voters Approve—L¹	294,099	324,458
2. Amends Constitution; Allows Pollution Control Bond Use for Related Activities—L¹	*352,922	248,123
3. Amends State Constitution; Requires Annual Legislative Sessions of Limited Duration—L¹	294,664	299,831
4. Amends Laws on Organization of International Port of Coos Bay—L²	4,234	4,745
5A. Advisory Vote: Changing the School Finance System—L⁵	*462,090	140,747
5B. Advisory Vote: Income Tax Increase Reducing Homeowner School Property Taxes—L⁵	177,964	408,842
5C. Advisory Vote: Income Tax Increase Eliminating Homeowner School Property Taxes—L⁵	128,642	449,725
5D. Advisory Vote: Sales Tax Reducing School Property Taxes—L⁵	202,367	385,820
5E. Advisory Vote: Sales Tax Eliminating School Property Taxes—L⁵	222,611	374,466
November 6, 1990		
1. Grants Metropolitan Service District Electors Right to Home Rule—L¹	*510,947	491,170
2. Constitutional Amendment Allows Merged School Districts to Combine Tax Bases—L¹	*680,463	354,288
3. Repeals Tax Exemption, Grants Additional Benefit Payments for PERS Retirees—R	406,372	617,586
4. Prohibits Trojan Operation Until Nuclear Waste, Cost, Earthquake Standards Met—I²	446,795	660,992
5. State Constitutional Limit on Property Taxes for Schools, Government Operations—I¹	*574,833	522,022

Election Date/Measure Number/Ballot Title	Yes	No
6. Product Packaging Must Meet Recycling Standards or Receive Hardship Waiver—I[2]	467,418	636,804
7. Six-County Work in Lieu of Welfare Benefits Pilot Program—I[2]	*624,744	452,853
8. Amends Oregon Constitution to Prohibit Abortion With Three Exceptions—I[1]	355,963	747,599
9. Requires the Use of Safety Belts—I[2]	*598,460	512,872
10. Doctor Must Give Parent Notice Before Minor's Abortion—I[2]	530,851	577,806
11. School Choice System, Tax Credit for Education Outside Public Schools—I[1]	351,977	741,863
May 19, 1992		
1. Amends Constitution: Future Fuel Taxes May Go to Police—L[1]	244,173	451,715
November 3, 1992		
1. Bonds May be Issued for State Parks—L[1]	653,062	786,017
2. Future Fuel Taxes May Go to Parks—L[1]	399,259	1,039,322
3. Limits Terms for Legislature, Statewide Offices, Congressional Offices—I[1]	*1,003,706	439,694
4. Bans Operation of Triple Truck-Trailer Combinations on Oregon Highways—I[2]	567,467	896,778
5. Closes Trojan Until Nuclear Waste, Cost, Earthquake, Health Conditions Met—I[2]	585,051	874,636
6. Bans Trojan Power Operation Unless Earthquake, Waste Storage Conditions Met—I[2]	619,329	830,850
7. Raises Tax Limit on Certain Property; Residential Renters' Tax Relief—I[1]	362,621	1,077,206
8. Restricts Lower Columbia Fish Harvests to Most Selective Means Available—I[2]	576,633	828,096
9. Government Cannot Facilitate, Must Discourage Homosexuality, Other "Behaviors"—I[1]	638,527	828,290
June 29, 1993 (Special Election)		
1. Allows Voter Approval of Urban Renewal Bond Repayment Outside Limit—L[1]	180,070	482,714
November 9, 1993 (Special Election)		
1. Should We Pass A 5% Sales Tax for Public Schools with these Restrictions?—L[1]	240,991	721,930
May 17, 1994[6]		
2. Allows New Motor Vehicle Fuel Revenues for Dedicated Purposes—L[1]	158,028	446,665
November 8, 1994[6]		
3. Amends Constitution: Changes Deadline for Filling Vacancies at General Election—L[1]	*776,197	382,126
4. Amends Constitution: Creates Vacancy if State Legislator Convicted of Felony—L[1]	*1,055,111	145,499
5. Amends Constitution: Bars New or Increased Taxes without Voter Approval—I[1]	543,302	671,025
6. Amends Constitution: Candidates May Use Only Contributions from District Residents—I[1]	*628,180	555,019
7. Amends Constitution: Guarantees Equal Protection: Lists Prohibited Grounds of Discrimination—I[1]	512,980	671,021
8. Amends Constitution: Public Employees Pay Part of Salary for Pension—I[1]	*611,760	610,776
9. Adopts Contribution and Spending Limits, Other Campaign Finance Law Changes—I[2]	*851,014	324,224

Election Date/Measure Number/Ballot Title	Yes	No
10. Amends Constitution: Legislature Cannot Reduce Voter-Approved Sentence Without 2/3 Vote—I[1]	*763,507	415,678
11. Mandatory Sentences for Listed Felonies; Covers Persons 15 and Up—I[2]	*788,695	412,816
12 Repeals Prevailing Rate Wage Requirement for Workers on Public Works—I[2]	450,553	731,146
13. Amends Constitution: Governments Cannot Approve, Create Classifications Based on, Homosexuality—I[1]	592,746	630,628
14. Amends Chemical Process Mining Laws: Adds Requirements, Prohibitions, Standards, Fees—I[1]	500,005	679,936
15. Amends Constitution: State Must Maintain Funding for Schools, Community Colleges—I[1]	438,018	760,853
16. Allows Terminally Ill Adults to Obtain Prescription for Lethal Drugs—I[2]	*627,980	596,018
17. Amends Constitution: Requires State Prison Inmates to Work Full Time—1[1]	*859,896	350,541
18. Bans Hunting Bears with Bait, Hunting Bears, Cougars with Dogs—I[2]	*629,527	586,026
19. Amends Constitution: No Free Speech Protection for Obscenity, Child Pornography—I[1]	549,754	652,139
20. Amends Constitution: "Equal Tax" on Trade Replaces Current Taxes—I[1]	284,195	898,416
May 16, 1995 (Special Election)		
21. Dedication of Lottery Funds to Education—L[1]	*671,027	99,728
22. Inhabitancy in State Legislative Districts—L[1]	*709,931	45,311
May 21, 1996		
23. Amends Constitution: Increases Minimum Value in Controversy Required to Obtain Jury Trial—L[1]	*466,580	177,218
24. Amends Constitution: Initiative Petition Signatures Must Be Collected From Each Congressional District—L[1]	279,399	360,592
25. Amends Constitution: Requires 3/5 Majority in Legislature to Pass Revenue-Raising Bills—L[1]	*349,918	289,930
November 5, 1996		
26. Amends Constitution: Changes the Principles that Govern Laws for Punishment of Crime—L[1]	*878,677	440,283
27. Amends Constitution: Grants Legislature New Power Over Both New, Existing Administrative Rules—L[1]	349,050	938,819
28. Amends Constitution: Repeals Certain Residency Requirements for State Veterans' Loans—L[1]	*708,341	593,136
29. Amends Constitution: Governor's Appointees Must Vacate Office If Successor Not Timely Confirmed—L[1]	335,057	958,947
30. Amends Constitution: State Must Pay Local Governments Costs of State-Mandated Programs—L[1]	*731,127	566,168
31. Amends Constitution: Obscenity May Receive No Greater Protection Than Under Federal Constitution—L[1]	630,980	706,974
32. Authorizes Bonds for Portland Region Light Rail, Transportation Projects Elsewhere—R[2]	622,764	704,970
33. Amends Constitution: Limits Legislative Change to Statutes Passed by Voters—I[1]	638,824	652,811
34. Wildlife Management Exclusive to Commission; Repeals 1994 Bear/Cougar Initiative—I[2]	570,803	762,979
35. Restricts Bases for Providers to Receive Pay for Health Care—I[2]	441,108	807,987
36. Increases Minimum Hourly Wage to $6.50 Over Three Years—I[2]	*769,725	584,303
37. Broadens Types of Beverage Containers Requiring Deposit and Refund Value—I[2]	540,645	818,336

Election Date/Measure Number/Ballot Title	Yes	No
38. Prohibits Livestock in Certain Polluted Waters or on Adjacent Lands—I[2]	479,921	852,661
39. Amends Constitution: Government, Private Entities Cannot Discriminate Among Health Care Provider Categories—I[1]	569,037	726,824
40. Amends Constitution: Gives Crime Victims Rights, Expands Admissible Evidence, Limits Pretrial Release—I[1]	*778,574	544,301
41. Amends Constitution: States How Public Employee Earnings Must Be Expressed—I[1]	446,115	838,088
42. Amends Constitution: Requires Testing of Public School Students; Public Report—I[1]	460,553	857,878
43. Amends Collective Bargaining Law for Public Safety Employees—I[2]	547,131	707,586
44. Increases, Adds Cigarette and Tobacco Taxes; Changes Tax Revenue Distribution—I[2]	*759,048	598,543
45. Amends Constitution: Raises Public Employees' Normal Retirement Age; Reduces Benefits—I[1]	458,238	866,461
46. Amends Constitution: Counts Non-Voters As "No" Votes on Tax Measures—I[1]	158,555	1,180,148
47. Amends Constitution: Reduces and Limits Property Taxes; Limits Local Revenues, Replacement Fees—I[1]	*704,554	642,613
48. Amends Constitution: Instructs State, Federal Legislators to Vote for Congressional Term Limits—I[1,3]	624,771	671,095

[0]Repeal of federal prohibition amendment.
[1]Constitutional amendment.
[2]Statutory enactment.
[3]Required communication to federal officials on behalf of people of Oregon.
[4]Tri-county measure voted on in Clackamas, Multnomah and Washington Counties.
[5]Advisory vote for legislators' information.

Earliest Authorities in Oregon

Pacific Fur Company*
Fort Astoria

Name	Term of Service	By What Authority/Remarks
McDougall, Duncan	Mar. 22, 1811-Feb. 15, 1812 Aug. 4, 1812-Aug. 20, 1813 Aug. 26, 1813-Oct. 16, 1813	Acting agent and partner; served in absence of Wilson Price Hunt by agreement with partners
Hunt, Wilson Price	Feb. 15, 1812-Aug. 4, 1812 Aug.20, 1813-Aug. 26, 1813	Agent and partner by Articles of Agreement, June 23, 1810, Article 21

*Sold to John George McTavish and John Stuart, partners of the North West Company, Oct. 16, 1813; sale confirmed by Wilson Price Hunt, agent, March 10, 1814.

North West Company
Headquarters, Columbia District, Fort George (Astoria)

Name	Term of Service	By What Authority/Remarks
McTavish, John George	Oct. 16, 1813-Dec. 1, 1813	Acting governor and partner
McDonald, John (of Garth)	Dec. 1, 1813-Apr. 4, 1814	Governor and partner, Alexander Henry, trader
McTavish, Donald	Apr. 23, 1814-May 22, 1814	Governor and partner; with Alexander Henry, drowned in the Columbia River
Keith, James	May 22, 1814-June 7, 1816	Acting governor and partner

Chief of the Coast	Term of Service	Chief of the Interior
Keith, James	June 7, 1816-Mar. 21, 1821	McKenzie, Donald

Hudson's Bay Company*

Headquarters, Columbia District, Fort George (Astoria) 1821-1825; Fort Vancouver, 1825-1846

Chief Factor		Junior Chief Factor
McMillan, James	Spring, 1821-Fall, 1821	Cameron, John Dougald
Cameron, John Dougald	Fall, 1821-Spring, 1824	Kennedy, Alexander
Kennedy, Alexander	Spring, 1824-Mar. 18, 1825	McLoughlin, John
McLoughlin, John	Mar. 18, 1825-May 31, 1845	None appointed

*Appointments in 1821 by agreement with North West Company; and 1822-1825 by council of Northern Department, Sir George Simpson, Governor.

Oregon (WALAMET) Mission of the Methodist Episcopal Church

Mission Bottom 1834-1841; Chemeketa (Salem) 1841-1847

Lee, Jason	Oct. 6, 1834-Mar. 26, 1838	Appointed superintendent upon recommendation of the Board of Managers of the Missionary Society
Leslie, David	Mar. 26, 1838-May 27, 1840	Acting superintendent in absence of Lee
Lee, Jason	May 27, 1840-Dec. 25, 1843	Superintendent
Leslie, David	Dec. 25, 1843-June 1, 1844	Acting superintendent in absence of Lee
Gary, George	June 1, 1844-July 18, 1847	Appointed superintendent; instructed to dissolve the mission properties

Provisional Government Executive Committee

Hill, David; Beers, Alanson; Gale, Joseph	July 5, 1843-May 25, 1844	Elected by meeting of inhabitants of the Oregon Territory
Stewart, P.G.; Russell, Osborn; Bailey, W.J.	May 25, 1844-July 14, 1845	By vote of the people

Governors of Oregon

Under Provisional Government

Name/Political Party[1]	Term of Service	By What Authority/Remarks
Abernethy, George	July 14, 1845-Mar. 3, 1849	By people at 1845 general election; reelected 1848

Under Territorial Government

Lane, Joseph—D	Mar. 3, 1849-June 18, 1850	Appointed by President Polk; resigned
Prichette, Kintzing—D	June 18, 1850-Aug. 18, 1850	Acting governor, was secretary
Gaines, John P.—W	Aug. 18, 1850-May 16, 1853	Appointed by President Taylor
Lane, Joseph—D	May 16, 1853-May 19, 1853	Appointed by President Pierce; resigned
Curry, George L.—D	May 19, 1853-Dec. 2, 1853	Acting governor, was secretary
Davis, John W.—D	Dec. 2, 1853-Aug. 1, 1854	Appointed by President Pierce; resigned
Curry, George L.—D	Aug. 1, 1854-Mar. 3, 1859	Acting governor, was secretary; appointed by President Pierce, Nov. 1, 1854

Under State Government

Name/Political Party	Term of Service	By What Authority/Remarks
Whiteaker, John—D	Mar. 3, 1859-Sept. 10, 1862	Elected 1858
Gibbs, A.C.—R	Sept. 10, 1862-Sept. 12, 1866	Elected 1862
Woods, George L.—R	Sept. 12, 1866-Sept. 14, 1870	Elected 1866
Grover, LaFayette—D	Sept. 14, 1870-Feb. 1, 1877	Elected 1870; reelected 1874; resigned
Chadwick, Stephen F.—D	Feb. 1, 1877-Sept. 11, 1878	Was secretary of state
Thayer, W.W.—D	Sept. 11, 1878-Sept. 13, 1882	Elected 1878
Moody, Z.F.—R	Sept. 13, 1882-Jan. 12, 1887	Elected 1882
Pennoyer, Sylvester—DP	Jan. 12, 1887-Jan. 14, 1895	Elected 1886; reelected 1890
Lord, William Paine—R	Jan. 14, 1895-Jan. 9, 1899	Elected 1894
Geer, T.T.—R	Jan. 9, 1899-Jan. 14, 1903	Elected 1898
Chamberlain, George E.—D	Jan. 15, 1903-Feb. 28, 1909	Elected 1902; reelected 1906; resigned
Benson, Frank W.—R	Mar. 1, 1909-June 17, 1910	Was secretary of state; resigned
Bowerman, Jay[2]—R	June 17, 1910-Jan. 8, 1911	Was president of Senate
West, Oswald—D	Jan. 11, 1911-Jan. 12, 1915	Elected 1910
Withycombe, James—R	Jan. 12, 1915-Mar. 3, 1919	Elected 1914; reelected 1918; died in office
Olcott, Ben W.—R	Mar. 3, 1919-Jan. 8, 1923	Was secretary of state
Pierce, Walter M.—D	Jan. 8, 1923-Jan. 10, 1927	Elected 1922
Patterson, I.L.—R	Jan. 10, 1927-Dec. 21, 1929	Elected 1926; died in office
Norblad, A.W.[3]—R	Dec. 22, 1929-Jan. 12, 1931	Was president of Senate
Meier, Julius L.—I	Jan. 12, 1931-Jan. 14, 1935	Elected 1930
Martin, Charles H.—D	Jan. 14, 1935-Jan. 9, 1939	Elected 1934
Sprague, Charles A.—R	Jan. 9, 1939-Jan. 11, 1943	Elected 1938
Snell, Earl—R	Jan. 11, 1943-Oct. 28, 1947	Elected 1942; reelected 1946; died in office
Hall, John H.[4]—R	Oct. 30, 1947-Jan. 10, 1949	Was speaker of House
McKay, Douglas—R	Jan. 10, 1949-Dec. 27, 1952	Elected 1948; reelected 1950; resigned
Patterson, Paul L.—R	Dec. 27, 1952-Jan. 31, 1956	Was president of Senate; elected 1954; died in office
Smith, Elmo—R	Feb. 1, 1956-Jan. 14, 1957	Was president of Senate
Holmes, Robert D.—D	Jan. 14, 1957-Jan. 12, 1959	Elected 1956
Hatfield, Mark O.—R	Jan. 12, 1959-Jan. 9, 1967	Elected 1958; reelected 1962
McCall, Tom—R	Jan. 9, 1967-Jan 13, 1975	Elected 1966; reelected 1970
Straub, Robert W.—D	Jan. 13, 1975-Jan. 8, 1979	Elected 1974
Atiyeh, Victor G.—R	Jan. 8, 1979-Jan. 12, 1987	Elected 1978; reelected 1982
Goldschmidt, Neil—D	Jan. 12, 1987-Jan. 14, 1991	Elected 1986
Roberts, Barbara—D	Jan. 14, 1991-Jan. 9, 1995	Elected 1990
Kitzhaber, John—D	Jan. 9, 1995	Elected 1994

[1]D-Democrat; R-Republican; DP-Democrat People's; I-Independent; W-Whig.

[2]Jay Bowerman became governor when Frank Benson, who was serving as both governor and secretary of state, became incapacitated. Benson resigned as governor but continued as secretary of state until his death.

[3]In 1920, the Constitution was changed to allow the president of the Senate to succeed as governor.

[4]A plane crash on October 28, 1947 killed Governor Earl Snell, Secretary of State Robert S. Farrell Jr., President of the Senate Marshall E. Cornett and the pilot, Cliff Hogue. John Hall, speaker of the House and next in line of succession, automatically became governor. Earl Newbry was appointed by John Hall to the position of secretary of state.

Secretaries of State

Under Provisional Government

Name/Political Party	Term of Service	By What Authority/Remarks
LeBreton, George W.	Feb. 18, 1841-Mar. 4, 1844	Elected by meeting of inhabitants of the Willamette Valley to office of clerk of courts and public recorder, thus served as first secretary; reelected 1843; died in office.
Johnson, Overton	Mar. 4, 1844-May 25, 1844	Appointed clerk and recorder
Long, Dr. John E.	May 25, 1844-June 21, 1846	Elected clerk and recorder by people at first 1844 general election; reelected 1845 general election; reelected 1845 by Legislature; drowned
Prigg, Frederick	June 26, 1846-Sept. 16, 1848	Appointed secretary to succeed Long; elected 1846 by Legislature; resigned
Holderness, Samuel M.	Sept. 19, 1848-Mar. 10, 1849	Appointed to succeed Prigg; elected 1848 by Legislature

Under Territorial Government

Name/Political Party	Term of Service	By What Authority/Remarks
Magruder, Theophilus	Mar. 10, 1849-Apr. 9, 1849	Elected by Legislature
Prichette, Kintzing—D	Apr. 9, 1849-Sept. 18, 1850	Appointed by President Polk
Hamilton, Gen. E.D.—W	Sept. 18, 1850-May 14, 1853	Appointed by President Taylor
Curry, George L.—D	May 14, 1853-Jan. 27, 1855	Appointed by President Pierce
Harding, Benjamin—D	Jan. 27, 1855-Mar. 3, 1859	Appointed by President Pierce

Under State Government

Name/Political Party	Term of Service	By What Authority/Remarks
Heath, Lucien—D	Mar. 3, 1859-Sept. 8, 1862	Elected 1858
May, Samuel E.—R	Sept. 8, 1862-Sept. 10, 1870	Elected 1862; reelected 1866
Chadwick, Stephen F.[1]—D	Sept. 10, 1870-Sept. 2, 1878	Elected 1870; reelected 1874
Earhart, R.P.—R	Sept. 2, 1878-Jan. 10, 1887	Elected 1878; reelected 1882
McBride, George W.—R	Jan. 10, 1887-Jan. 14, 1895	Elected 1886; reelected 1890
Kincaid, Harrison R.—R	Jan. 14, 1895-Jan. 9, 1899	Elected 1894
Dunbar, Frank I.—R	Jan. 9, 1899-Jan. 14, 1907	Elected 1898; reelected 1902
Benson, Frank W.[2]—R	Jan. 15, 1907-Apr. 14, 1911	Elected 1906; reelected 1910; died in office
Olcott, Ben W.[3]—R	Apr. 17, 1911-May 28, 1920	Appointed by Governor West; elected 1912; reelected 1916; resigned
Kozer, Sam A.—R	May 28, 1920-Sept. 24, 1928	Appointed by Governor Olcott; elected 1920; reelected 1924; resigned
Hoss, Hal E.—R	Sept. 24, 1928-Feb. 6, 1934	Appointed by Governor Patterson; elected 1928; reelected 1932; died in office
Stadelman, P.J.—R	Feb. 9, 1934-Jan. 7, 1935	Appointed by Governor Meier
Snell, Earl—R	Jan. 7, 1935-Jan. 4, 1943	Elected 1934; reelected 1938
Farrell, Robert S. Jr.—R	Jan. 4, 1943-Oct. 28, 1947	Elected 1942; reelected 1946; died in office
Newbry, Earl T.—R	Nov. 3, 1947-Jan. 7, 1957	Appointed by Governor Hall; elected 1948; reelected 1952
Hatfield, Mark—R	Jan. 7, 1957-Jan. 12, 1959	Elected 1956; resigned

Name/Political Party	Term of Service	By What Authority/Remarks
Appling, Howell, Jr.—R	Jan. 12, 1959-Jan. 4, 1965	Appointed by Governor Hatfield; elected 1960
McCall, Tom L.—R	Jan. 4, 1965-Jan. 9, 1967	Elected 1964; resigned
Myers, Clay—R	Jan. 9, 1967-Jan. 3, 1977	Appointed by Governor McCall; elected 1968; reelected 1972
Paulus, Norma—R	Jan. 3, 1977-Jan. 7, 1985	Elected 1976; reelected 1980
Roberts, Barbara—D	Jan. 7, 1985-Jan. 14, 1991	Elected 1984, reelected 1988, resigned
Keisling, Phil—D	Jan. 14, 1991	Appointed by Governor Roberts; elected 1992; reelected 1996

[1]When Stephen Chadwick succeeded L. F. Grover as governor in 1877, he did not resign as secretary of state. He signed documents and proclamations twice—as governor and as secretary of state—until September 1878.

[2]Frank Benson served as both secretary of state and governor; see Footnote 2 under Governors.

[3]When James Withycombe died in office on March 3, 1919, Ben W. Olcott succeeded him as governor. However, Governor Olcott did not resign or appoint a new secretary of state until May 28, 1920.

Treasurers of Oregon

Under Provisional Government

Name/Political Party	Term of Service	By What Authority/Remarks
Gray, W.H.	Mar. 1, 1843-July 5, 1843	Elected by meeting of citizens of the Willamette Valley
Willson, W.H.	July 5, 1843-May 14, 1844	Elected by meeting of the inhabitants of the Willamette settlements
Foster, Phillip	July 2, 1844-July 7, 1845	Elected by people at first 1844 general election
Ermatinger, Francis	July 7, 1845-Mar. 3, 1846	Elected by people at 1845 general election; reelected 1845 by Legislature; resigned
Couch, John H.	Mar. 4, 1846-Sept. 27, 1847	Appointed to succeed Ermatinger; elected by Legislature 1846; resigned
Kilbourn, William K.	Oct. 11, 1847-Sept. 28, 1849	Appointed to succeed Couch; elected by Legislature 1849

Under Territorial Government

Taylor, James	Sept. 28, 1849-Feb. 8, 1851	Elected by Legislature
Rice, L.A.	Feb. 8, 1851-Sept. 22, 1851	Elected by Legislature; resigned
Buck, William W.	Sept. 27, 1851-Dec. 16, 1851	Appointed to succeed Rice
Boon, John D.—D	Dec. 16, 1851-Mar. 1, 1855	Elected by Legislature
Lane, Nat H.—D	Mar. 1, 1855-Jan. 10, 1856	Elected by Legislature
Boon, John D.—D	Jan. 10, 1856-Mar. 3, 1859	Elected by Legislature

Under State Government

Boon, John D.—D	Mar. 3, 1859-Sept. 8, 1862	Elected 1858
Cooke, E.N.—R	Sept. 8, 1862-Sept. 12, 1870	Elected 1862; reelected 1866
Fleischner, L.—D	Sept. 12, 1870-Sept. 14, 1874	Elected 1870
Brown, A.H.—D	Sept. 14, 1874-Sept. 9, 1878	Elected 1874
Hirsch, E.—R	Sept. 9, 1878-Jan. 10, 1887	Elected 1878; reelected 1882
Webb, G.W.—D	Jan. 10, 1887-Jan. 12, 1891	Elected 1886
Metschan, Phil—R	Jan. 12, 1891-Jan. 9, 1899	Elected 1890; reelected 1894

Name/Political Party	Term of Service	By What Authority/Remarks
Moore, Charles S.—R	Jan. 9, 1899-Jan. 14, 1907	Elected 1898; reelected 1902
Steel, George A.—R	Jan. 15, 1907-Jan. 3, 1911	Elected 1906
Kay, Thomas B.—R	Jan. 4, 1911-Jan. 6, 1919	Elected 1910; reelected 1914
Hoff, O.P.—R	Jan. 6, 1919-Mar. 18, 1924	Elected 1918; reelected 1922; died in office
Myers, Jefferson—D	Mar. 18, 1924-Jan. 4, 1925	Appointed by Governor Pierce
Kay, Thomas B.—R	Jan. 4, 1925-April 29, 1931	Elected 1924; reelected 1928; died in office
Holman, Rufus C.—R	May 1, 1931-Dec. 27, 1938	Appointed by Governor Meier; elected 1932; reelected 1936; resigned
Pearson, Walter E.—D	Dec. 27, 1938-Jan. 6, 1941	Appointed by Governor Martin
Scott, Leslie M.—R	Jan. 6, 1941-Jan. 3, 1949	Elected 1940; reelected 1944
Pearson, Walter J.—D	Jan. 3, 1949-Jan. 5, 1953	Elected 1948
Unander, Sig—R	Jan. 5, 1953-Dec. 31, 1959	Elected 1952; reelected 1956; resigned
Belton, Howard C.—R	Jan. 4, 1960-Jan. 4, 1965	Appointed by Governor Hatfield; elected 1960
Straub, Robert—D	Jan. 4, 1965-Jan. 1, 1973	Elected 1964; reelected 1968
Redden, James A.—D	Jan. 1, 1973-Jan. 3, 1977	Elected 1972
Myers, Clay—R	Jan. 3, 1977-Apr. 1, 1984	Elected 1976; reelected 1980; resigned
Rutherford, Bill—R	Apr. 1, 1984-July 9, 1987	Appointed by Governor Atiyeh; elected 1984; resigned
Meeker, Tony—R	July 9, 1987-Jan. 4, 1993	Appointed by Governor Goldschmidt; elected 1988
Hill, Jim—D	Jan. 4, 1993	Elected 1992; reelected 1996

Oregon Supreme Court Justices[1]

Under Provisional Government

Name	Term of Service	By What Authority/Remarks
Babcock, Dr. Ira L.	Feb. 18, 1841-May 1, 1843	Supreme judge with probate powers elected at meeting of inhabitants of the Willamette Valley
Wilson, W.E.	No record of service	Supreme judge with probate powers; elected at meeting of inhabitants of the Willamette Settlements, May 2, 1843
Russell, Osborn	Oct. 2, 1843-May 14, 1844	Supreme judge and probate judge; appointed by the Executive Committee
Babcock, Dr. Ira L.	June 27, 1844-Nov. 11, 1844	Presiding judge, Circuit Court; elected at first general election May 1844; resigned
Nesmith, James W.	Dec. 25, 1844-Aug. 9, 1845	Presiding judge, Circuit Court; appointed by Executive Committee; elected by people 1845
Ford, Nathaniel	Declined service	Supreme judge; elected by Legislature Aug. 9, 1845; declined to serve
Burnett, Peter H.	Sept. 6, 1845-Dec. 29, 1846	Supreme judge; elected by Legislature; declined appointment to Supreme Court 1848
Thornton, J. Quinn	Feb. 20, 1847-Nov. 9, 1847	Supreme judge; appointed by Governor Abernethy; resigned
Lancaster, Columbia	Nov. 30, 1847-Apr. 9, 1849	Supreme judge; appointed by Governor Abernethy
Lovejoy, A.L.	No record of service	Supreme judge; elected by Legislature Feb. 16, 1849

Under Territorial[2] and State Government[3]

Name	Term of Service	By What Authority/Remarks
Bryant, William P.	1848-1850	Appointed 1848; resigned 1850 chief justice 1848-1850
Pratt, Orville C.	1848-1852	Appointed 1848; term ended 1852
Nelson, Thomas	1850-1853	Appointed 1850 to succeed Bryant; term ended 1853; chief justice 1850-1853
Strong, William	1850-1853	Appointed 1850 to succeed Burnett; term ended 1853
Williams, George H.	1853-1858	Appointed 1853, 1857; resigned 1858; chief justice 1853-1858
Olney, Cyrus	1853-1858	Appointed 1853, 1857; resigned 1858
Deady, Matthew P.	1853-1859	Appointed 1853, 1857; elected 1858; resigned 1859
McFadden, Obadiah B.	1853-1854	Appointed 1853; term ended 1854
Boise, Reuben P.	1858-1870 1876-1880	Appointed 1858 to succeed Olney; elected 1859; reelected 1864; term ended 1870; elected 1876; term ended 1878; appointed 1878; term ended 1880; chief justice 1862-1864, 1867-1870
Wait, Aaron E.	1859-1862	Elected 1858; resigned May 1, 1862; chief justice 1859-1862
Stratton, Riley E.	1859-1866	Elected 1858, 1864; died Dec. 26, 1866
Prim, Paine Page	1859-1880	Appointed 1859 to succeed Deady; elected 1860; reelected 1866, 1872; term ended 1878; appointed 1878; term ended 1880; chief justice 1864-1866, 1870-1872, 1876-1878
Page, William W.	1862	Appointed May 1862 to succeed Wait; term ended Sept. 1862
Shattuck, Erasmus D.	1862-1867 1874-1878	Elected 1862; resigned Dec. 1867; elected 1874; term ended 1878; chief justice 1866-1867
Wilson, Joseph G.	1862-1870	New appointment Oct. 17, 1862; elected 1864; resigned May 1870
Skinner, Alonzo A.	1866-1867	Appointed 1866 to succeed Stratton; term ended 1867
Upton, William W.	1867-1874	Appointed Dec. 1867 to succeed Shattuck; elected 1868; term ended 1874; chief justice 1872-1874
Kelsay, John	1868-1870	Elected 1868 to succeed Stratton; term ended 1870
Whitten, Benoni	1870	Appointed May 1870 to succeed Wilson; term ended Sept. 1870
McArthur, Lewis L.	1870-1878	Elected 1870; reelected 1876; term ended 1878
Thayer, Andrew J.	1870-1873	Elected 1870; died Apr. 26, 1873
Bonham, Benjamin F.	1870-1876	Elected 1870; term ended 1876; chief justice 1874-1876
Moser, Lafayette F.	1873-1874	Appointed May 1873 to succeed A. J. Thayer; term ended 1874
Burnett, John	1874-1876	Elected 1874; term ended 1876
Watson, James F.	1876-1878	Elected 1876; term ended 1878
Kelly, James K.	1878-1880	Appointed 1878; term ended 1880; chief justice 1878-1880
Lord, William P.	1880-1894	Elected 1880; reelected 1882, 1888; term ended 1894; chief justice 1880-1882, 1886-1888, 1892-1894

Name	Term of Service	By What Authority/Remarks
Watson, Edward B.	1880-1884	Elected 1880; term ended 1884; chief justice 1882-1884
Waldo, John B.	1880-1886	Elected 1880; term ended 1886; chief justice 1884-1886
Thayer, William W.	1884-1890	Elected 1884; term ended 1890; chief justice 1888-1890
Strahan, Reuben S.	1886-1892	Elected 1886; term ended 1892; chief justice 1890-1892
Bean, Robert S.	1890-1909	Elected 1890; reelected 1896, 1902, 1908; resigned May 1, 1909; chief justice 1894-1896, 1900-1902, 1905-1909
Moore, Frank A.	1892-1918	Elected 1892; reelected 1898, 1904, 1910, 1916; died Sept. 25, 1918; chief justice 1896-1898, 1902-1905, 1909-1911, 1915-1917
Wolverton, Charles E.	1894-1905	Elected 1894, 1900; resigned Dec. 4, 1905; chief justice 1898-1900, 1905
Hailey, Thomas G.	1905-1907	Appointed Dec. 5, 1905 to succeed Wolverton; term ended Jan. 15, 1907
Eakin, Robert	1907-1917	Elected 1906, 1912; resigned Jan. 8, 1917; chief justice 1911-1913
King, William R.	1909-1911	Appointed Feb. 12, 1909; term ended Jan. 1, 1911
Slater, Woodson T.	1909-1911	Appointed Feb. 12, 1909; term ended Jan. 1, 1911
McBride, Thomas A.	1909-1930	Appointed May 1, 1909 to succeed Robert S. Bean; elected 1914; reelected 1920, 1926; died Sept. 9, 1930; chief justice 1913-1915, 1917-1921, 1923-1927
Bean, Henry J.	1911-1941	Elected 1910; reelected 1914, 1920, 1926, 1932, 1938; died May 8, 1941; chief justice 1931-1933, 1937-1939
Burnett, George H.	1911-1927	Elected 1910; reelected 1916, 1922; died Sept. 10, 1927; chief justice 1921-1923, 1927
McNary, Charles L.	1913-1915	Appointed June 3, 1913; term ended Jan. 4, 1915
Ramsey, William M.	1913-1915	Appointed June 3, 1913; term ended Jan. 4, 1915
Benson, Henry L.	1915-1921	Elected 1914; reelected 1920; died Oct. 16, 1921
Harris, Lawrence T.	1915-1924	Elected 1914; reelected 1920; resigned Jan. 15, 1924
McCamant, Wallace	1917-1918	Appointed Jan. 8, 1917 to succeed Eakin; resigned June 4, 1918
Johns, Charles A.	1918-1921	Appointed June 4, 1918 to succeed McCamant; elected 1918; resigned Oct. 7, 1921
Olson, Conrad P.	1918-1919	Appointed Sept. 27, 1918 to succeed Moore; term ended Jan. 7, 1919
Bennett, Alfred S.	1919-1920	Elected 1918; resigned Oct. 5, 1920
Brown, George M.	1920-1933	Appointed Oct. 14, 1920 to succeed Bennett; elected 1920; reelected 1926; term ended 1933
McCourt, John	1921-1924	Appointed Oct. 8, 1921 to succeed Johns; elected 1922; died Sept. 12, 1924

Name	Term of Service	By What Authority/Remarks
Rand, John L.	1921-1942	Appointed Oct. 18, 1921 to succeed Benson; elected 1922; reelected 1928, 1934, 1940; died Nov. 19, 1942; chief justice 1927-1929, 1933-1935, 1939-1941
Coshow, Oliver P.	1924-1931	Appointed Jan. 15, 1924 to succeed Harris; elected 1924; term ended 1931; chief justice 1929-1931
Pipes, Martin L.	1924	Appointed Sept. 1924 to succeed McCourt; term ended Dec. 31, 1924
Belt, Harry H.	1925-1950	Elected 1924; reelected 1930, 1936, 1942, 1948; died Aug. 6, 1950; chief justice 1945-1947
Rossman, George	1927-1965	Appointed Sept. 13, 1927 to succeed George H. Burnett; elected 1928; reelected 1934, 1940, 1946, 1952, 1958; term ended 1965; chief justice 1947-1949
Kelly, Percy R.	1930-1949	Appointed Sept. 24, 1930 to succeed McBride; elected 1930; reelected 1936, 1942, 1948; died June 14, 1949; chief justice 1941-1943
Campbell, James U.	1931-1937	Elected 1930; reelected 1936; died July 16, 1937; chief justice 1935-1937
Bailey, John O.	1933-1950	Elected 1932; reelected 1938, 1944; resigned Nov. 15, 1950; chief justice 1943-1945
Lusk, Hall S.	1937-1960	Appointed July 22, 1937 to succeed Campbell; elected 1938; reelected 1944, 1950, 1956; resigned Mar. 15, 1960;
	1961-1968	recalled to temporary active service 1961 through 1968; chief justice 1949-1951
Brand, James T.	1941-1958	Appointed May 14, 1941 to succeed Henry J. Bean; elected 1942; reelected 1948, 1954; resigned June 30, 1958; chief justice 1951-1953
Hay, Arthur D.	1942-1952	Appointed Nov. 28, 1942 to succeed Rand; elected 1944; reelected 1950; died Dec. 19, 1952
Page, E.M.	1949-1950	Appointed July 8, 1949 to succeed Percy R. Kelly; resigned Jan. 18, 1950
Latourette, Earl C.	1950-1956	Appointed Jan. 19, 1950 to succeed E. M. Page; elected 1950; died Aug. 18, 1956; chief justice 1953-1955
Warner, Harold J.	1950-1963	Appointed Sept. 5, 1950 to succeed Belt; elected 1950; reelected 1956; term ended 1963; chief justice 1955-1957
Tooze, Walter L.	1950-1956	Appointed Nov. 16, 1950 to succeed Bailey; elected 1950; reelected 1956; died Dec. 21, 1956
Perry, William C.	1952-1970	Appointed Dec. 26, 1952 to succeed Hay; elected 1954; reelected 1960, 1966; resigned June 1, 1970; chief justice 1957-1959, 1967-1970
McAllister, William M.	1956-1976	Appointed Aug. 24, 1956 to succeed Latourette; elected 1956; reelected 1962, 1968, 1974; resigned Dec. 31, 1976; chief justice 1959-1967

Name	Term of Service	By What Authority/Remarks
Kester, Randall B.	1957-1958	Appointed Jan. 3, 1957 to succeed Tooze; resigned Mar. 1, 1958
Sloan, Gordon	1958-1970	Appointed Mar. 1, 1958 to succeed Kester; elected 1958; reelected 1964; resigned Oct. 1, 1970
O'Connell, Kenneth J.	1958-1977	Appointed July 1, 1958 to succeed Brand; elected 1958; reelected 1964, 1970; term ended 1977; chief justice 1970-1976
Goodwin, Alfred T.	1960-1969	Appointed Mar. 18, 1960 to succeed Lusk; elected 1960; reelected 1966; resigned Dec. 19, 1969
Denecke, Arno H.	1963-1982	Elected 1962; reelected 1968, 1974, 1980; resigned June 30, 1982; chief justice 1976-1982
Holman, Ralph M.	1965-1980	Elected 1964; reelected 1970, 1976; resigned Jan. 20, 1980
Tongue, Thomas H.	1969-1982	Appointed Dec. 29, 1969 to succeed Goodwin; elected 1970; reelected 1976; resigned Feb. 7, 1982
Howell, Edward H.	1970-1980	Appointed June 1, 1970 to succeed Perry; elected 1970; reelected 1976; resigned Nov. 30, 1980
Bryson, Dean F.	1970-1979	Elected 1970; appointed Oct. 23, 1970 (before elective term began) to succeed Sloan; reelected 1976; resigned April 1, 1979
Lent, Berkeley	1977-1988	Elected 1976; reelected 1982; resigned Sept. 30, 1988; chief justice 1982-1983
Linde, Hans	1977-1990	Appointed Jan. 3, 1977 to succeed McAllister; elected 1978; reelected 1984; resigned Jan. 31, 1990
Peterson, Edwin J.	1979 -1993	Appointed May 15, 1979 to succeed Bryson; elected 1980; reelected 1986, 1992; resigned Dec. 31, 1993; chief justice 1983 to 1991
Tanzer, Jacob	1980-1982	Appointed Jan. 21, 1980 to succeed Holman; elected 1980; resigned Dec. 31, 1982
Campbell, J.R.	1980-1988	Appointed Dec. 1, 1980 to succeed Howell; elected 1982; resigned Dec. 31, 1988
Roberts, Betty	1982-1986	Appointed Feb. 8, 1982 to succeed Tongue; elected 1982; resigned Feb. 7, 1986
Carson, Wallace P., Jr.	1982	Appointed July 14, 1982 to succeed Denecke; elected 1982; reelected 1988, 1994; chief justice 1991 to date
Jones, Robert E.	1983-1990	Appointed Dec. 16, 1982 to succeed Tanzer; elected 1984; resigned April 30, 1990
Gillette, W. Michael	1986	Appointed Feb. 10, 1986 to succeed Roberts; elected 1986; reelected 1992
Van Hoomissen, George	1988	Elected May 17, 1988 to succeed Lent; reelected 1994
Fadeley, Edward N.	1988	Elected Nov. 8, 1988 to succeed Campbell; reelected 1994

Name	Term of Service	By What Authority/Remarks
Unis, Richard	1990-1996	Appointed Feb. 1, 1990 to succeed Linde; elected 1990; resigned June 30, 1996
Graber, Susan P.[4]	1990	Appointed May 2, 1990 and Jan. 7, 1991 to succeed Jones; elected 1992
Durham, Robert D.	1994	Appointed Jan. 4, 1994 to succeed Peterson; elected 1994
Kulongoski, Ted	1997	Elected May, 1996

[1]Unless otherwise noted, justices took office in the year in which elected until 1905. Since then, terms have started on the first Monday in January and continued until the first Monday six years hence or until a successor has been sworn in, if later.

[2]Appointments under territorial government were made by the president of the United States.

[3]From 1859 to 1862, there were four Supreme Court justices. In 1862, a fifth justice was added. The justices at that time also rode circuit. In 1878, the Supreme Court and Circuit Court were separated; the Supreme Court then had three justices. In 1910, the number increased to five. The final increase to the present seven occurred in 1913.

[4]When Justice Jones resigned, he had already filed to run for another term and his name appeared on the ballot at the 1990 primary election. Because he was elected for another term, which began January 7, 1991, he had to resign from his new term, and Justice Graber was appointed again at that time.

Judges of the Court of Appeals

Oregon's Court of Appeals was established July 1, 1969 with five members; expanded to six members October 5, 1973; and to ten members September 1, 1977.

Name	Term of Service	By What Authority/Remarks
Langtry, Virgil	1969-1976	Appointed July 1, 1969; elected 1970; resigned Sept. 15, 1976
Foley, Robert H.	1969-1976	Appointed July 1, 1969; elected 1970; resigned Aug. 16, 1976
Schwab, Herbert M.	1969-1980	Appointed July 1, 1969; elected 1970; reelected 1976; resigned Dec. 31, 1980; chief judge 1969-1980
Fort, William S.	1969-1977	Appointed July 1, 1969; elected 1970; term ended 1977
Branchfield, Edward H.	1969-1971	Appointed July 1, 1969; term ended 1971
Thornton, Robert Y.	1971-1983	Elected 1970; reelected 1976; term ended 1983
Tanzer, Jacob	1973-1975	Appointed to new seat Oct. 5, 1973;
	1976-1980	term ended Jan. 6, 1975; elected 1976; appointed Aug. 16, 1976 (before elective term began) to succeed Foley; resigned Jan. 21, 1980
Lee, Jason	1975-1980	Elected 1974; died Feb. 19, 1980
Johnson, Lee	1977-1978	Elected 1976; resigned Dec. 18, 1978
Richardson, William L.	1976	Elected 1976; appointed Oct. 15, 1976 (before elective term began) to succeed Langtry; reelected 1982, 1988, 1994; chief judge 1993 to date
Buttler, John H.	1977-1992	Appointed to new seat Sept. 1, 1977; elected 1978; reelected 1984, 1990; resigned Dec. 31, 1992

Name	Term of Service	By What Authority/Remarks
Joseph, George M.	1977-1992	Appointed to new seat Sept. 1, 1977; elected 1978; reelected 1984, 1990; resigned Dec. 31, 1992; chief judge 1981-1992
Gillette, W. Michael	1977-1986	Appointed to new seat Sept. 1, 1977; elected 1978; reelected 1984; resigned Feb. 10, 1986
Roberts, Betty	1977-1982	Appointed to new seat Sept. 1, 1977; elected 1978; resigned Feb. 8, 1982
Campbell, J.R.	1979-1980	Appointed Mar. 19, 1979 to succeed Johnson; elected 1980; resigned Nov. 30, 1980
Warden, John C.	1980-1988	Appointed Feb. 19, 1980 to succeed Tanzer; term ended Jan. 5, 1981; appointed Jan. 6, 1981 to succeed Schwab; elected 1982; resigned Dec. 30, 1988
Warren, Edward H.	1980	Appointed Mar. 10, 1980 to succeed Lee; elected 1980; reelected 1986, 1992
Van Hoomissen, George A.	1981-1988	Elected 1980; reelected 1986; resigned Sept. 30, 1988
Young, Thomas F.	1981-1988	Appointed Jan. 5, 1981 to succeed Campbell; elected 1982; died Jan. 3, 1988
Rossman, Kurt C.	1982-1994	Appointed Mar. 2, 1982 to succeed Roberts; elected 1982; reelected 1988; resigned Dec. 31, 1994
Newman, Jonathan	1983-1991	Elected 1982; reelected 1988; resigned Aug. 31, 1991
Deits, Mary J.	1986	Appointed Feb. 28, 1986 to succeed Gillette; elected 1986; reelected 1992
Riggs, R. William	1988	Appointed Oct. 24, 1988 to fill Van Hoomissen position; elected 1988 to succeed Warden; reelected 1994
Graber, Susan P.	1988-1990	Appointed Feb. 11, 1988 to succeed Young; elected 1988; resigned May 2 1990
Edmonds, Walter I. Jr.	1989	Appointed Jan. 1, 1989 to succeed Van Hoomissen; elected 1990; reelected 1996
De Muniz, Paul J.	1990	Appointed May 11, 1990 to succeed Graber; elected 1990; reelected 1996
Durham, Robert D.	1991-1994	Appointed Nov. 14, 1991 to succeed Newman; elected 1992; resigned Jan. 4, 1994
Landau, Jack L.	1993	Appointed Dec. 15, 1992 to succeed Joseph; elected 1994
Leeson, Susan M.	1993	Appointed Dec. 15, 1992 to succeed Buttler; elected 1994
Haselton, Rick	1994	Appointed Mar. 4, 1994 to succeed Durham; elected 1994
Armstrong, Rex	1995	Elected 1994

Judges of the Oregon Tax Court

Oregon Tax Court was established January 1, 1962

Name	Term of Service	By What Authority/Remarks
Gunnar, Peter M.	1962-1965	Appointed by Governor Hatfield Jan. 1, 1962; elected 1962; resigned Feb. 18, 1965
Howell, Edward H.	1965-1970	Appointed by Governor Hatfield Feb. 19, 1965; elected 1966; resigned May 31, 1970
Roberts, Carlisle B.	1970-1983	Appointed by Governor McCall June 1, 1970; elected 1970; reelected 1976; term ended 1983
Stewart, Samuel B.	1983-1985	Elected 1982; died Feb. 25, 1985
Byers, Carl N.	1985	Appointed by Governor Atiyeh Mar. 6, 1985; elected 1986; reelected 1992

Attorneys General of Oregon

Name/Political Party	Term of Service	By What Authority/Remarks
Chamberlain, George E.—D	May 20, 1891- Jan. 14, 1895	Appointed by Governor Pennoyer; elected June 1892
Idleman, Cicero M.—R	Jan. 14, 1895- Jan. 9, 1899	Elected 1894
Blackburn, D.R.N.—R	Jan. 9, 1899- Jan. 12, 1903	Elected 1898
Crawford, Andrew M.—R	Jan. 13, 1903- Jan. 3, 1915	Elected 1902; reelected 1906, 1910
Brown, George M.—R	Jan. 4, 1915- Oct. 14, 1920	Elected 1914; reelected 1918; resigned
Van Winkle, Isaac H.—R	Oct. 14, 1920- Dec. 14, 1943	Appointed by Governor Olcott; elected 1920; reelected 1924, 1928, 1932, 1936, 1940; died in office
Neuner, George—R	Dec. 21, 1943- Jan. 5, 1953	Appointed by Governor Snell; elected 1944; reelected 1948
Thornton, Robert Y.—D	Jan. 5, 1953- May 20, 1969	Elected 1952; reelected 1956, 1960, 1964
Johnson, Lee—R	May 20, 1969- Jan. 3, 1977	Elected 1968; reelected 1972
Redden, James—D	Jan. 3, 1977- Mar. 24, 1980	Elected 1976
Brown, James M.—D	Mar. 24, 1980- Jan. 4, 1981	Appointed by Governor Atiyeh
Frohnmayer, David B.—R.	Jan. 5, 1981- Dec. 31, 1991	Elected 1980; reelected 1984, 1988; resigned 1991
Crookham, Charles S.—R	Jan 2, 1992- Jan. 3, 1993	Appointed by Governor Roberts
Kulongoski, Ted—D	Jan. 4, 1993- Jan. 4, 1997	Elected 1992
Myers, Hardy—D	Jan. 6, 1997	Elected 1996

Commissioners, Labor & Industries[1]

Hoff, O.P.—R	June 2, 1903- Jan. 6, 1919	Appointed by Governor Chamberlain; elected 1906; reelected 1910, 1914
Gram, C.H.—R	Jan. 6, 1919- Jan. 4, 1943	Elected 1918; reelected 1922, 1926, 1930, 1934, 1938
Kimsey, W.E.—R	Jan. 4, 1943- Jan. 3, 1955	Elected 1942; reelected 1946, 1950

Name/Political Party	Term of Service	By What Authority/Remarks
Nilsen, Norman O.—D	Jan. 3, 1955- Jan. 6, 1975	Elected 1954; reelected 1958, 1962, 1966, 1970
Stevenson, Bill—D	Jan. 6, 1975- Jan. 1, 1979	Elected 1974
Roberts, Mary Wendy—D.	Jan. 1, 1979- Jan 2, 1995	Elected 1978; reelected 1982, 1986, 1990
Roberts, Jack—R	Jan. 2, 1995	Elected 1994

[1]This position, originally called Labor Commissioner, was changed to Commissioner of the Bureau of Labor Statistics and Inspector of Factories and Workshops in 1918. In 1930, the name changed to Commissioner of the Bureau of Labor. The 1979 Legislature changed the name to Commissioner of Labor and Industries.

Superintendents of Public Instruction[1]

Simpson, Sylvester C.—D	Jan. 29, 1873- Sept. 14, 1874	Appointed by Governor Grover
Rowland, L.L.—R	Sept. 14, 1874- Sept. 9, 1878	Elected 1874
Powell, J.L.—R	Sept. 9, 1878- Sept. 11, 1882	Elected 1878
McElroy, E.B.—R	Sept. 11, 1882- Jan. 14, 1895	Elected 1882; reelected 1886, 1890
Irwin, G.M.—R	Jan. 14, 1895- Jan. 9, 1899	Elected 1894
Ackerman, J.H.—R	Jan. 9, 1899- Jan. 3, 1911	Elected 1898; reelected 1902, 1906
Alderman, L.R.—R	Jan. 4, 1911- Jan. 28, 1913	Elected 1910; resigned
Churchill, J.A.—R	July 1, 1913- June 1, 1926	Appointed by Governor West; elected 1914; reelected 1918, 1922; resigned
Turner, R.R.—D	June 1, 1926- Jan. 3, 1927	Appointed by Governor Pierce
Howard, Charles A.—R	Jan. 3, 1927- Sept. 1, 1937	Elected 1926; reelected 1930, 1934; resigned
Putnam, Rex—D	Sept. 1, 1937- Jan. 31, 1961	Appointed by Governor Martin; elected 1938; reelected 1942, 1946, 1950, 1954, 1958; resigned
Minear, Leon P.	Feb. 1, 1961- Mar. 31, 1968	Appointed by Governor Hatfield; elected 1966; resigned
Fasold, Jesse V.	Apr. 8, 1968- June 30, 1968	Appointed by Governor McCall; resigned
Parnell, Dale	July 1, 1968- Mar. 31, 1974	Appointed by Governor McCall; elected 1968; reelected 1970; resigned
Fasold, Jesse V.	Apr. 1, 1974- Jan. 6, 1975	Appointed by Governor McCall
Duncan, Verne A.	Jan. 6, 1975- Nov. 15, 1989	Elected 1974; reelected 1978, 1982, 1986; resigned 1989
Erickson, John	Dec. 18, 1989- Sept. 30, 1990	Appointed by Governor Goldschmidt; resigned
Paulus, Norma	Oct. 1, 1990	Elected 1990; appointed by Governor Goldschmidt (before elective term began); reelected 1994

[1]From 1942 to 1961, this office was filled by election on nonpartisan ballot. In 1961, the state Legislature passed a statute making the office appointive by the State Board of Education. The Supreme Court declared this unconstitutional in 1965, and a constitutional amendment to place the method of selection in the hands of the state Legislature was defeated in 1966. Another attempt to repeal the constitutional provision requiring election was defeated in 1980.

Presidents of the Senate

Session	Name/Political Party	City	County
1860	Elkins, Luther—D		Linn
1862	Bowlby, Wilson—R		Washington
1864	Mitchell, J.H.—R	Portland	Multnomah
1865[1]	Mitchell, J.H.—R	Portland	Multnomah
1866	Cornelius, T.R.—R		Washington
1868	Burch, B.F.—D		Polk
1870	Fay, James D.—D		Jackson
1872	Fay, James D.—D		Jackson
1874	Cochran, R.B.—D		Lane
1876	Whiteaker, John—D		Lane
1878	Whiteaker, John—D		Lane
1880	Hirsch, Sol—R	Portland	Multnomah
1882	McConnell, W.J.—R		Yamhill
1885[2]	Waldo, William—R	Salem	Marion
1887	Carson, John C.—R	Portland	Multnomah
1889	Simon, Joseph—R	Portland	Multnomah
1891	Simon, Joseph—R	Portland	Multnomah
1893	Fulton, C.W.—R	Astoria	Clatsop
1895	Simon, Joseph—R	Portland	Multnomah
1897	Simon, Joseph—R	Portland	Multnomah
1898[1]	Simon, Joseph—R	Portland	Multnomah
1899	Taylor, T.C.—R	Pendleton	Umatilla
1901	Fulton, C.W.—R	Astoria	Clatsop
1903[2]	Brownell, George C.—R	Oregon City	Clackamas
1905	Kuykendall, W.—R	Eugene	Lane
1907	Haines, E.W.—R	Forest Grove	Washington
1909[2]	Bowerman, Jay—R	Condon	Gilliam
1911	Selling, Ben—R	Portland	Multnomah
1913	Malarkey, Dan J.—R	Portland	Multnomah
1915	Thompson, W. Lair—R	Lakeview	Lake
1917	Moser, Gus C.—R	Portland	Multnomah
1919	Vinton, W.T.—R	McMinnville	Yamhill
1920[1]	Vinton, W.T.—R	McMinnville	Yamhill
1921[2]	Ritner, Roy W.—R	Pendleton	Umatilla
1923	Upton, Jay—R	Prineville	Crook
1925	Moser, Gus C.—R	Portland	Multnomah
1927	Corbett, Henry L.—R	Portland	Multnomah
1929	Norblad, A.W.—R	Astoria	Clatsop
1931	Marks, Willard L.—R	Albany	Linn
1933[3]	Kiddle, Fred E.—R	Island City	Union
1935[2]	Corbett, Henry L.—R	Portland	Multnomah
1937	Franciscovich, F.M.—R	Astoria	Clatsop
1939	Duncan, Robert M.—R	Burns	Harney
1941	Walker, Dean H.—R	Independence	Polk
1943	Steiwer, W.H.—R	Fossil	Wheeler
1945	Belton, Howard C.—R	Canby	Clackamas
1947	Cornett, Marshall E.—R	Klamath Falls	Klamath
1949	Walsh, William E.—R	Coos Bay	Coos
1951	Patterson, Paul L.—R	Hillsboro	Washington
1953	Marsh, Eugene E.—R	McMinnville	Yamhill
1955	Smith, Elmo—R	John Day	Grant
1957[2]	Overhulse, Boyd R.—D	Madras	Jefferson
1959	Pearson, Walter J.—D	Portland	Multnomah
1961	Boivin, Harry D.—D	Klamath Falls	Klamath
1963[2]	Musa, Ben—D	The Dalles	Wasco
1965[2]	Boivin, Harry D.—D	Klamath Falls	Klamath
1967[2]	Potts, E.D.—D	Grants Pass	Josephine

Session	Name/Political Party	City	County
1969	Potts, E.D.—D	Grants Pass	Josephine
1971[2]	Burns, John D.—D	Portland	Multnomah
1973	Boe, Jason—D	Reedsport	Douglas
1974[1]	Boe, Jason—D	Reedsport	Douglas
1975	Boe, Jason—D	Reedsport	Douglas
1977	Boe, Jason—D	Reedsport	Douglas
1978[1]	Boe, Jason—D	Reedsport	Douglas
1979	Boe, Jason—D	Reedsport	Douglas
1980[1]	Boe, Jason—D	Reedsport	Douglas
1981[4]	Heard, Fred W.—D	Klamath Falls	Klamath
1983[3]	Fadeley, Edward N.—D	Eugene	Lane
1985	Kitzhaber, M.D., John A.—D	Roseburg	Douglas
1987	Kitzhaber, M.D., John A.—D	Roseburg	Douglas
1989[2]	Kitzhaber, M.D., John A.—D	Roseburg	Douglas
1991	Kitzhaber, M.D., John A.—D	Roseburg	Douglas
1993	Bradbury, Bill—D	Bandon	Coos
1995[2]	Smith, Gordon H.—R	Pendleton	Umatilla
1997	Adams, Brady—R	Grants Pass	Josephine

[1]Special session
[2]Regular and special session
[3]Regular and two special sessions
[4]Regular and four special sessions

Speakers of the House of Representatives

Session	Name/Political Party	City	County
1860	Harding, B.F.—D		Marion
1862	Palmer, Joel—R		Yamhill
1864	Moores, I.R.—R		Marion
1865[1]	Moores, I.R.—R		Marion
1866	Chenoweth, F.A.—R		Benton
1868	Whiteaker, John J.—D		Lane
1870	Hayden, Benjamin—D		Polk
1872	Mallory, Rufus—R		Marion
1874	Drain, J.C.—R		Douglas
1876	Weatherford, J.K.—D	Albany	Linn
1878	Thompson, J.M.—D		Lane
1880	Moody, Z.F.—R	The Dalles	Wasco
1882	McBride, George W.—R		Columbia
1885[2]	Keady, W.P.—R	Corvallis	Benton
1887	Gregg, J.T.—R	Salem	Marion
1889	Smith, E.L.—R	Hood River	Hood River
1891	Geer, T.T.—R	Macleay	Marion
1893	Keady, W.P.—R	Portland	Multnomah
1895	Moores, C.B.—R	Salem	Marion
1897[4]	House failed to organize		
1898[1]	Carter, E.V.—R	Ashland	Jackson
1899	Carter, E.V.—R	Ashland	Jackson
1901	Reeder, L.B.—R	Pendleton	Umatilla
1903[2]	Harris, L.T.—R	Eugene	Lane
1905	Mills, A.L.—R	Portland	Multnomah
1907	Davey, Frank—R	Salem	Marion
1909[2]	McArthur, C.N.—R	Portland	Multnomah
1911	Rusk, John P.—R	Joseph	Wallowa
1913	McArthur, C.N.—R	Portland	Multnomah
1915	Selling, Ben—R	Portland	Multnomah
1917	Stanfield, R.N.—R	Stanfield	Umatilla
1919	Jones, Seymour—R	Salem	Marion

Session	Name/Political Party	City	County
1920[1]	Jones, Seymour—R	Salem	Marion
1921[2]	Bean, Louis E.—R	Eugene	Lane
1923	Kubli, K.K.—R	Portland	Multnomah
1925	Burdick, Denton G.—R	Redmond	Deschutes
1927	Carkin, John H.—R	Medford	Jackson
1929	Hamilton, R.S.—R	Bend	Deschutes
1931	Lonergan, Frank J.—R	Portland	Multnomah
1933[3]	Snell, Earl W.—R	Arlington	Gilliam
1935	Cooter, John E.—D	Toledo	Lincoln
1935[1]	Latourette, Howard—D	Portland	Multnomah
1937	Boivin, Harry D.—D	Klamath Falls	Klamath
1939	Fatland, Ernest R.—R	Condon	Gilliam
1941	Farrell, Robert S. Jr.—R	Portland	Multnomah
1943	McAllister, William M.—R	Medford	Jackson
1945	Marsh, Eugene E.—R	McMinnville	Yamhill
1947	Hall, John H.—R	Portland	Multnomah
1949	Van Dyke, Frank J.—R	Medford	Jackson
1951	Steelhammer, John F.—R	Salem	Marion
1953	Wilhelm, Rudie Jr.—R	Portland	Multnomah
1955	Geary, Edward A.—R	Klamath Falls	Klamath
1957[2]	Dooley, Pat—D	Portland	Multnomah
1959	Duncan, Robert B.—D	Medford	Jackson
1961	Duncan, Robert B.—D	Medford	Jackson
1963[2]	Barton, Clarence—D	Coquille	Coos
1965[2]	Montgomery, F.F.—R	Eugene	Lane
1967[2]	Montgomery, F.F.—R	Eugene	Lane
1969	Smith, Robert F.—R	Burns	Harney
1971[2]	Smith, Robert F.—R	Burns	Harney
1973	Eymann, Richard O.—D	Springfield	Lane
1974[1]	Eymann, Richard O.—D	Springfield	Lane
1975	Lang, Philip D.—D	Portland	Multnomah
1977	Lang, Philip D.—D	Portland	Multnomah
1978[1]	Lang, Philip D.—D	Portland	Multnomah
1979	Myers, Hardy—D	Portland	Multnomah
1980[1]	Myers, Hardy—D	Portland	Multnomah
1981[5]	Myers, Hardy—D	Portland	Multnomah
1983[3]	Kerans, Grattan—D	Eugene	Lane
1985	Katz, Vera—D	Portland	Multnomah
1987	Katz, Vera—D	Portland	Multnomah
1989[2]	Katz, Vera—D	Portland	Multnomah
1991	Campbell, Larry—R	Eugene	Lane
1993	Campbell, Larry—R	Eugene	Lane
1995[2]	Clarno, Bev—R	Bend	Deschutes
1997	Lundquist, Lynn—R	Powell Butte	Deschutes

[1]Special session
[2]Regular and special session
[3]Regular and two special sessions
[4]E. J. Davis was elected speaker by less than a quorum. Subsequently, Henry L. Benson was elected speaker by less than a quorum. The Supreme Court revised an 1871 decision and ordered the secretary of state to audit claims and draw warrants for all claims which the Legislature, through its enactments, permitted and directed, either expressly or by implication.
[5]Regular and four special sessions.

U.S. Senators from Oregon

First Position[2]

Name/Political Party	Term of Service[1]	By What Authority/Remarks
Smith, Delazon[3]—D	Feb. 14- Mar. 3, 1859	Elected by Legislature 1858
Baker, Edward[4]—R	Dec. 5, 1860- Oct. 21, 1861	Elected by Legislature 1860; died in office
Stark, Benjamin—D	Oct. 29, 1861- Sept. 11, 1862	Appointed by Governor Whiteaker to succeed Baker
Harding, Benjamin F.—D	Sept. 11, 1862- 1865	Elected by Legislature to succeed Baker
Williams, George H.—R	1865-1871	Elected by Legislature 1864
Kelly, James K.—D	1871-1877	Elected by Legislature 1870
Grover, LaFayette—D	1877-1883	Elected by Legislature 1876
Dolph, Joseph N.—R	1883-1895	Elected by Legislature 1882; reelected 1889
McBride, George W.—R	1895-1901	Elected by Legislature 1895
Mitchell, John H.—R	1901- Dec. 8, 1905	Elected by Legislature 1901; died in office
Gearin, John M.—D	Dec. 12, 1905- Jan. 23, 1907	Appointed by Governor Chamberlain to succeed Mitchell
Mulkey, Fred W.—R	Jan. 23- Mar. 2, 1907	Selected by general election 1906 for short term; elected by Legislature to serve remaining term of Mitchell and Gearin
Bourne, Jonathan Jr.—R	1907-1913	Selected by general election 1906; elected by Legislature 1907
Lane, Harry—D	1913- May 23, 1917	Selected by general election 1912; elected by Legislature 1913; died in office
McNary, Charles L.—R	May 29, 1917- Nov. 5, 1918	Appointed by Governor Withycombe to succeed Lane
Mulkey, Fred W.—R	Nov. 5- Dec. 17, 1918	Elected 1918 for short term; resigned to permit reappointment of McNary
McNary, Charles L.—R	Dec. 17, 1918- Feb. 24, 1944	Appointed 1918 for unexpired short term; elected 1918; reelected 1924, 1930, 1936, 1942; died in office
Cordon, Guy—R	Mar. 4, 1944- 1955	Appointed by Governor Snell to succeed McNary; elected 1944; reelected 1948
Neuberger, Richard L.—D	1955- Mar. 9, 1960	Elected 1954; died in office
Lusk, Hall S.—D	Mar. 16, 1960- Nov. 8, 1960	Appointed by Governor Hatfield to succeed Neuberger
Neuberger, Maurine—D	Nov. 8, 1960-1967	Elected 1960 for short and full terms
Hatfield, Mark O.—R.	1967-1996	Elected 1966; reelected 1972, 1978, 1984, 1990
Smith, Gordon H.—R	1997	Elected 1996

Second Position[2]

Name/Political Party	Term of Service	By What Authority/Remarks
Lane, Joseph—D	Feb. 14, 1859- 1861	Elected by Legislature 1858
Nesmith, James W.—D	1861-1867	Elected by Legislature 1860
Corbett, Henry W.—R	1867-1873	Elected by Legislature 1866
Mitchell, John H.—R	1873-1879	Elected by Legislature 1872
Slater, James H.—D	1879-1885	Elected by Legislature 1878
Mitchell, John H.—R	1885-1897	Elected by Legislature 1885; reelected 1891

Name/Political Party	Term of Service[1]	By What Authority/Remarks
Corbett, Henry W.—R[5]	March, 1897	Appointed by Governor Lord, not seated
Simon, Joseph—R	Oct. 6, 1898-1903	Elected by Legislature to fill vacancy
Fulton, Charles W.—R	1903-1909	Elected by Legislature 1903
Chamberlain, George E.—D[6]	1909-1921	Selected by general election 1908; elected by Legislature; reelected by people 1914
Stanfield, Robert N.—R	1921-1927	Elected 1920
Steiwer, Frederick—R	1927-Feb. 1, 1938	Elected 1926; reelected 1932; resigned
Reames, Alfred Evan—D	Feb. 1-Nov. 9, 1938	Appointed by Governor Martin to succeed Steiwer
Barry, Alex G.—R	Nov. 9, 1938-1939	Elected 1938 for short term
Holman, Rufus C.—R	1939-1945	Elected 1938
Morse, Wayne[7]—D	1945-1969	Elected 1944; reelected 1950, 1956, 1962
Packwood, Robert—R	1969-1995	Elected 1968; reelected 1974, 1980, 1986, 1992; resigned 1995
Wyden, Ron[8]—D	1996	Elected 1996

[1]Unless otherwise noted, normal terms of office began on the fourth day of March and ended on the third day of March until 1933, when terms were changed to begin and end on the third day of January unless a different date was set by Congress.

[2]Delazon Smith and Joseph Lane drew lots in 1859 for the short and long term senate seats. Smith won the short term of only 17 days expiring March 3, 1859 (designated first position). Lane won the long term expiring March 3, 1861 (designated second position).

[3]When the Legislature first met after statehood in May 1859, Smith was defeated for reelection, and no successor was named. Consequently, Oregon had only one U.S. senator from March 3, 1859 until Baker was elected October 1, 1860.

[4]Senator Edward Baker was killed in the Battle of Balls Bluff, Va. while serving as a colonel in the Civil War, the only U.S. senator to serve in military action while a senator. His statue, cast of horatio stone and marble, stands 6 ft. 5 in. tall in the Capitol rotunda in Washington, D.C.

[5]When the Legislature failed to elect a successor to Mitchell, Governor Lord appointed Henry Corbett. After conflict, however, the U.S. Senate decided the governor did not have this authority and refused to seat Corbett. Therefore, Oregon was represented by only one U.S. senator from March 4, 1897 to October 6, 1898.

[6]Direct election of U.S. senators resulted from Oregon's ratification of Article XVII of the U.S. Constitution January 23, 1913 (effective May 31, 1913). Oregon initiated a direct primary for selecting candidates in 1904.

[7]Wayne Morse was elected as a Republican in 1944 and reelected as a Republican in 1950. He changed to Independent in 1952 and to Democrat in 1955. He was reelected as a Democrat in 1956 and 1962.

[8]Elected to fill the unexpired term of Robert Packwood due to Senator Packwood's resignation. The elections, both primary and general, to fill Senator Packwood's seat were conducted by mail. The primary vote-by-mail election was the first statewide vote-by-mail to fill a federal office in United States history. Subsequent to Senator Wyden's election, vote-by-mail elections were conducted to fill the House seat vacated by Senator Wyden.

U.S. Representatives from Oregon

Name/Political Party	Term of Service[1]	By What Authority/Remarks
Thurston, Samuel R.—D	June 6, 1849-Apr. 9, 1851	Territorial Delegate elected 1849; died at sea returning home from 1st session
Lane, Joseph—D	June 2, 1851-Feb. 14, 1859	Territorial Delegate elected 1851; reelected 1853, 1855, 1857
Grover, LaFayette—D	Feb. 15-Mar. 3, 1859	First Representative at large, elected 1858 for short term

Name/Political Party	Term of Service[1]	By What Authority/Remarks
Stout, Lansing—D	1859-1861	Elected 1858
Shiel, George K.—D	1861-1863	Elected 1860
McBride, John R.—R	1863-1865	Elected 1862
Henderson, J.H.D.—R	1865-1867	Elected 1864
Mallory, Rufus—R	1867-1869	Elected 1866
Smith, Joseph S.—D	1869-1871	Elected 1868
Slater, James H.—D	1871-1873	Elected 1870
Wilson, Joseph G.—R	1873	Elected 1872; died in July, 1873 before qualifying
Nesmith, James W.—D	1873-1875	Elected 1873
La Dow, George A.—D	1875	Elected 1874; died Mar. 4, 1875 before qualifying
Lane, Lafayette—D	Oct. 25, 1875-1877	Elected 1875
Williams, Richard—R	1877-1879	Elected 1876
Whiteaker, John—D	1879-1881	Elected 1878
George, Melvin C.—R	1881-1885	Elected 1880; reelected 1882
Hermann, Binger—R	1885-1893	Elected 1884; reelected 1886, 1888, 1890

1st District

Name/Political Party	Term of Service	By What Authority/Remarks
Hermann, Binger—R	1893-1897	Elected 1892; reelected 1894
Tongue, Thomas H.—R	1897-Jan. 11, 1903	Elected 1896; reelected 1898, 1900, 1902; died in office
Hermann, Binger—R	June 1, 1903-1907	Elected 1903 to succeed Tongue; reelected 1904
Hawley, Willis C.—R	1907-1933	Elected 1906; reelected 1908, 1910, 1912, 1914, 1916, 1918, 1920, 1922, 1924, 1926, 1928, 1930
Mott, James W.—R	1933-Nov. 12, 1945	Elected 1932; reelected 1934, 1936, 1938, 1940, 1942, 1944; died in office
Norblad, A. Walter Jr.—R	Jan. 11, 1946-Sept. 20, 1964	Elected 1945 to succeed Mott; reelected 1946, 1948, 1950, 1952, 1954, 1956, 1958, 1960, 1962; died in office
Wyatt, Wendell—R	Nov. 3, 1964-1975	Elected 1964 to succeed Norblad; reelected 1966, 1968, 1970, 1972
AuCoin, Les—D	1975-1993	Elected 1974; reelected 1976, 1978, 1980, 1982, 1984, 1986, 1988, 1990
Furse, Elizabeth—D	1993	Elected 1992; reelected 1994, 1996

2nd District

Name/Political Party	Term of Service	By What Authority/Remarks
Ellis, William R.—R	1893-1899	Elected 1892; reelected 1894, 1896
Moody, Malcolm A.—R	1899-1903	Elected 1898; reelected 1900
Williamson, John N.—R	1903-1907	Elected 1902; reelected 1904
Ellis, William R.—R	1907-1911	Elected 1906; reelected 1908
Lafferty, Abraham W.—R.	1911-1913	Elected 1910
Sinnott, N.J.—R	1913-May 31, 1928	Elected 1912; reelected 1914, 1916, 1918, 1920, 1922, 1924, 1926; resigned
Butler, Robert R.—R	Nov. 6, 1928-Jan. 7, 1933	Elected 1928 to succeed Sinnott; reelected 1930; died in office
Pierce, Walter M.—D	1933-1943	Elected 1932; reelected 1934, 1936, 1938, 1940
Stockman, Lowell—R	1943-1953	Elected 1942; reelected 1944, 1946, 1948, 1950
Coon, Samuel H.—R	1953-1957	Elected 1952; reelected 1954

Name/Political Party	Term of Service[1]	By What Authority/Remarks
Ullman, Albert C.—D	1957-1981	Elected 1956; reelected 1958, 1960, 1962, 1964, 1966, 1968, 1970, 1972, 1974, 1976, 1978
Smith, Denny—R	1981-1983	Elected 1980
Smith, Robert F.—R	1983-1995	Elected 1982; reelected 1984, 1986, 1988, 1990, 1992
Cooley, Wes—R	1995-1997	Elected 1994
Smith, Robert F.—R	1997	Elected 1996

3rd District

Lafferty, Abraham W.—R	1913-1915	Elected 1912
McArthur, Clifton N.—R	1915-1923	Elected 1914; reelected 1916, 1918, 1920
Watkins, Elton—D	1923-1925	Elected 1922
Crumpacker, Maurice E.—R	1925-July 25, 1927	Elected 1924; reelected 1926; died in office
Korell, Franklin F.—R	Oct. 18, 1927-1931	Elected 1927; reelected 1928
Martin, Charles H.—D	1931-1935	Elected 1930; reelected 1932
Ekwall, William A.—R	1935-1937	Elected 1934
Honeyman, Nan Wood—D	1937-1939	Elected 1936
Angell, Homer D.—R	1939-1955	Elected 1938; reelected 1940, 1942, 1944, 1946, 1948, 1950, 1952
Green, Edith S.—D	1955-1975	Elected 1954; reelected 1956, 1958, 1960, 1962, 1964, 1966, 1968, 1970, 1972
Duncan, Robert B.—D	1975-1981	Elected 1974; reelected 1976, 1978
Wyden, Ron—D	1981-1996	Elected 1980; reelected 1982, 1984, 1986, 1988, 1990, 1992, 1994
Blumenauer, Earl—D[2]	1996	Elected 1996; reelected 1996

4th District

Ellsworth, Harris—R	1943-1957	Elected 1942; reelected 1944, 1946, 1948, 1950, 1952, 1954
Porter, Charles O.—D	1957-1961	Elected 1956; reelected 1958
Durno, Edwin R.—R	1961-1963	Elected 1960
Duncan, Robert B.—D	1963-1967	Elected 1962; reelected 1964
Dellenback, John—R	1967-1975	Elected 1966; reelected 1968, 1970, 1972
Weaver, James—D	1975-1987	Elected 1974; reelected 1976, 1978, 1980, 1982, 1984
DeFazio, Peter A.—D	1987	Elected 1986; reelected 1988, 1990, 1992, 1994, 1996

5th District

Smith, Denny—R	1983-1991	Elected 1982; reelected 1984, 1986, 1988
Kopetski, Mike—D	1991-1995	Elected 1990, reelected 1992
Bunn, Jim—R	1995-1997	Elected 1994
Hooley, Darlene—D	1997	Elected 1996

[1]Unless otherwise noted, normal terms of office began on the fourth day of March and ended on the third day of March until 1933, when terms were changed to begin and end on the third day of January unless a different date was set by Congress.

[2]Elected to fill the unexpired term of Representative Ron Wyden. The term ended January 3, 1997. Reelected to a full term at the November 5, 1996 General Election.

HISTORY

A gap in the tracks marks the site of the break in the railroad dike that caused the Columbia River to flood the city of Vanport in 1948. The city was destroyed by the flood.
Photo courtesy of the Oregon Historical Society. Negative number OrHi 68784.

THE splendor of Oregon began well before it became a territory or a state. Historian Terence O'Donnell's finely executed history introduces the reader to the physical and geological changes that created the land we know as Oregon. He escorts us through the peaceful times when the Northwest was occupied by the native people, and the events that have occurred since Lewis and Clark spread word of the Columbia River to the rest of the nation.

Oregon History

Oregon Historical Society; 1200 SW Park Ave.,
Portland 97205; 503-222-1741

Written by Terence O'Donnell

The great cataclysmic events were
mainly over; exploding mountains, lava
floods, draining seas, the massive drag-
ging glaciers—all this cosmic tumult,
breaking up the land and reforming it,
eon after eon, had finally spent itself.
Rivers, rain, the wind and pounding surf
continued to age the earth's face but, by
and large, what we now see and call
Oregon is what finally came to rest
about ten thousand years ago.

Then, as now, the Pacific drove in to
crash against the high-cliffed coast while
the ocean clouds drifting east paused to
drench with rain the seaward slopes of
what we since have come to call the
coast range. To the east and north lay
the long valley with its meander of
river—though here there was a difference between then and now, for it is
believed that before man came, the
valley floor was forest rather than the
present open plain. Beyond, however,
the land lay much as we see it today:
the Cascades soaring up to the arid lava
plains of the interior high country—
rimrock, deep canyons and massifs to
the northeast and southwest, dense with
mountain peaks. From the estuaries and
rain forests of the coast to the valley—
lush, humid, almost tropical—to the
interior with its distances and skies and
tingling sage-scented air, it was a landscape of ravishing variety, as it is today.

There is one respect, however, in
which it was a profoundly different place
from now; it was silent. The only sounds
were the sounds of the place itself:
falling rain, the singing rush of rivers
and avalanche's crash; the boom and
hiss of surf; fire, and its roar and crackle
in a forest tindered by a lightning strike;
and wind, screaming through the gul-
lies, creaking the giant oaks, whispering
the prairie grass—and bird song, thunder and the cries of animals.

This was the world into which one day
more than 10,000 years ago human
beings stepped—Asiatics from what is
now Siberia. Why they left we do not
know—famine, drought, more likely
hunters following their prey. In any
event they crossed by an Alaskan land
bridge—and probably by boat as well—
to North America. Settlement appears to
have first occurred in the interior, later
along the Columbia and finally on the
coast.

The natives of the coast lived in small
villages of plank houses strung along
the banks of the streams, which poured
down from the coastal mountains into
the Pacific. These streams, as well as a
vegetation almost tropical in its impene-
trability, isolated the coastal tribes, and
thus, a diversity of languages developed.
All, however, lived by the land and the
sea, berries and game, salmon and
shellfish. To the people of the Columbia
and lower Willamette, the most populous
of these first Oregonians, salmon was of
greater importance and used for trade as
well as sustenance. For the tribes of the
inland valleys, however, nuts and roots
and game took salmon's place. A pleas-
ing and literally fragrant aspect of the
culture of these three peoples was their
use of cedar for almost all their material
needs—clothing, shelter, utensils, con-
tainers, and of course, their superb
canoes. South, in the vicinity of the
present Klamath Lakes, the native people were marsh and lakeside dwellers,
subsisting on plants and waterfowl and
living in semisubterranean, earth-domed
lodges. Their neighbors to the east, in
what is now called the Great Basin, also
subsisted on waterfowl and plants—
when they could be found, for the
natives of the Great Basin often faced
near starvation—but these people were
few in number, mainly nomadic, and
lived in little bell-shaped huts made
of willow whips. Finally there were the
plateau tribes of northeastern Oregon.
Horsemen by about the 18th century,
they were a vigorous people and wide-
ranging, from the barren steppes of the
upper Columbia to the high alpine valleys of the Wallowas, living, when settled, in long teepee-type mat houses.

Such were the first Oregonians.
By the time of their contact with whites
in the early 19th century, they numbered tens of thousands, these divided
into nearly 100 bands and tribes.
Though a people of many differences, in
physique and language for example, they
did to some degree share a common
culture. Most were animists, believing
that all things, whether rock or tree,
stream or star, animal or man, were
imbued with spirit. Thus, for them, all
the world was living. And with this living

world they, in turn, lived in close communion. Weather, animals, the earth, its fruits—they mingled with these things, becoming one with them: the flesh and skin of animals; the berries, bulbs and nuts of earth; the cleansing water; the shade of trees; the warmth of fire. There were no separate orders: man, animals, matter. All were one.

Many of them held, too, that the creator of this world was the coyote demigod, Spilyai. Spilyai, in whose belly lived his three wise sisters in the form of huckleberries, is clever, capricious, lascivious, mischievous, and endlessly inventive—surely one of the most human and entertaining of the gods mankind has created.

Spilyai, as well as many other figures, animal and human, formed the subject of a large body of folk tales. A portion of these were rescued in the nick of time from their oral sources, translated and published. Most of the tales tell how Oregon began, how the ocean, the rivers and the lakes, the mountains and the valleys, the prairies and the deserts came to be—in the process giving us an unequaled sense of our natural world. If Oregon has a true folk literature in the sense of being distinct to the region and worthy of esteem, it is this rich gift to us from those who came here first.

◆ ◆ ◆

It probably happened somewhere on the southern coast. Exactly when it happened is difficult to say—four to five hundred years ago. One day a woman, straightening up from tearing mussels from the rock and gazing out across the sea—"the river with one bank," as the natives called the ocean—perhaps it was such a woman who saw it first, the great black-bodied bird with its strangely configured wings riding the swells, its beak, pole thin, jutting up at an angle from the head. As the years passed the people were to see more and more of these great black-bodied birds. One wonders if they knew that, for them at least, these were birds of ill omen, which would one day bring their doom.

It began with a myth. According to the myth there was a passage or strait on the north coast of North America, which connected the Atlantic and Pacific Oceans, i.e., that long-sought-for advantage, a direct sea route from Western Europe to Asia. Around this central myth clustered others. "Marine lying reached the climax and borders on the heroic," wrote the historian Hubert Howe Bancroft. For example, somewhere on the Oregon coast there flourished the kingdom of Fu Sang, founded by a Buddhist monk and his disciples from Afghanistan. Here they had created a great civilization centered on the Fu Sang tree and its magic powers.

It was the desire to see and plunder such marvelous places, but in particular to find that passage to the East, that accounts for the presence off the Oregon coast in the 16th century and thereafter of the great black-bodied birds, the ships of the explorers.

So far as can be determined, the first of these was a Spanish expedition sailing from Acapulco in 1542 under the command of Cabrillo. Following many mishaps, including the death of Cabrillo, his pilot, Ferrelo, reached the Rogue River in the spring of 1543. Torrential storms prohibited a landing and indeed were so severe that the crew was assembled to take their death vows. Perhaps this was the first of the great black-bodied birds, which the natives on the shore observed with bafflement and fear.

Indian petroglyphs stand out on these rocks on the Upper Owyhee River at Half Mile Rapid. Photo by Eric W. Valentine.

A few years later, Spain's great enemy, that "merry, careful" buccaneer, Sir Francis Drake, searching in the Golden Hind for the Northwest Passage—as well as Spanish treasure ships to plunder—also anchored off the southern Oregon coast before being driven south by storms.

It was another Spaniard, however, Martin d'Aguilar, thought to have been off present-day Port Orford, who gives us our first description of the Oregon coast, "... a rapid and abundant river, with ash trees, willows and brambles and other trees of Castile on its banks." But he too, for reasons of weather and currents, was unable to land. It was about this time also, that the galleon trade between Spain's new possessions in the Philippines and Mexico began. The course of the ships was south of the Oregon latitudes, but occasionally some were blown off their course. For example, the *San Francisco Xavier*, wrecked at the base of Neahkahnie Mountain in 1707. Its cargo of beeswax may still be found on the nearby beaches.

It was in the last quarter of the 18th century, however, that exploration began in earnest, navigators searching not only for the Northwest Passage but also for "the great river of the West," sometimes called the "Oregon," now known, of course, as the Columbia. In August of 1775 the distinguished Spanish explorer Bruno Heceta located the mouth of the river, but his crew was so weakened by

scurvy they were unable to man the sails and cross the bar. Regretfully, Heceta was forced to sail away. Two years later an even greater mariner, Captain Cook, searching for the river, passed it unknowingly on a stormy night. He was followed in 1778 by John Meares who deemed it no river at all and so named its estuary Deception Bay and its northern promontory Cape Disappointment. Finally, George Vancouver, commissioned by the British admiralty to make an official survey of the Northwest coast, passed by the mouth of the river in the spring of 1792. He too denied the river's existence despite the evidence—gulls, earthen-colored water, drifting logs and cross-currents. "Not considering the opening worthy of more attention I continued our pursuit to the N.W.," wrote Vancouver, one of the world's great maritime explorers.

At fault was Vancouver's skepticism. He believed the great river and the Northwest Passage to be no more than sailors' yarns, thus finding it particularly appropriate that he sailed from England in search of both on April 1. However, if Vancouver failed to find the Columbia, he did prove later that the Northwest Passage, which cartographers had mapped and mariners had sought for 400 years, did not, after all, exist.*

For all practical purposes this is still the case. With the aid of an ice-breaker, however, passage through the Arctic can be made.

Visitors enjoy the calm beauty of the Painted Hills in the John Day Fossil Beds National Monument. Photo by Hanne Madsen.

But the Columbia again and again resisted discovery. How at last it was discovered is a roundabout tale indeed. The merchants of Boston, like merchants elsewhere, were anxious to trade with the Chinese but were prevented by the simple fact that they produced little the far-off Chinese wanted. By now, however, these merchant circles had heard of the great profits made by irregular traders, Russian and British, selling Northwest furs to the Orient. Why not join them in the pickings? Thus was born the Pacific triangular trade.

In October of 1787 Captains Kendrick and Gray were sent out by their backers from Boston with a cargo of buttons and beads, blue cloth, and bits of iron and copper. Arriving on the Oregon coast 10 months later, they bargained with the natives for the pelts of sea otters, sold these in the Orient, bought tea and perhaps some silk and spices, after which Gray, the first American merchant sailor to circumnavigate the globe, set sail for Boston.

Gray's name, however, would be relatively unknown had it not been for his second voyage to the Oregon coast and a certain decision he made at 8 o'clock on the morning of May 11, 1792.

A few weeks before this day, so crucial to American expansionism, Gray, like Vancouver, was off the Oregon coast. Like Vancouver, he too noted at latitude 46 degrees 53 minutes a great flow of muddy water fanning from the shore. Passing on to the straits of San Juan de Fuca, Gray encountered Vancouver and informed him of his belief that these muddy waters might well signify the mouth of the great river of the west. The eminent navigator was not about to entertain such notions from this unknown American trader. No "reason to alter our opinions," wrote Vancouver.

But Gray was not about to alter his opinions either and started out to confirm his belief and find his river.

At four in the morning on May 11, Gray arrived at the river's mouth. Then, more than now, the Columbia bar was one of the most treacherous on earth. They waited, four hours they waited, until there came that right convergence of currents, tide and wind. Gray gave the command and the prow of his ship, the Columbia Rediviva, its figurehead holding before her the escutcheon of the Republic, crashed through the breakers into the waters of the great river of the west, which from then on would be known as the Columbia.

Robert Gray's discovery did much to encourage other American fur traders, who used the Columbia as a winter haven and who, by the end of the century, controlled the sea otter trade. Of more universal significance is the fact that this rather offhand happenstance of a discovery was, outside of Arctic regions, among the last major coastal geographical features of the world to be revealed. But more immediate and long lasting in its consequences is that, with Gray and his discovery, the presence of the United States was for the first time established in western America as well as on the Pacific, a presence on which the United States would later base its claim to possession.

After a week or so of trading with the Indians, Gray left without investigating the interior into which the river led. This was carried out several months later by Lieutenant William Broughton who, as Vancouver's second in command, had arrived to verify Gray's discovery. Broughton spent three weeks on the river, proceeding as far as the mouth of the Columbia Gorge. The log of this small boat voyage provides us with our first real description of the Oregon country. It was, Broughton wrote, "The most beautiful landscape that can be imagined." And he goes on to describe the wooded islands and water meadows, the sand spits, bluffs and beaches, the river banks thick with wild lavender and mint, the groves of alder, maple, birch, willow, poplar, oak, the long slopes of fir. He remarks as well on the wild life—flights of duck and geese, brown cranes, white swans, the otter, beaver, deer and elk. Finally, there were the mountains, in their perfect white repose, supreme above it all.

Broughton, like the Americans before him, was quite taken by the natives. John Boit of Gray's crew had written, "The Men at Columbia's River are strait limb'd, fine looking fellows, and the women are very pretty." Broughton found that they surpassed other tribes in their "paints of different colors, feathers and other ornaments," and in all instances they were civil and often helpful. One old chief was so much so that Broughton named the stretch of river that passed his village (in the vicinity

of present-day Vancouver) "Friendly Reach."

There was, however, one disquieting feature in this Edenic scene. All up and down the river, on bluff and sandspit, and trestled high beyond the reach of animals, stood the funerary canoes, great and small, which held the dead. With their black prows silhouetted somberly against the sky, they were a kind of prefigurement of what was to come, the disease, killing and heartsickness that would go on for a century and end by almost obliterating the native peoples from the face of their lovely earth.

Such then was the penetration of Oregon from the sea. The next would be by land. The idea had originated with the American Philosophical Association, and to promote it, Jefferson and Hamilton had contributed $12.50 each. It was Jefferson, however, who finally followed through, who persuaded Congress to fund an expedition across the continent to the Northwest coast. To head the expedition he chose his secretary, Meriwether Lewis. Lewis, in turn, chose William Clark, an army comrade, to share the command.

Their purposes were three: to determine a route between the Missouri and Columbia rivers and thereby facilitate travel and trade; to report on the flora and fauna and geography of the region; to establish friendly relations with the Indians. Another purpose, though not stated, was to lay further basis for new territorial claims should the United States decide to make them.

The expedition departed from St. Louis in the spring of 1804. They proceeded upstream in a leisurely fashion though not without incident, for there were desertions and thievery, all severely punished with the lash. On arriving at the Platte they had reached the end, as it were, of their world— "... we were now about to penetrate," wrote Lewis, "a country at least 2,000 miles in width, on which the foot of civilized man has never trodden; the good or evil it had in store for us was for experiment yet to determine."

More good than evil was their lot on the westward trek. Despite the cold, they wintered comfortably near present-day Bismarck, North Dakota. What difficulties they suffered were minor, as for example, the behavior of the Indians they encountered after crossing the Divide. "... we were caressed and besmeared with their grease and paint till I was heartily tired of the national hug," wrote Lewis. Also, they grew weary of a diet consisting of so much fish, but this they remedied on reaching the Columbia by purchasing forty dogs.

On November 15, 1805, 19 months after their departure from St. Louis, the expedition saw the Pacific at the mouth of the Columbia. Here they spent a miserable winter in a little log stockade (Fort Clatsop), which they built on a low hill above a bog of tidal creeks. It rained every day but six. They spent these dreary days making salt at present-day Seaside, hunting the scarce game and fighting the abundant fleas. On Christmas they celebrated with "pore

Elk, so much Spoiled that we eate it thro mear necessity, Some Spoiled Pounded fish and a fiew roots."

There was also much sickness: colds, dysentery, rheumatism. Many of the men acquired venereal diseases from the natives who, in turn, had been infected by the sailors of the fur trade. Indeed, in the scant 13 years since Gray and Broughton, there had been a shocking deterioration in the natives, far fewer of the "fine looking fellows" and "women very pretty" than Gray's party had noted. And instead of the "deer and otter skin" garments reported by Broughton, many now wore the tattered castoffs of the foreign sailors. One native woman wore a more permanent adornment: the name "J. Bowman," tattooed on her arm.

With spring the expedition was only too happy to be on its way, departing the Columbia in March of 1806, arriving in St. Louis in September, thus completing one of the most remarkable journeys of exploration in the history of the Americas and establishing another basis for eventual U.S. claims in the west. Of more immediate importance was the fact that Lewis and Clark's reports now made known to all that here was a place suitable for settlement.

In the winter of 1784 a German immigrant named John Jacob Astor arrived in Baltimore with seven flutes, which he sold at a profit and thence went on to more and greater profits—though through the sale of furs, not flutes. By 1810 and now a magnate in the trade, he decided to establish his new subsidiary, the Pacific Fur Company, at the mouth of the Columbia. His scheme was to sell goods to the Indians and the Russians in Alaska, and in return buy furs from them to sell in the Orient. It could not have been a more promising scheme. In operation it could have hardly been more disastrous.

One contingent of the staff Astor sent to the Columbia traveled by land, the other by sea, the latter in the *Tonquin* captained by Jonathan Thorn. Captain Thorn turned out to be a psychopath, and through his madness, eight men were lost at sea before the *Tonquin* reached its destination. This destination lay on the south side of the Columbia's mouth, a rise of land at the end of a little bay—present-day Astoria.

At first glance it seemed most inviting. "The weather was magnificent," wrote Gabriel Franchere, one of the company clerks, "and all Nature smiled. The forest looked like pleasant groves and the leaves like flowers." The trees in this forest, however, often had a girth of 50 feet, grew densely together, and were interspersed by giant boulders. Few of the company clerks had ever felled a tree and none under such conditions. After planting the 12 potatoes that had survived the journey, the company set to work. Two months later barely an acre had been cleared, two men had been badly injured by falling trees and one had blown his hand off. Morale was not helped by the fact that in the same period three of the company were killed by the natives.

At about this time—the spring of 1811—Captain Thorn set off in the Tonquin for a trading expedition up the coast while, at St. Louis, Astor's over-land contingent set off for the Columbia. On Vancouver Island, Thorn, acting with his usual intemperance, struck a native chief across the face with a roll of fur. A few days later, in retaliation, the natives massacred Thorn and his crew, during which the ship blew up. The overland contingent was plagued by disaster as well. One party, lost in the uplands of the Snake River, was reduced for nourishment to their own moccasins and quenched their thirst with urine.

The coup de grace to Astor's scheme occurred in June of 1812, when the United States declared war on Britain.

An old leather horse harness rests on a timber fence near the Clackamas County town of Molalla. Photo by Kurt Ridley.

This put the Astorians in an awkward position. At any time the British might arrive and seize the post. Also, more and more men of the British-owned North West Fur Company, "those strutting and plumed bullies of the north," were showing up at the post, waiting for the prize to drop into their hands. But there was uncertainty as to when the British would arrive, and the outcome of the war, and so the Astorians succeeded in persuading the Nor'Westerners to buy the post. In December of 1813 the stars and stripes came down, the Union Jack went up and Astoria became Fort George.

The Astorian enterprise resulted in some benefits. The overland parties explored new territory. The fur-collection stations established in various locales of the Pacific Northwest, including the Willamette Valley, provided a more extensive knowledge of the region. And finally the settlement of Astoria, along with Gray and Lewis and Clark's activities, would be another basis for the American territorial claim to the Northwest. But the price was very high. All told, the Astorian enterprise took the lives of over 60 adventurers.

The sale of Astoria had much to do with the fact that for the next three decades Britons, rather than Americans, dominated the American country. This occurred through the agency of the Hudson's Bay Company. The company, operating by royal charter in the vicinity of Hudson's Bay in eastern Canada, gradually moved westward—a move that culminated in its merger with the North West Company and the acquisition of Fort George in 1821. The company's principal activity was the trading of articles such as blankets, ironwork and firearms for pelts mainly sold in England. The specific reason for its interest in the Northwest lay in a fashion—the fashion for beaver hats. This, a simple fad rather than some grand strategy, lay behind the British presence in the Northwest.

The headquarters for this presence was Fort Vancouver, established in 1825 near the confluence of the Willamette and the Columbia. Sir George Simpson, the company's governor in the West, used to say that no great English country house occupied a site more beautiful—there on the gently sloping downs above the river with the mountains and the valley beyond. Here was finally erected a stockade 20 feet high,

150 yards wide, 215 yards long. It contained some 40 buildings. Among these was Bachelor Hall, a residence for the company's unmarried officers, which boasted a wine cellar as well as a library with the latest London journals. The environment might have been primitive, but that was no reason why the life lived in it should be so as well.

The most impressive of the fort's structures lay at its center, a manorhouse in the French Canadian style, flower beds before it, cannon to either side, and pacing sentries. This was the residence of the Chief Factor of the District—Alaska to California— Dr. John McLoughlin.

McLoughlin is called the Father of Oregon. We could hardly have been more fortunate in our genesis. He was a man of remarkable intelligence, vigor, color, character and those qualities from which our pioneer predecessors benefited greatly: generosity and compassion. Born downriver from Quebec of an Irish farmer father and a mother half-Scottish, half-French, he had in his youth two great advantages. On the one hand he knew the hard work and hardships of a poor farmer's son. On the other he had the good fortune to spend time at the estate of his maternal grandfather, a man of cultivation. From these two experiences he acquired that balance so rare– the balance of toughness and grace. When McLoughlin arrived at Fort Vancouver he was 41, a big man, 6 feet 4 inches, his white hair parted in the middle and falling to the shoulders, his steely eyes the color of gun metal, the mouth firm. He looked equally capable of administering the lash or holding up to the sunlight a goblet of port.

McLoughlin had three principal duties at the fort. The first was to make money —to trap out the whole of the Northwest, bring in the pelts, dress them and send them off to London. He did, and the company profited handsomely.

A second duty was to control the natives. He did this by prohibiting certain earlier practices. For example, it had been common practice to offer rum to the natives and then—after they were well addicted—to trade with them, a little rum for many furs. Also, McLoughlin always kept his word, whether for reward or punishment— always. In return for all these things the natives called their children after

Celebrating its 60th birthday in 1997, Timberline Lodge was dedicated by President Franklin D. Roosevelt on September 28, 1937. Photo by Paul Callicotte, courtesy of the Oregon Historical Society. Negative number OrHi 80369.

him, made him a chief, "White-Headed Eagle," and, it is said, carved his face, this white man's face, into their totem poles.

McLoughlin's third duty was a vexing one; it was to prevent settlement in the Oregon country for the following reasons. By now the region was claimed both by the United States and Britain by right of discovery—Britain basing its claim on Broughton's voyage to the Columbia Gorge. Since these claims could not be reconciled, the two countries concluded a treaty in 1818 which provided that the region be open to the citizens of both countries until 1828, when once again the problem would be discussed.

Such was the treaty, but McLoughlin's instructions were to discourage the American presence in any way possible. For one thing there was the truth of the old adage that where the ax of the settler rang, the trapper must certainly disappear, and trapping and the selling of furs was, after all, the company's business. Also, it was obvious that if the Americans settled in any number, American claims to the region would be strengthened.

By seeing to it that the area south of the Columbia would be thoroughly trapped out, McLoughlin did succeed in discouraging the encroachments of American trappers, but in forestalling settlement he failed. In a sense this failure began within, for the fort itself was a settlement in several respects.

In the year of its establishment, grain was sown, orchards planted and cattle allowed to multiply—resulting in a farm of 1,500 acres. Then there was the population of the fort, no camp at the crossing of forest paths but a community of several hundred with schools, churches and the other attributes of permanence.

More fundamental than this was an act of McLoughlin's compassion. Upon retirement, the company's French Canadian trappers were required by their contracts to return to Quebec for mustering out. Beginning in 1829, McLoughlin permitted them to take land and farm on the banks of the Willamette near present-day St. Paul. Thus did settlement begin in Oregon—with French Canadian trappers, not American pioneers, a fact sometimes forgotten.

◆ ◆ ◆

The Americans, however, were coming, but through a circumstance that initially had no connection with Oregon whatsoever. In the years 1824-36 there occurred in the eastern United States a born-again, evangelical movement, which placed great emphasis on missionary work. In 1831 four Nez Perce tribesmen journeyed to St. Louis seeking knowledge, it was said, of Christianity. Thus was kindled that fire of evangelicalism that would bring, in numbers, the first Americans to Oregon. "Let two suitable men, unencumbered with families, and possessing the spirit of martyrs throw themselves into the nation (the natives of Oregon). Live with them—

learn their language—preach Christ to them and, as the way opens, introduce schools, agriculture, and the arts of civilized life." So proclaimed the great Methodist Divine Wilbur Fisk in 1833.

His call was answered the following year by a 31-year-old Methodist, Jason Lee, a dedicated evangelist ready to suffer all hardships to save the natives of Oregon from damnation. Two years later, in 1836, four missionaries, Marcus and Narcissa Whitman and Henry and Eliza Spalding, sponsored by the Congregational, Presbyterian and Dutch Reformed churches, departed for Oregon—like Lee with trapping parties. Both groups were treated kindly by Dr. McLoughlin and given sound advice on where best to establish their respective missions. Lee and his associates settled near Salem while the Whitmans and Spaldings began their work in the vicinity of Walla Walla and Lewiston. Over the next decade these mission stations not only gained in population due to periodic reinforcements from the East, they also created substations—the Methodists at The Dalles of the Columbia, Oregon City and Clatsop Plains, and the Whitman-Spalding group at Spokane. In other words, by the early 1840s, the American missionaries had established seven settlements in the Oregon country.

This major contribution to the settlement of Oregon by the American missionaries is beyond dispute. Their success in Christianizing and civilizing the natives of Oregon is another matter, a tale of basically good intentions frustrated at every turn.

In the first place the missionaries were distracted by their own internal difficulties: frequent squabbling among themselves, little understanding from their distant headquarters in the East, and finally the necessity of devoting much of their time to providing for their own needs, thus leaving little energy for the instruction of the natives.

It was, however, their problems with the natives themselves that were insurmountable. Many of the latter were to some degree migratory, so sustained instruction at the mission sites was often difficult. Far more distressing was the fact that the missionaries were obliged to love a people whose habits they abhorred—gambling, drinking, stealing, irregular sexual conduct, the near nakedness, and an almost total indifference to cleanliness, bodily or otherwise. Worse, the missionaries were signally unsuccessful in convincing the Indians that in practicing these habits they were sinning.

If the missionaries had problems with the natives, so too did the natives have problems with the missionaries. In the beginning the missionaries were a novelty, but the novelty rather soon wore off. In the beginning also, the missionaries had been distributors of material rewards, but these soon dwindled, provoking one Cayuse to complain that "God is stingy." Baptism, as far as the natives could see, had not improved their prowess in the hunt, in war or in love. The missionaries' continued descriptions of the torments of hell both puzzled and depressed them. Soon, too, doubts developed as to the divine origins

Horses and carts jam the streets of downtown Heppner just before the turn of the century. This Morrow County town was founded in 1873.

Photo courtesy of the city of Heppner.

of the missionaries' message. "Where are these laws from?" asked a Walla Walla chief. "Are they from God or from the earth? ... I think they are from the earth, because, from what I know of white men, they do not honor these laws." Finally, the natives had reason to question one of Christianity's cardinal tenets. In 1839 two Catholic priests, Fathers Blanchet and Demers, arrived in Oregon evangelizing in competition with the Protestants. The antagonism that flared between the two religious bodies was fierce and often waspish, none of which deterred these men of God from haranguing the natives on the absolute necessity of brotherly love.

It took no more than a decade for the Protestant missionary effort to founder. In 1844 Jason Lee was removed from his post, while in the following year the Methodist Annual Report confessed that, "The hopes of the mission for the future depend primarily upon the success of the Gospel among the immigrants." As for the Whitmans and the Spaldings, in November of 1847 the Cayuse, convinced that Dr. Whitman was purposely infecting them with smallpox, slaughtered him, his wife, and 12 of their associates.*

Though failing in their mission to Christianize and civilize the native Oregonians, the missionaries nonetheless had a profound effect. For one thing they established schools, which became colleges, such as Willamette, Pacific, Linfield, and Lewis and Clark (formerly Albany College), which continue after nearly a century and a half to enrich the state. Also, by reason of their letters and reports concerning the virtues of Oregon country, they encouraged immigration. Finally, they planted the seed in 1838 that was to bear fruit with statehood. This was a memorial carried by Lee to Washington asking Congress to establish its jurisdiction over the Oregon Country. "We flatter ourselves we are the germe (sic) of a great State."

◆ ◆ ◆

The immigration encouraged by the missionaries began in the early 1840s, for a number of reasons. The Mississippi, Missouri and Ohio river valleys

from which so many of the pioneers started out was the most economically depressed region of the country, and this, combined with the promise of free land in the West, was a weighty incentive. Also, no region in the country was more unhealthy than these valleys, malaria endemic and a scourge; whereas Oregon already had its reputation of being a tonic place. Finally there was the plain American restlessness.

As there were different reasons for the immigration, so there were different kinds of immigrants. There were the enterprising, but there were also the failures and the lawless. Also, there was one large body of pioneers, nearly a half, who in many cases set out with much reluctance—the women. On the whole, however, the wagon-train pioneers were a fairly homogenous body. Except for the bachelor drovers and household hands, most were families. Almost all were Protestants. Very few were people of means, and very few were impoverished, since it took money to buy the gear to get to Oregon. Finally, the great majority were farmers.

A distinction is sometimes made between the kinds of people who went to Oregon and those who favored California. And some say the distinction is valid. From the beginning California tended to attract the single adventurer, particularly with the advent of the Gold Rush. Oregon, on the other hand, from the beginning often attracted sober and respectable individuals. Hall J. Kelley, the Boston schoolteacher who first encouraged immigration to Oregon, called for "pious and educated young men," and, as we have seen, the first American settlers in Oregon were in fact missionaries. Also, that memorial carried by Lee to Congress in 1838 made it clear that the settlers did not care to be joined by the "reckless adventurer," by the "renegade of civilization" or by the unprincipled sharpers of Spanish America," i.e., Californians. Some of the diaries and letters of the immigrants tend to confirm this attitude. Charles Pitman, traveling with a group bound for California who had begun to have second thoughts, wrote, "If things are not as anticipated when we left, in fact the Aristocracy or respectable portion of the companies will go to this valley" (in Oregon). And Jesse Applegate wrote to his brother, "... almost all the respectable

The natives had less resistance than whites and thus more often died. Also, Dr. Whitman had in fact poisoned the natives' dogs and also injected his melons with an emetic to discourage thievery.

portion of the California immigrants are going on the new road to Oregon—and nearly all the respectable immigrants that went last year to California came this year to Oregon." It is all marvelously summed up in the apocryphal story of the branch in the Oregon Trail, the route south to California marked by a cairn of gold quartz, the one north by a sign lettered "To Oregon." Those who could read came here.

The trek started in the spring at Independence, Missouri, that "great Babel upon the border of the wilderness." Here the wagons—on the average 10 feet long with 2-foot sides—were stocked: tools and clothes, seed, perhaps a harmonium, a clock; and the staples, bacon, beans, sugar, salt, coffee and probably a keg of whiskey. They had 2,000 miles to go and it would take about six months.

Before starting out, or shortly thereafter, captains were chosen and, because they were entering a land where no civil authority existed, it was necessary to draw up regulations covering all aspects of behavior. "... No profane swearing, no obscene conversation, or immoral conduct, allowed in this company." There was also the very thorny problem of whether to travel on the Sabbath.

The first four-fifths of the journey was ordinarily not a hardship, at least for the men who, relieved of the routine of farm chores, often found it a lark. It was decidedly less so for the women because it was hard to keep house and manage children in a jolting 10-foot box, and there were almost always the clouds of asphyxiating dust kicked up by the vanguard. Then there were the camp-

sites. These could be a pleasant grove of trees but usually well back from the river bottoms to avoid dampness and mosquitoes; this meant for the women long distances over which to haul the water. Then, too, the campsites had often been occupied the night before by a forward party and so could be rankly odoriferous with animal and human feces.

There were other problems as well, shortages of grass for the cattle, raging rivers to cross, sometimes bitter hand-to-hand fighting on the part of the men. Death by drowning and by the accidental discharge of firearms was far from uncommon and killed more of the immigrants than the natives. Indeed it is estimated that between 1840-60 more natives were slaughtered by the immigrants than vice versa.

But there were pleasures too. Despite the fights, there was considerable camaraderie. "This trip finds us together like a band of brothers." Many of the women might have said the same. At night there were prayer meetings to attend or a fiddle to dance to or friends with whom to share a jug. And as 17-year-old Susan Parish wrote, "... Where there are young people together there is always lovemaking."

On the last leg of the journey, however—from Fort Hall in Idaho to the Willamette Valley—the pleasures were few indeed. Now food supplies were low, and both immigrants and animals exhausted by the long months of the trek. Worst of all there lay before them the dreaded Blue Mountains, which, because of the steepness of the grades, could only be crossed with the aid of block and tackle. The immigrants prayed that now in late September the snows of winter would not come early to the mountains.

On finally reaching the valleys of Oregon, the immigrants—53,000 of them between 1840 and 1860—without exception were glad the journey was over.

And what did they find? The geography of the Willamette Valley was the same then as now; roughly 100 miles long, 20 to 30 miles wide, flat green prairie swelling here and there into buttes, oak savannas, streams pouring from both ranges of mountains through slopes of hemlock, spruce, fir and incense cedar to feed the river, which meandered the whole of the valley's length and gave the place its name. What astonished the immigrants, however, was not so much the valley, about as Edenic as they had expected, but rather something above it, that great white escarpment against the blue of the eastern sky, the mountains.

There were other surprises too, some pleasant, some not. By the mid-1840s the valley was pretty well hunted out, so there was a scarcity of game. Also, the immigrants were disappointed that the wild plum of their native forests did not grow here. More disappointing yet, there were no bee trees filled with honey. On the other hand, hazel nuts abounded as did a variety of berries. The climate, too, was welcome, the temperate winters, the gentle summers, the relative absence of thunder and lightning, but—and a novelty and delight to all—the frequency of rainbows.

This then was the world where the immigrants settled, most typically or anyway most ideally claiming land— the expected 640 acres for a man and wife—on the prairie margins, close to both timber and the open land. They needed the timber to build their houses and barns, the open land for their animals to graze on and to plant the wheat —shelter and food, the bases of their life.

But these things could take time and the beginnings were difficult. Peter Burnett, an immigrant of 1843 and first governor of California, provides us with a picture. "At every public meeting, it was easy to distinguish the new from the old settlers. They were lank, lean, hungry and tough. We were ruddy, ragged and rough. They were dressed

in broadcloth, wore linen-bosomed shirts and black cravats while we wore very coarse patched clothes; the art of patching was understood to perfection in Oregon. But while they dressed better than we did, we fed better than they. They wanted our provisions while we wanted their material for clothing."*

"Many of the men immigrants were childish, most of them discouraged, and all of them more or less embarrassed. There was necessarily, under the circumstances, a great hurry to select claims; and the newcomers had to travel over the country in the rainy season in search of homes. Their animals being poor, they found it difficult to get along as fast as they desired. There were no hotels in the country ... the old settlers had necessarily to open their doors to the new immigrants ... our families were often overworked in waiting upon others and our provisions vanished before the keen appetites of our new guests. They bred famine wherever they went."

No single person aided the immigrants more than did John McLoughlin. Touched by the hardships they had endured, he helped them again and again with money, supplies and good counsel even though his instructions were to discourage settlement. But finally the instructions were adamant; he was to discontinue all assistance. "Gentlemen," it is said he replied, "if such is your order I will serve you no longer." And he did not, resigning in 1846 to retire to the town which he had founded in 1829, the first in Oregon, indeed the first to be incorporated in the west, Oregon City.

As mentioned earlier, the wagontrain immigrants were in their makeup remarkably homogenous. The people among whom they settled were far less so. On the Tualatin Plains lived the "Rocky Mountain Boys," aging American trappers, rugged types with Indian wives and children. Across the Columbia in their library were ensconced the gentlemen of the Hudson's Bay Company with their ruby port and London journals. In the vicinity of St. Paul, those first settlers, the French Canadians, remained

---

Due to the absence of wool, cotton or flax there was a great shortage of cloth. Provisions were usually adequate for the old settlers but badly taxed by the sudden yearly increases in population brought on by the migrations.

History

on. With them now were those two very sharp thorns in the Protestant side, Fathers Blanchet and Demers. Upriver at Mission Bottom struggled the Methodists.

In the towns lived yet another type—New England merchants, most of whom had arrived with their goods by ship. This was not the only respect in which these New Englanders differed from the wagontrain emigrants who, for the most part, embodied the traditions and attitudes of the southern small farmer. Finally, there were the vanishing natives. By 1845 the Willamette Valley's 2,000 settlers had outnumbered them. Such then was the diversity with which Oregon began.

There was, however, one common characteristic. Only seven percent of these 2,000 settlers were over the age of 45. In other words, it was a remarkably young community and, like all young communities, was boisterous and thus required restraint, or that is to say laws—particularly laws relating to land title and claim jumping.

This was recognized in 1843 at Champoeg on the Willamette. Here about 100 settlers met to see if they could form a provisional government—"provisional" since the boundary question had not been solved. They succeeded, though not without considerable confusion and dissension. One of the more candid of those present, Dr. Robert Newell, wrote, "After a few days experience I became satisfied that I knew but little about the business of Legislating as the majority of my colleagues." As for the dissension, McLoughlin and a majority of the French Canadians were understandably chary of this attempt to form a government on American lines in a region still jointly occupied by Britain and the United States. The so-called American party prevailed by a narrow margin.

Thus was created a body of law and a government of three branches—legislative, executive (a committee of three), and a judiciary. Despite the fact that it did not have the power to tax, and when it did acquire the power had great difficulty in collecting the tax—even from its own executive committee—and despite the fact that it was not officially recognized by the majority over whom it presumed to rule, still, the laws it enacted were by and large observed, though on occasion in a curious fashion. In Polk County, for example, a man was

sentenced to three years imprisonment but, there being no jail and no taxes with which to build one, it was decided to sell him at auction. A local farmer bought the criminal, worked him for three years, after which he was given a horse and saddle and twenty dollars, and released.

This then, with its capital at Oregon City, was Oregon's government until 1849. As time passed its provisions were revised. In 1845 the executive committee of three was replaced by a governor—George Abernethy, a former mission employee. Also in '45 changes were made to allow local British participation. Still there were stresses and strains. Some were content with the provisional nature of the government; others wanted immediate American intervention. There were also those who favored an entirely independent republic, neither American nor British.

The "English Party" and the "American Party" were the two principal factions in these disputes. The English Party consisted of the Hudson's Bay Company and the Catholic French Canadians. The American Party was an uneasy alliance of the Rocky Mountain Boys, the New England merchants, the wagontrain immigrants, and the Methodists. It was because of this dissension in the American Party that the English Party usually held the balance, at least until 1846 when the boundary question was finally solved. After a generation of bickering, the British demanding everything north of the Columbia, the Americans demanding everything south of Alaska, the present boundaries were finally agreed upon by negotiation.

The 1846 treaty was not popular in Oregon. In particular, the provision permitting the Hudson's Bay Company to keep its land at Fort Vancouver was resented—that fort where so many of the missionaries and settlers had received succor from the hands of Dr. McLoughlin. "Man is a preposterous pig; probably the greediest animal that crawls upon this planet," wrote Mrs. Frances Fuller Victor, Oregon's first historian, in commenting on this desire to grab Fort Vancouver too.

◆ ◆ ◆

Between the boundary settlement and the end of the decade three events occurred that had a profound effect on

Oregon. The first of these had its beginning on the morning of December 8, 1847 when George Abernethy addressed the legislature, gathered in the Methodist church by the falls at Oregon City. "Our relations with the Indians becomes every year more embarrassing," warned the governor. "They see the white man occupying their lands, rapidly filling up the country, and they put in a claim for pay. They have been told that a chief would come out from the United States and treat with them for their lands; they have been told this so often that they begin to doubt the truth of it."

That afternoon the legislators, obliged to leave off their game of horse billiards (a kind of shuffleboard) because of falling snow, assembled again in the church, and it was then that they heard the news. The Cayuse Indians had slaughtered the Whitmans together with 12 members of their mission and were holding captive 53 women and children. The legislators acted immediately by moving that a volunteer army be formed with three objectives—rescue of the captives, punishment of the murderers and prevention of a coalition of the Cayuse with other interior tribes. Thus began the Cayuse War, the first of the Oregon Indian wars, a bungle and a waste from beginning to end.

First of all, there was a shortage of both money and men. The Provisional Government's treasury contained forty-three dollars and seventy-two cents and,

as for volunteers, one settler remarked that when the war was over "We will have great *Patriots* as we now have great chimney-corner warriors."

Next, to the considerable chagrin of the Americans, before they could get themselves together and proceed to the scene of the massacre, the Hudson's Bay Company had rescued the prisoners and delivered them to Oregon City. As was feared, some of the women had been violated. The wrath this provoked can be gauged from an editorial in the Oregon City Spectator: "... Let them (the Indians) be pursued with unrelenting hatred and hostility, until their lifeblood has atoned for their infamous deed; let them be hunted as beasts of prey; let their name and race be blotted from the face of the earth, and the places that once knew them, know them no more forever."

The formal campaign began with the arrival at The Dalles of the volunteers' commander, Colonel Cornelius Gilliam, veteran of the Black Hawk and Seminole wars, famed tracker of runaway slaves, Baptist preacher, and a man of whom it has been said that he "preferred the smoke of gunpowder to the smoke of peace pipes." The first casualty of this campaign occurred on the evening of his arrival and was reported by him in a letter to his wife: "... One of the Garde shot a Squaw in the thy thinking that She was an Indian man. It apperes that she was acrolling (crawling) along on

Students in a ski conditioning class learn some of the fundamentals on straw before heading to the slopes in a 1947 class at Oregon State College. Photo courtesy of the Oregon Historical Society. Negative number OrHi 94586.

Floodwaters surging down Willow Creek in 1903 destroyed a large part of the town of Heppner, county seat of Morrow County.

Photo courtesy Oregon Historical Society. Negative number OrHi 1445.

the ground so that she get to plaice of appointment between her and some of our young men which I am very sorry to (say) such things do frequently occurs ..."

Colonel Gilliam's young men, in a manner most haphazard, fought their little war for the next six months, their ranks reduced by dysentery, drunkenness and desertions, the latter particularly frequent when spring planting came around. Also, they had some difficulty in finding the Indians and, when they did, some difficulty in determining which were enemies and which friends. They never did succeed in apprehending, let alone identifying, Whitman's murderers. Finally, Colonel Gilliam by accident shot himself dead, which more or less ended the hostilities.

Though the casualties were not particularly high since both sides were chronically short of gunpowder, it exacerbated those already difficult relations between Americans and British, Protestants and Catholics and, most seriously, Indians and whites. The only blessing in disguise lay in the fact that Oregon at last gained some attention from Washington City, as the capital was then called. At the outset of the war the sheriff of Oregon, retired Rocky Mountain trapper Joseph Meek, was dispatched to Washington where he presented himself as "envoy extraordinary and minister plenipotentiary from the Republic of Oregon to the Court of the United States—" the "Court" a sarcastic reference by Sheriff Meek to what he no doubt considered an effete and decadent capital compared with his own

at Oregon City. This prejudice notwithstanding, Meek had come to request assistance in the Cayuse War and, in particular, to urge on President Polk, a shirttail relation, territorial status for the Oregon Country. Eventually his efforts, along with others, would prove successful but, in the meantime, the second event so important to early Oregon had occurred.

One day in August of 1848 a Captain Newell sailed up the Willamette, buying as he went along all the spades he could find—a circumstance found puzzling. When his ship would hold no more of spades, wheat and other provisions, Captain Newell informed the gulled locals that gold had been discovered in California.

It is estimated that two-thirds of the able-bodied men of Oregon threw down what was in hand—axes, awls, chisels, plows, pens, scales, forceps, tankards, and Bibles—and departed for California. The most serious of the derelictions was the plow for, after all, the people left behind had to eat. The Oregon City Spectator pled with Oregonians to stay on the farm—until, that is, the paper's own printer departed and ended for the time being the paper's publication.

It is possible that the Oregon settlement would not have survived, or if so but lamely, without the California goldrush. Now for the first time there was a nearby market for Oregon products. Also, many Oregonians returned with gold to replace what had been an awkward currency to say the least; wheat, one bushel = one dollar.

Finally, there were those who, going off to the goldrush, never returned. Good riddance. Such could not be persons of worth for otherwise they would not have elected to remain in California. Here is Mrs. Victor on the subject of the gold-rush: "... After all it will be seen that the distance of Oregon from the Sierra Foothills proved at this time the greatest of blessings, being near enough for commercial communication, and yet so far away as to escape the more evil consequences attending the mad scramble for wealth, such as social dissolutions, the rapine of intellect and principle, an overruling spirit of gambling—a delirium of development, attended by robbery, murder, and all uncleanness, and followed by reaction and death." From such wickedness Oregon, unlike its unfortunate neighbor to the south, had been preserved.

The third and last important happening in Oregon's 1840s was the culmination of the settlers' repeated requests for a U.S. presence. On March 3, 1849, the Mexican war hero Joseph Lane of Indiana, appointed governor by President Polk, arrived in Oregon City to proclaim that the Oregon Country was now an official Territory of the United States.

At last, the settlers and their land were under U.S. protection. What stuck in the craw of many, however, was that they were also under U.S. authority. Heretofore the people had enacted their own laws and elected their own officials. Hereafter all principal officials could be appointed in Washington—political spoils, strangers ruling over Oregon. Also, Washington might review and pass on Oregon legislation. The sop was one locally elected delegate to Congress. And the sop really fell short of even that, for the delegate had no vote.

Finally, the settlers began to wonder if the protection itself was worth territorial status in view of the form that protection first took. This was the appearance in Oregon City, following Lane's arrival, of a U.S. force called the Mounted Rifle Regiment. According to Mrs. Victor they were "quartered at great expense, and to the disturbance of peace and order of that moral and temperate community." After a winter of racket, drunkenness and random shots, they were removed to Fort Vancouver, a departure the citizens of Oregon City celebrated by burning down their barracks. Thus began the rather equivocal relations between the Territory of Oregon and the government of the United States.

"America is change," wrote Lord Bryce. Certainly that was the case in the Oregon of the 1850s. Population at the beginning of the decade was 13,000, at its end 52,000. One result of this increase was that settlement spread from the valley into the foothills, some of it in the bottoms of the tributary streams pouring down from the two mountain ranges, some higher up where the falling water could be utilized to power mills. The valley floor itself was no longer burned over by the Indians and so the oak savannas multiplied, and here and there—invaders from the mountain slopes—there were groves of pointy firs. The greatest change, however, lay in the extent of cultivated land—wheat and oats, hay, potatoes, onions, the young orchards finally beginning to bear, all protected from the growing herds of cattle by the zigzag of split-rail fences. Finally, now that there were mills, the crude cabins of chinked logs were giving way to the white simplicity of Greek revival farm houses, lilac at the door and inside things almost unknown in the '40s—a cookstove, a sewing machine, perhaps a settee and some fiddle-backed chairs brought around the Horn.

Growth and change were reflected in another significant development as well: the towns. By the middle of the decade over 30 had been registered in the valley; hardly a valley town today that does not have its origins in the 1850s. What is more, many of these towns were now linked, for by the middle '50s, 14 steamboats made scheduled runs up and down the river. The towns themselves were not much, the buildings of a flimsy, slapdash sort, much clutter and muck about, but here and there a columned courthouse went up. And there was also the occasional academy where a youth could learn a little Latin and how to play the flute. As for the capital, one commentator tells us that, "A sort of gay and fashionable air was imparted to Society in Oregon City by the families of the territorial officers ... which was a new thing in the Willamette Valley, and provoked not a little jealousy among the more sedate and surly."

History

There was development as well at either end of the valley. In 1850 gold was discovered in the Rogue River valley, which led to the founding of Jacksonville and to which Ashland supplied lumber and flour, while Roseburg had its beginnings in 1852 as a waystation on the Oregon-California immigrant trail. It was, however, at the other end of the valley, at the Willamette's final bend, that the most competitive developments occurred.

Portland's dream began in 1845, 16 blocks platted out along the river bank and a coin flipped to give the place the name of Portland. Two advantages gave Portland the eventual edge over the other river towns. It was the head of navigation, the farthest point on the river to which ocean-going ships could proceed at all seasons of the year. Thus were upriver the towns of Milwaukie, Gladstone and Oregon City cut out.

On the other hand Portland had a low-grade pass—the route of the present Canyon road—built through the hills to the rich wheatlands of the Tualatin valley. Thus were downriver towns such as Linton and St. Helens cut out, for their accesses to the valley were over very steep grades indeed. In short, Portland was a place where the wagons could meet the ships—and, during the California goldrush, many wagons met many ships. Wheat and gold, the wharf and the road, sawmill, tannery and blacksmith shop, and a population of about 800, "a small and beautiful village," a local judge described it. In fact, it was a raw, disheveled place, gangling and awkward in the spurt of its first

growth. "Rather gamey," said a lady passing through on her way south.

By 1851, however, the town was incorporated. A brick building with arches went up at the waterfront, classic revival cottages with tiny pillared porches appeared on the now elm-planted blocks, land was set aside for parks, and there was a "library" and a music shop. By 1858 there were 100 stores and a population of about 2,000. Oregon had its "metropolis."

Portland, Oregon City, the smaller river towns, in these were centered Oregon's trade and commerce, but they were also centers of something else— faction. As a California journalist of the time wrote, "The Oregonians have two occupations, agriculture and politics." This interest in politics arose in part from the fact that in the 19th century, politics could be about as dear to a man as life, and in part from the fact that politics was the trough in which the slop of spoils flowed. It was the crowding at this trough that accounts for the rough and tumble of Oregon politics in the decade of the 1850s.

The principal contestants in the melee were the Democrats, the Whigs (predecessors of the Republicans), the Temperance Party, and the Know Nothings, the latter a secret society of nativists out to foul Roman Catholics, the foreignborn and the Democrats. The Democrats were the majority party and tended to be agrarian in membership; whereas their principal adversaries, the Whigs, were town-oriented. The two parties disagreed over just about everything except the spoils and voiced their disagreement

An "Oregon" huskie after a climb of Brown Mountain with Arnie Klott who took this spectacular photo of Mt. McLoughlin in Jackson County.

loudly and abusively in their respective papers, the Whig *Oregonian* and the Democratic *Oregon Statesman*. The latter always referred to the *Oregonian* as "the Sewer" and on one occasion stigmatized it as "a complete tissue of gross profanity, obscenity, falsehood and meanness" whose editor seldom told the truth "even by mistake." Editor Dryer of the *Oregonian* responded by labeling Editor Bush of the *Statesman*, "pimp generalissimo of a small, cheap paper."

One of the main issues on which the two parties disagreed was the location of the state capital, a controversy that raged for some 15 years. Initially at Oregon City, it was moved to Salem, then to (Marysville) Corvallis, next back again to Salem, where a statehouse was finally completed, only to burn down.

Another serious issue was statehood. The Democrats favored it since as the majority party they could be sure of capturing the elective offices as well as patronage. The Whigs—by 1857 the Republicans—opposed it for the same reason. The people on the whole were not interested, not sure by any means they wished to join the Union, and on three occasions voted the proposition down. But finally, and due mainly to the will and work of the Democratic Party machine, the measure was carried and on March 15, 1859 the *Brother Jonathan* sailed into Portland with the news that Oregon had become the 33rd state.*

The 1850s in Oregon was a decade of growth and also of refinement of what was at hand. There was achievement in all areas—the economy, transportation, education, government, the amenities of everyday life. But overlaying all of this,

---

In 1853 the northern portion of the Oregon Territory had been detached by Congress to form Washington Territory. When Oregon became a state in 1859, its eastern boundary began on the north at the intersection of the Snake River and the 46th parallel, extended south up the middle channel of the south Snake to its junction with the Owyhee River near the present town of Nyssa, and thence south to the present northern boundary of Nevada. This was the final change in Oregon's boundaries. The remainder of the old Oregon country—a region bounded east and west by the Rocky Mountains and the Pacific Ocean, ranging from 54° 40' (the southern boundary of Alaska) to 42° (the northern border of California)—was included in Washington Territory.

there was a stain, and it was the stain of blood. From 1851-53 and again from 1855-56, Indian wars plagued both southern and northeastern Oregon.

The problem was land. With the Donation Land Law of 1850, Congress offered free land to the immigrants before arranging for its purchase from the natives—treaty after treaty negotiated for such a purpose and never ratified. Some of the settlers sympathized with the Indians in their plight, but many urged their extermination. "Indeed, this seems to be the only alternative left," editorialized the Oregonian in the fall of 1853. Certain individuals took it upon themselves to do just that, but others, such as Joseph Lane and Joel Palmer, sought to gain fair treatment for the natives. Palmer, superintendent of Indian affairs, 1853-56, initiated the reservation system in Oregon as a means of protecting the natives from the whites and to bring peace to the two races. In a limited way his policy was effective, but it was not to be the end of Indian hostilities.

Though proudly independent and often critical of the federal government and its claims, Oregon remained basically Unionist during the Civil War. There were pockets of Oregonians sympathetic to the South and slavery, but their support was limited to such acts as throwing the Albany municipal cannon into the river so that it could not be fired to celebrate Lincoln's election. By and large Oregon was little touched by the war; its attention concentrated instead on an event and region far closer to home, the discovery of gold in eastern Oregon, Idaho and Montana.

Eastern Oregon had not created a favorable first impression. "The plains smoked with dust and dearth," remarked Thomas Farnham in 1839. A later immigrant agreed. "This is a barren, God-forsaken country, fit for nothing but to receive the footprints of the savage and his universal associate the coyote." Yet only eight years later a process began—summarized by D.W. Meinig as "Gold, Grass and Grain"—which was to make the interior one of the richest regions in the new state.

The gold strikes themselves, in 1861 and '62 in Baker and Grant Counties, were enormously lucrative, an estimated $20 million taken from the mines in 1862 alone. Like the previous strikes in

California in the '40s and in southern Oregon in the '50s, the economy of the whole state benefited immensely from this infusion.

Of more permanent importance was the fact that cattle began to be driven across the Cascades from the valley to feed the miners—over 100,000 head in the decade of the '60s. It was just at this time that grazing land was growing short in the valley, whereas in the interior there was an abundance of bunch grass, not to mention the wild rye and flax and meadow grass of the bottoms. Here were later born the great cattle empires of Oregon with their barons, men like Pete French and Henry Miller, and so too the beginnings of cattle towns—Burns, Prineville, Lakeview and others.

Cattle were followed by sheep with consequences that in time would prove lamentable. Great sheep empires were created as well, most of these in northeastern Oregon between The Dalles and the Umatilla. These too contributed much to the founding and growth of towns like Heppner, Pendleton and Condon. In this region also was the Hay Creek Ranch, largest Merino breeding station in the world. Not far away was Shaniko, which, when the railroad came, handled at one point more wool than any railhead in the world. It was the railroad, too, that carried sheep-raising into southeastern Oregon. This gradual encroachment by the sheepmen and their close-cropping flocks on the cattle ranges led to the sheep and cattle wars, which were not settled until the present century, and in which thousands of sheep and cattle, and some men as well, were shot.

Many factors brought about the relative decline in the sheep and cattle business. The valley with its late springs had never been entirely ideal for the raising of wheat, whereas the high country, particularly in the northeast with its warmer climate but moisture-holding soil, seemed meant for wheat. It was a suitability, however, which could not be realized until the railroads of the 1880s made possible cheap, convenient transportation. When that happened it was an increasingly apparent matter of economics. More money could be made from an acre sown than an acre grazed. In 1869 the first wheat shipment went to Liverpool. By 1890 a grain ship left Portland on the average of once a week for foreign ports.

Thus the development of the interior, "gold, grass and grain." By the turn of the century—with its 16 counties, dozens of towns, its wheat, cattle, sheep, and still here and there, some gold—the interior had come into its own, enriching and broadening a state, which for so long had lived both literally and figuratively in that narrowness called "the valley."

◆ ◆ ◆

No region could be in greater contrast to the high country of the interior than the Oregon coast. Though the first region to be visited by whites, it was the last to be developed, in part because of its isolation. The waters off the Oregon coast are among the roughest in the world. Furthermore, there are few harbors, and those few are obstructed by dangerous bars. Inland, on the other hand, are the mountains, which until the era of good roads, a very recent era, were difficult to cross except in summer. The remainder of the year the passes were deep in snow and mud. There was, too, the fact that in the valley and in areas of the interior good agricultural land abounded, whereas on the coast there was little. Finally, during those years when so much development was taking place in the interior, all the central Oregon coast was closed, since it had been set aside as an Indian reservation.

In the beginning, and for many years thereafter, what development occurred tended to take place at the northern and southern ends of the coast. Following the removal of Hudson's Bay Company to Fort Vancouver in 1825, Astoria languished until the late '40s when emigrants began to settle there. In 1864 the first salmon-canning factory was established and from then on Astoria served as the center of the industry. Not long after, Ben Holladay, the railroad entrepreneur, built the luxurious Seaside House in present-day Seaside, and the north coast began its years as a popular resort.

Tillamook was settled early as well. It was the site of the first American landing on the Oregon coast—by Captain Robert Gray on his initial voyage in 1788. He, however, called it Murderer's Bay, since it was here that his black cabin boy was killed by local natives. The first actual settler was Joseph Champion, who arrived in 1851 and made his home in a tree, which he referred to as his "Castle." Tillamook's growth was slow. Not until 1871 was there a road of sorts to the valley and not until 1884 did a stage begin to run. Scandinavians, drawn in part by the fishing, now began to predominate on the coast—large numbers of Finns, for example, at Astoria—but at Tillamook and at a few other places, Swiss settled and developed a cheese-making industry.

South of Tillamook the Siletz Indian Reservation began, the reservation established by Joel Palmer in the 1850s for the several thousand displaced natives of Southern Oregon and the Willamette Valley. It extended 125 miles down the coast and from the sea to the mountains, roughly 1.3 million acres. Forty years later it had been reduced to 47,000 acres and, of the natives, there were only a few hundred left. Disease, famine and greed had done their work.

The first bite out of these Indian lands was taken in 1865 at what is now Newport. The year before, oysters, for which there was a ravenous market in the grill rooms and saloons of San Francisco, had been found in great numbers in Yaquina Bay. Two years later, in 1866, a regular stage began to operate on the new military road from Corvallis and the Ocean House, a resort hotel, was built. Newport was on its way.

Certain areas of the southern coast, like the northern coast, were early populated—the former because of "soft gold," pelts, the latter because of hard gold,

the real stuff. Both Port Orford and Gold Beach began in the early 1850s as mining communities, the latter aptly named since grains of gold and grains of sand were literally intermixed there at the mouth of the Rogue. These communities also drew population because of the Rogue River Indian wars of the 1850s—and lost population too. It was at Gold Beach that one of the worst incidents of the war took place, the Rogue River Indians murdering 23 whites, among them the controversial Indian agent, Ben Wright, whom they killed and whose heart they then cooked and ate. However, the south coast community which was to know the greatest growth, did not trace its origins to wars and gold but to settlement and the good use of its port and timbered interland. This was Coos Bay, for years the largest lumber-shipping port in the world. There was, as well, R.D. Hume's salmon fisheries at Rogue River.

Finally, one other kind of development took place on the coast which must not be overlooked. In 1863, during the Civil War, Fort Stevens was constructed and remained on for the next 84 years as the principal guardian of the Columbia. It was also in these last decades of the century that those nine structures, symbolizing as well as anything the Oregon coast—its lighthouses—were built.

Despite the little resorts and the industries—the lumbering, the salmon and the oysters, the cheese and other dairy products—the coast at the turn

A parade wends its way down Main Street in downtown Clatskanie about 1910.

Photo courtesy of Debbie Hazen, Clatskanie Chief.

of the century remained an isolated, largely undeveloped place, far more so than the interior. It was to remain so until the 1930s when good, hard-surfaced roads finally made it over the mountains from the valley, and in particular with the completion in 1933 of the Coast Highway, which before had been in many places simply the beach—when the tide was out. Yet this delayed development of the coast has been a great boon to Oregon, for now—with public ownership of the beaches and more than 50 percent of the ocean-front land in public hands—no scenic coast in the world is better preserved and protected.

◆ ◆ ◆

If development was slow at the coast, it was not so in the valley, particularly at Portland. The gold finds and Indian wars of the 1850s in Southern Oregon had stimulated its economy considerably, but it was the gold finds of the 1860s east of the Cascades that really filled the Portland pocket. This good fortune was followed by another in the following decade—wheat. Beginning in the 1870s, Portland was on its way to becoming one of the major wheat ports of the world.

With these economic changes came others as well. Like any thriving city, Portland attracted foreign immigrants: Irish, German, Jewish, Scottish, Scandinavian, Chinese—grafts on the American stock that had founded the town. Also, that white and wooden New England look was passing and was replaced by stone and brick and the prefabricated

splendor of cast-iron fronts. Likewise the classical cottages of the neighborhoods were here and there giving way to the bay-windowed "mansions" of the Italian Villa style, the walls of these grander houses hung with the trophies of European tours, for Portland was no longer "rather gamey" as the woman bound for California had so unkindly said. By the '70s the town, having survived two major conflagrations, boasted an opera house, several theaters, a library, a concert orchestra and four academies. Culture had arrived.

It had arrived in other places too. Salem, Forest Grove, Albany, Corvallis and Eugene all had their colleges by the 1870s. Literary societies were popular in many places and libraries had been established in all the major valley towns. Like Portland, these towns had their touches of grandness too; a Gothic castle or Italian Villa taking up the whole of an elm-lined block, an opera house perhaps, almost certainly a large impressive hotel, the latter the sign in the last decades of the century that a town had "arrived."

The basis of all this thriving townlife was, of course, the farmland of the Willamette Valley. Until the middle of the 1870s, wheat continued to be the major crop, but now flax and, in particular, hops began to be cultivated, while better transportation encouraged the raising of more perishable produce such as fruits and vegetables.

The most visible changes, however, were in the landscape itself. With the invention of barbed wire in the '70s, the

412

rail fences began to disappear. Farm machinery called for larger barns and larger fields as well. Roads had greatly improved. The lone rider was still to be seen—a politician on his rounds, a preacher on his circuit, a young man a-courting, a woman bound for camp-meeting, the children up behind—but far more common now were the buckboard and the surrey. One-room schoolhouses were everywhere, and there were the little country churches, often crowning a hilltop in a grove of oak, the few that remain today among the most touching and beautiful remnants of early Oregon life. There were too, beginning in the 1880s, those most emblematic of rural structures, the grange halls. Finally, and like the churches often situated on a little rise, there was a feature that more than any other reflected change and the passing of time, and specifically the passing of the pioneer era—the graveyards. Each year more and more of the headstones marked the journey's end of those who had set out across the plains in the middle decades of the century and who, with their dreams and work, began to form the place in which we live today.

Some of course were still alive, for having survived the trail they tended to die old. One day in the autumn of 1883, 50 of them gathered in Portland to lead a parade. The purpose of the parade was to honor the end of their era and to celebrate the beginning of another, for behind the old men steamed a transcontinental locomotive, the first to reach Oregon.

Since settlement, no single event did more to transform Oregon than did the railroads. The first, promoted by Ben Holladay in 1868, was to link Portland with San Francisco. By 1872 it had reached Roseburg and thus, by that date, was the valley served. With the arrival in 1883 of that first transcontinental train in Portland and the completion of Holladay's line to San Francisco in 1887, Portland was, as the president of the Portland Board of Trade put it, "incorporated with the rest of the world." In the next years local lines were constructed to the coast, in the interior and all through the valley. By the turn of the century Oregon, excepting the southeast corner, was fully integrated by its rails.

A number of consequences followed. Now agriculture was no longer limited to areas served by water routes. In the interior the railroads affected the transition from a cattle-raising economy to one of wheat and wool. The coast at Astoria, Newport and Coos Bay was relieved to some degree of its isolation. New towns developed at important junctions, and more than one county seat was moved to be closer to the locomotives' toot. Portland, where all rails met, became more than ever the economic center of the state. Finally, the railroads facilitated immigration into Oregon from all regions of the country.

There was, however, one consequence of the railroads not foreseen or, at any rate, not desired—the high freight rates. For farmers these could be prohibitive. Efforts to have them lowered were initially defeated due to the alliance between the railroads and government. In the last decades of the century, government in Oregon was largely in the hands of the colorful but conservative wing of the Republican party. The color came from such figures as John Mitchell. When U.S. Senator Mitchell, for example, died in office in 1905, he had been convicted of both bigamy and bribery. It was in response to such escapades, but in particular to the freight rates, that the first, but unsuccessful, protests were mounted in the new Oregon Grange in the 1870s.

In time the protest movement broadened its base to include small businessmen as well as farmers, conservatives as well as liberals. Much of this protest was expressed through the new political party called the Populists. With the election of the Populist candidate, Sylvester Pennoyer, to the governorship in 1886, reform achieved a significant victory. With the appearance of the Progressive W.S. U'Ren and his Direct Legislation League in 1898, political corruption was finally at bay.

U'Ren believed that reform could only be achieved by citizens taking a more direct role in legislation. To this end U'Ren and his supporters succeeded in passing the initiative and referendum bills in 1902, the direct primary in 1904, an effective corrupt practices act in 1908, and also in 1908, the recall. Thus was the Oregon System of direct participation by the electorate completed—a model subsequently adopted by many other states.

This was also a period of progressive labor legislation, though labor organization began in Oregon in 1853 with the creation of the Typographical Society. The Portland Protection Union, the second union organized in the state, was formed in 1868. By the 1880s there were some 20 trade unions, with the American Federation of Labor appearing in Portland in 1887. The reform period in the first years of the century saw the enactment in 1913 of a worker's compensation law and the first effective minimum-wage and maximum-hour law for women in the nation. The reform movement's concern for women had also been expressed the previous year when a suffrage amendment was finally added to the state constitution.

It was in this rush of reform that Oregon left the old century and entered the next, almost all segments of society affected by the new provisions. One group, however, as usual, was not touched by these improvements, the native Oregonians.

The reservation system had not proved a solution to "the Indian problem." Often bands hostile to each other were placed on the same reserve. Government administrators could be corrupt and incompetent. The natives were encouraged to farm on land which in many instances was unsuited to agriculture. The Modoc war of 1872 south of Klamath, the Nez Perce war of 1877 rising in northeastern Oregon, and the Bannock war of 1878 in southeastern Oregon, the last of the Indian wars, all arose out of resistance to reservation life. In 1887 the Dawes Act abolished the natives' communal ownership of their reservation, giving them individual parcels instead, with the hope that this would encourage them to be independent farmers. The principal result of the act was an enormous reduction in the amount of Indian-held land. As Gordon Dodds has written, "By the 1880s Oregon Indians, for the white majority, were literally out-of-sight and out-of-mind, consigned to fringe regions, unworthy in their impotence even of hatred."

◆ ◆ ◆

Excepting, then, the status of native Oregonians, it was with a bang of reform that Oregon entered the 20th century. It entered with another bang as well or, more accurately, a bash, indeed a colossal bash, the Lewis and Clark Centennial and American Pacific Exposition and Oriental Fair of 1905. First promoted by the Oregon Historical Society, the purpose of this international exposition was to celebrate the centenary of the arrival of the two intrepid explorers and their party and the first official U.S. presence in the West. There was another motive as well; visitors, overwhelmed by paradise, might settle and invest.

Laid out near the river in northwest Portland, the fair was said to be a "scene of unparalleled splendor"; the flowing turf and balustraded terraces, a sunken garden, stately staircases descending to a lake, a cornucopia of agricultural produce, the flywheels of a hundred new inventions, exotic gewgaws from the East, lots of roses and electric lights— Eden up-to-date. The fair with its nearly three million visitors was an enormous success. Though not the only factor, the fair did play an important part in Portland's population leap. In 1900 a good-sized town of 90,000, it was by 1910 a city of almost a quarter of a million, while the state itself now numbered over 400,000.

One feature of the fair was prophetic. It served as the terminus for the country's first transcontinental auto race. The automobile had come and with it the beginning of changes that would outstrip even those of the railroad. In 1906, Portland grudgingly raised the speed limit from eight to 10 miles an hour. The real breakthrough came in 1910 when the Meier and Frank Company switched from horse delivery to trucks. In the same year the Oregon Automobile Association called on the counties to put up road signs, "so that auto-tourists ... might be able to find their way anywhere in Oregon." It was now, too, that the "good roads movement" increased its activity with its slogan, "Get Oregon out of the mud." In 1919 the state published its first official road map.

The canoe, the horse, the river boat, the stagecoach, even the railroads, impinged lightly on the Oregon landscape whereas the impact of the automobile was major. Among its many other effects, it continued and greatly augmented what the railroads had helped to begin, the gradual urbanization of the state. In 1880 only 15 percent of the population lived in towns; in 1910,

44 percent. By 1993, 62 percent of Oregonians lived in incorporated towns and cities.

In addition to these important developments in the first years of the century—the reform movement, the growth and increasing urbanization of the population, the building of more and better roads—there was another, which from then until now has been a prime determinant of the state's economic health: lumbering. A lumber mill was built by Dr. McLoughlin at Oregon City in 1831. With the Gold Rush, lumber became the state's principal export. Thereafter the industry went into decline until the turn of the century and the depletion of eastern forests. The industry continued to grow and in 1938 Oregon became the major lumber state in the Union.

◆ ◆ ◆

By the time of the first World War, the reform movement had pretty well petered out, though Oregon continued to send reform-minded senators to Washington, men like Harry Lane and Charles McNary. As for the war itself, Oregon's response was whole-hearted. In keeping with the Spanish-American War record established by the "tall men of Oregon," Portland's National Guard Unit was the first in the nation to mobilize, and Oregon as a whole, due to the extraordinary number of volunteers, became known as "the volunteer state." As is so often the case, however, the coin of patriotism had its other side. Vigilante groups prowled Portland and other towns in search of dissidents. Pacifists refusing to buy war bonds were roughly treated. Even German street names were changed to the names of presidents and flowers.

Certain elements of the war years carried over into the next decade. The wartime shipyards did much to stimulate the timber trade, while war needs greatly increased food production and processing. Both industries contributed significantly to the prosperity of the state in the 1920s. But the intolerance of the war years came into the '20s as well. The Portland Police Department created a Red Squad, which, in its enthusiasm, tended on occasion to overlook the law. Anti-Japanese sentiment surfaced in Klamath Falls, Redmond and Hood River. The flaming crosses of the Ku Klux Klan flared from many a hill and butte. In the end, discriminatory legislation was passed adversely

"Moby Dick," a 184-foot long cyclo-crane, is moored to its mast after a short flight from the hangar at the former U.S. Naval Air Station in Tillamook. Photo courtesy of the Oregon Historical Society. Negative number CN 020049.

affecting Orientals and Roman Catholics. It was an unlovely combination, the bigotry and boom.

The following decade brought some unlovely combinations, too—desperate men, frightened women, hungry children. Oregon was not as afflicted as many other states by the Depression —less dependent as we were on such hard-hit industries as automotives, steel and textiles. Nonetheless Oregonians too had their soup kitchens and Hoovervilles and CCC camps. On the docks and in the logging camps there were bitter and violent labor disputes. The numbers of unemployed were increased as well by the arrival of migrants from the dustbowl states and the south, a new admixture to the Oregon population. In 1934 Governor Julius Meier summed up the general situation: "Oregon is dead broke."

As elsewhere, we grasped at panaceas such as the Townsend Plan and Technocracy. In 1937, however, a true, if partial, panacea did appear—Bonneville Dam. A cheap and plentiful source of power, it was in time to have a profound effect on the character of the state's economy.

True economic revival did not occur until World War II. As in the first war, shipbuilding, lumber and food production were greatly stimulated and now, too, a new industry came to Oregon— aluminum. The war also brought new additions to Oregon's population, drawing 160,000 workers to the war industries, among these a large number of blacks, giving to the state for the first time a black population of significant size. Likewise increased food production

offered jobs to Spanish-speaking migrants, many of whom settled and who now constitute the state's largest minority. The effect of the war on the character of Oregon's population and economy was to be both profound and lasting.

Paradoxically, native Oregonians remained alien among the rest of the population, although in the first decades of the century certain advances were made. In 1924 the natives were finally made full citizens of the United States. In 1934 the Indian Reorganization Act provided for tribal councils and prohibited the sale of Indian lands to non-Indians, while a decade later a court of treaty claims was established. In the 1950s and early '60s, however, the government—operating on the premise that the natives should be assimilated into white society—terminated three Oregon reservations. The results, on the whole, did not contribute to the natives' welfare. By the late '60s, perhaps in reaction to the dispersion caused by termination, there was a revival of tribalism. At the same time government policy began to provide for self-determination, with lessened government and bureau influence in tribal affairs.

Five reservations exist in Oregon: Warm Springs, Umatilla, Burns Paiute, Siletz and Grand Ronde. Eight tribes are recognized by the government as having sovereign rights and a trust relationship with the U.S. government: Warm Springs, Umatilla, Burns Paiute, Siletz, Grand Ronde, Cow Creek, the Confederated Tribes of Coos, Lower Umpqua and Siuslaw, and the Klamath Tribe. The present policy with regard to native Oregonians

The historic Sumpter Valley Railroad Depot which once served a bustling railroad carrying logs, gold ore, cattle and passengers between Prairie City and Baker City from 1891 to 1947, is now home to the Dewitt Museum.

Photo courtesy of Grant County.

and the hope for the future is well summed up in the 1983 Oregon Historical Society publication, *Oregon Indians: Culture, History, and Current Affairs.* "The continuing acknowledgment of tribal sovereignty and the support for self-determination is a policy approach that rests solidly on the most basic points of Indian and United States legal history, and it holds much promise for the future. It may be that now, after more than two centuries, the right of Indian people to live their own lives, and determine their own destiny, will finally be respected.

"Like any object held too close, the recent past is difficult to see. Events in postwar Oregon are still too near to be perceived with any true perspective. Still, from the present vantage point, there are certain events and trends which would appear to be of permanent significance."

◆ ◆ ◆

Oregon's economy continues to depend heavily on lumber and agriculture. Two new industries, however, have developed, which have broadened the economic base—electronics and tourism. Oregon is an ideal location for the former since the electronics industry is not dependent upon raw materials or close proximity to markets but, on the other hand, does require the skilled labor force Oregon can provide. Tourism, only recently thought of as an industry, has vastly increased since the war and is now the state's third-largest source of revenue. Both electronics and tourism are fortunate new directions for the state's economy since neither threaten Oregon's most important resource after its people—the land on which they live.

For most of Oregon's history, the Republican party was in the majority, supported by the state's primarily rural population. As demographics changed through the fifties and sixties, with migration from other parts of the nation and a move to the cities, a majority of Oregon voters registered as Democrats. In 1957, the Oregon State Senate elected its first Democratic president since 1878, and Democrats held the majority until 1995. Similarly, after decades of Republican control, the Oregon House held Democratic majorities for all but four sessions between 1957 and 1991, when Larry Campbell became the speaker of the House.

In 1994, Oregon elected a new Democratic governor and a Republican legislature. At the same general election, voters considered twenty ballot measures. Political observers noted that voters were selective and thoughtful about their decisions in support or rejection of various measures.

The results of the election indicate that Oregon voters continue to show independence and give careful consideration to the policy issues facing the state.

Over the years, the state's political activity has been greatly concerned with environmental legislation, with strong bipartisan support.

As at the beginning of the century, when Oregon led the nation with the "Oregon System" of legislative reform, so in the area of environmental protection it has taken the lead with such citizen-supported measures as the Scenic Rivers Act, the Land Conservation and Development Commission and the Bottle Bill. The first settlers believed Oregon to be a kind of Eden. Now, a century and a half later, their descendants appear determined to see that it remains so.

Driving down the roads of Oregon today, whether in the valley, the interior or the coast, and looking at the landscape and all the things that we so recently have put upon it, it is easy to forget that it all began more than 10,000 years ago when the land mainly came to rest and man arrived to live from it. Cruising the freeway hardly brings to mind those first 100 centuries of native life, only in detail different from our own, at bottom the same—shelter, food, some ornament and myth, birth, growing and decay. History, it is said, is a pageant, a procession which never pauses, both the figures and the backdrops always changing. Thus, with the long, slow centuries of native life did the pageant of this place begin.

Processions, though they never pause, do proceed at different rates—the rate in history determined by the rate of change —and so it is that the pageant of our history begins to quicken with the first appearance off the coast of those great black-bodied birds, the ships of the explorers. Heceta retiring, disappointed, from the mouth of the Columbia; Gray, triumphant, crashing through the breakers at the bar; Lewis and Clark, water-borne as well, celebrating Christmas with "Spoiled pounded fish and a fiew roots."

The backdrop changes to Fort Vancouver and Dr. McLoughlin belaboring his cane on someone's back or holding up that goblet of port to the sunlight, while 30 miles along the Willamette the French Canadian trappers with their squaws are sowing wheat and children. Enter the grave, dedicated missionaries, their faces finally cast with bafflement and failure; followed by the immigrants, "lank, lean and tough." They are best backdropped by the falls at Oregon City, where most of them arrived, or searching for claims in the mud of the Oregon winter. Next there is a confusion of gold and blood, Indian wars and miners, and at the same time someone burns down the statehouse and both Whigs and Democrats are hanged in effigy. Meanwhile, the general background to all of this—the long, green valley with its meander of river—is filling up with houses, barns, churches, schoolhouses, taverns, shops, here and there a huddle of them, the largest huddle at the last bend of the Willamette.

No sooner has one begun to take in all of this than the backdrop begins to broaden. At the top appears a scene, half plain, half sky, vast herds of cattle moving through it, though soon to dwindle as the green of grazing passes to the gold of wheat, while at the bottom little lighthouses go up at the ends of the headlands, and the natives lose their land and die.

For some time it has been a noisy pageant—laughter, gunfire, war whoops, the intoning of sermons, a politician's blast, the cries of love and pain, ironshod wheels on cobblestones, all in all a terrible racket. But now there comes a sound that splits the air like the bugles of perdition—except that it's a whistle. The railroad has arrived.

From now on the speed of the procession is such that one can hardly keep up with it. Wheat pours down on Portland. New towns are built. A horde of immigrants descend. The people capture the statehouse. Women get the vote. The automobile appears. And before we know it we are flying down the freeway, gazing out across this time-deep land where, as we sometimes forget, so much has happened.

Chronological History of Oregon

Oregon's history contains many more significant dates than space will permit, but this list should prove helpful to those embarking on a study of the state.

Oregon Country 1542-1847

1542—Bartolome Ferrelo, pilot for Juan Rodrigues Cabrillo, sails north as far as southwest coast of Oregon.

1579—Sir Francis Drake sails north to the southern part of Oregon.

1603—Martin d'Aguilar sails along the Oregon coast and sights a river where the Columbia was later discovered.

1765—"Ouragon," first known use of Oregon, in a proposal by Major Robert Rogers.

1774—Juan Perez, first known Spanish Explorer in 170 years, sails along the coast.

1775—Bruno Heceta and Juan Francisco de Bodega y Quadra land on what is now Washington soil. First recorded Europeans known to stand on Northwest soil.

1778—Captain James Cook visits the Northwest coast on a voyage of discovery and, via the sea-otter trade with China, starts heavy fur trading by many nations in this area.

1779—"Oregon" first used in print by Jonathan Carver.

1788—Capt. Robert Gray, first American landing in Oregon, arrives at Tillamook. Markus Lopius, first black to set foot on Oregon soil, is aboard Robert Gray's sloop *Lady Washington.*

1792—Captain Robert Gray discovers the river of the West, naming it the Columbia, after his ship, the *Columbia Rediviva.*

1793—Sir Alexander Mackenzie, the first white man to cross the North American continent, canoes down the Bella Coola River to the Pacific Ocean.

1803—President Jefferson purchases Louisiana from France. American interests now turn to this new land of Louisiana and the unknown wilderness beyond it, called Oregon Country.

1804-1806—Captains Lewis and Clark and party travel from St. Louis to the mouth of the Columbia. A Shoshone Indian, Sacajawea, and her husband,

The city of Vanport was built in 1942 to accommodate war workers in shipyards along the Columbia River. In 1948 it was completely destroyed by flooding.

Photo courtesy of Oregon Historical Society. Negative number OrHi 68813.

Toussaint Charbonneau, serve as guides and interpreters from what is now North Dakota to the Pacific.

1807-1812—David Thompson, a British fur trader of the North West Company and explorer, is the first white man to travel the entire length of the Columbia River.

1811—The Pacific Fur Company, financed by John Jacob Astor, is established near the mouth of the Columbia River, where Astoria now stands.

1812—South Pass, the gateway through the Rocky Mountains, is discovered by Robert Stuart of the Pacific Fur Company and is later used by pioneers on the Oregon Trail.

1813—Astoria is sold to the North West Fur Co., a British enterprise, and later is taken by the British and considered a prize of the War of 1812. It is later renamed Fort George.

1814—Jane Barnes, first white woman to land in the Pacific Northwest, arrives at Fort George.

1814—First livestock in the Pacific Northwest is brought from California by ship.

1817—William Cullen Bryant uses the name "Oregon" in his poem *Thanatopsis*.

1818—Fort George returns to American ownership, by Treaty of 1814. A treaty of joint occupancy is signed by U.S. and Great Britain for this Pacific Northwest territory.

1824—Hudson's Bay Co. headquarters moves from Fort George to newly selected Fort Vancouver site on north bank of Columbia. Dr. John McLoughlin becomes chief factor at the post, where he remained for 22 years.

1827—First sawmill in the Pacific Northwest built by Dr. McLoughlin.

1828—Jedediah Smith, fur trapper, reaches the Pacific Northwest from California, the first party to come overland from California. Fifteen of his 18 men were massacred by Indians on the Umpqua River.

1828—First grist mills built by Hudson's Bay Co. at Fort Vancouver and Fort Colville.

1829—Hudson's Bay Co. post established at Willamette Falls, present site of Oregon City.

1831—Four Indians of the Flathead and Nez Perce tribes travel to St. Louis seeking missionaries to come to Oregon.

1832—Captain Bonneville and party of 110 men, come west via the Rocky Mountains and travel to Fort Walla Walla.

1832—First expedition of Nathaniel Wyeth travels into Columbia River country. Hudson's Bay Co. establishes fort on the Umpqua River.

1833—First school in the Pacific Northwest at Fort Vancouver. Teacher is John Ball, member of Wyeth's party. Same year, first timber to be shipped from Oregon is sent to China.

1834—Fort Hall, in what is now Idaho, is established by Nathaniel Wyeth on his second expedition. This same year, the Jason Lee party of the first Protestant missionaries to the Oregon Country arrives at Fort Vancouver with Wyeth. Later established the Willamette Mission near present-day Salem.

1836—*The Beaver*, first steamboat on the Pacific Ocean, is brought to Fort Vancouver. Protestant missionaries,

Dr. Marcus Whitman, H.H. Spalding, their wives, and W.H. Gray, arrive in Oregon Country. Mrs. Whitman and Mrs. Spalding are the first white women to come across the continent to Oregon Country. This is the first group to bring wagons west of Fort Hall. Waiilatpu Mission (Protestant) is established by Dr. Whitman at this time. Alice Clarissa, the Whitman's daughter, was the first white American child born here.

1838—Congress is asked to extend United States jurisdiction over Oregon. The Reverends Francis Blanchet and Modesti Demers celebrate the first Catholic Mass in the Pacific Northwest. The first cattle drive of the West arrives from California.

1839—First printing press in the Northwest brought to Lapwai (now Idaho) from Honolulu and used to print a Nez Perce primer, the first book produced in the Pacific Northwest. Father Blanchet establishes the first actual Catholic mission in St. Paul, Oregon.

1841—American settlers in the Willamette Valley meet to create a government, but fail. The *Star of Oregon*, first ship built by Americans in the Oregon Country, is launched this year.

1842—Dr. John McLoughlin designs plans for what is now Oregon City. Willamette University, first university west of the Mississippi, founded by Jason Lee.

1843—Civil government established in Oregon Country. The first large group of Americans arrives over the Oregon Trail; approximately 900 settlers come to the Willamette Valley.

1844—National election slogan "54-40 or Fight" is proof of growing American interest in Oregon. First American taxes on the Pacific Coast were collected on a voluntary basis.

1845—Second provisional government in Oregon Country is organized. George Abernethy is elected provisional governor.

1846—Treaty between the U.S. and Great Britain establishes the Oregon boundary at 49 degrees north latitude. First newspaper, *Oregon Spectator*, is printed at Oregon City.

1847—Whitman Massacre at Waiilatpu. The Cayuse War, first Indian war, follows.

The Oregon Territory 1848-58

1848—Oregon Territory is organized on August 14 (Abraham Lincoln is asked to be governor of the Territory of Oregon).

1849—Gen. Joseph Lane, first appointed territorial governor, arrives. Vancouver made military headquarters for Pacific Northwest.

1850—Donation Land Claim law is enacted. Mail service between San Francisco and the Columbia River is established. Rogue River Indian War begins.

1851—Portland is incorporated. (Named after Portland, Maine, by flipping a coin to decide between "Boston" and "Portland.")

1851—Territorial Government enacts a law allowing black pioneer and humanitarian, George Washington Bush, to settle in Oregon.

1851—The first person of Chinese ancestry to settle in Portland, Sung Sung.

1853—Washington Territory created from part of Oregon Territory. Southern boundary is marked by the Columbia River.

1853—The Typographical Society is the first labor union in Oregon.

1855—The Yakima Indian War begins, fought on both sides of the mid-Columbia. First telegraph company is operated in Oregon.

1855—Oregon's first State Capitol, erected in 1854, burns.

1856—Eastern Washington and Oregon are closed to settlers by Army order, due to Indian war.

1858—First election of Oregon state officers.

State of Oregon 1859-Present

1859—February 14: Congress ratifies Oregon State Constitution. This is the formal birthday of the state.

June 3: Congressional proposal to admit Oregon into the Union is accepted by the state. John Whiteaker becomes the first elected governor of Oregon. Ladd and Tilton Bank, first in the state, is founded.

1860—Daily stagecoach service inaugurated between Portland and Sacramento.

1861—Historic village of Champoeg destroyed by one of worst floods in Northwest history.

1863—Idaho Territory created, eventually making three full states out of original Oregon Country.

1864—Salem becomes the State Capital by popular vote. Transcontinental telegraph lines into Portland via California are first existent.

1867—The first Chinese Temple or "Jess House" built and dedicated to Kuan-yin, a revered Buddhist saint.

1868—Corvallis College, designated as Agricultural College of Oregon (now Oregon State University), is first state-supported institution of higher education in Oregon.

1869—First public high school is established in Oregon.

1871—Abigail Scott Duniway first introduces Susan B. Anthony in Oregon to help galvanize a woman suffrage crusade.

1872—Modoc Indian War.

1873—Oregon Pioneer Association, the state's first historical society, founded in Butteville.

1876—University of Oregon opens in Eugene.

1877—Nez Perce War.

1878—Bannock Indian War.

1880—Miyo Iwakoshi is the first person of Japanese ancestry to settle in Oregon.

1882—State normal schools for training teachers established at Monmouth and Ashland.

1883—Transcontinental railroad is completed.

1886—Mary Leonard becomes the first woman admitted to the bar to practice law in Oregon.

1888—Oregon Volunteer group is in the first military expedition to the Philippines.

1888—Oregon Historical Society incorporated.

1890—The Chinese Consolidated Benevolent Association is established; reorganized in 1910; incorporated in 1911.

1892—Portland Art Association is founded.

1902—Initiative and referendum laws adopted allowing people of Oregon to place measures on ballot and recall existing laws by popular vote. Oregon is first state to adopt such laws.

1903—McCants Stewart, first Black admitted to Oregon Bar.

1903—Voters' Pamphlet first published.

1904—George Hardin is the first Black officer appointed to the Portland Police Bureau.

1905—Lewis and Clark Centennial Exposition is held in Portland, celebrating 100 years since the visit of Lewis and Clark.

1905—Sarah A. Evans, appointed first City Market Inspector in the U.S., marks the beginning of the consumer-protection movement.

1906—Association of Oregon Counties first organized.

1908—Lola Baldwin is named head of the newly formed Women's Division (Portland), becoming first female Civil Service police officer in United States.

1912—Women's suffrage is adopted in Oregon.

1913—South jetty at the mouth of the Columbia is completed to facilitate shipping on the Columbia and Willamette Rivers.

1920—Oregon League of Women Voters formed.

1921—Ku Klux Klan organized in Oregon.

1922—Compulsory education law passed.

1922—Beatrice Cannady, first Black woman admitted to Oregon Bar.

1922—Japanese American Citizen's League is established.

1925—League of Oregon Cities formed.

1933—The Tillamook Burn, one of the nation's worst forest disasters, wipes out 240,000 acres of Oregon's finest timber.

1935—State Capitol, built in 1876, is destroyed by fire.

1936—Nan Wood Honeyman elected, Oregon's first woman representative in Congress.

1937—Bonneville Dam completed, providing Oregon with a great source of hydroelectric power.

1939—New Capitol at Salem is completed.

1941—Shipbuilding boom starts at Portland.

1942—First women are called to jury duty in a federal court in Oregon.

1946—Rural School Bill passed. Equalization measure encourages consolidation and raises standards of rural schools.

History

1947—Gov. Earl Snell, Sec. of State Robert S. Farrell Jr. and Pres. of the Senate Marshall E. Cornett killed in private plane crash.

1948—Memorial Day Flood completely destroys Vanport, suburban Portland city of 17,500 built to house wartime workers.

1949—Fair Employment Practices Commission, first in a series of State Civil Rights Legislation.

1949—First woman mayor in Portland, Dorothy McCullough Lee.

1952—Constitutional amendment approved assuring equal representation in State Legislature.

1954—McNary Dam on Columbia River dedicated by U.S. President Dwight D. Eisenhower.

1960—Maurine Neuberger, Oregon's first woman elected to U.S. Senate—3rd in U.S.

1961—Freeway completed connecting Salem and Portland.

1962—October 12 (Columbus Day) storm causes extensive damage.

1966—Opening of Astoria Bridge linking Oregon and Washington at the mouth of the Columbia. Ceremony marks completion of I-5 freeway, nonstop, Washington to California.

1967—Beach Bill approved.

1968—John Day Dam, last remaining damsite on Columbia River, dedicated by Vice President Hubert Humphrey.

1971—Bottle Bill approved—first in nation. Single member district reapportionment for Oregon Legislature.

1973—Statewide Land Use Planning approved. Equal Rights Amendment to the U.S. Constitution ratified; reaffirmed in 1977.

1976—Norma Paulus elected Oregon's first woman secretary of state.

1977—March 1, ban on aerosol sprays. Capitol Wings Addition completed.

1977—Confederated Tribe of Siletz won restoration of trust relationship.

1978—Congress lists the Oregon Trail as a National Historic Trail.

1980—Mt. St. Helens erupts with cataclysmic force in southwestern Washington, devastating 200 sq. mi. of popular forestland and triggering destructive ash, floods, mud flows and river silt. The busy Columbia River is temporarily closed to deep-draft ships at Portland and Vancouver.

1982—Cow Creek Band of Upper Umpqua Indians win restoration of trust relationship.

1982—Betty Roberts is the first woman justice of the Supreme Court of Oregon.

1983—Confederated Tribes of Grand Ronde win restoration of trust relationship.

1984—Confederated Tribes of Coos, Lower Umpqua and Siuslaw Indians win restoration of trust relationship.

1985—Vera Katz becomes first woman speaker of Oregon House of Representatives.

1986—Klamath Tribe wins restoration of trust relationship.

1986—MAX (Metropolitan Area Express) light rail begins operation.

1986—China Gateway, the second largest in the United States, is dedicated.

1987—Oregon Vietnam Veterans' Living Memorial dedicated in Portland.

1988—State Capitol is 50 years old, officially listed in Historic Register.

1988—Grand Ronde Reservation Act signed into law, reestablishing a 9,811 acre reservation for the Confederated Tribes of the Grand Ronde Community.

1990—The Northern Spotted Owl listed as a threatened species by the U.S. Department of Fish and Wildlife.

1990—Oregon Convention Center is opened.

1990—Voters passed Ballot Measure 5, limiting property taxes for schools and government operations.

1991—Barbara Roberts inaugurated as Oregon's first woman governor.

1992—James A. Hill Jr. elected as first black state official.

1993—Oregon Trail 150th Anniversary Celebration.

1993—Oregon holds the nation's first statewide vote-by-mail election.

1995—Beverly Clarno becomes first Republican woman to serve as speaker of the Oregon House of Representatives.

1996—Oregon conducts the first vote-by-mail election for a federal office.

1996—Douglas Franklin Wright is executed at the Oregon State Penitentiary—the state's first in 34 years.

Act of Congress Admitting Oregon into the Union

Preamble

Whereas the people of Oregon have framed, ratified and adopted a constitution of state government which is republican in form, and in conformity with the Constitution of the United States and have applied for admission into the Union on an equal footing with the other states; therefore —

1. Admission of State—Boundaries

That Oregon be, and she is hereby, received into the Union on an equal footing with the other states in all respects whatever, with the following boundaries: In order that the boundaries of the state may be known and established, it is hereby ordained and declared that the State of Oregon shall be bounded as follows, to wit: Beginning one marine league at sea, due west from the point where the forty-second parallel of north latitude intersects the same, thence northerly, at the same distance from the line of the coast lying west and opposite the state, including all islands within the jurisdiction of the United States, to a point due west and opposite the middle of the north ship channel of the Columbia River; thence easterly, to and up the middle channel of said river, and, where it is divided by islands, up the middle and widest channel thereof,

to a point near Fort Walla Walla, where the forty-sixth parallel of north latitude crosses said river, thence east, on said parallel, to the middle of the main channel of the Shoshone or Snake River; thence up the middle of the main channel of said river, to the mouth of the Owyhee River; thence due south, to the parallel of latitude forty-two degrees north; thence west, along said parallel, to the place of beginning, including jurisdiction in civil and criminal cases upon the Columbia River and Snake River, concurrently with states and territories of which those rivers form a boundary in common with this state.

2. Concurrent Jurisdiction on Columbia & Other Rivers—Navigable Waters to be Common Highways

The said State of Oregon shall have concurrent jurisdiction on the Columbia and all other rivers and waters bordering on the said State of Oregon, so far as the same shall form a common boundary to said state, and any other state or states now or hereafter to be formed or bounded by the same; and said rivers and waters, and all the navigable waters of said state, shall be common highways and forever free, as well as to the inhabitants of said state as to all other citizens of the United States, without any tax, duty & impost, or toll thereof.

3. Representation in Congress

Until the next census and apportionment of representatives, the State of

The Umatilla County Clock Tower and Courtyard in Pendleton were dedicated in 1989. Construction was funded in part by selling name-inscribed bricks which were used to pave the pathway and courtyard at the base of the tower.

Photo courtesy of Umatilla County Commissioners.

History

Oregon shall be entitled to one representative in the Congress of the United States.

4. Propositions Submitted to People of State

The following propositions be and the same are hereby offered to the said people of Oregon for their free acceptance or rejection, which, if accepted, shall be obligatory on the United States and upon the said State of Oregon, to wit:

School Lands

First, that sections numbered sixteen and thirty-six in every township of public lands in said state, and where either of said sections, or any part thereof, has been sold or otherwise disposed of, other lands equivalent thereto, and as contiguous as may be, shall be granted to said state for the use of schools.

University Lands

Second, the seventy-two sections of land shall be set apart and reserved for the use and support of a state university, to be selected by the Governor of said state, subject to the approval of the Commissioner of the General Land Office, and to be appropriated and applied in such manner as the legislature of said state may prescribe for the purpose aforesaid, but for no other purpose.

Lands For Public Buildings

Third, that ten entire sections of land, to be selected by the Governor of said state, in legal subdivisions, shall be granted to said state for the purpose of completing the public buildings, or for the erection of others at the seat of government, under the direction of the legislature thereof.

Salt Springs & Contiguous Lands

Fourth, that all salt springs within said state, not exceeding twelve in number, with six sections of land adjoining, or as contiguous as may be to each, shall be granted to said state for its use, the same to be selected by the Governor thereof within one year after the admission of said state, and when so selected, to be used or disposed of on such terms, conditions and regulations as the legislature shall direct; provided, that no salt spring or land, the right whereof is now vested in any individual or individuals, or which may be hereafter confirmed or adjudged to any individual or individuals, shall by this article be granted to said state.

Percentage on Land Sales

Fifth, that 5 per centum of the net proceeds of sales of all public lands lying within said state which shall be sold by Congress after the admission of said state into the Union, after deducting all the expenses incident to the same, shall be paid to said state, for the purpose of making public roads and internal improvements, as the legislature shall direct; provided, that the foregoing propositions, hereinbefore offered, are on the condition that the people of Oregon shall provide by an ordinance, irrevocable without the consent of the United States, that said state shall never interfere with the primary disposal of the soil within the same by the United States, or with any regulations Congress may find necessary for securing the title in said soil to bona fide purchasers thereof; and that in no case shall nonresident proprietors be taxed higher than residents.

Conditions on Which Propositions Are Offered

Sixth, and that the state shall never tax the lands or the property of the United States in said state; provided, however, that in case any of the lands herein granted to the State of Oregon have heretofore been confirmed to the Territory of Oregon for the purposes specified in this act, the amount so confirmed shall be deducted from the quantity specified in this act.

5. Residue of Territory

Until Congress shall otherwise direct, the residue of the Territory of Oregon shall be and is hereby incorporated into and made a part of the Territory of Washington.

Approved February 14, 1859.

Proposition of Congress accepted by the Legislative Assembly of the State of Oregon on June 3, 1859.

CONSTITUTION

Yak herd grazes below the Elkhorn Mountains in Union County. Thee Farm has the largest all black yak herd in North America. Photo courtesy of Thee Farm.

S INCE 1859, Oregon's Constitution has provided the framework for the state's government and judicial systems. Over the years, Oregonians have voted numerous times to amend the Constitution. Since the adoption of the initiative process in 1902, Oregon's citizens have had the right to place Constitutional amendments on the statewide ballot by circulating petitions among residents of the state. The following pages contain the Constitution of Oregon, including amendments resulting from the November 1996 election.

Constitution of Oregon
1996 EDITION

The Oregon Constitution was framed by a convention of 60 delegates chosen by the people. The convention met on the third Monday in August 1857 and adjourned on September 18 of the same year. On November 9, 1857, the Constitution was approved by the vote of the people of Oregon Territory. The Act of Congress admitting Oregon into the Union was approved February 14, 1859, and on that date the Constitution went into effect.

The Constitution is here published as it is in effect following the approval of amendments on November 5, 1996. The text of the original signed copy of the Constitution filed in the office of the Secretary of State is retained unless it has been repealed or superseded by amendment. Where the original text has been amended or where a new provision has been added to the original Constitution, the source of the amendment or addition is indicated in the source note immediately following the text of the amended or new section. Notations also have been made setting out the history of repealed sections.

Unless otherwise specifically noted, the lead lines for the sections have been supplied by the Legislative Counsel.

PREAMBLE

We the people of the State of Oregon to the end that Justice be established, order maintained, and liberty perpetuated, do ordain this Constitution.—

Section 1. Natural rights inherent in people. We declare that all men, when they form a social compact are equal in right: that all power is inherent in the people, and all free governments are founded on their authority, and instituted for their peace, safety, and happiness; and they have at all times a right to alter, reform, or abolish the government in such manner as they may think proper.—

Section 2. Freedom of worship. All men shall be secure in the Natural right, to worship Almighty God according to the dictates of their own consciences.—

Section 3. Freedom of religious opinion. No law shall in any case whatever control the free exercise, and enjoyment of religeous (sic) opinions, or interfere with the rights of conscience.—

Section 4. No religious qualification for office. No religious test shall be required as a qualification for any office of trust or profit.—

Section 5. No money to be appropriated for religion. No money shall be drawn from the Treasury for the benefit of any religeous (sic), or theological institution, nor shall any money be appropriated for the payment of any religeous (sic) services in either house of the Legislative Assembly.—

Section 6. No religious test for witnesses or jurors. No person shall be rendered incompetent as a witness, or juror in consequence of his opinions on matters of religeon (sic); nor be questioned in any Court of Justice touching his religeous (sic) belief to affect the weight of his testimony.—

Section 7. Manner of administering oath or affirmation. The mode of administering an oath, or affirmation shall be such as may be most consistent with, and binding upon the conscience of the person to whom such oath or affirmation may be administered.—

Section 8. Freedom of speech and press. No law shall be passed restraining the free expression of opinion, or restricting the right to speak, write, or print freely on any subject whatever; but every person shall be responsible for the abuse of this right.—

Section 9. Unreasonable searches or seizures. No law shall violate the right of the people to be secure in their persons, houses, papers, and effects, against unreasonable search, or seizure; and no warrant shall issue but upon probable cause, supported by oath, or affirmation, and particularly describing the place to be searched, and the person or thing to be seized.—

Section 10. Administration of justice. No court shall be secret, but justice shall be administered, openly and without purchase, completely and without delay, and every man shall have remedy by due course of law for injury done him in his person, property, or reputation.—

Section 11. Rights of accused in criminal prosecution. In all criminal prosecutions, the accused shall have the right to public trial by an impartial jury in the county in which the offense shall have been committed; to be heard by himself and counsel; to demand the nature and cause of the accusation against him, and to have a copy thereof; to meet the witnesses face to face, and to have compulsory process for obtaining witnesses in his favor; provided, however, that any accused person, in other than capital cases, and with the consent of the trial judge, may elect to waive trial by jury and consent to be tried by the judge of the court alone, such election to be in writing; provided, however, that in the circuit court ten members of the jury may render a verdict of guilty or not guilty, save and except a verdict of guilty of first degree murder, which shall be found only by a unanimous verdict, and not otherwise; provided further, that the existing laws and constitutional provisions relative to criminal prosecutions shall be continued and remain in effect as to all prosecutions for crimes committed before the taking effect of this amendment. [Constitution of 1859; Amendment proposed by S.J.R. No. 4, 1931, and adopted by people Nov. 8, 1932; Amendment proposed by S.J.R. No. 4, 1933 (2d s.s.), and adopted by people May 18, 1934]

Note: The lead line to section 11 was a part of the measure submitted to the people by S.J.R. No. 4, 1933 (2d s.s.).

Section 12. Double jeopardy; compulsory self-incrimination. No person shall be put in jeopardy twice for the same offence (sic), nor be compelled in any criminal prosecution to testify against himself.—

Section 13. Treatment of arrested or confined persons. No person arrested, or confined in jail, shall be treated with unnecessary rigor.—

Section 14. Bailable offenses. Offences (sic), except murder, and treason, shall be bailable by sufficient sureties. Murder or treason, shall not

Constitution

be bailable, when the proof is evident, or the presumption strong.—

Section 15. Foundation principles of criminal law.
Laws for the punishment of crime shall be founded on these principles: protection of society, personal responsibility, accountability for one's actions and reformation. [Constitution of 1859; Amendment proposed by S.J.R. 32, 1995, and adopted by the people Nov. 5, 1996]

Section 16. Excessive bail and fines; cruel and unusual punishments; power of jury in criminal case.
Excessive bail shall not be required, nor excessive fines imposed. Cruel and unusual punishments shall not be inflicted, but all penalties shall be proportioned to the offense.—In all criminal cases whatever, the jury shall have the right to determine the law, and the facts under the direction of the Court as to the law, and the right of new trial, as in civil cases.

Section 17. Jury trial in civil cases.
In all civil cases the right of Trial by Jury shall remain inviolate.—

Section 18. Private property or services taken for public use.
Private property shall not be taken for public use, nor the particular services of any man be demanded, without just compensation; nor except in the case of the state, without such compensation first assessed and tendered; provided, that the use of all roads, ways and waterways necessary to promote the transportation of the raw products of mine or farm or forest or water for beneficial use or drainage is necessary to the development and welfare of the state and is declared a public use. [Constitution of 1859; Amendment proposed by S.J.R. No. 17, 1919, and adopted by people May 21, 1920; Amendment proposed by S.J.R. No. 8, 1923, and adopted by people Nov. 4, 1924]

Section 19. Imprisonment for debt.
There shall be no imprisonment for debt, except in case of fraud or absconding debtors.—

Section 20. Equality of privileges and immunities of citizens.
No law shall be passed granting to any citizen or class of citizens privileges, or immunities, which, upon the same terms, shall not equally belong to all citizens.—

Section 21. Ex-post facto laws; laws impairing contracts; laws depending on authorization in order to take effect; laws submitted to electors.
No ex-post facto law, or law impairing the obligation of contracts shall ever be passed, nor shall any law be passed, the taking effect of which shall be made to depend upon any authority, except as provided in this Constitution; provided, that laws locating the Capitol of the State, locating County Seats, and submitting town, and corporate acts, and other local, and Special laws may take effect, or not, upon a vote of the electors interested.—

Section 22. Suspension of operation of laws.
The operation of the laws shall never be suspended, except by the Authority of the Legislative Assembly.

Section 23. Habeas corpus.
The privilege of the writ of habeas corpus shall not be suspended unless in case of rebellion, or invasion the public safety require it.—

Section 24. Treason.
Treason against the State shall consist only in levying war against it, or adhering to its enemies, giving them aid or comfort.—No person shall be convicted of treason unless on the testimony of two witnesses to the same overt act, or confession in open Court.—

Section 25. Corruption of blood or forfeiture of estate.
No conviction shall work corruption of blood, or forfeiture of estate.—

Section 26. Assemblages of people; instruction of representatives; application to legislature.
No law shall be passed restraining any of the inhabitants of the State from assembling together in a peaceable manner to consult for their common good; nor from instructing their Representatives; nor from applying to the Legislature for redress of greviances (sic).—

Section 27. Right to bear arms; military subordinate to civil power.
The people shall have the right to bear arms for the defence (sic) of themselves, and the State, but the Military shall be kept in strict subordination to the civil power[.]

Section 28. Quartering soldiers.
No soldier shall, in time of peace, be quartered in any house, without the consent of the owner, nor in time of war, except in the manner prescribed by law.

Section 29. Titles of nobility; hereditary distinctions.
No law shall be passed granting any title of Nobility, or conferring hereditary distinctions.—

Section 30. Emigration.
No law shall be passed prohibiting emigration from the State.—

Section 31. Rights of aliens; immigration to state.
[Constitution of 1859; repeal proposed by H.J.R. 16, 1969, and adopted by people May 26, 1970]

Section 32. Taxes and duties; uniformity of taxation.
No tax or duty shall be imposed without the consent of the people or their representatives in the Legislative Assembly; and all taxation shall be uniform on the same class of subjects within the territorial limits of the authority levying the tax. [Constitution of 1859; Amendment proposed by H.J.R. No. 16, 1917, and adopted by people June 4, 1917]

Section 33. Enumeration of rights not exclusive.
This enumeration of rights, and privileges shall not be construed to impair or deny others retained by the people.—

Section 34. Slavery or involuntary servitude.
There shall be neither slavery, nor involuntary servitude in the State, otherwise than as a punishment for crime, whereof the party shall have been duly convicted.—[Added to Bill of Rights as unnumbered section by vote of people at time of adoption of the Oregon Constitution in accordance with section 4 of Article XVIII thereof]

Section 35. Free negroes and mulattoes.
[Added to Bill of Rights as unnumbered section by vote of people at time of adoption of the Oregon Constitution in accordance with Section 4 of Article XVIII thereof; Repeal proposed by H.J.R. No. 8, 1925, and adopted by people Nov. 2, 1926]

Section 36. Liquor prohibition.
[Created through initiative petition filed July 1, 1914, adopted by people Nov. 3, 1914; Repeal proposed by initiative petition filed March 20, 1933, and adopted by people July 21, 1933]

Section 36. Capital punishment abolished.
[Created through initiative petition filed July 2, 1914, adopted by people Nov. 3, 1914; Repeal proposed by S.J.R. No. 8, 1920 (s.s.), and adopted by people May 21, 1920, as Const. Art. I, §38]

Note: At the general election in 1914 two sections, each designated as section 36, were created and added to the Constitution by separate initiative petitions. One of these sections was the prohibition section and the other abolished capital punishment.

Section 36a. Prohibition of importation of liquors.
[Created through initiative petition filed July 6, 1916, adopted by people Nov. 7, 1916; Repeal proposed by initiative petition filed March 20, 1933, and adopted by people July 21, 1933]

Section 37. Penalty for murder in first degree.
[Created through S.J.R. No. 8, 1920, adopted by people

May 21, 1920; Repeal proposed by S.J.R. No. 3, 1963, and adopted by people Nov. 3, 1964]

Section 38. Laws abrogated by amendment abolishing death penalty revived. [Created through S.J.R. No. 8, 1920, adopted by people May 21, 1920; Repeal proposed by S.J.R. No. 3, 1963, and adopted by people Nov. 3, 1964]

Section 39. Sale of liquor by individual glass. The State shall have power to license private clubs, fraternal organizations, veterans' organizations, railroad corporations operating interstate trains and commercial establishments where food is cooked and served, for the purpose of selling alcoholic liquor by the individual glass at retail, for consumption on the premises, including mixed drinks and cocktails, compounded or mixed on the premises only. The Legislative Assembly shall provide in such detail as it shall deem advisable for carrying out and administering the provisions of this amendment and shall provide adequate safeguards to carry out the original intent and purpose of the Oregon Liquor Control Act, including the promotion of temperance in the use and consumption of alcoholic beverages, encourage the use and consumption of lighter beverages and aid in the establishment of Oregon industry. This power is subject to the following:

(1) The provisions of this amendment shall take effect and be in operation sixty (60) days after the approval and adoption by the people of Oregon; provided, however, the right of a local option election exists in the counties and in any incorporated city or town containing a population of at least five hundred (500). The Legislative Assembly shall prescribe a means and a procedure by which the voters of any county or incorporated city or town as limited above in any county, may through a local option election determine whether to prohibit or permit such power, and such procedure shall specifically include that whenever fifteen per cent (15%) of the registered voters of any county in the state or of any incorporated city or town as limited above, in any county in the state, shall file a petition requesting an election in this matter, the question shall be voted upon at the next regular November biennial election, provided said petition is filed not less than sixty (60) days before the day of election.

(2) Legislation relating to this matter shall operate uniformly throughout the state and all individuals shall be treated equally; and all provisions shall be liberally construed for the accomplishment of these purposes. [Created through initiative petition filed July 2, 1952, adopted by people Nov. 4, 1952]

Section 40. Penalty for aggravated murder. Notwithstanding sections 15 and 16 of this Article, the penalty for aggravated murder as defined by law shall be death upon unanimous affirmative jury findings as provided by law and otherwise shall be life imprisonment with minimum sentence as provided by law. [Created through initiative petition filed July 6, 1983, adopted by people Nov. 6, 1984]

Section 41. Work and training for corrections institution inmates. (1) Whereas the people of the state of Oregon find and declare that inmates who are confined in corrections institutions should work as hard as the taxpayers who provide for their upkeep; and whereas the people also find and declare that inmates confined within corrections institutions must be fully engaged in productive activity if they are to successfully re-enter society with practical skills and a viable work ethic; now, therefore, the people declare:

(2) All inmates of state corrections institutions shall be actively engaged full-time in work or on-the-job training. The work or on-the-job training programs shall be established and overseen by the corrections director, who shall ensure that such programs are cost-effective and are designed to develop inmate motivation, work capabilities and cooperation. Such programs may include boot camp prison programs. Education may be provided to inmates as part of work or on-the-job training so long as each inmate is engaged at least half-time in hands-on training or work activity.

(3) Each inmate shall begin full-time work or on-the-job training immediately upon admission to a corrections institution, allowing for a short time for administrative intake and processing. The specific quantity of hours per day to be spent in work or on-the-job training shall be determined by the corrections director, but the overall time spent in work or training shall be full-time. The corrections director may reduce or exempt participation in work or training programs by those inmates deemed by corrections officials as physically or mentally disabled, or as too dangerous to society to engage in such programs.

(4) There shall be sufficient work and training programs to ensure that every eligible inmate is productively involved in one or more programs. Where an inmate is drug and alcohol addicted so as to prevent the inmate from effectively participating in work or training programs, corrections officials shall provide appropriate drug or alcohol treatment.

(5) The intent of the people is that taxpayer-supported institutions and programs shall be free to benefit from inmate work. Prison work programs shall be designed and carried out so as to achieve net cost savings in maintaining government operations, or so as to achieve a net profit in private sector activities.

(6) The provisions of this section are mandatory for all state corrections institutions. The provisions of this section are permissive for county or city corrections facilities. No law, ordinance or charter shall prevent or restrict a county or city governing body from implementing all or part of the provisions of this section. Compensation, if any, shall be determined and established by the governing body of the county or city which chooses to engage in prison work programs, and the governing body may choose to adopt any power or exemption allowed in this section.

(7) The corrections director shall contact public and private enterprises in this state and seek proposals to use inmate work. The corrections director may: (a) install and equip plants in any state corrections institution, or any other location, for the employment or training of any of the inmates therein; or (b) purchase, acquire, install, maintain and operate materials, machinery and appliances necessary to the conduct and operation of such plants. The corrections director shall use every effort to enter into contracts or agreements with private business concerns or government agencies to accomplish the production or marketing of products or services produced or performed by inmates.

(8) Compensation, if any, for inmates who engage in prison work programs shall be determined and established by the corrections director. Such compensation shall not be subject to

existing public or private sector minimum or prevailing wage laws, except where required to comply with federal law. Inmate compensation from enterprises entering into agreements with the state shall be exempt from unemployment compensation taxes to the extent allowed under federal law. Inmate injury or disease attributable to any inmate work shall be covered by a corrections system inmate injury fund rather than the workers compensation law. Any compensation earned through prison work programs shall only be used for the following purposes: (a) reimbursement for all or a portion of the costs of the inmate's rehabilitation, housing, health care, and living costs; (b) restitution or compensation to the victims of the particular inmate's crime; (c) restitution or compensation to the victims of crime generally through a fund designed for that purpose; (d) financial support for immediate family of the inmate outside the corrections institution; and (e) payment of fines, court costs, and applicable taxes.

(9) All income generated from prison work programs shall be kept in a separate account and shall only be used for implementing, maintaining and developing prison work programs. Prison industry work programs shall be exempt from statutory competitive bid and purchase requirements. Expenditures for prison work programs shall be exempt from the legislative appropriations process to the extent the programs rely on income sources other than state taxes and fees. Where state taxes or fees are the source of capital or operating expenditures, the appropriations shall be made by the legislative assembly. The state programs shall be run in a businesslike fashion and shall be subject to regulation by the Prison Industries Board, consisting of the Governor, Secretary of State, and State Treasurer. The Board shall meet at least quarterly and shall act by vote of any two of the three members. Expenditures from the state prison work programs account must be approved by the Board. Agreements with private enterprise as to state prison work programs must be approved by the Board. The corrections director shall make all state records available for public scrutiny and the records shall be subject to audit by the Secretary of State.

(10) Prison work products or services shall be available to any public agency and to any private enterprise without restriction imposed by any state or local law, ordinance or regulation as to competition with other public or private sector enterprises. The products and services of corrections work programs shall be provided on such terms as are approved by the corrections director.

(11) Inmate work shall be used as much as possible to help operate the corrections institutions themselves and to support other government operations. This work includes, but is not limited to, institutional food production; maintenance and repair of buildings, grounds, and equipment; office support services, including printing; prison clothing production and maintenance; prison medical services; training other inmates; agricultural and forestry work, in parks and public forest lands; and environmental clean-up projects. Every state agency shall cooperate with the corrections director in establishing inmate work programs.

(12) As used throughout this section, unless the context requires otherwise: "full-time" means the equivalent of at least forty hours per seven day

week; "corrections director" means the person in charge of the state corrections system.

(13) This section is self-implementing and supersedes all existing inconsistent statutes. This section shall become effective April 1, 1995. If any part of this section or its application to any person or circumstance is held to be invalid for any reason, then the remaining parts or applications to any persons or circumstances shall not be affected but shall remain in full force and effect. [Created through initiative petition filed Jan. 12, 1994, adopted by people Nov. 8, 1994]

Note: Added to Article I as unnumbered section by initiative petition (Measure No. 17) adopted by people Nov. 8, 1994.

Note: The text of subsection (1) of section 42 is preceded by a preamble that reads as follows:

PREAMBLE: This initiative is designed to preserve and protect crime victims' rights to justice and due process and to ensure the prosecution and conviction of persons who have committed criminal acts. It shall be interpreted to accomplish these ends.

Section 42. Crime victims' rights. (1) To ensure crime victims a meaningful role in the criminal and juvenile justice system, to accord them due dignity and respect, and to ensure that persons who violate laws for the punishment of crime are apprehended, convicted and punished, the following rights are hereby granted to victims in all prosecutions for crimes and juvenile delinquency proceedings:

(a) The right to be reasonably protected from the criminal defendant or the convicted criminal throughout the criminal justice process; decisions as to the pretrial release of the defendant are to be based on the principle of reasonable protection of the victim and the public; any person arrested for a crime for which the People have set a mandatory minimum sentence shall not be released prior to trial unless a court determines by clear and convincing evidence that the person will not commit new criminal offenses while on release;

(b) The right to be present at, to be heard at, and, upon specific request, to be informed in advance of any critical stage of the proceedings where the criminal defendant is present, including trial;

(c) The right, upon request, to information about the conviction, sentence, imprisonment, criminal history and future release from physical custody of the criminal defendant or convicted criminal;

(d) The right to refuse an interview, deposition or other discovery request by the defendant, the defendant's attorney, or other person acting on behalf of the defendant;

(e) The right to receive prompt restitution from the person or persons convicted of the criminal conduct that caused the victim's loss or injury.

(f) The right to have all relevant evidence admissible against the criminal defendant;

(g) The right, in a criminal prosecution, to a public trial without delay by a jury selected from registered voters and composed of persons who have not been convicted of a felony or served a felony sentence within the last 15 years, except that no court shall hold that a jury is required in juvenile court delinquency proceedings.

(h) The right to have eleven members of the jury render a verdict of guilty of aggravated murder or murder, notwithstanding any other law or provision of this Constitution;

(i) The right to have a copy of a transcript of any court proceeding, if one is otherwise prepared;

(j) The right that no law shall permit a sentence imposed by a judge in open court to be set aside or otherwise not carried out except through the reprieve, commutation, and pardon power of the governor or pursuant to appellate or post-conviction relief;

(k) The right that no law shall limit the court's authority to sentence a criminal defendant consecutively for crimes against different victims;

(l) The right to have all charges against a criminal defendant tried in a single trial; subject to rules regarding venue;

(m) The right to be consulted, upon request, regarding plea negotiations involving any violent felony; and

(n) The right to be informed of these rights as soon as reasonably practicable.

(2) The rights conferred on victims by this section shall be limited only to the extent required by the United States Constitution; Section 9, Article I and Section 12, Article I of this Constitution shall not be construed more broadly than the United States Constitution and in criminal cases involving a victim, the validity of prior convictions shall not be litigated except to the extent required by the United States Constitution.

(3) This section shall not reduce a criminal defendant's rights under the United States Constitution, reduce any existing right of the press, or affect any existing statutory rule relating to privilege or hearsay.

(4) As to the decision to initiate criminal or juvenile proceedings and as to the conduct and prosecution of such proceedings, it is the district attorney who is authorized to assert the rights conferred on victims by this section.

(5) "Victim" means persons who have suffered financial, social, psychological or physical harm as a result of a crime or juvenile offense, and includes, in the case of a homicide, a member of the immediate family of the decedent, and, in the case of a minor victim, the legal guardian of the minor. In no event shall the criminal defendant be considered a victim. In criminal cases not involving a victim, the people of the State of Oregon, represented by the State of Oregon, shall have the same rights conferred by this section on victims.

(6) "Relevant evidence" means evidence having any tendency to prove the charge against the criminal defendant or establish the proper sentence for the criminal defendant.

(7) In criminal cases prosecuted by a municipality, "district attorney" as used in this section includes the city attorney.

(8) "Criminal defendant" includes juvenile offenders in juvenile court delinquency proceedings.

(9) This section creates no new civil liabilities.
[Created through initiative petition filed Oct. 19, 1995, and adopted by people Nov. 5, 1996]

Note: Added to Article I as unnumbered section by initiative petition (Measure No. 40, 1996) adopted by people Nov. 5, 1996.

ARTICLE II
SUFFRAGE AND ELECTIONS

Section 1. Elections free. All elections shall be free and equal.—

Section 2. Qualifications of electors. (1) Every citizen of the United States is entitled to vote in all elections not otherwise provided for by this Constitution if such citizen:

(a) Is 18 years of age or older;

(b) Has resided in this state during the six months immediately preceding the election, except that provision may be made by law to permit a person who has resided in this state less than 30 days immediately preceding the election, but who is otherwise qualified under this subsection, to vote in the election for candidates for nomination or election for President or Vice President of the United States or elector of President and Vice President of the United States; and

(c) Is registered not less than 20 calendar days immediately preceding any election in the manner provided by law.

(2) Except as otherwise provided in section 6, Article VIII of this Constitution with respect to the qualifications of voters in all school district elections, provision may be made by law to require that persons who vote upon questions of levying special taxes or issuing public bonds shall be taxpayers. [Constitution of 1859; Amendment proposed by initiative petition filed Dec. 20, 1910, and adopted by people Nov. 5, 1912; Amendment proposed by S.J.R. No. 6, 1913, and adopted by people Nov. 3, 1914; Amendment proposed by S.J.R. No. 6, 1923, and adopted by people Nov. 4, 1924; Amendment proposed by H.J.R. No. 7, 1927, and adopted by people June 28, 1927; Amendment proposed by H.J.R. No. 5, 1931, and adopted by people Nov. 8, 1932; Amendment proposed by H.J.R. No. 26, 1959, and adopted by people Nov. 8, 1960; Amendment proposed by H.J.R. No. 41, 1973, and adopted by people Nov. 5, 1974; Amendment proposed by initiative petition filed July 20, 1986, and adopted by people Nov. 4, 1986]

Section 3. Rights of certain electors. A person suffering from a mental handicap is entitled to the full rights of an elector, if otherwise qualified, unless the person has been adjudicated incompetent to vote as provided by law.

Constitution

431

The privilege of an elector, upon conviction of any crime which is punishable by imprisonment in the penitentiary, shall be forfeited, unless otherwise provided by law. [Constitution of 1859; Amendment proposed by S.J.R. No. 9, 1943, and adopted by people Nov. 7, 1944; Amendment proposed by S.J.R. No. 26, 1979, and adopted by people Nov. 4, 1980]

Section 4. Residence. For the purpose of voting, no person shall be deemed to have gained, or lost a residence, by reason of his presence, or absence while employed in the service of the United States, or of this State; nor while engaged in the navigation of the waters of this State, or of the United States, or of the high seas; nor while a student of any Seminary of Learning; nor while kept at any alms house, or other assylum (sic), at public expence (sic); nor while confined in any public prison.—

Section 5. Soldiers, seamen and marines; residence; right to vote. No soldier, seaman, or marine in the Army, or Navy of the United States, or of their allies, shall be deemed to have acquired a residence in the state, in consequence of having been stationed within the same; nor shall any such soldier, seaman, or marine have the right to vote.—

Section 6. Negroes, Chinamen and mulattoes. [Constitution of 1859; Repeal proposed by H.J.R. No. 4, 1927, and adopted by people June 28, 1927]

Section 7. Bribery at elections. Every person shall be disqualified from holding office, during the term for which he may have been elected, who shall have given, or offered a bribe, threat, or reward to procure his election.—

Section 8. Regulation of elections. The Legislative Assembly shall enact laws to support the privilege of free suffrage, prescribing the manner of regulating, and conducting elections, and prohibiting under adequate penalties, all undue influence therein, from power, bribery, tumult, and other improper conduct.—

Section 9. Penalty for dueling. Every person who shall give, or accept a challenge to fight a duel, or who shall knowingly carry to another person such challenge, or who shall agree to go out of the State to fight a duel, shall be ineligible to any office of trust, or profit.—

Section 10. Lucrative offices; holding other offices forbidden. No person holding a lucrative office, or appointment under the United States, or under this State, shall be deemed to be eligible to a seat in the Legislative Assembly; nor shall any person hold more than one lucrative office at the same time, except as in this Constitution (sic) expressly permitted; Provided, that Officers in the Militia, to which there is attached no annual salary, and the Office of Post Master, where the compensation does not exceed One Hundred Dollars per annum, shall not be deemed lucrative.—

Section 11. When collector or holder of public moneys ineligible to office. No person who may hereafter be a collector, or holder of public moneys, shall be eligible to any office of trust or profit, until he shall have accounted for, and paid over according to law, all sums for which he may be liable. -

Section 12. Temporary appointments to office. In all cases, in which it is provided that an office shall not be filled by the same person, more than a certain number of years continuously, an appointment pro tempore shall not be reckoned a part of that term.—

Section 13. Privileges of electors. In all cases, except treason, felony, and breach of the peace, electors shall be free from arrest in going to elections, during their attendance there, and in returning from the same; and no elector shall be obliged to do duty in the Militia on any day of election, except in time of war, or public danger.—

Section 14. Time of holding elections and assuming duties of office. The regular general biennial election in Oregon for the year A. D. 1910 and thereafter shall be held on the first Tuesday after the first Monday in November. All officers except the Governor, elected for a six year term in 1904 or for a four year term in 1906 or for a two year term in 1908 shall continue to hold their respective offices until the first Monday in January, 1911; and all officers, except the Governor elected at any regular general biennial election after the adoption of this amendment shall assume the duties of their respective offices on the first Monday in January following such election. All laws pertaining to the nomination of candidates, registration of voters and all other things incident to the holding of the regular biennial election shall be enforced and be effected the same number of days before the first Tuesday after the first Monday in November that they have heretofore been before the first Monday in June biennially, except as may hereafter be provided by law. [Constitution of 1859; Amendment proposed by H.J.R. No. 7, 1907, and adopted by people June 1, 1908]

Section 14a. Time of holding elections in incorporated cities and towns. Incorporated cities and towns shall hold their nominating and regular elections for their several elective officers at the same time that the primary and general biennial elections for State and county officers are held, and the election precincts and officers shall be the same for all elections held at the same time. All provisions of the charters and ordinances of incorporated cities and towns pertaining to the holding of elections shall continue in full force and effect except so far as they relate to the time of holding such elections. Every officer who, at the time of the adoption of this amendment, is the duly qualified incumbent of an elective office of an incorporated city or town shall hold his office for the term for which he was elected and until his successor is elected and qualified. The Legislature, and cities and towns, shall enact such supplementary legislation as may be necessary to carry the provisions of this amendment into effect. [Created through H.J.R. No. 22, 1917, and adopted by people June 4, 1917]

Section 15. Method of voting in legislature. In all elections by the Legislative Assembly, or by either branch thereof, votes shall be given openly or viva voce, and not by ballot, forever; and in all elections by the people, votes shall be given openly, or viva voce, until the Legislative Assembly shall otherwise direct.—

Section 16. Election by plurality; proportional representation. In all elections authorized by this constitution until otherwise provided by law, the person or persons receiving the highest number of votes shall be declared elected, but provision may be made by law for elections by equal proportional representation of all the voters for every office which is filled by the election of two or more persons whose official duties, rights and powers are equal and concurrent. Every qualified elector resident in his precinct and registered as may be required by law, may vote for one person under the title for each office.

Provision may be made by law for the voter's direct or indirect expression of his first, second or additional choices among the candidates for any office. For an office which is filled by the election of one person it may be required by law that the person elected shall be the final choice of a majority of the electors voting for candidates for that office. These principles may be applied by law to nominations by political parties and organizations. [Constitution of 1859; Amendment proposed by initiative petition filed Jan. 29, 1908, and adopted by people June 1, 1908]

Section 17. Place of voting. All qualified electors shall vote in the election precinct in the County where they may reside, for County Officers, and in any County in the State for State Officers, or in any County of a Congressional District in which such electors may reside, for Members of Congress.—

Section 18. Recall; meaning of words "the legislative assembly shall provide." (1) Every public officer in Oregon is subject, as herein provided, to recall by the electors of the state or of the electoral district from which the public officer is elected.

(2) Fifteen per cent, but not more, of the number of electors who voted for Governor in the officer's electoral district at the most recent election at which a candidate for Governor was elected to a full term, may be required to file their petition demanding the officer's recall by the people.

(3) They shall set forth in the petition the reasons for the demand.

(4) If the public officer offers to resign, the resignation shall be accepted and take effect on the day it is offered, and the vacancy shall be filled as may be provided by law. If the public officer does not resign within five days after the petition is filed, a special election shall be ordered to be held within 35 days in the electoral district to determine whether the people will recall the officer.

(5) On the ballot at the election shall be printed in not more than 200 words the reasons for demanding the recall of the officer as set forth in the recall petition, and, in not more than 200 words, the officer's justification of the officer's course in office. The officer shall continue to perform the duties of office until the result of the special election is officially declared. If an officer is recalled from any public office the vacancy shall be filled immediately in the manner provided by law for filling a vacancy in that office arising from any other cause.

(6) The recall petition shall be filed with the officer with whom a petition for nomination to such office should be filed, and the same officer shall order the special election when it is required. No such petition shall be circulated against any officer until the officer has actually held the office six months, save and except that it may be filed against a senator or representative in the legislative assembly at any time after five days from the beginning of the first session after the election of the senator or representative.

(7) After one such petition and special election, no further recall petition shall be filed against the same officer during the term for which the officer was elected unless such further petitioners first pay into the public treasury which has paid such special election expenses, the whole amount of its expenses for the preceding special election.

(8) Such additional legislation as may aid the operation of this section shall be provided by the legislative assembly, including provision for payment by the public treasury of the reasonable special election campaign expenses of such officer. But the words, "the legislative assembly shall provide," or any similar or equivalent words in this constitution or any amendment thereto, shall not be construed to grant to the legislative assembly any exclusive power of lawmaking nor in any way to limit the initiative and referendum powers reserved by the people. [Created through initiative petition filed Jan. 29, 1908, adopted by people June 1, 1908; Amendment proposed by S.J.R. No. 16, 1925, and adopted by people Nov. 2, 1926; amendment proposed by H.J.R. No. 1, 1983, and adopted by people Nov. 6, 1984]

Note: The word "Recall" constituted the lead line to section 18 and was a part of the measure submitted to the people by S.J.R. No. 16, 1925.

Section 19. Limits on Oregon Terms. To promote varied representation, to broaden the opportunities for public service, and to make the electoral process fairer by reducing the power of incumbency, terms in Oregon elected offices are limited as follows:

(1) No person shall serve more than six years in the Oregon House of Representatives, eight years in the Oregon Senate, and twelve years in the Oregon Legislative Assembly in his or her lifetime.

(2) No person shall serve more than eight years in each Oregon statewide office in his or her lifetime.

(3) Only terms of service beginning after this Act [sections 19 to 21 of this Article] goes into effect [December 3, 1992] shall count towards the limits of this Section.

(4) When a person is appointed or elected to fill a vacancy in office, then such service shall be counted as one term for the purposes of this Section.

(5) A person shall not appear on the ballot as a candidate for elected office or be appointed to fill a vacancy in office if serving a full term in such office would cause them to violate the limits in this Section.

(6) This Section does not apply to judicial offices. [Created through initiative petition filed April 23, 1991, and adopted by the people Nov. 3, 1992.]

Note: The lead line to section 19 was a part of the measure proposed by initiative petition filed April 23, 1991, and adopted by the people Nov. 3, 1992.

Section 20. Limits on Congressional Terms. To promote varied representation, to broaden the opportunities for public service, and to make the electoral process fairer by reducing the power of incumbency, terms in the United States Congress representing Oregon are limited as follows:

(1) No person shall represent Oregon for more than six years in the U.S. House of Representatives and twelve years in the U.S. Senate in his or her lifetime.

(2) Only terms of service beginning after this Act [sections 19 to 21 of this Article] goes into effect [December 3, 1992] shall count towards the limits of this Section.

(3) When a person is appointed or elected to fill a vacancy in office, then such service shall be counted as one term for the purposes of this Section.

(4) A person shall not appear on the ballot as a candidate for elected office or be appointed to fill

Constitution

a vacancy in office if serving a full term in such office would cause them to violate the limits in this section. [Created through initiative petition filed April 23, 1991, and adopted by the people Nov. 3, 1992.]

Note: The lead line to section 20 was a part of the measure proposed by initiative petition filed April 23, 1991, and adopted by the people Nov. 3, 1992.

Section 21. Severability; standing. (1) If any part of this Act [sections 19 to 21 of this Article] is held to be invalid for any reason, then the remaining parts shall not be affected but shall remain in full force and effect. If any part of this Act is held to be invalid, it is the expressed intent of the People of Oregon that their elected officials should respect the limits within this Act.

(2) Any person residing in Oregon or non-profit entity doing business in Oregon has standing to bring suit to enforce this measure [sections 19 to 21 of this Article]. [Created through initiative petition filed April 23, 1991, and adopted by the people Nov. 3, 1992]

Note: Section 21 was designated as Paragraphs 2 and 4 in Measure No. 3, 1992, adopted by the people Nov. 3, 1992. Paragraph 3 was temporary in nature.

Note: The leadline to section 21 was a part of the measure proposed by initiative petition filed April 23, 1991, and adopted by the people Nov. 3, 1992.

Section 22. Political campaign contribution limitations. Section (1) For purposes of campaigning for an elected public office, a candidate may use or direct only contributions which originate from individuals who at the time of their donation were residents of the electoral district of the public office sought by the candidate, unless the contribution consists of volunteer time, information provided to the candidate, or funding provided by federal, state, or local government for purposes of campaigning for an elected public office.

Section (2) Where more than ten percent (10%) of a candidate's total campaign funding is in violation of Section (1), and the candidate is subsequently elected, the elected official shall forfeit the office and shall not hold a subsequent elected public office for a period equal to twice the tenure of the office sought. Where more than ten percent (10%) of a candidate's total campaign funding is in violation of Section (1) and the candidate is not elected, the unelected candidate shall not hold a subsequent elected public office for a period equal to twice the tenure of the office sought.

Section (3) A qualified donor (an individual who is a resident within the electoral district of the office sought by the candidate) shall not contribute to a candidate's campaign any restricted contributions of Section (1) received from an unqualified donor for the purpose of contributing to a candidate's campaign for elected public office. An unqualified donor (an entity which is not an individual and who is not a resident of the electoral district of the office sought by the candidate) shall not give any restricted contributions of Section (1) to a qualified donor for the purpose of contributing to a candidate's campaign for elected public office.

Section (4) A violation of Section (3) shall be an unclassified felony. [Created through initiative petition filed Jan. 25, 1993, adopted by people Nov. 8, 1994]

Note: Initiative petition (Measure No. 6) proposed constitutional amendment as unnumbered section. Sections (1), (2), (3) and (4) were designated SECTION 1., SECTION 2., SECTION 3. and SECTION 4., respectively, by

initiative petition (Measure No. 6) adopted by people Nov. 8, 1994.

ARTICLE III
DISTRIBUTION OF POWERS

Sec. 1. Separation of powers
2. Budgetary control over executive and administrative officers and agencies
3. Joint legislative committee to allocate emergency fund appropriations and to authorize expenditures beyond budgetary limits
4. Senate, confirmation of executive appointments

Section 1. Separation of powers. The powers of the Government shall be divided into three seperate (sic) departments, the Legislative, the Executive, including the administrative, and the Judicial; and no person charged with official duties under one of these departments, shall exercise any of the functions of another, except as in this Constitution expressly provided.—

Section 2. Budgetary control over executive and administrative officers and agencies. The Legislative Assembly shall have power to establish an agency to exercise budgetary control over all executive and administrative state officers, departments, boards, commissions and agencies of the State Government. [Created through S.J.R. No. 24, 1951, adopted by people Nov. 4, 1952]

Note: Section 2 was designated as "Sec. 1" by S.J.R. No. 24, 1951, adopted by people Nov. 4, 1952.

Section 3. Joint legislative committee to allocate emergency fund appropriations and to authorize expenditures beyond budgetary limits. (1) The Legislative Assembly is authorized to establish by law a joint committee composed of members of both houses of the Legislative Assembly, the membership to be as fixed by law, which committee may exercise, during the interim between sessions of the Legislative Assembly, such of the following powers as may be conferred upon it by law:

(a) Where an emergency exists, to allocate to any state agency, out of any emergency fund that may be appropriated to the committee for that purpose, additional funds beyond the amount appropriated to the agency by the Legislative Assembly, or funds to carry on an activity required by law for which an appropriation was not made.

(b) Where an emergency exists, to authorize any state agency to expend, from funds dedicated or continuously appropriated for the uses and purposes of the agency, sums in excess of the amount of the budget of the agency as approved in accordance with law.

(c) In the case of a new activity coming into existence at such a time as to preclude the possibility of submitting a budget to the Legislative Assembly for approval, to approve, or revise and approve, a budget of the money appropriated for such new activity.

(d) Where an emergency exists, to revise or amend the budgets of state agencies to the extent of authorizing transfers between expenditure classifications within the budget of an agency.

(2) The Legislative Assembly shall prescribe by law what shall constitute an emergency for the purposes of this section.

(3) As used in this section, "state agency" means any elected or appointed officer, board, commission, department, institution, branch or other agency of the state government.

(4) The term of members of the joint committee established pursuant to this section shall run from the adjournment of one regular session to the organization of the next regular session. No member of a committee shall cease to be such member solely by reason of the expiration of his term of office as a member of the Legislative Assembly. [Created through S.J.R. No. 24, 1951, adopted by people Nov. 4, 1952]

Note: Section 3 was designated as "Sec. 2" by S.J.R. No. 24, 1951, adopted by people Nov. 4, 1952.

Section 4. Senate confirmation of executive appointments. (1) The Legislative Assembly in the manner provided by law may require that all appointments and reappointments to state public office made by the Governor shall be subject to confirmation by the Senate.

(2) The appointee shall not be eligible to serve until confirmed in the manner required by law and if not confirmed in that manner, shall not be eligible to serve in the public office.

(3) In addition to appointive offices, the provisions of this section shall apply to any state elective office when the Governor is authorized by law or this Constitution to fill any vacancy therein, except the office of judge of any court, United States Senator or Representative and a district, county or precinct office. [Created through S.J.R. 20, 1977, adopted by people Nov. 7, 1978]

ARTICLE IV
LEGISLATIVE DEPARTMENT

Section 1. Legislative power; initiative and referendum. (1) The legislative power of the state, except for the initiative and referendum powers reserved to the people, is vested in a Legislative Assembly, consisting of a Senate and a House of Representatives.

(2)(a) The people reserve to themselves the initiative power, which is to propose laws and amendments to the Constitution and enact or reject them at an election independently of the Legislative Assembly.

(b) An initiative law may be proposed only by a petition signed by a number of qualified voters equal to six percent of the total number of votes cast for all candidates for Governor at the election at which a Governor was elected for a term of four years next preceding the filing of the petition.

(c) An initiative amendment to the Constitution may be proposed only by a petition signed by a number of qualified voters equal to eight percent of the total number of votes cast for all candidates for Governor at the election at which a Governor was elected for a term of four years next preceding the filing of the petition.

(d) An initiative petition shall include the full text of the proposed law or amendment to the Constitution. A proposed law or amendment to the Constitution shall embrace one subject only and matters properly connected therewith.

(e) An initiative petition shall be filed not less than four months before the election at which the proposed law or amendment to the Constitution is to be voted upon.

(3)(a) The people reserve to themselves the referendum power, which is to approve or reject at an election any Act, or part thereof, of the Legislative Assembly that does not become effective earlier than 90 days after the end of the session at which the Act is passed.

(b) A referendum on an Act or part thereof may be ordered by a petition signed by a number of qualified voters equal to four percent of the total number of votes cast for all candidates for Governor at the election at which a Governor was elected for a term of four years next preceding the filing of the petition. A referendum petition shall be filed not more than 90 days after the end of the session at which the Act is passed.

(c) A referendum on an Act may be ordered by the Legislative Assembly by law. Notwithstanding section 15b, Article V of this Constitution, bills ordering a referendum and bills on which a referendum is ordered are not subject to veto by the Governor.

(4)(a) Petitions or orders for the initiative or referendum shall be filed with the Secretary of State. The Legislative Assembly shall provide by law for the manner in which the Secretary of State shall determine whether a petition contains the required number of signatures of qualified voters. The Secretary of State shall complete the verification process within the 15-day period after the last day on which the petition may be filed as provided in paragraph (e) of subsection (2) or paragraph (b) of subsection (3) of this section.

(b) Initiative and referendum measures shall be submitted to the people as provided in this section and by law not inconsistent therewith.

Constitution

(c) All elections on initiative and referendum measures shall be held at the regular general elections, unless otherwise ordered by the Legislative Assembly.

(d) Notwithstanding section 1, Article XVII of this Constitution, an initiative or referendum measure becomes effective 30 days after the day on which it is enacted or approved by a majority of the votes cast thereon. A referendum ordered by petition on a part of an Act does not delay the remainder of the Act from becoming effective.

(5) The initiative and referendum powers reserved to the people by subsections (2) and (3) of this section are further reserved to the qualified voters of each municipality and district as to all local, special and municipal legislation of every character in or for their municipality or district. The manner of exercising those powers shall be provided by general laws, but cities may provide the manner of exercising those powers as to their municipal legislation. In a city, not more than 15 percent of the qualified voters may be required to propose legislation by the initiative, and not more than 10 percent of the qualified voters may be required to order a referendum on legislation. [Created through H.J.R. No. 16, 1967, adopted by people May 28, 1968 (this section adopted in lieu of former sections 1 and 1a of this Article); Amendment proposed by S.J.R. 27, 1985, and adopted by people May 20, 1986]

Section 1. Legislative authority vested in assembly; initiative and referendum; style of bills. [Constitution of 1859; Amendment proposed by H.J.R. No. 1, 1901, and adopted by people June 2, 1902; Amendment proposed by S.J.R. No. 6, 1953, and adopted by people Nov. 2, 1954; Repeal proposed by H.J.R. No. 16, 1967, and adopted by people May 28, 1968 (present section 1 of this Article adopted in lieu of this section)]

Section 1a. Initiative and referendum on parts of laws and on local, special and municipal laws. [Created through initiative petition filed Feb. 3, 1906, adopted by people June 4, 1906; Repeal proposed by H.J.R. No. 16, 1967, and adopted by people May 28, 1968 (present section 1 of this Article adopted in lieu of this section)]

Section 2. Number of Senators and Representatives. The Senate shall consist of sixteen, and the House of Representatives of thirty four members, which number shall not be increased until the year Eighteen Hundred and Sixty, after which time the Legislative Assembly may increase the number of Senators and Representatives, always keeping as near as may be the same ratio as to the number of Senators, and Representatives: Provided that the Senate shall never exceed thirty and the House of Representatives sixty members.—

Section 3. How Senators and Representatives chosen; filling vacancies; qualifications. (1) The senators and representatives shall be chosen by the electors of the respective counties or districts or subdistricts within a county or district into which the state may from time to time be divided by law.

(2) If a vacancy in the office of senator or representative from any county or district or subdistrict shall occur, such vacancy shall be filled as may be provided by law. A person who is appointed to fill a vacancy in the office of senator or representative shall have been an inhabitant of the district the person is appointed to represent for at least one year next preceding the date of the appointment. However, for purposes of an appointment occurring during the period beginning on January 1 of the year next following the operative date of an apportionment under section 6 of this Article, the person must have

been an inhabitant of the district for one year next preceding the date of the appointment or from January 1 of the year following the reapportionment to the date of the appointment, whichever is less. [Constitution of 1859; Amendment proposed by S.J.R. No. 20, 1929, and adopted by people Nov. 4, 1930; Amendment proposed by H.J.R. No. 20, 1953, and adopted by people Nov. 2, 1954; Amendment proposed by S.J.R. 14, 1995, and adopted by people May 16, 1995]

Section 3a. Applicability of qualifications for appointment to legislative vacancy. (1) The amendment to section 3 of this Article by Senate Joint Resolution 14 (1995) applies to any person appointed to the office of state Senator or state Representative on or after the effective date of the amendment to section 8 of this Article by Senate Joint Resolution 14 (1995).

(2) This section is repealed December 31, 1999. [Section 3a was designated section 1b, which was created by S.J.R. 14, 1995, and adopted by people May 16, 1995]

Section 4. Term of office of legislators; classification of Senators. (1) The Senators shall be elected for the term of four years, and Representatives for the term of two years. The term of each Senator and Representative shall commence on the second Monday in January following his election, and shall continue for the full period of four years or two years, as the case may be, unless a different commencing day for such terms shall have been appointed by law.

(2) The Senators shall continue to be divided into two classes, in accordance with the division by lot provided for under the former provisions of this Constitution, so that one-half, as nearly as possible, of the number of Senators shall be elected biennially.

(3) Any Senator or Representative whose term, under the former provisions of this section, would have expired on the first Monday in January 1961, shall continue in office until the second Monday in January 1961. [Constitution of 1859; Amendment proposed by S.J.R. No. 23, 1951, and adopted by people Nov. 4, 1952; Amendment proposed by S.J.R. No. 28, 1959, and adopted by people Nov. 8, 1960]

Section 5. Census. [Constitution of 1859; Repeal proposed by H.J.R. No. 16, 1971, and adopted by people May 23, 1972]

Section 6. Apportionment of Senators and Representatives. [Constitution of 1859; Amendment proposed by initiative petition filed July 3, 1952, and adopted by people Nov. 4, 1952; repeal proposed by H.J.R. 6, 1985, and adopted by people Nov. 4, 1986 (present section 6 of this Article adopted in lieu of this section)]

Section 6. Apportionment of Senators and Representatives. (1) At the regular session of the Legislative Assembly next following an enumeration of the inhabitants by the United States Government, the number of Senators and Representatives shall be fixed by law and apportioned among legislative districts according to population. A senatorial district shall consist of two representative districts. Any Senator whose term continues through the next regular legislative session after the effective date of the reapportionment shall be specifically assigned to a senatorial district. The ratio of Senators and Representatives, respectively, to population shall be determined by dividing the total population of the state by the number of Senators and by the number of Representatives. A reapportionment by the Legislative Assembly shall become operative no sooner than September 1 of the year of reapportionment.

(2) This subsection governs judicial review and correction of a reapportionment enacted by the Legislative Assembly.

(a) Original jurisdiction is vested in the Supreme Court, upon the petition of any elector of the state filed with the Supreme Court on or before August 1 of the year in which the Legislative Assembly enacts a reapportionment, to review any reapportionment so enacted.

(b) If the Supreme Court determines that the reapportionment thus reviewed complies with subsection (1) of this section and all law applicable thereto, it shall dismiss the petition by written opinion on or before September 1 of the same year and the reapportionment shall become operative on September 1.

(c) If the Supreme Court determines that the reapportionment does not comply with subsection (1) of this section and all law applicable thereto, the reapportionment shall be void. In its written opinion, the Supreme Court shall specify with particularity wherein the reapportionment fails to comply. The opinion shall further direct the Secretary of State to draft a reapportionment of the Senators and Representatives in accordance with the provisions of subsection (1) of this section and all law applicable thereto. The Supreme Court shall file its order with the Secretary of State on or before September 15. The Secretary of State shall conduct a hearing on the reapportionment at which the public may submit evidence, views and argument. The Secretary of State shall cause a transcription of the hearing to be prepared which, with the evidence, shall become part of the record. The Secretary of State shall file the corrected reapportionment with the Supreme Court on or before November 1 of the same year.

(d) On or before November 15, the Supreme Court shall review the corrected reapportionment to assure its compliance with subsection (1) of this section and all law applicable thereto and may further correct the reapportionment if the court considers correction to be necessary.

(e) The corrected reapportionment shall become operative upon November 15.

(3) This subsection governs enactment, judicial review and correction of a reapportionment if the Legislative Assembly fails to enact any reapportionment by July 1 of the year of the regular session of the Legislative Assembly next following an enumeration of the inhabitants by the United States Government.

(a) The Secretary of State shall make a reapportionment of the Senators and Representatives in accordance with the provisions of subsection (1) of this section and all law applicable thereto. The Secretary of State shall conduct a hearing on the reapportionment at which the public may submit evidence, views and argument. The Secretary of State shall cause a transcription of the hearing to be prepared which, with the evidence, shall become part of the record. The reapportionment so made shall be filed with the Supreme Court by August 15 of the same year. It shall become operative on September 15.

(b) Original jurisdiction is vested in the Supreme Court upon the petition of any elector of the state filed with the Supreme Court on or before September 15 of the same year to review any reapportionment and the record made by the Secretary of State.

(c) If the Supreme Court determines that the reapportionment thus reviewed complies with subsection (1) of this section and all law applica-

ble thereto, it shall dismiss the petition by written opinion on or before October 15 of the same year and the reapportionment shall become operative on October 15.

(d) If the Supreme Court determines that the reapportionment does not comply with subsection (1) of this section and all law applicable thereto, the reapportionment shall be void. The Supreme Court shall return the reapportionment by November 1 to the Secretary of State accompanied by a written opinion specifying with particularity wherein the reapportionment fails to comply. The opinion shall further direct the Secretary of State to correct the reapportionment in those particulars, and in no others, and file the corrected reapportionment with the Supreme Court on or before December 1 of the same year.

(e) On or before December 15, the Supreme Court shall review the corrected reapportionment to assure its compliance with subsection (1) of this section and all law applicable thereto and may further correct the reapportionment if the court considers correction to be necessary.

(f) The reapportionment shall become operative on December 15.

(4) Any reapportionment that becomes operative as provided in this section is a law of the state except for purposes of initiative and referendum. A reapportionment shall not be operative before the date on which an appeal may be taken therefrom or before the date specified in this section, whichever is later.

(5) Notwithstanding section 18, Article II of this Constitution, after the convening of the next regular legislative session following the reapportionment, a Senator whose term continues through that legislative session is subject to recall by the electors of the district to which the Senator is assigned and not by the electors of the district existing before the latest reapportionment. The number of signatures required on the recall petition is 15 percent of the total votes cast for all candidates for Governor at the most recent election at which a candidate for Governor was elected to a full term in the two representative districts comprising the senatorial district to which the Senator was assigned. [Created through H.J.R. 6, 1985, adopted by people Nov. 4, 1986 (this section adopted in lieu of former section 6 of this Article)]

Section 7. Senatorial districts; senatorial and representative subdistricts. A senatorial district, when more than one county shall constitute the same, shall be composed of contiguous counties, and no county shall be divided in creating such senatorial districts. Senatorial or representative districts comprising not more than one county may be divided into subdistricts from time to time by law. Subdistricts shall be composed of contiguous territory within the district; and the ratios to population of senators or representatives, as the case may be, elected from the subdistricts, shall be substantially equal within the district.
[Constitution of 1859; Amendment proposed by H.J.R. No. 20, 1953, and adopted by people Nov. 2, 1954]

Section 8. Qualification of Senators and Representatives; effect of felony conviction.
(1) No person shall be a Senator or Representative who at the time of election is not a citizen of the United States; nor anyone who has not been for one year next preceding the election an inhabitant of the district from which the Senator or Representative may be chosen. However, for purposes of the general election next following the operative date

of an apportionment under section 6 of this Article, the person must have been an inhabitant of the district from January 1 of the year following the reapportionment to the date of the election.

(2) Senators and Representatives shall be at least twenty one years of age.

(3) No person shall be a Senator or Representative who has been convicted of a felony during:

(a) The term of office of the person as a Senator or Representative; or

(b) The period beginning on the date of the election at which the person was elected to the office of Senator or Representative and ending on the first day of the term of office to which the person was elected.

(4) No person is eligible to be elected as a Senator or Representative if that person has been convicted of a felony and has not completed the sentence received for the conviction prior to the date that person would take office if elected. As used in this subsection, "sentence received for the conviction" includes a term of imprisonment, any period of probation or post-prison supervision and payment of a monetary obligation imposed as all or part of a sentence.

(5) Notwithstanding sections 11 and 15, Article IV of this Constitution:

(a) The office of a Senator or Representative convicted of a felony during the term to which the Senator or Representative was elected or appointed shall become vacant on the date the Senator or Representative is convicted.

(b) A person elected to the office of Senator or Representative and convicted of a felony during the period beginning on the date of the election and ending on the first day of the term of office to which the person was elected shall be ineligible to take office and the office shall become vacant on the first day of the next term of office.

(6) Subject to subsection (4) of this section, a person who is ineligible to be a Senator or Representative under subsection (3) of this section may:

(a) Be a Senator or Representative after the expiration of the term of office during which the person is ineligible; and

(b) Be a candidate for the office of Senator or Representative prior to the expiration of the term of office during which the person is ineligible.

(7) No person shall be a Senator or Representative who at all times during the term of office of the person as a Senator or Representative is not an inhabitant of the district from which the Senator or Representative may be chosen or has been appointed to represent. A person shall not lose status as an inhabitant of a district if the person is absent from the district for purposes of business of the Legislative Assembly. Following the operative date of an apportionment under section 6 of this Article, until the expiration of the term of office of the person, a person may be an inhabitant of any district. [Amendment proposed by H.J.R. 6, 1985, and adopted by people Nov. 4, 1986; Amendment proposed by S.J.R. 33, 1993, and adopted by people Nov. 8, 1994; Amendment proposed by S.J.R. 14, 1995, and adopted by people May 16, 1995]

Section 8a. Applicability of qualification for legislative office. (1) The amendment to section 8 of this Article by Senate Joint Resolution 14 (1995) applies to any person holding the office of state Senator or state Representative on or after

the effective date of the amendment to section 8 of this Article by Senate Joint Resolution 14 (1995).

(2) This section is repealed December 31, 1999. [Created by S.J.R. 14, 1995, and adopted by people May 16, 1995]

Section 9. Legislators free from arrest and not subject to civil process in certain cases; words uttered in debate. Senators and Representatives in all cases, except for treason, felony, or breaches of the peace, shall be privileged from arrest during the session of the Legislative Assembly, and in going to and returning from the same; and shall not be subject to any civil process during the session of the Legislative Assembly, nor during the fifteen days next before the commencement thereof: Nor shall a member for words uttered in debate in either house, be questioned in any other place.—

Section 10. Regular sessions of the Legislative Assembly. The sessions of the Legislative Assembly shall be held biennially at the Capitol of the State commencing on the second Monday of September, in the year eighteen hundred and fifty eight, and on the same day of every second year thereafter, unless a different day shall have been appointed by law.—

Section 10a. Emergency sessions of the Legislative Assembly. In the event of an emergency the Legislative Assembly shall be convened by the presiding officers of both Houses at the Capitol of the State at times other than required by section 10 of this Article upon the written request of the majority of the members of each House to commence within five days after receipt of the minimum requisite number of requests. [Created through H.J.R. No. 28, 1975, and adopted by the people Nov. 2, 1976]

Section 11. Legislative officers; rules of proceedings; adjournments. Each house when assembled, shall choose its own officers, judge of the election, qualifications, and returns of its own members; determine its own rules of proceeding, and sit upon its own adjournments; but neither house shall without the concurrence of the other, adjourn for more than three days, nor to any other place than that in which they may be sitting.—

Section 12. Quorum; failure to effect organization. Two thirds of each house shall constitute a quorum to do business, but a smaller number may meet; adjourn from day to day, and compel the attendance of absent members. A quorum being in attendance, if either house fail to effect an organization within the first five days thereafter, the members of the house so failing shall be entitled to no compensation from the end of the said five days until an organization shall have been effected.—

Section 13. Journal; when yeas and nays to be entered. Each house shall keep a journal of its proceedings.—The yeas and nays on any question, shall at the request of any two members, be entered, together with the names of the members demanding the same, on the journal; provided that on a motion to adjourn it shall require one tenth of the members present to order the yeas, and nays.

Section 14. Deliberations to be open; rules to implement requirement. The deliberations of each house, of committees of each house or joint committees and of committees of the whole, shall be open. Each house shall adopt rules to implement the requirement of this section and the houses jointly shall adopt rules to implement the requirements of this section in any joint activity that the two houses may undertake. [Amendment proposed by S.J.R. No. 36, 1973, and adopted by people Nov. 5, 1974; Amendment proposed by H.J.R. No. 29, 1977, and adopted by people May 23, 1978]

Section 15. Punishment and expulsion of members.
Either house may punish its members for disorderly behavior, and may with the concurrence of two thirds, expel a member; but not a second time for the same cause.—

Section 16. Punishment of nonmembers.
Either house, during its session, may punish by imprisonment, any person, not a member, who shall have been guilty of disrespect to the house by disorderly or contemptious (sic) behavior in its presence, but such imprisonment shall not at any time, exceed twenty (sic) twenty four hours.—

Section 17. General powers of Legislative Assembly.
Each house shall have all powers necessary for a branch of the Legislative Department, of a free, and independant (sic) State.—

Section 18. Where bills to originate.
Bills may originate in either house, but may be amended, or rejected in the other; except that bills for raising revenue shall originate in the House of Representatives.—

Section 19. Reading of bills; vote on final passage.
Every bill shall be read by title only on three several days, in each house, unless in case of emergency two-thirds of the house where such bill may be pending shall, by a vote of yeas and nays, deem it expedient to dispense with this rule; provided, however, on its final passage such bill shall be read section by section unless such requirement be suspended by a vote of two-thirds of the house where such bill may be pending, and the vote on the final passage of every bill or joint resolution shall be taken by yeas and nays. [Constitution of 1859; Amendment proposed by S.J.R. No. 15, 1945, and adopted by people Nov. 5, 1946]

Section 20. Subject and title of Act.
Every Act shall embrace but one subject, and matters properly connected therewith, which subject shall be expressed in the title. But if any subject shall be embraced in an Act which shall not be expressed in the title, such Act shall be void only as to so much thereof as shall not be expressed in the title.

This section shall not be construed to prevent the inclusion in an amendatory Act, under a proper title, of matters otherwise germane to the same general subject, although the title or titles of the original Act or Acts may not have been sufficiently broad to have permitted such matter to have been so included in such original Act or Acts, or any of them. [Constitution of 1859; Amendment proposed by S.J.R. No. 41, 1951, and adopted by people Nov. 4, 1952]

Section 21. Acts to be plainly worded.
Every act, and joint resolution shall be plainly worded, avoiding as far as practicable the use of technical terms.—

Section 22. Mode of revision and amendment.
No act shall ever be revised, or amended by mere reference to its title, but the act revised, or section amended shall be set forth, and published at full length. However, if, at any session of the Legislative Assembly, there are enacted two or more acts amending the same section, each of the acts shall be given effect to the extent that the amendments do not conflict in purpose. If the amendments conflict in purpose, the act last

signed by the Governor shall control. [Constitution of 1859; Amendment proposed by S.J.R. No. 28, 1975, and adopted by people Nov. 2, 1976]

Section 23. Certain local and special laws prohibited.
The Legislative Assembly, shall not pass special or local laws, in any of the following enumerated cases, that is to say:-

Regulating the jurisdiction, and duties of justices of the peace, and of constables;

For the punishment of Crimes, and Misdemeanors;

Regulating the practice in Courts of Justice;

Providing for changing the venue in civil, and Criminal cases;

Granting divorces;

Changing the names of persons;

For laying, opening, and working on highways, and for the election, or appointment of supervisors;

Vacating roads, Town plats, Streets, Alleys, and Public squares;

Summoning and empanneling (sic) grand, and petit jurors;

For the assessment and collection of Taxes, for State, County, Township, or road purposes;

Providing for supporting Common schools, and for the preservation of school funds;

In relation to interest on money;

Providing for opening, and conducting the elections of State, County, and Township officers, and designating the places of voting;

Providing for the sale of real estate, belonging to minors, or other persons laboring under legal disabilities, by executors, administrators, guardians, or trustees.—

Section 24. Suit against state.
Provision may be made by general law, for bringing suit against the State, as to all liabilities originating after, or existing at the time of the adoption of this Constitution; but no special act authorizeing (sic) such suit to be brought, or making compensation to any person claiming damages against the State, shall ever be passed.—

Section 25. Majority necessary to pass bills and resolutions; special requirements for bills raising revenue; signatures of presiding officers required.
(1) Except as otherwise provided in subsection (2) of this section, a majority of all the members elected to each House shall be necessary to pass every bill or Joint resolution.

(2) Three-fifths of all members elected to each House shall be necessary to pass bills for raising revenue.

(3) All bills, and Joint resolutions passed, shall be signed by the presiding officers of the respective houses. [Amendment proposed by H.J.R. 14, 1995, and adopted by people May 21, 1996]

Section 26. Protest by member.
Any member of either house, shall have the right to protest, and have his protest, with his reasons for dissent, entered on the journal.—

Section 27. All statutes public laws; exceptions.
Every Statute shall be a public law, unless otherwise declared in the Statute itself.—

Section 28. When Act takes effect.
No act shall take effect, until ninety days from the end of the session at which the same shall have been passed, except in case of emergency; which

emergency shall be declared in the preamble, or in the body of the law.

Section 29. Compensation of members. The members of the Legislative Assembly shall receive for their services a salary to be established and paid in the same manner as the salaries of other elected state officers and employes. [Constitution of 1859; Amendment proposed by S.J.R. No. 3, 1941, and adopted by people Nov. 3, 1942; Amendment proposed by H.J.R. No. 5, 1949, and adopted by people Nov. 7, 1950; Amendment proposed by H.J.R. No. 8, 1961, and adopted by people May 18, 1962]

Section 30. Members not eligible to other offices. No Senator or Representative shall, during the time for which he may have been elected, be eligible to any office the election to which is vested in the Legislative Assembly; nor shall be appointed to any civil office of profit which shall have been created, or the emoluments of which shall have been increased during such term; but this latter provision shall not be construed to apply to any officer elective by the people.—

Section 31. Oath of members. The members of the Legislative Assembly shall before they enter on the duties of their respective offices, take and subscribe the following oath or affirmation;—I do solemnly swear (or affirm as the case may be) that I will support the Constitution of the United States, and the Constitution of the State of Oregon, and that I will faithfully discharge the duties of Senator (or Representative as the case may be) according to the best of my Ability, And such oath may be administered by the Govenor (sic), Secretary of State, or a judge of the Supreme Court.—

Section 32. Income tax defined by federal law; review of tax laws required. Notwithstanding any other provision of this Constitution, the Legislative Assembly, in any law imposing a tax or taxes on, in respect to or measured by income, may define the income on, in respect to or by which such tax or taxes are imposed or measured, by reference to any provision of the laws of the United States as the same may be or become effective at any time or from time to time, and may prescribe exceptions or modifications to any such provisions. At each regular session the Legislative Assembly shall, and at any special session may, provide for a review of the Oregon laws imposing a tax upon or measured by income, but no such laws shall be amended or repealed except by a legislative Act. [Created through H.J.R. 3, 1969, and adopted by people Nov. 3, 1970]

Section 33. Reduction of criminal sentences approved by initiative or referendum process. Notwithstanding the provisions of section 25 of this Article, a two-thirds vote of all the members elected to each house shall be necessary to pass a bill that reduces a criminal sentence approved by the people under section 1 of this Article. [Created through initiative petition filed Nov. 16, 1993, adopted by people Nov. 8, 1994]

ARTICLE V
EXECUTIVE DEPARTMENT

Section 1. Governor as chief executive; term of office; period of eligibility. The cheif (sic) executive power of the State, shall be vested in a Governor, who shall hold his office for the term of four years; and no person shall be eligible to such office more than Eight, in any period of twelve years.—

Section 2. Qualifications of Governor. No person except a citizen of the United States, shall be eligible to the Office of Governor, nor shall any person be eligible to that office who shall not have attained the age of thirty years, and who shall not have been three years next preceding his election, a resident within this State. The minimum age requirement of this section does not apply to a person who succeeds to the office of Governor under section 8a of this Article. [Amendment proposed by H.J.R. No. 52, 1973, and adopted by people Nov. 5, 1974]

Section 3. Who not eligible. No member of Congress, or person holding any office under the United States, or under this State, or under any other power, shall fill the Office of Governor, except as may be otherwise provided in this Constitution.—

Section 4. Election of Governor. The Governor shall be elected by the qualified Electors of the State at the times, and places of choosing members of the Legislative Assembly; and the returns of every Election for Governor, shall be sealed up, and transmitted to the Secretary of State; directed to the Speaker of the House of Representatives, who shall open, and publish them in the presence of both houses of the Legislative Assembly.—

Section 5. Greatest number of votes decisive; election by legislature in case of tie. The person having the highest number of votes for Governor, shall be elected; but in case two or more persons shall have an equal and the highest number of votes for Governor, the two houses of the Legislative Assembly at the next regular session thereof, shall forthwith by joint vote, proceed to elect one of the said persons Governor.—

Section 6. Contested elections. Contested Elections for Governor shall be determined by the Legislative Assembly in such manner as may be prescribed by law.—

Section 7. Term of office. The official term of the Governor shall be four years; and shall commence at such times as may be prescribed by this constitution, or prescribed by law.—

Section 8. Vacancy in office of Governor. [Constitution of 1859; Amendment proposed by S.J.R. No. 10, 1920 (s.s.), and adopted May 21, 1920; Amendment proposed by S.J.R. No. 8, 1945, and adopted by people Nov. 5, 1946; Repeal proposed by initiative petition filed July 7, 1972, and adopted by people Nov. 7, 1972 (present section 8a of this Article adopted in lieu of this section)]

Section 8a. Vacancy in office of Governor.

In case of the removal from office of the Governor, or of his death, resignation, or disability to discharge the duties of his office as prescribed by law, the Secretary of State; or if there be none, or in case of his removal from office, death, resignation, or disability to discharge the duties of his office as prescribed by law, then the State Treasurer; or if there be none, or in case of his removal from office, death, resignation, or disability to discharge the duties of his office as prescribed by law, then the President of the Senate; or if there be none, or in case of his removal from office, death, resignation, or disability to discharge the duties of his office as prescribed by law, then the Speaker of the House of Representatives, shall become Governor until the disability be removed, or a Governor be elected at the next general biennial election. The Governor elected to fill the vacancy shall hold office for the unexpired term of the outgoing Governor. The Secretary of State or the State Treasurer shall appoint a person to fill his office until the election of a Governor, at which time the office so filled by appointment shall be filled by election; or, in the event of a disability of the Governor, to be Acting Secretary of State or Acting State Treasurer until the disability be removed. The person so appointed shall not be eligible to succeed to the office of Governor by automatic succession under this section during the term of his appointment. [Created through initiative petition filed July 7, 1972, adopted by people Nov. 7, 1972 (this section adopted in lieu of former section 8 of this Article)]

Section 9. Governor as commander in chief of state military forces.

The Governor shall be commander in chief (sic) of the military, and naval forces of this State, and may call out such forces to execute the laws, to suppress insurrection (sic), or to repel invasion.

Section 10. Governor to see laws executed.

He shall take care that the Laws be faithfully executed.—

Section 11. Recommendations to legislature.

He shall from time to time give to the Legislative Assembly information touching the condition of the State, and reccommend (sic) such measures as he shall judge to be expedient[.]

Section 12. Governor may convene legislature.

He may on extraordinary occasions convene the Legislative Assembly by proclamation, and shall state to both houses when assembled, the purpose for which they shall have been convened.—

Section 13. Transaction of governmental business.

He shall transact all necessary business with the officers of government, and may require information in writing from the offices of the Administrative, and Military Departments upon any subject relating to the duties of their respective offices.—

Section 14. Reprieves, commutations and pardons; remission of fines and forfeitures.

He shall have power to grant reprieves, commutations, and pardons, after conviction, for all offences (sic) except treason, subject to such regulations as may be provided by law. Upon conviction for treason he shall have power to suspend the execution of the sentence until the case shall be reported to the Legislative Assembly, at its next meeting, when the Legislative Assembly shall either grant a pardon, commute the sentence, direct the execution of the sentence, or grant a farther (sic) reprieve.—

He shall have power to remit fines, and forfeitures, under such regulations as may be prescribed by law; and shall report to the Legislative Assembly at its next meeting each case of reprieve, commutation, or pardon granted, and the reasons for granting the same; and also the names of all persons in whose favor remission of fines, and forfeitures shall have been made, and the several amounts remitted [.]

Section 15. [This section of the Constitution of 1859 was redesignated as section 15b by the amendment proposed by S.J.R. No. 12, 1915, and adopted by people Nov. 7, 1916]

Section 15a. Single item and emergency clause veto.

The Governor shall have power to veto single items in appropriation bills, and any provision in new bills declaring an emergency, without thereby affecting any other provision of such bill. [Created through S.J.R. No. 12, 1915, adopted by people Nov. 7, 1916; Amendment proposed by S.J.R. No. 13, 1921, and adopted by people June 7, 1921]

Section 15b. Legislative enactments; approval by Governor; notice of intention to disapprove; disapproval and reconsideration by legislature; failure of Governor to return bill.

(1) Every bill which shall have passed the Legislative Assembly shall, before it becomes a law, be presented to the Governor; if the Governor approve, the Governor shall sign it; but if not, the Governor shall return it with written objections to that house in which it shall have originated, which house shall enter the objections at large upon the journal and proceed to reconsider it.

(2) If, after such reconsideration, two-thirds of the members present shall agree to pass the bill, it shall be sent, together with the objections, to the other house, by which it shall likewise be reconsidered, and, if approved by two-thirds of the members present, it shall become a law. But in all such cases, the votes of both houses shall be determined by yeas and nays, and the names of the members voting for or against the bill shall be entered on the journal of each house respectively.

(3) If any bill shall not be returned by the Governor within five days (Saturdays and Sundays excepted) after it shall have been presented to the Governor, it shall be a law without signature, unless the general adjournment shall prevent its return, in which case it shall be a law, unless the Governor within thirty days next after the adjournment (Saturdays and Sundays excepted) shall file such bill, with written objections thereto, in the office of the Secretary of State, who shall lay the same before the Legislative Assembly at its next session in like manner as if it had been returned by the Governor.

(4) Before filing a bill after adjournment with written objections, the Governor must announce publicly the possible intention to do so at least five days before filing the bill with written objections. However, nothing in this subsection requires the Governor to file any bill with objections because of the announcement. [Created through S.J.R. No. 12, 1915, adopted by people Nov. 7, 1916; Amendment proposed by H.J.R. No. 9, 1937, and adopted by people Nov. 8, 1938; amendment proposed by S.J.R. 4, 1987, and adopted by people Nov. 8, 1988]

Note: See Article V §15 note.

Constitution

Section 16. Governor to fill vacancies by appointment.
When during a recess of the legislative assembly a vacancy occurs in any office, the appointment to which is vested in the legislative assembly, or when at any time a vacancy occurs in any other state office, or in the office of judge of any court, the governor shall fill such vacancy by appointment, which shall expire when a successor has been elected and qualified. When any vacancy occurs in any elective office of the state or of any district or county thereof, the vacancy shall be filled at the next general election, provided such vacancy occurs more than sixty-one (61) days prior to such general election. [Constitution of 1859; Amendment proposed by H.J.R. No. 5, 1925, and adopted by people Nov. 2, 1926; Amendment proposed by H.J.R. 30, 1985, and adopted by people May 20, 1986; Amendment proposed by S.J.R. 4, 1993, and adopted by people Nov. 8, 1994]

Note: The lead line to section 16 was a part of the measure submitted to the people by H.J.R. No. 5, 1925.

Section 17. Governor to issue writs of election to fill vacancies in legislature.
He shall issue writs of Election to fill such vacancies as may have occured (sic) in the Legislative Assembly.

Section 18. Commissions.
All commissions shall issue in the name of the State; shall be signed by the Govenor (sic), sealed with the seal of the State, and attested by the Secretary of State.—

ARTICLE VI
ADMINISTRATIVE DEPARTMENT

Sec. 1. Election of Secretary and Treasurer of state; terms of office; period of eligibility

2. Duties of Secretary of State

3. Seal of state

4. Powers and duties of Treasurer

5. Offices and records of executive officers

6. County officers

7. Other officers

8. County officers' qualifications; location of offices of county and city officers; duties of such officers

9. Vacancies of county, township, precinct and city offices

10. County home rule under county charter

Section 1. Election of Secretary and Treasurer of state; terms of office; period of eligibility.
There shall be elected by the qualified electors of the State, at the times and places of choosing Members of the Legislative Assembly, a Secretary, and Treasurer of State, who shall severally hold their offices for the term of four years; but no person shall be eligible to either of said offices more than Eight in any period of Twelve years.—

Section 2. Duties of Secretary of State.
The Secretary of State shall keep a fair record of the official acts of the Legislative Assembly, and Executive Department of the State; and shall when required lay the same, and all matters relative thereto before either branch of the Legislative Assembly. He shall be by virtue of his office, Auditor of public Accounts, and shall perform such other duties as shall be assigned him by law.—

Section 3. Seal of state.
There shall be a seal of State, kept by the Secretary of State for official purposes, which shall be called "The seal of the State of Oregon".—

Section 4. Powers and duties of Treasurer.
The powers, and duties of the Treasurer of State shall be such as may be prescribed by law.—

Section 5. Offices and records of executive officers.
The Governor, Secretary of State, and Treasurer of State shall severally keep the public records, books and papers at the seat of government in any manner relating to their respective offices. [Amendment proposed by S.J.R. 13, 1985, and adopted by people Nov. 4, 1986]

Section 6. County officers.
There shall be elected in each county by the qualified electors thereof at the time of holding general elections, a county clerk, treasurer and sheriff who shall severally hold their offices for the term of four years. [Constitution of 1859; Amendment proposed by initiative petition filed June 9, 1920, and adopted by people Nov. 2, 1920; Amendment proposed by H.J.R. No. 7, 1955, and adopted by people Nov. 6, 1956]

Section 7. Other officers.
Such other county, township, precinct, and City officers as may be necessary, shall be elected, or appointed in such manner as may be prescribed by law.—

Section 8. County officers' qualifications; location of offices of county and city officers; duties of such officers.
Every county officer shall be an elector of the county, and the county assessor, county sheriff, county coroner and county surveyor shall possess such other qualifications as may be prescribed by law. All county and city officers shall keep their respective offices at such places therein, and perform such duties, as may be prescribed by law. [Constitution of 1859; Amendment proposed by H.J.R. No. 7, 1955, and adopted by people Nov. 6, 1956; Amendment proposed by H.J.R. No. 42, 1971, and adopted by people Nov. 7, 1972; Amendment proposed by H.J.R. No. 22, 1973, and adopted by people Nov. 5, 1974]

Section 9. Vacancies in county, township, precinct and city offices.
Vacancies in County, Township, precinct and City offices shall be filled in such manner as may be prescribed by law.—

Section 9a. County manager form of government.
[Created through H.J.R. No. 3, 1943, adopted by people Nov. 7, 1944; Repeal proposed by H.J.R. No. 22, 1957, and adopted by people Nov. 4, 1958]

Section 10. County home rule under county charter.
The Legislative Assembly shall provide by law a method whereby the legal voters of any county, by majority vote of such voters voting thereon at any legally called election, may adopt, amend, revise or repeal a county charter. A county charter may provide for the exercise by the county of authority over matters of county concern. Local improvements shall be financed only by taxes, assessments or charges imposed on benefited property, unless otherwise provided by law or charter. A county charter shall prescribe the organization of the county government and shall provide directly, or by its authority, for the number, election or appointment, qualifications, tenure, compensation, powers and duties of such officers as the county deems necessary. Such officers shall among them exercise all the powers and perform all the duties, as distributed by the county charter or by its authority, now or hereafter, by the Constitution or laws of this state, granted to or imposed upon any county officer. Except as expressly provided by general law, a county charter shall not affect the selection, tenure, compensation, powers or duties prescribed by law for judges in their judicial capacity, for justices of the peace or for district attorneys. The initiative and referendum powers reserved to

the people by this Constitution hereby are further reserved to the legal voters of every county relative to the adoption, amendment, revision or repeal of a county charter and to legislation passed by counties which have adopted such a charter; and no county shall require that referendum petitions be filed less than 90 days after the provisions of the charter or the legislation proposed for referral is adopted by the county governing body. To be circulated, referendum or initiative petitions shall set forth in full the charter or legislative provisions proposed for adoption or referral. Referendum petitions shall not be required to include a ballot title to be circulated. In a county a number of signatures of qualified voters equal to but not greater than four percent of the total number of all votes cast in the county for all candidates for Governor at the election at which a Governor was elected for a term of four years next preceding the filing of the petition shall be required for a petition to order a referendum on county legislation or a part thereof. A number of signatures equal to but not greater than six percent of the total number of votes cast in the county for all candidates for Governor at the election at which a Governor was elected for a term of four years next preceding the filing of the petition shall be required for a petition to propose an initiative ordinance. A number of signatures equal to but not greater than eight percent of the total number of votes cast in the county for all candidates for Governor at the election at which a Governor was elected for a term of four years next preceding the filing of the petition shall be required for a petition to propose a charter amendment. [Created through H.J.R. No. 22, 1957, adopted by people Nov. 4, 1958; Amendment proposed by S.J.R. No. 48, 1959, and adopted by people Nov. 8, 1960; Amendment proposed by H.J.R. No. 21, 1977, and adopted by people May 23, 1978]

ARTICLE VII (Amended)
JUDICIAL DEPARTMENT

Sec. 1.   Courts; election of judges; term of office; compensation
1a.   Retirement of judges; recall to temporary active service
2.   Amendment's effect on courts, jurisdiction and judicial system; Supreme Court's original jurisdiction
2a.   Temporary appointment and assignment of judges
2b.   Inferior courts may be affected in certain respects by special or local laws
3.   Jury trial; re-examination of issues by appellate court; record on appeal to Supreme Court; affirmance notwithstanding error; determination of case by Supreme Court
4.   Supreme Court; terms; statements of decisions of court
5.   Juries; indictment; information; verdict in civil cases
6.   Incompetency or malfeasance of public officer
7.   Oath of office of Judges of Supreme Court
8.   Removal, suspension or censure of judges
9.   Juries of less than 12 jurors

Section 1. Courts; election of judges; term of office; compensation. The judicial power of the state shall be vested in one supreme court and in such other courts as may from time to time be created by law. The judges of the supreme and other courts shall be elected by the legal voters of the state or of their respective districts for a term of six years, and shall receive such compensation as may be provided by law, which compensation shall not be diminished during the term for which

they are elected. [Created through initiative petition filed July 7, 1910, adopted by people Nov. 8, 1910]

Section 1a. Retirement of judges; recall to temporary active service. Notwithstanding the provisions of section 1, Article VII (Amended) of this Constitution, a judge of any court shall retire from judicial office at the end of the calendar year in which he attains the age of 75 years. The Legislative Assembly or the people may by law:

(1) Fix a lesser age for mandatory retirement not earlier than the end of the calendar year in which the judge attains the age of 70 years;

(2) Provide for recalling retired judges to temporary active service on the court from which they are retired; and

(3) Authorize or require the retirement of judges for physical or mental disability or any other cause rendering judges incapable of performing their judicial duties.

This section shall not affect the term to which any judge shall have been elected or appointed prior to or at the time of approval and ratification of this section. [Created through S.J.R. No. 3, 1959, adopted by people Nov. 8, 1960]

Section 2. Amendment's effect on courts, jurisdiction and judicial system; Supreme Court's original jurisdiction. The courts, jurisdiction, and judicial system of Oregon, except so far as expressly changed by this amendment, shall remain as at present constituted until otherwise provided by law. But the supreme court may, in its own discretion, take original jurisdiction in mandamus, quo warranto and habeas corpus proceedings. [Created through initiative petition filed July 7, 1910, adopted by people Nov. 8, 1910]

Section 2a. Temporary appointment and assignment of judges. The Legislative Assembly or the people may by law empower the Supreme Court to:

(1) Appoint retired judges of the Supreme Court or judges of courts inferior to the Supreme Court as temporary members of the Supreme Court.

(2) Appoint members of the bar as judges pro tempore of courts inferior to the Supreme Court.

(3) Assign judges of courts inferior to the Supreme Court to serve temporarily outside the district for which they were elected.

A judge or member of the bar so appointed or assigned shall while serving have all the judicial powers and duties of a regularly elected judge of the court to which he is assigned or appointed. [Created through S.J.R. No. 30, 1957, adopted by people Nov. 4, 1958]

Section 2b. Inferior courts may be affected in certain respects by special or local laws. Notwithstanding the provisions of section 23, Article IV of this Constitution, laws creating courts inferior to the Supreme Court or prescribing and defining the jurisdiction of such courts or the manner in which such jurisdiction may be exercised, may be made applicable:

(1) To all judicial districts or other subdivisions of this state; or

(2) To designated classes of judicial districts or other subdivisions; or

(3) To particular judicial districts or other subdivisions. [Created through S.J.R. No. 34, 1961, adopted by people Nov. 6, 1962]

Section 3. Jury trial; re-examination of issues by appellate court; record on appeal to Supreme Court; affirmance notwithstanding error; determination of case by Supreme Court. In actions at law, where the value in controversy shall exceed $750, the right of trial by jury shall be preserved, and no fact tried by a jury shall be otherwise re-examined in any court of this state, unless the court can affirmatively say there is no evidence to support the verdict. Until otherwise provided by law, upon appeal of any case to the supreme court, either party may have attached to the bill of exceptions the whole testimony, the instructions of the court to the jury, and any other matter material to the decision of the appeal. If the supreme court shall be of opinion, after consideration of all the matters thus submitted, that the judgment of the court appealed from was such as should have been rendered in the case, such judgment shall be affirmed, notwithstanding any error committed during the trial; or if, in any respect, the judgment appealed from should be changed, and the supreme court shall be of opinion that it can determine what judgment should have been entered in the court below, it shall direct such judgment to be entered in the same manner and with like effect as decrees are now entered in equity cases on appeal to the supreme court. Provided, that nothing in this section shall be construed to authorize the supreme court to find the defendant in a criminal case guilty of an offense for which a greater penalty is provided than that of which the accused was convicted in the lower court. [Created through initiative petition filed July 7, 1910, adopted by people Nov. 8, 1910; Amendment proposed by H.J.R. No. 71, 1973, and adopted by people Nov. 5, 1974; Amendment proposed by H.J.R. 47, 1995, and adopted by people May 21, 1996]

Section 4. Supreme Court; terms; statements of decisions of court. The terms of the supreme court shall be appointed by law; but there shall be one term at the seat of government annually. At the close of each term the judges shall file with the secretary of state concise written statements of the decisions made at that term. [Created through initiative petition filed July 7, 1910, adopted by people Nov. 8, 1910]

Section 5. Juries; indictment; information. [Created through initiative petition filed July 7, 1910, adopted by people Nov. 8, 1910; Amendment proposed by S.J.R. No. 23, 1957, and adopted by people Nov. 4, 1958; Repeal proposed by S.J.R. No. 1, 1973, and adopted by people Nov. 5, 1974 (present section 5 of this Article adopted in lieu of this section)]

Section 5. Juries; indictment; information; verdict in civil cases. (1) The Legislative Assembly shall provide by law for:

(a) Selecting juries and qualifications of jurors;

(b) Drawing and summoning grand jurors from the regular jury list at any time, separate from the panel of petit jurors;

(c) Empaneling more than one grand jury in a county; and

(d) The sitting of a grand jury during vacation as well as session of the court.

(2) A grand jury shall consist of seven jurors chosen by lot from the whole number of jurors in attendance at the court, five of whom must concur to find an indictment.

(3) Except as provided in subsections (4) and (5) of this section, a person shall be charged in a circuit court with the commission of any crime punishable as a felony only on indictment by a grand jury.

(4) The district attorney may charge a person on an information filed in circuit court of a crime punishable as a felony if the person appears before the judge of the circuit court and knowingly waives indictment.

(5) The district attorney may charge a person on an information filed in circuit court if, after a preliminary hearing before a magistrate, the person has been held to answer upon a showing of probable cause that a crime punishable as a felony has been committed and that the person has committed it, or if the person knowingly waives preliminary hearing.

(6) An information shall be substantially in the form provided by law for an indictment. The district attorney may file an amended indictment or information whenever, by ruling of the court, an indictment or information is held to be defective in form.

(7) In civil cases three-fourths of the jury may render a verdict. [Created through S.J.R. No. 1, 1973, and adopted by people Nov. 5, 1974 (this section adopted in lieu of former section 5 of this Article)]

Section 6. Incompetency or malfeasance of public officer. Public officers shall not be impeached; but incompetency, corruption, malfeasance or delinquency in office may be tried in the same manner as criminal offenses, and judgment may be given of dismissal from office, and such further punishment as may have been prescribed by law. [Created through initiative petition filed July 7, 1910, adopted by people Nov. 8, 1910]

Section 7. Oath of office of Judges of Supreme Court. Every judge of the supreme court, before entering upon the duties of his office, shall take and subscribe, and transmit to the secretary of state, the following oath:

"I, _____, do solemnly swear (or affirm) that I will support the constitution of the United States, and the constitution of the State of Oregon, and that I will faithfully and impartially discharge the duties of a judge of the supreme court of this state, according to the best of my ability, and that I will not accept any other office, except judicial offices, during the term for which I have been elected." [Created through initiative petition filed July 7, 1910, adopted by people Nov. 8, 1910]

Section 8. Removal, suspension or censure of judges. (1) In the manner provided by law, and notwithstanding section 1 of this Article, a judge of any court may be removed or suspended from his judicial office by the Supreme Court, or censured by the Supreme Court, for:

(a) Conviction in a court of this or any other state, or of the United States, of a crime punishable as a felony or a crime involving moral turpitude; or

(b) Wilful misconduct in a judicial office where such misconduct bears a demonstrable relationship to the effective performance of judicial duties; or

(c) Wilful or persistent failure to perform judicial duties; or

(d) Generally incompetent performance of judicial duties; or

(e) Wilful violation of any rule of judicial conduct as shall be established by the Supreme Court; or

(f) Habitual drunkenness or illegal use of narcotic or dangerous drugs.

(2) Notwithstanding section 6 of this Article, the methods provided in this section, section 1a of this Article and in section 18, Article II of this Constitution, are the exclusive methods of the removal, suspension, or censure of a judge.
[Created through S.J.R. No. 9, 1967, adopted by people Nov. 5, 1968; Amendment proposed by S.J.R. No. 48, 1975, and adopted by people May 25, 1976]

Section 9. Juries of less than 12 jurors.
Provision may be made by law for juries consisting of less than 12 but not less than six jurors.
[Created through S.J.R. No. 17, 1971, adopted by people Nov. 7, 1972]

ARTICLE VII (Original)
THE JUDICIAL DEPARTMENT

Note: Original Article VII, compiled below, has been supplanted in part by amended Article VII and in part by statutes enacted by the Legislative Assembly. The provisions of original Article VII relating to courts, jurisdiction and the judicial system, by the terms of section 2 of amended Article VII, are given the status of a statute and are subject to change by statutes enacted by the Legislative Assembly, except so far as changed by amended Article VII.

Section 1. Courts in which judicial power vested.
The Judicial power of the State shall be vested in a Suprume (sic) Court, Circuits (sic) Courts, and County Courts, which shall be Courts of Record having general jurisdiction, to be defined, limited, and regulated by law in accordance with this Constitution.—Justices of the Peace may also be invested with limited Judicial powers, and Municipal Courts may be created to administer the regulations of incorporated towns, and cities.—

Section 2. Supreme Court.
The Supreme Court shall consist of Four Justices to be chosen in districts by the electors thereof, who shall be citizens of the United States, and who shall have resided in the State at least three years next preceding their election, and after their election to reside in their respective districts:—The number of Justices, the Districts may be increased, but shall not exceed five until the white population of the State shall amount to One Hundred Thousand, and shall never exceed seven; and the boundaries of districts may be changed, but no Change of Districts, shall have the effect to remove a Judge from office, or requre (sic) him to change his residence without his consent.—

Section 3. Terms of office of Judges.
The Judges first chosen under this Constitution shall allot among themselves, their terms of office, so that the term of one of them shall expire in Two years, one in Four years, and Two in Six years, and thereafter, one or more shall be chosen every Two years to serve for the term of Six years.—

Section 4. Vacancy.
Every vacancy in the office of Judge of the Supreme Court shall be filled by election for the remainder of the vacant term, unless it would expire at the next election, and until so filled, or when it would so expire, the Governor shall fill the vacancy by appointment.—

Section 5. Chief Justice.
The Judge who has the shortest term to serve, or the oldest of several having such shortest term, and not holding by appointment shall be the Cheif (sic) Justice.—

Section 6. Jurisdiction.
The Supreme Court shall have jurisdiction only to revise the final decisions of the Circuit Courts, and every cause shall be tried, and every decision shall be made by those Judges only, or a majority of them, who did not try the cause, or make the decision in the Circuit Court.—

Section 7. Term of Supreme Court; statements of decisions of court.
The terms of the Supreme Court shall be appointed by Law; but there shall be one term at the seat of Government annually:—

And at the close of each term the Judges shall file with the Secretary of State, Concise written Statements of the decisions made at that term.—
Note: Section 7 is in substance the same as section 4 of amended Article VII.

Section 8. Circuit court.
The Circuits (sic) Courts shall be held twice at least in each year in each County organized for judicial purposes, by one of the Justices of the Supreme Court at times to be appointed by law; and at such other times as may be appointed by the Judges severally in pursuance of law.—

Section 9. Jurisdiction of circuit courts.
All judicial power, authority, and jurisdiction not vested by this Constitution, or by laws consistent therewith, exclusively in some other Court shall belong to the Circuit Courts, and they shall have appellate jurisdiction, and supervisory control over the County Courts, and all other inferior Courts, Officers, and tribunals.—

Section 10. Supreme and circuit judges; election in classes.
When the white population of the State shall amount to Two Hundred Thousand the Legislative Assembly, may provide for the election of Supreme, and Circuit Judges, in distinct classes, one of which classes shall consist of three Justices of the Supreme Court, who shall not perform Circuit duty, and the other

class shall consist of the necessary number of Circuit Judges, who shall hold full terms without allotment, and who shall take the same oath as the Supreme Judges.—

Section 11. County judges and terms of county courts. There shall be elected in each County for the term of Four years a County Judge, who shall hold the County Court at times to be regulated by law.—

Section 12. Jurisdiction of county courts; county commissioners. The County Court shall have the jurisdiction pertaining to Probate Courts, and boards of County Commissioners, and such other powers, and duties, and such civil Jurisdiction, not exceeding the amount or value of five hundred dollars, and such criminal jurisdiction not extending to death or imprisonment in the penitentiary, as may be prescribed by law.—But the Legislative Assembly may provide for the election of Two Commissioners to sit with the County Judge whilst transacting County business, in any, or all of the Counties, or may provide a seperate (sic) board for transacting such business.—

Section 13. Writs granted by county judge; habeas corpus proceedings. The County Judge may grant preliminary injuctions (sic), and such other writs as the Legislative Assembly may authorize him to grant, returnable to the Circuit Court, or otherwise as may be provided by law; and may hear, and decide questions arising upon habeas corpus; provided such decision be not against the authority, or proceedings of a Court, or Judge of equal, or higher jurisdiction.—

Section 14. Expenses of court in certain counties. The Counties having less than ten thousand white inhabitants, shall be reimbersed (sic) wholly or in part for the salary, and expcnses of the County Court by fees, percentage, & other equitable taxation, of the business done in said Court & in the office of the County Clerk.—

Section 15. County clerk; recorder. A County Clerk shall be elected in each County for the term of Two years, who shall keep all the public records, books, and papers of the County; record conveyances, and perform the duties of Clerk of the Circuit, and County Courts, and such other duties as may be prescribed by law:—But whenever the number of voters in any County shall exceed Twelve Hundred, the Legislative Assembly may authorize the election of one person as Clerk of the Circuit Court, one person as Clerk of the County Court, and one person Recorder of conveyances.—

Section 16. Sheriff. A sheriff shall be elected in each County for the term of Two years, who shall be the ministerial officer of the Circuit, and County Courts, and shall perform such other duties as may be prescribed by law.—

Section 17. Prosecuting attorneys. There shall be elected by districts comprised of one, or more counties, a sufficient number of prosecuting Attorneys, who shall be the law officers of the State, and of the counties within their respective districts, and shall perform such duties pertaining to the administration of Law, and general police as the Legislative Assembly may direct.—

Section 18. Juries; indictment; information. [Constitution of 1859; Amendment proposed by initiative petition filed January 30, 1908, and adopted by people June 1, 1908; Amendment proposed by H.J.R. No. 14, 1927, and adopted by people June 28, 1927; Repeal proposed by S.J.R. No. 23, 1957, and adopted by people Nov. 4, 1958]

Section 19. Official delinquencies. Public Officers shall not be impeached, but incompetency, corruption, malfeasance, or delinquency in office may be tried in the same manner as criminal offences (sic), and judgment may be given of dismissal from Office, and such further punishment as may have been prescribed by law.—

Note: Section 19 is the same as section 6 of amended Article VII.

Section 20. Removal of Judges of Supreme Court and prosecuting attorneys from office. The Govenor (sic) may remove from Office a Judge of the Supreme Court, or Prosecuting Attorney upon the Joint resolution of the Legislative Assembly, in which Two Thirds of the members elected to each house shall concur, for incompetency, Corruption, malfeasance, or delinquency in office, or other sufficient cause stated in such resolution.—

Section 21. Oath of office of Supreme Court Judges. Every judge of the Supreme Court before entering upon the duties of his office shall take, subscribe, and transmit to the Secretary of State the following oath.—I _____ do solemnly swear (or affirm) that I will support the Constitution of the United States, and the constitution of the State of Oregon, and that I will faithfully, and impartially discharge the duties of a Judge of the Supreme, and Circuits (sic) Courts of said, State according to the best of my ability, and that I will not accept any other office, except Judicial offices during the term for which I have been elected.—

ARTICLE VIII
EDUCATION AND SCHOOL LANDS

Sec. 1. Superintendent of Public Instruction
    2. Common School Fund
    3. System of common schools
    4. Distribution of school fund income
    5. State Land Board; land management
    6. Qualifications of voters in school elections
    7. Prohibition of sale of state timber processed in Oregon

Section 1. Superintendent of Public Instruction. The Governor shall be superintendent of public instruction, and his powers, and duties in that capacity shall be such as may be prescribed by law; but after the term of five years from the adoption of this Constitution, it shall be competent for the Legislative Assembly to provide by law for the election of a superintendent, to provide for his compensation, and prescribe his powers and duties.—

Section 2. Common School Fund. (1) The sources of the Common School Fund are:

(a) The proceeds of all lands granted to this state for educational purposes, except the lands granted to aid in the establishment of institutions of higher education under the Acts of February 14, 1859 (11 Stat. 383) and July 2, 1862 (12 Stat. 503).

(b) All the moneys and clear proceeds of all property which may accrue to the state by escheat.

(c) The proceeds of all gifts, devises and bequests, made by any person to the state for common school purposes.

(d) The proceeds of all property granted to the state, when the purposes of such grant shall not be stated.

(e) The proceeds of the five hundred thousand acres of land to which this state is entitled under the Act of September 4, 1841 (5 Stat. 455).

(f) The five percent of the net proceeds of the sales of public lands to which this state became entitled on her admission into the union.

(g) After providing for the cost of administration and any refunds or credits authorized by law, the proceeds from any tax or excise levied on, with respect to or measured by the extraction, production, storage, use, sale, distribution or receipt of oil or natural gas and the proceeds from any tax or excise levied on the ownership of oil or natural gas. However, the rate of such taxes shall not be greater than six percent of the market value of all oil and natural gas produced or salvaged from the earth or waters of this state as and when owned or produced. This paragraph does not include proceeds from any tax or excise as described in section 3, Article IX of this Constitution.

(2) All revenues derived from the sources mentioned in subsection (1) of this section shall become a part of the Common School Fund. The State Land Board may expend moneys in the Common School Fund to carry out its powers and duties under subsection (2) of section 5 of this Article. Unexpended moneys in the Common School Fund shall be invested as the Legislative Assembly shall provide by law and shall not be subject to the limitations of section 6, Article XI of this Constitution. The State Land Board may apply, as it considers appropriate, income derived from the investment of the Common School Fund to the operating expenses of the State Land Board in exercising its powers and duties under subsection (2) of section 5 of this Article. The remainder of the income derived from the investment of the Common School Fund shall be applied to the support of primary and secondary education as prescribed by law. [Constitution of 1859; amendment proposed by H.J.R. No. 7, 1967, and adopted by people May 28, 1968; amendment proposed by H.J.R. No. 6, 1979, and adopted by people Nov. 4, 1980; amendment to subsection (2) proposed by S.J.R. 1, 1987, and adopted by people Nov. 8, 1988; amendment to paragraph (b) of subsection (1) proposed by H.J.R. 3, 1989, and adopted by people June 27, 1989]

Section 3. System of common schools. The Legislative Assembly shall provide by law for the establishment of a uniform, and general system of Common schools.

Section 4. Distribution of school fund income. Provision shall be made by law for the distribution of the income of the common school fund among the several Counties of this state in proportion to the number of children resident therein between the ages, four and twenty years.—

Section 5. State Land Board; land management. (1) The Governor, Secretary of State and State Treasurer shall constitute a State Land Board for the disposition and management of lands described in section 2 of this Article, and other lands owned by this state that are placed under their jurisdiction by law. Their powers and duties shall be prescribed by law.

(2) The board shall manage lands under its jurisdiction with the object of obtaining the greatest benefit for the people of this state, consistent with the conservation of this resource

under sound techniques of land management. [Constitution of 1859; Amendment proposed by H.J.R. No. 7, 1967, and adopted by people May 28, 1968]

Section 6. Qualifications of voters in school elections. In all school district elections every citizen of the United States of the age of twenty-one years and upward who shall have resided in the school district during the six months immediately preceding such election, and who shall be duly registered prior to such election in the manner provided by law, shall be entitled to vote, provided such citizen is able to read and write the English language. [Created through initiative petition filed June 25, 1948, adopted by people Nov. 2, 1948]

Section 7. Prohibition of sale of state timber unless timber processed in Oregon. (1) Notwithstanding subsection (2) of section 5 of this Article or any other provision of this Constitution, the State Land Board shall not authorize the sale or export of timber from lands described in section 2 of this Article unless such timber will be processed in Oregon. The limitation on sale or export in this subsection shall not apply to species, grades or quantities of timber which may be found by the State Land Board to be surplus to domestic needs.

(2) Notwithstanding any prior agreements or other provisions of law or this Constitution, the Legislative Assembly shall not authorize the sale or export of timber from state lands other than those described in section 2 of this Article unless such timber will be processed in Oregon. The limitation on sale or export in this subsection shall not apply to species, grades or quantities of timber which may be found by the State Forester to be surplus to domestic needs.

(3) This section first becomes operative when federal law is enacted allowing this state to exercise such authority or when a court or the Attorney General of this state determines that such authority lawfully may be exercised. [Created through S.J.R. 8, 1989, adopted by people June 27, 1989]

ARTICLE IX
FINANCE

Section 1. Assessment and taxation; uniform rules; uniformity of operation of laws. The

Constitution

Legislative Assembly shall, and the people through the initiative may, provide by law uniform rules of assessment and taxation. All taxes shall be levied and collected under general laws operating uniformly throughout the State. [Constitution of 1859; Amendment proposed by H.J.R. No. 16, 1917, and adopted by people June 4, 1917]

Section 1a. Poll or head tax; declaration of emergency in tax laws.
No poll or head tax shall be levied or collected in Oregon. The Legislative Assembly shall not declare an emergency in any act regulating taxation or exemption. [Created through initiative petition filed June 23, 1910, adopted by people Nov. 8, 1910; Amendment proposed by S.J.R. No. 10, 1911, and adopted by people Nov. 5, 1912]

Section 1b. Ships exempt from taxation until 1935.
All ships and vessels of fifty tons or more capacity engaged in either passenger or freight coasting or foreign trade, whose home ports of registration are in the State of Oregon, shall be and are hereby exempted from all taxes of every kind whatsoever, excepting taxes for State purposes, until the first day of January, 1935. [Created through S.J.R. No. 18, 1915, adopted by people Nov. 7, 1916]

Section 1c. Financing redevelopment and urban renewal projects.
The Legislative Assembly may provide that the ad valorem taxes levied by any taxing unit, in which is located all or part of an area included in a redevelopment or urban renewal project, may be divided so that the taxes levied against any increase in the true cash value, as defined by law, of property in such area obtaining after the effective date of the ordinance or resolution approving the redevelopment or urban renewal plan for such area, shall be used to pay any indebtedness incurred for the redevelopment or urban renewal project. The legislature may enact such laws as may be necessary to carry out the purposes of this section. [Created through S.J.R. No. 32, 1959, adopted by people Nov. 8, 1960]

Section 2. Legislature to provide revenue to pay current state expenses and interest.
The Legislative Assembly shall provide for raising revenue sufficiently to defray the expenses of the State for each fiscal year, and also a sufficient sum to pay the interest on the State debt, if there be any.—

Section 3. Laws imposing taxes; gasoline and motor vehicle taxes.
[Constitution of 1859; Amendment proposed by S.J.R. No. 11, 1941, and adopted by people Nov. 3, 1942; repealed by S.J.R. No. 7, 1979, and adopted by people May 20, 1980]

Section 3. Tax imposed only by law; statement of purpose.
No tax shall be levied except in accordance with law. Every law imposing a tax shall state distinctly the purpose to which the revenue shall be applied. [Created through S.J.R. No. 7, 1979, adopted by people May 20, 1980 (this section and section 3a adopted in lieu of former section 3 of this Article)]

Section 3a. Use of revenue from taxes on motor vehicle use and fuel.
(1) Except as provided in subsection (2) of this section, revenue from the following shall be used exclusively for the construction, reconstruction, improvement, repair, maintenance, operation and use of public highways, roads, streets and roadside rest areas in this state:

(a) Any tax levied on, with respect to, or measured by the storage, withdrawal, use, sale, distribution, importation or receipt of motor vehicle fuel or any other product used for the propulsion of motor vehicles; and

(b) Any tax or excise levied on the ownership, operation or use of motor vehicles.

(2) Revenues described in subsection (1) of this section:

(a) May also be used for the cost of administration and any refunds or credits authorized by law.

(b) May also be used for the retirement of bonds for which such revenues have been pledged.

(c) If from levies under paragraph (b) of subsection (1) of this section on campers, mobile homes, motor homes, travel trailers, snowmobiles, or like vehicles, may also be used for the acquisition, development, maintenance or care of parks or recreation areas.

(d) If from levies under paragraph (b) of subsection (1) of this section on vehicles used or held out for use for commercial purposes, may also be used for enforcement of commercial vehicle weight, size, load, conformation and equipment regulation. [Created through S.J.R. No. 7, 1979, adopted by people May 20, 1980 (this section and section 3 adopted in lieu of former section 3 of this Article)]

Section 3b. Rate of levy on oil or natural gas; exception.
Any tax or excise levied on, with respect to or measured by the extraction, production, storage, use, sale, distribution or receipt of oil or natural gas, or the ownership thereof, shall not be levied at a rate that is greater than six percent of the market value of all oil and natural gas produced or salvaged from the earth or waters of this state as and when owned or produced. This section does not apply to any tax or excise the proceeds of which are dedicated as described in sections 3 and 3a of this Article. [Created through H.J.R. No. 6, 1979, adopted by people Nov. 4, 1980]

Note: Section 3b was designated as "Section 3a" by H.J.R. 6, 1979, adopted by people Nov. 4, 1980.

Section 4. Appropriation necessary for withdrawal from treasury.
No money shall be drawn from the treasury, but in pursuance of appropriations made by law.—

Section 5. Publication of accounts.
An accurate statement of the receipts, and expenditures of the public money shall be published with the laws of each regular session of the Legislative Assembly.—

Section 6. Deficiency of funds; tax levy to pay.
Whenever the expenses, of any fiscal year, shall exceed the income, the Legislative Assembly shall provide for levying a tax, for the ensuing fiscal year, sufficient, with other sources of income, to pay the deficiency, as well as the estimated expense of the ensuing fiscal year.—

Section 7. Appropriation laws not to contain provisions on other subjects.
Laws making appropriations, for the salaries of public officers, and other current expenses of the State, shall contain provisions upon no other subject.—

Section 8. Stationery for use of state.
All stationary (sic) required for the use of the State shall be furnished by the lowest responsible

bidder, under such regulations as may be prescribed by law. But no State Officer, or member of the Legislative Assembly shall be interested in any bid, or contract for furnishing such stationery.—

Section 9. Taxation of certain benefits prohibited. Benefits payable under the federal old age and survivors insurance program or benefits under section 3(a), 4(a) or 4(f) of the federal Railroad Retirement Act of 1974, as amended, and their successors, shall not be considered income for the purposes of any tax levied by the state or by a local government in this state. Such benefits shall not be used in computing the tax liability of any person under any such tax. Nothing in this section is intended to affect any benefits to which the beneficiary would otherwise be entitled. This section applies to tax periods beginning on or after January 1, 1986. [Created through H.J.R. 26, 1985, adopted by people May 20, 1986]

Section 10. Retirement plan contributions by governmental employees. (1) Notwithstanding any existing State or Federal laws, an employee of the State of Oregon or any political subdivision of the state who is a member of a retirement system or plan established by law, charter or ordinance, or who will receive a retirement benefit from a system or plan offered by the state or a political subdivision of the state, must contribute to the system or plan an amount equal to six percent of their salary or gross wage.

2. On and after January 1, 1995, the state and political subdivisions of the state shall not thereafter contract or otherwise agree to make any payment or contribution to a retirement system or plan that would have the effect of relieving an employee, regardless of when that employee was employed, of the obligation imposed by subsection (1) of this section.

3. On and after January 1, 1995, the state and political subdivisions of the state shall not thereafter contract or otherwise agree to increase any salary, benefit or other compensation payable to an employee for the purpose of offsetting or compensating an employee for the obligation imposed by subsection (1) of this section. [Created through initiative petition filed May 10, 1993, adopted by people Nov. 8, 1994]

Section 11. Retirement plan rate of return contract guarantee prohibited. (1) Neither the state nor any political subdivision of the state shall contract to guarantee any rate of interest or return on the funds in a retirement system or plan established by law, charter or ordinance for the benefit of an employee of the state or a political subdivision of the state. [Created through initiative petition filed May 10, 1993, adopted by people Nov. 8, 1994]

Section 12. Retirement not to be increased by unused sick leave. (1) Notwithstanding any existing Federal or State law, the retirement benefits of an employee of the state or any political subdivision of the state retiring on or after January 1, 1995, shall not in any way be increased as a result of or due to unused sick leave. [Created through initiative petition filed May 10, 1993, adopted by people Nov. 8, 1994]

Section 13. Retirement plan restriction severability. If any part of Sections 10, 11 or 12 of this Article is held to be unconstitutional under the Federal or State Constitution, the remaining parts shall not be affected and shall remain in full force and effect. [Created through initiative petition filed May 10, 1993, adopted by people Nov. 8, 1994]

ARTICLE X
THE MILITIA

Section 1. State militia. The Legislative Assembly shall provide by law for the organization, maintenance and discipline of a state militia for the defense and protection of the State. [Constitution of 1859; Amendment proposed by H.J.R. No. 5, 1961, and adopted by people Nov. 6, 1962]

Section 2. Persons exempt. Persons whose religious tenets, or conscientious scruples forbid them to bear arms shall not be compelled to do so. [Constitution of 1859; Amendment proposed by H.J.R. No. 5, 1961, and adopted by people Nov. 6, 1962]

Section 3. Officers. The Governor, in his capacity as Commander-in-Chief of the military forces of the State, shall appoint and commission an Adjutant General. All other officers of the militia of the State shall be appointed and commissioned by the Governor upon the recommendation of the Adjutant General. [Constitution of 1859; Amendment proposed by H.J.R. No. 5, 1961, and adopted by people Nov. 6, 1962]

Section 4. Staff officers; commissions. [Constitution of 1859; Repeal proposed by H.J.R. No. 5, 1961, and adopted by people Nov. 6, 1962]

Section 5. Legislature to make regulations for militia. [Constitution of 1859; Repeal proposed by H.J.R. No. 5, 1961, and adopted by people Nov. 6, 1962]

Section 6. Continuity of government in event of enemy attack. [Created through H.J.R. No. 9, 1959, adopted by people Nov. 8, 1960; repeal proposed by H.J.R. No. 24, 1975, and adopted by people Nov. 2, 1976]

ARTICLE XI
CORPORATIONS AND INTERNAL IMPROVEMENTS

Section 1. Prohibition of state banks.

The Legislative Assembly shall not have the power to establish, or incorporate any bank or banking company, or monied (sic) institution whatever; nor shall any bank company, or instition (sic) exist in the State, with the privilege of making, issuing, or putting in circulation, any bill, check, certificate, prommisory (sic) note, or other paper, or the paper of any bank company, or person, to circulate as money.—

Note: The semicolon appearing in the signed Constitution after the word "whatever" in section 1, was not in the original draft reported to, and adopted by the convention and is not part of the Constitution. State v. H.S. & L.A., (1880) 8 Or. 396, 401.

Section 2. Formation of corporations; municipal charters; intoxicating liquor regulation.

Corporations may be formed under general laws, but shall not be created by the Legislative Assembly by special laws. The Legislative Assembly shall not enact, amend or repeal any charter or act of incorporation for any municipality, city or town. The legal voters of every city and town are hereby granted power to enact and amend their municipal charter, subject to the Constitution and criminal laws of the State of Oregon, and the exclusive power to license, regulate, control, or to suppress or prohibit, the sale of intoxicating liquors therein is vested in such municipality; but such municipality shall within its limits be subject to the provisions of the local option law of the State of Oregon. [Constitution of 1859; Amendment by initiative petition, adopted by people June 4, 1906; Amendment by initiative petition filed June 23, 1910, and adopted by people Nov. 8, 1910]

Section 2a. Merger of adjoining municipalities; county-city consolidation.

(1) The Legislative Assembly, or the people by the Initiative, may enact a general law providing a method whereby an incorporated city or town or municipal corporation may surrender its charter and be merged into an adjoining city or town, provided a majority of the electors of each of the incorporated cities or towns or municipal corporations affected authorize the surrender or merger, as the case may be.

(2) In all counties having a city therein containing over 300,000 inhabitants, the county and city government thereof may be consolidated in such manner as may be provided by law with one set of officers. The consolidated county and city may be incorporated under general laws providing for incorporation for municipal purposes. The provisions of this Constitution applicable to cities, and also those applicable to counties, so far as not inconsistent or prohibited to cities, shall be applicable to such consolidated government. [Created through H.J.R. No. 10, 1913, adopted by people Nov. 3, 1914; Amendment proposed by S.J.R. 29, 1967, and adopted by people Nov. 5, 1968]

Section 3. Liability of stockholders.

The stockholders of all corporations and joint stock companies shall be liable for the indebtedness of said corporation to the amount of their stock subscribed and unpaid and no more, excepting that the stockholders of corporations or joint stock companies conducting the business of banking shall be individually liable equally and ratably and not one for another, for the benefit of the depositors of said bank, to the amount of their stock, at the par value thereof, in addition to the par value of such shares, unless such banking corporation shall have provided security through membership in the federal deposit insurance corporation or other instrumentality of the United States or otherwise for the benefit of the depositors of said bank equivalent in amount to such double liability of said stockholders. [Constitution of 1859; Amendment proposed by S.J.R. No. 13, 1911, and adopted by people Nov. 5, 1912; Amendment proposed by H.J.R. No. 2, 1943, and adopted by people Nov. 7, 1944]

Section 4. Compensation for property taken by corporation.

No person's property shall be taken by any corporation under authority of law, without compensation being first made, or secured in such manner as may be prescribed by law.

Section 5. Restriction of municipal powers in Acts of incorporation.

Acts of the Legislative Assembly, incorporating towns, and cities, shall restrict their powers of taxation, borrowing money, contracting debts, and loaning their credit.—

Section 6. State not to be stockholder in company; exception of gifts for higher education purposes.

The state shall not subscribe to, or be interested in the stock of any company, association or corporation. However, as provided by law the state may hold and dispose of stock, including stock already received, that is donated or bequeathed; and may invest in the stock of any company, association or corporation, any funds or moneys that:

(1) Are donated or bequeathed for higher education purposes; or

(2) Are the proceeds from the disposition of stock that is donated or bequeathed for higher education purposes, including stock already received; or

(3) Are dividends paid with respect to stock that is donated or bequeathed for higher education purposes, including stock already received. [Constitution of 1859; Amendment proposed by H.J.R. No. 11, 1955, and adopted by people Nov. 6, 1956; Amendment proposed by H.J.R. 27, 1969, and adopted by people Nov. 3, 1970]

Section 7. Credit of state not to be loaned-limitation upon power of contracting debts.

The Legislative Assembly shall not lend the credit of the state nor in any manner create any debt or liabilities which shall singly or in the aggregate with previous debts or liabilities exceed the sum of fifty thousand dollars, except in case of war or to repel invasion or suppress insurrection or to build and maintain permanent roads; and the Legislative Assembly shall not lend the credit of the state nor in any manner create any debts or liabilities to build and maintain permanent roads which shall singly or in the aggregate with previous debts or liabilities incurred for that purpose exceed one percent of the true cash value of all the property of the state taxed on an ad valorem basis; and every contract of indebtedness entered into or assumed by or on behalf of the state in violation of the provisions of this section shall be void and of no effect. This section does not apply to any agreement entered into pursuant to law by the state or any agency thereof for the lease of real property to the state or agency for any period not exceeding 20 years and for a public purpose. [Constitution of 1859; Amendment proposed by initiative petition filed July 2, 1912, and adopted by people Nov. 5, 1912; Amendment proposed by H.J.R. No. 11, 1920 (s.s.), and adopted by people May 21, 1920; Amendment proposed by S.J.R. No. 4, 1961, and adopted by people Nov. 6, 1962; Amendment proposed by S.J.R. 19, 1963, and adopted by people Nov. 3, 1964]

Section 8. State not to assume debts of counties, towns or other corporations. The State shall never assume the debts of any county, town, or other corporation whatever, unless such debts, shall have been created to repel invasion, suppress insurrection, or defend the State in war.—

Section 9. Limitations on powers of county or city to assist corporations. No county, city, town or other municipal corporation, by vote of its citizens, or otherwise, shall become a stock-holder in any joint company, corporation or association, whatever, or raise money for, or loan its credit to, or in aid of, any such company, corporation or association. Provided, that any municipal corporation designated as a port under any general or special law of the state of Oregon, may be empowered by statute to raise money and expend the same in the form of a bonus to aid in establishing water transportation lines between such port and any other domestic or foreign port or ports, and to aid in establishing water trans-portation lines on the interior rivers of this state, or on the rivers between Washington and Oregon, or on the rivers of Washington and Idaho reached by navigation from Oregon's rivers; any debts of a municipality to raise money created for the aforesaid purpose shall be incurred only on approval of a majority of those voting on the question, and shall not, either singly or in the aggregate, with previous debts and liabilities incurred for that purpose, exceed one per cent of the assessed valuation of all property in the municipality. [Constitution of 1859; Amendment proposed by S.J.R. No. 13, 1917, and adopted by people June 4, 1917]

Section 10. County debt limitation. No county shall create any debt or liabilities which shall singly or in the aggregate, with previous debts or liabilities, exceed the sum of $5,000; provided, however, counties may incur bonded indebtedness in excess of such $5,000 limitation to carry out purposes authorized by statute, such bonded indebtedness not to exceed limits fixed by statute. [Constitution of 1859; Amendment proposed by initiative petition filed July 7, 1910, and adopted by people Nov. 8, 1910; Amendment proposed by initiative petition filed July 2, 1912, and adopted by people Nov. 5, 1912; Amendment proposed by S.J.R. No. 11, 1919, and adopted by people June 3, 1919; Amendment proposed by H.J.R. No. 7, 1920 (s.s.), and adopted by people May 21, 1920; Amendment proposed by S.J.R. No. 1, 1921 (s.s.), and adopted by people Nov. 7, 1922; Amendment proposed by S.J.R. No. 5, 1921 (s.s.), and adopted by people Nov. 7, 1922; Amendment proposed by H.J.R. No. 3, 1925, and adopted by people Nov. 2, 1926; Amendment proposed by S.J.R. No. 18, 1925, and adopted by people Nov. 2, 1926; Amendment proposed by H.J.R. No. 19, 1925, and adopted by people Nov. 2, 1926; Amendment proposed by H.J.R. No. 21, 1957, and adopted by people Nov. 4, 1958]

Section 11. Tax and indebtedness limitation.
[Created through initiative petition filed July 6, 1916, and adopted by people Nov. 7, 1916; Amendment proposed by H.J.R. No. 9, 1931, and adopted by people Nov. 8, 1932; Amendment proposed by H.J.R. No. 9, 1951, and adopted by people Nov. 4, 1952; Repeal proposed by S.J.R. No. 33, 1961, and adopted by people Nov. 6, 1962 (present section 11 of this Article adopted in lieu of this section)]

Section 11. Tax base limitation. (1) Except as provided in subsection (3) of this section, no taxing unit, whether it be the state, any county, municipality, district or other body to which the power to levy a tax has been delegated, shall in any year so exercise that power to raise a greater amount of revenue than its tax base as defined in subsection (2) of this section. The portion of any tax levied in excess of any limitation imposed by this section shall be void.

(2) The tax base of each taxing unit in a given year shall be one of the following:

(a) The amount obtained by adding six percent to the total amount of tax lawfully levied by the taxing unit, exclusive of amounts described in paragraphs (a) and (b) of subsection (3) of this section, in any one of the last three years in which such a tax was levied by the unit; or

(b) An amount approved as a new tax base by a majority of the legal voters of the taxing unit voting on the question submitted to them in a form specifying in dollars and cents the amount of the tax base in effect and the amount of the tax base submitted for approval. The new tax base, if approved, shall first apply to the levy for the fiscal year next following its approval.

(3) The limitation provided in subsection (1) of this section shall not apply to:

(a) That portion of any tax levied which is for the payment of bonded indebtedness or interest thereon.

(b) That portion of any tax levied which is specifically voted outside the limitation imposed by subsection (1) of this section by a majority of the legal voters of the taxing unit voting on the question.

(4) Notwithstanding the provisions of subsections (1) to (3) of this section, the following special rules shall apply during the periods indicated:

(a) During the fiscal year following the creation of a new taxing unit which includes property previously included in a similar taxing unit, the new taxing unit and the old taxing unit may not levy amounts on the portions of property received or retained greater than the amount obtained by adding six percent to the total amount of tax lawfully levied by the old taxing unit on the portion received or retained, exclusive of amounts described in paragraphs (a) and (b) of subsection (3) of this section, in any one of the last three years in which such a tax was levied.

(b) During the fiscal year following the annexa-tion of additional property to an existing taxing unit, the tax base of the annexing unit established under subsection (2) of this section shall be increased by an amount equal to the equalized assessed valuation of the taxable property in the annexed territory for the fiscal year of annexation multiplied by the millage rate within the tax base of the annexing unit for the fiscal year of annexa-tion, plus six percent of such amount.

(c) Whenever any taxing unit merges with one or more other taxing units without expanding its territory, in the first fiscal year of the merger, the tax base of the merged taxing unit shall be equal to the tax bases of all of the taxing units included in the merger for the prior fiscal year, plus six percent thereof.

(5) The Legislative Assembly may provide for the time and manner of calling and holding elections authorized under this section. However, the question of establishing a new tax base by a taxing unit other than the state shall be submitted at a regular statewide general or primary election. [Created through S.J.R. No. 33, 1961, adopted by people Nov. 6, 1962 (this section adopted in lieu of former section 11 of this Article); Amendment proposed by H.J.R. 28, 1985, and adopted by people May 20, 1986]

Section 11a. School district tax levy. (1)
Notwithstanding section 11 of this Article, in any year, a school district may levy ad valorem property taxes for operating purposes in an amount that, together with other levies, is not in excess of the amount levied for operating purposes in the preceding year.

(2) A levy referred to in subsection (1) of this section shall not be considered in determining the limitation imposed under section 11 of this Article.

(3) Notwithstanding subsection (5) of section 11 of this Article, the question of establishing a new tax base by a school district may be submitted only once annually on a date specified by the Legislative Assembly.

(4) The Legislative Assembly shall by law implement this section. Notwithstanding sections 1 and 28, Article IV and section 1a, Article IX of this Constitution, the initial legislation, chapter 16, Oregon Laws 1987 (Enrolled Senate Bill 278), shall take effect on the effective date of this section. [Created through S.J.R. 3, 1987, adopted by people May 19, 1987]

Section 11b. Property tax categories; limitation on categories; exceptions. (1)
During and after the fiscal year 1991-92, taxes imposed upon any property shall be separated into two categories: One which dedicates revenues raised specifically to fund the public school system and one which dedicates revenues raised to fund government operations other than the public school system. The taxes in each category shall be limited as set forth in the table which follows and these limits shall apply whether the taxes imposed on property are calculated on the basis of the value of that property or on some other basis:

MAXIMUM ALLOWABLE TAXES
For Each $1000.00 of
Property's Real Market Value

Fiscal Year	School System	Other than Schools
1991-1992	$15.00	$10.00
1992-1993	$12.50	$10.00
1993-1994	$10.00	$10.00
1994-1995	$ 7.50	$10.00
1995-1996	$ 5.00	$10.00
and thereafter		

Property tax revenues are deemed to be dedicated to funding the public school system if the revenues are to be used exclusively for educational services, including support services, provided by some unit of government, at any level from pre-kindergarten through post-graduate training.

(2) The following definitions shall apply to this section:

(a) "Real market value" is the minimum amount in cash which could reasonably be expected by an informed seller acting without compulsion, from an informed buyer acting without compulsion, in an "arms-length" transaction during the period for which the property is taxed.

(b) A "tax" is any charge imposed by a governmental unit upon property or upon a property owner as a direct consequence of ownership of that property except incurred charges and assessments for local improvements.

(c) "Incurred charges" include and are specifically limited to those charges by government which can be controlled or avoided by the property owner.

(i) because the charges are based on the quantity of the goods or services used and the owner has direct control over the quantity; or

(ii) because the goods or services are provided only on the specific request of the property owner; or

(iii) because the goods or services are provided by the governmental unit only after the individual property owner has failed to meet routine obligations of ownership and such action is deemed necessary to enforce regulations pertaining to health or safety.

Incurred charges shall not exceed the actual costs of providing the goods or services.

(d) A "local improvement" is a capital construction project undertaken by a governmental unit

(i) which provides a special benefit only to specific properties or rectifies a problem caused by specific properties, and

(ii) the costs of which are assessed against those properties in a single assessment upon the completion of the project, and

(iii) for which the payment of the assessment plus appropriate interest may be spread over a period of at least ten years.

The total of all assessments for a local improvement shall not exceed the actual costs incurred by the governmental unit in designing, constructing and financing the project.

(3) The limitations of subsection (1) of this section apply to all taxes imposed on property or property ownership except

(a) Taxes imposed to pay the principal and interest on bonded indebtedness authorized by a specific provision of this Constitution.

(b) Taxes imposed to pay the principal and interest on bonded indebtedness incurred or to be incurred for capital construction or improvements, provided the bonds are offered as general obligations of the issuing governmental unit and provided further that either the bonds were issued not later than November 6, 1990, or the question of the issuance of the specific bonds has been approved by the electors of the issuing governmental unit.

(4) In the event that taxes authorized by any provision of this Constitution to be imposed upon

any property should exceed the limitation imposed on either category of taxing units defined in subsection (1) of this section, then, notwithstanding any other provision of this Constitution, the taxes imposed upon such property by the taxing units in that category shall be reduced evenly by the percentage necessary to meet the limitation for that category. The percentages used to reduce the taxes imposed shall be calculated separately for each category and may vary from property to property within the same taxing unit. The limitation imposed by this section shall not affect the tax base of a taxing unit.

(5) The Legislative Assembly shall replace from the State's general fund any revenue lost by the public school system because of the limitations of this section. The Legislative Assembly is authorized, however, to adopt laws which would limit the total of such replacement revenue plus the taxes imposed within the limitations of this section in any year to the corresponding total for the previous year plus 6 percent. This subsection applies only during fiscal years 1991-92 through 1995-96, inclusive. [Created through initiative petition filed May 8, 1990, adopted by people Nov. 6, 1990]

Section 11c. Limits in addition to other tax limits. The limits in section 11b of this Article are in addition to any limits imposed on individual taxing units by this Constitution. [Created through initiative petition filed May 8, 1990, adopted by people Nov. 6, 1990]

Section 11d. Effect of section 11b on exemptions and assessments. Nothing in sections 11b to 11e of this Article is intended to require or to prohibit the amendment of any current statute which partially or totally exempts certain classes of property or which prescribes special rules for assessing certain classes of property, unless such amendment is required or prohibited by the implementation of the limitations imposed by section 11b of this Article. [Created through initiative petition filed May 8, 1990, adopted by people Nov. 6, 1990]

Section 11e. Severability of sections 11b, 11c and 11d. If any portion, clause or phrase of sections 11b to 11e of this Article is for any reason held to be invalid or unconstitutional by a court of competent jurisdiction, the remaining portions, clauses and phrases shall not be affected but shall remain in full force and effect. [Created through initiative petition filed May 8, 1990, adopted by people Nov. 6, 1990]

Section 11f. School district tax levy following merger. (1) If a school district merges with one or more other school districts and the merger is first effective for a fiscal year beginning on or after January 1, 1991, the tax base of the school district shall be equal to the sum of the tax base amounts for each of the school districts included in the merger, as otherwise determined under subsection (2) of section 11 of this Article.

(2) Subsection (4) of section 11 of this Article does not apply to a school district. The Legislative Assembly shall enact legislation to carry out the provisions of this section, including the circumstances under which mergers occur. [Created through H.J.R. 14, 1989, adopted by people Nov. 6, 1990]

Note: Section 11f was designated as "Section 11b" by H.J.R. 14, 1989, adopted by people Nov. 6, 1990.

Section 11g. Tax increase limitation; exceptions. Notwithstanding Section 32, Article I,

Section 1, Article IX, Section 11, Article 11, or any other provision of this Constitution;

(1) Except as provided in subsections (3), (4), and (5) of this section, the ad valorem property tax on each property for the tax year 1997-98, excluding the portion of the tax that is levied to pay bonded indebtedness or interest thereon, shall not exceed the lesser of the following: (i) the ad valorem property tax on the same property for the tax year ending June 30, 1996, reduced by ten percent (10%), or (ii) the ad valorem property tax on the same property for the tax year ending June 30, 1995.

(2)(a) For tax years following tax year 1997-98, except as provided in subsections (3), (4), and (5) of this section, the ad valorem property tax on each property shall not exceed the tax for the previous year, plus three percent (3%).

(b) The portion of the property tax that is levied on each property for the payment of bonded indebtedness or interest thereon is exempted from the three percent (3%) annual increase limitation set forth in (a) of this subsection.

(3)(a) On and after the effective date of this section, there shall be no new or additional ad valorem property tax levies against real property unless the question of the levy has been approved by not less than fifty percent (50%) of voters voting in a general election in an even numbered year, or other election in which not less than fifty percent (50%) of the registered voters eligible to vote on the question cast a ballot.

(b) Nothing in this subsection shall affect taxes levied for the repayment of bonded indebtedness approved by voters in an election held prior to the effective date of this Act, or the issuance of refunding bonds to pay such bonded indebtedness. This subsection shall not require voter approval for the issuance of, or the levy of taxes to pay, bonds issued to refund bonds issued in conformance with this subsection.

(c) For purposes of this Article, capital construction and improvements for which bonded indebtedness may be authorized shall not include maintenance and repairs, the need for which could reasonably be anticipated, supplies and equipment which are not intrinsically part of the structure, but shall include public safety and law enforcement vehicles with a projected useful life of not less than five years or the period established for repayment of the bonds, whichever is greater.

(d) The ballot title of a bond measure which is subject to this section shall include a reasonably detailed, simple and understandable description as to the use of the proceeds and the approximate percentage each use is of the whole.

(e) If an election is conducted by mail and includes a question, the approval of which would result in a new or additional ad valorem property tax levy against real property, the front of the outer envelope mailed to electors shall be clearly and boldly printed in red with the following statement: CONTAINS VOTE ON PROPOSED TAX INCREASE.

(f) When an election includes a question regarding a new or additional ad valorem property tax levy, elections officers shall provide a timely notice of deadlines for the filing of voters pamphlet statements to each person who has requested in writing that they receive such notices.

(4)(a) In the event a property is improved during or after the 1994-1995 tax year, the ad valorem property taxes on that property may be increased, by reason of such improvements, in excess of the three percent (3%) limitation of subsection (2) of this section, except that the tax shall not exceed the lesser of (i) the average ad valorem property taxes paid on similar properties similarly valued and located in the same taxing code area, or (ii) the ad valorem property taxes on the property without regard to the new or additional improvements, plus the ad valorem property taxes on the improvements at the same dollar to value ratio as paid on the property without the improvements.

Once the new improvements are added to a property and the ad valorem property tax attributable to the new or additional improvements is determined, the ad valorem property tax attributable to the improvements may be increased in subsequent tax years in the manner allowed under subsection (2) of this section.

For the purpose of this subsection, "improvements" mean new construction, reconstruction or major additions, remodeling, renovation or rehabilitation of real property including siting, installation or rehabilitation of manufactured structures, but shall not include minor construction or general, on-going maintenance and repair.

(b) In the event a property is rezoned, resulting in a higher assessed valuation, ad valorem property taxes on that property may be increased in excess of the limitation set forth in subsection (2) of this section, except the tax shall not exceed the average ad valorem property taxes paid on similar properties similarly valued and located in the same taxing code area, and the ad valorem property tax increase exceeding three percent (3%) per annum shall not be in effect until the first tax year after the property is actually used in a manner or for a purpose consistent with the new zoning unless the zone change was requested in writing by the property owner(s).

If prior to the effective date of this Act the ad valorem property taxes on a property have been increased due to a zone change not requested by the owner of the property, and the property has not been used in a manner or for a purpose consistent with the new zoning, and there has not been a transfer of ownership, the property shall be reassessed for the tax year 1997-98 consistent with the zoning effective immediately prior to the unrequested zone change or the actual use of the property, whichever results in the greater tax. Thereafter, the tax may be increased only within the limitations of this Act until there is a transfer of ownership or the property is used in a manner consistent with the new zoning. Transfer of ownership by inheritance shall not be considered transfer of ownership for purposes of this subsection.

(c) If a property is subdivided into two or more separate parcels, the tax on each newly created parcel shall not exceed the average tax paid on property similarly valued to the newly created parcel and located in the same taxing code area.

(d) If there is a lot line adjustment between existing, adjacent properties that does not create a new lot of record, the tax on each newly created parcel shall be adjusted according to any increase

or decrease in value, but the combined ad valorem property tax on the properties shall not be increased more than is permitted under subsection (2) of this section for the tax year in which the lot line adjustment is taken into account.

(e) If a property is placed in a different taxing code area, the ad valorem property tax on that property may be increased in excess of the limitation set forth in subsection (2) of this section if:

(A) The taxing district annexation that resulted in the property being placed in the different taxing code area was approved by a majority of voters casting a ballot in a general election in an even numbered year or other election in which not less than fifty percent (50%) of the registered voters eligible to vote in the election cast a ballot, and

(B) the increased tax on the property does not exceed the average ad valorem property tax paid on similar property similarly valued in the same taxing code area.

(5) For the first year following disqualification for exemption or special assessment, or in the event a property is added to the assessment and tax rolls as omitted property, ad valorem property taxes on that property may be increased in excess of the three percent (3%) increase limitation set forth in subsection (2) of this section, except the tax shall not exceed the average ad valorem property taxes paid on similar property similarly valued in the same taxing code area.

(6) In no case shall the assessed valuation of any property exceed its real market value.

(7) If it is necessary to allocate among political subdivisions of the state, or departments or agencies within those political subdivisions, any revenue reductions resulting from this Act, redistribution of revenues shall be done in a manner so as to (i) prioritize public safety and public education, and (ii) minimize any loss of local control of cities and counties to state government;

(8)(a) No government product or service that on or after June 30, 1995 was wholly or partially paid for by ad valorem property taxes, shall be shifted, transferred, or otherwise converted so as to be wholly or partially paid for by a fee, assessment, or other charge except state income taxes, without prior voter approval. If such a shift, transference or conversion of a property tax to a fee, assessment, or other charge except state income taxes, occurred without voter approval after June 30, 1995 and prior to the effective date of this Act, for tax year 1997-98 and subsequent years, the ad valorem property tax on each such property, the owner or user of which continues to be subject to such a fee, assessment, or other charge except state income taxes, shall be decreased by an additional amount equal to the portion of the fee, assessment, or other charge which was formerly paid through property taxes until such time as voters approve the fee, assessment, or other charge.

(b) The limitations of (a) of this subsection shall not apply to a new or increased fee, assessment or other charge, the imposition or enactment of which directly results in an equal or greater offsetting reduction in property taxes levied in the same taxing district, providing that the reduction is in addition to the reductions and limitations set forth elsewhere in this Act. [Created through initiative petition filed Dec. 8, 1995, and adopted by the people Nov. 5, 1996]

Note: Measure No. 47, 1996, as adopted by the people, included two paragraphs in section 11g (3) designated as paragraph (c). Sequential paragraph lettering was substituted editorially.

"This Act," in section 11g, refers to Measure No. 47, 1996, which created sections 11g, 11h, 11i and 11j of this Article. The effective date of Measure No. 47, 1996, is December 5, 1996.

Section 11h. Voluntary contributions for support of schools or other public entities.
Whereas some property owners may prefer not to have their property taxes reduced by this Act, and voluntarily would provide support for public schools in excess of the limitations of this Act; to facilitate their doing so, the state legislature shall adopt legislation to implement a mechanism whereby a property owner may conveniently make an annual, voluntary contribution in conjunction with property tax payments, and designate the school or other public entity to which the additional revenue shall be disbursed as a voluntary contribution. [Created through initiative petition filed Dec. 8, 1995, and adopted by people Nov. 5, 1996]

Note: "This Act," in section 11h, refers to Measure No. 47, 1996, which created sections 11g, 11h, 11i and 11j of this Article.

Section 11i. Legislation to implement limitation and contribution provisions.
The Legislative Assembly may adopt and amend legislation to implement the provisions of sections 11g and 11h of this Article. [Created through initiative petition filed Dec. 8, 1995, and adopted by people Nov. 5, 1996]

Section 11j. Severability of sections 11g, 11h and 11i.
SEVERABILITY of Sections 11g, 11h, and 11i of this Article. If any portion, clause or phrase of Sections 11g, 11h, and 11i of this Article is for any reason held to be invalid or unconstitutional by a court of competent jurisdiction, the remaining portions, clauses and phrases shall not be affected but shall remain in full force and effect. [Created through initiative petition filed Dec. 8, 1995, and adopted by people Nov. 5, 1996]

Section 12. Peoples' utility districts.
Peoples' Utility Districts may be created of territory, contiguous or otherwise, within one or more counties, and may consist of an incorporated municipality, or municipalities, with or without unincorporated territory, for the purpose of supplying water for domestic and municipal purposes; for the development of water power and/or electric energy; and for the distribution, disposal and sale of water, water power and electric energy. Such districts shall be managed by boards of directors, consisting of five members, who shall be residents of such districts. Such districts shall have power:

(a) To call and hold elections within their respective districts.

(b) To levy taxes upon the taxable property of such districts.

(c) To issue, sell and assume evidences of indebtedness.

(d) To enter into contracts.

(e) To exercise the power of eminent domain.

(f) To acquire and hold real and other property necessary or incident to the business of such districts.

(g) To acquire, develop, and/or otherwise provide for a supply of water, water power and electric energy.

Such districts may sell, distribute and/or otherwise dispose of water, water power and electric energy within or without the territory of such districts.

The legislative assembly shall and the people may provide any legislation, that may be necessary, in addition to existing laws, to carry out the provisions of this section. [Created through initiative petition filed July 3, 1930, adopted by people Nov. 4, 1930]

Section 13. Interests of employes when operation of transportation system assumed by public body.
Notwithstanding the provisions of section 20, Article I, section 10, Article VI, and sections 2 and 9, Article XI, of this Constitution, when any city, county, political subdivision, public agency or municipal corporation assumes responsibility for the operation of a public transportation system, the city, county, political subdivision, public agency or municipal corporation shall make fair and equitable arrangements to protect the interests of employes and retired employes affected. Such protective arrangements may include, without being limited to, such provisions as may be necessary for the preservation of rights, privileges and benefits (including continuation of pension rights and payment of benefits) under existing collective bargaining agreements, or otherwise. [Created through H.J.R. No. 13, 1965, adopted by people Nov. 8, 1966]

Section 14. Metropolitan service district charter.
(1) The Legislative Assembly shall provide by law a method whereby the legal electors of any metropolitan service district organized under the laws of this state, by majority vote of such electors voting thereon at any legally called election, may adopt, amend, revise or repeal a district charter.

(2) A district charter shall prescribe the organization of the district government and shall provide directly, or by its authority, for the number, election or appointment, qualifications, tenure, compensation, powers and duties of such officers as the district considers necessary. Such officers shall among them exercise all the powers and perform all the duties, as granted to, imposed upon or distributed among district officers by the Constitution or laws of this state, by the district charter or by its authority.

(3) A district charter may provide for the exercise by ordinance of powers granted to the district by the Constitution or laws of this state.

(4) A metropolitan service district shall have jurisdiction over matters of metropolitan concern as set forth in the charter of the district.

(5) The initiative and referendum powers reserved to the people by this Constitution hereby are further reserved to the legal electors of a metropolitan service district relative to the adoption, amendment, revision or repeal of a district charter and district legislation enacted thereunder. Such powers shall be exercised in the manner provided for county measures under section

10, Article VI of this Constitution. [Created by S.J.R. 2, 1989, adopted by people Nov. 6, 1990]

Section 15. Funding of programs imposed upon local governments; exceptions. (1) Except as provided in subsection (7) of this section, when the Legislative Assembly or any state agency requires any local government to establish a new program or provide an increased level of service for an existing program, the State of Oregon shall appropriate and allocate to the local government moneys sufficient to pay the ongoing, usual and reasonable costs of performing the mandated service or activity.

(2) As used in this section:

(a) "Enterprise activity" means a program under which a local government sells products or services in competition with a nongovernment entity.

(b) "Local government" means a city, county, municipal corporation or municipal utility operated by a board or commission.

(c) "Program" means a program or project imposed by enactment of the Legislative Assembly or by rule or order of a state agency under which a local government must provide administrative, financial, social, health or other specified services to persons, government agencies or to the public generally.

(d) "Usual and reasonable costs" means those costs incurred by the affected local governments for a specific program using generally accepted methods of service delivery and administrative practice.

(3) A local government is not required to comply with any state law or administrative rule or order enacted or adopted after January 1, 1997, that requires the expenditure of money by the local government for a new program or increased level of service for an existing program until the state appropriates and allocates to the local government reimbursement for any costs incurred to carry out the law, rule or order and unless the Legislative Assembly provides, by appropriation, reimbursement in each succeeding year for such costs. However, a local government may refuse to comply with a state law or administrative rule or order under this subsection only if the amount appropriated and allocated to the local government by the Legislative Assembly for a program in a fiscal year:

(a) Is less than 95 percent of the usual and reasonable costs incurred by the local government in conducting the program at the same level of service in the preceding fiscal year; or

(b) Requires the local government to spend for the program, in addition to the amount appropriated and allocated by the Legislative Assembly, an amount that exceeds one-hundredth of one percent of the annual budget adopted by the governing body of the local government for that fiscal year.

(4) When a local government determines that a program is a program for which moneys are required to be appropriated and allocated under subsection (1) of this section, if the local government expended moneys to conduct the program and was not reimbursed under this section for the usual and reasonable costs of the program, the local government may submit the issue of reimbursement to nonbinding arbitration by a panel of three arbitrators. The panel shall consist of one representative from the Oregon Department of Administrative Services, the League of Oregon Cities and the Association of Oregon Counties. The panel shall determine whether the costs incurred by the local government are required to be reimbursed under this section and the amount of reimbursement. The decision of the arbitration panel is not binding upon the parties and may not be enforced by any court in this state.

(5) In any legal proceeding or arbitration proceeding under this section, the local government shall bear the burden of proving by a preponderance of the evidence that moneys appropriated by the Legislative Assembly are not sufficient to reimburse the local government for the usual and reasonable costs of a program.

(6) Except upon approval by three-fifths of the membership of each house of the Legislative Assembly, the Legislative Assembly shall not enact, amend or repeal any law if the anticipated effect of the action is to reduce the amount of state revenues derived from a specific state tax and distributed to local governments as an aggregate during the distribution period for such revenues immediately preceding January 1, 1997.

(7) This section shall not apply to:

(a) Any law that is approved by three-fifths of the membership of each house of the Legislative Assembly.

(b) Any costs resulting from a law creating or changing the definition of a crime or a law establishing sentences for conviction of a crime.

(c) An existing program as enacted by legislation prior to January 1, 1997, except for legislation withdrawing state funds for programs required prior to January 1, 1997, unless the program is made optional.

(d) A new program or an increased level of program services established pursuant to action of the Federal Government so long as the program or increased level of program services imposes costs on local governments that are no greater than the usual and reasonable costs to local governments resulting from compliance with the minimum program standards required under federal law or regulations.

(e) Any requirement imposed by the judicial branch of government.

(f) Legislation enacted or approved by electors in this state under the initiative and referendum powers reserved to the people under section 1, Article IV of this Constitution.

(g) Programs that are intended to inform citizens about the activities of local governments.

(8) When a local government is not required under subsection (3) of this section to comply with a state law or administrative rule or order relating to an enterprise activity, if a nongovernment entity competes with the local government by selling products or services that are similar to the products and services sold under the enterprise activity, the nongovernment entity is not required to comply with the state law or administrative rule or order relating to that enterprise activity.

(9) Nothing in this section shall give rise to a claim by a private person against the State of Oregon based on the establishment of a new program or an increased level of service for an existing program without sufficient appropriation and allocation of funds to pay the ongoing, usual and reasonable costs of performing the mandated service or activity.

(10) Subsection (4) of this section does not apply to a local government when the local government is voluntarily providing a program four years after the effective date of the enactment, rule or order that imposed the program.

(11) In lieu of appropriating and allocating funds under this section, the Legislative Assembly may identify and direct the imposition of a fee or charge to be used by a local government to recover the actual cost of the program. [Created through H.J.R. 2, 1995, and adopted by people Nov. 5, 1996]

Section 15a. Subsequent vote for reaffirmation of section 15. (1) Section 15 of this Article is repealed on June 30, 2001, unless, at the general election held in 2000, a majority of the electors voting on the question of whether or not to retain section 15 of this Article as part of the Oregon Constitution vote to retain the section. If the electors vote to retain the section, section 15 of this Article remains in effect. If the electors do not vote to retain section 15 of this Article, then that section is repealed on June 30, 2001. The Legislative Assembly may provide for the disposition of any matters remaining unresolved with respect to the appropriation and allocation of moneys under section 15 of this Article.

(2) By appropriate action of the Legislative Assembly and the Secretary of State, the question described in subsection (1) of this section shall be submitted to the people for their decision at the statewide general election held in 2000.

(3) This section is repealed on January 1, 2002. [Created through H.J.R. 2, 1995, and adopted by people Nov. 5, 1996]

ARTICLE XI-A
RURAL CREDITS

[Created through initiative petition filed July 6, 1916, adopted by people Nov. 7, 1916; Repeal proposed by S.J.R. No. 1, 1941, and adopted by people Nov. 3, 1942]

ARTICLE XI-A
FARM AND HOME LOANS TO VETERANS

Sec. 1. State empowered to make farm and home loans to veterans
2. Bonds
3. Eligibility to receive loans
4. Tax levy
5. Repeal of conflicting constitutional provisions
6. Refunding bonds

Section 1. State empowered to make farm and home loans to veterans. Notwithstanding the limits contained in section 7, article XI of the Constitution, the credit of the State of Oregon may be loaned and indebtedness incurred in an amount not to exceed eight percent of the true cash value of all the property in the state, for the purpose of creating a fund, to be known as the "Oregon War Veterans' Fund," to be advanced for the acquisition of farms and homes for the benefit of male and female residents of the State of Oregon who served in the Armed Forces of the United States. Secured repayment thereof shall be and is a prerequisite to the advancement of money from such fund, except that moneys in the Oregon War Veterans' Fund may also be appropriated to the Director of Veterans' Affairs to be expended, without security, for the following purposes:

(1) Aiding war veterans' organizations in connection with their programs of service to war veterans;

(2) Training service officers appointed by the counties to give aid as provided by law to veterans and their dependents;

(3) Aiding the counties in connection with programs of service to war veterans;

(4) The duties of the Director of Veterans' Affairs as conservator of the estates of beneficiaries of the United States Veterans' Administration; and

(5) The duties of the Director of Veterans' Affairs in providing services to war veterans, their dependents and survivors. [Created through H.J.R. No. 7, 1943, adopted by people Nov. 7, 1944; Amendment proposed by H.J.R. No. 1, 1949, and adopted by people Nov. 7, 1950; Amendment proposed by H.J.R. No. 14, 1951, and adopted by people Nov. 4, 1952; Amendment proposed by S.J.R. No. 14, 1959, and adopted by people Nov. 8, 1960; Amendment proposed by H.J.R. No. 9, 1967, and adopted by people Nov. 5, 1968; Amendment proposed by H.J.R. No. 33, 1969, and adopted by people Nov. 3, 1970; Amendment proposed by H.J.R. No. 12, 1973, and adopted May 28, 1974; Amendment proposed by H.J.R. No. 10, 1977, and adopted by people May 17, 1977; Amendment proposed by S.J.R. No. 53, 1977, and adopted by people May 17, 1977]

Section 2. Bonds. Bonds of the state of Oregon containing a direct promise on behalf of the state to pay the face value thereof, with the interest therein provided for, may be issued to an amount authorized by section 1 hereof for the purpose of creating said "Oregon War Veterans' Fund." Said bonds shall be a direct obligation of the state and shall be in such form and shall run for such periods of time and bear such rates of interest as provided by statute. [Created through H.J.R. No. 7, 1943, adopted by people Nov. 7, 1944; Amendment proposed by H.J.R. No. 1, 1949, and adopted by people Nov. 7, 1950]

Section 3. Eligibility to receive loans. No person shall receive money from the Oregon War Veterans' Fund except the following:

(1) A person who:

(a) Resides in the State of Oregon at the time of applying for a loan from the fund;

(b) Served honorably in active duty in the Armed Forces of the United States for a period of not less than 210 days, any part of which occurred between September 15, 1940, and December 31, 1976 or who was, prior to completion of such period of service, discharged or released from active duty on account of service-connected injury or illness;

(c) Has been honorably separated or discharged from the Armed Forces of the United States or has been furloughed to a reserve; and

(d) Makes application for a loan either within the 30-year period immediately following the date on which the person was released from active duty in the Armed Forces of the United States, or not later than January 31, 1985, whichever occurs last.

(2)(a) The spouse of a person who is qualified to receive a loan under subsection (1) of this section but who has either been missing in action or a prisoner of war while on active duty in the Armed Forces of the United States even though the status of missing or being a prisoner occurred prior to completion of the minimum length of service or residence set forth in subsection (1) of this section, provided the spouse resides in this state at the time of application for the loan.

(b) The surviving spouse of a person who was qualified to receive a loan under subsection (1) of this section but who died while on active duty in the Armed Forces of the United States even though the death occurred prior to completion of the minimum length of service or residence set forth in subsection (1) of this section, provided the surviving spouse resides in this state at the time of application for the loan.

(c) The eligibility of a surviving spouse under this subsection shall terminate on his or her remarriage. [Created through H.J.R. No. 7, 1943, adopted by people Nov. 7, 1944; Amendment proposed by H.J.R. No. 1, 1949, and adopted by people Nov. 7, 1950; Amendment proposed by H.J.R. No. 14, 1951, and adopted by people Nov. 4, 1952; Amendment proposed by S.J.R. No. 14, 1959, and adopted by people Nov. 8, 1960; Amendment proposed by H.J.R. No. 9, 1967, and adopted by people Nov. 5, 1968; Amendment proposed by S.J.R. No. 23, 1971, and adopted by people Nov. 7, 1972; Amendment proposed by H.J.R. No. 23, 1975, and adopted by people May 25, 1976; Amendment proposed by H.J.R. No. 23, 1979, adopted by people May 20, 1980; Amendment proposed by S.J.R. 3, 1995, and adopted by people Nov. 5, 1996]

Section 4. Tax levy. There shall be levied each year, at the same time and in the same manner that other taxes are levied, a tax upon all property in the state of Oregon not exempt from taxation, not to exceed two (2) mills on each dollar valuation, to provide for the payment of principal and interest of the bonds authorized to be issued by this article. The two (2) mills additional tax herein provided for hereby is specifically authorized and shall not be computed as a part of the revenue raised by taxation which is subject to the tax limitation of section 11, article XI of the constitution of the state of Oregon, and said tax levy hereby authorized shall be in addition to all other taxes which may be levied according to law. [Created through H.J.R. No. 7, 1943, adopted by people Nov. 7, 1944]

Section 5. Repeal of conflicting constitutional provisions. The provisions of the constitution in conflict with this amendment hereby are repealed so far as they conflict herewith. [Created through H.J.R. No. 7, 1943, adopted by people Nov. 7, 1944]

Section 6. Refunding bonds. Refunding bonds may be issued and sold to refund any bonds issued under authority of sections 1 and 2 of this article. There may be issued and outstanding at any one time bonds aggregating the amount authorized by section 1 hereof, but at no time shall the total of all bonds outstanding, including refunding bonds, exceed the amount so authorized. [Created through H.J.R. No. 7, 1943, adopted by people Nov. 7, 1944]

ARTICLE XI-B
STATE PAYMENT OF IRRIGATION AND DRAINAGE DISTRICT INTEREST

[Created through H.J.R. No. 32, 1919, adopted by people June 3, 1919; Repeal proposed by H.J.R. No. 1, 1929, and adopted by people Nov. 4, 1930]

ARTICLE XI-C
WORLD WAR VETERANS' STATE AID SINKING FUND

[Created through H.J.R. No. 12, 1921, adopted by people June 7, 1921; Amendment proposed by H.J.R. No. 7, 1923, adopted by people Nov. 4, 1924; Repeal proposed by S.J.R. No. 12, 1951, and adopted by people Nov. 4, 1952]

ARTICLE XI-D
STATE POWER DEVELOPMENT

Sec. 1. State's rights, title and interest to water and water-power sites to be held in perpetuity
2. State's powers enumerated
3. Legislation to effectuate article
4. Construction of article

Section 1. State's rights, title and interest to water and water-power sites to be held in perpetuity. The rights, title and interest in and to all water for the development of water power and to water power sites, which the state of Oregon now owns or may hereafter acquire, shall be held by it in perpetuity. [Created through initiative petition filed July 7, 1932, adopted by people Nov. 8, 1932]

Section 2. State's powers enumerated. The state of Oregon is authorized and empowered:

1. To control and/or develop the water power within the state;

2. To lease water and water power sites for the development of water power;

3. To control, use, transmit, distribute, sell and/or dispose of electric energy;

4. To develop, separately or in conjunction with the United States, or in conjunction with the political subdivisions of this state, any water power within the state, and to acquire, construct, maintain and/or operate hydroelectric power plants, transmission and distribution lines;

5. To develop, separately or in conjunction with the United States, with any state or states, or political subdivisions thereof, or with any political subdivision of this state, any water power in any interstate stream and to acquire, construct, maintain and/or operate hydroelectric power plants, transmission and distribution lines;

6. To contract with the United States, with any state or states, or political subdivisions thereof, or with any political subdivision of this state, for the purchase or acquisition of water, water power and/or electric energy for use, transmission, distribution, sale and/or disposal thereof;

7. To fix rates and charges for the use of water in the development of water power and for the sale and/or disposal of water power and/or electric energy;

8. To loan the credit of the state, and to incur indebtedness to an amount not exceeding one and one-half percent of the true cash value of all the property in the state taxed on an ad valorem

basis, for the purpose of providing funds with which to carry out the provisions of this article, notwithstanding any limitations elsewhere contained in this constitution;

9. To do any and all things necessary or convenient to carry out the provisions of this article. [Created through initiative petition filed July 7, 1932, adopted by people Nov. 8, 1932; Amendment proposed by S.J.R. No. 6, 1961, and adopted by people Nov. 6, 1962]

Section 3. Legislation to effectuate article. The legislative assembly shall, and the people may, provide any legislation that may be necessary in addition to existing laws, to carry out the provisions of this article; Provided, that any board or commission created, or empowered to administer the laws enacted to carry out the purposes of this article shall consist of three members and be elected without party affiliation or designation. [Created through initiative petition filed July 7, 1932, adopted by people Nov. 8, 1932]

Section 4. Construction of article. Nothing in this article shall be construed to affect in any way the laws, and the administration thereof, now existing or hereafter enacted, relating to the appropriation and use of water for beneficial purposes, other than for the development of water power. [Created through initiative petition filed July 7, 1932, adopted by people Nov. 8, 1932]

ARTICLE XI-E
STATE REFORESTATION

Section 1. State empowered to lend credit for forest rehabilitation and reforestation; bonds; taxation. The credit of the state may be loaned and indebtedness incurred in an amount which shall not exceed at any one time 3/16 of 1 percent of the true cash value of all the property in the state taxed on an ad valorem basis, to provide funds for forest rehabilitation and reforestation and for the acquisition, management, and development of lands for such purposes. So long as any such indebtedness shall remain outstanding, the funds derived from the sale, exchange, or use of said lands, and from the disposal of products therefrom, shall be applied only in the liquidation of such indebtedness. Bonds or other obligations issued pursuant hereto may be renewed or refunded. An ad valorem tax outside the limitation imposed by section 11, article XI, of this constitution shall be levied annually upon all the property in the state of Oregon taxed on an ad valorem basis, in sufficient amount to provide for the payment of such indebtedness and the interest thereon. The legislative assembly may provide other revenues to supplement or replace the said tax levies. The legislature shall enact legislation to carry out the provisions hereof. This amendment shall supersede all constitutional provisions in conflict herewith. [Created through H.J.R. No. 24, 1947, adopted by people Nov. 2, 1948; Amendment proposed by S.J.R. No. 7, 1961, and adopted by people Nov. 6, 1962]

ARTICLE XI-F(1)
HIGHER EDUCATION BUILDING PROJECTS

Section 1. State empowered to lend credit for higher education building projects. The credit of the state may be loaned and indebtedness incurred in an amount which shall not exceed at any one time three-fourths of one percent of the true cash value of all the taxable property in the state, as determined by law to provide funds with which to redeem and refund outstanding revenue bonds issued to finance the cost of buildings and other projects for higher education, and to construct, improve, repair, equip, and furnish buildings and other structures for such purpose, and to purchase or improve sites therefor. [Created through H.J.R. No. 26, 1949, adopted by people Nov. 7, 1950; Amendment proposed by H.J.R. No. 12, 1959, and adopted by people Nov. 8, 1960]

Section 2. Only self-liquidating projects authorized. The buildings and structures hereafter constructed for higher education pursuant to this amendment shall be such only as conservatively shall appear to the constructing authority to be wholly self-liquidating and self-supporting from revenues, gifts, grants, or building fees. All unpledged net revenues of buildings and other projects may be pooled with the net revenues of new buildings or projects in order to render the new buildings or projects self-liquidating and self-supporting. [Created through H.J.R. No. 26, 1949, adopted by people Nov. 7, 1950]

Section 3. Sources of revenue. Ad valorem taxes shall be levied annually upon all the taxable property in the state of Oregon in sufficient amount, with the aforesaid revenues, gifts, grants, or building fees, to provide for the payment of such indebtedness and the interest thereon. The legislative assembly may provide other revenues to supplement or replace such tax levies. [Created through H.J.R. No. 26, 1949, adopted by people Nov. 7, 1950]

Section 4. Bonds. Bonds issued pursuant to this article shall be the direct general obligations of the state, and be in such form, run for such periods of time, and bear such rates of interest, as shall be provided by statute. Such bonds may be refunded with bonds of like obligation. Unless provided by statute, no bonds shall be issued pursuant to this article for the construction of buildings or other structures for higher education until after all of the aforesaid outstanding revenue bonds shall have been redeemed or refunded. [Created through H.J.R. No. 26, 1949, adopted by people Nov. 7, 1950]

Section 5. Legislation to effectuate Article. The legislative assembly shall enact legislation to carry out the provisions hereof. This article shall supersede all conflicting constitutional provisions. [Created through H.J.R. No. 26, 1949, adopted by people Nov. 7, 1950]

ARTICLE XI-F(2)
VETERANS' BONUS

Constitution

Section 1. State empowered to lend credit to pay veterans' bonus; issuance of bonds.

Notwithstanding the limitations contained in Section 7 of Article XI of the constitution, the credit of the State of Oregon may be loaned and indebtedness incurred to an amount not exceeding 5 percent of the assessed valuation of all the property in the state, for the purpose of creating a fund to be paid to residents of the State of Oregon who served in the armed forces of the United States between September 16, 1940, and June 30, 1946, and were honorably discharged from such service, which fund shall be known as the "World War II Veterans' Compensation Fund."

Bonds of the State of Oregon, containing a direct promise on behalf of the state to pay the face value thereof with the interest thereon provided for may be issued to an amount authorized in Section 1 hereof for the purpose of creating said World War II Veterans' Compensation Fund. Refunding bonds may be issued and sold to refund any bonds issued under authority of Section 1 hereof. There may be issued and outstanding at any one time bonds aggregating the amount authorized by Section 1, but at no time shall the total of all bonds outstanding, including refunding bonds, exceed the amount so authorized. Said bonds shall be a direct obligation of the State and shall be in such form and shall run for such periods of time and bear such rates of interest as shall be provided by statute. No person shall be eligible to receive money from said fund except the veterans as defined in Section 3 of this act [sic]. The legislature shall and the people may provide any additional legislation that may be necessary, in addition to existing laws, to carry out the provisions of this section. [Created through initiative petition filed June 30, 1950, adopted by people Nov. 7, 1950]

Section 2. Definitions.
The following words, terms, and phrases, as used in this act [sic] shall have the following meaning unless the text otherwise requires:

1. "Domestic service" means service within the continental limits of the United States, excluding Alaska, Hawaii, Canal Zone and Puerto Rico.

2. "Foreign Service" means service in all other places, including sea duty.

3. "Husband" means the unremarried husband, and "wife" means the unremarried wife.

4. "Child or Children" means child or children of issue, child or children by adoption or child or children to whom the deceased person has stood in loco parentis for one year or more immediately preceding his death.

5. "Parent or Parents" means natural parent or parents; parent or parents by adoption; or, person or persons, including stepparent or stepparents, who have stood in loco parentis to the deceased person for a period of one year or more immediately prior to entrance into the armed service of the United States.

6. "Veterans" means any person who shall have served in active duty in the armed forces of the United States at any time between September 16, 1940, and June 30, 1946, both dates inclusive, and who, at the time of commencing such service, was and had been a bona fide resident of the State of Oregon for at least one year immediately preceding the commencement of such service, and who shall have been separated from such service under honorable conditions, or who is still in

such service, or who has been retired. [Created through initiative petition filed June 30, 1950, adopted by people Nov. 7, 1950]

Section 3. Amount of bonus.
Every veteran who was in such service for a period of at least 90 days shall be entitled to receive compensation at the rate of Ten Dollars ($10.00) for each full month during which such veteran was in active domestic service and Fifteen Dollars ($15.00) for each full month during which such veteran was in active foreign service within said period of time. Any veteran who was serving on active duty in the armed forces between September 16, 1940, and June 30, 1946, whose services were terminated by reason of service-connected disabilities, and who, upon filing a claim for disabilities with the United States Veterans' Administration within three months after separation from the armed service, was rated not less than 50% disabled as a result of such claim, shall be deemed to have served sufficient time to entitle him or her to the maximum payment under this act [sic] and shall be so entitled. The maximum amount of compensation payable under this act [sic] shall be six hundred dollars ($600.00) and no such compensation shall be paid to any veteran who shall have received from another state a bonus or compensation because of such military service. [Created through initiative petition filed June 30, 1950, adopted by people Nov. 7, 1950]

Section 4. Survivors of certain deceased veterans entitled to maximum amount.
The survivor or survivors, of the deceased veteran whose death was caused or contributed to by a service-connected disease or disability incurred in service under conditions other than dishonorable, shall be entitled, in the order of survivorship provided in this act [sic], to receive the maximum amount of said compensation irrespective of the amount such deceased would have been entitled to receive if living. [Created through initiative petition filed June 30, 1950, adopted by people Nov. 7, 1950]

Section 5. Certain persons not eligible.
No compensation shall be paid under this act [sic] to any veteran who, during the period of service refused on conscientious, political or other grounds to subject himself to full military discipline and unqualified service, or to any veteran for any periods of time spent under penal confinement during the period of active duty, or for service in the merchant marine: Provided, however, that for the purposes of this act [sic], active service in the chaplain corps, or medical corps shall be deemed unqualified service under full military discipline. [Created through initiative petition filed June 30, 1950, adopted by people Nov. 7, 1950]

Section 6. Order of distribution among survivors.
The survivor or survivors of any deceased veteran who would have been entitled to compensation under this act [sic], other than those mentioned in Section 4 of this act [sic], shall be entitled to receive the same amount of compensation as said deceased veteran would have received, if living, which shall be distributed as follows:

1. To the husband or wife, as the case may be, the whole amount.

2. If there be no husband or wife, to the child or children, equally; and

3. If there be no husband or wife or child or children, to the parent or parents, equally. [Created through initiative petition filed June 30, 1950, adopted by people Nov. 7, 1950]

Section 7. Bonus not saleable or assignable; bonus free from creditors' claims and state taxes. No sale or assignment of any right or claim to compensation under this act [sic] shall be valid, no claims of creditors shall be enforcible against rights or claims to or payments of such compensation, and such compensation shall be exempt from all taxes imposed by the laws of this state. [Created through initiative petition filed June 30, 1950, adopted by people Nov. 7, 1950]

Section 8. Administration of article; rules and regulations. The director of Veterans' Affairs, State of Oregon, referred to herein as the "director" hereby is authorized and empowered, and it shall be his duty, to administer the provisions of this act [sic], and with the approval of the veterans advisory committee may make such rules and regulations as are deemed necessary to accomplish the purpose hereof. [Created through initiative petition filed June 30, 1950, adopted by people Nov. 7, 1950]

Section 9. Applications. All applications for certificates under this act [sic] shall be made within two years from the effective date hereof and upon forms to be supplied by the director. Said applications shall be duly verified by the claimant before a notary public or other person authorized to take acknowledgments, and shall set forth applicant's name, residence at the time of entry into the service, date and place of enlistment, induction or entry upon active federal service, beginning and ending dates of foreign service, date of discharge, retirement or release from active federal service, statement of time lost by reason of penal confinement during the period of active duty; together with the applicant's original discharge, or certificate in lieu of lost discharge, or certificate of service, or if the applicant has not been released at the time of application, a statement by competent military authority that the applicant during the period for which compensation is claimed did not refuse to subject himself to full military discipline and unqualified service, and that the applicant has not been separated from service under circumstances other than honorable. The director may require such further information to be included in such application as deemed necessary to enable him to determine the eligibility of the applicant. Such applications, together with satisfactory evidence of honorable service, shall be filed with the director. The director shall make such reasonable requirements for applicants as may be necessary to prevent fraud or the payment of compensation to persons not entitled thereto. [Created through initiative petition filed June 30, 1950, adopted by people Nov. 7, 1950]

Section 10. Furnishing forms; printing, office supplies and equipment; employes; payment of expenses. The director shall furnish free of charge, upon request, the necessary forms upon which applications may be made and may authorize the county clerks, Veterans organizations and other organizations, and notaries public willing to assist veterans without charge, to act for him in receiving application under this act [sic], and shall furnish such clerks, organizations and notaries public, with the proper forms for such purpose. The director hereby is authorized and directed with the approval of the veterans' advisory committee, to procure such printing, office supplies and equipment and to employ such persons as may be necessary in order to properly carry out the provisions of this

act [sic], and all expense incurred by him in the administration thereof shall be paid out of the World War II Veterans' Compensation Fund, in the manner provided by law for payment of claims from other state funds. [Created through initiative petition filed June 30, 1950, adopted by people Nov. 7, 1950]

ARTICLE XI-G
HIGHER EDUCATION INSTITUTIONS AND ACTIVITIES; COMMUNITY COLLEGES

Sec. 1. State empowered to lend credit for financing higher education institutions and activities, and community colleges
2. Bonds
3. Sources of revenue

Section 1. State empowered to lend credit for financing higher education institutions and activities, and community colleges. (1) Notwithstanding the limitations contained in section 7, Article XI of this Constitution, and in addition to other exceptions from the limitations of such section, the credit of the state may be loaned and indebtedness incurred in an amount not to exceed at any time three-fourths of one percent of the true cash value of all taxable property in the state, as determined by law.

(2) Proceeds from any loan authorized or indebtedness incurred under this section shall be used to provide funds with which to construct, improve, repair, equip and furnish those buildings, structures and projects, or parts thereof, and to purchase or improve sites therefor, designated by the Legislative Assembly for higher education institutions and activities or for community colleges authorized by law to receive state aid.

(3) The amount of any loan authorized or indebtedness incurred under this section by means of bonds to be issued in any biennium shall not exceed the dollar amount appropriated from the General Fund for the same or similar purposes. Any dollar amounts appropriated to meet the requirements of this subsection shall be specifically designated therefor by the Legislative Assembly.

(4) Nothing in this section prevents the financing of buildings, structures and projects, or parts thereof, by a combination of the moneys available under this section, under Article XI-F(1) of this Constitution, and from other lawful sources. However, moneys available under this section shall not be expended on or for any buildings, structures or projects, or parts thereof, that are wholly self-liquidating and self-supporting. [Created through H.J.R. No. 8, 1963 (s.s.), adopted by people May 15, 1964; Amendment proposed by H.J.R. No. 2, 1967 (s.s.), and adopted by people May 28, 1968]

Section 2. Bonds. Bonds issued pursuant to this Article shall be the direct general obligations of the state and shall be in such form, run for such periods of time, and bear such rates of interest as the Legislative Assembly provides. Such bonds may be refunded with bonds of like obligation. [Created through H.J.R. No. 8, 1963 (s.s.), adopted by people May 15, 1964]

Section 3. Sources of revenue. Ad valorem taxes shall be levied annually upon the taxable property within the State of Oregon in sufficient amount to provide for the prompt payment of bonds issued pursuant to this Article and the interest thereon. The Legislative Assembly may

Constitution

provide other revenues to supplement or replace, in whole or in part, such tax levies. [Created through H.J.R. No. 8, 1963 (s.s.), adopted by people May 15, 1964]

ARTICLE XI-H
POLLUTION CONTROL

Sec. 1. State empowered to lend credit for financing pollution control facilities or related activities
2. Only facilities seventy percent self-supporting and self-liquidating authorized; exceptions
3. Authority of public bodies to receive funds
4. Source of revenue
5. Bonds
6. Legislation to effectuate Article

Section 1. State empowered to lend credit for financing pollution control facilities or related activities. In the manner provided by law and notwithstanding the limitations contained in sections 7 and 8, Article XI, of this Constitution, the credit of the State of Oregon may be loaned and indebtedness incurred in an amount not to exceed, at any one time, one percent of the true cash value of all taxable property in the state:

(1) To provide funds to be advanced, by contract, grant, loan or otherwise, to any municipal corporation, city, county or agency of the State of Oregon, or combinations thereof, for the purpose of planning, acquisition, construction, alteration or improvement of facilities for or activities related to, the collection, treatment, dilution and disposal of all forms of waste in or upon the air, water and lands of this state; and

(2) To provide funds for the acquisition, by purchase, loan or otherwise, of bonds, notes or other obligations of any municipal corporation, city, county or agency of the State of Oregon, or combinations thereof, issued or made for the purposes of subsection (1) of this section. [Created through H.J.R. No. 14, 1969, and adopted by people May 26, 1970; amendment proposed by S.J.R. 41, 1989, and adopted by people May 22, 1990]

Section 2. Only facilities seventy percent self-supporting and self-liquidating authorized; exceptions. The facilities for which funds are advanced and for which bonds, notes or other obligations are issued or made and acquired pursuant to this Article shall be only such facilities as conservatively appear to the agency designated by law to make the determination to be not less than 70 percent self-supporting and self-liquidating from revenues, gifts, grants from the Federal Government, user charges, assessments and other fees. This section shall not apply to any activities for which funds are advanced and shall not apply to facilities for the collection, treatment, dilution, removal and disposal of hazardous substances. [Created through H.J.R. No. 14, 1969, and adopted by people May 26, 1970; amendment proposed by S.J.R. 41, 1989, and adopted by people May 22, 1990]

Section 3. Authority of public bodies to receive funds. Notwithstanding the limitations contained in section 10, Article XI of this Constitution, municipal corporations, cities, counties, and agencies of the State of Oregon, or combinations thereof, may receive funds referred to in section 1 of this Article, by contract, grant, loan or otherwise and may also receive such funds through disposition to the state, by sale, loan or otherwise, of bonds, notes or other obligations issued or made for the purposes set forth in section 1 of this Article. [Created through H.J.R. No. 14, 1969, and adopted by people May 26, 1970]

Section 4. Source of revenue. Ad valorem taxes shall be levied annually upon all taxable property within the State of Oregon in sufficient amount to provide, together with the revenues, gifts, grants from the Federal Government, user charges, assessments and other fees referred to in section 2 of this Article for the payment of indebtedness incurred by the state and the interest thereon. The Legislative Assembly may provide other revenues to supplement or replace such tax levies. [Created through H.J.R. No. 14, 1969, and adopted by people May 26, 1970]

Section 5. Bonds. Bonds issued pursuant to section 1 of this Article shall be the direct obligations of the state and shall be in such form, run for such periods of time, and bear such rates of interest, as shall be provided by law. Such bonds may be refunded with bonds of like obligation. [Created through H.J.R. No. 14, 1969, and adopted by people May 26, 1970]

Section 6. Legislation to effectuate Article. The Legislative Assembly shall enact legislation to carry out the provisions of this Article. This Article shall supersede all conflicting constitutional provisions and shall supersede any conflicting provision of a county or city charter or act of incorporation. [Created through H.J.R. No. 14, 1969, and adopted by people May 26, 1970]

ARTICLE XI-I(1)
WATER DEVELOPMENT
PROJECTS

Sec. 1. State empowered to lend credit to established Water Development Fund; eligibility; use
2. Bonds
3. Refunding bonds
4. Source of revenue
5. Legislation to effectuate Article

Section 1. State empowered to lend credit to establish Water Development Fund; eligibility; use. Notwithstanding the limits contained in sections 7 and 8, Article XI of this Constitution, the credit of the State of Oregon may be loaned and indebtedness incurred in an amount not to exceed one and one-half percent of the true cash value of all the property in the state for the purpose of creating a fund to be known as the Water Development Fund. The fund shall be used to provide financing for loans for residents of this state for construction of water development projects for irrigation, drainage, fish protection, watershed restoration and municipal uses and for the acquisition of easements and rights of way for water development projects authorized by law. Secured repayment thereof shall be and is a prerequisite to the advancement of money from such fund. As used in this section, "resident" includes both natural persons and any corporation or cooperative, either for profit or nonprofit, whose principal income is from farming in Oregon or municipal or quasi-municipal or other body subject to the laws of the State of Oregon. Not less than 50 percent of the potential amount available from the fund will be reserved for irrigation and drainage projects. For municipal use, only municipalities and communities with populations less than 30,000 are eligible for loans from the fund. [Created through S.J.R. No. 1, 1977, adopted by people Nov. 8, 1977; amendment proposed by S.J.R. No. 6, 1981, adopted by people May 18, 1982; amendment proposed by H.J.R. 45, 1987, adopted by people May 17, 1988]

Section 2. Bonds. Bonds of the State of Oregon containing a direct promise on behalf of the state to pay the face value thereof, with the interest therein provided for, may be issued to an amount authorized by section 1 of this Article for the purpose of creating such fund. The bonds shall be a direct obligation of the state and shall be in such form and shall run for such periods of time and bear such rates of interest as provided by statute. [Created through S.J.R. No. 1, 1977, adopted by people Nov. 8, 1977]

Section 3. Refunding bonds. Refunding bonds may be issued and sold to refund any bonds issued under authority of sections 1 and 2 of this Article. There may be issued and outstanding at any time bonds aggregating the amount authorized by section 1 of this Article but at no time shall the total of all bonds outstanding, including refunding bonds, exceed the amount so authorized. [Created through S.J.R. No. 1, 1977, adopted by people Nov. 8, 1977]

Section 4. Source of revenue. Ad valorem taxes shall be levied annually upon all the taxable property in the State of Oregon in sufficient amount to provide for the payment of principal and interest of the bonds issued pursuant to this Article. The Legislative Assembly may provide other revenues to supplement or replace, in whole or in part, such tax levies. [Created through S.J.R. No. 1, 1977, adopted by people Nov. 8, 1977]

Section 5. Legislation to effectuate Article. The Legislative Assembly shall enact legislation to carry out the provisions of this Article. This Article supersedes any conflicting provision of a county or city charter or act of incorporation. [Created through S.J.R. No. 1, 1977, adopted by people Nov. 8, 1977]

ARTICLE XI-I(2)
MULTIFAMILY HOUSING FOR ELDERLY AND DISABLED

Sec. 1. State empowered to lend credit for multifamily housing for elderly and disabled persons
2. Source of revenue
3. Bonds
4. Legislation to effectuate Article

Section 1. State empowered to lend credit for multifamily housing for elderly and disabled persons. In the manner provided by law and notwithstanding the limitations contained in section 7, Article XI of this Constitution, the credit of the State of Oregon may be loaned and indebtedness incurred in an amount not to exceed, at any one time, one-half of one percent of the true cash value of all taxable property in the state to provide funds to be advanced, by contract, grant, loan or otherwise, for the purpose of providing additional financing for multifamily housing for the elderly and for disabled persons. Multifamily housing means a structure or facility designed to contain more than one living unit. Additional financing may be provided to the elderly to purchase ownership interest in the structure or facility. [Created through H.J.R. No. 61, 1977, adopted by people May 23, 1978; amendment proposed by S.J.R. No. 34, 1979, adopted by people May 20, 1980; amendment proposed by H.J.R. No. 1, 1981, adopted by people May 18, 1982]

Section 2. Source of revenue. The bonds shall be payable from contract or loan proceeds; bond reserves; other funds available for these purposes; and, if necessary, state ad valorem taxes. [Created through H.J.R. No. 61, 1977, adopted by people May 23, 1978]

Section 3. Bonds. Bonds issued pursuant to section 1 of this Article shall be the direct obligations of the state and shall be in such form, run for such periods of time and bear such rates of interest as shall be provided by law. The bonds may be refunded with bonds of like obligation. [Created through H.J.R. No. 61, 1977, adopted by people May 23, 1978]

Section 4. Legislation to effectuate Article. The Legislative Assembly shall enact legislation to carry out the provisions of this Article. This Article shall supersede all conflicting constitutional provisions. [Created through H.J.R. No. 61, 1977, adopted by people May 23, 1978]

ARTICLE XI-J
SMALL SCALE LOCAL ENERGY LOANS

Sec. 1. State empowered to loan credit for small scale local energy loans; eligibility; use
2. Bonds
3. Refunding bonds
4. Source of revenue
5. Legislation to effectuate Article

Section 1. State empowered to loan credit for small scale local energy loans; eligibility; use. Notwithstanding the limits contained in sections 7 and 8, Article XI of this Constitution, the credit of the State of Oregon may be loaned and indebtedness incurred in an amount not to exceed one-half of one percent of the true cash value of all the property in the state for the purpose of creating a fund to be known as the Small Scale Local Energy Project Loan Fund. The fund shall be used to provide financing for the development of small scale local energy projects. Secured repayment thereof shall be and is a prerequisite to the advancement of money from such fund. [Created through S.J.R. No. 24, 1979, adopted by people May 20, 1980]

Section 2. Bonds. Bonds of the State of Oregon containing a direct promise on behalf of the state to pay the face value thereof, with the interest therein provided for, may be issued to an amount authorized by section 1 of this Article for the purpose of creating such fund. The bonds shall be a direct obligation of the state and shall be in such form and shall run for such periods of time and bear such rates of interest as provided by statute. [Created through S.J.R. No. 24, 1979, adopted by people May 20, 1980]

Section 3. Refunding bonds. Refunding bonds may be issued and sold to refund any bonds issued under authority of sections 1 and 2 of this Article. There may be issued and outstanding at any time bonds aggregating the amount authorized by section 1 of this Article but at no time shall the total of all bonds outstanding including refunding bonds, exceed the amount so authorized. [Created through S.J.R. No. 24, 1979, adopted by people May 20, 1980]

Section 4. Source of revenue. Ad valorem taxes shall be levied annually upon all the taxable property in the State of Oregon in sufficient amount to provide for the payment of principal and interest of the bonds issued pursuant to this Article. The Legislative Assembly may provide other revenues to supplement or replace, in whole or in part, such tax levies. [Created through S.J.R. No. 24, 1979, adopted by people May 20, 1980]

Section 5. Legislation to effectuate Article. The Legislative Assembly shall enact legislation to carry out the provisions of this Article. This Article supersedes any conflicting provision of a county or city charter or act of incorporation. [Created through S.J.R. No. 24, 1979, adopted by people May 20, 1980]

ARTICLE XII
STATE PRINTING

Section 1. State printing; State Printer. Laws may be enacted providing for the state printing and binding, and for the election or appointment of a state printer, who shall have had not less than ten years' experience in the art of printing. The state printer shall receive such compensation as may from time to time be provided by law. Until such laws shall be enacted the state printer shall be elected, and the printing done as heretofore provided by this constitution and the general laws. [Constitution of 1859; Amendment proposed by S.J.R. No. 1, 1901, and adopted by people June 6, 1904; Amendment proposed by initiative petition filed Feb. 3, 1906, and adopted by people June 4, 1906]

ARTICLE XIII
SALARIES

Section 1. Salaries or other compensation of state officers. [Constitution of 1859; Repeal proposed by S.J.R. No. 12, 1955, and adopted by people Nov. 6, 1956]

ARTICLE XIV
SEAT OF GOVERNMENT

Sec. 1. Seat of government
2. Erection of state house prior to 1865

Section 1. Seat of government. [Constitution of 1859; Repeal proposed by S.J.R. No. 41, 1957, and adopted by people Nov. 4, 1958 (present section 1 and former 1958 section 3 of this Article adopted in lieu of this section and former original section 3 of this Article)]

Section 1. Seat of government. The permanent seat of government for the state shall be Marion County. [Created through S.J.R. No. 41, 1957, adopted by people Nov. 4, 1958 (this section and former 1958 section 3 of this Article adopted in lieu of former original sections 1 and 3 of this Article)]

Section 2. Erection of state house prior to 1865. No tax shall be levied, or money of the State expended, or debt contracted for the erection of a State House prior to the year eighteen hundred and sixty five.—

Section 3. Limitation on removal of seat of government; location of state institutions. [Constitution of 1859; Amendment proposed by S.J.R. No. 1, 1907, and adopted by people June 1, 1908; Repeal proposed by S.J.R. No. 41, 1957, and adopted by people Nov. 4, 1958 (present section 1 and former 1958 section 3 of this Article adopted in lieu of this section and former section 1 of this Article)]

Section 3. Location and use of state institutions. [Created through S.J.R. No. 41, 1957, adopted by people Nov. 4, 1958 (this section, designated as "Section 2" by S.J.R. No. 41, 1957 and present section 1 of this Article adopted in lieu of former original sections 1 and 3 of this Article); Repeal proposed by S.J.R. No. 9, 1971, and approved by people Nov. 7, 1972]

ARTICLE XV
MISCELLANEOUS

Sec. 1. Officers to hold office until successors elected; exceptions; effect on defeated incumbent
2. Tenure of office; how fixed; maximum tenure
3. Oaths of office
4. Regulation of lotteries
5. Property of married women not subject to debts of husband; registration of separate property

6. Minimum area and population of counties
7. Officers not to receive fees from or represent claimants against state
8. Persons eligible to serve in legislature
9. When elective office becomes vacant

Section 1. Officers to hold office until successors elected; exceptions; effect on defeated incumbent. (1) All officers, except members of the Legislative Assembly and incumbents who seek reelection and are defeated, shall hold their offices until their successors are elected, and qualified.

(2) If an incumbent seeks reelection and is defeated, he shall hold office only until the end of his term; and if an election contest is pending in the courts regarding that office when the term of such an incumbent ends and a successor to the office has not been elected or if elected, has not qualified because of such election contest, the person appointed to fill the vacancy thus created shall serve only until the contest and any appeal is finally determined notwithstanding any other provision of this constitution. [Constitution of 1859; Amendment proposed by H.J.R. 51 (1969), and adopted by people Nov. 3, 1970]

Section 2. Tenure of office; how fixed; maximum tenure. When the duration of any office is not provided for by this Constitution, it may be declared by law; and if not so declared, such office shall be held during the pleasure of the authority making the appointment. But the Legislative Assembly shall not create any office, the tenure of which shall be longer than four years.

Section 3. Oaths of office. Every person elected or appointed to any office under this Constitution, shall, before entering on the duties thereof, take an oath or affirmation to support the Constitution of the United States, and of this State, and also an oath of office,—

Section 4. Regulation of lotteries. (1) Except as provided in subsections (2), (3), (4) and (5) of this section, lotteries and the sale of lottery tickets, for any purpose whatever, are prohibited, and the Legislative Assembly shall prevent the same by penal laws.

(2) The Legislative Assembly may provide for the establishment, operation, and regulation of raffles and the lottery commonly known as bingo or lotto by charitable, fraternal, or religious organizations. As used in this section, charitable, fraternal or religious organizations means such organizations or foundations as defined by law because of their charitable, fraternal, or religious purposes. The regulations shall define eligible organizations or foundations, and may prescribe the frequency of raffles, bingo or lotto, set a maximum monetary limit for prizes and require a statement of the odds on winning a prize. The Legislative Assembly shall vest the regulatory authority in any appropriate state agency.

(3) There is hereby created the State Lottery Commission which shall establish and operate a State Lottery. All proceeds from the State Lottery, including interest, but excluding costs of administration and payment of prizes, shall be used for any of the following purposes: creating jobs, furthering economic development or financing public education in Oregon.

(4)(a) The State Lottery Commission shall be comprised of five members appointed by the Governor and confirmed by the Senate who shall serve at the pleasure of the Governor. At least one of the Commissioners shall have a minimum of five years experience in law enforcement and at least one of the Commissioners shall be a certified public accountant. The Commission is empowered to promulgate rules related to the procedures of the Commission and the operation of the State Lottery. Such rules and any statutes enacted to further implement this article shall insure the integrity, security, honesty, and fairness of the Lottery. The Commission shall have such additional powers and duties as may be provided by law.

(b) The Governor shall appoint a Director subject to confirmation by the Senate who shall serve at the pleasure of the Governor. The Director shall be qualified by training and experience to direct the operations of a state-operated lottery. The Director shall be responsible for managing the affairs of the Commission. The Director may appoint and prescribe the duties of no more than four Assistant Directors as the Director deems necessary. One of the Assistant Directors shall be responsible for a security division to assure security, integrity, honesty, and fairness in the operation and administration of the State Lottery. To fulfill these responsibilities, the Assistant Director for security shall be qualified by training and experience, including at least five years of law enforcement experience, and knowledge and experience in computer security.

(c) The Director shall implement and operate a State Lottery pursuant to the rules, and under the guidance, of the Commission. The State Lottery may operate any game procedure authorized by the Commission, except parimutuel racing, Social games, and the games commonly known in Oregon as bingo or lotto, whereby prizes are distributed using any existing or future methods among adult persons who have paid for tickets or shares in that game; provided that, in lottery games utilizing computer terminals or other devices, no coins or currency shall ever be dispensed directly to players from such computer terminals or devices.

(d) There is hereby created within the General Fund the Oregon State Lottery Fund which is continuously appropriated for the purpose of administering and operating the Commission and the State Lottery. The State Lottery shall operate as a self-supporting revenue-raising agency of state government and no appropriations, loans, or other transfers of state funds shall be made to it. The State Lottery shall pay all prizes and all of its expenses out of the revenues it receives from the sale of tickets or shares to the public and turn over the net proceeds therefrom to a fund to be established by the Legislative Assembly from which the Legislative Assembly shall make appropriations for the benefit of any of the following public purposes: creating jobs, furthering economic development or financing public education in Oregon. Effective July 1, 1997, 15 percent of the net proceeds from the State Lottery shall be deposited, from the fund created by the Legislative Assembly under this paragraph, in an education endowment fund. Earnings on moneys in the education endowment fund shall be retained in the fund or expended for the public purpose of financing public education in Oregon as provided by law. Moneys in the education endowment fund shall be invested as provided by law and shall not be subject to the limitations of section 6, Article XI of this Constitution. The Legislative Assembly may appropriate other moneys or revenue to the education endowment fund. The Legislative Assembly shall appropriate amounts sufficient to pay lottery bonds before appropriating the net proceeds from the State Lottery for any other purpose. At least 84% of the total annual revenues from the sale of all lottery tickets or shares shall be returned to the public in the form of prizes and net revenues benefiting the public purposes.

(5) Only one state lottery operation shall be permitted in the State.

(6) The Legislative Assembly has no power to authorize, and shall prohibit, casinos from operation in the State of Oregon. [Constitution of 1859; Amendment proposed by H.J.R. No. 14, 1975, and adopted by people Nov. 2, 1976; Amendment proposed by initiative petition filed April 3, 1984, adopted by people Nov. 6, 1984. (Paragraph designations in subsection (4) were not included in the petition.); Amendment proposed by H.J.R. 20, 1985, and adopted by people Nov. 4, 1986; Amendment proposed by H.J.R. 15, 1995, and adopted by people May 16, 1995]

Section 5. Property of married women not subject to debts of husband; registration of separate property. The property and pecuniary rights of every married woman, at the time of marriage or afterwards, acquired by gift, devise, or inheritance shall not be subject to the debts, or contracts of the husband; and laws shall be passed providing for the registration of the wife's seperate (sic) property.

Section 6. Minimum area and population of counties. No county shall be reduced to an area of less than four hundred square miles; nor shall any new county be established in this State containing a less area, nor unless such new county shall contain a population of at least twelve hundred inhabitants.

Section 7. Officers not to receive fees from or represent claimants against state. No State officers, or members of the Legislative Assembly, shall directly or indirectly receive a fee, or be engaged as counsel, agent, or Attorney in the prosecution of any claim against this State.—

Section 8. Chinamen not to hold real estate or mining claims; working mining claims. [Constitution of 1859; Repeal proposed by S.J.R. No. 14, 1945, and adopted by people Nov. 5, 1946]

Section 8. Persons eligible to serve in legislature. Notwithstanding the provisions of section 1 article III and section 10 article II of the Constitution of the State of Oregon, a person employed by the State Board of Higher Education, a member of any school board or employee thereof, shall be eligible to a seat in the Legislative Assembly and such membership in the Legislative Assembly shall not prevent such person from being employed by the State Board of Higher Education or from being a member or employee of a school board. [Created through initiative petition filed June 13, 1958, adopted by people Nov. 4, 1958]

Section 9. When elective office becomes vacant. The Legislative Assembly may provide that any elective public office becomes vacant, under such conditions or circumstances as the Legislative Assembly may specify, whenever a person holding the office is elected to another public office more than 90 days prior to the expiration of the term of the office he is holding. For the purposes of this section, a person elected is considered to be elected as of the date the election is held. [Created through S.J.R. No. 41, 1959, adopted by people Nov. 8, 1960]

ARTICLE XVI
BOUNDARIES

Section 1. State boundaries. The State of Oregon shall be bounded as provided by section 1 of the Act of Congress of February 1859, admitting the State of Oregon into the Union of the United States, until:

(1) Such boundaries are modified by appropriate interstate compact or compacts heretofore or hereafter approved by the Congress of the United States; or

(2) The Legislative Assembly by law extends the boundaries or jurisdiction of this state an additional distance seaward under authority of a law heretofore or hereafter enacted by the Congress of the United States. [Constitution of 1859; Amendment proposed by S.J.R. No. 4, 1957, and adopted by people Nov. 4, 1958; Amendment proposed by H.J.R. No. 24, 1967, and adopted by people Nov. 5, 1968]

ARTICLE XVII
AMENDMENTS AND REVISIONS

Sec. 1.   Method of amending Constitution
     2.   Method of revising Constitution

Section 1. Method of amending Constitution. Any amendment or amendments to this Constitution may be proposed in either branch of the legislative assembly, and if the same shall be agreed to by a majority of all the members elected to each of the two houses, such proposed amendment or amendments shall, with the yeas and nays thereon, be entered in their journals and referred by the secretary of state to the people for their approval or rejection, at the next regular general election, except when the legislative assembly shall order a special election for that purpose. If a majority of the electors voting on any such amendment shall vote in favor thereof, it shall thereby become a part of this Constitution. The votes for and against such amendment, or amendments, severally, whether proposed by the legislative assembly or by initiative petition, shall be canvassed by the secretary of state in the presence of the governor, and if it shall appear to the governor that the majority of the votes cast at said election on said amendment, or amendments, severally, are cast in favor thereof, it shall be his duty forthwith after such canvass, by his proclamation, to declare the said amendment, or amendments, severally, having received said majority of votes to have been adopted by the people of Oregon as part of the Constitution thereof, and the same shall be in effect as a part of the Constitution from the date of such proclamation. When two or more amendments shall be submitted in the manner aforesaid to the voters of this state at the same election, they shall be so submitted that each amendment shall be voted on separately. No convention shall be called to amend or propose amendments to this Constitution, or to propose a new Constitution, unless the law providing for such convention shall first be approved by the people on a referendum vote at a regular general election. This article shall not be construed to impair the right of the people to amend this Constitution by vote upon an initiative petition therefor. [Created through initiative petition filed Feb. 3, 1906, adopted by people June 4, 1906]

Note: The above section replaces sections 1 and 2 of Article XVII of the original Constitution.

Section 2. Method of revising Constitution.

(1) In addition to the power to amend this Constitution granted by section 1, Article IV, and section 1 of this Article, a revision of all or part of this Constitution may be proposed in either house of the Legislative Assembly and, if the proposed revision is agreed to by at least two-thirds of all the members of each house, the proposed revision shall, with the yeas and nays thereon, be entered in their journals and referred by the Secretary of State to the people for their approval or rejection, notwithstanding section 1, Article IV of this Constitution, at the next regular state-wide primary election, except when the Legislative Assembly orders a special election for that purpose. A proposed revision may deal with more than one subject and shall be voted upon as one question. The votes for and against the proposed revision shall be canvassed by the Secretary of State in the presence of the Governor and, if it appears to the Governor that the majority of the votes cast in the election on the proposed revision are in favor of the proposed revision, he shall, promptly following the canvass, declare, by his proclamation, that the proposed revision has received a majority of votes and has been adopted by the people as the Constitution of the State of Oregon or as a part of the Constitution of the State of Oregon, as the case may be. The revision shall be in effect as the Constitution or as a part of this Constitution from the date of such proclamation.

(2) Subject to subsection (3) of this section, an amendment proposed to the Constitution under section 1, Article IV, or under section 1 of this Article may be submitted to the people in the form of alternative provisions so that one provision will become a part of the Constitution if a proposed revision is adopted by the people and the other provision will become a part of the Constitution if a proposed revision is rejected by the people. A proposed amendment submitted in the form of alternative provisions as authorized by this subsection shall be voted upon as one question.

(3) Subsection (2) of this section applies only when:

(a) The Legislative Assembly proposes and refers to the people a revision under subsection (1) of this section; and

(b) An amendment is proposed under section 1, Article IV, or under section 1 of this Article; and

(c) The proposed amendment will be submitted to the people at an election held during the period between the adjournment of the legislative session at which the proposed revision is referred to the people and the next regular legislative session. [Created through H.J.R. No. 5, 1959, adopted by people Nov. 8, 1960]

ARTICLE XVIII
SCHEDULE

Sec. 1.   Election to accept or reject Constitution
     2.   Questions submitted to voters
     3.   Majority of votes required to accept or reject Constitution
     4.   Vote on certain sections of Constitution
     5.   Apportionment of Senators and Representatives
     6.   Election under Constitution; organization of state
     7.   Former laws continued in force
     8.   Officers to continue in office
     9.   Crimes against territory
    10.   Saving existing rights and liabilities
    11.   Judicial districts

Section 1. Election to accept or reject Constitution.
For the purpose of taking the vote of the electors of the State, for the acceptance or rejection of this Constitution, an election shall be held on the second Monday of November, in the year 1857, to be conducted according to existing laws regulating the election of Delegates in Congress, so far as applicable, except as herein otherwise provided.

Section 2. Questions submitted to voters.
Each elector who offers to vote upon this Constitution, shall be asked by the judges of election this question:

Do you vote for the Constitution? Yes, or No.

And also this question:

Do you vote for Slavery in Oregon? Yes, or No.

And also this question:

Do you vote for free Negroes in Oregon? Yes, or No.

And in the poll books shall be columns headed respectively.

"Constitution, Yes."   "Constitution, No"

"Free Negroes, Yes"   "Free Negroes, No."

"Slavery, Yes."   "Slavery, No".—

And the names of the electors shall be entered in the poll books, together with their awnsers (sic) to the said questions, under their appropriate heads. The abstracts of the votes transmitted to the Secretary of the Territory, shall be publicly opened, and canvassed by the Governor and Secretary, or by either of them in the absence of the other; and the Governor, or in his absence the Secretary, shall forthwith issue his proclamation, and publish the same in the several newspapers printed in this State, declaring the result of the said election upon each of said questions.—

Section 3. Majority of votes required to accept or reject Constitution.
If a majority of all the votes given for, and against the Constitution, shall be given for the Constitution, then this Constitution shall be deemed to be approved, and accepted by the electors of the State, and shall take effect accordingly; and if a majority of such votes shall be given against the Constitution, then this Constitution shall be deemed to be rejected by the electors of the State, and shall be void.—

Section 4. Vote on certain sections of Constitution.
If this Constitution shall be accepted by the electors, and a majority of all the votes given for, and against slavery, shall be given for slavery, then the following section shall be added to the Bill of Rights, and shall be part of this Constitution:

"Sec. _____ "Persons lawfully held as slaves in any State, Territory, or District of the United States, under the laws thereof, may be brought into this State, and such Slaves, and their descendants may be held as slaves within this State, and shall not be emancipated without the consent of their owners."

And if a majority of such votes shall be given against slavery, then the foregoing section shall not, but the following sections shall be added to the Bill of Rights, and shall be a part of this Constitution.

"Sec. _____ There shall be neither slavery, nor involuntary servitude in the State, otherwise than as a punishment for crime, whereof the party shall have been duly convicted."—

And if a majority of all the votes given for, and against free negroes, shall be given against free negroes, then the following section shall be added to the Bill of Rights, and shall be part of this Constitution:

"Sec. :_____ No free negro, or mulatto, not residing in this State at the time of the adoption of this Constitution, shall come, reside, or be within this State, or hold any real estate, or make any contracts, or maintain any suit therein; and the Legislative Assembly shall provide by penal laws, for the removal, by public officers, of all such negroes, and mulattoes, and for their effectual exclusion from the State, and for the punishment of persons who shall bring them into the State, or employ, or harbor them."

Note: See sections 34 and 35 of Article I, Oregon Constitution.

Section 5. Apportionment of Senators and Representatives.
Until an enumeration of the white inhabitants of the State shall be made, and the senators and representatives apportioned as directed in the Constitution, the County of Marion shall have two senators, and four representatives.—

Linn two senators, and four representatives.

Lane two senators, and three represtatives (sic).

Clackamas and Wasco, one senator jointly, and Clackamas three representatives, and Wasco one representative.—

Yamhill one senator, and two representatives[.]

Polk one senator, and two representatives[.]

Benton one senator, and two representatives[.]

Multnomah, one senator, and two representatives.

Washington, Columbia, Clatsop, and Tillamook one senator jointly, and Washington one representative, and Washington and Columbia one representative jointly, and Clatsop and Tillamook one representative jointly.—

Douglas, one senator, and two representatives.—

Jackson one senator, and three representatives.—

Josephine one senator, and one repsentative (sic).—

Umpqua, Coos and Curry, one senator jointly, and Umpqua one representative, and Coos and Curry one representative jointly.—

Section 6. Election under Constitution; organization of state.
If this Constitution shall be ratified, an election shall be held on the first Monday of June 1858, for the election of members of the Legislative Assembly, a Representative in Congress, and State and County officers, and the Legislative Assembly shall convene at the Capital on the first Monday of July 1858, and proceed to elect two senators in Congress, and make such further provision as may be necessary to the complete organization of a State government.—

Section 7. Former laws continued in force.
All laws in force in the Territory of Oregon when this Constitution takes effect, and consistent therewith, shall continue in force until altered, or repealed.—

Section 8. Officers to continue in office.
All officers of the Territory of Oregon, or under its laws, when this Constitution takes effect, shall continue in office, until superseded by the State authorities.—

Section 9. Crimes against territory.
Crimes and misdemeanors committed against the Territory of Oregon shall be punished by the

State, as they might have been punished by the Territory, if the change of government had not been made.—

Section 10. Saving existing rights and liabilities. All property and rights of the Territory, and of the several counties, subdivisions, and political bodies corporate, of, or in the Territory, including fines, penalties, forfeitures, debts and claims, of whatsoever nature, and recognizances, obligations, and undertakings to, or for the use of the Territory, or any county, political corporation, office, or otherwise, to or for the public, shall inure to the State, or remain to the county, local division, corporation, officer, or public, as if the change of government had not been made. And private rights shall not be affected by such change.—

Section 11. Judicial districts. Until otherwise provided by law, the judicial districts of the State, shall be constituted as follows: The counties of Jackson, Josephine, and Douglas, shall constitute the first district. The counties of Umpqua, Coos, Curry, Lane, and Benton, shall constitute the second district.—The counties of Linn, Marion, Polk, Yamhill and Washington, shall constitute the third district.—The counties of Clackamas, Multnomah, Wasco, Columbia, Clatsop, and Tillamook, shall constitute the fourth district— and the County of Tillamook shall be attached to the county of Clatsop for judicial purposes.—

INDEX

A

B

C

H

I

J

K

L